DECADE
OF DECISION

The Supreme Court and the Constitutional Revolution

1954–1964

DECADE

of

DECISION

THE SUPREME COURT AND THE CONSTITUTIONAL
REVOLUTION 1954–1964

G. THEODORE MITAU

James Wallace Professor of Political Science
MACALESTER COLLEGE

CHARLES SCRIBNER'S SONS · NEW YORK

To Charlotte

Preface

The years since 1954 represent one of the most fascinating and crucial periods in the development of American constitutional law. Hopefully this book can contribute towards an understanding of the complex interactions of Court, Constitution and Congress and can elucidate the enormity of the policy-dilemmas that confronted the justices in the process of decision-making.

A political system that reserves to a written Constitution and its judicial interpreters as much power as the American exudes great faith in the possibilities of peaceful intergroup accommodations and conflict management. This author believes that careful analysis of the Supreme Court's reasoning and actions offers a superb opportunity to study how the Court reconciles competing perceptions of justice and how it proceeds to adapt traditional constitutional norms to contemporary demands for social and political changes.

Most readers may find it difficult not to acknowledge their profound respect for the high quality of argument with which members of the Court advanced their differing views and convictions in cases that involved issues of major principle and far-reaching consequence. Some readers might even approve decisions that before seemed to lack both reason and wisdom. All readers, this author pleads, will forgive him for any error of judgment and interpretation for which he alone must bear responsibility.

Special appreciation is due Professor Harold Chase of the University of Minnesota for his wise counsel and encouragement and Mr. Quentin Johnson of Macalester College for his invaluable research assistance.

G. THEODORE MITAU
Macalester College

Contents

DECADE
OF DECISION

The Supreme Court and the Constitutional Revolution

1954–1964

Introduction

During the past decade the Supreme Court of the United States rendered a number of critically important decisions which vastly expanded constitutional protections for the politically weak, the socially disliked and the criminally suspect. More than ever before, the Court forced majorities to extend consideration and respect to the rights of unpopular minorities and to their consensus-disrupting causes and conduct.

This short book is designed to sketch a few of the major cases —to probe the nature of the issues that confronted the Court, to discern the precedents that were broken, to examine the legal theories that emerged in the opinions and to delineate the judicial dilemmas that persist.

Legislative committees expressed more than annoyance with Supreme Court rulings that blocked certain types of investigations aimed at the disclosure of organizational membership or with decisions that seemed to shield individuals from questions judicially deemed to lack relevance or pertinency to the announced purpose of the inquiry. A number of state loyalty oaths became constitutionally invalid or suspect for their interference with personal liberty; the mere "advocacy" of the overthrow of the government was judged insufficient to sustain criminal conviction; and Communist party membership itself could not, under the Bill of Rights, legally bar the privileges of obtaining a United States passport.

The political and social consequences of these precedent-shattering cases were profound. In public education the doctrine of "separate but equal" was found to be no longer constitutionally

3

valid and with it came down other legally established systems
of segregation which had governed the relations of the races
throughout the South for so many years.

State legislative and congressional apportionment laws were
held to be subject to judicial review and to the judicially promulgated "one man, one vote" principle. As a result political power
formerly held disproportionately by a rural America was now
shifted to the cities and the suburbs.

While vigorously denying hostility to religion and explicitly
acknowledging the place of religion to be an "exalted one" in
our society, the Court interpreted the establishment clause (as
applied to the states through the Fourteenth Amendment) to
prohibit the recital of prayers or the reading of Bible passages
at the opening of daily classroom activity in the nation's public
schools—practices long established and deeply cherished in thousands of communities.

Law enforcement officials of state and local governments were
greatly disturbed when the Court determined that the commands
of due process of law called for rules of criminal procedure which
required the states to provide counsel for indigent defendants,
which exacted assurances that the accused be made aware of his
right to be advised by counsel throughout the course of an
accusatorial investigation, and which tested confessions against
direct as well as indirect forms of police coercion and persuasion.

Traditional concepts of private property and private choice
received severe blows, and civil rights demonstrations gained
new legal status, when the Court struck down convictions of
trespass imposed on Negro sit-ins protesting segregated lunch
counters and other segregated places of public accommodation.
A national determination to end a wide variety of governmentally
sanctioned forms of discrimination was then further underscored
when the Court upheld unanimously the Civil Rights Act of 1964.

Supreme Court decisions dealing with questions of such magnitude involved major questions of public policy. It has long been
a truism in American government to assert that although legislatures enact laws and executives execute them, it is left to the
judiciary to say what is and what is not constitutional. The
Constitution itself is what the judges construe it to be. Not quite.

When a Supreme Court decision is handed down, that does not mean that automatic compliance can be expected—far from it. In the final analysis, it is the judges, state and federal, the governors, state legislators, policemen, prosecuting attorneys, boards of education, superintendents of instruction—the over-whelming majority of politicians and citizens who must be willing to live up to the norms of conduct that such legal pronounce-ments stipulate. To the outcomes of judicial decision-making there is no neutrality. In this process of accommodation of con-flicting interests and values, usually someone gains and someone loses. Broadly speaking, those who gained from the libertarian decisions of the last decade were the poor, the ill-educated, the underprivileged and the underrepresented. Their legal victories necessarily entailed losses in privilege and power to many Amer-icans who viewed these constitutional developments with much apprehension and intense hostility.

How highly controversial and widely resented some of the Supreme Court decisions were was brought out by Louis Harris in his survey published in November, 1966.

. . .

HIGH COURT APPROVAL[1]

The U.S. Supreme Court has become a highly controversial branch of government and is able to muster an over-all vote of confidence from less than half the American people. The public, whatever constitutional principles may be involved, is most critical of two key decisions: the banning of prayers in public schools and the refusal to accept confessions made by suspects before they can obtain legal counsel.

In a survey the public gives a negative rating to the job done by the nation's highest court by 52–48 per cent. This is largely the result of the court's extreme unpopularity in the South, although the Midwest approximates the national average of disapproval.

"Popular" decisions by the court include three landmark cases decided in recent years. For example, every group by a 3-to-1 ratio

1 The Harris Survey, November 14, 1966. Copyright © 1966, The Washington Post Company. Reprinted with permission.

specifically supports the "one-man, one-vote" decision which required many states to reapportion legislative districts on a population basis. Furthermore, with the exception of the South, the decisions to outlaw segregation in the schools and in public accommodations met with close to 2-to-1 public approval.

A sixth decision—that which forbids the State Department from denying passports to Communists—splits the public almost down the middle.

A consistent pattern in the results reveals that younger people, Negroes and the better educated tend to back the court while white Southerners, older people and the less well-educated tend to be the court's severest critics.

Rating of the U.S. Supreme Court

The special cross section of the public was asked:

"How would you rate the job the U.S. Supreme Court has been doing—excellent, pretty good, only fair or poor?

A young husband in Columbia, Miss., said: "I have two school-age children. Therefore, I don't like what the court is doing—

	Good-Excellent Per cent	Only Fair-Poor Per cent
Nationwide	48	52
By region		
East	52	48
Midwest	48	52
South	35	65
West	55	45
By age		
Under 35	58	42
35-49	51	49
50 and over	42	58
By education		
8th grade or less	44	56
High school	46	54
College	53	47

period." Said an Illinois housewife: "I'm disturbed about this bending over backward to take care of the single individual. What about the majority who want the opposite?"

The court, however, is not without supporters. "They are trying to eliminate some of the bigotry," said a 64-year-old woman from Los Angeles. "They have put the churches on their toes," added a neighbor: "They've stuck their necks out and taken stands when they could have avoided it."

Six Key Decisions

Here is the roster of approval and disapproval by the public on six key Supreme Court decisions:

	Approve Per cent	Disapprove Per cent
Reapportionment: one man, one vote	76	24
Desegregation of schools	64	36
Desegregation of public accommodations	64	36
Allowing Communists passports	49	51
Disallowing confessions without counsel	35	65
Outlawing prayers in classrooms	30	70

In the South, only the reapportionment decision meets with public approval. The public accommodations decision, upholding the 1964 Civil Rights Act, is opposed more than 2 to 1. It is significant, however, that the 1954 court decision on school integration is now supported by 44 per cent of all Southerners, indicating that opposition tends to dwindle with time.

By contrast, Negroes heartily support five out of six of the key decisions. They are heavily influenced by the forthright position of the court on racial equality, but they are opposed to the school prayer ban by 3 to 1, indicating the strong religious feeling that exists in the Negro community.

Young people appear to be far more aroused about individual civil liberties than their elders. This is undoubtedly a reflection of the feelings of this younger generation that nonconformity is vital to a free society. Clearly, the issue of dissent has split the generations in America in the mid-1960's.

.   .   .

For the sake of constitutional government and orderly national development, it will increasingly become the responsibility of political leadership to demonstrate with imagination and vigor that the new protections and opportunities offered in the name of civil liberty represent not an invitation to license and chaos, but a constructive effort to adapt the individualistic faith of the Founding Fathers to the pluralistic society of the twentieth century—that they represent constitutional implementations of the American dream of equality for all people, irrespective of race, religion or economic status.

I

Freedom of Association—
Communists and
Internal Subversion

"His Name Just Happened To Come Up"

From *Herblock's Special For Today* (Simon & Schuster, 1958).

As Cold War pressures intensified in the years following World War II, so did the fervor and intensity of congressional investigations. World Communism was seen as a challenge to American interests and foreign policy on different fronts and continents. There was Stalin's sullen intransigence in negotiations and the ruthless consolidation of the Soviet empire behind an Iron Curtain in Eastern Europe. Berlin had become a divided city with Russian and American tanks and soldiers facing each other in battle readiness across barbed wire and walls. After a long and bloody civil war, Communist armies forced Chiang Kai-shek and his nationalist regime out of China and brought to power a dictatorship of the peasant proletariat under the leadership of Mao Tse-Tung. On June 25, 1950, North Korean Communist troops crossed the 38th parallel leading to massive Chinese and United States military involvements in a strenuous three-year war which proved politically unpopular in this country and divisive in the Western Alliance. Meanwhile the atomic and nuclear armaments race grew more competitive, and the United States-Soviet propaganda war more acrimonious.

What had happened to the dreams of a peaceful world, to the assurances of the United Nations Charter, to the promises of the Four Freedoms? Americans were apprehensive, frustrated and disillusioned. To many there seemed to be one central and coordinating force guiding the course of events towards the ultimate destruction of this country, its institutions, and its way of life—the Communist world revolution directed and supported by Moscow. To these Americans, Communist moves were met by responses of the United States government that appeared inexplicably inept and ineffective. On the face of it, neither the President, nor his advisors in the State Department, nor the other officials instrumental in the making or implementing of foreign policy seemed to evidence a proper understanding of the enemy and of his operations.

In Congress powerful forces were prepared to share and further articulate these convictions, suspicions and anxieties. Testimony by former Communists and undercover agents before the House Committee on Un-American Activities, the Senate Internal Security Subcommittee and the Senate Permanent Investigations Subcommittee charged infiltrations in the labor movement, in the entertainment industry and in colleges and universities. Communist cells were shown to have operated in Washington even in the pre-war years and certain espionage agents were alleged to have been linked to Communist contacts working for the Office of Strategic Services (OSS), the State Department, Treasury Department and other governmental agencies.

As twenty years of Democratic administration came to an end, these congressional investigating committees and their activities moved aggressively to the center of the political stage. Committee Chairmen like Senators Joseph R. McCarthy, William Jenner, and Pat McCarran dominated the headlines with their accusations of Communist subversion and duplicity in and out of government. Widest possible coverage and publicity was given to heated exchanges between witnesses who refused to testify on constitutional grounds and hostile questioners who claimed it to be their patriotic duty to force into the open revelations of conspiratorial conduct and associations.

Tons of newsprint and thousands of pages of committee hearings were filled with the charges and counter-charges that surrounded such prominent names as Harry Dexter White, Alger Hiss, Whittaker Chambers, Elizabeth Bentley, Louis F. Budenz, William W. Remington and Owen Lattimore. Attempts by Congress to sort out truth from falsehood, to balance the rights of ideological dissent with the requirements of national security and to ascertain realistically "the clear and present danger" that Communism posed proved most difficult under the circumstances.

Its decisions had to be taken against a background of unresolved conflicts characterized by nostalgic memories of a simpler and more satisfying isolationist past, by genuine concerns with America's stance against Communist expansionism, by failures of presidential and executive leadership and by the harshest demands of partisan politics.

Such, essentially, was the temper and setting in which Congress legislated against the Communist menace.

Laws Against Internal Subversion

When Congress in 1954 passed the Communist Control Act, this nation's arsenal was already brimming with legal weapons that could be used in battles against those who sought the violent overthrow of government. Anti-sedition laws were available in forty-four states, in Alaska and in Hawaii. On the federal level, treason was defined in Article III of the United States Constitution and enforced by legislation going back to 1790. Anti-insurrectionist and anti-conspiracy statutes were added in 1861 and 1862. World War I saw the enactment of laws dealing with espionage, with the dissemination of subversive doctrines and with efforts to obstruct the draft or military recruiting. Legislation aimed at the registration of aliens, of agents serving foreign governments and of organizations operating under foreign control made its first appearance on the eve of World War II. Of such measures, the Smith Act of 1940 stood out as the most comprehensive and controversial. Title I of the Act had made it a crime (1) to advocate, "the duty, necessity, desirability or propriety of overthrowing or destroying any government in the United States by force or violence"; (2) to print, publish, distribute, or issue any seditious materials with the intent of causing "the overthrow or destruction of any government in the United States"; and (3) "to organize or help organize any society, group or assembly of persons" or to become a member of such a group, committed to the destruction of this country's governmental institutions.

In 1950 came the first major postwar statute to incorporate the investigative results of various congressional committees that had conducted hearings on Communist subversion. The Internal Security Act was passed on September 19, but vetoed by the President three days later with a message that expressed his objections in most forceful terms. He warned that the measure was so "broad and vague" that it would "make a mockery of the Bill of Rights," that it "would open a Pandora's box of opportunities for official condemnation of organizations and individuals for perfectly honest opinions which happen to be stated also by Communists" and that its provision for the registration of Communists was "about as practical as requiring thieves to register with the sheriff." Congress was unimpressed. Next day, after a short and bitter debate the veto was overridden with heavy, bipartisan majorities.

As to the Act itself, Title I introduced congressional "findings" which reflected the basic presuppositions and understandings concerning the nature of Communism that dominated most of the arguments of its principal framers and supporters—Senators Karl Mundt, Richard Nixon, McCarran, and Homer Ferguson.

There exists a world Communist movement which, in its origins, its development, and its present practice, is a worldwide revolutionary movement whose purpose it is, by treachery, deceit, infiltration into other groups (governmental and otherwise), espionage, sabotage, terrorism and any other means deemed necessary, to establish a Communist totalitarian dictatorship in the countries throughout the world through the medium of a worldwide Communist organization. . . .

The direction and control of the world Communist movement is vested in and exercised by the Communist dictatorship of a foreign country. . . .

The world Communist movement establishes . . . in various countries, action organizations which are not free and independent organizations, but are sections of a worldwide Communist organization and are controlled, directed and subject to the discipline of the Communist dictatorship of such foreign country. . . .

The Communist action organizations . . . acting under such control, direction and discipline endeavor to carry out the objectives of the world Communist movement by bringing about the overthrow of the existing government by any available means. . . . Although such organizations usually designate themselves as political parties, they are in fact constituent elements of the worldwide Communist movement and promote the objectives of such movement by conspiratorial and coercive tactics, instead of through the democratic processes of a free elective system. . . .

Communist organizations in various countries . . . operate to a substantial extent through organizations, commonly known as "Communist fronts," which in most instances are created and maintained, or used, in such manner as to conceal the facts as to their true character and purposes and membership. One result of this method of operation is that such affiliated organizations are able to obtain financial and other support from persons who would not extend such support if they knew the true purposes of and the actual nature of the control and influence exerted upon, such "Communist fronts". . . .

In the United States those individuals who knowingly and willfully participate in the world Communist movement . . . in effect repudiate their allegiance to the United States, and in effect transfer their allegiance to the foreign country in which is vested the direction and control of the world Communist movement. . . .

The Communist movement in the United States is an organization numbering thousands of adherents, rigidly and ruthlessly disciplined. Awaiting and seeking to advance a moment when the United States may be so far extended by foreign engagements, so far divided in counsel or so far in industrial or financial straits, that overthrow of the Government of the United States by force and violence may seem possible of achievement, it seeks converts far and wide by an extensive system of schooling and indoctrination. . . . The Communist organization in the United States, pursuing its stated objectives, the recent successes of Communist methods in other countries and the nature and control of the world Communist movement itself, presents a clear and present danger to the security of the United States and to the existence of free American institutions. . . .

Given these characteristics of the Communist movement, the Internal Security Act provisions aimed at the registration, restriction and public exposure of its members, organs and fellow conspirators.

A five-member, presidentially-appointed Subversive Activities

Control Board was given power to conduct hearings and to determine (subject to judicial review) whether a particular organization was a Communist action or "front" group and whether it served the Communist movement and its conspiratorial objectives. In deciding what constituted a "Communist-action organization," the Board was to weigh a number of factors. First, the extent to which the policies, leadership, activities and finances of a suspect group were under the domination, discipline or direction of the world Communist movement or of foreign governments controlled by it; second, the extent to which the organization concealed the nature of the foreign direction or the details of its membership; and third, the extent to which "its principal leaders or substantial number of its members" subordinate their loyalty to the United States "to such foreign government or foreign organization."

An affirmative conclusion called for the registration (with the Attorney General) of the Communist organization, its officers and membership, and for the imposition of special restrictions and disabilities. Thus members of such groups were legally barred from employment with the federal government, from applying for or using passports and from working in defense establishments. Alien members could be denied entry into the United States, deported, rejected from naturalization or even denaturalized. Failure to register was made subject to heavy fines and to long terms of imprisonment. Section 4(a) of the law made it a criminal act for any person "knowingly to combine, conspire, or agree with any other person to perform any act which would substantially contribute to the establishment within the United States of a totalitarian dictatorship."

One additional provision required that mail, television or broadcasts emanating from "action" or "front" groups had to be labeled Communist propaganda, and another authorized the President to declare an "internal security emergency" in the event of war, invasion or insurrection. Under such circumstances the Attorney General could detain anyone "as to whom there is reasonable ground to believe that such person probably will engage . . ." in acts of conspiracy or sabotage.

Congressional demands for still more drastic restraints persisted. Hearings and reports during 1952 and 1953 further high-lighted allegations of Communist infiltrations in government, labor, education and defense industries. Charges of "twenty years of treason" and of governmental "softness on Communism" increased legislative pressures for openly outlawing the Communist party and for making membership in it criminal.

This campaign was joined to the surprise and chagrin of many civil libertarians by persons with such impeccable credentials of liberalism as Senators Hubert Humphrey, Herbert Lehman and J. William Fulbright. For both tactical and substantive reasons, these Senators seemed persuaded that anti-Communist legislation could no longer be permitted to remain the monopoly of the "professional" Communist haters—let the country know that liberals too objected to subversion and to totalitarianism whether it originated from the right or from the left. Moreover, once it became clear to all that the Communist party was really not a party at all but a criminal conspiracy, then the center of attention could be shifted from the partisanly inclined investigative committees to the less politically charged atmosphere of the Department of Justice and of the courts.

As finally approved by the Senate (79–0) and by the House (265–2) in August of 1954, the Communist Control Act did not technically outlaw the party as such but brought its membership along with members of "Communist-infiltrated organizations" under the restrictions and penalties of the Internal Security Act of 1950.

What the Communist Control Act of 1954 did was to (1) deny to the Communist party ("or any successors of such party regardless of the assumed name") all the rights, privileges and immunities granted to other legal (including political) bodies under American law, (2) bar Communists from holding office in unions or serving as representatives in bargaining negotiations, (3) deprive Communist-infiltrated labor organizations of their bargaining rights under the National Labor Relations Act (as a condition of recourse to the machinery of the National Labor Relations Board, the Taft-Hartley Law of 1947 had already required officers of a union to certify by affidavit [oath] that they were not affiliated with, or members of the Communist party and that they did not believe in the overthrow of government by violent, illegal, or unconstitutional methods) and (4) provide a set of thirteen factors that "a jury, under instructions from the court," should consider in ascertaining "membership or participation" in the Communist party or its organizations. This included whether a person to his knowledge

> had been listed as a member; made a financial contribution; subjected himself to party discipline; carried out any orders of the party; acted as an agent or courier; conferred with officers or members "in behalf of any plan . . ."; had been accepted as an officer or member; communicated with the party; prepared documents or books for the party; mailed or distributed propaganda on its behalf; advised or counseled the officers; indicated by "word, action, conduct, . . . or in any other way a willingness to carry out . . . purposes of the organization."

To round out the legislative picture, briefest reference needs to be made also to a number of additional measures aimed at the control of Communism enacted by the 83rd and subsequent Congresses.

> Witnesses testifying in national security investigations could be given immunity from prosecution (by action of a two-thirds majority and after issuance of a court order at which time the Attorney General must also be heard); Communist action or front groups were required to register their printing equipment; naturalized or native born Americans could be stripped of their citizenship upon conviction of conspiracy to overthrow or destroy by force the government of the United States; penalties were increased for sedition, conspiracy, for harboring fugitives from court action, for persons forfeiting or jumping bail, and for committing sabotage or espionage in peace times as well as during periods of national emergency; the Foreign Agents Registration Act was strengthened and the Post Office Department was authorized to intercept Communist propaganda emanating from foreign sources and not deliver such mail until formally requested to do so by the addressee.

Parallelling these legislative efforts and at times goaded by Congress, the executive branch also adopted various programs designed to battle Communist infiltration and subversion of the federal service. President Truman's Executive Order 9835 (1947) provided for loyalty investigations, for loyalty boards and for hearing and review procedures. Government employment could be refused individuals or their dismissal ordered on evidence that there were reasonable grounds "for the belief that the person involved is disloyal to the government of the United States." A Loyalty Review Board within the Civil Service Commission was given authority to promulgate the necessary rules which were to guide the departments and to state the policies that would govern requests for appeals by employees. In subsequent rulings this Board refused to impose on the government the duty to grant hearings in all circumstances, to disclose its confidential informants or to require the confrontation of the accuser or his cross-examination by the accused. A government job was deemed to be a privilege—not a right. Specifically exempted from referral to the Review Board, moreover, were certain "sensitive" agencies where department heads were given the power by Congress to summarily discharge suspected persons or preclude their employment when considered "necessary or advisable in the interest of national security." This more inclusive and even tougher concept of "security" formed the core of the Eisenhower administration's program under Executive Order 10450. In addition to considerations of loyalty, an individual could henceforth be removed from federal employment as a "security risk" for reasons of personal behavior, sexual misconduct, excessive use of drugs or alcohol or for other mental or physical disorders which could subject him "to coercion, influence, or pressure which may cause him to act contrary to the best interests of national security." By the end of 1954, approximately five million loyalty forms had been processed, 3,000 persons had been discharged as security risks, and another 5,000 had resigned their positions while their security status was under challenge.

Republican claims of having ousted from the government "thousands" of security risks while the previous administration fired only "hundreds" combined with Democratic resentments at what they called the "numbers game" gave the 1954 mid-term elections a peculiar bitterness. Subsequent bipartisan efforts led to the establishment of a national commission to review the federal loyalty and security program (its recommendations did

not, however, become law) and to an order by the Department
of Justice under which the accused was granted rights of limited
confrontation. In cases not involving national security, he or
his counsel were permitted to cross-examine witnesses whose
negative testimony had proved relevant to the charges. More
substantial changes in the official approach to the security problem in federal employment, however, came largely as a result of
judicial rather than executive or legislative decisions.

Dennis v. United States— The Court Sustains Congress

Many Americans, for whom the preservation of dissent ranked
foremost among civil liberties, grew increasingly apprehensive
about what Congress, in the name of fighting Communism,
seemed to be doing in the country and to the Constitution. Were
the methods employed in this battle properly adapted to the
preservation of freedom against totalitarian assaults from abroad
or from within or were these means destroying the very ends
they were supposed to serve? Had not Wisconsin's Senator Mc-
Carthy through his inquisitorial and tempestuous hearings
pointed up the emotional intensity of the Communist issue and
the extent to which public opinion could be aroused and divided?
With a Senate nearly paralyzed through bitter personal controversy and partisan recriminations and an executive either unwilling or unable to contain forces angrily committed to exposure
and accusation, much of the reconciliation of the "means and
ends" dilemma surrounding the nation's quest for security from
Communism was bound to be significantly affected by decisions
of the United States Supreme Court.

   Dennis v. *United States* (1951) presented the first major test.
Eleven top Communist party leaders had been indicted and convicted of conspiracy under the Smith Act (1) for teaching and
advocating and (2) for organizing the Communist party to teach
and advocate the violent overthrow of the United States government. After a widely publicized, seven-months district court trial

in New York, a 6 to 2 vote of the Supreme Court sustained their convictions and upheld the constitutionality of the Act. In the district court, Judge Medina had charged the jury that they could not convict unless they decided that the defendants intended "to overthrow . . . the Government of the United States by force and violence as speedily as circumstances would permit." Justice Fred M. Vinson writing for the Supreme Court held this instruction to be thoroughly compatible with the "clear and present danger" standard formulated by Justice Oliver W. Holmes in the *Schenck* case (1919). As now construed by Vinson, the standard did not require (1) "that before a Government may act, it must wait until the *putsch* is about to be executed," (2) that a "conspiracy to advocate . . ." is beyond constitutional restraint "because it comprises only the preparation" and (3) that a judge must submit to the jury the question whether there was enough substantive danger in this Communist conspiracy to permit Congress to exempt it from the protections of the First Amendment.

In affirming for the Circuit Court of Appeals, Judge Learned Hand had declared that courts "must ask whether the gravity of the 'evil', discounted by its improbability, justifies such invasion of free speech as is necessary to avoid the danger." Vinson agreed with this modification of the "clear and present danger" rule, and concluded that the world crisis and the readiness of the Communist party to exploit it was of sufficient immediacy to warrant a finding of criminal conspiracy.

Lengthy concurrences were entered by Justices Felix Frankfurter and Robert Jackson. Frankfurter stressed that primary responsibility for the complex process of balancing the interests of national security with the guarantees of freedom enshrined in the Bill of Rights must lie with Congress and not with the Courts: "[A]ll the Court says is that Congress was not forbidden by the Constitution to pass this enactment and that a prosecution under it may be brought against a conspiracy such as the one before us."

Born of a different age, the "clear and present danger" doctrine was held by Jackson to be entirely inapplicable to the coup d'etat type of power seizure which Communists have adopted

in overturning free governments. Reliance on the law of conspiracy would have been a more appropriate remedy since
"[t]here is no constitutional right to 'gang up' on the Government."

Justice Hugo Black dissented and so did Justice William
Douglas. As Black saw the issue, defendants were indicted for a
conspiracy "to organize the Communist party and to use speech
or newspapers and other publications *in the future* to teach and
advocate the forcible overthrow of the Government" (*emphasis
supplied*). This he viewed as a form of prior restraint incompatible with the First Amendment and as a repudiation of the
"clear and present danger" test. He concluded his brief statement
with a rejection of Frankfurter's "balancing of interests" thesis
and with this admonition to his fellow citizens:

> Public opinion being what it now is, few will protest the conviction
> of these Communist petitioners. There is hope, however, that in
> calmer times, when present pressures, passions and fears subside, this
> or some later Court will restore the First Amendment liberties to the
> high preferred place where they belong in a free society.

Douglas, in his dissent, based major emphasis on the failure
of the government to provide any evidence whatever that Communists constituted an internal threat to the United States.
Speech, in the absence of any showing of sabotage or unlawful
conduct, was treated as "the equivalent of overt acts of treasonable or seditious character." In a country such as ours where
Communism has been thoroughly exposed, where the party has
never attained much of a following, where the doctrines of revolution have gained few adherents, where people are neither starving
nor disillusioned, where literacy is high and democratic traditions
strong—in such a country, Communists "are miserable merchants
of unwanted ideas; their wares remain unsold. The fact that their
ideas are abhorrent does not make them powerful."

With majorities in Congress and Court thus legally proscribing
Communist party membership, the Department of Justice and
federal district attorneys initiated fourteen additional conspiracy
suits leading to a total of 104 convictions.

Nor did *Dennis* stand alone. Its conclusions had important
ramifications in at least seven other cases in which the Court

upheld various state and federal measures of Communist control between 1951 and 1956.

Garner v. *Board of Public Works of Los Angeles* (1951)—Upheld the right of the City of Los Angeles to inquire into past memberships and loyalty of its employees. The city's charter had forbidden the employment of persons affiliated with organizations which advocate the forceful overthrow of govemnent.

Adler v. *Board of Education* (1952)—New York's Feinberg law made it unlawful for public school employees to be members of organizations advocating overthrow of government by violence. Listing of such organizations (after hearing) and refusal to retain or employ persons belonging to such groups (after hearing and subject to judicial review) was upheld.

Harisiades v. *Shaughnessy* (1952)—Sustained the power of Congress, under the Alien Registration Act of 1940, to authorize deportation of aliens because of membership in the Communist party, even if membership tei ninated before the Act was passed.

Carlson v. *Landon* (1952)—Detention of an alien Communist taken into custody and held without bail as authorized under thc Internal Security Act did not constitute a denial of due process of law.

Barsky v. *Board of Regents* (1954)—Failure of defendant to respond to a subpoena of a congressional committee and his subsequent conviction became the basis for a six-month suspension of his medical license by New York. Supreme Court held that this did not deny him any constitutional rights.

Galvan v. *Press* (1954)—Upheld deportation of a resident alien under the Internal Security Act for having been a member of the Communist party (1944–1946) although it was not shown that he was aware of its advocating the overthrow of government by use of violence.

The Warren Court Asserts Itself, 1955-1957

With President Eisenhower's Supreme Court appointments of Earl Warren and William J. Brennan there emerged notable changes in the reception given by the Court to those federal legislative and executive actions against Communism which lib-

erals saw as impinging on individual freedoms. Much has been
written about the peculiar ideological unpredictability of a judge
newly coming to the bench. Frankfurter had greatly disappointed
his liberal supporters and Warren, the new Chief Justice—former
Republican Governor of California and Vice-Presidential nominee
of the Republican party—soon caused equal anguish to conservatives. (See Chapter II for reactions to the *Brown* v. *Board
of Education* decision.)

When the Eisenhower security program came up for judicial
review in *Cole* v. *Young* (1956), a majority of the Court concluded that the petitioner, a food and drug administrator in the
Department of Health, Education and Welfare, could not be
discharged as a security risk under authority of Executive Order
10450 and the Personnel Suspension Act of 1950. These provisions
were designed to give summary discharge powers to heads of
federal departments and agencies when in their judgment the
continued retention of an employee was no longer "clearly consistent with the interests of national security." Petitioner had
been charged for having had a "close association with individuals
reliably reported to be Communists," for having contributed
funds to a group on the Attorney General's list, and for having
"attended social gatherings of an allegedly subversive organization." Upon refusal to respond to the accusations and failing to
request a hearing, petitioner's employment was ordered termin-
ated.

With HEW not having been one of the specifically selected
eleven "sensitive" agencies included in the Act of 1950, the Court
found the Executive Order unreasonably ambiguous and vague
in that it required discharge of any employee "regardless of the
character of his position in the government service." Moreover,
it noted that there was no formal determination by the department head of the "effect which continuance of his employment
might have upon 'national security'." Since Congress could not
have intended such excessive discretion, the majority decided
to resolve the doubt in favor of the petitioner and against the
government.

Justice Tom Clark, joined by Justices Stanley Reed and Sherman Minton, objected to the interpretation by the majority that

the Act of 1950 applied to "sensitive agencies" only and that there had to be a finding not merely "that a particular person is subversive, but also that he occupies a sensitive job." As far as the dissenters were concerned, "[t]he janitor might prove to be in as important a spot security-wise as the top employee in the building." Matters pertaining to security under the Act were left to presidential judgment; he rightfully expected "complete and unswerving loyalty"; the Court should not "subvert" this intent by "technical interpretation."

Public and congressional reactions to *Cole* were mild in comparison to the storm of criticisms and vituperations that whirled around the Supreme Court as a result of its decisions in *Pennsylvania* v. *Nelson* (1956), *Watkins* v. *United States* (1957) and *Yates* v. *United States* (1957).

In *Nelson,* Warren, holding for the Court, stated that the aggregate of congressional anti-Communist legislation was "intended to occupy the field of sedition" and therefore "superseded" Pennsylvania's sedition statute under which Steve Nelson, an acknowledged Communist, had been tried and convicted. Without such federal preemption, he reasoned, the forty-three states with similar sedition laws might wish to exercise concurrent jurisdiction. This would greatly complicate federal law enforcement and raise substantial constitutional issues of multiple or double punishment. Justices Reed, Harold Burton and Minton argued to the contrary, that the Court "should not void state legislation without a clear mandate from Congress." That law enforcement difficulties might arise gives the courts "no valid reason for ousting a state from exercise of its police power." Owing to the federal structure of our government, criminal law, in the absence of specific congressional intent to the contrary, has always depended on the widest participation of state law enforcement officials, concluded the Reed dissent.

Watkins produced a major frontal collision between the Court and the Congress. At issue was the scope of inquiry in an investigation conducted by the House Un-American Activities Committee of alleged Communist subversion in the labor movement.

Petitioner, who had been identified by two committee witnesses as a card-carrying Communist, complied with the subpoena, testified "freely and without reservation" as to his own background of union activities and acknowledged that he cooperated with Communists, that he contributed to Communist causes, that he attended meetings at which Communists were present, but that he "never carried a Communist party card" and never submitted himself to the discipline of the party.

"A more complete and candid statement . . . could hardly be imagined," was the assessment that the government's brief rendered of the degree of cooperation that Watkins gave to the Committee. But when Committee counsel read a list of names of alleged Communists and asked petitioner to identify those whom he knew, the witness balked.

> I will answer any questions which this committee puts to me about myself. I will also answer questions about those persons whom I knew to be members of the Communist party and whom I believe still are. I will not, however, answer any questions with respect to others with whom I associated in the past. I do not believe that any law in this country requires me to testify about persons who may in the past have been Communist party members or otherwise engaged in Communist party activity but who to my best knowledge and belief have long since removed themselves from the Communist movement.

Rejecting these grounds for silence, Congress voted a contempt citation and the Department of Justice initiated proceedings which led to Watkins' conviction.

On review, Chief Justice Warren examined (1) the constitutional status of congressional investigations in general and (2) the scope of the resolution which guided this particular inquiry. After tracing historical origins and precedents, he readily granted that constitutionally there could be no question that the lawmaking powers of Congress included the power to carry out legislative investigations. Encompassed were inquiries to expose corruption, waste or inefficiencies in government as well as inquiries to furnish the informational basis on which Congress could predicate its laws. This power was traditional, it was pervasive and general—but was it unlimited? No, insisted Warren. To hold so "would be to abdicate the responsibility placed by the Constitution upon the judiciary to insure that the Congress does not unjustifiably encroach upon an individual's right to privacy . . ." and to other freedoms granted him by the Bill of Rights. An inquiry is not an end in itself; it must further "a legitimate task of Congress." It cannot be conducted "solely for the personal aggrandizement of the investigators or to 'punish' those investigated . . . ; there is no congressional power to expose for the sake of exposure." Under the Constitution, Congress is neither charged with the enforcement of the law nor with its adjudication. These are functions reserved to the executive and to the courts.

When conducting investigations and compelling testimony, a committee functions as "the eyes and the ears of the Congress." It receives its power under an authorizing resolution—its charter, which defines the investigative purpose and sets the limits. In this case, the Committee was charged with investigating ". . . the extent, character, and objects of un-American propaganda activities in the United States . . . [and] the diffusion within the United States of subversive and un-American propaganda that . . . attacks the principle of the form of government as guaranteed by our Constitution. . . ." Warren queried, "[W]ho can define the meaning of 'un-American'? What is that single, solitary 'principle of the form of government . . .'?" He concluded that "[i]t would be difficult to imagine a less explicit authorizing resolution."

With such an excessively vague charter, the committee or its subcommittee was left to define its own authority, direction and focus, and the witness was left without any standard with which to judge the pertinence of the questions he was required to answer. "Fundamental fairness demands that no witness be compelled to make such a determination with so little guidance." Warren ordered the judgment of the Court of Appeals reversed and the dismissal of the indictment by the district court.

Justice Clark was the only dissenter. The majority, it seemed to him, engaged in a "mischievous curbing of the informing function of the Congress." Watkins did have "complete knowledge and understanding of the hearings. . . . " The questions were "entirely pertinent to the announced purpose of the Committee's inquiry," and his refusal to furnish the necessary identifications prevented the Committee from learning more about the techniques and extent of Communist infiltration in the labor movement. While the meaning of "un-American" may not be precise, "these are fairly well understood terms" which the Court should construe not critically but supportively under the presumption that Congress had full power to inquire into such subject matter. Courts are not made "supervisors of congressional investigations" under the separation of power principle, nor must the conduct of the committee system meet the standards of exactness or explicitness required in criminal proceedings. "So long as the object of a legislative inquiry is legitimate and the questions propounded are pertinent thereto, it is not for the courts to interfere with the committee system of inquiry." Watkins was not entitled to remain silent in order to protect himself or his former associates on "the grounds that his rights were being abridged." The Constitution acknowledges "no general privilege of silence."

Yates, the third in this group of "reaction-provoking" cases involved the conspiracy convictions of fourteen "second-string" California Communists. Defendants were charged with (1) organizing the Communist party and (2) conspiring "to advocate and teach the duty and necessity of overthrowing the Government of the United States by force and violence." As to the first charge, Justice John M. Harlan, speaking for the majority of the Court, rejected the government's contention that the term "organizing" as used in the Smith Act connotes "a continuing process"—an on-going activity unaffected by the three-year statute of limitations. Since the indictment was not brought until 1951, while the Communist party had been organized in 1945, and since criminal statutes under "the familiar rule . . . are to be strictly construed," that phase of the government's case had to be thrown out. (Actually the party was first founded in 1919; its reorganization as the Communist Political Association occurred in 1942; out of this emerged, three years later, the new Communist party.)

As far as the development of the law of free association is concerned, the second part of the indictment posed the most significant issue. Did the Smith Act prohibit

> advocacy and teaching of forcible overthrow *as an abstract principle, divorced from any effort to instigate action* to that end, so long as such advocacy or teaching is engaged in with evil intent (*emphasis supplied*)?

Having stipulated the question in this form, the Court replied
"[w]e hold that it does not."

Why was *Dennis* which had upheld the Act not controlling? In
comparing the two cases Harlan distinguished *Yates* for the failure
of the judge to instruct the jury that the Smith Act aimed not
at ideas or at the discussion of revolutionary goals but more
precisely at the advocacy of action.

> . . . The District Court appears to have been led astray by the holding
> in *Dennis* that advocacy of violent action to be taken at some future
> time was enough. It seems to have considered that, since inciting
> speech is usually thought of as something calculated to induce im-
> mediate action, and since *Dennis* held advocacy of action for future
> overthrow sufficient, this meant that advocacy, irrespective of its
> tendency to generate action, is punishable, provided only that it is
> uttered with a specific intent to accomplish overthrow . . . ; the Dis-
> trict Court apparently thought that *Dennis* obliterated the traditional
> dividing line between advocacy of abstract doctrine and advocacy of
> action.

What the jury in *Dennis* found was a seditious group ready for
action at a time considered "propitious," and what the Supreme
Court held was that the government did not need to await the
completion of the "putsch." In this case, however, "mere doctrinal
justification" of forcible overthrow was held punishable *per se*.
It was not made adequately clear to the jury that those "to whom
the advocacy is addressed must be urged to *do* something, now or
in the future, rather than merely to believe in something" (*emphasis supplied by Court*).

There was more to the "reconstruction" of *Dennis* or to what
competent scholars of the Court have labeled the "Retreat from
Dennis." Government evidence to the effect that five of the defendants were merely members, officers or functionaries of the
Communist party, Harlan stressed, "would not permit a jury to
find that they were members of such a conspiracy." On the ground
that the government's evidence was much "too meagre" to justify
another trial, he ordered their immediate acquittal. As to the
nine other defendants, from the fact that they conducted classes
and engaged in "systematic teaching and advocacy of illegal"
action, a jury could find that "one of the purposes of such classes

was to develop in the members of the group a readiness to engage at the crucial time . . ." in moments of national crisis "in such activities as sabotage and street fighting, in order to divert and diffuse the resistance of the authorities and if possible to seize local vantage points." For these and some additional similar reasons, the Court felt justified to order their retrial.

Black and Douglas, no doubt pleased that the Court seemed to be moving closer to their dissents in *Dennis,* would have reversed all of the convictions outright. Black, who wrote the partial concurrence and dissent in *Yates* observed that the Smith Act trials allowed as evidence Marxist "books, tracts, pamphlets, newspapers, and manifestoes," much of it written over a hundred years ago which were introduced to drown a jury in a "turgid, diffuse, abstruse, and just plain dull . . . jungle of verbiage." In the absence of proof showing an overt act of treasonable conspiracy, Black placed his trust in the values of the First Amendment which he interpreted as assuring all Americans of complete freedom to advocate causes and forms of government, however repugnant and "obnoxious" to the majority. Justice Clark dissented again. He would have affirmed the convictions on the grounds that the conspiracy in *Yates* was in its essentials parallel to that condemned in *Dennis*—the California setting being the only difference. These defendants, though lower in the party hierarchy, "served in the same army and were engaged in the same mission." They were organizing the party as the indictment charged, and despite the frustrating construction that the Court placed on "organizing," their activities were precisely what the Smith Act sought to proscribe. There was no doubt in Clark's mind that *Yates* would significantly weaken the government's future efforts to inflict criminal sanctions on Communists.

His prophecy came close to the mark. Largely as a result of *Yates,* the government moved to cease proceedings or to dismiss Smith Act indictments which meant that less than a third of all the Communists convicted under it served their prison terms. With the Act's "organizing" and "advocating" provisions thus narrowly construed there still remained the "membership" clause. Its demise, for practical purposes, came in *Noto* v. *United States* (1961). Once more relying heavily on *Yates,* the Court further restrained government prosecutions by stipulating that before criminality can be established under that clause, there must be substantial proof that the defendant wished to attain the objectives of the party by his own personal willingness to "resort to violence." Such concrete evidence was provided in one case, in *Scales* v. *United States* (1961), decided on the same day as *Noto*. Here a divided Court did affirm the conviction of a defendant who had been a director of a Communist training school in which detailed instruction was given as to how the forceful overthrow of government was to be accomplished.

Before concluding the survey of the remarkably liberal decisions of the 1956–1957 terms, at least three additional cases should be mentioned—all of them cases in which a divided Court supported the rights of individuals against the actions of state government.

Konigsberg v. *State Bar of California* (1957)—Petitioner's refusal to answer questions by the state bar examiners concerning his past political affiliations and membership in the Communist party had led to the rejection of his application for admission to the California Bar on the ground that there was substantial doubt with regard to his moral character and loyalty. In the absence of reliable evidence of immoral conduct or subversive activity, conviction was reversed and remanded as an infringement of First Amendment rights.

Sweezy v. *New Hampshire* (1957)—Defendant was questioned by New Hampshire's Attorney General under a law authorizing this official to investigate subversive activities as a "one-man legislative committee." Questions were asked concerning defendant's past political associations, those of his wife and those of certain named individuals. He was also queried about the treatment given to the subject of socialism in one of his lectures at the University of New Hampshire. Although testifying to never having been a member of the Communist Party, he declined, under the First Amendment and as a matter of principle, to answer questions regarding his political beliefs and opinions. Conviction for contempt was reversed as an invasion of academic freedom, "enshrined" by the First Amendment.

Slochower v. *Board of Higher Education of City of New York* (1956) —Petitioner, a tenured associate professor of German at Brooklyn College, was summarily dismissed from his position shortly after he invoked the Fifth Amendment against self-incrimination at a hearing before the Senate Internal Security Subcommittee. Slochower testified that he was not a Communist party member, but refused to answer questions regarding his political associations between 1940 and 1941. Reversed and remanded. "The privilege against self-incrimination would be reduced to a hollow mockery if its exercise could be taken as equivalent either to a confession of guilt or a conclusive presumption of perjury."

The Court in Precarious and Ambiguous Balance, 1958–1962

Anti-Court feelings in Congress rose to new heights in 1958. Grievances were deep and supported by powerful political pressures and politicians. Earlier Court decisions pertaining to school desegregation contributed to these anti-Court feelings. Court rulings that seemed to strengthen the powers and prerogatives of the federal government at the expense of the states and their rights when it came to fighting Communism and subversion were bitterly resented by conservatives of both political parties. Equally resented were judicial censures and strictures of congressional and state investigations and of laws against Communism and sedition. Ceaseless attacks on these controversial decisions by hostile critics in the Congress, press and, on occasion, in the pulpit once again spurred legislative demands to curb the Court and its jurisdiction.

S. 2646, co-sponsored in the 85th Congress by Senators Jenner (*R.*, Indiana) and John Butler (*R.*, Maryland), represented the strongest of the anti-Court bills. It would have denied judicial review in cases involving

(1) any proceedings of Congress or of one of its committees against a witness charged with contempt;

(2) any federal executive or administrative program adopted under congressional authority for the purpose of removing individuals that may "impair the security of the United States Government";

(3) any state law or executive regulation aimed at controlling "subversive activities" within such a state;

(4) any rules, by-laws, or regulations of any state school authority "concerning subversive activities of its teaching body";

(5) "any law, rule, or regulation of any State, or of any board of bar examiners . . . pertaining to the admission of persons to the practice of law. . . ."

On August 20, 1958, when the measure came to the floor, the Senate voted 49–41 to table it. Major support for the Jenner-Butler proposal came from a coalition of Southern Democrats and conservative Republicans (see Table 1). Its narrow defeat served as a telling reminder that under the Constitution, the appellate jurisdiction of the Supreme Court is very much dependent upon the will of Congress. Ever since *Ex parte McCardle* (1869), it has been a well-established principle of American constitutional law that this congressional will could be exercised at full discretion to contract, to expand or even to abolish opportunities for judicial review in all areas not specifically enumerated in Article III as properly belonging to the Court's original jurisdiction.

Without in any way attempting to account for judicial motivations or presuming the existence of causative links, it is nonetheless true that beginning with the 1958 Court term there could be noted, especially in certain decisions affecting internal security, a significant shift to the ideological right. This shift meant that the Court's majoritarian balance inclined more towards the positions of Frankfurter, Harlan and Clark and less towards those of Warren, Black and Douglas. While this trend certainly could not begin to still all the criticisms of the Court on Capitol Hill, it contributed inevitably to cool, somewhat, legislative tempers and ardors for resorting to radical jurisdictional surgery in the realm of internal security. *Barenblatt* v. *United States* (1958) was one of the major cases that signaled the change.

A thirty-one-year-old psychology professor from Vassar College, Lloyd Barenblatt, was summoned in 1954 by the House Un-American Activities Committee to testify about his political activities while a graduate student at the University of Michigan between 1947 and 1950. His name as a member of an "alleged Communist student organization" had come to the attention of the Committe through the testimony of an ex-Communist. Baren-

TABLE 1

SENATE VOTE ON THE JENNER-BUTLER BILL
AUGUST 20, 1958*

(Defeated 49 to 41; Democrats divided 30 to 16;
Republicans, 19 to 25)

Southern Coalition Support Score†	Southern Democrats		Northern Democrats		Republicans	
	Yes	No	Yes	No	Yes	No
0–20	0	3	0	18	0	1
21–40	0	0	0	3	2	7
41–60	4	1	0	5	10	10
61–80	5	0	0	0	12	1
81–100	7	0	0	0	1	0
Totals	16	4	0	26	25	19

* A "Yes" on this table indicates a vote against a motion to table the Jenner amendment to a minor court bill. A "No" indicates a vote in favor of the motion to table.

† Each senator's individual support score for the coalition is found in *Congressional Quarterly,* February 13, 1959, p. 276. Major issues that involved a split between Northern Democrats and Southern Democrats in 1958 comprised the following: taxation, federal aid programs, "Court-curbing" measures, foreign aid, farm policy, civil rights, labor legislation, and billboard regulation. For further details, see *Congressional Quarterly,* February 13, 1959, p. 271 and the 1958 *Congressional Quarterly Almanac,* p. 767.

PARTY FACTION AND THE VOTE ON THE JENNER-BUTLER BILL*

	% Yes	% No	Total Number of Senators Voting
Northern Democrats	0	100	26
Southern Democrats	80	20	20
All Democrats	35	65	46
All Republicans	57	43	44

* A "Yes" on this table indicates a vote against a motion to table the Jenner amendment to a minor court bill. A "No" indicates a vote in favor of the motion to table.

blatt refused to reply to questions dealing with his political and religious beliefs, and with his private and "associational activities."

In an opinion which sharply delineated the division on the Court, Harlan affirmed the conviction for contempt of Congress. He predicated his argument on three major premises. (1) While *Watkins* was critical of the vagueness of the Committee's basic charter (its authorizing resolution), the Court did not mean to prohibit investigations of this type altogether. (2) Petitioner could not seriously contend that Communist influences in education were not properly within the Committee's purview and that the questions asked were not pertinent. (Sweezy had "not been shown ever to have been connected with the Communist party.") (3) The First Amendment was not violated because

> . . . the balance between the individual and the governmental interests here at stake must be struck in favor of the latter. . . .

Black's dissent in this case has often been cited by civil libertarians as one of his most eloquent ones in the defense of the First Amendment's "preferred position." As he perceived Harlan's argument, the majority would enforce the Bill of Rights only if it was "*reasonable* to do so." But that was not what the written Constitution demanded. These rights were to guard against "*every* encroachment" (*emphasis supplied by Court*), legislative or executive. Even if the balancing thesis were to be applied, Black found the majority's case to be very weak. Our nation's security certainly did not require "stifling the voice of opposition," destroying "the right to err politically," or punishing people "because of those with whom they associate for political purposes." His greatest scorn, however, was reserved for the Un-American Activities Committee itself. As he saw it, the Committee purposefully punished and held up to public scorn and humiliation witnesses who were Communists or who refused to "admit or deny Communist affiliations." Its own acknowledged policy of "pitiless publicity and exposure" led Black to conclude:

> Ultimately all the questions in this case really boil down to one— whether we as a people will try fearfully and futilely to preserve

democracy by adopting totalitarian methods, or whether in accordance with our traditions and our Constitution we will have the confidence and courage to be free.

The influence from *Watkins* took on quite a momentum as the last two Eisenhower appointees, both former circuit judges, made their impact on the Court. With Charles Whittaker (1957, *R.*, Missouri) and Potter Stewart (1959, *R.*, Ohio) joining Frankfurter, Harlan and Clark, a new majority crystallized which held in a number of cases, as it did in *Barenblatt,* that the public interest for disclosure and compelled testimony outweighed the rights of witnesses to remain silent. Three cases will serve to illustrate this point.

Uphaus v. *Wyman* (1959)—Defendant, executive director of World Fellowship, Inc. operating a summer camp in New Hampshire, refused to produce the names of guests for the state's Attorney General who was conducting a one-man legislative investigation of subversion in the state. Court (Clark) held that (1) the New Hampshire Subversive Activities Act was not superseded by the Smith Act (defendant's reliance on *Nelson* "sweeps too broad") and (2) "nexus between World Fellowship and subversive activities disclosed by the record . . ." justified investigation in the interest of the state's "self-preservation" and is "sufficiently compelling to subordinate the interest in . . . privacy. . . ." Conviction affirmed; Brennan and Warren dissented largely on the basis of *Watkins;* Black and Douglas, on the grounds that defendant was deprived of his rights under the First and Fourteenth Amendments.

Wilkinson v. *United States* (1961)—Defendant, a vocal critic of the House Un-American Activities Committee, a suspected Communist and organizer of "intense hostility" to the Committee, refused to answer subcommittee questions including one pertaining to his Communist party membership "as a matter of conscience and responsibility." Committee's inquiry dealt with Communist propaganda and infiltration into basic industries in the South. Court (Stewart) held that (1) Committee resolution authorizing Atlanta hearings was "explicit" and the questions pertinent; (2) that *Barenblatt* had settled the basic competence and validity of HUAC's power to carry out such inquiries; and (3) that the First Amendment claims were inapplicable. Conviction affirmed. Black, Douglas, Brennan and Warren dissented stressing that the record revealed to them that HUAC resorted to its contempt power to harass, expose and punish its critics.

In *Braden* v. *United States* (1961), a companion case to *Wilkinson,* the defendant was an uncooperative witness who had been active in the Emergency Civil Liberties Committee and in the Southern Conference Educational Fund—organizations charged with being connected to the Communist party and with opposing the Committee and its investigations. The Court, dividing as in *Wilkinson,* affirmed his conviction. Relying on *Watkins* and *Sweezy,* defendant had refused to answer questions concerning his activities in these organizations and concerning his membership in the Communist party when he "affixed" his signature on a letter sent out by the Southern Conference opposing congressional bills aimed at nullifying certain Supreme Court decisions. Such reliance, the majority reasoned, was unwarranted where the witness' "refusal to answer was deliberate."

Conservative critics of the Court were particularly reassured when Frankfurter sustained the registration requirements of the Internal Security Act of 1950. In *Communist Party of the United States* v. *Subversive Activities Control Board,* decided June 5, 1961, speaking for Justices Clark, Harlan, Whittaker and Stewart, Frankfurter (in a one hundred page opinion) turned back the Communist party's contention that this requirement of the law (registration) constituted a bill of attainder and that it violated the First Amendment.

Reduced to its core, Frankfurter found that (1) on the basis of the government's briefs which included testimony by such prominent Communist and ex-Communist leaders as Gitlow, Budenz, Browder, voluminous records of the F.B.I., as well as ample evidence of consistent adherence to Soviet programs and policies, the Board could reasonably hold that the Communist party was a Communist action group substantially directed, dominated and controlled by the Soviet Union and the world Communist movement within the meaning of Title II of the Internal Security Act; (2) the Board's reliance on the party's conduct prior to the passage of the Act was not in error, as the defendant contended, but formed the necessary context "within which the implications of present conduct may be known"; (3) the registration provisions which Congress adopted did not outlaw the party but made for its exposure and scrutiny—these were methods reasonably adapted to legislative objectives which were not subject to judicial revision; (4) the law was not a bill of attainder since it failed to single out particular individuals or specified organizations, but merely "described activities in which an organization may or may not engage"; (5) unlike *N.A.A.C.P.* v. *Alabama* and other cases where the Court discovered "no rational relation" in requirements to compel disclosure of membership to a legitimate state interest, the Communist movement's threat to the security of this nation, especially its foreign involvements, poses problems of an entirely different magnitude; (6) where "an existing government is menaced by a worldwide integrated movement which employs every combination of possible means . . . to destroy the government itself . . . ," the First Amendment limitations do not entitle courts to set aside congressional judgments as to how best to meet that threat; (7) there is adequate precedent to hold that a legislature has the power to remove secrecy from organizations and associations if the public interest should make this necessary as illustrated by the Federal Corrupt Practices Act, the Foreign Agents Registration Act and the Federal Regulation of Lobbying Act; and (8) any judicial determination of the party's claim that the registration order subjected it to self-incrimination in repugnance to the Fifth Amendment was premature.

Separate dissents by Warren, Black, Douglas and Brennan encompassed eighty-six pages. They covered the spectrum from a procedural attack on the Board's failure to properly cross-examine certain key witnesses (Gitlow and Budenz) through a direct challenge of the constitutional foundations of the Title II of the Internal Security Act (Subversive Activities Control Act) to the incompatibility of the Act's registration provisions with the Fifth Amendment protections against self-incrimination. Much of it was familiar ground—the dissents in *Dennis* and the rule in *Yates* which viewed the "advocacy directed at promoting unlawful action" necessarily distinguished from the advocacy of forceful overthrow "as an abstract doctrine."

Rights of Free Association for Negroes and Communists

One of the clearest statements of what is meant by freedom of association under the Constitution was enunciated by Justice Harlan in *N.A.A.C.P.* v. *State of Alabama* (1958).

Effective advocacy of both public and private points of view, particularly controversial ones, is undeniably enhanced by group association, as this Court has more than once recognized by remarking upon the close nexus between the freedoms of speech and assembly. . . . It is beyond debate that freedom to engage in association for the advancement of beliefs and ideas is an inseparable aspect of the "liberty" assured by the Due Process Clause of the Fourteenth Amendment which embraces freedom of speech. . . . [I]t is immaterial whether the beliefs sought to be advanced by association pertain to political, economic, religious or cultural matters, and state action which may have the effect of curtailing the freedom to associate is subject to closest scrutiny.

What the Court struck down as an unwarranted abridgment of liberty in this case was an attempt by Alabama to force the N.A.A.C.P. to produce its membership lists or face a heavy fine ($100,000). While the petitioner was willing to cooperate with the other general registration requirements imposed on it as a foreign (New York) corporation seeking to do business in the state, the demand for names was resisted. This in turn earned it a contempt conviction by the Alabama courts. Upon an "uncontroverted showing" that the identification of its members in the past "exposed these members to economic reprisal, loss of employment, threat of physical coercion, and other manifestations of public hostility," Harlan found nothing in the state's request for business records to justify the infraction of the N.A.A.C.P.'s right "to associate freely with others"—a right safeguarded by the Fourteenth Amendment.

Controversies surrounding the organizational efforts of the N.A.A.C.P. gave rise to at least three further important elaborations of associational freedoms.

Bates v. *City of Little Rock* (1960)—Defendant refused to turn over to city clerk names and addresses of local N.A.A.C.P. members as part of information required under local occupation license tax registration procedure; conviction reversed. "When it is shown that state action threatens significantly to impinge upon constitutionally protected freedom it becomes the duty of the Court to determine whether the action bears a reasonable relationship to the achievement of the governmental purpose asserted as its justification." City failed to give any reasons for subjecting the organization to the occupation tax or for the need to know its membership.

Shelton v. *Tucker* (1960)—Teachers in the Arkansas public school system challenged the constitutionality of a statute under which they were required to file an affidavit listing their "organizational connections over the previous five years." While the right to investigate the fitness and competence of its instructional personnel, the disclosure of all associational activities, church, civic, political, etc., was adjudged to be "an unlimited and indiscriminate sweep . . . beyond what was necessary to achieve a legitimate governmental purpose." Reversed: Frankfurter, Harlan, Clark and Whittaker, maintaining that the statute on its face and in the absence of evidence of abuse did not represent an infringement on the Fourteenth Amendment, dissented.

N.A.A.C.P. v. *Button* (1963)—A 1956 Virginia statute prohibited any person or organization not having a direct litigational interest from soliciting legal business. N.A.A.C.P. and its counsel were convicted of violating this law for having assisted Negro litigants in whom they had no direct personal interest, with proceedings aimed at breaking down racial barriers. Conviction reversed—(1) litigation here became "a form of political expression"; (2) in the light of intense hostility to N.A.A.C.P. for its numerous litigations, such law "may easily become a weapon of oppression"; (3) the law violates the Fourteenth Amendment "by unduly inhibiting protected freedoms of expression and association." Dissent—Harlan, Clark and Stewart—"striking down this . . . statute cannot be squared with accepted constitutional doctrine in the domain of state regulatory power over the legal profession."

Extending the "right of association" to Communists, of course, was something else again. Despite small membership (an estimated 10,000 in 1962), American government, law, political and public opinion, for reasons already noted, had placed this group in a special category of disapproval and legal debility. By the early 1960's, however, changes in the political climate at home and abroad permitted some further reassessment of how profound a danger Communists actually posed to the internal security of this nation. Stalin had gone, and world Communism had become polycentric and deeply divided; President Kennedy had called for a "reexamination of the Cold War" and Khrushchev for "peaceful coexistence"; a partial nuclear test-ban treaty had been signed; Soviet preoccupation with Red China had eased Western tensions; successful "consensus politics" and long months of economic prosperity had brought a domestic sense of tranquility and optimism; political power and interest alignments within the Congress had shifted and such well-known fighters of Communism as Senators McCarthy, Jenner and McCarran had disappeared from the Washington scene; F.B.I. surveillance of Communists had been thorough, so thorough it has been rumored that dues from undercover agents constitute a significant item in the party's budget—and, most important for the purpose of this discussion, the membership of the Supreme Court had also undergone change. In 1962, President Kennedy had appointed Byron White (*D.,* Colorado) to succeed Whittaker and Arthur Goldberg (*D.,* Illinois) to succeed Frankfurter. The Warren, Black, Douglas and Brennan bloc gained a pivotal fifth, occasionally even a sixth vote, and the law of "free association" expanded its coverage through a series of highly controversial decisions.

Aptheker v. *Secretary of State,* one of the earliest of the group, was handed down on June 22, 1964. Appellants, admittedly members of the Communist party, had their passports revoked by the Secretary of State under authority of Paragraph 6 of the Subversive Activities Control Act of 1950. The Court was asked to declare Paragraph 6 unconstitutional. "Protection of national security" was the major governmental contention. Goldberg attacked Paragraph 6 for failing to distinguish between (1) degrees of active membership and commitment, (2) purpose of travel (sick relative, etc.) and (3) "security-sensitivity" of the area of travel. He concluded that Paragraph 6 "sweeps too widely and too indiscriminately across the liberty guaranteed in the Fifth

Amendment." Appellants, countered Clark, with whom Harlan and White concurred in the dissent, were not just any ordinary "unknowing" Communists. Elizabeth Gurley Flynn, was Chairman of the Communist party of the United States and Herbert Aptheker served as editor of *Political Affairs,* the party's "theoretical organ." Congress had ample evidence to find that Communists travel on numerous party missions to give orders, exchange secrets and engage in sabotage and espionage. Paragraph 6 was a reasonable congressional plan to deny passports in the interests of national security.

Next to fall in *United States* v. *Brown* (1965) was Paragraph 504 of the Labor-Management Reporting and Disclosure Act of 1959 which barred anyone "who is or has been a member of the Communist party" from serving as an officer or employee of a labor union. Respondent, "an avowed Communist," had been working as a longshoreman on the San Francisco docks. After his election to the executive board of his local he was convicted of having violated that section.

Warren found Paragraph 504 to be a bill of attainder expressly forbidden by Art. I, Sect. 9, Cl. 3 of the Constitution. Instead of using general language and rules to bar persons who "commit certain acts" from interfering with interstate commerce (such as instigating political strikes), Congress explicitly named such individuals "members of the Communist Party." Whether these people actually would cause such strikes is a question which, under the Constitution and the principle of separation of powers, cannot be legislatively ascertained but must be left to the determination of "courts and juries."

Since the Communist party as such has never been outlawed (that, too, would constitute a bill of attainder), mere membership cannot be taken as a "convenient shorthand term" or as an equivalent "for a list of undesirable characteristics."

White dissented, joined by Clark, Harlan and Stewart. As he read Warren's opinion, *American Communications Association* v. *Douds,* a 1950 case which sustained the "predecessor statute of 504" and which should have guided the decision in the present case, was overruled incorrectly and with it the right of Congress to "rationally draw inferences about probable conduct on the basis of political affiliations and beliefs. . . ." What alarmed White even more was that the decision of the Chief Justice could well raise constitutional doubts about any statute that disqualified Communists from sensitive security positions in government unless such a law made explicit provision for individual adjudication proving personal acts of disloyalty. "The basic flaw in the Court's reasoning, however, is its too narrow view of the legislative process." He saw Paragraph 504 "reasonably related to a permissible legislative objective," and therefore would have upheld its constitutionality.

Following these decisions, it came as no great surprise to observers of the Supreme Court, that governmental efforts to register the Communist party under the Acts of 1950 and 1954 were about to come to an unsuccessful end after years of litigation and prodigious investitures of money, legal talent and testimony. In 1961, it may be recalled, the Court had upheld the registration provisions of these acts in *Communist Party of the United States* v. *Subversive Activities Control Board.* There, after the party failed to comply and no membership lists were filed, the Board, following a hearing, instructed the Attorney General to seek the registration of certain named party members.

Later, in 1965, in *Albertson* v. *Subversive Activities Control Board* petitioners challenged the registration order of the Board (which the Court of Appeals had affirmed) on the grounds that it violated their Fifth Amendment rights against self-incrimination. Squarely before the Court was the question of the constitutionality of one of the focal devices in the congressional policy of identifying and exposing Communists. The decisional outcome was not unexpected. If "mere association with the Communist party presents sufficient threat of prosecution" under the membership clause of the Smith Act, and if such admission "cannot be compelled in oral testimony" (on the witness stand), Brennan reasoned for a unanimous Court, then the registration provisions which require such admission in writing must be adjudged "inconsistent with the protection of the self-incrimination clause." Justice White did not participate in this case and Clark wrote a concurrent opinion recalling his doubts as to the constitutionality of the registration provisions first expressed in a 1948 memorandum to the Senate Judiciary Committee while he was Attorney General in President Truman's administration.

Albertson held that the privilege against self-incrimination acted as a shield against the registration of individual Communists. Could this protection be invoked also by officers of the party ordered to register it as a Communist action organization under the terms of the Subversive Activities Act of 1950? The Circuit Court of Appeals for the District of Columbia, decided on March 3, 1957, that they could.

American law does not generally grant such impersonal or artificial legal entities as corporations and unincorporated associations the right to plead the Fifth Amendment when governmental agencies demand certain information regarding their economic activities and decisions. In regulatory inquiries addressed to such entities the public interest is usually considered "paramount." But when Congress subjected Communist party members who were to register to heavy penalties and when the appellant (an unincorporated voluntary association) cannot act except through persons who may not be denied the protections against self-incrimination (*Albertson*) then, concluded the Court, the party's officers too could properly exercise this right and refuse to supply the required data.

Two undercover agents who served as paid informers for the F.B.I. since 1953 and who indicated willingness to sign were ruled unqualified to have "the requisite authority and capacity to supply the information called for. . . ." Judge Prettyman added in his concurrence, "[i]t seems to me close to frivolous to suggest that a person protected by the Fifth Amendment can be compelled to hire an agent, . . . [and] furnish him with the means to instigate a criminal prosecution against him. . . ."

While the Court would not deny Congress the constitutional right to regulate and expose the party, such laws could not simultaneously seek the unconstitutional incrimination of its members. These twin legislative objectives proved constitutionally irreconcilable. On April 4, the Department of Justice formally announced that it would not appeal the decision of the Circuit Court of Appeals—thus concluding a seventeen-year legal battle without the registration of either the Communist party or of a single Communist.

That "second sober look," with which the Warren Court's new liberal majority began to view internal security sanctions that had been purposely designed to restrict the right of free association, was by no means limited to the federal government and its laws or activities. Cases involving state investigations probing into associations, state loyalty oaths and state laws disqualifying Communists from public service also received critical judicial review with results equally favorable to the defendants.

Gibson v. *Florida Legislative Investigating Committee* (1963)— Local N.A.A.C.P. officer was compelled to bring records to committee hearings "to refer to them to determine whether specific individuals, otherwise identified as, or 'suspected of being,' Communists, were N.A.A.C.P. members." This he refused to do. Justice Goldberg argued since the committee failed to establish a "nexus" between the N.A.A.C.P., a legitimate organization, and Communist subversive activities, there was nothing to justify governmental intervention into associational rights protected by the First and Fourteenth Amendments; contempt conviction was reversed. White, Clark, Harlan and Stewart dissenting; Justice White: "The net effect of the Court's decision is . . . to insulate from effective legislative inquiry and preventive legislation the time-proven skills of the Communist party in subverting and eventually controlling legitimate organizations."

Baggett v. *Bullitt* (1964)—Defendants, members of the faculty, staff and student body of the University of Washington brought this action to invalidate that state's loyalty oath as "unduly vague, uncertain, and broad." State employee had to swear that he was not subversive, that he did not belong to the Communist party, or was a "knowing member" of any other subversive organization, and that he would not advocate, abet, advise or teach "any person to commit, attempt to commit, or aid in the commission of any act intended to overthrow, destroy or alter . . . the constitutional form of the government . . . by revolution, force or violence. . . ." According to Justice White, "a person is subversive not only if he himself commits the specified acts but if he abets . . . a third person to commit an act which will assist yet a fourth person . . ." to engage in a proscribed course of action nor is the meaning of "revolution" clear within the context of altering forms of government. The oath was found invalid inasmuch as it does not provide to him, who must solemnly swear, "an ascertainable standard of conduct . . . ; free speech may not be so inhibited. . . ." Reversed: Clark and

Harlan would have affirmed (1) the act was no more vague than the
Maryland "Ober law" which the Court had upheld in an earlier
case and (2) the Supreme Court of Washington should have been
given the first opportunity to construe the meaning of the oath.

Elfbrandt v. *Russell* (1966)—Petitioner, a Quaker and teacher in
the Arizona school system, challenged the constitutionality of the
state's loyalty oath which "subjected to a prosecution anyone who
took the oath and who 'knowingly and wilfully becomes or remains
a member of the Communist party . . . or its subordinate organizations.' " Justice Douglas reversed the decision of the Supreme Court
of Arizona which had upheld the act, on the basis that (1) this
type of law fails to acknowledge that there may be those "who join
an organization but do not share its unlawful purposes" nor intend
"to participate in its unlawful activities"; (2) this law by not requiring a showing of "specific intent" is predicated "on the doctrine of
'guilt by association.' " Dissenting were Justices White, Clark, Harlan
and Stewart who countered that previous cases had unequivocally
guaranteed to states the right to "condition public employment upon
its employees abstaining from knowing membership in the Communist party and other organizations advocating the violent overthrow of the government which employs them. . . ."

Then, on January 23, 1967, in *Keyishian* v. *Board of Regents
of the University of the State of New York,* the Court following
the law of *Aptheker, Baggett* and *Elfbrandt,* declared unconstitutional major provisions in New York's famous Feinberg Act under
which "subversive" teachers and administrators were subject
to summary dismissal from the state's educational system. In a
very real sense *Keyishian* rang down the legal curtain on an epoch
that was stirred by issues and controversies that had few if any
parallels in the development of American civil liberties. Clark
dissented emphatically in *Keyishian:* "No court has ever reached
out so far to destroy so much with so little."

It was an era in which Supreme Court decisions greatly enhanced the rights of the nation's severest critics, in which a
majority of the Court was willing to expound theories of freedom
which were shared neither by majorities in the Congress nor in
public opinion. Some Communists and some suspected of Communism were freed from prison and legal sanction while the

penumbra of permissible governmental intervention and restriction was notably narrowed. It is still true, of course, that the Congress and state legislatures can question witnesses on their past political activities and associations but committee interrogations must meet certain standards of relevance and pertinence. Security risks can still be removed from government employment but here too procedural rights must be safeguarded and summary dismissals limited to truly sensitive positions. Loyalty oaths, however, are constitutionally suspect and—most significant of all for an understanding of the Court's impact on the law of the land—Communist party membership as such can no longer be considered prima facie evidence of subversive conduct. Advocacy of abstract ideas, even revolutionary ideas, was judicially distinguished from actual incitement to unlawful action. Evidence of sedition has to be factual, substantial and concrete—not merely indirect or associational—and if so determined, the practitioners of sedition will receive full punishment. Lacking, however, a clear showing of a "clear and present danger" to a legitimate public interest, the First Amendment's freedom of speech and its corollary, freedom to organize and agitate, were held to be too sacred to sacrifice to governmental restraint.

Notwithstanding the Court's libertarian standard, operational freedom for "miserable merchants of unwanted ideas," as Douglas labeled Communists in his *Dennis* dissent, is not easily attainable in the reality of American political life. Hostility to Communists and to what they stand for runs deep and strong. New domestic or foreign policy crises could easily reinvigorate repressive measures towards Communists, the Supreme Court or both. Fears of Communist undercover involvement in the racial struggle, in the demonstrations of the New Left, and more particularly, in the movements bitterly opposing the war in Viet Nam could readily rekindle congressional pressure for new investigations, exposures, and sanctions. Nine lonely, black-robed men sitting in that magnificent temple of justice across from the nation's Capitol can promulgate constitutional law but can do little to insure compliance or constraint. They can teach lofty concepts of the Constitution but many Americans may not wish to be so instructed. As in all areas of law, the Court, in the final analysis, depends on others to implement its decisions. In affording protection to those who preach the overthrow of the very government which gives them the right to so speak, the Court must count on this country's majority and on those who represent, or act for it, to exercise a degree of social discipline that the Constitution may demand but that only responsible leadership can assure.

SUGGESTED READINGS

R. S. Brown, Jr. *Loyalty and Security. Employment Tests in the United States.* New Haven, 1958.

Zechariah Chafee, Jr. *The Blessings of Liberty.* Ann Arbor, 1956.

Harold W. Chase. *Security and Liberty.* Garden City, New York, 1955.

Thomas I. Emerson. "Freedom of Association and Freedom of Expression," *Yale Law Journal,* November, 1964, 1–35.

Thomas I. Emerson. *Toward a General Theory of the First Amendment.* New York, 1966.

Walter Gellhorn. *The States and Subversion.* Ithaca, 1952.

M. R. Konvitz. *Fundamental Liberties of a Free People.* Ithaca, 1957.

Earl Latham. *The Communist Controversy in Washington.* Cambridge, 1966.

Alexander Meiklejohn. "The Barenblatt Opinion," *University of Chicago Law Review,* Winter, 1960, 329–340.

Wallace Mendelson. "On the Meaning of the First Amendment: Absolutes in the Balance," *California Law Review,* December, 1962, 821–828.

Nathaniel L. Nathanson. "The Communist Trial and the Clear-and-Present Danger Test," *Harvard Law Review,* May, 1950, 1167–1175.

Wilson Record. *Race and Radicalism: The NAACP and the Communist Party in Conflict.* Ithaca, 1964.

David A. Shannon. *The Decline of American Communism.* New York, 1959.

II

Desegregation and the Public Schools

Handwriting On The Wall

From *Straight Herblock* (Simon & Schuster, 1964).

On May 17, 1954, in *Brown* v. *Board of Education,* the United States Supreme Court ruled unanimously that segregation of public schools "solely on the basis of race" denied Negro children "equal educational opportunities" even though "physical facilities and other 'tangible' factors" may have been equal. "Separate educational facilities," insisted Chief Justice Warren in the decade's most far-reaching decision, "are inherently unequal." With this remarkable economy of words and unconcealed bluntness the Court struck down one of the most deeply rooted principles in American constitutional law.

Any attempt to trace the constitutional development of the "separate but equal" concept in American public education must at least go back to *Roberts* v. *The City of Boston* (1849). This case represented one of the earliest judicial efforts to reconcile a segregated school system for white and Negro children with the high ideological promise of the equality of all men before the law regardless of race and color. The facts were simple. A five-year-old Negro child was refused admission to an all-white school nearest to her home after her father had declined to send her to the school for colored children located about a fifth of a mile further down the street. Specifically at issue in this case was the policy of the Boston School Committee which considered separate schools for Negroes as "not only legal and just, but [as] . . . best adapted to promote the instruction of that class of the population" and the compatibility of that policy with the command of the Declaration of Rights and Constitution of the Commonwealth of Massachusetts which required nondiscrimination in all matters legal and political. By the simple device of ignoring the constitutional issue, Chief Justice Shaw of the Supreme Judicial Court of Massachusetts seemed to encounter no great difficulty in turning back the challenge and maintaining the status quo. Since the state had given the Boston School Committee the power to regulate the system, the Committee's judgment (being "reasonable" and arrived at "upon great deliberation") was to be considered binding and conclusive upon the court. "Prejudice," he added, "if it exists, is not created by law and probably cannot be changed by law."

Although the petitioner and his illustrious counsel, Charles Sumner, lost their plea for desegregation, Roberts, unlike the members of his race in the ante-bellum South, was at least fortunate enough to have had legal standing in a court. As personal chattel, Southern Negro slaves had no civil rights, no political rights, no power to enter into enforceable contracts. Like other chattel they could be bought and sold, bartered and devised, seized and auctioned. As Kenneth Sharp put it so succinctly, "They were, in short, property in fact as well as in law." There was no slavery in the North, to be sure, but as the *Roberts* case demonstrated, this did not mean that there prevailed in Boston the kind of effective equality to which some men aspired even then.

Abolition of slavery and the grant of national citizenship following the Civil War radically transformed the legal position of the Negro throughout the South. Yet by the end of the nineteenth century discriminatory practices and Jim Crow laws, enacted in many of the Southern states, effectively emasculated the promises of the Fourteenth and Fifteenth Amendments. The technically freed Negro was left without much personal dignity and safety in a highly structured society. Law and custom prevented the intermingling of the races in restaurants, hotels, schools and all other places of public accommodation. White primaries robbed the Negro of his vote and racially hostile sheriffs and courts left him frequently without even the most elemental concepts of justice and fair play.

Congressional attempts to make the Fourteenth Amendment meaningful to the Negro by extending to him the protections of the national government were soon frustrated by the Supreme Court in a series of decisions that developed the concepts of dual citizenship within a dual federalism. This narrow interpretation of the Amendment was first applied to the *Slaughterhouse* cases in 1871; the question of Negro rights as such was not involved. A challenge to the Fourteenth Amendment in that instance grew out of a suit for an injunction by a group of butchers who claimed an abridgment of their equal rights and privileges by a company in the slaughtering business which had been granted a monopoly through the actions of a reconstructionist legislature in Louisiana. Justice Samuel Miller speaking for a five to four majority, claimed an important distinction between the privileges and immunities that belong to a citizen of the United States and those that belong to the citizen of the state. The Fourteenth Amendment was designed to guard only against state violations of "privileges or immunities of citizens of the *United States*"; there was no language to protect "the citizen of a state against the legislative power of his own state." To Justice Stephen Field and his fellow dissenters this interpretation denied the very purpose of the Amendment which was to protect the citizens of the United States "against the deprivation of their common rights by state legislation." If this was not to be its objective, "it was a vain and idle enactment, which accomplished nothing, and most unnecessarily excited Congress and the people on its passage."

Unfortunately for the Negro whose civil rights were thus left to the mercies of state and local officialdom (most of whom were committed to the perpetuation of white power and privilege), it was the Miller and not the Field position that was to triumph when the Court ten years later reviewed the constitutionality of the Civil Rights Act of 1875. The Act which the Court struck down represented a congressional attempt to establish by law that regardless of race, color or previous condition of servitude, "all persons within the jurisdiction of the United States shall be entitled to the full and equal enjoyment of the accommodations, advantages, facilities, and privileges of inns, public conveyances, and theatres. . . ."

Justice Joseph Bradley, for the majority of the Court, considered the provisions to constitute mere expressions of social and not of legal rights, matters over which Congress had no constitutional control under either the Thirteenth or Fourteenth Amendment. What these Amendments forbid, and what Congress may constitutionally seek to bar through prohibitory legislation, are direct state interferences with *fundamental* rights. In the traditionalist view of Justice Bradley a catalogue of such rights included the right to hold property, to buy and sell, to receive equal treatment in the courts and those basic rights which constituted the distinction between freedom and slavery; failure to gain admission to an inn, to a public conveyance or amusement did not belong in this category; no "badges of slavery" were imposed.

Such discriminations do constitute a "badge of servitude" countered Justice John Harlan in a lengthy and vigorous dissent the essence of which found its way into the Court's majority opinions eighty years later.

The rights which Congress sought to secure under the Act of 1875 were "legal, not social rights." Unless these Amendments "be splendid baubles," the national grant of citizenship to the American Negro demanded that there can be no discrimination by the "state, nor the officers of any state, nor any corporation or individual wielding power under state authority for the public benefit or the public convenience. . . ."

With Congress judicially blocked from effectively implementing the guarantees of national citizenship, many of the Southern states proceeded to enact a wide variety of segregationist codes as legitimate exercises of their state police power. One of these, a Louisiana railroad segregation law, came into litigation and finally reached the Supreme Court in 1896. It provided that railroad companies operating within the state were to furnish separate railway cars for white and colored travelers. Plessy, an American citizen and resident of Louisiana who was of "seven-eights Caucasian and one-eighth African blood," had violated the regulations by taking a vacant seat in a coach reserved for whites only. Under the terms of the act such passengers were subject to ejection or imprisonment. On review, a majority of the Court insisted that statutes of this type were thoroughly reconcilable with the Fourteenth Amendment since the Amendment "could not have been intended to abolish distinctions based upon color, or to enforce social, as distinguished from political, equality." Louisiana law could be considered a "reasonable regulation," not unlike the laws of Congress for the District of Columbia and those of many other states of the Union which provided separate schools for colored children; such laws "have been generally, if not uniformly, sustained by the courts. . . ." According to the social and psychological theories then dominant on the Court, the separation of the races did "not necessarily imply the inferiority of either race to the other." If it is claimed that enforced segregation "stamps the colored race with a badge of inferiority," replied Justice Henry B. Brown in terms distinctly reminiscent of the Bradley opinion in the Civil Rights Cases, "it is not by reason of anything found in the act, but solely because the colored race chooses to put that construction upon it." In other words, the sense of social degradation that flowed from the acts of discrimination was invented by those against whom the discrimination was practiced.

Justice Harlan again found himself a dissenter. While there was no gainsaying the white man's dominance in prestige, achievement, education, wealth and power, Harlan insisted that under American laws a caste system was unthinkable. "Our Constitution is colorblind, and neither knows nor tolerates classes among citizens." Separating citizens on the basis of race, "while they are on a public highway, is a badge of servitude wholly inconsistent . . . with equality before the law established by the Constitution. . . . The thin disguise of equal accommodations for passengers in railroad coaches will not mislead anyone, nor atone for the wrong this day done. . . ."

Perhaps most relevant to the 1960's was Harlan's premonition of the broader socio-political implication of segregation. "The destinies of the two races, in this country, are indissolubly linked together, and the interests of both require that fhe common government of all shall not permit the seeds of race hate to be planted under the sanction of law. What can more certainly arouse race hate, what can more certainly create and perpetuate a feeling of distrust between these races, than state enactments which, in fact, proceed on the ground that colored citizens are so inferior and degraded that they cannot be allowed to sit in public coaches occupied by whites?"

Although the *Plessy* case dealt with the issue of segregation in public transportation specifically, the legal rationale advanced by the Court that coerced separateness in no way implied a constitutionally defective inequality and actually had much broader and more serious consequences. State and federal courts were quick to invoke this case as a precedent in order to immunize state regulatory legislation and police powers from the equality requirements of the Fourteenth Amendment in many additonal areas of public accommodations and services affecting Negroes—most prominently, however, in education, an area traditionally reserved to the control of the states. Even the United States Supreme Court, when confronted on appeal or review with a direct challenge that segregated educational facilities constituted clear violations of the Fourteenth Amendment, simply avoided the central constitutional question altogether and dealt with the issue in procedural or nonsubstantive terms. As late as 1927 Chief Justice William Taft in *Gong Lum* v. *Rice* upheld an order under which a child of Chinese descent, but of United States citizenship, was assigned to attend a Negro school in accordance with the segregation laws of Mississippi on the basis that "this same question has been many years decided to be within the constitutional power of the state legislatures to settle, without interference of the federal courts under the federal Constitution."

The first break with the uncritical application of the "separate but equal" doctrine to segregated education occurred in 1938, when the Court led by Chief Justice Charles E. Hughes began to question the extent to which separate facilities offered Negro students were, in fact, equal to those available to whites. In *Missouri ex rel. Gaines* v. *Canada* the Court struck down as not affording equal protection of laws a Missouri provision which would have paid for the legal education of Negro students in "any adjacent state" pending the establishment of a law school at its Negro university. Sending Negroes out of the state while white students were admitted to the Law School of the University of Missouri was termed a "resort" that "may mitigate the inconvenience of the discrimination but cannot serve to validate it." Ten years later, in *Sipuel* v. *Oklahoma,* the Court compelled the State of Oklahoma under the equal protection clause to provide legal education "as soon as it does for applicants of any other group" for a qualified Negro whose admission had been put off.

An even more significant constitutional development was reached in *Sweatt* v. *Painter* (1950), a case involving the University of Texas Law School. Not only did the Court for the first time realistically scrutinize the quantitative factors in a segregated educational arrangement, but it then went on to raise the much broader issue—whether separate facilities could ever offer a Negro law student the type of professional preparation which would truly be on a par with that made available to his fellow white students. Compared with the University of Texas Law School, the newly established law school at Texas State University for Negroes was found clearly deficient in terms of the quality of its curriculum, faculty, library, size of student body, opportunity for law review work and professional specialization. Moreover, it was inferior in a number of important considerations which made a law school great—"qualities which are incapable of objective measurement but . . . include reputation of the faculty, experience of the administration, position and influence of alumni, standing in the community, traditions and prestige." Still more basic objections were raised. If legal education is to equip the future attorney with the practical skills and experiences which will prepare him to practice his profession in the courts of the State of Texas, how could this ever be accomplished equitably in a setting which "excludes from its student body members of the racial group which number 85% of the population of the State and include most of the lawyers, witnesses, jurors, judges and other officials with whom the petitioner will inevitably be dealing when he becomes a member of the Texas Bar"? These were the considerations that persuaded the Court to conclude that the equal protection clause entitled the petitioner to be admitted immediately to the formerly all-white University of Texas Law School.

Brown v. Board of Education

The constitutional law enunciated in *Sweatt* led directly to *Brown* and its reversal of *Plessy*. To satisfy the Fourteenth Amendment, the Court now demanded that equal protection include more than physical factors—more than bricks and mortar, books and curriculum. Schools represent a microcosm of a larger world which is both multiracial and racially interdependent. An education which seeks to prepare young people to live effective lives in a contemporary America could no longer be obtained in segregated schools. This was the essence of the thesis advanced in *Brown* by Chief Justice Warren on behalf of all his "brothers" on the Court. In developing his argument, Warren found the early history and intent of the Fourteenth Amendment to be "inconclusive," "elusive" and not particularly relevant since the role and scope of public education is vastly different today from what it was at the time when the Amendment was adopted. "Today, education is perhaps the most important function of state and local government . . . it is a principal instrument of awakening the child to cultural values, in preparing him for later professional training and in helping him to adjust normally to his environment."

As to the quality of the educational facilities in *Brown* (which consolidated appeals from the courts in South Carolina, Virginia, Delaware, Kansas and the District of Columbia), Warren found that the Negro and white schools that were involved were in fact "equalized or being equalized with respect to buildings, curricula, qualifications and salaries of teachers and other 'tangible' factors." But these factors did not tell the entire story of such a separation based on race. What about the "effect of segregation" on public education in general and on the Negro child in particular? By posing this profound and encompassing question the *Brown* Court proceeded to place the equality standard of the Fourteenth Amendment into a context of social reality which looks for verification to empiricism rather than to the norms of precedent and history. Warren's opinion incorporated judicial findings employing the language and concepts of social psychology from the Kansas case (one of the cases on appeal) to the effect that:

> Segregation of white and colored children in public schools has a detrimental effect upon the colored children. The impact is greater when it has the sanction of law; for the policy of separating the races is usually interpreted as denoting the inferiority of the Negro

group. A sense of inferiority affects the motivation of a child to learn. Segregation with the sanction of law, therefore, has a tendency to [retard] the educational and mental development of Negro children and to deprive them of some of the benefits they would receive in a racial[ly] integrated school system.

However much these observations may differ from the knowledge of psychology in *Plessy*'s day, the sense of inferiority induced by segregated education now seemed "amply supported by modern authorities." Among the authorities referred to in Warren's famous "Footnote 11" were eight texts, journal articles and special studies which discussed the psychologically detrimental effects of segregation on the personality development of the Negro child. "We now conclude," wrote Warren in explicit repudiation of *Plessy*, "that in the field of public education the doctrine of 'separate but equal' has no place. Separate educational facilities are inherently unequal." Thus one hundred and five years after *Roberts,* segregation was finally found to constitute a denial of the equal protection clause of the Fourteenth Amendment.

In view of the enormous consequences of this decision to the seventeen Southern and border states where 2.5 million Negro children were attending 15,000 segregated schools, the Court ordered a rehearing of *Brown* (already briefed and argued twice) in order to determine the specific nature of the implemental decree. The second *Brown* case (1955) enunciated the measures by which the new interpretation of the equal protection clause was to find its realization. Primary responsibility for carrying out desegregation was placed in the hands of local school boards; federal district courts were charged to see to it that local school authorities implemented the *Brown* decision in "good faith." For the purpose of "adjusting and reconciling public and private needs," these courts were to retain jurisdiction over desegregation proceedings "during the transition period" and be guided by the principles of equity law.

Mere disagreement wtih the Supreme Court's decision could not be permitted to vitiate the declared constitutional principles. There had to be a "prompt and reasonable start towards full compliance." If more time was needed it was the defendant's responsibility to demonstrate that such delay was "in the public interest and . . . consistent with good faith compliance at the earliest practicable date."

In assessing local efforts, courts could consider such factors as the administrative problems, the physical conditions of the school plants, the school transportation system, personnel, the necessary redrawing of school districts and the revision of local laws and regulations. Desegregation was to proceed "with all deliberate speed."

Compliance Problems in the South

Brown shook Southern opinion as no other case in recent constitutional history. In countless editorials, political pronouncements, legislative resolutions and memorials the Warren Court was assailed for abuse of power, encroachment upon the rights of the states, defiance of long established constitutional principles and precedents and substitution of "personal political and social ideas for the established law of the land." A withering indictment of the *Brown* decision reflecting and expanding these reactions in further detail was presented to the United States Congress on March 12, 1956 by a group of 101 Southern senators and representatives in the form of the *Southern Manifesto: Declaration of Constitutional Principles.* A few of the more outstanding arguments went as follows: The Supreme Court unwarrantedly interfered with the rights of the states and of Congress; education was not mentioned in either the original Constitution or in the Fourteenth Amendment; nothing in the history of the Fourteenth Amendment indicates a congressional attempt to disrupt patterns of segregated education which have either prevailed or were subsequently approved in twenty-six out of thirty-seven states of the Union; segregated facilities were upheld in *Plessy* and in the *Lum* case; the Supreme Court of the United States saw no conflict between the Fourteenth Amendment and the discretionary right of the states to operate their schools on the "separate but equal" principle; "this interpretation, restated time and again, became part of the life of the people of many of the states and confirmed their habits, customs, tradition and way of life"; government must not deprive parents of "the right to direct the lives and education of their own children"; by this unconstitutional exercise of power the Court has created "chaos and confusion" in the South; the amicable relations between the races are destroyed; "hatred and suspicion" reign in place of "friendship and understanding"; "outside agitators are threatening immediate and revolutionary changes in our public school system." While continuing to rely on the Constitution, the signers of this statement declared that they would seek to reverse this unconstitutional decision, use lawful means to prevent its implementation and appeal to those states not directly affected "to consider the constitutional principles involved against the time when they too, on issues vital to them, may be the victims of judicial encroachment."

Among the many other charges hurled at *Brown* by its critics, there was at least one more that received wide circulation and support. The Court was accused of buttressing its argument with "pseudo-scientific" evidence which presumed to prove socio-psychological damage to the personality growth of minority youth attending racially segregated schools. Warren's reference to the studies of Professors K. B. Clark and Gunnar Myrdahl came under particularly heavy attack. Findings of such behavioral sciences—"very young, imprecise and changeable . . ."—were deemed as yet unworthy of judicial cognizance.

Supporters of the Court stressed the lawfulness and morality of the *Brown* decision. Far from constituting a revolutionary break with constitutional precedents, many of them viewed the opinion as pointing towards the realistic fulfillment of the American dream of equality for all which the Fourteenth Amendment was purposely planned to effectuate. As far back as 1880 in *Strauder* v. *West Virginia* (which declared unconstitutional a state law barring Negroes from jury service), the Supreme Court fully appreciated the equal protection guarantees of the Fourteenth Amendment:

What is this but declaring that the law in the States shall be the same for the blacks as for the white; that all persons, whether colored or white, shall stand equal before the laws of the States, and, in regard to the colored race, for whose protection the amendment was primarily designed, that no discrimination shall be made against them by law because of their color? The words of the amendment, it is true, are prohibitory, but they contain a necessary implication of a positive immunity, or right, most valuable to the colored race—the right of exemption from unfriendly legislation against them distinctively as colored—exception from legal discriminations, implying inferiority in civil society, lessening the security of their enjoyment of the rights which others enjoy, and discriminations which are steps towards reducing them to the condition of a subject race.

This was the constitutional theory underlying the Harlan dissents in the Civil Rights Cases and in *Plessy;* it was channelled into *Brown* more immediately through the opinions in *Missouri ex. rel. Gaines* v. *Canada, Sipuel* v. *Oklahoma, Sweatt* v. *Painter* and *McCaurin* v. *Oklahoma State Regents.* Thus *Brown* largely reaffirmed lines of constitutional interpretations for which there was ample precedent and logic. To argue, as the majority of the Court attempted to do in *Plessy,* that segregated public conveyances could humiliate Negroes "solely if the colored race chooses to put that construction upon it," revealed the extent to which members of the Court failed to see these laws for what they really were, parts of a complex superstructure of caste and class which had as its main objective the perpetuation of the Negro's sense of inferiority, dependence and helplessness.

The argument that separate facilities never were truly equal required little proof of anyone who had experienced Southern segregation as he rode the trains, attended theaters, ate in restaurants, looked for hotel accommodations, went to the public beaches or visited Negro schools and colleges in the area. Social scientists studying the impact of segregation on Negroes were just beginning to reduce to scientific prose what American writers and poets had portrayed for years as the cost of segregation to both races.

Brown acknowledged judicially what many people had known or felt for a long time: Segregation was morally indefensible, socially irrational and politically undemocratic. It perpetuated a racial myth which imprisoned American values at home and weakened America's leadership abroad. Equally important to many, it defiled this country's claim to stand as a world model of freedom and human dignity in defense of which whites and Negroes had fought side by side in all of this nation's major wars.

Southern resistance to *Brown* took forms other than mere rhetorical expressions of defiance. As federal and state courts began to strike down compulsory segregation statutes in Arkansas, Florida, Kentucky, Missouri, North Carolina, Oklahoma and Texas, some Southern states launched legislative efforts aimed at circumventing or avoiding compliance. South Carolina ordered cessation of state aid for teachers' salaries to schools arranging for pupil transfers "pursuant to . . . an order of any court"; Louisiana amended its Constitution to require that "all public elementary and secondary schools . . . shall be operated separately for white and colored children" and provided for the withholding of all public funds from any school which violated the state's segregation policy; Virginia in its General Assembly passed a declaration of "Interposition and Nullification" labeling the Supreme Court interpretation of the Constitution "as a clear and present threat to the several states" and ordering continued adherence to segregation on the ground that "until such time as the Constitution of the United States may be amended in the manner provided by that Constitution, . . . [the] commonwealth is under no obligation to accept supinely an unlawful decree of the Supreme Court of the United States. . . ." Alabama, Arkansas, Florida, Georgia and Mississippi repealed their compulsory school attendance laws and empowered local districts to close the state's public schools and make available tuition grants from public school funds to children attending private schools.

Measures of "massive resistance" against *Brown* received their severest legal blow in 1958 when the Supreme Court ruled unconstitutional in *Cooper* v. *Aaron* certain actions of Governor Faubus which had resulted in preventing the admission of a small group of Negro students to Central High School in Little Rock, Arkansas, under a locally approved desegregation plan.

The facts in the case showed that while the local school board was willing to move in "good faith" towards the implementation of the constitutional requirements imposed by *Brown,* the state's governmental leadership worked in an opposite direction: The Arkansas state constitution was amended directing the legislature to oppose the "unconstitutional desegregation decisions" of the Supreme Court in "every constitutional manner"; laws were enacted to prevent racial integration of the public schools; Governor Faubus dispatched units of the National Guard "forcibly preventing nine Negro students . . . from entering," although neither the mayor, nor the chief of police, nor the school board requested such intervention; a district court enjoined the Governor from interfering with the orderly process of desegregation.

As tensions continued to rise, President Eisenhower finally decided, on September 25, 1957, to order Regular Army units to proceed to Central High School to assure the personal safety of the Negro students and to maintain law and order.

As the Supreme Court saw it, the issue in *Cooper* was the question of whether the local board, under such conditions of "chaos, bedlam and turmoil" and in a setting of intense public hostility which endangered the educational process of all children, should be permitted to postpone its desegregation program and order its recently admitted Negroes to segregated schools or whether the constitutional rights of these students were of such significance that they could not be made to yield to "the violence and disorder which have followed upon the actions of the Governor and Legislature."

In a unanimous, short and forceful decision the Court declared that "law and order are not here to be preserved by depriving the Negro children of their constitutional rights"; under the supremacy clause of the United States Constitution and on the basis of other well established case law, the commands of the Fourteenth Amendment and of *Brown* must be considered binding on the state and all of its officers and agencies and cannot be nullified by the actions of state governors, legislators or courts.

Following *Cooper,* open defiance of desegregation through the tactics of "massive resistance" began to recede. There were prominent exceptions, of course. In Virginia, for example, the school board of Prince Edward County abandoned its public school system under a state enabling law and continued for years to make tuition grants to parents who would send their children to private, nonsectarian schools attended by whites only. Protracted litigation did not end until 1964 when the Court in *Griffin* v. *Board of Supervisors of Prince Edward County* finally declared unconstitutional this policy of attempted noncompliance with *Brown* by closing schools in one county while schools in others remained open.

Governor Wallace's attempt in 1963 to circumvent federal court orders desegregating schools in Mobile, Birmingham and Macon County, Alabama, led him to activate the National Guard and stand in open defiance of federal authorities. President Kennedy declaring an "obstruction of justice" federalized the Guard, and two weeks later five federal district judges in Alabama issued an injunction forbidding the Governor to interfere with the lawful operation of these schools.

The admission of James Meredith in September of 1962 to the University of Mississippi led to such violence, despite President Kennedy's appeal to the students to remain calm, that two men were killed and a number injured in the resulting demonstrations which did not end until nearly 16,000 federal troops were deployed around the Oxford campus. Subsequent legal actions initiated by the United States Attorney General caused the Fifth Circuit Court of Appeals to issue restraining orders prohibiting Governor Barnett and other state officials from interfering with the enrollment of Meredith at the university.

The more moderate and responsible leaders in Southern government and politics, however, followed a different course. Direct federal-state confrontations resulting in violence and loss of life had to be halted. One solution to avoid such violence was found in the school placement or pupil assignment laws which had been enacted within a year of *Brown* by legislatures in Alabama, Florida and North Carolina; by the end of the nineteen-fifties they had proved so attractive that many other Southern states followed their example and adopted similar statutes. Under such laws local school authorities were empowered to admit, assign or transfer students to elementary and secondary schools within their jurisdiction by applying and weighing a variety of quantitative and qualitative criteria including the availability of rooms, transportation facilities and instructional personnel; adequacy of a student's academic preparation; suitability of the curriculum; the student's home environment, intelligence, psychological qualifications, health, social adaptability, personality and morals; and the likely effect of the transfer on other pupils, on teachers and on the general peace, order and good will of the school community.

Alabama's school placement law was sustained by a federal court in *Shuttlesworth* v. *Birmingham Board of Education* as furnishing "the legal machinery for an orderly administration of the public schools in a constitutional manner by the admission of qualified pupils upon a basis of individual merit without regard to their race or color. We must presume that it will be so administered. If not, in some future proceeding it is possible that it may be declared unconstitutional in its application." In 1958 the United States Supreme Court affirmed the judgment (in a per curiam memorandum) "upon the limited ground on which the District Court rested its decision."

Such placement laws, with their complex administrative machinery and with the frequently added requirement that petitioners had to exhaust all administrative remedies before seeking judicial relief, proved highly effective, especially in Arkansas, North Carolina, South Carolina and Virginia. Without ever referring to the subject of race or color they did much to block the impact of *Brown*. The United States Civil Rights Commission in its 1962 Report termed them "the principal obstacle to desegregation in the South." Although 27.3 per cent of all school districts in the seventeen Southern and border States (including the District of Columbia) were desegregated by the end of the 1961-1962 school year, statistical data from the highly respected Southern Education Reporting Service showed that only .241 per cent of the region's Negroes actually attended classes with whites.

With "Due Deliberation"

By 1962, district-court-approved grade-a-year integration plans came under increasingly critical scrutiny in the Courts of Appeals encompassing much of the Deep South, as they began to note too many of them reflecting tactics of "tokenism" that could not be reconciled with the "good faith" test imposed by *Brown*.

An indication that the United States Supreme Court did not consider the prevailing moves towards desegregation to constitute sufficient progress emerged clearly from two cases handed down at the end of the 1963 term, *Goss* v. *Board of Education of the City of Knoxville* and *Watson* v. *City of Memphis*. In *Goss* the Court struck down a pupil transfer plan under which a student could apply for a transfer to attend a school where his race was "in the majority." This provision was held unconstitutional for resting on race classification and as involving an "obvious one-way operation" of ill-concealed efforts to continue segregationist practices. While acknowledging the existence of "deeprooted problems" and "multifarious local difficulties," the Court pointedly noted that nine years had already passed since *Brown* and therefore "the context in which we must interpret and apply (its) . . . language to plans for desegregation has been significantly altered." *Watson* gave even more direct evidence of the Court's growing impatience with desegregation schemes that showed more regard for due deliberation than for speed. A group of Negro petitioners sought an injunction calling for the immediate and complete desegregation of parks and recreational facilities owned and operated by the City of Memphis. A federal district court denied their petition on the grounds that the city needed more time to complete its gradual desegregation plan, that the plan was consistent with the public interest and that it was carried out in good faith. An appeals court sustained the decision.

In reversing this judgment on further review and ordering the immediate and complete desegregation of all of the city's parks and recreational areas, Justice Goldberg declared for a unanimous Supreme Court: (1) "*Brown* never contemplated that the concept of 'deliberate speed' would countenance indefinite delay in eliminating racial barriers in the schools, let alone other public facilities not involving the same physical problems or comparable conditions; (2) the rights here asserted are, like all such rights, *present* rights . . . not merely hopes for some future enjoyment of some formalistic constitutional promise; (3) . . . neither the asserted fears of violence and tumult nor the asserted inability to preserve the peace were demonstrated at trial to be anything more than personal speculations or vague disquietudes of city officials."

Those who saw the *Brown* decision as a long overdue rectification of a wrong done their fellow man were disappointed at the slow pace of desegregation. Only a few major cities—for example, Louisville, Kentucky, and Atlanta, Georgia—undertook voluntarily to comply. After ten years and more than three hundred litigations, only about 6% or 183,000 Negroes out of a Negro school population of over three million attended integrated classes with whites in 1965, and half of them had started as late as 1964. The Southern Education Reporting Service, in its findings of 1966, revealed very little progress in Alabama (.43%), Mississippi (.59%) and Louisiana (.69%); the highest level of compliance in the South was in Virginia (11.49%). In the border states, by contrast, nearly 70% of all Negro students went to desegregated schools.

Impatience with the slow rate of desegregation contributed to the demand for federal incentives and sanctions. Title IV of the Civil Rights Act of 1964 authorized the federal government:

(1) To make surveys and report to Congress and the President on the progress of school desegregation;

(2) To give technical and financial assistance, if necessary, to local public school systems engaged in the process of desegregation;

(3) To file suit upon receipt of complaint for the desegregation of public schools and colleges where aggrieved individuals are unable to initiate and sustain legal proceedings, and where local authorities have had reasonable time to correct the offending conditions.

An even more effective instrument was Title VI which permitted Washington, after appropriate notice and hearing, to terminate financial assistance or grants to any recipient of federal aid engaged in discriminatory practices. The Department of Health, Education and Welfare implemented this Title by requiring applicants for federal assistance to execute an assurance of compliance showing that the school system (1) is subject to a final court order of desegregation, or (2) has adopted a desegregation plan, determined to be adequate by the Commissioner of Education. In April, 1965, the Commissioner set the fall of 1967 as the target date for total desegregation for applicant school systems; for schools beginning in 1965, four grades would have to be desegregated by June, 1966.

Major judicial support for more rapid compliance came in March, 1967, when the United States Court of Appeals for the Fifth Circuit affirmed a decision which had the effect of demanding that Alabama, Florida, Georgia, Louisiana, Mississippi and Texas integrate their public schools from kindergarten up beginning in the fall of the year. Adopting the guidelines and standards of the Department of Health, Education and Welfare for schools that accept federal funds, the Court further held that "[t]he necessity of overcoming the effects of the dual school system in this circuit requires integration of faculties, facilities and activities, as well as of students." On April 16, 1967, the United States Supreme Court formally rejected an appeal to stay the implementation of that far-reaching decision.

How vigorously federal authorities will use their newly obtained powers remains to be seen. Much depends on whether politically powerful groups in the South are now willing to move from token desegregation to acceptance of the new order. As the formerly disenfranchised Negro electorate becomes more articulate and its voting power more decisive in Southern constituencies, pressure on local governments and the federal government will increase.

Full Faith Compliance Outside of the South— De Facto Segregation

According to the 1962 Report of the United States Civil Rights Commission, school authorities in twenty-two cities throughout eleven Northern and Western states had received formal complaints of segregation or discrimination. Charges included: "gerrymander of school zone lines, transfer policies and practices, discriminatory feeder pattern of elementary to secondary schools, overcrowding of predominantly Negro schools and underutilization of schools attended by whites; site selection to create or perpetuate segregation, discrimination in vocational and distributive education programs and in the employment and assignment of Negro teachers." Some impressive statistical testimony of the extent of racial imbalance in major Northern cities was brought together by Will Maslow in his widely cited study, "De Facto Public School Segregation."

> In New York City . . . there are 75 public elementary schools (out of a total of 570) with Negro or Puerto Rican enrollments of 90% or more. . . .

> In Chicago, 102,000 Negro children, 87% of the city's elementary students, are said to be attending practically all-Negro public schools in the black belt. . . .

> . . . [F]ive elementary public schools in San Francisco had a Negro enrollment and two an Asian enrollment of more than 80%.

> . . . [I]n Cleveland, where about 30% of the city's 130,000 public school children were Negroes, 27 of the city's 127 elementary schools were "predominantly Negro."

> In Philadelphia . . . 47% of the students in the public schools are Negroes. In each of 38 public schools, 14% of the total number, the Negro enrollment is 99+%.

> In Los Angeles, expert estimates indicate that in 43 of the city's 404 elementary schools the percentage of Negroes and in 34 the percentage of Mexican-Americans is 85 or higher.

> In Indianapolis, seven of the city's 89 elementary schools are "all Negro," although 56 are "mixed". . . .[1]

An absence of statutes compelling outright segregation posed constitutional problems obviously quite different in nature from those that arose in the South where racially separate educational facilities were sired by public law and policy.

Beginning in the early nineteen-sixties, school authorities and courts in the North were petitioned by civil rights leaders and by Negro parents on behalf of their children to declare that the

[1] Will Maslow, "De Facto Public School Segregation," *Villanova Law Review* (Spring, 1961), pp. 353–376.

existence of racial imbalance in the schools, usually referred to as de facto segregation, was equally as repugnant to the Constitution as were the once formally segregated schools of the South.

The Neighborhood School Policy Defended and Attacked

De facto segregation without the expressed sanction of law but reinforced nevertheless through a policy of maintaining neighborhood schools was attacked for contributing to conditions where Negro children became second-class citizens in the educational order of the community. It was felt that the system consigned Negroes to overcrowded and dilapidated slum schools, where poor teachers, poor facilities and low expectations of performance further undermined their lack of confidence and motivation to ever become effective participants in the American democracy, where white and Negro students were permitted to grow into adulthood without learning how to understand each other, and where educational experiences which might demonstrate how little a person's color had to do with intelligence, talent, skill or character were utterly lacking.

Friends of the neighborhood school rallied to the defense of an institution they considered historically proven, socially desirable, administratively efficient and academically sound; local school districts if compactly drawn in response to population densities, distances of travel, pupil safety, teacher availability and building capacity were likely to offer people a feeling of neighborliness and stability; transferring students to schools outside their neighborhoods might subject them to undesirable associations and learning situations and additionally involve expenditures that could more profitably be channelled into the improvement and upgrading of schools for the less advantaged; middle-class parents faced with the prospect of having their children forced to attend different or inferior schools would move to the suburbs or turn to private education with either alternative resulting in consequences detrimental to public education in general. These in brief were some of the contentions as petitioners turned to the courts for legal answers that would formally delineate the neighborhood school's constitutional status.

While resistance to policies aimed at achieving a racially more balanced educational system generally never reached the intensities of opposition that it did in the South, it was true that in a considerable number of Northern communities conflicts between anxious parents and school authorities erupted at times into angry exchanges and occasionally even into demonstrations, sit-ins and marches on city hall.

What faced the courts in a constitutional sense was the question of whether the Fourteenth Amendment forbidding states to deny anyone the equal protection of the laws, as now interpreted by *Brown*, merely enjoined positive acts of discrimination or segregation or whether it also placed positive responsibilities on local school authorities to adopt measures for the redress of racially imbalanced schools. Should the concept and tradition of the neighborhood school be made to yield to the higher value of racial equity in situations where residential living patterns, population movements and ethnic prejudices were the major factors that made these neighborhoods nearly all black or all white? How much of a role, as a result of *Brown*, must now be assigned to the school in the social engineering of a racially more just American society?

By way of assisting local school boards and administrators with their response to these complicated challenges and questions, at least four states were willing to furnish some policy guidance.

New York's Board of Regents stated in 1960 "that even adventitious segregation of Negro pupils in public schools may adversely affect their motivation to learn and is, therefore, a denial of equal educational opportunity under state law." The New York City Board of Education later that year announced an "open enrollment" plan which was designed to bring about a greater racial balance in schools with extraordinarily heavy Negro and Puerto Rican enrollments. The plan was prefaced by a statement which stressed that "racial integration in our schools is an essential and imperative element of democratic education. . . ."

California's State Board of Education affirmed its agreement with *Brown* and urged that "in all areas under our control or subject to our influence, the policy of elimination of existing segregation and curbing of any tendency toward its growth must be given serious and thoughtful consideration by all persons involved at all levels."

Under an act passed by the 1963 legislature, local school boards in Illinois were directed to change, revise or create school districts "in a manner which will take into consideration the prevention of segregation . . ." and were prohibited from "erecting, purchasing or otherwise acquiring buildings for school purposes . . . in such a manner as to promote segregation and separation of children in public schools because of color, race or nationality."

A Massachusetts law of 1965 represents perhaps the toughest policy against de facto segregation.

> It is hereby declared to be the policy of the Commonwealth to encourage all school committees to adopt as educational objectives the promotion of racial balance and the correction of existing racial imbalance in the public schools. The prevention or elimination of racial imbalance shall be an objective in all decisions involving the drawing or altering of school attendance lines and the selection of new school sites.

A local school committee which did "not show progress within a reasonable time in eliminating racial imbalance in its schools" stood the risk of losing its share of state financial aid.

Unaided by further Supreme Court decisions, state and federal courts were largely left to themselves to work out their own interpretations of these broad policy objectives and of the standards set forth by *Brown* as they adjudicated particular allegations of de facto segregation in Northern cities where there were heavy concentrations of Negro enrollments.

As one would anticipate, multiple jurisdictions were not conducive to lend either symmetry or uniformity to the development of constitutional law. Courts formulated decrees which significantly reflected different theories of what school boards could be expected to do by way of eliminating racial imbalance. A few principal cases suffice to point up clearly some of the dissimilarities in judicial approach.

In *Bell* v. *School, City of Gary* (1963), a group of Negro parents presented charges against the city's school board whose policy included, among other things, discriminatory school attendance zones, discriminatory patterns of new school construction and failure "affirmatively to provide" a racially integrated school system. From a study of the evidence supplied, the court found the problem in Gary to be "not one of segregated schools but rather one of segregated housing" with the result that Negroes lived in high population concentrations "[e]ither by choice or design." The neighborhood school policy was defended as a "long and well established institution in American public education," with many social, cultural and administrative advantages. Judge Beamer saw nothing in constitutional law that required "a school system developed on the neighborhood school plan, honestly and conscientiously constructed with no intention or purpose to segregate" to be abandoned "because the resulting effect is to have a racial imbalance in certain schools where the district is populated almost entirely by Negroes or whites." The opinion concluded with the declaration that "the defendant had no affirmative duty to balance the races in the various schools under its jurisdiction, regardless of the residence of students involved."

In *Lynch* v. *Kenston School Board* (1964), for example, an attack by Negro parents on de facto segregation, due to residential living patterns, in Kenston, Ohio, where a rigid application of the neighborhood school policy resulted in an "inherently unequal" school situation, was turned back by a federal district court on the grounds that *Brown* stood not for integration but merely for the end of coerced segregation. Plaintiffs were held to have no "constitutional right to attend or to refrain from attending a particular school on the basis of racial consideration when there has been no actual discrimination against them." Their right to be protected against racial discrimination "at the same time denies them the right to consideration on a racial basis," to be assigned to schools "composed of a sufficient number of the Caucasian race." This was a form of segregation in reverse totally incompatible with the Fourteenth Amendment.

A significantly different line of reasoning was employed in *Taylor* v. *Board of Education of New Rochelle* (1961). Here a

New York federal district court found that the board of education had "intentionally created and maintained" an elementary school with a 94% Negro enrollment by the gerrymandering of district lines, by the transferring out of white students, by an overly inflexible adherence to the neighborhood school policy and by refusing to adopt plans which would have alleviated segregation. Having thus contributed by its own actions to the de facto segregation, the board was held constitutionally obligated to end segregation in "good faith" and "with dispatch." When the board under protest subsequently adopted a transfer plan with one of the restrictions providing that the classroom teacher and principal would have to certify that such a pupil wishing to transfer would be "able to perform in an academically satisfactory fashion on the grade level to which he is assigned" (with additional testimony given to the effect that "emotional stability" was one of the factors to be weighed), the court struck down this condition on grounds that (1) the "plan does not contain any specific test by which one can define and clarify the rather ambiguous standard . . . ," and (2) the "Constitution does not provide that only academically superior or emotionally well adjusted Negroes are to have an opportunity to secure an education from officially-created segregation." The decision was affirmed by the Second Circuit Court of Appeals and the Supreme Court denied certiorari.

One noteworthy aspect of Judge Kaufman's opinion in *Taylor* dealt with the allegation by the defendant school board that the neighborhood school policy was "reasonable and educationally sound," and adherence to it was not in conflict with the Constitution. While insisting that such policy as an "abstract proposition" was not on trial, the court first quoted Justice Frankfurter's language from *Cooper* that "[l]ocal customs, however hardened by time, are not decreed in heaven," and then went on to express its own position in these terms:

> The neighborhood school policy is certainly not sacrosanct. It is valid only insofar as it is operated within the confines established by the Constitution. It cannot be used as an instrument to confine Negroes within an area artificially delineated in the first instance by official acts. If it is so used, the Constitution has been violated and the courts must intervene.

While *Taylor* can certainly not be cited to support the proposition that the neighborhood school policy was unconstitutional *per se,* courts following its approach could easily suspect such a system wherever school enrollments revealed a picture of inordinately high racial imbalance. Various courts in California, Massachusetts, New Jersey and New York did just that. Among many others, *Barksdale* v. *Springfield School Committee,* a Massachusetts case, illustrates this point well. Petitioners sought an injunction in the federal court to bar the local school committee from continuing the operations of racially imbalanced schools that were operating under a neighborhood school plan. In the absence of any evidence that these neighborhood districts were drawn with any intent to segregate, segregation was found nonetheless to have resulted "from rigid adherence" to the neighborhood school concept. On the basis that the education of Negro children was impaired "in racially concentrated schools," Judge Sweeney considered "it . . . [to be] neither just nor sensible to proscribe the segregation having its basis in affirmative state action while at the same time failing to provide a remedy for segregation which grows out of discrimination in housing or other economic or social factors." In this context, the court concluded, neighborhood school policy was to be either "abandoned or modified when it results in segregation in fact."

Among such "modifications" upheld by courts in New York, for example, were desegregation plans adopted by school authorities in New York City, Rochester and Long Island (often over the determined opposition of white parents and after protracted litigation) which endeavored to correct racial imbalance by "pairing," transferring or transporting pupils from their neighborhood schools to other schools within the general school district. In their decrees courts left considerable discretion with local administrations to implement such policies and reserved judicial review only to claims of arbitrary and capricious actions.

A survey of the voluminous amount of litigation that followed *Brown* in the North readily reveals not only the complexity of the issues involved in defining and correcting de facto segregation but also the limitations that necessarily inhere in the judicial process as such. This latter problem persuaded a number of judges to follow the examples of New Jersey and New York where courts seemed to place increasing reliance and responsibility on local administrative channels and processes for the design and execution of desegregation plans appropriate to local conditions and problems.

What becomes also quite apparent is the stubborn persistence of a number of important questions concerning the "proper" applications of *Brown* to de facto school segregation which the Supreme Court as of 1966 still left in constitutional limbo. What were the appropriate numerical criteria or statistical methods for determining the existence of racial balance in multiracial urban communities? Were local school boards authorized, under the equality provisions of the Fourteenth Amendment, to adopt compulsory transfer and bussing policies for the purpose of correcting racial imbalance? Which of two major approaches to the neighborhood school concept reflected the intent of *Brown* most accurately, *Taylor* or *Bell*?

Whether the Court's unwillingness to speak denotes a conviction that there are no pressing needs for a national resolution of the existing uncertainties and divergences or whether it merely amounts to an implied admission that these problems are at this juncture judicially insoluble is not disclosed by the record. It could well be true that as a matter of constitutional principle, the Court may deem it propitious and reasonable to leave to legislatures, to state boards of education and to local school authorities the writing of the final chapter on the American Negro's road to equality in education.

How long a road lies ahead was impressively underscored recently again by the most comprehensive survey on the subject, *Equality of Educational Opportunity,* a study conducted by the United States Office of Education for the President and the Congress in compliance with Section 402 of the Civil Rights Act of 1964. These were some of the relevant findings concerning the extent of segregation ten years after *Brown.*

> The great majority of American children attend schools that are largely segregated. . . . Almost 80% of all white pupils in 1st grade and 12th grade attend schools that are from 90 to 100 percent white. . . . More than 65 percent of all Negro pupils in the first grade attend

schools that are between 90 and 100 percent Negro. . . . For the
nation as a whole, the average Negro elementary pupil attends a
school in which 65 percent of the teachers are Negro; the average
white elementary pupil attends a school in which 97 percent of the
teachers are white. . . .

The 1967 Report of the United States Civil Rights Commission,
Racial Isolation in the Public Schools, offered further supporting documentation. Nationally, racial imbalance was found to
be growing, to be "typical of major metropolitan areas," to be
"severe within the central cities," to be prevalent "regardless of
the size of the school system," to be relatively unaffected by the
proportion of Negroes that are enrolled in the schools, to be
"intense whether the cities are large or small" and not to be
"markedly" different "from that in the South."

SUGGESTED READINGS

Monroe Berger. "Desegregation, Law, and Social Science: What Was the
Basis of the Supreme Court's Decision?" *Commentary,* May, 1957, 471–
477.

Charles L. Black, Jr. "The Lawfulness of the Segregation Decisions,"
Yale Law Journal, January, 1960, 421–430.

Kenneth B. Clark. *Prejudice and Your Child.* Boston, 1963.

Kenneth B. Clark. "The Desegregation Cases: Criticism of the Social
Scientist's Role," *Villanova Law Review,* Winter, 1959–1960, 224–240.

M. Richard Cramer. "School Desegregation and New Industry: The
Southern Community Leader's Viewpoint," *Social Forces,* May, 1963,
384–389.

"De Facto Segregation: A New Storm over the Public Schools Divides the
Opinions of Educators," *John Hopkins Magazine,* October, 1963, 6–9.

W. E. Gandy. "Implications of Integration for the Southern Teacher,"
Journal of Negro Education, Spring, 1962, 191–197.

James Jackson Kilpatrick. *The Southern Case for School Segregation.*
New York, 1962.

Erwin Knoll. "Ten Years of Deliberate Speed," *American Education,*
December, 1964–January, 1965, 1–3.

Samuel Krislov. "Constituency v. Constitutionalism: The Desegregation

Issue and Tensions and Aspirations of Southern Attorney Generals," *Midwest Journal of Political Science*, February, 1959, 75–92.

Jack Walter Peltason. *Fifty-Eight Lonely Men: Southern Federal Judges and School Desegregation*. New York, 1961.

Reed Sarratt. "Educational Segregation-Desegregation in the United States (1961–1963)," *American Review*, Autumn, 1963, 48–65.

Ralph L. Smith. "The South's Pupil Placement Laws: Newest Weapon Against Integration," *Commentary*, October, 1960, 326–329.

III

Reapportionment and Political Power

'Nag, Nag! That's all you and the
Supreme Court ever do!'

CONRAD, *Los Angeles Times*. Reprinted by permission
of the Register and Tribune Syndicate.

In American politics and public law the issue of equality in legislative representation, and the question of who shall represent whom and what, is certainly not a novel one. During the colonial period when representation was frequently based on political subdivisions with towns and counties entitled to fixed numbers of assembly delegates, considerable tension developed between the tidewater aristocrats of the older and more established coastal regions and the more democratically inclined frontiersmen of the western sections who demanded a stronger voice in councils and legislatures. When, therefore, the spokesmen of the Stamp Congress insisted that there could be "no taxation without representation," this constituted far more than rebellious rhetoric assailing the unrepresentativeness of the House of Commons or an attack on the organization of the British Empire. It articulated an eighteenth century faith in popular government, in government by the consent of the governed, in principles which subsequently found their most succinct expressions in the political theories enunciated in the Declaration of Independence and the Northwest Ordinance.

When the Founding Fathers deliberated on the frame of government in the Convention of 1787, the problem of representation once again proved to be a most difficult one. Among the delegates the feelings on the subject of "equal representation for equal numbers of peoples" was so intense and ideological cleavage so pronounced that had it not been for the Great Compromise, William Paterson's famous "New Jersey Plan," the assemblage might well have ended up in an irreconcilable deadlock. The

scheme that finally commanded a consensus between the pro-
tagonists of little Delaware and populous Virginia provided for
equal representation of states in the Senate while the House
of Representatives was to be chosen "by the People of the several
States . . . [and] apportioned among the several States . . .
according to their respective numbers." (Art. I, Sec. 2).

At the state level, with federal complexities lacking, the
forces of popular sovereignty were sufficiently powerful to overcome anti-egalitarian objections and the fears of "mobocracy."
They adopted the concept of popular representation (with slight
modifications), made it applicable to both houses and incorporated it into the constitutions of the majority of the original
states and of nearly all those joining the Union between 1790
and 1860. Post-civil war state constitutions, by way of contrast,
reveal a distinct shift away from primary reliance on the population principle. At that time representational patterns emerged
in which political subdivisions such as towns and counties found
great prominence in one of the legislative chambers while in the
other, though technically based on population also, disparities
in voting strength between districts continued to increase and
multiply.

By the turn of the century these constitutional provisions helped
to reinforce the political power, views and attitudes of rural and
small town America as it struggled with the challenges of burgeon-
ing cities, expanding industries and rapidly changing conceptions
of the role and functions of government.

In 1910, some 45% of this country's population was classified
as being urban; fifty years later, the 1960 census revealed that
63% of the American people resided in Standard Metropolitan
Statistical Areas defined by the Bureau of the Census as including
"a central city or cities with a population in excess of 50,000 and
the surrounding counties which form an integrated community
with such city or cities."

In the face of such a radically changing population picture,
the strength of the city vote was progressively diluted. Just how
imbalanced the rural-urban representational ratios had actually
become by 1960 in nearly all of the fifty states can be readily
illustrated in a number of ways.

TABLE 1

NUMBER AND POPULATION OF COUNTIES IN THE UNITED STATES, GROUPED BY CATEGORIES OF POPULATION SIZE*

(Population in thousands)

Categories	1910		1930		1950		1960	
	No.	Pop.	No.	Pop.	No.	Pop.	No.	Pop.
Under 25,000	2,149	27,421	2,062	26,331	1,954	24,261	1,942	23,064
25,000–99,999	796	32,203	869	37,411	901	40,757	884	41,247
100,000–499,999	87	17,154	142	29,911	200	40,088	238	48,542
500,000 and over	15	14,853	23	28,634	41	44,789	64	65,705
Total	3,047	91,631	3,096	122,287	3,096	149,895	3,128	178,558

* Independent cities not contained within a county, such as exist in a few states, are treated as counties and are included in the above tabulations. The District of Columbia, which is not a part of any state and which had no locally elective legislative representation in any of the years studied, is omitted from this table. Totals include only areas with representation in state legislatures.

Source: Paul T. David and Ralph Eisenberg, *Devaluation of the Urban and Suburban Vote* (Charlottesville: Bureau of Public Administration, University of Virginia, 1961), p. 8.

Table 1 demonstrates clearly that on a national average in 1960 voters living in the least populous counties possessed more than twice the vote given those in the sixty-four counties with populations of 500,000 and over. Also quite apparent is a remarkably stable and persistent trend since 1910 which reflects the systematic depreciation of the value of the urban vote when compared to that of the rural vote. Based on research findings underlying another set of tables, not included here, Professors David and Eisenberg were able to conclude that within the metropolitan areas it is not primarily the central city but the

T A B L E 2

STATES WITH SENATE DISTRICTS SHOWING VARIATIONS IN
POPULATION FROM SMALLEST TO LARGEST IN A RATIO
OF 1 TO 10 OR MORE. STATES ARE RANKED
FROM LARGEST TO SMALLEST RATIO

	State	*Smallest District*	*Largest District*	*Ratio*
1.	California	14,294	6,038,771	422.47 to 1
2.	Nevada	568	127,016	223.62 to 1
3.	New Mexico	1,874	262,199	139.91 to 1
4.	Idaho	915	93,460	102.14 to 1
5.	Florida	9,543	935,047	97.98 to 1
6.	Rhode Island	486	47,080	96.87 to 1
7.	Montana	894	79,016	88.38 to 1
8.	Arizona	3,868	331,755	85.77 to 1
9.	Georgia	13,050	556,326	42.63 to 1
10.	Alabama	15,417	643,864	41.76 to 1
11.	Maryland	15,481	492,428	31.81 to 1
12.	Oklahoma	13,125	346,038	26.37 to 1
13.	South Carolina	8,629	216,382	25.08 to 1
14.	Kansas	16,083	343,231	21.34 to 1
15.	New Jersey	48,555	923,545	19.02 to 1
16.	Delaware	4,177	70,000	16.76 to 1
17.	Alaska	4,603	57,431	12.48 to 1
18.	Michigan	55,806	690,259	12.37 to 1
19.	Pennsylvania	51,793	553,154	10.68 to 1
20.	Illinois	53,500	565,300	10.57 to 1
21.	Iowa	29,696	266,314	8.97 to 1

TABLE 2 (Continued)

VARIATIONS IN POPULATION OF HOUSE DISTRICTS FROM SMALLEST TO LARGEST. STATES ARE RANKED FROM LARGEST TO SMALLEST RATIO

	State	Smallest District	Largest District	Ratio
1.	Vermont	38	33,155	872.50 to 1
2.	Connecticut	191	81,089	424.55 to 1
3.	New Hampshire	8	1,179	147.38 to 1
4.	Florida	2,868	311,682	108.68 to 1
5.	Georgia	1,876	185,422	98.84 to 1
6.	West Virginia	4,391	252,925	57.60 to 1
7.	Rhode Island	486	18,977	39.05 to 1
8.	Delaware	1,643	58,228	35.44 to 1
9.	Kansas	2,069	68,646	33.18 to 1
10.	Pennsylvania	4,485	139,293	31.06 to 1
11.	Utah	1,164	32,380	27.82 to 1
12.	Tennessee	3,454	79,031	22.88 to 1
13.	Nevada	568	12,525	22.05 to 1
14.	North Carolina	4,520	82,059	18.15 to 1
15.	Louisiana	6,909	120,205	17.40 to 1
16.	Idaho	915	15,576	17.02 to 1
17.	Iowa	7,910	133,157	16.83 to 1
18.	Mississippi	3,576	59,542	16.65 to 1
19.	Alabama	6,731	104,767	15.56 to 1
20.	New Mexico	1,874	29,133	15.55 to 1
21.	Montana	894	12,537	14.02 to 1
22.	Oklahoma	4,496	62,787	13.97 to 1
23.	Massachusetts	3,559	49,478	13.90 to 1
24.	Missouri	3,960	52,970	13.38 to 1
25.	New York	14,974	190,343	12.71 to 1
26.	Maryland	6,541	82,071	12.55 to 1
27.	Minnesota	8,343	99,446	11.92 to 1
28.	Arizona	5,754	30,438	5.29 to 1
29.	Michigan	34,006	135,268	3.98 to 1

Source: Adapted from National Municipal League, *Compendium on Legislative Apportionment* (New York, 1962).

suburbs which, over the years, experienced the most serious loss in voting power.

Another method of showing the extent and scope of legislative malapportionment seeks to discover the smallest percentage of a state's population which could theoretically elect a majority of the members of either chamber. Based on a study of the National Municipal League, as of July 1, 1961, there were thirty state senates and twenty-five state assemblies in which 35% or less of the population could elect a majority of the membership. States in which even less than 15% of the people could achieve such results in the upper house included Arizona, Florida, California, Maryland, Nevada and New Mexico.

Enormous differences in population between districts were also common in a large number of states (see Table 2).

Efforts by urban interests to force legislative reapportionment had run into major legal and political roadblocks. About three-quarters of all state constitutions contained a provision which modified the population basis of representation or which alloted a specific number of seats to counties, towns or other political subdivisions irrespective of populations in either one or in both houses of the legislature. Legislators were disinclined to redraw district lines which could easily eliminate or endanger their own seats or those of friends or fellow partisans. To merely increase the size of the legislature—a favorite nineteenth century device —proved politically unfeasible in view of the fact that most assemblies were already excessively large and the parliamentary processes unduly cumbersome. Even in the dozen or so states where constitutions did provide that representation in both houses should be based substantially on population and where districts were to be subjected to periodic reapportionment as in forty-one states, urban voters after exhausting all other political remedies found most of the state courts unwilling to order compliance or to declare existing apportionment statutes to be null and void. The general reluctance of the courts to interject themselves into the reapportionment struggles was well exemplified by two widely cited cases from Illinois and Minnesota.

In *Ferguson* v. *Marks* (1926) petitioners sought a writ of mandamus to force the Illinois legislature "to meet and apportion the state," in pursuance of a state constitutional requirement that stipulated periodic reapportionment following each decennial federal census. Such reapportionment had not taken place since 1901. Quoting with approval from an earlier case, the state Supreme Court rejected the request on the grounds that (1) the "duty to reapportion . . . is a specific legislative duty imposed solely on the legislative department . . . ; it alone is responsible to the people for a failure to perform that duty . . ." and (2) while mandamus may be invoked to compel an executive officer to perform a certain act, "the judical department cannot compel by mandamus the legislative department to perform any duty imposed upon it by law. . . ."

Largely relying on this precedent, and in the absence of reliance on the equality provisions of the Fourteenth Amendment, a Minnesota Supreme Court nineteen years later turned back a request to declare void that state's apportionment act of 1913 despite gross malapportionment that had resulted from major population changes. Although the Minnesota constitution made population the basis of representation for both houses, the court refused to accept the petition contending that the originally valid district law could not be subsequently judicially disturbed. "The remedy lies in the political conscience of the legislature," wrote the chief justice, "where lies the burden of the constitutional mandate. It is not within the province of this court to prompt the action of that conscience. It is usually sensitive enough to the prompting from the electorate." Unfortunately, from the point of view of a heavily underrepresented urban electorate, the distinguished jurist's optimistic faith in the political responsiveness of lawmakers was badly misplaced. Ultimately, it took the threat of direct intervention by the federal judiciary—and a far-reaching reversal in decision-making at the level of the United States Supreme Court—to bring about legislative reapportionment, so long delayed in Minnesota and throughout much of the nation.

As of November 1, 1961 there had been no reapportionment for half a century or more in Alabama, Connecticut, Iowa (Senate) and Tennessee and none for at least ten years in sixteen other states. Finally, even where legislatures were reapportioned with some regularity, substantial equality between legislative districts was, of course, rarely if ever achieved.

Enter the Federal Courts

Like their colleagues at the state level, a majority of the United States Supreme Court was most reluctant to provide judicial redress for underrepresented and disfavored voters and thus do for legislators what legislators refused to do themselves.

As late as 1946 a suit (*Colegrove* v. *Green*) assailing congressional districts in Illinois for lack of "compactness" and "approximate equality of population" was dismissed for want of equity by Justice Frankfurter on the grounds that the issue was of a "peculiarly political nature" and therefore not "for judicial determination." Justices Black, Douglas and Murphy dissented. While admitting that the districts then in existence failed to reflect great changes in the distribution of population, the majority opinion insisted that "no court can affirmatively remap the Illinois districts so as to bring them more in conformity with the standards of fairness for a representative system." If, on the other hand, the existing system were to be declared invalid, then the state would have to elect its congressional delegation on an at-large basis, which would either be "worse" or violative of a long-standing congressional intent.

In addition, the Court stated that since the Constitution left apportionment matters to the exclusive control of Congress and state legislatures, the failure of these bodies to take corrective action in no way warrants federal court intervention into such a deeply partisan and political "embroilment." In controversies of this kind "the remedy ultimately lies with the people. . . . Courts ought not to enter this political thicket."

Writing a dissent which some years later was to become the prevailing opinion of the Court, Justice Black argued that the petitioners had standing to sue, that the issue was justiciable, that this was not a "political question" removed from judicial determination, and that petitioners were merely asserting rights guaranteed them by Article I of the federal Constitution and by the equality clause of the Fourteenth Amendment. To give "all the people an equally effective voice in electing their representatives," federal courts have an obligation to exercise their equity powers and to enjoin state officers from enforcing an act which resulted "in a wholly indefensible discrimination against petitioners and all other voters in heavily populated areas."

Further reinforcement of the doctrine of judicial non-intervention in apportionment controversies came in quick order. *McDougall* v. *Green* (1948) upheld an Illinois statute requiring a statewide distribution of signatures on petitions seeking the formation of a new political party which the Court found was designed to give voters in the least populous areas of the state an effective veto over the "nomination of candidates whose support is confined to geographically limited areas." In a *per curiam* memo (with Justices Douglas and Murphy dissenting) the contention was advanced that "[i]t would be strange indeed, and doctrinaire, for this Court, applying such broad constitutional concepts as due process and equal protection of the laws, to deny a State the power to assure a proper diffusion of political initiative as between its thickly populated counties and those having concentrated masses, in view of the fact that the latter have practical opportunities for exercising their political weight at the polls not available to the former." To the voters of Cook County whose legislative underrepresentation, especially in the state Senate was notorious, the Court's reasoning must have appeared as something of a caricature of political realities.

Two years later the law of *Colegrove* and *McDougall* was invoked once again by a similarly divided Court to sustain Georgia's admittedly inequitable county unit system for the selection of candidates in statewide primaries. "Federal courts" ordered the *per curiam* memorandum in *South* v. *Peters* affirming precedent and tradition, "consistently refuse to exercise their equity powers in cases posing political issues arising from a state's geographic distribution of electoral strength among its political subdivisions."

In the light of *Colegrove* and these other cases federal district courts in Alabama, Oklahoma and Pennsylvania continued to reject petitions for judicial assistance that endeavored to void or correct imbalances in state legislative representation on the basis of federal constitutional guarantees.

The first major break with this line of approach occurred in 1956. Speaking through Chief Justice McLaughlin in *Dyer* v. *Kazuhisa Abe,* the federal district court of Hawaii held that the failure of the territorial legislature to reapportion itself for fifty-five years, despite a requirement of the Hawaiian Organic Act which demanded apportionment "from time to time," violated the fundamental law of the Territory and deprived plaintiffs of the equal protection and due process of law guarantees of the United States Constitution. Going beyond a frank assertion that equity jurisdiction should be exercised to force territorial reapportionment, the court added that classifications which discriminate geographically are just as indefensible as those that discriminate racially. "The people of Hawaii need no court intervention to insure a democratic school system. They do need judicial aid in achieving a democratic legislature. . . . The time has come, and the Supreme Court has marked the way . . . [in decisions affecting discriminatory practices in the schools and franchise] when serious considerations should be given to a reversal of the traditional reluctance of judicial intervention in legislative reapportionment."

When petitioners in other states attempted to rely on *Dyer* for support, courts were disinclined to follow the activist role distinguishing that case on the grounds that Hawaii, being at that time a political subdivision of the United States, had a legal relationship to the nation quite unlike that of any other state.

In at least one instance, however, a federal court in Minnesota in *Magraw* v. *Donovan* (1958) did acknowledge the power under the Fourteenth Amendment to be able to take positive remedial action upon a showing of gross legislative inequalities between districts under a state constitution which imposed an "unmistakable duty on the State Legislature to reapportion." While retaining jurisdiction in the matter, the court decided to give the upcoming legislature one more chance to "heed the constitutional mandate . . ." (this time it did!).

The Supreme Court Decides to Decide

At the level of the Supreme Court it turned out to be a reapportionment case from Tennessee, *Baker* v. *Carr* (1962), that began a revolution in judicial-legislative relations of such magnitude as to affect ultimately the distribution of political power throughout every state of the nation. As a consequence of this pivotal decision all election districts were now subject to close federal scrutiny and to federally promulgated standards of equality.

Dissenters in *Colegrove* had become a majority in *Baker*. Justice Brennan now speaking for the Court decided that petitioners' complaint alleging deprivation of equal protection under the Fourteenth Amendment, growing out of Tennessee's failure to redistrict for sixty years, was improperly denied by a federal district court. In reversing the dismissal order, he found that (1) the trial court did have jurisdiction to hear the case, (2) this was a justiciable cause for which appropriate relief could be available and (3) petitioners were in the position to challenge the constitutionality of the 1901 apportionment statute.

The central thrust of the argument stressed this: When petitioners suing for themselves and others similarly situated could show that "arbitrary" state action "placed them in a constitutionally unjustified inequality vis à vis voters in irrationally favored counties," then this sufficiently constitutes an "impairment" of rights secured them under the equal protection clause of the Fourteenth Amendment. It constitutes personal injury which affords petitioners judicial standing and remedy. Even in *Colegrove,* a majority of the seven justices participating in the decision seemed disinclined to dismiss the suit "for want of equity." Protection of "political rights" such as these does not involve the guarantee clause of the Constitution or the type of "political questions" which courts must necessarily eschew.

Having established "jurisdiction," "justiciability" and "standing," the opinion remanded to the district court the nature of the relief which was to be "fashioned in the light of well-known principles of equity."

Baker had broken the dike. Georgia's unique method of nominating candidates for statewide office and for the United States Senate—the county unit system that had served so well to dilute the political power of the urban electorate by assigning preferential weights to the smaller rural counties—reached the Supreme Court once again. In *Gray* v. *Sanders* (1963) it was invalidated. Justice Douglas rejected the urgings of the defense that the Georgia system was analogous to the federal Electoral College on the grounds that the latter grew out of "specific historical concerns" and that the wording of the Seventeenth Amendment calling for senators to be elected "by the people" left "no constitutional way by which the equality of voting power could be voided." Then came the sentence which has left its impact on all subsequent reapportionment cases. "The conception of political equality from the Declaration of Independence, to Lincoln's Gettysburg Address, to the Fifteenth, Seventeenth, and Nineteenth Amendments can mean only one thing—one person, one vote."

Implications apparent already in *Baker* and *Gray* become more fully explicit in 1964 when the Supreme Court through a series of decisions proceeded to incorporate the one man, one vote principles into the law of the land. In February of that year came *Wesberry* v. *Sanders,* another case from the Peach State, this one attacking wide population disparities in congressional districts. Justice Black for the majority construed Constitutional Convention debates and constitutional history to mean that the intent of Article I, Section 2 ordering that the House of Representatives shall be chosen "by the People of the several States" and be "apportioned among the several States . . . according to their respective numbers," would require "equal representation for equal numbers." To meet this intent districts need not be drawn "with mathematical precision" yet to deny the goal of equality would deny the "high standard of justice and common sense which the Founders set for us."

What *Wesberry* accomplished for congressional districts, *Reynolds* v. *Sims* did for state legislative districts four months later when Chief Justice Warren, over the lengthy and strenuous dissent of Justice Harlan, applied the one man, one vote standard to Alabama's legislature. Here representational inequalities stemming "from legislative inaction for [sixty years] coupled with the unavailability of any political or judicial remedies" were found to have "resulted in a minority stranglehold on the State Legislature." Going considerably beyond the broad principles laid down in *Baker, Gray* and *Wesberry,* the Court began to address itself to the need for more specific guidelines. Following *Baker* and encouraged by the opportunities it seemed to offer "disinherited" voters, a large number of reapportionment suits had ushered in a series of contradictory and unreconcilable decisions as federal and state courts went about implementing the new Supreme Court rulings. Under the equal protection clause of the Fourteenth Amendment, could there be any "constitutionally cognizable principles which could justify departures from the basic standard of equality among the voters in the apportionment of seats in state legislatures"? Could states, for example, in their apportionment patterns "rationally" use such factors other than population as cities, towns or counties? No, said the Court; neither history, nor area, nor economic interests, nor groups, nor geography, nor political subdivision nor bicameralism itself can be permitted to warrant deviation from the substantial population equality required of all districts—"people, not land or trees or pastures, vote."

On the other hand, a bicameral state legislature, in which each house is apportioned equally so as not to thwart the will of the majority through a "veto" in its unrepresentative chamber, is neither necessarily "anachronistic" nor "meaningless." Bicameralism can still perform its "prime" function of insuring "mature and deliberate consideration of" and to prevent "precipitate action on, proposed legislation." House and Senate could represent different constituencies and be of differing sizes. Single-member districts might be used in one and multimember or "floterial" districts (combining political subdivisions) in the other. Minor malapportionments in one chamber could be balanced off in the other. "Differing complexions and collective attitudes" could be reflected in the two bodies as long as "both are apportioned substantially on a population basis . . . and the weight of the vote of each citizen is approximately equal in weight to that of any other citizen in the state." In a succession of decisions handed down on June 15 and June 22 of 1964, the Supreme Court, applying the standards of *Reynolds,* sustained challenges to the districting systems of Colorado, Connecticut, Delaware, Florida, Idaho, Illinois, Iowa, Maryland, Michigan, New York, Ohio, Oklahoma, Virginia and Washington.

Prodded by judicial activism and by the new precedents, state reapportionment proceeded at a phenomenal rate. Among the most interesting innovations in the process of implementing the one man, one vote rule, was the use of electronic computers for the location and design of new districts. A number of courts (especially a federal court in Delaware), legislatures and non-partisan reapportionment commissions began to avail themselves of "advice" which such machines could render. While no single program emerged as the definitive one, sufficient research had already been done to demonstrate the considerable usefulness of computer techniques in maximizing the numerical equality, compactness and contiguity of districts. Electronic computers, if so instructed, could also assist in reducing the effectiveness of the political gerrymander.

As of the 1966 election, only two years after *Reynolds, Congressional Quarterly* was able to report that thirty states had apportioned their entire legislatures; fifteen, their entire lower House; and thirteen, one-half of their Senates. Even more important on the basis of data available for forty-seven state houses all but nine now showed 46% or more of the population being able to elect a majority of representatives. The picture in the new state Senates was even more encouraging for those concerned with attaining majority rule. Evidence from forty-six states revealed only five upper houses falling below the 46% figure. Among other still unsettled questions are (1) the constitutional position of the multimember district, (2) the role of the judiciary with respect to the old and reliable gerrymander, (3) the absolute and total extension of the one man, one vote concept to city councils, counties and other political subdivisions and (4) the degree of mathematical deviation from the "ideal" district that may be judicially tolerated.

(1) Federal courts in Pennsylvania, Texas and Virginia held multimember districts permissible; the Supreme Court of Iowa

had urged their use for subdividing urban areas, but Tennessee's highest court deemed them incompatible with the state constitution. Floterial districts were ruled a deprivation of equal protection of laws by an Indiana federal district court. One form of the multimember district reached the United States Supreme Court in 1965 when Georgia's 1962 senatorial apportionment statute was attacked for providing county-wide voting in multimember districts established "among the seven most populous counties." Contrary to the district court which found this to constitute "an invidious discrimination," Justice Brennan in *Fortson* v. *Dorsey* reaffirmed the *Reynolds* view that in the absence of "mathematic disparity" the mere requirement that a senator reside in a district within the county "while his tenure depends on a county-wide electorate" does not by itself indefensibly dilute the weight of the vote "of the people in his home district." Most relevant for future litigation was the dictum that a different conclusion might have been reached if it were shown that the multimember constituency pattern was designed or operated in a way "to minimize or cancel out the voting strength of racial or political elements of the voting population." In *Burns* v. *Richardson* (1966) the Supreme Court upheld Hawaii's multimember Senate districts largely on the basis of *Fortson*'s dictum and so converted it into a constitutionally significant test. Whether the Court may in some future instance insist on the subdistricting of multimember districts remains to be seen. Such a system has much to recommend itself. Minorities living in concentrated neighborhoods or ghettoes would be less in danger of being outvoted, the representatives could be kept close to their constituents and interparty competition might be sharpened.

(2) The issue of a racially motivated gerrymander was raised in *Gomillion* v. *Lightfoot* back in 1958. A group of Negro voters in Tuskegee charged an Alabama redistricting act as having transformed a formerly square city boundary "into a strangely irregular twenty-eight sided figure . . . with the inevitable effect" of removing "from the city all save four or five of its four hundred Negro voters while not removing a single white voter or resident." Reversing dismissals decreed by a district court and affirmed by a Circuit Court of Appeals, Justice Frankfurter overruled

defendant's contention claiming unrestricted power in the states "to establish, destroy, or reorganize by contraction or expansion its political subdivisions. . . ." Unlike *Colegrove* on which the state also relied, this case, it was held, instead of merely relating to unequal weighing of voting strengths, rested on a legislature singling "out a readily isolated segment of a racial minority for special discriminatory treatment. . . ." Courts cannot remain silent when legislatures through the manipulation of districts seek to impair voting rights guarantees contained in the federal Constitution.

Another charge of a racially inspired gerrymander confronted the Court in *Wright* v. *Rockefeller* (1964). Under attack was the constitutionality of the 18th Congressional district in Harlem— population 86.3% Negro and Puerto Rican. Justice Black for the majority agreed with the district court on a lack of factual proof to the effect that the district situated in the "ghettoized Island of Manhattan" was drawn "on racial lines or that the Legislature was motivated by considerations of race, creed or country of origin."

Justice Douglas (joined by Justice Goldberg) took a much less sanguine view of the gerrymander. To him the "twists and turns producing an 11-sided, step-shaped boundary" between the 18th and neighboring districts could, even in the absence of district court findings, reasonably justify an inference of intentional segregation. "The fact" that Congressman Powell representing the district and other "Negro political leaders . . . [as intervenors for the defense] find advantage in this nearly solid Negro and Puerto Rican district is irrelevant. . . ." Segregation, however benevolent, violates the democratic ideal. "When racial or religious lines are drawn by the State," summarized Justice Douglas in his dissent, "the multiracial, multireligious communities that our Constitution seeks to weld together as one become separatist; antagonisms that relate to race or to religion rather than to political issues are generated; communities seek not the best representative but the best racial or religious partisan."

(3) Yet to be decided by the Supreme Court is the question of extending the "reapportionment revolution" to local government. The one man, one vote concept was judged not applicable

by federal courts in Michigan with regard to local legislatures and in Georgia with regard to electing state judges and members of school boards. Opposite conclusions were reached in California, New Jersey, New York and Wisconsin as to county board membership, in Maryland, New York and Virginia as to city councils and in Pennsylvania as to school board districts.

Two unanimous decisions foreshadowing possibly more limited applications of the one man, one vote rule to local governments were handed down by the United States Supreme Court on May 22, 1967. In a Michigan case, *Sailors* v. *Board of Education of the County of Kent,* the Court held that members of a school board which was "not legislative in the classical sense" (board membership was "basically appointive rather than elective") need not come from districts which were equal in population. "Viable local governments," wrote Justice Douglas, "may need many innovations, numerous combinations of old and new devices, great flexibility in municipal arrangements to meet changing urban conditions."

In the other case, *Dusch* v. *Davis,* the Supreme Court reversed a lower court ruling which had declared unconstitutional the representational scheme under which councilmen were elected in Virginia Beach, Virginia. Against charges of violating the equality requirements of the Fourteenth Amendment, the Court upheld the community's "7–4 plan" where four members of the council came from a city-wide constituency and seven from separate and greatly varying districts. According to Douglas, the plan "reflected a detente between urban and rural communities that may be important in resolving the complex problems of the modern megalopolis in relation to the city, suburbia and the rural countryside."

(4) So far the Court has refused to indicate the precise range of deviation from an absolute numerical equality that may be held to conform to the one man, one vote standard. In the latest decision on this point, *Swann* v. *Adams* (1967), the Court turned back for the third time a Florida apportionment law "for failure of the State to present or the district court to articulate acceptable reasons" that could account for inequalities between districts. The plan that was declared invalid contained population variations

of 30% among Senate districts and 40% among House districts. Using percentage deviations from the average district as the measure, the Court noted overrepresentations of 15.09% in the Senate and 18.28% in the House. Underrepresented districts in the Senate deviated as much as 10.56% and those of the House as much as 15.27%. As to interstate comparisons, the Court pointedly emphasized that approval of a 10% or 15% deviation from the norm in one state "has little bearing on the validity of a similar variation in another State." What seemed relevant here was that appellants had demonstrated "that a closer approximation to equally populated districts was a feasible undertaking." Justice Harlan dissented. To him, Florida's plan seemed to be in "substantial compliance" with *Reynolds,* and appellants had failed to show "any invidious" purpose or effect underlying the mathematical deviations.

Meanwhile lower federal courts have permitted some elasticity although it is generally understood that a population deviation should not exceed by more than 15% the size of an average district. If a mathematically stricter compliance is required, reapportionment laws in a considerable number of states would be open to challenge.

Critical Reactions to the Reapportionment Revolution

MAJOR VOICES FROM WITHIN THE COURT

Dissents from the majority positions were thoroughly detailed, ideologically consistent, occasionally strident in tone. *Baker,* in the view of Justice Frankfurter, the spokesman of judicial self-restraint, represented "a massive repudiation of the past . . . disregard of inherent limits in the effective exercise of the Court's judicial power. . . ." To avoid loss of "public confidence," the Court should not interject itself into these areas of intense feelings where political forces clash "in political settlements." *Colegrove* properly stated the rule. "From its earliest opinions this

Court has consistently recognized a class of controversies which do not lend themselves to judicial standards and judicial remedies." State apportionment systems belong to this category of questions basically political in nature. Courts should not be asked "to choose among competing bases of representation"—choices ultimately rooted deeply in differing concepts of "political philosophy." Furthermore, the claim that the equal protection clause of the Fourteenth Amendment dictates a standard under which representative government would have to be predicated on a man to man equality "is to put it bluntly, not true." Unlike the majority, Justice Frankfurter saw nothing in American constitutional history to demand such a stringent egalitarianism. While supported by some of the Founding Fathers and praised by great political thinkers, equality in representation was not practiced in England nor in the colonies; it was not made part of the national government, nor put into effect by the states when the Fourteenth Amendment was ratified; ". . . it has never been generally practiced, today or in the past."

It was the *Reynolds* case which occasioned Justice Harlan's most vigorous and lengthy exposition of disagreement although previously he had entered dissents in *Baker* and *Wesberry*. In his view the majority stood accused of completely misreading the wording of the Fourteenth Amendment, especially its second section which explicitly reserved to the states the right to deny or abridge "the right of their inhabitants to vote for the members of their legislatures" leaving to Congress the power of remedy. There was nothing in the history of the debate, adoption or ratification of the Amendment to "inhibit the States in choosing any democratic method they pleased for the apportionment of their legislatures." By "straying from the appropriate bounds of its authority" the Court has now wielded its new "constitutional" doctrine to preclude use by the states in establishing districts of such important rational factors as "history . . . 'economic or other sorts of group interests' . . . area . . . geographic considerations . . . a desire to 'insure effective representation for sparsely settled areas' . . . theories of bicameralism [except those approved by the Court] . . . occupation . . . 'an attempt to balance urban and rural power' . . . the preference of a majority of the voters in the States." In a paragraph that received wide public attention, particularly among the critics of the Court, Justice Harlan concluded that this assault on federalism reflects a dangerous view currently prevailing in the Court "that every major social ill in this country can find its cure in some constitutional 'principle,' and that this Court should 'take the lead' in promoting reform when other branches of government fail to act. The Constitution is not a panacea for every blot upon the public welfare, nor should this Court, ordained as a judicial body, be thought of as a general haven for reform movements."

The constitutional law enunciated by the Court in *Reynolds* to the effect that both houses of a legislature must be based on population drew a stinging rebuke from Justice Stewart in his dissent in *Lucas* v. *Forty-Fourth General Assembly of Colorado* (1964). A majority of the Court in this case had rejected as failing to meet the equal protection clause of the Fourteenth Amendment a reapportionment plan taking the form of a constitutional amendment to the Colorado constitution under which senatorial districts would have been structured on a basis combining population and area.

The Stewart dissent, joined by Justice Clark, criticized the Court for enshrining a particular theory of representation into a constitutional principle and then imposing this on the state of Colorado along with every other of the "fifty States from Maine to Hawaii, from Alaska to Texas, without regard and respect for the many individualized and differentiated characteristics of each state. . . ." The Court's interpretation of the equal protection clause, reasoned Stewart, had brought it to the point when a state can only meet its requirements "by the uncritical, simplistic, and heavy-handed application of sixth-grade arithmetic." Throughout our history legislatures have always had to balance regional, social and economic interests in order to attain the public interest. What is wanted is "a medley of competing voices" not "the majority's monolithic command." Within such a setting of diversity and complexity, "legislators do not represent faceless numbers. They represent people . . . with needs and interests . . . which can often be related to the geographic areas in which these people live." It was entirely "rational" for a state like Colorado, with distinct geographic regions, with the Continental Divide crossing the state, with some areas nearly inaccessible during the winter months, with districts of "substantially differing interests" to conclude "that effective representation . . . was unlikely to be achieved if the rule of equal population . . . were mechanically imposed." Colorado's Senate apportionment formula, rather than defying the principle of majority rule, manifested a conscious choice by which majorities wished to protect the interests of minorities.

CONGRESSIONAL REACTIONS

To the critics of the Court the reapportionment decisions, beginning with *Baker,* constituted further examples of unwarranted federal intervention into the affairs and rights of states, as judicial precedents were cast aside and local wishes ignored. Pressures on Congress to reverse the Supreme Court or to exempt from federal jurisdiction state apportionment systems mounted steadily. To further these objectives, legislatures in over half of the states formally called for the convening of a national constitutional convention; in more than a dozen additional states either both or at least one of the houses had enacted resolutions petitioning Congress to initiate procedures for changes in the Constitution. The General Assembly of the Council of State Governments, a group of influential state legislators, endorsed proposals which would have barred federal courts from hearing apportionment disputes and would have established a new "Court of the Union," composed of all of the state chief justices. This court would function as a tribunal superior to the Supreme Court on questions pertaining to federal-state relations.

In Congress, over one hundred measures were introduced, mostly by Southern Democrats and Republicans, to curb the role of the Supreme Court in suits affecting state patterns of representation. Among the strongest of such anti-Court bills, originating in the House, the one sponsored by Representative William Tuck, a Democrat from Virginia, met approval on August 19, 1964 when strongly backed by a coalition of Southern Democrats and Republicans. It passed by a vote of 218 to 175. The Tuck

TABLE 3

HOUSE VOTING ON THE TUCK BILL
(H.R. 11926)

	Yea-Nay	Yea Votes		Nay Votes		Yea Percentage Dem. Repub.		Nay Percentage Dem. Repub.	
		Dem.	Repub.	Dem.	Repub.	%	%	%	%
North	126–155	12	114	124	31	9	91	80	20
South	92–20	84	8	16	4	91	9	80	20
Total	218–175	96	122	140	35	44	56	80	20

Source: *Congressional Quarterly Weekly Report*, August 21, 1964, pp. 1952–53.

POPULATION AREA BREAKDOWN OF HOUSE REPUBLICANS VOTING AGAINST THE TUCK BILL

Congressional District Classification	Number	Percentage of Those Republicans Voting No
Urban Areas	9	26%
Suburban Areas	15	43%
Rural Areas	10	28%
At Large	1	3%
Total	35	100%

Note: Classification of congressional districts was made on the basis of data presented in the *Congressional Quarterly* and *The Congressional District Data Book—88th Congress,* cited above.

Source: *Congressional Quarterly Weekly Report,* August 21, 1964, pp. 1953–1954.

Bureau of the Census, *The Congressional District Data Book—88th Congress,* 1963.

bill was less successful in the Senate where moderates and liberals combined to defeat it 56 to 21. Essentially, the Tuck bill would have denied jurisdiction to all federal courts in matters pertaining to state legislative reapportionment.

As shown in Table 3, of those voting against the Tuck bill in the House, 144 were Democrats and 35 were Republicans, 69%

of the Republican members representing urban or suburban constituencies.

On January 6, 1965, Senator Everett M. Dirksen, Republican minority leader in the Senate, introduced S.J. Res. 2, an amendment to the Constitution allowing the states to include factors other than population in the apportionment of either the Senate or the House. Cosponsored by thirty-seven senators (thirty-two Republicans and five Democrats) and overwhelmingly approved by the Judiciary Subcommittee on Constitutional Amendments, this resolution quickly became the rallying point for the foes of the Court's reapportionment decisions. In the form that the Dirksen Amendment finally emerged on the floor of the Senate it provided:

> Section 1. The people of a state may apportion one house of a bicameral legislature using population, geography, and political subdivisions as factors, giving each factor such weight as they deem appropriate, or giving reasonable weight to the same factors in apportioning a unicameral legislature, if in either case such plan or apportionment has been submitted to a vote of the people in accordance with law and with the provisions of this Constitution and has been approved by a majority of those voting on that issue. When a plan of apportionment based on factors of population, geography, and political subdivisions is submitted to a vote of the people under this Section there shall also be submitted, at the same election, an alternative plan of apportionment based upon substantial equality of population.
>
> Section 2. Any plan of apportionment which has been approved under this article shall be resubmitted to a vote of the people, or another plan may be submitted under the provisions of Section 1, at the November general election held two years following each year in which there is commenced any enumeration provided for in Section 2 of Article I, and upon approval by a majority of those voting thereon, such plan of apportionment shall continue in effect until changed in accordance with law and with the provisions of this Constitution.

Major organizational support for the amendment included representatives of the American Farm Bureau Federation, the National Grange, the United States Chamber of Commerce, the National Association of Manufacturers, the Citizens Committee for Balanced Legislative Representation (organized originally in California), and the National Commission on Constitutional Government (comprising members of various state legislatures). Among those lobbying against the Dirksen proposal were spokesmen for the National Committee for Fair Representation (including leaders from the AFL-CIO, the Americans for Democratic Action and the American Civil Liberties Union), the National Catholic Conference for Interracial Justice, the National Council of Jewish Women, the United Presbyterian Church (Office of Church and Society), the Southern Christian Leadership Conference, the United States Conference of Mayors and the National League of Cities.

During the 1964 campaign, Senator Goldwater criticized the Court severely, viewing the reapportionment decisions as further evidence of unwarranted judicial lawmaking in violation of states' rights and constitutional traditions. While the Republican platform contained a plank supporting a constitutional amendment which would have permitted the states to apportion one house of their legislatures on factors other than population, the Democratic presidential candidate and his party's convention studiously avoided taking a position on the issue.

Arguments favoring the Dirksen proposal before the Subcommittee on Constitutional Amendments and on the floor of the Senate stressed a number of common themes. *Baker* and *Reynolds,* as so well demonstrated by Justices Frankfurter and Harlan, had shattered constitutional precedents, federal-state relations and judicial respect for matters left to legislative determination; in these cases the majority misapplied the Fourteenth Amendment, misunderstood the intentions of the Founding Fathers and misread American constitutional history. A rigid application of the one man, one vote principle in both legislative houses would break down the traditions of moderation, check and balance and a republican form of government and would inevitably lead to a domination of rural America by the cities and their political bosses who neither understood nor showed concern for the needs of the farmer, his roads, schools or local government; Chicago would rule downstate Illinois and the four metropolitan counties of California the rest of that state. Nothing gave the Supreme

Court the right to impose a theory of representation requiring both houses to be based on population when the people of a number of states (such as California, Colorado, Illinois, Missouri and Ohio) explicitly ratified a federal plan under which one house at least allowed districts and representation voting distributions in which political subdivisions and area factors were given consideration. The Dirksen Amendment would return to the people the power which was properly theirs by enabling them to adopt free from judicial interference patterns of representation indigenous to the peculiar conditions of each state.

Opponents of the Dirksen Amendment rested their arguments on contentions such as these: The Supreme Court through its reapportionment decisions at last brought equitable representation to America's cities and metropolitan areas. Long ignored and denied their fair share of political power by conservative rural legislatures, urban voters (especially Negroes), organized labor and the poor were forced to turn away from their own state legislatures and seek assistance in Washington to help finance their enormously expanding needs in education, housing, transportation, welfare and other service areas. "Rotten borough" state legislatures greatly enhanced and accelerated the trend towards federal centralization and a progressively weakened state government.

Fundamental to a democratic government, to political justice and equity, suggested the critics, is the principle that the weight of every person's vote must be equal, regardless of his race, sex, religion, residence, wealth or occupation. This is what the Supreme Court reaffirmed and this is what the Amendment is designed precisely to negate. It gives to a majority the right to adopt a system of apportionment which may legitimately discriminate by distributing the vote in favor of the residents of one region of the state over those living in another. Under our Constitution one's right to freedom of speech and religion and to all the other civil liberties cannot be abridged even by a majority voting on such rights at a referendum; the Amendment would not only make it possible to abridge a man's vote—a most precious civil right—simply because he may happen to live in a metropolitan area of a state, but would also keep the federal courts from ex-

ercising their powers of judicial review over these newly encouraged experimentations in anti-majoritarian electoral engineering.

Widely heralded as a countermeasure to meet the threat of an
urban mass electorate bent on destroying rural America, the
Amendment perpetuates and reinforces a well-known political
myth. There is nothing homogeneous or unified about the politics
of metropolitania. It is and will likely continue to be a complex
fabric of political accommodations and compromises between
conflicting interests of core city and suburb, rich and poor, whites
and blacks, employers and employees, Democrats and Republicans. Equalizing the vote throughout the state and terminating
the political discriminations based on geography and residence
of the type actually invited by the Amendment would bring a
new vitality to the operations of state and local government and
to the effectiveness with which these units could function within
the framework of a contemporary federalism.

After considerable debate, Senator Paul Douglas leading the
anti-Dirksen forces, the Amendment came up for decision on
August 4, 1965. The vote was 57 to 39, seven short of the two-
thirds required to pass a constitutional Amendment. Republicans
favoring the measure divided 29 to 3 and Democrats 28 to 36;
Northern Democrats broke 10 to 33, and Southern Democrats
18 to 3. Table 4 reveals the sectional urban-rural and ideological
divisions on the issue. Cutting across party lines 78% of senators
coming from Northern states and 78% of senators coming from
states classified as 60% or more urban opposed the proposal. Not
surprisingly, the ideological dimensions of the vote on the Dirksen Amendment became equally clear. Based on "ratings" by the
Americans for Democratic Action, a liberal group strongly supporting the Supreme Court and the anti-Amendment cause, 28
of the 39 Senators who voted "nay" received a rating of 81–100
on an index of "liberalism" including such other controversial
legislation as housing and urban development, voting rights,
Appalachian regional development and anti-poverty programs.

When an undiscouraged Senator Dirksen renewed his battle
in 1966, nearly forty states had already complied or were in the
process of complying with the one man, one vote standard. Never-

T A B L E 4

SENATE VOTING ON THE DIRKSEN AMENDMENT
(S.J. Res. 66, August 4, 1965)

	Yea-Nay	Yea Votes		Nay Votes		Yea Percentage		Nay Percentage	
		Dem.	Repub.	Dem.	Repub.	Dem. %	Repub. %	Dem. %	Repub. %
North	37–36	10	27	33	3	27	73	91	9
South	20–3	18	2	3	0	90	10	100	0
Total	57–39	28	29	36	3	49.9	50.1	92	8

Source: *Congressional Quarterly Weekly Report*, August 6, 1965, p. 1587.

URBAN-RURAL ANALYSIS OF VOTING ON THE DIRKSEN AMENDMENT

	Yea	Nay	% Yea	% Nay
Urban States (60% and above urbanized)	4	14	22	78
Rural States (below 60% urbanized)	53	25	68	32
Total	57	39	59	41

Note: States were classified on the basis of data presented in an urban-suburban-rural breakdown of all states in *Congressional Quarterly Weekly Report*, February 2, 1962, pp. 156–169.

BREAKDOWN OF A.D.A. RATINGS OF NAY VOTERS ON THE DIRKSEN AMENDMENT

A.D.A. Rating	Number	Percent
00–20	0	00
21–40	1	3
41–60	1	3
61–80	9	23
81–100	28	71
Total	39	100

Source: *Congressional Quarterly Weekly Report*, August 6, 1965, p. 1587 and February 25, 1966, p. 474.

theless the 1965 Amendment in only slightly revised form was again brought to a vote. On April 20, in the face of hardened senatorial positions, the Amendment was once more defeated 55 to 38, seven votes short of the required two-thirds margin.

One Man, One Vote— *In Search for a Middle Position*

In testimony before Congress and in various professional journals, Professor Robert G. Dixon of the George Washington University Law School, has effectively and cogently pleaded his case for compromise between the extremes of the Dirksen and anti-Dirksen reapportionment positions.

Briefly stated, this is his argument. The essence of American traditions, governmental structures and political practices has never been strictly majoritarian. Federalism, separation of powers, written constitutions, committee systems, executive veto, extraordinary majorities to override vetoes or to amend constitutions, the state-based nature of the political party system—these and other features of the American system of government were specifically designed to protect minorities, to assure diversity and to force majorities to build coalitions of a democratic consensus. In such a system the reapportionment issue arises primarily in connection with the need to establish an effective and democratic pattern of legislative representation and not, as the Court mistakenly insisted, with instituting the mere quantitative equality of individual voters. Inasmuch as American politics is essentially group politics, the central concern in apportionment must be the guarantee of fair representation for all groups. What is important is not whether all districts are structured mathematically equal but whether the makeup of the legislature realistically reflects the complex and heterogenous composition of community life and whether it has wide popular acceptance.

A "winner take all" system (see Table 5) based on population alone views people as stripped of political allegiances and group identifications.

TABLE 5

EQUALIZING APPORTIONMENT AND EXPRESSING THE "POPULAR WILL"

	Party X	Party Y	Total Popula- tion	Seats Before Reappor- tionment	Seats After Reappor- tionment
County A	5,000	20,000	25,000	1	1
County B	55,000	45,000	100,000	1	4

Before reapportionment: Each party, one seat. Party vote split 60,000 to 65,000. After reapportionment: Party X, 60,000—four seats; Party Y, 65,000 votes—one seat.

Source: Robert G. Dixon, Jr., "Representation Goals," *National Civic Review* (November, 1963), 545.

Professor Dixon has no major quarrel with *Baker* and with the necessity of occasional judicial intervention when apportionments are frozen and electors left with no viable political alternative to redress gross imbalances. Such actions can aid in "returning politics to the people." Constitutionally, the Court in *Baker* would have been on firmer grounds had it invoked the due process of law or guarantee of republican form of government clauses rather than the equal protection of law provision. Use of the Fourteenth Amendment brought the Court to a rigid egalitarianism which critically oversimplified the problems of representation and ignored the depth of the political thickets in which the federal judiciary would soon find itself.

However, instead of curbing the jurisdiction of the federal courts Dixon preferred the type of amendment (supporting, in the main, proposals introduced by Senators Javits and Church) under which one house would be based on numerical equality and the other on a mixed representation formula with fixed limits of deviation and a decennial popular review. In this manner representative democracy could avoid the excesses of majoritarianism and the irresponsibilities of minority rule.

A substantially similar concern that the representational problems were oversimplified in the reapportionment cases was also ably expressed by Professor Alexander M. Bickel of Yale in his *Politics and the Warren Court.* He contended that Justice Brennan's assertion in *Baker* to the effect that the discrimination reflected "no policy, but simply arbitrary and capricious action" represented not so much a quarrel with the legislature's logic as with its value judgment. Tennessee may have been unwise, but there was nothing necessarily irrational in providing greater voting strength to its rural than to its populous urban areas. Democratic government essentially rests on consent.

> This means that the institutions must not merely represent a numerical majority, which is a shifting and uncertain quantity anyway, but must reflect the people in all their diversity, so that all the people may feel that their particular interests and even prejudices, that all their diverse characteristics, were brought to bear on the decision-making process.[1]

Representative institutions in a "reflective" democratic government must be something more than mere "animated voting machines." To Bickel it seems ironic "that the superdemocrats look to the unrepresentative courts for an arbitrary decision which they resent when it is made by a faultily representative legislature, acting in concert with a majoritarian governor."[2]

Emphasis on the interest group concept of representation in apportionment has, of course, come under criticism for a variety of reasons. It has been suggested that it is extremely difficult to determine criteria by which such groups could be singled out for attention, that it is politically unwise to assign fixed electoral weights on such a basis and that there is no democratically sound method of formally allotting to any one group a dominant role within a particular district. Opponents of the group concept prefer to place their faith in the one man, one vote principle as the best available defense against renewed efforts aimed at building protective walls around favored minorities whose claims to special treatment have in the past generally proved specious and transitory.

---

[1] Alexander M. Bickel, *Politics and the Warren Court* (New York: Harper and Row, 1965), p. 184.
[2] *Ibid.*, p. 188.

Political Consequences of Reapportionment

For some time American liberals had bitterly indicted malapportionment as one of the major causes for the failures of this country's governmental machinery to adapt itself to the demands of a rapidly changing society. Were it not for the disproportionate power possessed by legislators from rural areas and the smaller towns, the problems and fiscal needs of big cities would have received more sympathetic consideration and treatment.

There were many specific charges. When it came to the distribution of statewide revenues in order to aid schools, highways, streets, mass transit, air pollution or welfare programs, malapportioned legislatures devised ingenious formulas that shortchanged their urban constituents. Rural and urban rates of tax assessment and tax burden were found inequitable and discriminatory. Necessary structural changes in government to permit a metropolitan approach to metropolitan problems were resisted. Conservative legislators from sparsely populated districts, whose seniority placed them in strategically significant posts, were inclined to slow down or block legislation that could have helped cities to redevelop, to clear up their slums or to increase their volume of low cost public housing. Welfare programs to improve the lot of the poor, the unemployed, the sick or the disabled were either underfinanced or viewed with suspicion. It seemed more important to minimize the role of government than to use its potential as a regulator, promoter or partner. Political apologists of the *status quo* were strengthened, and the likelihood of effective interparty competition was reduced as malapportioned state legislatures "gerrymandered" their districts and those of their favored congressmen.

Malapportionment helped to obstruct party government and party responsibility as governors elected from statewide constituencies confronted committee chairmen who came from thinly populated counties enabling them to attain the long legislative tenures that gave them commanding positions from which to attack proposals backed by the executive.

Liberals were able to demonstrate that this phenomenon was

not peculiar to the states. Prior to the reapportionment decisions it was not at all unusual for three-fourths of the committee chairmen in Congress to represent the least populous districts while representatives from the most populous districts had to be satisfied with only one-fourth of such chairmanships.

Surveying these complex political configurations in federal, state and local governments, it is doubtful whether they could all fairly be attributed solely to the failure of legislative reapportionment. Operating within a system so enormously complicated and diverse as that of the United States, patterns of apportionment are necessarily interwoven with other political, social and structural factors which vary greatly from state to state and from section to section and which cannot be isolated. Equally difficult, in the absence of much more research, are generalizations about the immediate political outcomes of reapportionment.

Sufficient fragmentary evidence, however, is available already to indicate that between 1962 and 1965, reapportionment benefits accrued to the distinct advantage of Democrats in Michigan, New York and most of the New England states, while Republicans gained in California, Minnesota and in an impressive number of the bigger cities of the South. Residents in suburban communities throughout the country fared much better than did those living in the core city. Within the metropolitan areas legislative reapportionment intensified rivalries between cities as well as within the ranks of the dominant party. Interparty competition in general seems to have been enhanced. Legislative logjams were broken, for example, in Colorado and Michigan, facilitating increases in school aid and workmen's compensation, and nearly half of all states took major steps towards constitutional and governmental reform.

In the congressional election of 1966, according to *Congressional Quarterly,* redistricting played a decisive role in the Virginia Democratic primary defeat of Representative (Judge) Howard W. Smith, longtime chairman of the House Rules Committee, in the Tennessee Democratic primary defeat of Representative Thomas Murray, Chairman of the House Post Office and Civil Service Committee, and in the Massachusetts Republican primary defeat of Joe Martin, former Speaker of the House. Reapportionment was noted to have contributed significantly to the congressional victories of a Democrat in Indiana and of a Republican in Ohio.

With the sharp Republican resurgence in 1966, Democratic strategists for their part can find little in reapportionment itself on which to build hopes for an early reversal in political fortunes.

Those who were confident that reapportionment would insure a more generous and liberal legislative attitude or policy towards education, welfare and state revenue structures may also have to face some disappointments.

A number of recent scholarly studies using interstate comparisons revealed no statistically significant correlation between malapportioned legislatures and the extent to which states were willing to finance certain public policies. Employing such indices as state expenditures for unemployment compensation, for educational purposes and for welfare recipients, these researchers could not discern mathematically any direct effect of unrepresentative legislatures upon the particular policy outcomes. Socioeconomic variables rather than malapportionment may have to account for most of the interstate differences.

While such studies are as yet much too limited and tentative in scope and findings, they do suggest caution in any interpretation concerning the measurable quantitative consequences of reapportionment. The revolution is still too young to have earned an epitaph. Through the reapportionment decisions the Court has been instrumental in shifting power to urban and suburban America. What the residents of our cities and suburbs will now accomplish with their newly won political leverage will determine greatly for many years to come the direction and quality of American life. The one man, one vote doctrine offers political opportunities without reciprocal guarantees that the "new" majority will necessarily respect the wishes and rights of the minorities which compose it or protect the interest of the "new" minority which once ruled so firmly in capitols and courthouses.

SUGGESTED READINGS

James B. Atleson. "Aftermath of Baker v. Carr—An Adventure in Judicial Experimentation," *California Law Review*, August, 1963, 535–572.

William J. D. Boyd. "Suburbia Takes Over," *National Civic Review*, June, 1965, 294–298.

Paul T. David. "1 Member vs. 2, 3, 4, or 5," *National Civic Review*, February, 1966, 75–81.

Robert G. Dixon, Jr. "Reapportionment in the Supreme Court and Congress: Constitutional Struggle for Fair Representation," *Michigan Law Review*, December, 1964, 209–242.

Howard D. Hamilton (ed.). *Reapportioning Legislatures: A Consideration of Criteria and Computers.* Columbus, 1966.

Richard I. Hofferbert. "The Relation Between Public Policy and Some Structural and Environmental Variables in the American States," *American Political Science Review*, March, 1966, 73–82.

Malcolm E. Jewell (ed.). *The Politics of Reapportionment.* New York, 1962.

Robert B. McKay, "Political Thickets and Crazy Quilts: Reapportionment and Equal Protection," *Michigan Law Review*, February, 1963, 645–710.

Robert B. McKay, *Reapportionment: The Law and Politics of Equal Representation.* New York, 1965.

"Note on Reapportionment," *Harvard Law Review*, April, 1966, 1226–1287.

James K. Pollock. "Considering All Angles," *National Civic Review*, July, 1966, 374–379.

C. Herman Pritchett. "Equal Protection and the Urban Majority," *American Political Science Review*, December, 1964, 869–875.

Glendon Schubert. *Reapportionment.* New York, 1965.

"Symposium on Legislative Reapportionment," *Law and Contemporary Problems*, Spring, 1952, 253–469.

James B. Weaver and Sidney W. Hess. "Districting by Machine," *National Civic Review*, June, 1964, 293–296.

Belle Zeller (ed.). *American State Legislatures,* Report of the Committee on American Legislatures. Washington, 1954.

IV

*Church, State and
Public Education*

"What Do They Expect Us To Do——Listen To The Kids Pray At <u>Home</u>?"

From *Straight Herblock* (Simon & Schuster, 1964).

On July 8, 1958, the Board of Education of a New Hyde Park, New York, school district adopted, as part of its educational program on "America's Moral and Spiritual Heritage," the following twenty-two word prayer, composed and recommended by the New York Board of Regents:

> Almighty God, we acknowledge our dependence upon Thee, and beg Thy blessing upon us, our parents, our teachers, and our Country.

After the pledge of allegiance to the flag and as an act of reverence to God, each school day was to begin with the public recital of this prayer in the presence of the teacher. Approximately four months later a group of petitioners, taxpayers and parents of children in the district requested a court order to compel the Board of Education to discontinue the use of the prayer on the grounds that by interfering with their religious practices and those of their children as believers and nonbelievers, it violated rights guaranteed them under the First Amendment of the United States Constitution and under the constitution of the State of New York.

While no provision in New York's statutes specifically called for prayers or for the reading of the Bible in public schools, the laws of a number of other states did just that.

Pennsylvania statutes, for example, required at least ten verses of the Bible to be read at the opening of each public school day. Non-complying teachers were to be fired. In Arkansas the Lord's Prayer or "any prayer" could be offered; failure of teachers to comply entailed a $25 penalty for the first offense and a second conviction constituted grounds for removal. Alabama stipulated that the teacher's report must show daily Bible reading otherwise public funds were to be withheld. Five verses from the Bible were the order in Delaware; a $25 fine was the sanction for the first violation and in instances of a second infringement, a teacher's credentials were to be revoked. Maine demanded readings from the scriptures with special emphasis upon the Ten Commandments, the Psalms of David, the Proverbs of Solomon, the Sermon on the Mount and the Lord's Prayer. Teachers were to inculcate "Christian virtue" along with daily Bible readings in Florida.

All in all, at the time when New York's prayer was challenged in the courts, the reading of the Bible without comment by the teacher and with the general provision that students should not be forced to participate against their will was considered mandatory in twelve states—Alabama, Arkansas, Delaware, Florida, Georgia, Idaho, Kentucky, Maine, Massachusetts, New Jersey, Pennsylvania and Tennessee.

In another group of about thirty states Bible reading or prayers were either permitted or made a matter of local option by statute, by judicial action (beginning mostly at the end of the nineteenth century), by rulings of the attorney general or by the law's silence. Court decisions barring the Bible and prayers from classroom devotional exercises for constitutional reasons were reported, on the other hand, in California, Illinois, Louisiana, Nebraska, South Dakota, Washington and Wisconsin.

These considerable differences in legal policy and approach probably reflect accurately this country's cultural pluralism and the historical, philosophical, religious and ethnic factors which helped to shape and direct it. They also reveal something of the profound divergences with which Americans viewed the role of religion and, more particularly in this context, the place of the Bible and prayer in tax-supported public schools.

Additional statistical evidence of this diversity in approach was brought to light in connection with a 1960 survey by Professor Dierenfield of Macalester College which was designed to ascertain the extent to which religious influences are overtly manifested and acknowledged in public education. On the basis of returns from approximately 2,500 school superintendents to the question "Is Bible reading conducted in the schools of your system?," the following responses were received:

TABLE 1

BIBLE READING IN THE SCHOOLS, 1960

By Area	Yes	No
United States	41.74	58.26
Western states	11.03	88.97
Midwestern states	18.26	81.74
Southern states	76.84	23.16
Eastern states	67.56	32.44
By Size of Community	Yes	No
500– 2,500	30.84	69.16
2,500– 5,000	43.11	56.89
5,000– 25,000	52.73	47.27
25,000–100,000	40.11	59.89
100,000 and over	54.17	45.83

Source: R. D. Dierenfield, *Religion in American Public Schools* (Washington: Public Affairs Press, 1962), p. 51.

In the light of such variegated practices, New York with its plural and strongly self-conscious religious cultures and its deeply rooted heritage of political liberalism was a peculiarly appropriate locale within which to raise the issue of the constitutionality of prayer. Was the Regents' prayer a permissible means of teaching spiritual values? Finding the rationale for the prayer incompatible with the establishment clause of the United States Constitution, the New York trial court in *Engel* v. *Vitale* (1959) decided that it was nevertheless possible to hold for the defendant school board since prayers in the public schools were traditional and accepted by the people at the time of the adoption of the First and Fourteenth Amendments.

What the Founding Fathers wished to guard against, insisted Judge Meyer in a scholarly opinion, was the type of church establishment as then known in Connecticut, Maryland, Massachusetts, New York or South Carolina. In this spirit they vigorously opposed religious conformity and forced contributions for the propagation of sectarian faiths. Still, Benjamin Franklin suggested the appropriateness of a daily public prayer at the Convention, and both Madison and Jefferson participated in the formulation of regulations at the University of Virginia under which students were expected to attend services conducted by their respective sects. With schools largely operating under church auspices, prayers were routine and generally unquestioned. McGuffey's ubiquitous nineteenth century *Readers* always included the Lord's Prayer and children's hymns. Such was the "sense of the nation." Even the United States Supreme Court in applying the Constitution to state regulations affecting religious liberties acknowledged the necessity of accommodating the separation of power doctrine to the religious needs of the people and to their institutions which "presuppose a Supreme Being." The Constitution could not have contemplated a separation between Church and State "in every and all respects," nor could it be made to sanction "a preference of nonbelievers over believers."

Tested against such a reading of constitutional history and interpretation, Judge Meyer justified the prayer not as constituting religious instruction but as a simple, non-sectarian, devotional exercise of a character fully within the power of the Regents to recommend for incorporation into the opening observances of each school day.

Charges that these devotional exercises might offend some students or their parents, that they might represent a form of pressure to conform to majority standards or that they could exacerbate interreligious tensions were turned back by the court as being unwarranted or unsound.

> To recognize subtle pressures as compulsion under the Amendment is to stray far afield from the oppressions the Amendment was designed to prevent . . . it is to raise the psychology of dissent, which produces pressure on every dissenter, to the level of governmental force, and to subordinate the spiritual needs of believers to the psychological needs of nonbelievers. The equality of treatment which the Amendment was designed to produce does not require, indeed proscribes, so doing.

. . . [T]he existence of religious differences is one of the facts of life of which school children are every day made aware by absences for religious holidays, differences in clothing, in dietary habits and in other observances. Religious tensions are part of every day living and competition among creeds is advantageous. . . .

An otherwise "unhappy" day for the petitioners might have been made a little brighter when the court ordered the Board of Education to circulate widely to parents and children the content of the prayer and the procedures that would govern nonparticipating students in cases where this should be the parental demand.

The Court of Appeals of New York sustained the use of the prayer, and after a grant of certiorari, the case finally reached the United States Supreme Court in 1962. There Justice Black held that the classroom invocation and the recital of the prayer promulgated by the Board of Regents did constitute a religious activity in direct conflict with the establishment clause of the First Amendment made applicable to the states through the Fourteenth Amendment.

There were essentially three main parts to Black's argument. First, by the time the Constitution was adopted, "there was a widespread awareness among many Americans of the dangers of a union of Church and State." The people of this country "knew the anguish, hardship and bitter strife" that accompanied religious struggles for government support and control. One of the very purposes of the First Amendment was to keep away from this land the kind of controversies that raged in England over the Book of Common Prayer.

Second, as a "solemn avowal of divine faith and supplication to the blessing of the Almighty," the Regents' prayer was clearly of a religious nature. It thus offends the establishment clause which must mean "at least . . . that in this country it is no part of the business of government to compose official prayers for any group of the American people to recite as part of a religious program carried on by government."

Third, to violate the establishment clause there need not be a showing of "direct governmental compulsion." What the clause forbids "is a union of government and religion" which as history has amply demonstrated "tends to destroy government and degrade religion." Although New York permits children to remain silent or to be excused, the arrangement is fundamentally defective by failing to appreciate that "[w]hen the power, prestige and financial support of government is placed behind a particular religious belief, the indirect coercive pressure upon religious minorities to conform to the prevailing officially approved religion is plain."

That the Court was aware of the highly sensitive and controversial nature of its ruling was quite obvious. Nothing in the decision, argued Black, should be construed as indicating hostility to either religion or prayer. "The history of man is inseparable from the history of religion. . . . 'More things are wrought by prayer than this world dreams of'. . . . It is neither sacrilegious nor antireligious to say that each separate government in this country should stay out of the business of writing or sanctioning official prayers and leave that purely religious function to the people themselves and to those the people choose to look to for religious guidance." To underscore this point further the Court added a footnote which explicitly exempts from the range of its opinion references to the Deity in "officially espoused anthems," in the reciting of historical documents or at patriotic or ceremonial functions.

Justice Stewart dissented briefly but pointedly. "I cannot see how an 'official religion' is established by letting those who want to say a prayer say it. On the contrary, I think that to deny the wish of these school children to join in reciting this prayer is to deny them the opportunity of sharing in the spiritual heritage of our Nation." He went on to point out that presidential messages, invocational prayers opening sessions of the Court and of Congress, public chaplains, the Pledge of Allegiance, a congressionally ordered National Day of Prayer, inscriptions on our coins—none of these establish an "official religion." They merely express what was already recognized in *Zorach* v. *Clauson* (1952), "We are a religious people whose institutions presuppose a Supreme Being." In *Engel* the majority now "misapplied" a great constitutional principle.

Public Controversy and Congressional Reactions

Engel deeply disturbed and divided American opinion. Former President Hoover was quoted as saying: "This interpretation of the Constitution is a disintegration of one of the most sacred of American heritages." He urged the immediate adoption of a constitutional amendment to reestablish "the right to religious devotion." Former President Eisenhower was reported as "shocked" by the decision while President Kennedy counseling restraint asked for the support of the Court and the constitutional principles it enunciated. Cardinal Spellman of New York viewed the decision "as strik[ing] at the very heart of the godly tradition in which America's children have for so long been raised." Evangelist Billy Graham believed the "Constitution meant we were to have freedom of religion not freedom from religion." Georgia's Senator Herman Talmadge was acrid in his condemnation.

> For some years now the members of the Supreme Court have persisted in reading alien meanings into the Constitution; . . . they have sought in effect, to change our form of government. But never in the wildest of their excesses . . . have they gone as far as they did on yesterday.

In the House, the remarks by Representative L. Mendel Rivers of South Carolina, Chairman of the Committee on Armed Services, ranked among the most indignant.

> What is wrong with this prayer? Only a court composed of agnostics could find its defects . . . ; the Court has now officially stated its disbelief in God Almighty. This, to me, represents the most serious blow that has ever been struck at the Constitution of the United States. I know of nothing in my lifetime that could give more aid and comfort to Moscow than this bold, malicious, atheistic, and sacrilegious twist of this unpredictable group of uncontrolled despots. . . ."

A plea for a conciliatory attitude came from New York's senior senator, Kenneth B. Keating, who disagreed with the ruling but expressed his concern at the bitterness of the reaction to the Supreme Court itself.

It should not be used as an excuse for another massive assault upon the institution of the Court. Right or wrong, the Supreme Court is a vital part of our Republic, and it does not serve any point of view in this controversy to heap abuse upon its members or to undermine its status.

Representative Emanuel Celler of New York, Chairman of the House Judiciary Committee, approved of the decision.

All parties agreed that the prayer was religious in nature. This being so, it ran contrary to the First Amendment—which is well grounded in history and has served to save the United States from religious strife.

Editorials sympathic to the Court's decision appeared in the New York *Times,* St. Louis *Post Dispatch,* Cleveland *Plain Dealer,* Pittsburgh *Post Gazette,* Milwaukee *Journal,* Louisville *Courier-Journal,* Chicago *Sun-Times,* Washington *Post,* New York *Post* and Detroit *News.* "Monday's decision," wrote the Atlanta *Constitution,* "has not dealt a blow to religion. . . . On the contrary, it has fortified constitutional guarantees that our Government must leave each individual free to worship in his own way." A similar note was struck by the New York *Herald Tribune.*

If we accept the ruling with respect, and calm, we will not stumble to the conclusion that a serious blow has been struck to the very core of religious teaching. If we seek ways to live with the decree against official prayer, to understand it, we certainly can reach an accommodation less troublesome than some see possible in these first hours when striking headlines leave many in a state of disbelief. The court's intent—and eventually, we trust, its great achievement —is to strengthen the foundation of religious heritage by limiting secular intrusions that could become a mischievous and enervating force. . . .

Then there were the editorials in varying degrees critical of the Court and its decision. San Francisco's *News Call Bulletin* termed the decision "narrow legalism." The Kansas City *Star* thought the Court's action "was out of proportion to any danger," and the New York *Journal-American* editorialized that "the Hearst Newspapers believe the decision . . . [to be] a misinterpretation of the Constitution. . . . We urge immediate use of the recourse provided by the Constitution—formal amendment—to insure that the letter of the law is not again used to negate the intent of the Founding Fathers. . . ." Among the most stinging attacks were those of the Los Angeles *Times* which insisted that the six judges "persuaded by a small group of guardhouse sophists" made a "burlesque show of the world's first complete declaration of religious toleration" and the following editorial observation found in the New York *Mirror*:

> It is difficult to understand how any six men in the United States could agree on this decision, written by Justice Hugo Black, who started his political career in the Ku Klux Klan but who, on the bench, became the leader of the radical left. Here is a decision without a quoted precedent, with no roots in law, with no historic basis.

Additional anti-Court editorials appeared in the New York *Daily News*, Baltimore *Sun*, Boston *Globe*, Chicago *Tribune* and the Washington *Star*. According to a study appearing in the *Western Political Quarterly* (March, 1964) of the nation's principal dailies from the forty-two largest metropolitan areas taking editorial positions, a majority opposed the *Engel* decision. Opposition was most intense among papers in the Northern Midwest.

The Holy Bible Before the Court

Only one year later, an even more comprehensive church-state conflict confronted the Court in *School District of Abington* v. *Schempp*. Two companion cases from Pennsylvania and Maryland questioned the constitutionality of classroom readings from the Bible and recitations of the Lord's Prayer. These were the facts. Based on authority provided by Pennsylvania statutes, each school day at Abington High School opened with a fifteen-minute devotional exercise conducted under the supervision of a teacher and broadcast over an intercommunication system into every schoolroom in the building. Selected students, without comment or interpretation, read ten verses from the Bible (the King James version, the Douay Bible, the Revised Standard version or the

Jewish Holy Scriptures). This recitation was followed by the Lord's Prayer repeated in unison by all pupils standing in the various rooms. A salute to the flag and miscellaneous announcements ended the proceedings. Students and parents were informed that participation was voluntary and that those not wishing to remain could be excused and wait in the hall near their homerooms until the services were completed.

In testimony given at the time of the trial, Edward Schempp, a member of the Unitarian Church, emphasized that he decided not to have his children excused from participation in the exercises on the grounds that they would be "labeled as 'odd balls' " by teachers or students, that their classmates "were liable to 'lump all particular religious difference[s] or religious objections [together] as atheism' and that today the word 'atheism' is often connected with 'atheistic communism'. . . ." By standing and waiting outside in the hall (which "carried with it the imputation of punishment for bad conduct"), they might furthermore fail to hear the important announcements which followed the flag salute.

The constitutional issues raised and the factual setting in the Maryland case in which Mrs. Murray and her son, "both professed atheists," challenged the practice of Bible reading and the use of the Lord's Prayer were substantially similar.

Did these religious activities by the schools breach the wall of separation between church and state and violate the petitioners' freedom of religion and conscience safeguarded by the terms of the First and Fourteenth Amendments? The Schempps averred that Bible reading and the Lord's Prayer were clearly contrary to "their familial teachings" and to "the religious beliefs which they held." The Murrays viewed the school regulation as contravening their religious rights "by placing a premium on belief as against non-belief" and as subjecting "their freedom of conscience to the rule of the majority . . ."; furthermore, they insisted "it pronounces belief in God as the source of all moral and spiritual values, equating these values with religious values, and thereby renders sinister, alien and suspect . . . [their] beliefs and ideals, . . . promoting doubt and question of their morality, good citizenship and good faith."

Agreeing with the petitioners, Justice Clark found the religious exercises under review constitutionally clearly invalid. Ever since *Cantwell* v. *Connecticut* (1940) held that the Fourteenth Amendment absorbed and applied to the states the liberties guaranteed by the First Amendment, the concept of governmental "neutrality" according to Clark seemed to have emerged as the unifying theme consistently adhered to by the Court in cases alleging denials of freedom of religion.

Major opinions aside from *Engel* from which he cited supportive language included:

Everson v. *Board of Education* (1947)—Sustained a New Jersey law that authorized reimbursement to parents of money expended by them to transport their children to public as well as to parochial schools.

McCollum v. *Board of Education* (1948)—Struck down an Illinois program under which privately employed instructors conducted weekly religion classes in the public schools.

Zorach v. *Clauson* (1952)—Upheld New York City's released time program where public school students during the school day were excused to attend regular periods of religious instruction away from the school buildings at special centers supported by religious organizations and by parents.

Without attempting to reconcile or harmonize the Court's conclusions in each of these three cases, a task which some of the members of the bench had found impossible, Clark was nevertheless able to point to the frequently repeated motif, common to both majority and minority opinions—the Constitution prohibits the comingling of governmental and religious activities.

From *Everson* came this interpretation of the First Amendment's establishment clause:

Neither a state nor the Federal Government can set up a church. Neither can pass laws which aid one religion, aid all religions, or prefer one religion over another.

It was further elaborated in Justice Frankfurter's concurrent opinion to *McCollum:*

Separation is a requirement to abstain from fusing functions of Government and of religious sects, not merely to treat them all equally.

Zorach added another refinement:

> There cannot be the slightest doubt that the First Amendment reflects the philosophy that Church and State should be separated. . . .
> The First Amendment, however, does not say that in every and all respects there shall be separation of Church and State. Rather, it studiously defines the manner, the specific ways, in which there shall be no concert or union or dependency one on the other. . . .

Then follows Clark's own exposition for the need of "neutrality." History teaches that "powerful sects" might wish to achieve union of "governmental and religious functions" so that the "official support" of government could be given to religious tenets. "This the Establishment Clause prohibits." The demand for "neutrality" is also stipulated by the "Free Exercise Clause which recognizes . . . the right of every person to freely choose his own course . . . free of any compulsion from the state." The test, therefore, for any legislation, is this, "what are the purpose and the primary effect of the enactment?" Enactments must fall if, instead of being secular in purpose, their primary effect is the advancement or inhibition of religion, he concluded.

Pennsylvania and Maryland contended that within their secular programs of instruction they sought through Bible reading to promote "moral values" in contrast to "the materialistic trends of our times." Since the states, however, also admitted the "religious character" of the exercises and since the Bible is certainly a religious instrument, it cannot then be consistently claimed "that the Bible is here used either as an instrument for nonreligious moral inspiration or as a reference for the teaching of secular subjects." The states could not have it both ways.

Would the denial of the programs of Pennsylvania and Maryland establish a "religion of secularism"? Clark did not think so. Admittedly, as already made clear in *Zorach,* the state cannot establish a "religion of secularism," show hostility to religion or prefer disbelief over belief. Then he added, "One's education is not complete without a study of comparative religion, or the history of religion and its relationship to the advancement of civilization." Nor is there any conflict with the First Amendment or with this opinion that there could not be such a "study of the Bible or of religion, when presented objectively as part of a secular program of education. . . ." The exercises employed by Pennsylvania and Maryland, however, "do not fall into these categories." They thus violate "the command of the First Amendment that the Government maintain strict neutrality, neither aiding nor opposing religion."

Nor is the unconstitutionality of such programs diminished by the fact that they may represent the wishes of the majority of the people who claim their rights to worship under the free exercise clause of the First Amendment. In his argument for placing limits upon American majoritarianism when individual liberties are involved, Clark referred to Justice Jackson's famous defense of Jehovah's Witnesses convicted of failing to salute the flag—*West Virginia Board of Education* v. *Barnette* (1943). "The very purpose of the Bill of Rights was to withdraw certain subjects from the vicissitudes of political controversy, to place them beyond the reach of majorities and officials and to establish them as legal principles to be applied by the courts. One's right to . . . freedom of worship . . . and other fundamental rights may not be submitted to vote; they depend on the outcome of no elections."

As was true of *Engel,* the Court once again showed concern that its libertarian stand might be construed as indicative of anti-religious judicial predispositions. Reemphasizing what was said earlier about the educational significance of the objective and literary study of the Bible and of comparative religion, Clark ended his opinion on the following note:

> The place of religion in our society is an exalted one, achieved through a long tradition of reliance on the home, the church and the inviolable citadel of the human heart and mind. We have come to recognize through bitter experience that it is not within the power of government to invade that citadel, whether its purpose or effect be to aid or oppose, to advance or retard. In the relationship between man and religion, the State is firmly committed to a position of neutrality.

Three members of the Court wrote concurrent opinions. Justice Douglas briefly added one point. The instructional programs were constitutionally defective and "must fall under [the establishment clause] . . . for the additional reason that public funds, though small in amount, are being used to promote a religious exercise." Through the instrumentality of the state, religious exercises desired by "only some of the people" are financed by "all of the people." The use of such public funds, however indirect, would make a "mockery" of the establishment clause.

Justice Goldberg stressed that the majority position with respect to "neutrality" does not contemplate a constitutional climate of "noninterference and noninvolvement" to the extent of a "brooding and pervasive devotion to the secular and a passive, or even active, hostility to the religious." With a "vast portion of our people" believing in and worshipping God, "[g]overnment must inevitably take cognizance of the existence of religion and, indeed, under certain circumstances the First Amendment may require that it do so." Among the instances of such "accommodation" Goldberg specifically mentioned the providing of military chaplains and "the teaching *about* religion, as distinguished from teaching *of* religion." There could still be numerous other examples of delicate "accommodation between state and church . . . free of hostility or favor and productive of religious and political harmony, but without undue involvement of one in the concerns or practices of the other."

The concurrent opinion of Justice Brennan filled seventy-four pages in *U.S. Reports.* His primary concern was not how the Founding Fathers themselves would have adjudged the devotional exercises with respect to the Constitution, but whether the challenged practices "threaten those consequences which the Framers deeply feared; whether, in short, they tend to promote that type of interdependence between religion and state which the First Amendment was designed to prevent." To rely too heavily on "the advice of the Founding Fathers" seemed to Brennan "futile" and "misdirected." The records are ambiguous; the "precise problem" of devotional exercises in public schools was obviously not given "distinct consideration"; the religious composition of contemporary America "makes us a vastly more diverse people than were our forefathers"; and the modern secular public school system "available to all children" supported by public funds collected from citizens with differing views on religion was then entirely unknown.

What made the Pennsylvania and Maryland practices constitutionally deficient to Brennan is that they represented "involvements of religious with secular institutions which (a) serve the essentially religious activities of religious institutions; (b) employ the organs of government for essentially religious purposes; or (c) use essentially religious means to serve governmental ends where secular means would suffice."

Tested by such standards, administrative justifications that "morning devotional exercises may foster better discipline in the classroom and elevate the spiritual level" which might be educationally true, would still not satisfy the Constitution. Nor would the use of different versions of the Bible make the exercises any less sectarian—"[t]here are persons in every community—often deeply devout—to whom any version of the Judaeo-Christian Bible is offensive." Others may object to the "manner" in which the Bible is used; and still others "have always regarded prayer as a necessarily private experience." As to the so-called "voluntary" quality of the morning services and the procedures for nonparticipation, the disinclination of children to deviate from their "peer group norms," testified to by experts on child behavior, helps to create the kind of climate and conditions where fear of stigmatization and pressures of conformity "may well deter those children who do not wish to participate for any reason based upon the dictates of conscience from exercising an indisputable constitutional right to be excused."

To Justice Stewart, the lone dissenter, the records in the two cases seemed "wholly inadequate" especially as to evidence of the degree of coercion to which nonparticipating students were subjected under the "excusal provisions." At the root of his quarrel with the majority lay the extent of cooperation permissible between church and state. "We err . . . if we do not recognize, as a matter of history and as a matter of the imperative of our free society, that religion and government must necessarily interact in countless ways." When applying the free exercise clause great weight must be given to the "claim on the part of those who affirmatively desire to have their children's school day open with the reading of passages from the Bible." It is not enough to say that those who wish to have their children exposed to religious influences should "fulfill that wish off school property and outside school time." The public school system "so structures a child's life that if religious exercises are held to be an impermissible activity in schools, religion is placed at an artificial and state-created disadvantage." Rather than maintaining and realizing the desired "neutrality" the state would in effect contribute to the "establishment of a religion of secularism" or at least would sanction "the beliefs of those who think that religious exercises should be conducted only in private."

The demands of governmental neutrality in the intricate inter-actions of government and religion cannot be meaningfully met by the mechanical or "ritualistic invocation of the nonconstitu-tional phrase 'separation of church and state'."

Congress Acts

Congressional demands to "do something about" the Supreme Court's interpretation of the First Amendment received new vigor and impetus with the *Schempp* decision of 1963. After months of pressure, Representative Emanuel Celler, Chairman of the House Judiciary Committee, finally consented to open hear-ings on proposals to amend the Constitution. When the Com-mittee met on April 22, it was presented with 150 resolutions aimed at offering constitutional sanctions to prayers and Bible reading in the public schools; fifty-eight of them were identical to H.J. Res. 693, introduced during the first session of the 89th Congress by Representative Frank J. Becker of New York.

Analysis of the political profile of the 115 congressmen who introduced prayer amendments reveals that

> Forty-eight were Democrats; 67, Republicans; all but 19 of the Democrats came from the states of the old Confederacy. Nine of the Republicans came from the South.

> These measures had strong conservative backing; 67% of all the Republican congressmen and 15% of all the Democratic congressmen scored 80% or better on the rating scale of the Americans for Consti-tutional Action.

More congressional support came from rural than urban areas with 69% of the congressmen elected from predominantly rural constituencies.

Most representative of all the prayer proposals and most widely discussed, was the "Becker Amendment." Its substance emerged from three short paragraphs.

Section 1. Nothing in this Constitution shall be deemed to prohibit the offering, reading from, or listening to prayers or biblical scriptures, if participation therein is on a voluntary basis, in any governmental or public school, institution or place.

Section 2. Nothing in this Constitution shall be deemed to prohibit making reference to belief in, reliance upon, or invoking the aid of God or a Supreme Being in any governmental, or public document, proceeding, activity, ceremony, school, institution, or place, or upon any coinage, currency, or obligation of the United States.

Section 3. Nothing in this article shall constitute an establishment of religion.

Hearings on this amendment quickly revealed its overwhelming rejection by the religious leadership of many of the major Protestant and Jewish groups; Episcopalians, Methodists and America's Catholic hierarchy, however, seemed to be divided on the issue. Testifying against the Becker Amendment were officials of the National Council of Churches (an organization composed of thirty-one member communions and approximately forty million American Christians), as well as national spokesmen for Presbyterians, Baptists, Lutherans, Seventh Day Adventists, Unitarians and the United Church of Christ. Similarly opposed to the amendment was the Synagogue Council of America composed of Orthodox, Conservative and Reform Jewish congregations. The Greek Orthodox Archdiocese of North and South America, one of the constituent communions of the N.C.C. did not, however, share the National Council's position and refused to associate itself with its pronouncements on this issue.

Reducing and paraphrasing the chorus of arguments to the barest essentials, the opponents seemed to advance four fundamental types of contentions: (1) The First Amendment served America well; it permitted the development of a religious pluralism that proved vital, spiritually enriching, and capable of offering each citizen true freedom of religion; (2) the Becker Amendment would undermine the historic traditions of separation of church and state. It would lead to bitter, divisive and dangerous struggles for governmental power in order to control religious practices, programs and institutions; (3) there is nothing in all of the Supreme Court's First Amendment interpretations that can be reasonably construed as precluding religious expressions in the home, in the church or in private prayer, nor has the Court ever denied references to God in public documents, ceremonies or exercises—an issue gratuitously and provocatively interjected by the Becker Amendment to arouse public fears and resentments; (4) Becker's "voluntarism" transparently ignores the pressures of conformity in a public setting where governmental influence and sponsorship strengthen the will and beliefs of the majority to the disadvantage of minority creeds and sects.

Warnings against any "tampering" with the Constitution also were voiced by 223 of this country's leading constitutional lawyers and experts. "If the first clause of the Bill of Rights, forbidding laws respecting the establishment of religion should prove so easily susceptible to impairment by amendment, none of the succeeding clauses will be secure." Editorials embodying similar anti-Becker Amendment sentiments appeared in the *Christian Science Monitor,* the *Christian Century,* the Jesuit weekly *America, Commonweal,* the *Catholic World* and *Christianity Today,* as well as in a major share of the general press.

For support of his amendment, Congressman Becker could count on some of the dissenters from within the National Council of Churches and on a substantial number of the smaller and the more "fundamentalist inclined" churches. Strong endorsements, for example, came from the National Association of Evangelicals with a membership of two million comprising the Assemblies of God, the Brethren in Christ, the Church of God, the Evangelical Mennonite Church, the Free Methodist Church, the International Pentecostal Assemblies and the United Fundamentalist Church along with more than thirty other specific denominations, conferences and associations, reflecting a similar theological orientation. Dr. Carl McIntire, President of the International Council of Christian Churches, a well-known fundamentalist leader, worked indefatigably with the national prayer lobby, the Citizens Congressional Committee and the Constitutional Prayer Foundation to enlist one million signatures on petitions requesting Congress to pass the Becker Amendment. Evangelist Billy Graham was quoted as strongly commending the amendment and as favoring daily reading of the Ten Commandments throughout the nation's public schools. "Protestants, Catholics, and Jews all agree on the Ten Commandments." A statement on behalf of Francis Cardinal Spellman of New York importuned Congress "that the one sure, effective, and early solution is an amendment to our Constitution which would remedy the result of the Regents' prayer case by correcting the Court's misreading of the no-establishment clause."

Among proponents of the amendment sensitive to the legal dimensions of the issue, wide circulation was given to an article appearing in the *Utah Law Review* by Erwin N. Griswold, the distinguished Dean of the Harvard Law School, attacking the "absolutist approach" of the Supreme Court to the prayer and other civil liberties cases.

The most well-known congressional patrons of the amendment included the nominees for the Republican presidential ticket of 1964, Senator Goldwater and Representative William Miller, the present Republican Minority Leader in the House, Representative Gerald R. Ford, his predecessor in that position, Representative Charles Halleck of Indiana, and a former Democratic vice-presidential nominee, Senator John Sparkman of Alabama.

The nation's governors also expressed approval. From their Fifty-fourth Annual Meeting at Hershey, Pennsylvania, came a call for Congress "to propose an amendment to the Constitution . . . that will make clear and beyond challenge the acknowledgement by our Nation and people of their faith in God and permit the free and voluntary participation in prayer in public schools."

One of the governors, George Wallace of Alabama, who had testified earlier before the House Judiciary Committee, displayed considerable passion in his indictment of the Court's prayer ruling:

It is the bitter fruit of the liberal dogma that worships human intelligence and scorns the concept of divinity . . . It is a part of the deliberate design to subordinate the American people, their faith, their customs, and their religious traditions to a godless state.

On local and state levels meanwhile, the "right to public prayer" campaigns and the Project America crusades were eagerly advanced by their devoted followers, many of them members of the American Legion, the Catholic War Veterans, the National Catholic Youth Organization, the International Christian Youth in the United States and by such state groups as the Massachusetts Citizens for Public Prayer. Assisting their efforts were sympathetic editorials in *U.S. News and World Report,* the Philadelphia *Sunday Bulletin,* the Baltimore *News American,* the New York *Journal-American* and other Hearst newspapers.

Friends of the amendment in Congress, pulpits and editorial chairs echoed and elaborated arguments similar in tenor and substance to those developed by Becker in his appearances before the Celler Committee.

The Members of this Congress surely are aware of the fact that the vast majority of our people favor a constitutional amendment which will guarantee permanently their right of privacy and Scriptural devotions in our public schools.

It has been argued by some that children "mumbling" a prayer in school is meaningless, and reading passages from the Bible, which they do not understand, a "waste of time." If this be true, then many of our educational programs involving the memorizing of poems and the reciting of classics are also meaningless.

I am further impressed by the fact that this fraternity of cynics, atheists and unbelievers who would abolish any mention of the deity in our schools and other public institutions manifest opposition to what we call patriotism.

I yield to no one in my support of religious freedom, and I can remember no dilemma faced by any student during my years in school when the Lord's Prayer was said every day I attended school. No one suffered a dilemma when passages were read from the King James version of the Bible, although I am a Roman Catholic. There were Catholics, Protestants, and Jews in my school, but we never thought of one another as such.

Despite the fervor of grass roots support and the persistent efforts of Becker and his associates, the Judiciary Committee refused to report the measure to the House. A discharge petition was filed but fell short of the required minimum of 218 by 51 signatures. Aroused by another disallowance of prayer in *Stein* v. *Oshinsky* (1965) decided by the United States Court of Appeals in New York (a case which the Supreme Court refused to review), Senator Everett Dirksen with forty-seven other senators as co-sponsors introduced S.J. Res. 148 on March 22, 1966.

> Nothing contained in this Constitution shall prohibit the authority administering any school system, educational institution or other public building supported in whole or in part through the expenditure of public funds from providing for or permitting the voluntary participation by students or others in prayer. Nothing contained in this article shall authorize any such authority to prescribe the form or content of any prayer.

Much narrower in scope than the Becker Amendment, Dirksen's proposal was aimed specifically at school boards and administrators. It also omitted all explicit references to the Bible or to the inclusion of appeals to the deity in governmental documents, ceremonies and exercises. Mindful, moreover, of the Court's ruling in *Engel*, the resolution pointedly precluded school authorities from "prescribing" any particular prayer. Still, hearings on the resolution before the Senate Judiciary Committee's Subcommittee on Constitutional Amendment quickly divulged no major differences in either the basic arguments or alignments which had centered around the Becker Amendment and the constitutional issues it had raised. When the Committee declined to bring S.J. Res. 148 to the floor, another prayer amendment seemed destined for legislative oblivion, but a determined Senator Dirksen refused to let the matter rest. A resolution empowering the President to designate a National UNICEF Day each year to honor the United Nation's Children's Fund which the Judiciary Committee did report became the parliamentary vehicle through which the minority leader attained his objective of forcing a Senate vote.

After substituting the Dirksen Amendment for the UNICEF resolution, the Senate considered the proposed constitutional change for three days. Dirksen led off the debate by questioning the representativeness of the National Council of Churches and other religious organizations which had testified in opposition.

> Instead of the pastors and ministers for the common man, we had as witnesses the social engineers of the church, the world savers, those who are constantly advancing anesthesia for every ill and ache of the body politic, not only in this country, but in the whole wide world. . . . The humble ministers and pastors and priests and rabbis had neither the time nor money to come to Washington and present their views in behalf of this amendment; only the church hierarchy in the ivory towers of Washington and places close by were heard at the hearing. . . . They are the semantic theologians who long ago have forgotten the common touch. . . .

Senator Milward Simpson of Wyoming argued that the amendment "will help satisfy the need which this Nation has for a return to the religious faith of our Founding Fathers," while Senators James Eastland of Mississippi and Leverett Saltonstall of Massachusetts both emphasized that the amendment would assure America's children the right to worship in their schools.

Speaking in opposition and stressing the amendment's threat to religious freedom were Senators Samuel Ervin of North Carolina, Senator Joseph Tydings of Maryland, and Senator Mike Mansfield of Montana. By September 21 the "sound and fury" of senatorial debate had died down. A conservative coalition of fifteen Southern Democrats, seven Northern Democrats and twenty-seven Republicans failed by nine votes to win the two-thirds majority that would have been required to approve Senator Dirksen's constitutional amendment. Illustrative of the broader ideological implications of the coalition alignments was the fact that of the thirty-seven senators voting against the amendment, thirty-two scored a 61% or better liberal voting record on the basis of ratings compiled by the Americans for Democratic Action for all the major roll calls of the 89th Congress. Of the forty-eight senators voting *yea* on the amendment, thirty ranked in the 00–20% A.D.A. liberal rating category; twenty-eight Senators voting *nay* out of a total of thirty-seven had scored ratings of from 00–20% on the scale of the Americans for Conservative Action. (See Table 2.)

T A B L E 2

BREAKDOWN OF A.D.A. AND A.C.A. RATINGS OF YEA AND
NAY VOTERS ON THE DIRKSEN PRAYER AMENDMENT

(S. J. Res. 144, September 21, 1966)

A.D.A. Rating	Yea Votes	Nay Votes
00–20	30	1
21–40	8	0
41–60	4	4
61–80	3	8
81–100	3	24
Total	48*	37
A.C.A. Rating	Yea Votes	Nay Votes
00–20	5	28
21–40	9	6
41–60	7	2
61–80	15	1
81–100	12	0
Total	48*	37

Source: *Congressional Quarterly Weekly Report*, September 23, 1966, p.
2259 and February 25, 1966, p. 474.

* Senator Griffin, of Michigan, voted yea on the amendment but was not
counted in the yea total because he had not yet been given an A.D.A. or A.C.A.
rating at the time the data for this table was compiled.

Compliance and Controversy

Obeying the *Schempp* decision, lower courts in quick succession
struck down offending daily Bible reading practices in Delaware,
Idaho, Massachusetts, New Jersey and Ohio. In only one case
was it necessary for the United States Supreme Court (in a *per
curiam* memorandum) to reverse a state tribunal on this issue.
Florida's highest court in *Chamberlain* v. *Dade County Board
of Instruction* persisted in sustaining a program of religious
exercises clearly in conflict with the emerging national standards.

That there would be continued resistance to the application
and enforcement of the doctrines of *Engel* and *Schempp* was to be

expected. What was to become equally obvious was the considerable extent to which courts would find themselves involved in problems of school administration as they were called on to test local patterns of accommodation in the light of the new rules. Two cases will illustrate the point.

(1) In Michigan, parents of the Jenison School District brought suit against the superintendent of schools and the board of education to enjoin the implementation of a plan of religious exercise under which students who wished to say a prayer or read scriptures would be permitted to do so each school day prior to and following their classes. At 8:45 a.m. a bell would ring indicating that the homerooms were open for prayer; another bell, five minutes later, would signify the end of the voluntary prayer period and constitute a warning that the actual start of classes would begin at 9:00 a.m.

Plaintiffs objected to these practices on the grounds that "they raised problems of excusal and segregation which are constitutionally prohibited." After reviewing the prayer case opinions of the Supreme Court, District Judge Fox in *Reed* v. *Van Hoven* detailed the following "accommodation" for students who would wish to engage in worship:

> . . . [T]hey meet in a room other than their regular homeroom, and complete their exercises at least five minutes before the regularly scheduled class day, or at least five minutes after their completion of the regular school class day. . . .

> [N]o bell signifying the start of a prayer exercise should be rung. This exercise is voluntary, and those wishing to avail themselves of the opportunity provided should learn the time when it is offered to them and appear at the designated location. . . .

To avoid any form of coercion and to assure complete separation of the official school activities from the prayer exercises, the court added that

> there be a general comingling of the entire student body on the way to class, just as there would be were there no exercises whatsoever. That is, all rooms will be empty before the bell rings for the start of the school day. . . . [T]hus no student will enter a room containing a group which has previously congregated there for the purpose of

prayer—all students will enter simultaneously upon the signal for the start of the school day. . . .

Those children who may themselves dissent, or whose parents may dissent from their participating in the exercises, would be required only to report for school at the regular opening time of school and would leave school at the regular closing time. . . .

If prayers were to be said at lunch, they would have to be silent prayers; if teachers were to assist, they could be assigned no other role of responsibility in all pre- and post-school sessions except that of maintaining order.

No teacher shall be called upon to select the prayer which should be said, or to select the readings which may be given. The students would determine by means of their own choosing what should be done in this respect.

Having offered this plan as "an attempt to avoid the nexus between official authority and religion," the court denied the request for the injunction and ordered the school board to incorporate these modifications into the existing practices.

(2) From Whitestone, New York, came a case in 1965 that rekindled the fire of the prayer controversy throughout Congress and the nation. A group of parents who were members of the Roman Catholic, Jewish, Armenian Apostolic and Episcopalian faiths sought a mandatory injunction ordering the defendant principal of Public School 184 to permit their twenty-one kindergarten children aged five to eleven to say the following prayers before partaking of milk and cookies:

For the morning classes:
   God is Great, God is Good
   And we thank Him for our Food. Amen.

For the afternoon classes:
   Thank You for the World so sweet
   Thank You for the Food we eat
   Thank You for the Birds that sing
   Thank You God for Everything.

A federal district court in *Stein* v. *Oshinsky* holding that these prayers voluntarily offered by the children did not constitute an establishment of religion had granted plaintiffs their motion.

On review Judge Friendly of the Circuit Court of Appeals reversed the district court on the premise that the constitutional rights of free exercise of religion do not require a state to permit "student initiated" prayers. Despite the plaintiff's desire that "their children be given an opportunity to acknowledge their dependence and love to Almighty God through a prayer each day in their respective classrooms," the court saw nothing in the First Amendment that denied school authorities the right

> to weigh the likely desire of other parents not to have their children present at such prayers, either because the prayers were too religious or not religious enough . . . [or to conclude] that plaintiffs must content themselves with having their children say these prayers before nine or after three . . . [or to permit] students to withdraw momentarily for such necessary observances—or to forego the milk and cookies, just as they excuse children on holidays important to their religion.

With reference to the administrative realities of the "voluntary" quality of prayers the court took special note of the defendant's contention that:

> . . . [I]n the context of closely organized schooling of young children, "student-initiated" prayers are an illusion and any effective routine requires the active participation of the teachers. . . .

For the purpose of settling the specific issue posed by the suit, the court imposed no positive duty on the public school authorities of New York to use their personnel and facilities to accommodate the religious needs of these children through this type of program.

With precisely how much reluctance local communities and school authorities proceed to adjust themselves to the "new" spirit of the First Amendment is difficult to document. Court records can only provide a very limited evidence of the extent of non-compliance. Dissenting minorities may not readily bring litigation for fear that they, or more directly their children, may be subjected to social disapproval or discrimination. Superintendents and principals, although fully aware that religious exercises in their own schools are constitutionally indefensible, might not be willing to incur hostility and resentment from powerful local interests strongly committed to the continuance of such practices. Communities with high religious and social homogeneity do not enthusiastically respond to the demands of pluralism perceived as externally "decreed."

T A B L E 3

DEVOTIONAL BIBLE READING IN THE SCHOOLS 1960 AND 1966

By Area	1966 Yes	1960 Yes	1966 No	1960 No
United States	13.78%	41.74%	86.22%	58.26%
Western states	02.38	11.03	48.13	88.97
Midwestern states	05.45	18.26	94.55	81.74
Southern states	51.87	76.84	97.62	23.16
Eastern states	04.35	67.56	95.65	32.44

By Size of Community	1966 Yes	1960 Yes	1966 No	1960 No
500– 2,500	09.04%	30.84%	90.96%	69.16%
2,500– 5,000	12.25	43.11	87.75	56.89
5,000– 25,000	15.82	52.73	84.18	47.27
25,000–100,000	20.43	40.11	79.57	59.89
Over 100,000	29.63	54.17	70.37	45.83

Source: R. D. Dierenfield, *Religion in American Public Schools* (Washington: Public Affairs Press, 1962), p. 51. Professor Dierenfield's 1966 survey is presently in the process of publication.

Based on inchoate and fragmentary field studies and surveys, compliance with *Engel* and *Schempp* must be assessed presently as falling far short of the court-enunciated standards for religious freedom.

According to findings recently reported by the Anti-Defamation League of B'nai B'rith, New York,

a survey by the State Superintendent of Kentucky disclosed that out of 204 school districts in the state, only 61 indicated discontinuance of prayers and Bible readings; 121 superintendents said "their schools had 'unwritten policies' that permitted Bible reading and classroom prayers";

a survey conducted by the Indiana School Board Association showed that "less than 6% of the school boards had changed their policies in compliance with the Supreme Court's rulings on devotional exercises";

a survey by the Texas Council of Churches reported "prayers were said in 51% of the secondary schools prior to the Supreme Court rulings and in 50% presently."[1]

More corroborative evidence of a somewhat limited compliance is offered by Professor Dierenfield's follow-up study (see p. 145) of the place of religion in public education. Table 3 shows responses to the question concerning devotional Bible readings in the schools on the basis of a 51% return by 2,000 school systems of the continental United States, selected from a random, stratified and proportional sample.

Separation of State and Church— Some Other Unsettled Questions

Bible reading and the recitation of prayers constitute, of course, only one aspect of an entire "complex of relationships" between government, religion and education upon which the First Amendment places certain restraints. Other related components of this complex pose issues and problems any detailed analysis of which is necessarily precluded here by considerations of space. The briefest mentioning of a few of the most important of the unsettled questions will have to suffice.

Next to Bible reading, baccalaureate exercises and the celebration of Christmas represent probably the most widely practiced and current forms of religious observances in America's public schools. High school baccalaureate is essentially a church service conducted in a public school setting. Where pressures for graduating seniors to participate is substantial, the constitutionality of such exercises will be patently doubtful.

[1] From a speech by Rabbi Arthur Gilbert at an Institute on the Role of Religion in Public Education, January 26, 1967, University of Minnesota.

Christmas has not only profoundly religious origins but is also rooted deeply in community custom and culture. Shared and honored by all the members of the dominant Christian religion, the observance of the birth of Christ cannot be entirely ignored in the schools. With all the media of communications stressing the theme of this holy day and with works of music, art and drama enriching and extolling the Christmas message, public school administrators, teachers and school boards find themselves in critical need for positive programs and guidelines if they are to retain their indispensably necessary community support. Whatever else a constitutionally "reasonable recognition" of Christmas may entail, school policies will have to aim at a climate of respect equally as strong for children who neither observe the holiday nor share its traditions as for those who do. As so cogently expressed in the report, *Religion in the Public Schools,* "[t]he non-Christian is not a guest in a Christian school—he is a fellow citizen in a public school which includes a good many Christian members."[2]

Whether parochial schools should be permitted to receive public aid has been debated for years and resolved differently throughout the states. Some state constitutions and laws contain explicit provisions against any form of aid to private, church-related schools; others prohibit only direct grants or transfers of public property. The federal-state confrontation on this issue was not fully explored by the Supreme Court until 1947. Then in *Everson* v. *Board of Education* the Court in a 5 to 4 decision sustained a New Jersey law permitting the reimbursement of parents for the bus transportation of their children irrespective of whether they attended parochial or public schools. A First Amendment that does not require a state to remove police and fire protection and other "general governmental" services from parochial schools will also not preclude, wrote Justice Black, "a general program to help parents get their children, regardless of their religion, safely and expeditiously to and from accredited schools." While the Court seemed persuaded that in this instance the government contributed no money to the schools, the case also contained language widely quoted in subsequent opinions

[2] American Association of School Administrators, 1964, p. 35.

for the purpose of reinforcing the "wall of separation" as demanded by the establishment clause.

> Neither a state nor the Federal Government . . . can pass laws which aid one religion, aid all religions, or prefer one religion over another. . . . No tax in any amount, large or small, can be levied to support any religious activities or institutions, whatever they may be called, or whatever form they may adopt to teach or practice religion. . . .

Still, *Everson* became the constitutional "parent" of the "child benefit theory." While states were not to be permitted to financially support parochial schools they need not become adversaries to the point of depriving students enrolled in them of benefits which the public may wish to extend to them though not to their schools. Supporters of P.L. 89–10, the Elementary and Secondary Education Act of 1965, considered this to be their constitutional rationale. Thus grants for the educationally deprived, including those with physical, mental or emotional handicaps, could reach children from low income families in private and parochial, as well as public, schools. Similarly, grants for the acquisition of school library resources, textbooks and other printed and published instructional materials were to be made available to children and teachers in the public as well as in the private sectors of elementary and secondary education. Many other phases of this act—calling for public and private joint participation, for "educational centers" and for shared special services—bring into constitutional focus numerous areas of potential controversy and litigation. Problems of a quite comparable nature are also posed by such measures as the Economic Opportunity Act, the National Defense Education Act and the Higher Education Act.

In one such challenge, *Horace Mann League of the United States* v. *Board of Public Works* (1966), Maryland's highest court struck down public laws that had granted construction funds of $2.5 million to four church-related colleges under a plan substantially similar to that employed by the federal government in its Higher Educational Facilities Act of 1963.

Considerable significance has been attached to this decision.

It did address itself to the central constitutional issue, and the Supreme Court, by refusing to review it, let the decision stand. What then makes a college a religious or sectarian college in the sense of the First Amendment and thus ineligible for public assistance? Chief Justice Prescott of Maryland selected six standards as relevant with which to test the sectarian or non-sectarian nature of the four church-connected colleges.

(1) the stated purposes of the college;

(2) the college personnel, which includes the governing board, the administrative officers, the faculty and the student body (with considerable stress being laid on the substantiality of religious control over the governing board as a criterion of whether the college is sectarian);

(3) the college's relationship with religious organizations and groups, which relationship includes the extent of ownership, financial assistance, the college's memberships and affiliations, religious purposes and miscellaneous aspects of the college's relationship with its sponsoring church;

(4) the place of religion in the college's program, which includes the extent of religious manifestations in the physical surroundings, the character and extent of religious observance sponsored or encouraged by the college, the required participation for any or all students, the extent to which the college sponsors or encourages religious activity of sects different from that of the college's own church and the place of religion in the curriculum and in the extra-curricular programs;

(5) the result or the "outcome" of the college program, such as accreditation and the nature and character of the activities of the alumni; and

(6) the work and image of the college in the community.

Using these criteria the court found the operative effect of such grants to constitute "aid of religion" in all but one of the institutions. Hood College, a liberal arts college for women, although related to the United Church of Christ was found not so religious in its purpose, operations and character as to make its support a coercive exercise on behalf of fostering religion. If accommodation rather than absolute "separationism" is to be the goal, this frankly elastic approach leaves a twilight zone of constitutional indeterminacy. Nevertheless this approach of adopting operational rather than semantic or conceptual tests with which to assess the religious components of non-public educational institutions has much to recommend itself in as complex a matrix as that of state-church relations.

Absolute separation in education of all things secular from all things religious does not seem to express the majority consensus in *Engel* or in *Schempp*. While Bible reading, prayers and devotional exercises were declared constitutionally impermissible, repeated emphasis was placed in these opinions on the conviction that there was room in the school, indeed need, for the moral message of the Bible and for respectful understanding and appreciation of the great cultural contributions religion has made to the finest values in American life. Admittedly the concept of "neutrality" which permeated the prayer cases so noticeably, represents no magic wand yielding concrete formulae that might reconcile easily conflicts between the expectations of the free exercise clause and the establishment clause or between the demands of the secular and the sectarian. While separationists may strongly applaud the results of the prayer cases, they may well be troubled by an unsophisticated or unqualified application of the neutrality concepts to the controversies revolving around the private school and public aid. There it could result in a significant strengthening of sectarian parochialism at the cost of the kind of integrative ecumenicism which the American public school system seemed to serve so well.

What was revolutionary about the prayer cases then, was not that the Supreme Court had changed so much or so radically or that the Bible or prayer were unimportant, but that the Court had proceeded to apply to the states once again standards of civil liberty that had long been indigenous to the American creed though not to the American practice. Religious pluralism has no doubt been strengthened by *Engel* and *Schempp*. Whether, however, the Court's concept of neutrality, as developed in these cases, will equally reinforce the public school as it struggles with the parochial school over the share of federal and state funds remains yet to be settled. This uncertainty may well constitute the political price paid by the public schools for increased federal aid to education.

SUGGESTED READINGS

R. S. Andursky. "First Amendment and Federal Aid to Church-Related Schools," *Syracuse Law Review,* Summer, 1966, 609–626.

Donald E. Boles. *The Bible, Religion and the Public Schools.* Ames, 1961.

Richard H. Dierenfield. *Religion in American Public Schools.* Washington, 1962.

David Fellman. "Religion in American Public Law," *Boston University Law Review,* Summer, 1964, 287–399.

M. R. Karpas. "The Schools and Religion: A Study to Identify the Advocates of Religious Instruction in the Public Schools," *Journal of Human Relations,* First Quarter, 1965, 13–20.

P. G. Kauper. "Prayer, Public Schools and the Supreme Court," *Michigan Law Review,* April, 1963, 1031–1068.

P. G. Kauper. "Released Time and Religious Liberty: A Further Reply," *Michigan Law Review,* November, 1954, 233–236.

W. J. Kenealy and W. B. Ball. "Proposed Prayer and Bible-Reading Amendments: Contrasting Views," *Catholic Lawyer,* Summer, 1964, 185–193.

Philip B. Kurland. *Religion and the Law of Church and State and the Supreme Court.* New York, 1962.

Irving Long. "Is the First Amendment made Applicable to the States by the Fourteenth?" *American Bar Association Journal,* April, 1963, 345–348.

Leo Pfeffer. *Church, State, and Freedom.* Boston, 1953.

Charles E. Rice. "Let Us Pray—An Amendment to the Constitution," *Catholic Lawyer,* Summer, 1964, 178–184.

Charles E. Rice. *The Supreme Court and Public Prayer: The Need for Restraint.* New York, 1964.

S. Rothman. "Politics of Catholic Parochial Schools: An Historical and Comparative Analysis," *Journal of Politics,* February, 1963, 49–71.

William W. Van Alstyne. "Constitutional Separation of Church and State: The Quest for a Coherent Position," *American Political Science Review,* December, 1963, 865–882.

V

The Defendant and
the Criminal Law

"Now, boys, before you begin—please keep
in mind the recent United States Supreme
Court decision in the case of Ernesto Miranda
v. Arizona on Writ of Certiorari from the Supreme
Court of Arizona."

From *Wall Street Journal,* February 9, 1967.

Crime in the United States represents a national tragedy and a national challenge of gigantic dimensions. Why this affluent society with its tremendous opportunities for personal achievement and development should also produce one of the world's most steeply rising crime rates constitutes one of the painfully depressing aspects of contemporary life. Compared with an increase in population of 8% between 1960 and 1965, statistics compiled by the Department of Justice (*Uniform Crime Reports*), for example, showed crimes of violence multiplying three times as fast while crimes against property rose still higher—the number of offenses per 100,000 population was up 36%. Although this frightening picture of lawlessness and violence has certainly not been a secret to anyone, and public lamentations have been most extensive, very little actually is known scientifically about the complex causes and possible cures of crime. General observations and polemics abound in this area. Slums cause crime—this may well be true but it does not necessarily account for the rising incidence of crimes committed by the children of "suburbia," by the "white collar" employees of stores and corporations, by bored and frustrated students on the campuses of highly reputable colleges and universities or by the Mafia and other "professional" syndicates.

Some have "blamed" crime largely on drug addiction, "soft" judges, short sentences, hobbled police, public apathy, urban living, broken homes, fatherless children, racial factors or Supreme Court decisions among others, as if crime were an occurrence easily yielding to direct and unidimensional explanations. In discussing "crime," the President's Commission on Law Enforcement and Administration of Justice (1967) properly pointed out that it is

> not a single simple phenomenon that can be examined, analyzed and described in one piece. It occurs in every part of the country and in every stratum of society. Its practitioners and its victims are people of all ages, incomes, and backgrounds. Its trends are difficult to ascertain. Its causes are legion. Its cures are speculative and controversial.

As the most comprehensive and professional national survey on this subject in over thirty years, the Commission's complex findings and more than two hundred recommendations add much light and no little controversy. Eschewing facile generalizations concerning the motivational elements in all of the diverse manifestations of criminal behavior, the Report nevertheless does place particularly heavy responsibility for crime on societal and environmental factors.

> Society insists that individuals are responsible for their actions, and the criminal process operates on that assumption. However, society has not devised ways for ensuring that all its members have the ability to assume responsibility. It has let too many of them grow up untaught, unmotivated, unwanted. The criminal justice system has a great potential for dealing with individual instances of crime, but it was not designed to eliminate the conditions in which most crime breeds. It needs help. Warring on poverty, inadequate housing and unemployment is warring on crime. A civil rights law is a law against crime. Money for schools is money against crime. Medical, psychiatric and family-counseling services are services against crime.

It is the system of justice, of course, with which this chapter is essentially concerned—more specifically, those major Supreme Court decisions that dramatically and controversially expanded certain important procedural rights of the accused in criminal proceedings.

Gideon's Triumph—An Indigent Defendant's Right to Counsel

For a legal system, which prides itself on such noble traditions as presuming an accused innocent unless proven guilty, to permit a defendant to be formally tried in a court without the benefit of counsel must seem strange to any fair-minded person. And yet for centuries the common law courts of Britain did not allow "a prisoner to be heard by counsel upon the general issue of guilt or innocence" either in felony cases or on charges of treason. Apparently on the theory that misdemeanors, by way of contrast, constituted less of a threat to crown and realm, assistance of counsel for such lesser charges was made available and ostensibly did not offend the system. Nearly a half a century before England changed these general rules, the Sixth Amendment to the United States Constitution already proclaimed that "[i]n all criminal prosecutions, the accused shall . . . have the Assistance of Counsel for his Defence." Until relatively recently, this Amendment was interpreted as restricting the federal government only; however, it is interesting to note that by 1789 only six of the original states judged it sufficiently important to incorporate such similar protection into their own constitutions. However, at the state level, moves towards copying or implementing the Sixth Amendment rights of counsel proceeded at a slow and uneven rate through constitutional changes, statutory enactment or judicial interpretation. More importantly, neither the states nor the federal government extended the procedural right readily to the indigent defendant. In federal jurisdictions, the right to counsel for defendants who were poor, and who did not "competently and intelligently" waive right to counsel, did not become mandatory until 1938 (*Johnson* v. *Zerbst*). Four years later, when the Supreme Court was asked to extend this principle to defendants in state courts, Justice Owen J. Roberts, writing for the majority, in *Betts* v. *Brady* refused. At that time, the law of as many as eleven states failed to provide counsel for indigent defendants in either capital or non-capital cases. Maryland and Texas went so far as to explicitly reject such assistance altogether. In other states constitutional and statutory provisions, to the contrary, had either been ignored, limited to certain types of offenses or left to judicial discretion. Having surveyed all the relevant practices, Roberts concluded: "In the great majority of the states, it has been the considered judgment of the people, their representatives and their courts that appointment of counsel is not a fundamental right, essential to a fair trial." Under these conditions "we are unable to say that the concept of due process incorporated in the Fourteenth Amendment obligates the states . . . to furnish counsel in every such case."

Justice Black, speaking for Justices Douglas and Frank Murphy, dissented. While not willing to go so far as requiring counsel for indigents in all cases and under all circumstances, he did contend that the defendant in this case—an uneducated and unemployed farm hand sentenced to an eight-year prison term for robbery—could not have obtained a fair trial without such aid. Subjecting a man "to increased dangers of conviction merely because of . . . [lack of] property," seemed to Black difficult to reconcile with "common and fundamental ideas of fairness and right."

It took yet another twenty years before a handwritten, badly misspelled petition from an inmate of a Florida state prison to the United States Supreme Court (proceeding *in forma pauperis*) led to the revolution in state criminal procedures that finally gave even to indigents the right to counsel. Anthony Lewis, in his excellent study of the case in *Gideon's Trumpet,* gives this succinct description of the man whose search for justice occasioned a most far-reaching Court reversal.

> Gideon was a fifty-one-year-old white man who had been in and out of prisons much of his life. He had served time for four previous felonies, and he bore the physical marks of a destitute life: a wrinkled, prematurely aged face, a voice and hands that trembled, a frail body, white hair. He had never been a professional criminal or a man of violence; he just could not seem to settle down to work, and so he made his way by gambling and occasional thefts. Those who had known him, even the men who had arrested him and those who were now his jailers, considered Gideon a perfectly harmless human being, rather likeable, but one tossed aside by life. Anyone meeting him for the first time would be likely to regard him as the most wretched of men. And yet a flame still burned in Clarence Earl Gideon. He had not given up caring about life or freedom; he had not lost his sense of injustice. Right now he had a passionate—some thought almost irrational—feeling of having been wronged by the State of Florida, and he had the determination to try to do something about it.[1]

[1]Anthony Lewis, *Gideon's Trumpet* (New York: Random House, 1964), pp. 5–6. Reprinted with permission.

Gideon had been charged, convicted and sentenced to a five-year term for "having broken and entered a poolroom (Bay Harbor Poolroom in Panama City, Florida) . . . with intent to commit a misdemeanor"; under Florida law this constituted a felonious offense. His request for counsel had been turned down by the trial court which informed him that according to the law of the state, counsel for indigent defendants could only be furnished in capital cases.

Also rejected was a habeas corpus petition to the Florida Supreme Court in which Gideon attacked his conviction on the grounds "that the trial court's refusal to appoint counsel for him denied him rights 'guaranteed by the Constitution and the Bill of Rights . . .'." It was at this point that Gideon wrote a pencilled request for review of his case by the United States Supreme Court. By granting certiorari, the Court indicated its willingness to face squarely the issue of whether or not *Betts* should be considered controlling and whether the failure to provide counsel was " 'offensive to the common and fundamental ideas of fairness'." Justice Black and a unanimous Court decided that it was, and that *Betts* "should be overruled." While it was true, he argued, that *Betts* considered the Sixth Amendment counsel guarantee not to be a "fundamental right" incorporated into the Fourteenth Amendment as, for example, such rights as freedom of speech, press, religion, assembly and petition, there were other cases such as *Powell* v. *Alabama* (1932) that could have been followed in which the Supreme Court did hold the aid of counsel to be indeed of such a fundamental nature as to be binding upon the states. To Black, therefore, *Betts* "made an abrupt break with its own well-considered precedents." But more than that, "in our adversary system of criminal justice," he added, "any person hailed into court, who is too poor to hire a lawyer cannot be assured a fair trial unless counsel is provided for him. This seems to us to be an obvious truth."

Actually Black overstated his case somewhat, as Harlan quite correctly pointed out in his concurrence. *Powell* v. *Alabama* had involved a capital offense which was obviously not true of either *Betts* or *Gideon*. In non-capital cases, on the other hand, the Court had employed the so-called "special circumstance" rule where the limitations and debilities of the defendant or the procedural complexities of a trial were generally invoked as justifying the appointment of counsel. To the *Betts* Court, however, these circumstances were apparently not of such a nature as to "establish a denial of due process." Since *Betts*, meanwhile, there were a number of decisions which held that "the mere existence of a serious criminal charge constituted in itself special circumstances." This meant to Harlan that it would be sounder for the overall administration of justice if the "special circumstances rule" should now be formally abandoned "at least as to offenses which . . . carry the possibility of a substantial prison sentence." While agreeing, therefore, that *Betts* should be overruled (although he thought it "was entitled to a more respectable burial"), Harlan also disassociated himself rather pointedly from the theory advanced by Douglas in his concurrent opinion in which he stated that the Sixth Amendment along with the rest of the Bill of Rights was made directly applicable to the states through absorption into the Fourteenth Amendment. This was going too far for Harlan's view of federalism. "Any such concept would disregard the frequently wide disparity between the legitimate interests of the States and of the Federal Government. . . ."

With the aid of his Court-selected counsel—the distinguished trial lawyer and future Supreme Court Justice Abe Fortas—Gideon thus had won a reversal and with it the right for a new trial. Then began some legal sparring and repeated postponements in the now familiar Circuit Court of Bay County, Florida while Gideon turned down a volunteered attorney from the American Civil Liberties Union and irascibly insisted on conducting his own defense. Finally he cooperated with a local counsel designated by Judge McCrary, the trial commenced and Gideon was given his second "day in court." This time a carefully conducted defense by a highly skilled attorney proved successful, and when the jury after deliberating sixty-five minutes returned with a verdict of "not guilty," Gideon, having spent about two years in prison, walked out, once again a free man.

The consequences of *Gideon* were immediate and enormous. Within thirteen months of that decision, the Court employing the new standard reversed and remanded for trial appeals from

Alabama (2), California (1), Florida (27), Illinois (2), Louisiana (2), Maryland (1), Missouri (1), New York (1), North Carolina (3), Ohio (2), Oklahoma (1), and Pennsylvania (3)—all cases in which indigent defendants vainly sought assistance of counsel. On October 14, 1963, in one summary disposition alone (*Dumond v. Wainwright*) the Court, over the objections of Justice Harlan, remanded to the Supreme Court of Florida ten cases for reconsideration "in light of *Gideon* v. *Wainwright.*"

Reports from Florida's director of prisons, indicated that within a few months of *Gideon,* about 1,000 prisoners were released from the state penitentiary because prosecutors could or would not retry them under the new procedural standard. Of another group of over three hundred prisoners who did receive a new trial, most had their sentences reduced, twelve received longer sentences and seventy-five inmates found that their terms were reaffirmed. While there are no reliable findings of results from *Gideon*-induced retrials for all of the states, there is sufficient evidence to indicate that the number of appeals from indigent prisoners, convicted without the benefit of counsel in state courts, has gone up throughout the nation. This, despite the fact that the possibility of an even harsher sentence as a consequence of a second trial could well have had a dissuasive effect in some jurisdictions.

To facilitate compliance with *Gideon* (and other subsequent implementing cases), legislatures and courts in twenty-three states took specific actions within twenty-four months to expand or improve their assigned counsel or public defender systems in varying degrees. This list included Arizona, Delaware, Florida, Idaho, Illinois, Kansas, Maine, Maryland, Massachusetts, Michigan, Minnesota, Mississippi, Missouri, Nebraska, Nevada, New Mexico, North Carolina, North Dakota, Oregon, Pennsylvania, Tennessee, Utah and Virginia.

Danny Escobedo and the Right to Counsel at the Station House

Gideon did not stand by itself. On the same day the Court remanded *Gideon,* two additional cases were decided in which the Court upheld counsel rights for indigent defendants. In *Draper* v. *State of Washington,* a trial judge had ruled a request for a free transcript of an appeal "patently frivolous," and in *Douglas* v. *People of the State of California,* a district court of appeal had concluded that "no good whatever could be served by appointment of counsel." The Supreme Court overruled both decisions. Four weeks later the Court reversed a conviction for murder where an indigent defendant had been left without the aid of counsel at the time of the "preliminary hearing" when he entered his plea. (*White* v. *Maryland*). This case was then followed by *Massiah* v. *United States* (1964), where the Court reversed a federal narcotics conviction because the federal agent solicited by electronic "surreptitious means" incriminating statements from the defendant while free on bail after his indictment —"at a time when he was clearly entitled to a lawyer's help." What the precise point should be at which counsel assistance becomes critical in a criminal proceeding was clearly a crucial consideration in *Escobedo* v. *Illinois* (1964). It helped to make that case—coming only a little over a year after *Gideon*—a landmark in American constitutional law.

Danny Escobedo, aged 22, never considered himself "the ideal teen-ager." Although he had not served time, his previous encounters with the Chicago police included two "investigative arrests" and three charges "ranging from assault to murder." After his brother-in-law was shot on the night of January 19, 1960 on Chicago's West Side, Danny was picked up by the police without a warrant, interrogated and released after some hours, when his attorney obtained a writ of habeas corpus. Then, ten days later, he was rearrested, handcuffed and, along with his sister, brought back to the police station. One of his "friends," Benedict DiGerlando, who had meanwhile been in custody for some days, had told the police that it was Danny who had "fired the fatal shots."

When his attorney arrived shortly afterwards, the police had already taken Danny to the interrogation room. Despite protestations that he wished to talk to his client (whom he had "spotted . . . in an office in the Homicide Bureau . . . waved to" and who had waved back before someone closed the door), the request was rejected. While being questioned Danny had indicated "repeatedly" that he wanted to "speak to his lawyer" but was informed by the detectives around him that "his lawyer 'didn't want to see' him." (There was some evidence in the record, acknowledged in Footnote 5 of Justice Goldberg's opinion, to the effect that Danny had conferred earlier with his attorney concerning what might generally occur in the course of the interrogation.)

What transpired during the course of the interrogation was in dispute. Danny testified that one of the police officers who spoke Spanish promised him that "my sister and I could go home if I pinned it on Benedict DiGerlando." This was contradicted by Officer Montejano. Danny's admission of complicity in the crime (which under Illinois law made him equally as guilty as if he had fired the bullet himself) came as a result of a direct confrontation, according to testimony, by one of the police officers:

> I informed him of what DiGerlando told me and when I did, he told me that DiGerlando was [lying] and I said, "Would you care to tell DiGerlando that?" and he said, "Yes, I will." So I brought . . . Escobedo in and he confronted DiGerlando and he told him that he was lying and said, "I didn't shoot Manuel, you did it."

Defense motions to strike this damaging admission, during the trial at which Escobedo was convicted of murder, were denied. After the Illinois Supreme Court affirmed the conviction, the United States Supreme Court granted certiorari "to consider whether the petitioner's statement was constitutionally admissible at his trial." It was found by Justice Goldberg not to be so. He saw the interrogation, although preceding the indictment, as an important and often decisive link to the subsequent trial.

> Petitioner had become the accused, and the purpose of the interrogation was to "get him" to confess his guilt despite his constitutional right not to do so. . . . Without informing him of his absolute right to remain silent in the face of . . . this accusation, the police urged him to make a statement.

> It would exalt form over substance to make the right to counsel, under these circumstances, depend on whether at the time of the

interrogation, the authorities had secured a formal indictment. Petitioner had, for all practical purposes, already been charged with murder.

Goldberg was not unmindful that the Court's insistence on the assistance of counsel at the preliminary stages of a trial could seriously stifle the willingness to confess and force the police to rely more heavily on "extrinsic evidence independently secured through skillful investigation." This he considered to be the necessary price required by the Constitution which "unlike some others, strikes the balance in favor of the right of the accused to be advised by his lawyer of his privilege against self-incrimination."

At what stage in the process must counsel then be provided? When "the investigation is *no longer a general inquiry* into an unresolved crime but has *begun to focus* on a particular suspect . . . , when its focus is on the accused and its *purpose* is to *elicit a confession* . . . , [when] our adversary system begins to operate . . ." (*emphasis supplied*). It is at that point that the defendant must have the opportunity to consult his lawyer. Such then was the gist of *Escobedo* to which the majority of the justices gave their assent.

There were three separate opinions for the four dissenters. Harlan thought the rule of *Escobedo* "ill-conceived" and as likely to obstruct "seriously and unjustifiably . . . perfectly legitimate methods of criminal law enforcement." As Stewart construed applicable legal precedents, the adversary proceedings which required assistance of counsel did not begin until the accused was arraigned, indicted or presented with a formal charge. During the investigative phase no such constitutional guarantees were necessary, and no previous cases had ever ruled to that effect. The majority's standard in *Escobedo* "perverts those precious constitutional guarantees and frustrates the vital interests of society in preserving the legitimate and proper function of honest and purposeful police investigation." Justice White was equally emphatic. Like his "colleagues-in-dissent," he challenged the new rule as an unwarranted and unworkable burden on criminal law enforcement. Police cars would have to be "equipped with public defenders and undercover agents and police informants [would need a] . . . defense counsel at their side." More funda-mental than that, he was unwilling to join the majority position which he perceived as barring "from evidence all admissions ob-tained from an individual suspected of crime, *whether involun-tarily made or not*" (*emphasis supplied*). What the Constitution prohibits are "inquisitions," "compelled" incriminations, but there is no constitutional right to remain silent or to preclude voluntary confessions. Danny's disclosure was not compelled; he "knew full well that he did not have to answer and . . . that his lawyer had advised him not to answer." Although the *Escobedo* decision will not destroy the criminal law enforcement machinery, concluded White, "it will be crippled and the task made a great deal more difficult."

Confessions and Warning— On the Way to Miranda

Only thirty years ago, a nation that always prided itself in affording "due process of law" to all its citizens was stunned to learn how confessions were obtained under particular circum-stances in at least one of the states of the Union. While some of the more critical students of American criminal procedure (as well as devotees of Tennessee Williams) have long suspected that police treatment given defendants in major crimes deeply offending community standards could occasionally be harsh, cruel and even arbitrary—especially if the defendants belong to unpopular minorities—the public revelation of such an instance (*Brown* v. *Mississippi*, 1936) in the stark and august atmosphere of the United States Supreme Court added special impact and drama.

> On that night (Friday, March 30, 1934) . . . a deputy sheriff, accompanied by others, came to the home of . . . one of the de-fendants, and requested him to accompany them to the house of the deceased, and there a number of white men were gathered, who began to accuse the defendant of the crime. Upon his denial they seized him, and with the participation of the deputy they hanged

him by a rope to the limb of a tree, and, having let him down, they hung him again, and when he was let down the second time, and he still protested his innocence, he was tied to a tree and whipped, and, still declining to accede to the demand that he confess, he was finally released, and he returned with some difficulty to his home, suffering intense pain and agony. The record of the testimony shows that the signs of the rope on his neck were plainly visible during the so-called trial. A day or two thereafter the . . . deputy, accompanied by another, returned to the home of the defendant and arrested him, and departed with the prisoner towards the jail . . . while on the way . . . the deputy stopped and again severely whipped the defendant, declaring that he would continue the whipping until he confessed, and the defendant then agreed to confess to such a statement as the deputy would dictate, and he did so, after which he was delivered to jail.

Another case (*Chambers* v. *Florida*, 1940), where twenty-five to forty Negro farm tenants were rounded up without a warrant, confined in the county jail for nearly a week, continuously questioned singly or in pairs, for several days and nights without being permitted to contact friends, families or counsel under "circumstances to break the strongest nerves and the stoutest resistance"—occasioned an outburst by Justice Black which rose above the terse language of the law to reach heights of classic universality.

The testimony of centuries, in governments of varying kinds over populations of different races and beliefs, stood as proof that physical and mental torture and coercion had brought about the tragically unjust sacrifices of some who were the noblest and most useful of their generations. The racks, the thumbscrew, the wheel, solitary confinement, protracted questioning and cross questioning, and other ingenious forms of entrapment of the helpless and unpopular had left their wake of mutilated bodies and shattered minds along the way to the cross, the guillotine, the stake and the hangman's noose. And they who have suffered most from secret and dictatorial proceedings have almost always been the poor, the ignorant, and the numerically weak, the friendless, and the powerless.

Such extreme cases as *Brown* and *Chambers* with their crude and brutal extractions of confessions clearly outrage the conscience of a civilized people and violate the standards of civilized criminal procedures. Fortunately, responsible and competent police investigators have long refused to avail themselves of such inhuman practices. Still, confessions allegedly given voluntarily, can in fact be the constitutionally unallowable outcomes of subtle psychological pressures, objectionable interrogational tactics and environmental conditioning to which the suspect has been subjected by law enforcement officers who were honestly convinced of his guilt and eager to rid society of one of its enemies.

Some of the important pre-*Miranda* cases which illustrated the Court's concern with delayed arraignments and abusive interrogative practices included the following:

McNabb v. *United States* (1943)—Defendants, none of whom had gone beyond the fourth grade or had ever left their Tennessee community, were arrested at their homes in the middle of the night and charged with the murder of an alcohol tax officer who had been killed "at a site where the NcNabbs had allegedly hidden untaxed whiskey." Defendants were placed in a detention room for "about 14 hours" and "subjected to unremitting questioning by numerous officers," eventually confessed without being permitted to contact their families or an attorney and without having been arraigned or granted a hearing as required by federal law. Reversed. ". . . [A] decent regard for the duty of courts as agencies of justice . . . forbids that men should be convicted upon evidence secured under the circumstances revealed here."

Mallory v. *United States* (1957)—Defendant, "a nineteen-year-old lad of limited intelligence" had been accused of having committed rape, was arrested in the afternoon and "detained at headquarters" where he could have easily been brought before a magistrate. Instead, he was questioned; when this "produced no confession" he was asked "to submit to a 'lie-detector' test," and after another five hours which included some additional questioning, he confessed. At no time was he warned of his rights to counsel, to an examination before a magistrate, or to remain silent. Reversed and remanded. "It is not the function of the police to arrest, as it were, at large and to use an interrogative process at police headquarters in order to determine whom they should charge before a committing magistrate on 'probable cause'."

Spano v. *People of the State of New York* (1959)—Petitioner, age 25, foreign born, and with no record of law violations, had voluntarily surrendered subsequent to admitting his crime over the phone to a friend [Bruno], a new member of the police department. In line with his attorney's advice, petitioner refused to talk as he was questioned by teams of interrogators for "virtually eight straight hours." Finally he confessed after having been repeatedly refused in his request for a conference with his counsel. One aspect of the strategy of questioning was found by the Court as especially offensive. To help obtain the confession Bruno was instructed "falsely to state that petitioner's telephone call had gotten him into trouble, that his job was in jeopardy, and that loss of his job would be disastrous to his three children, his wife and his unborn child." Reversed. "We conclude that petitioner's will was overborne by official pressure, fatigue and sympathy falsely aroused." As police "methods used to extract confessions [have become] . . . more sophisticated, our duty to enforce . . . constitutional protections does not cease."

The Court's 1963 and 1964 terms produced at least four important constitutional steppingstones towards *Miranda*. (1) *Malloy* v. *Hogan* (1964). This was a highly significant decision. By relying on precedents from forced confession and seizures cases (including *Mapp* v. *Ohio,* 1961, which extended to the states the rule against the introduction of evidence obtained by unconstitutional search and seizure), the Court incorporated the Fifth Amendment prohibition against self-incrimination against "abridgments by the States." To Justice Brennan and four of his colleagues, the application of the federal standard to a state proceeding where a defendant was committed to prison "until he was willing to answer . . . [certain] questions" represented "recognition that the American system of criminal prosecution is accusatorial, not inquisitorial" and that there cannot be unequal standards of justice for federal and for state proceedings.

While Justice White (joined by Stewart) aimed his dissent mostly at procedural points, Harlan (joined by Clark) entered objections which were much more substantive and clearly reflective of the widening split on the Court with respect to the constitutional status of criminal law. As Harlan interpreted the majority opinion it amounted to (a) "a disregard of all relevant differences which may exist between state and federal criminal law," (b) a "compelled uniformity . . . inconsistent with . . . our federal system . . ." and (c) a failure to understand that due process of law under the Fourteenth Amendment merely required "fairness." State criminal procedures could still be fair, Harlan insisted, without extending to defendants the Fifth Amendment safeguards against self-incrimination. *Murphy* v. *Waterfront Commission* (1964) further extended the privilege against self-incrimination by holding that witnesses who were granted immunity from prosecution under state laws (in order to obtain answers to certain questions concerning work stoppages at the piers) could still not be required to testify if their testimony "and its fruits" might tend to incriminate them under *federal* law. As a result of this decision, witnesses having nothing to fear henceforth from any subsequent federal prosecution that might grow out of information given to the Commission, could now, therefore, be required "to answer the questions propounded to them."

(2) *Jackson* v. *Denno* (1964). In at least one-third of the states (including New York) and in over half of the federal judicial circuits, questions pertaining to the voluntariness of a confession instead of being decided by the trial judge, have been referred, as a matter of procedural rule, to juries for their determination. In *Jackson,* the defendant held up a room clerk in Brooklyn and, after leaving the hotel, shot and killed a policeman in a struggle in which he too was severely wounded. While still under medication at the hospital, he was questioned by police officers to whom he eventually confessed to both the robbery and the homicide. At the trial, the judge left to the jury the task of reconciling conflicting testimony as to whether the confession was coerced. Such a policy, according to Justice White, who delivered the opinion of the Court ordering a reversal, required too much of the jury. They were expected to disregard or put out of their minds involuntary confession and also to "understand the policy of forbidding reliance upon a coerced, but true, confession . . ." as they weighed the question of guilt or innocence and arrived at a general verdict. Since there was no way of actually determining whether the jury improperly admitted an invalid confession in its decision, defendant's rights to a fair hearing under the due

process of law clause of the Fourteenth Amendment were placed in distinct jeopardy. Separate dissents by Justices Black, Clark and Harlan criticized the majority for reversing a rule approved only a few years ago in *Stein* v. *New York* (1953), for striking down a procedural principle widely adopted throughout the nation, for disrupting criminal administration and for constituting an unwarranted attack on "jury waywardness."

(3) *Griffin* v. *California* (1965). According to the law of six states (and by explicit state constitutional demand in California and Ohio), a defendant was at liberty to exercise his constitutional right not to take the stand, while prosecutors were permitted, however, to comment upon his failure to testify and call it to the attention of the jury. Did such provisions violate the Fifth Amendment protections against self-incrimination made binding upon states through the Fourteenth Amendment? Justice Douglas who delivered the majority opinion in this case decided that they did and consequently reversed a first-degree murder conviction. As the record revealed, "the prosecutor made much" of the defendant's unwillingness to testify.

> The defendant certainly knows whether Essie Mae had this beat up appearance at the time he left her apartment and went down the alley with her.
>
> What kind of a man is it that would want to have sex with a woman that beat up if she was beat up at the time he left?
>
> He would know that. He would know how she got down the alley. He would know how the blood got on the bottom of the concrete steps. He would know how long he was with her in that box. He would know how her wig got off. He would know whether he beat her or mistreated her. . . .
>
> These things he has not seen fit to take the stand and deny or explain.
>
> And in the whole world, if anybody would know, this defendant would know.
>
> Essie Mae is dead, she can't tell you her side of the story. The defendant won't.

Although the trial judge instructed the jury not to draw any inference of guilt concerning the defendant's failure to explain or deny particular evidence, Douglas saw in the prosecutor's comments "a remnant of the 'inquisitorial system of criminal justice', . . . a penalty imposed by courts for exercising constitutional privilege." While such inference by a jury may even be "natural and irresistible," courts should not be permitted to "solemnize the silence of the accused into evidence against him." Rejecting these arguments, Stewart (joined by White) pointed out that the majority rule had no precedent and that it "stretche[d] the concept of compulsion beyond all reasonable bounds." Rather than being a "coercive device," the prosecutive right of comment brings "into the light of rational discussion a fact inescapably impressed on the jury's consciousness." This should accrue to the mutual advantage of the defendant by protecting him against a jury's "uneducated assumptions" and inferences drawn from his silence—and the state's—by permitting this right of comment "to shape a legal process designed to ascertain the truth."

(4) *Henry* v. *State of Mississippi* (1965). The availability of habeas corpus proceedings to challenge the illegal restraint of defendants as a result of state court convictions has long been recognized in American constitutional law. Somewhat paralleling this principle has been an equally significant one. Under the doctrine of abstention which developed out of the federal formula with its dual court system, state rather than federal courts were to retain primary responsibility for much of the administration of criminal justice. Thus before defendants in most criminal proceedings could assert their federal rights in federal courts, state judicial remedies had to be exhausted. As a matter of comity, moreover, federal courts would ordinarily defer until state courts had been given an opportunity to pass on these contentions, nor would federal courts generally be inclined to review state court decisions which rest "on independent and adequate state grounds." During the last fifteen years, especially since *Brown* v. *Allen* (1953), applications for such habeas corpus petitions have, however, increased considerably. (Between fiscal 1963 and fiscal 1964 the Administrative Office of the United States

Courts noted an increase of 85.5%.) A trend accentuated, no doubt, by the more critical attitude with which a majority of the Supreme Court approached state criminal procedures and by a number of decisions through which such attitudes found forceful expression with results often beneficial to the defendant's side of a case. The power of the federal judiciary to grant judicial relief, despite appellant's failure to "exhaust state remedies" not available to him at the time he sought federal judicial assistance, was clearly delineated, for example, in *Fay* v. *Noia* (1963). During the same term, *Townsend* v. *Sain* (1963) imposed the affirmative duty on the federal courts to grant an evidentiary hearing where substantial state errors were alleged or where essential facts were not brought to the attention of the state court that originally tried the case.

Some of the more striking illustrations of the powerful role that the federal courts assumed vis-à-vis state criminal procedures occurred, of course, in connection with civil rights demonstrations in the South. In one such instance, *Aelony* v. *Pace* (1963), a state prosecutor of Sumter County, Georgia, was quoted as admitting that he filed insurrection charges against field organizers of the Student Nonviolent Coordinating Committee (S.N.C.C.), who had been campaigning for desegregation and voter registrations, in order to keep defendants in jail pending their presentment to the grand jury. Under Georgia law, persons charged with such a capital offense were not entitled to bail. Some of these individuals had been incarcerated for three months and there was considerable evidence that the prosecution was not about to permit their cases to come up for trial except on the condition that the defendants promise to cease their activities or leave the state immediately. On appeal, a three-judge federal district court declared the insurrection statute unconstitutional and granted an injunction staying further prosecution under other collateral charges brought against defendants to prevent them from exercising rights guaranteed to them under the federal Constitution and under the Civil Rights Acts of 1870 and 1957.

Finally, *Henry* v. *Mississippi* (1965) not only re-emphasized the availability of habeas corpus where it was shown that the defendant did not intelligently and deliberately waive his federal claims in a state court (such as a protest over "tainted evidence" or coerced confession) but went at least one step further. As a possible measure of ameliorating federal-state frictions, the Court "afforded" states the opportunity to make the "initial determination of waiver" and to fully "air federal claims" in their own courts subject, of course, to federal judicial review. Ultimately, then, federal courts would still test by "settled principles" whether or not challenged state criminal procedures complied with federal constitutional norms. Harlan dismissed this approach as a "watered down form of federalism . . . not congenial to the kind of federalism I had supposed was ours," and as not sufficiently respectful of the constitutional adequacy of state court processes (technically referred to as "state grounds").

Miranda v. Arizona and the Lawyer at the Station House

Perhaps no single Supreme Court decision affecting the administration of criminal law—certainly none during the last two decades—has had a more far-reaching impact or been more controversial than *Miranda* and its three companion cases (*Vignera* v. *New York, Westover* v. *United States* and *California* v. *Stewart*) decided June 13, 1966. For years to come, judges and scholars, prosecutors and defense counsels, the press, politicians and the public will debate the wisdom and utility of the constitutional concepts, policy choices, social theory, criminological principles and perceptions of law enforcement which were reflected in the opinion of the Chief Justice and in the dissents.

The facts of the case were not in dispute.

On March 13, 1963 . . . Ernesto Miranda, was arrested at his home and taken in custody to a Phoenix police station. He was there identified by the complaining witness. The police then took him to "Interrogation Room No. 2" of the detective bureau. There he was questioned by two police officers. The officers admitted at trial that Miranda was not advised that he had a right to have an attorney present. Two hours later, the officers emerged from the interrogation

room with a written confession signed by Miranda. At the top of the
statement was a typed paragraph stating that the confession was made
voluntarily, without threats or promises of immunity and "with full
knowledge of my legal right, understanding any statement I make
may be used against me."

At his trial before a jury, the written confession was admitted into
evidence over the objection of defense counsel, and the officers testified to the prior oral confession made by Miranda during the interrogation. Miranda was found guilty of kidnapping and rape. . . .

His conviction and sentence was affirmed by the Arizona Supreme
Court upon a finding that the confession was obtained by constitutionally valid means. Brought up for review on a writ of
certiorari, a 5-to-4 majority of the United States Supreme Court
voted to reverse the judgment.

Warren's opinion left no doubt that a majority of the Court
was now ready and eager to amplify what was begun in *Escobedo*
(which federal and state courts had applied quite differently
resulting in confusion and uncertainty) and to promulgate in
the light of that decision a fairly distinct and comprehensive
standard for constitutionally permissible forms of police questioning. Thus, before a statement by a defendant in police custody, "deprived of his freedom of action" and "cut off from the
outside world," can be admitted in evidence, the following procedural conditions had to be met:

(1) The defendant must have been warned "at the outset of the
interrogation process" that he had a right to consult an attorney.

(2) If indigent, the defendant must be assured that the public will provide him with counsel.

(3) The defendant must be apprised of his right to remain silent
and if he "indicated in any manner, at any time prior to or during questioning, that he wishes to remain silent, the interrogation
must cease."

(4) If defendant does give a statement he must be warned that anything he says "can and will be used" against him in court.

(5) Before a waiver of a defendant's rights will be held valid in an
interrogation conducted in the absence of an attorney, "a heavy

> burden rests on the Government to demonstrate that the defendant knowingly and intelligently waived his privilege against self-incrimination and his right to retained or appointed counsel."

Such then were the essential and necessary protections that Warren saw bestowed by the Constitution through the Fifth and Sixth Amendments on defendants in American police custody.

There were necessary protections, he argued, first because our judicial traditions insist that no person in a criminal case shall "be a witness against himself"; second, because the use of physical brutality, psychological pressures and other refined forms of the third degree employed by overly zealous law officers to extract confessions from prisoners kept incommunicado are still practiced as documented by special studies, by cases up to 1965 and in reports from governmental commissions (the Wickersham Commission, 1931 and the Commission on Civil Rights, 1961); third, because inquisitorial tricks and tactics (detailed in well-known texts and manuals for use by the police when alone with the accused in the privacy of the interrogation room) can easily "subjugate the individual to the will of his examiner"; and fourth, because individual "dignity" and "integrity" commands respect from our government, federal and state.

The procedures and warnings which Warren proposed were to be guidelines only—"the Constitution does not require any specific code . . . for protecting the privilege against self-incrimination during custodial interrogation." They were not designed to do away with all confessions (freely and voluntarily given, they "remain a proper element in law enforcement") nor with "[g]eneral on-the-scene questioning as to facts surrounding the crime. . . ." They were sufficiently practical—the F.B.I. has used rules consistent with this standard for years and so have some foreign countries—and sufficiently safe "not to constitute an undue interference with a proper system of law enforcement." Whether it will be the Court's interrogation model that Congress or state legislatures might wish to adopt, its operation must effectively meet the constitutional requirement of "informing accused persons of their right of silence and . . . [of] affording a continuous opportunity to exercise it."

When Warren applied the standard to *Miranda* (and to the other three cases) he found every one of them wanting. "They all . . . share salient features—incommunicado interrogation of individuals in a police-dominated atmosphere, resulting in self-incriminating statements without full warnings of constitutional rights."

The dissenting opinions were sharply worded and indicative of the deep division on the Court regarding the question of limits imposed by the Constitution on custodial interrogation. Common to the three separate dissents was a solemn rejection of the "new" code which was characterized in varying degrees of intensity as an unsound judicial experiment, as ignoring the legitimate considerations of public safety, as unnecessarily critical of the police and as dangerously compounding their already sufficiently difficult problems. There were additional objections and elaborations. Rather than imposing the absolute warning requirement that Warren stipulated as demanded by the Fifth Amendment, Clark would also have preferred the Court to go more slowly and retain the "totality of circumstances" test of "due process of law" under which failure of the police to give the necessary warning was only one of the factors to be weighed in determining whether the confession was "clearly voluntary."

Harlan disapproved of the new rules because they tended "ultimately to discourage any confession at all," because they failed to acknowledge that legitimate questioning of suspects was an important "instrument of law enforcement" and because they ignored considerable expert testimony attesting "that some crimes cannot be solved without confession." Like Clark, he adhered to the more flexible "due process of law" test contending that the Fifth Amendment applied only to judicial proceedings, not to police interrogation.

White's disagreements with the Court parallelled and augmented those of Clark and Harlan. He indicted the majority for making a new law without having empirically ascertained what the actual contemporary interrogation practices were and for unrealistically "escalating the requirements to prove waiver." Moreover, the Court's preoccupation with the "dignity of the accused" should have been balanced by another "desideratum"—

"the human personality of others; . . . society's interest in the general security is of equal weight." He quarreled with the Court's "deep-seated distrust of all confessions," insisting that voluntary confessions, especially "when corroborated" by the police, "have the highest reliability and significantly contribute to the certitude with which we may believe the accused is guilty." By practically precluding interrogation, by reducing the likelihood of confessions and the plea of guilty and by increasing the numbers of trials, criminal apprehension will become more difficult and the "similarly tempted" less deterred.

> "I have no desire, whatsoever," concluded Justice White with acerbity, "to share the responsibility for any such impact on the present criminal process. In some unknown number of cases the Court's rule will return a killer, a rapist or other criminal to the streets and to the environment which produced him, to repeat his crime whenever it pleases him. As a consequence, there will not be gain, but a loss, in human dignity. The real concern is not the unfortunate consequences of this new decision on the criminal law as an abstract, disembodied series of authoritative proscriptions but the impact on those who rely on the public authority for protection and who without it can only engage in violent self-help with guns, knives and the help of their neighbors similarly inclined. There is, of course, a saving factor: the next victims are uncertain, unnamed and unrepresented in this case."

Three of the dissenters, including Justice Stewart, decided against the defendants in each of the four cases; Clark concurred with the exception of *California* v. *Stewart,* in which case had it been separately decided, he would have voted with the majority of the Court.

As to the defendants themselves, a concluding footnote seems in order. At the second trial in February, 1967, Ernesto Miranda was convicted by a jury (deliberating less than two hours), following testimony by his common law wife that when she visited him in jail "he admitted to me that he had kidnapped the girl, and roped her up, then took her into the desert and raped her." Of the other three defendants, two have already been retried and sentenced to serve long prison terms; Roy Allen Stewart's case is still before the courts.

The availability of the *Escobedo* and *Miranda* rules to defendants tried and convicted prior to the announcement of these decisions was settled by the Court in *Johnson* v. *New Jersey* (1966). Chief Justice Warren explicitly rejected retroactivity. While this was in no way intended to "disparage" the new constitutional guarantees, the Court contended that their retroactive application "would seriously disrupt the administration of our criminal laws." *Gideon,* where the Court seemed not similarly restrained was distinguished on the grounds that the right to counsel "affected 'the very integrity of the fact finding process' " and that there was a "clear danger of convicting the innocent." Although *Escobedo* and *Miranda* thus authorized prospective application only, defendants not yet included under its provisions could still obtain justice by availing "themselves of the voluntariness test." Whatever the logical sufficiency of these distinctions, the long-term considerations of public policy and administrative efficacy appear to have been the more persuasive elements of the judicial arguments.

Should They Be Made to Talk?

Strong and not unexpected support for custodial interrogation and confessions has come from police officials, public prosecutors and state attorneys general as well as from certain segments of the bench and bar. There was ample testimony to that effect, for example, during the 1958 hearings of the House and Senate Judiciary Committees which at that time were considering legislative proposals to limit the applicability of the *McNabb* and *Mallory* rules. These were the decisions in which the Supreme Court held that confessions were inadmissible in evidence if there was an "unnecessary delay" in the arraignment of the accused. Critics from various law enforcement agencies who testified before these Committees termed the Court's position an obstruction to the effective control and apprehension of criminals. A few comments from the Washington scene will suffice as illustration.

To exclude voluntary confessions on any ground whatsoever is in my humble judgment detrimental to the cause of justice and permits guilty persons to escape conviction. (Judge Alexander Holtzoff, United States District Court, Washington D.C.)

. . . [P]ersons convicted of serious crimes are likely to go free unless there is consideration of remedial legislation. (Oliver Gasch, United States District Attorney, District of Columbia)

. . . [I]f a remedy is not found, the result will be disastrous to law enforcement in the District of Columbia and in all Federal courts throughout the land, and ultimately in the States also. (Edgar E. Scott, Deputy Chief of Detectives, Metropolitan Police Department, Washington, D.C.)

I think that . . . if the procedure [of arrest] . . . is to function properly there should be very considerable discretion given to the officers as to when they should charge. (Warren Olney, Assistant Attorney General, Criminal Division, United States Department of Justice)

Late in the summer of 1958, the 85th Congress almost enacted such a bill designed to limit the application of the *Mallory* rule. H.R. 11477 passed the House 294 to 79 (D. 125–75; R. 169–4), and in a slightly different version, the Senate voted 65 to 12 (D. 30–8; R. 35–4). Failure of the Senate to accept the conference report, however, caused the bill to die. Had the measure become law it would have amended Title 18 of the United States Criminal Code by adding this statutory rule for the admission of statements and confessions.

(1) Evidence, including statements and confessions, otherwise admissible, shall not be inadmissible solely because of delay in taking an arrested person before a commissioner or other officer empowered to commit persons charged with offenses against the laws of the United States.

(2) No statement, including a confession, made by an arrested person during an interrogation by a law-enforcement officer shall be admissible unless prior to such interrogation the arrested person had been advised that he is not required to make a statement and that any statement made by him may be used against him.

Although the Senate took no further formal legislative action on these proposals, an anti-*Mallory* measure did once more pass the House in 1959 and again in 1961 (but this time applicable only to the District of Columbia).

Congressional debates centered on the need to balance the community's natural quest for security with a defendant's constitutional right to due process of law. Pro-interrogation forces, while condemning threats, intimidations and recourse to brutality as indefensible police methods, emphasized the usefulness of the custodial arrangement to both the accused and the law enforcement effort. A person wrongly suspected could clear his name quickly and thus avoid the embarrassment of a formal arraignment. A reasonably short period of detention was needed, moreover, to enable the police to check out alibis, substantiate accusations or obtain statements from persons in certain crimes where it is difficult to secure evidence—this would be true particularly when the felony involved murder, rape or robbery.

Many of those who favored the retention of the *McNabb-Mallory* rule, on the other hand, readily admitted that the tasks of the police might have been made more difficult because of it but judged that worth the cost if constitutional protections for the accused were to remain viable and meaningful. What the Fourth Amendment demanded, it seemed to them, was that no one should be arrested or deprived of his liberty until or unless probable cause had been established. Measures, such as H.R. 11477, would have reversed the process with arrest preceding rather than following an evidence gathering process in which dragnet operations, easy detention or prolonged questioning could have played an ominously prominent role all too reminiscent of star chamber proceedings.

Nearly always intertwined with these discussions of custodial interrogation, of course, has been the problem of defining the limits within which it is permissible to employ psychological tactics in efforts to obtain confessions from a suspect.

Among the best known and most widely cited police texts on the subject are those written by Fred E. Inbau and John E. Reid whose association with the Chicago Police Scientific Crime Detection Laboratories has extended over a number of years. One of their most recent works, delineates its thesis in three succinct propositions.

(1) Many Criminal Cases, Even When Investigated by the Best Qualified Police Departments, Are Capable of Solution Only by Means of an Admission or Confession from the Guilty Individual or upon the Basis of Information Obtained from the Questioning of Other Criminal Suspects.

(2) Criminal Offenders, Except of Course, Those Caught in the Commission of Their Crimes, Ordinarily Will Not Admit Their Guilt unless Questioned under Conditions of Privacy, and for a Period of Perhaps Several Hours.

(3) In Dealing with Criminal Offenders, and Consequently Also with Criminal Suspects Who May Actually Be Innocent, the Interrogator Must of Necessity Employ Less Refined Methods Than Are Considered Appropriate for the Transaction of Ordinary, Everyday Affairs by and between Law-Abiding Citizens.[1]

For questioning to be effective there must be a proper setting. "The principal psychological factor contributing to a successful interrogation is privacy—being alone with the person under interrogation." Then comes the "Method." Among the "topics" outlined in the table of contents, were the following:

Display an Air of Confidence in the Subject's Guilt . . . Point out Some, but by no Means All, of the Circumstantial Evidence Indicative of a Subject's Guilt . . . Call Attention to the Subject's Physiological and Psychological Symptoms of Guilt . . . Sympathize with the Subject by Telling Him That Anyone Else under Similar Conditions or Circumstances Might Have Done the Same Thing . . . Sympathize with the Subject by (1) Condemning His Victim, (2) Condemning His Accomplice, or (3) Condemning Anyone Else upon Whom Some Degree of Moral Responsibility Might Conceivably Be Placed for the Commission of the Crime in Question . . . Point out the Possibility of Exaggeration on the Part of the Accuser or Victim or Exaggerate the Nature and Seriousness of the Offense Itself. . . .

When Co-Offenders Are Being Interrogated and the Previously Described Techniques Have Been Ineffective, "Play One Against the Other" . . . Refer to Some Non-Existing Incriminating Evidence to

[1] *Criminal Interrogation and Confessions* (Baltimore: Williams and Wilkens Co., 1962), pp. 204, 206, 207. Reprinted with permission.

Determine whether the Subject Will Attempt to Explain It Away; if He Does, That Fact Is Suggestive of His Guilt . . . Ask the Subject whether He Is Willing to Take a Lie-Detector Test. The Innocent Person Will Almost Always Steadfastly Agree to Take Practically Any Test to Prove His Innocence.[2]

Various specific suggestions for the conduct of the interrogation stressed the need for patience, persistence and "overtime periods." Two particular "bits of advice" with which the interrogator might be able to handle an accused person's insistence on his rights to silence, to contact his family or to request legal assistance, which Justice Warren cited verbatim in *Miranda,* deserve special attention:

"Joe, you have a right to remain silent. That's your privilege and I'm the last person in the world who'll try to take it away from you. If that's the way you want to leave this, O.K. But let me ask you this. Suppose you were in my shoes and I were in yours and you called me in to ask me about this and I told you, 'I don't want to answer any of your questions.' You'd think I had something to hide, and you'd probably be right in thinking that. That's exactly what I'll have to think about you, and so will everybody else. So let's sit here and talk this whole thing over."

If a subject expresses a desire to talk to a relative . . . or to any other person, the interrogator should respond by suggesting that the subject first tell the truth to the interrogator himself rather than get anyone else involved in that matter. If the request is for an attorney, the interrogator may suggest that the subject save himself or his family the expense of any such professional service, particularly if he is innocent of the offense under investigation. The interrogator may also add, "Joe, I'm only looking for the truth, and if you're telling the truth, that's it. You can handle this by yourself."[3]

To many of the critics of the *McNabb* and *Mallory* decisions, these physically non-coercive interrogation techniques for overcoming or persuading a suspect's reluctance to talk amounted to practical, morally defensive and highly effective weapons with which society should protect itself against crime and the criminal offender.

To others, however, the kinds of psychological tactics and

[2] *Ibid.,* pp. ix–x. Reprinted with permission.
[3] *Ibid.,* pp. 111, 112. Reprinted with permission.

tricks advocated by Inbau and Reid seemed equally as repre-
hensible as were the older and cruder forms of pressures with
which confessions were extracted from uncooperative subjects.
Most vulnerable to these newer, more sophisticated questioning
practices were again those naturally least able to resist—the
young, the poor, the ignorant, the illiterates. Even before *Miranda*
ruled so decisively and so controversially on the issue of custodial
interrogation in a "police-dominated atmosphere," strong voices
from within the legal profession seriously questioned the voluntariness of confessions obtained in such a setting. One who vigorously challenged what might be termed society's "double standard" with respect to the pre-trial criminal process has been Professor Yale Kamisar of the University of Michigan.

> The courtroom is a splendid place where defense attorneys bellow
> and strut and prosecuting attorneys are hemmed in at many turns. But
> what happens before an accused reaches the safety and enjoys the
> comforts of this veritable mansion? Ah, there's the rub. Typically he
> must first pass through a much less pretentious edifice, a police
> station with bare back rooms and locked doors.
>
> In this "gatehouse" of American criminal procedure—through
> which most defendants journey and beyond which many never get
> —the enemy of the state is a depersonalized "subject" to be "sized
> up" and subjected to "interrogation tactics and techniques most
> appropriate for the occasion"; he is "game" to be stalked and
> cornered. Here ideals are checked at the door, "realities" faced, and
> the prestige of law enforcement vindicated. Once he leaves the
> "gatehouse" and enters the "mansion"—if he ever gets there—the
> enemy of the state is repersonalized, even dignified, the public in-
> vited, and a stirring ceremony in honor of individual freedom from
> law enforcement celebrated.[4]

Impact and Reactions to Miranda— Cops, Confessions and Congress

In *Johnson* v. *New Jersey* (1966) the Supreme Court ruled that
unlike *Gideon* which was held to be retroactive (see p. 161) the

---

[4] Livingston Hall and Yale Kamisar, *Modern Criminal Procedure*, 2nd ed.
(St. Paul: West Publishing Co., 1966), p. 313. Reprinted with the permission
of the West Publishing Company.

protections set out in *Miranda* were available to only those individuals whose trials had not begun as of June 13, 1966. Nevertheless, when the consequences of *Gideon* (free counsel for indigent defendants in felonies and in some misdemeanors) are added to the principles stipulated in *Miranda* (warnings, right to remain silent and right to counsel at interrogations, if so desired), it becomes readily apparent that this country's pre-arraignment system will be forced to undergo major changes, if early compliance with these strikingly upsetting Court decisions is to be attained. *Gideon* alone with its demand for greatly expanded services by tax-supported public defenders or assigned counsels poses financial and administrative requirements of major proportions. In a recently completed survey sponsored by the American Bar Foundation, Lee Silverstein reveals something of the scope of the problem:

> Each year in American state courts' approximately 300,000 persons are charged with felonies.
>
> Of such persons, about 150,000 are indigent and cannot afford to retain counsel for their defense.
>
> To provide legal service for all indigents charged with a felony would cost about $25,000,000 annually [computed on average rates paid attorneys in 1962 by counties which assigned counsels].
>
> An educated guess places the number of persons charged with misdemeanors ["crimes punishable with imprisonment for a period of a year or less"] at 5,000,000, of which 1,250,000 would likely be indigent. If New Jersey's experience can be considered representative, "approximately 700,000 persons are sentenced to jail for misdemeanors each year, including those who are sentenced in default of paying fines." [Reports on misdemeanors were found quite incomplete and difficult to categorize because of lack of uniformity in state criminal definitions and procedures.][5]

While many states have begun to establish defender systems or enlarge those already in existence (with some aid coming from the federal government under the Criminal Justice Act of 1964 and with some professional expertise supplied by such organiza-

[5] Lee Silverstein, *Defense of the Poor in Criminal Cases in American State Courts* (Chicago: American Bar Foundation), p. 123.

tions as the National Legal Aid and Defender Association), much still remains to be done if the poor are to be given effective legal assistance. Professional staffs have to be recruited. Certain attitudes within the bar towards criminal work need to be revised. Standards of indigence have to be defined, physical facilities made available and extra funds secured for occasional special services from private investigators and experts. Such developments take time, necessitate financial support and depend on community understanding.

In January of 1967, New York City, for example, adopted "an around-the-clock arraignment system" which, according to the *Defender Newsletter*, March 1967 (a publication of the N.L.A.D.A.) "reduces by approximately 20 hours the time previously required to bring an arrested person before the committing judge and affords him an opportunity for release."

Even more far-reaching adjustments are called for by *Miranda*. That milestone decision demands much of the police—an overwhelming majority of this country's law enforcement officialdom believes far too much. Whether or not this contention is valid is, of course, debatable. What is beyond argument, however, is the enormity of the scope of contemporary police work. By way of illustration, here are some of the "highlights" of one police department's activities for 1963—those of the Los Angeles Police Department:

Investigated 183,299 crimes
Investigated 55,658 traffic accidents
Made 171,252 adult arrests
Made 24,663 juvenile arrests
Cited 1,550,773 traffic violations
Processed 200,763 misdemeanor warrants
Made 10,726 drunk driving arrests
Located 4,654 missing children
Transmitted 4,628,472 radio messages
Responded to 2,425,205 calls for service
Traveled 28,981,060 miles in providing police service
Conducted 15,363 Police Commission investigations.[6]

6 *The Courts, the Public and the Law Explosion*, ed. H. W. Jones (Englewood Cliffs: Prentice-Hall, Inc., 1965), p. 95.

Throughout most of the nation, police are generally overworked and underpaid, their departments understaffed and underequipped, as well as lacking wide public support. The President's Commission on Law Enforcement and Administration of Justice (1967) found median annual pay for patrolmen to be $5,300 for large cities and $4,600 for small cities; maximum for all positions was less than $1,000 over starting salary. Also noted by the Commission was a considerable amount of anti-police sentiment among certain groups within communities—this was especially true of Negroes, Puerto Ricans and juveniles.

But then, the police, too, expressed their resentments, and *Miranda* may well have been on their minds. In the words of the Commission's Report:

> [M]any police officers . . . believe that recent judicial interpretations of the Constitution and various statutes have unduly and inappropriately inhibited the work of the police and so have made it harder for police to protect the public. Part of this feeling stems, no doubt, from the sharp contrast between the tense, fast-moving situations in which policemen are called upon to make split-second decisions, and the calm that prevails in the appellate courts while lawyers and judges argue the merits of those decisions. . . .

One month after *Miranda*, the Executive Director of the International Association of Police Chiefs editorially referred to the new standard in these words:

> For the police such detachment is not possible. They must face the guns and knives of the unconvicted killers, and the anguished mothers of the . . . [raped].

What *Miranda* ordered the police to do, it may be remembered, was to inform a person arrested without a warrant of four basic protections: first, that he has the right to remain silent; second, that if he does talk, anything that he says can and will be used against him; third, that he has a right to consult a lawyer and have the lawyer with him during the interrogation; and fourth, that if he is indigent, a lawyer will be appointed to represent him. Ever since *McNabb*, law enforcement personnel commenting critically on the rules promulgated there, stressed the usefulness of incommunicado interrogation and the need for reasonable flexibility in arraignments. Implicit in their criticisms then and now was their strongly held conviction that confessions constituted an indispensable tool for the solution of major crimes.

Some significant dissents from this view should be noted, however. Based on a Los Angeles survey conducted shortly following *Miranda*, and covering over 1,000 felony complaints, the county's District Attorney Evelle J. Younger, was quoted as concluding "that a confession is essential to successful prosecution in only a small percentage of criminal cases." Similar findings were reported by the Chief of Detectives in Detroit, Vincent W. Piersante, and by Nathan R. Sobel, a New York State Supreme Court justice in Brooklyn.

Congressional reactions to *Miranda* with very few exceptions were predominantly hostile.

The Court's decision "will make confessions a thing of the past" (Senator Herman Talmadge, Georgia). Despite rising crime rates "we have sacrificed the rights of society and have placed additional shackles on the ability of the police to perform their duty." (Senator Karl Mundt, South Dakota). What *Miranda* demonstrated was "the majority's eager, crusading spirit, tipping the balance of justice towards the criminal—without equal regard for those against whom the criminal has offended . . ." (Representative Durward Hall, Missouri). This case "adds the finishing touch in stripping away police powers" (Representative Robert Sikes, Florida). The Supreme Court ". . . has become obsesssed with this overemphasis of individual rights as against the rights of society" (Senator Robert Byrd, West Virginia). Recounting a recent assault upon his secretary "[i]t is my sincere, solemn, and at the same time dismal prediction, that statistics for the increase in crime one year from now will show the disappointing, yes, even sickening results of the *Miranda* decision" (Representative William I. Randall, Missouri). "It seems to me . . . to be the height of folly to embark on fanciful new experiments limiting the powers of the police when crime is annually increasing at a disastrous rate" (Senator John C. Stennis, Mississippi). As a consequence of *Miranda*, ". . . multitudes of guilty suspects will escape conviction and punishment, and be turned loose upon society to repeat their crimes simply because many crimes cannot

be solved without confessions." (Senator Samuel Ervin, North
Carolina). The Senator also introduced a constitutional amendment which would have made binding on all appellate courts
(federal and state) the determination of a trial judge as to
whether a defendant's confession was voluntary or not.

Newspapers with anti-*Miranda* editorials included the Chicago
Tribune, June 14, 1966, "another roadblock in the path of police
and prosecutors"; the Columbus (Ohio) *Dispatch,* June 15, 1966,
"Rights of Lawful Society Shaken by Warren Opinion"; the New
York *Daily News,* June 15, 1966, "So Why Have Cops and DA's";
the Augusta (Georgia) *Chronicle,* July 27, 1966, "Police and
prosecuting attorneys all across the nation have protested . . .
the Supreme Court's rulings . . ."; and the Washington *Evening
Star,* June 15, 1966, "Green Light for Criminals." Among widely-
read commentators, David Lawrence and Richard Wilson devoted
vigorously critical essays to the *Miranda* decision.

Congressional debate and voting on the District of Columbia
"omnibus crime bill" during 1965 and 1966 offered an even more
ample and reliable opportunity to gauge legislative attitudes
to the constitutional principles which *Mallory* and *Miranda*
imposed on interrogations and confessions. As a matter of fact,
it was this constitutional issue which created a major conflict
between Senate and House versions of the bill. As passed by the
Senate, Section 101, Title I of H.R. 5688 was amended to reaffirm
the *Mallory* rule (arraignment without "unnecessary delay").
The House on the other hand specifically provided that no
"statements and confessions, otherwise admissible, shall not be
inadmissible solely because of delay in taking an arrested person
before a commissioner. . . ." Another point of disagreement arose
in connection with Section 301, Title III, "Detention of Persons."
While the House bill permitted the police to detain any person
on probable cause for interrogation up to a maximum time of
four hours prior to arraignment, the Senate bill contained no
such authorization. As finally reconciled by the Conference Committee, these two critical provisions were re-written with the
House version clearly dominant. Section 101, Title I, allowed
arrests (after warnings and with rights of counsel) and detention
prior to arraignment up to six hours; for Section 201, Title III,

the Committee adopted the wording of the House. On October 17, the Senate passed H.R. 5688 by voice vote, two days later a House coalition of Republicans and Southern Democrats approved the measure—208 to 79 (D. 128–68; R. 80–11). Northern Democrats divided 60 to 66 and Southern Democrats 68 to 2; Republicans split 80 to 11.

Senators Wayne Morse and Robert Kennedy who had refused to sign the conference report entered their minority views in the *Congressional Record*. Both of them saw Titles I and III dangerous and unwarranted legislative attempts to circumvent important constitutional safeguards provided in *Mallory* and *Miranda*.

President Johnson vetoed the bill, November 13, 1966, with a message which posed a number of objections. The matter of interrogation and confession ranked first in order.

> This bill provides that a policeman may pick up a person and question him for four hours without making an arrest—six hours exclusive of interrogation, after an arrest—perhaps ten hours of questioning—without taking him before a judicial officer. No one doubts the necessity of the police questioning persons on the street with respect to criminal activities. The law has always permitted this. The law properly provides, however, that after a person is deprived of his freedom—after he is arrested—the police must take him before a magistrate who will determine whether his arrest is arbitrary or based on probable cause. This must be done without unnecessary delay.

When the 90th Congress convened in 1967, the legislative battle against *Mallory* and *Miranda* resumed once again. Senator McClellan, chairman of a special Senate Judiciary Subcommittee on Criminal Laws and Procedures, who insisted that he "shared the views of the dissenting Justices" in *Miranda,* promised energetic action in his opening statement on this subject to the Senate on January 25. S. 674, which he introduced with the sponsorship of Senators Ervin, Roman L. Hruska and Byrd (West Virginia), would provide federal trial judges with broad discretion in ruling on the admissibility of confessions "because of delay in bringing such person before a commissioner. . . ." As sponsor of the Administration's safe street and crime control measures the Senator from Arkansas promises to play a prominent role in legislative efforts to restrict seriously or to reverse the *Mallory* and *Miranda* standards.

Even more pointed anti-Court language can be found in a proposal by Senator Ervin which received the wide co-sponsorship of nineteen senators. S. 1194, introduced March 7, 1967 provided:

> Sec. 1. That the sole test of the admissibility of an admission or confession of an accused in a criminal prosecution in any trial court

TABLE 1

RATINGS OF CO-SPONSORS OF S.1194

(Introduced March 7, 1967—90th Congress, 1st Session)

A bill "To define the jurisdiction of the Supreme Court and the Inferior Courts Ordained and Established by the Congress Under Article III of the Constitution of the United States."

Senator	State	Party	A.C.A. Rating*	A.D.A. Rating*
Ervin	N.C.	D	68	5
Jordan, E.	N.C.	D	70	0
Thurmond	S.C.	R	88	0
Fannin	Ariz.	R	88	0
Hickenlooper	Ia.	R	97	0
Talmadge	Ga.	D	63	0
Hollings†	S.C.	D	—	—
Byrd, H.	Va.	D	80	5
Bennett	Utah	R	94	0
Hansen†	Wy.	R	—	—
Long, R.	La.	D	8	45
Eastland	Miss.	D	71	0
McClellan	Ark.	D	65	0
Stennis	Miss.	D	69	0
Byrd	W.Va.	D	31	35
Hill	Ala.	D	38	10
Hayden	Ariz.	D	20	5
Ellender	La.	D	48	20
Dodd	Conn.	D	21	75

T A B L E 1 (Continued)

Distribution	A.C.A. Rating*	Percentage	A.D.A. Rating*	Percentage
00–20%	2	11.7%	13	76.5%
21–40	3	17.7	2	11.7
41–60	1	5.9	1	5.9
61–80	7	41.2	1	5.9
81–100	4	23.5	0	0.0
Total	17	100.0	17	100.0

* Based on compilations found in *Congressional Quarterly Weekly Report,* November 4, 1966, p. 2754.

† Both "freshman" senators are generally identified with the more conservative wing of the Republican party. They were not included in the ratings, however.

. . . shall be its voluntary character and neither the Supreme Court nor any inferior appellate court . . . established . . . under Article III of the Constitution of the United States shall have jurisdiction to reverse, vacate, modify, or disturb in any way a ruling of such a trial court . . . admitting in evidence as voluntarily made any admission or confession of an accused if such ruling is supported by any competent evidence admitted at the trial.

Section 2 of the bill placed identical jurisdictional limitations on the Supreme Court with reference to confessions admitted in state trial courts and sustained in state appellate courts.

The politically conservative leanings of most of the senators who sponsored these provisions is easily demonstrated (see Table 1). Whether the potential thrust which is embodied in this approach will receive favorable reception in this Congress with its notably more conservative predispositions is at the moment a matter of speculation.

What already seems quite evident, however, is that public opinion generally tends to back wider police authority for the purpose of obtaining statements of persons accused of crimes. For example, see the survey conducted by Louis Harris (p. 7) where almost two-thirds of those questioned "disapproved" of "disallowing" confessions obtained in the absence of counsel.

As the pressures "to do something" about the worsening crime situation intensify so will the search for new legislation to redress what many people seem to regard as an imbalance in the relationship between the rights of the accused and the rights of society. A code for pre-arraignment procedures drafted by the highly prestigious American Law Institute (March, 1966) suggests a "compromise." When arrests are made without a warrant, it would permit a four-hour "period of preliminary screening" when suspects could be questioned by the police without the required presence of an attorney unless such a person "has made it clear that he is unwilling to make a statement" or wishes to consult with counsel regarding it. After the first four hours, interrogation is allowed to proceed only in the presence of counsel or with counsel's consent. By providing for this concept of "preliminary screening," the A.L.I. draft does then deviate somewhat from the strict requirement of the *Mallory* rule—arraignment without "unnecessary delay." At the same time the model code explicitly forbids all incommunicado interrogation and—aside from other protections such as warning, free access and sound-recording of interrogation—prohibits all police questioning without the presence of counsel beyond the initial period of detention.

The President's Commission on Law Enforcement and the Administration of Justice shuns specific formal recommendations on this particular subject but expresses concern with the lack of systematic research "to assess the police need for confessions and the possibilities of establishing rules under which station house questioning would be permissible." It also emphasizes the urgent necessity for statutory clarification of contradictory and confused law with respect to such related aspects as wiretapping, electronic eavesdropping and the "frisking" of suspects by the police. Within the Johnson Administration itself, Attorney General Ramsey Clark opposes legislative reversals of *Mallory* or *Miranda* contending that the case has not been made proving that the Court-developed standards have, in fact, "hampered" law enforcement operations.

In view of the enormous complexity of crime and in view of the fundamental difficulties that have already emerged in efforts to strike a widely accepted balance between colliding claims of individual liberty with social order, this much appears certain. There are undeniable advantages inherent in the legislative process that could be brought to bear on a "proximate solution to an insoluble problem." While courts must proceed on a case-by-case basis, legislatures can bring together the diverse facets of the law enforcement technology, they can accommodate sharply competing community interests and values and they do operate within a much larger context of social engineering. Still, it must be observed that legislatures were slow to apply the libertarian values of the Bill of Rights to criminal procedures in general and to the "gatehouse" of the process in particular. Perhaps Congress through empirical investigation can discern better means with which to advance the cause of justice than could the Supreme Court. But as with all recommendations to redefine or reinterpret highly treasured constitutional provisions, the burden of proof rests on the innovator that advocated changes can be reconciled fairly with norms of individual liberty.

Many Americans would insist, it seems, that the understandable frustrations and failures encountered in an attempted abatement or control of a contemporary social crisis should not be permitted to serve as apologia for unwarranted or arbitrary exercises of governmental authority.

SUGGESTED READINGS

William M. Beaney. "Right to Counsel Before Arraignment," *Minnesota Law Review,* April, 1961, 771–782.

David Fellman. *The Defendant's Rights.* New York, 1958.

Livingston Hall and Yale Kamisar. *Modern Criminal Procedure.* St. Paul, 1966.

Fred E. Inbau and John E. Reid. *Criminal Interrogation and Confessions.* Baltimore, 1962.

Sanford H. Kadish. "Legal Norm and Discretion in the Police and Sentencing Processes," *Harvard Law Review,* March, 1962, 904–931.

Yale Kamisar. "What is an 'Involuntary' Confession? Some Comments on Inbau and Reid's *Criminal Interrogation and Confessions,*" *Rutgers Law Review,* Summer, 1963, 728–759.

Anthony Lewis. *Gideon's Trumpet*. New York, 1964.

Frank C. Newman. "Due Process, Investigations and Civil Rights," *U.C.L.A. Law Review*, Vol. 8, 1961, 735–767.

Monrad G. Paulsen. "The Fourteenth Amendment and the Third Degree," *Stanford Law Review*, Issue 3, 1954, 411–438.

Frank J. Remington. "The Law Relating to 'On the Street' Detention, Questioning, and Frisking of Suspected Persons and Police Arrest Privileges in General," *Journal of Criminal Law, Criminology, and Police Science*, November–December, 1960, 386–394.

Henry B. Rothblatt and Emma A. Rothblatt. "Police Interrogation: The Right to Counsel and to Prompt Arraignment," *Brooklyn Law Review*, December, 1960, 24–68.

VI

*Sit-Ins, Demonstrations
and Public
Accommodations*

"Who Says We're Not Willing To Sit Down Together?"

From *Straight Herblock* (Simon & Schuster, 1964).

M any Americans have been proudly asserting that "ours is a government of laws . . ."—that this country's basic representative institutions and processes give people a sense of participation, purpose and orderliness out of which grows community consensus and political stability. What has happened to that vaunted vision of the nation?

Over a thousand students riot at Berkeley.

5000 peace marchers in Chicago demonstrate against U.S. foreign policy.

Civil rights demonstrators threaten opening of the World's Fair.

About 500 students stage protest against Ambassador Goldberg at Harvard University.

Powell declines to return from Bimini to avoid bloodshed in Harlem.

Students and faculty boycott classes at Catholic University in Washington, D.C. until liberal professor is reinstated.

Rioting, violence, vandalism and fire bombs in Watts (Los Angeles) leave 34 dead, 1,032 wounded, and over $40 million in property damage.

Rochester, New York, reports four dead, 350 injured, and 800 arrested in racial demonstrations and rioting; theft and vandalism are estimated at $1 million.

Harlem demonstrations result in one death, 142 injured, and 528 arrests.

Kentucky National Guard is called to protect Derby against threatened mass demonstrations.

Twenty-six were killed in Newark and forty-two in Detroit; nearly 7,000 were arrested and property damage estimated at nearly half a billion dollars.

Thus certain segments of the population have within recent years resorted to direct action with some frequency. They have demonstrated, picketed, threatened violence and even engaged in violence itself in order to express hostility to specific policies, frustrations with the haplessness of politics, indignation over social injustice or defiance of particular laws judged inappropriate or morally indefensible. In the name of a higher law, the law of the community in selected instances was considered inapplicable, the will of the majority inadequately represented and urgent demands for public order and peace minimized or ignored.

As indicated by the preceding headlines, the causes endorsed by the demonstrators are as varied as the places of demonstration, the numbers of persons involved, and the types of demonstration. This chapter, however, deals with the use of demonstrations, sit-ins and protests for one cause only—equal public accommodations. It was in this context that various forms of protest resulted in bringing the cause to the attention of the Supreme Court and the Congress, and where the demonstrators involved came from easily identifiable groups.

To begin the account, it is necessary to go back to 1960. During that year various forms of protest against discriminatory practices in hotels, restaurants, lunch counters, parks, playgrounds, swimming beaches, libraries and theaters brought nearly 100,000 Negroes and whites to the streets of over a hundred cities in the Southern and border states. According to estimates supplied by the Southern Regional Council, by the end of 1963, nearly 24,000 of such civil rights demonstrators were arrested by the police, among them thousands of school-age children and college students.

These were the years when television and newspapers throughout the nation and much of the world's press reported in pictures and print almost daily clashes between civil rights marchers and hostile whites.

> In Jacksonville, Florida, one person was killed and 70 persons injured during a three-day riot; a white sit-in student was attacked in jail and suffered a fractured jaw; a 16-year old boy was pistol-whipped by Ku Klux Klansmen. . . .

> In Chattanooga, Tennessee, a massive three-day street brawl was described by the Chattanooga *Times* as "the most massive racial clash in the history of Chattanooga." In Nashville, a Negro defense lawyer's home was bombed; Negro sit-in students were burned with cigarettes; and a white sit-in student was beaten. . . .

> After a sit-in in Houston, Texas, a Negro man was stabbed by a white man in a parking lot. Another Negro was flogged with a chain by three whites; the symbol of the KKK was carved on his chest and stomach; and he was hung by the knees from an oak tree. . . .

In Mississippi where the brutal murder of three civil rights workers (Neshoba County, June, 1964) shocked the nation, reports of racial violence for the summer of 1964 in that state alone accounted for "35 shootings, 30 bombings, 35 church burnings, 80 beatings, and at least six murders."[1]

Riots and racial confrontations burned into national consciousness the names of such cities as Birmingham, Montgomery, Selma, St. Augustine, Greensboro, Tallahassee, Athens, Gadsden and Durham.

Inspired by the Reverend Martin Luther King and by the success of his bus boycott in Montgomery, Negro leaders seemed convinced that the principle of nonviolent resistance was the most appropriate and promising tactic with which to break open the racially closed society. Activists from the Southern Christian Leadership Conference, the Congress of Racial Equality (CORE) and the Student Nonviolent Coordinating Committee (SNCC) helped to plan and organize the protests. To further dramatize injustices and to expose or challenge segregationist practices in interstate travel and terminal facilities, CORE, beginning in the

---

[1] John Herbers, "*Communique* from Mississippi," *New York Times Magazine*, November 8, 1964, p. 34.

spring of 1961, recruited students from Northern college campuses
to travel by bus through the South in small biracial teams. At
Anniston, Alabama, the first of such groups of "freedom riders"
was attacked by a white mob and its bus set on fire while the
police, although warned of their impending arrival, provided
insufficient protection.

As more and more "freedom riders" and Northern civil rights
volunteers streamed southward, they quickly became objects of
hostility. Frequently arrested upon arrival or ordered out of
town, harassed by local gangs and official enmity, these student
protesters helped to bring the civil rights struggle of the Southern
Negro to the attention of the entire nation. They came to the
aid of a new generation of Negroes that had the courage to de-
nounce and violate long-established customs and patterns of
segregation. These protesters fully realized that those who opposed them had the protection of the economically and politically
powerful, that sheriffs and police officials would not or could
not hesitate to suppress protests and demonstrations; that bail
would be expensive and difficult to obtain; that jail conditions
were sometimes primitive and treatment harsh; that trials would
be postponed and charges pyramided; that outrages against Negroes often went uninvestigated and unpunished; that Negroes
were systematically excluded from jury service; that removal of
cases to federal jurisdiction and courts could rarely be achieved;
and that criminal sanctions under the federal Civil Rights Acts
then in force offered no effective remedies. They also knew that
local prosecutors and courts could try those who collectively
asserted their civil rights under a rich arsenal of statutes which
included violations for trespass, disorderly conduct, breach of
peace, unlawful assembly, "criminal mischief," incitement of
riots and obstruction of traffic. And still they dared to march, to
sit-in, to kneel-in, to wade-in, to picket, to demonstrate, to be
arrested, tried and convicted.

Out of the hundreds of cases which emerged from this struggle
for civil rights, only a few can be selected, those that illustrate
what the law was before the revolution began and how it was
changed through reversals in the United States Supreme Court
and through the enactments of the Congress.

Sit-Ins and Trespass

There was really nothing very unique about the ordinance of Greenville, North Carolina which required the separation of the races in the restaurants of the city. Hundreds of other communities throughout the South had enacted substantially similar provisions declaring integrated service to be "contrary to custom."

> It shall be unlawful for any person owning, managing or controlling any hotel, restaurant, cafe, eating house, boarding house or similar establishment to furnish meals to white persons and colored persons in the same room, or at the same table, or at the same counter. . . . Separate facilities shall be interpreted to mean:
>
> (a) Separate eating utensils and separate dishes for the serving of food, all of which shall be distinctly marked by some appropriate color scheme or otherwise;
>
> (b) Separate tables, counters or booths;
>
> (c) A distance of at least thirty-five feet shall be maintained between the area where white and colored persons are served. . . .
>
> (d) A separate facility shall be maintained and used for the cleaning of eating utensils and dishes furnished the two races.
>
> *Code of Greenville, 1953*
> as amended in 1958 #31–8.

To the civil rights demonstrators of 1960, however, segregated lunch counters in Greenville, South Carolina, and in numerous other Southern cities, represented important symbols of the American Negro's badge of inferiority and shame, vestiges of a social order that had to be exorcized in an effort to gain more effective freedom and equality.

Following a typical pattern of protest employed earlier in the year by students from North Carolina Agricultural and Technical College in Greensboro, a group of ten Negro boys and girls entered the S. H. Kress store in Greenville, South Carolina, on August 9, 1960. They seated themselves at a lunch counter reserved for white patrons and expected to be served. According to testimony read into the court record, "the manager of the store announced that the lunch counter was closed, the lights were extinguished, and all persons were requested to leave. The white persons present left, but all Negroes refused to leave. . . ." Still unwilling to depart, although informed by the manager that integrated service was "contrary to local customs" and to the Greenville ordinance, the police arrived. The sit-in demonstrators were arrested and subsequently convicted in the county court on the charge of having violated the state's trespass statutes. On appeal, the South Carolina State Supreme Court affirmed the convictions in *City of Greenville* v. *Peterson* (1961). It rejected the defendants' contention that their arrest and conviction "was in furtherance" of the customs and laws of racial segregation, and thus in conflict with the Fourteenth Amendment. At issue, according to the court, was not a constitutional question but merely the state's trespass statute which was applicable to "Any person . . . Who fails and refuses, without cause or good excuse, to leave immediately upon being ordered or requested to do so by the person in possession or his agent. . . ." This law made no reference to race or color; its purpose was simply to protect the owner and his property rights. As far as the state was concerned, the motivation for closing the counter was entirely irrelevant. What was decisive and conclusive was the evidence that "defendants were arrested because they chose to remain upon the premises after being requested to leave by the manager."

Unlike *Peterson,* a sit-in case from New Orleans presented a much more direct confrontation of constitutional guarantees. In *Louisiana* v. *Goldfinch* (subsequently known as *Lombard* v. *Louisiana*), defendants seeking to be served were arrested in McCrory's store, a member of a national chain, for their failure to comply with the order of a manager who, after asking them to leave a lunch counter reserved for white customers only, had summoned the police. Following conviction in a state district court under a "criminal mischief statute," the case was appealed to the Louisiana Supreme Court. There, defendants insisted that the statute "in its application against Negroes" was "discriminatory and unconstitutional" in that it violated the due process of law and equal protection clauses of both the federal as well as the state constitution and that it offended especially the safeguards offered them by the Fourteenth Amendment. Defendants also attempted to introduce evidence to the effect "that the action of the manager . . . was provoked or encouraged by the State, its policy, or officers. . . ."

As the Louisiana Supreme Court read the facts, the action of the manager "bringing about the arrest of the defendants . . . was the independent action . . . of the privately owned store, uninfluenced by any governmental action, design or policy—state or municipal." To sustain the conviction and the statute, the court sought to distinguish between private and public acts of discrimination. The latter were constitutionally clearly invalid, the former were not. As late as 1948, the United States Supreme Court had held that the Fourteenth Amendment "erects no shield against merely private conduct, however discriminatory or wrongful." Moreover, since neither the government of the state nor that of New Orleans required the segregation of the races in restaurants by any statutory or decisional law, whatever segregation does exist must necessarily be viewed as the "result of the business choice of the individual proprietors, both white and Negro, catering to the desires and wishes of their customers." If the defendants' contentions were to prevail this would mean that they could "impose upon the proprietor their own concept of the proper use of his property unsupported by any right under the law or Constitution to do so." The Court felt that taking rights from one group of citizens and giving them to another was a legislative function which it was unwilling to assume.

Neither in legal reasoning nor in outcome could these two cases from South Carolina and Louisiana be considered in any way extraordinary or unrepresentative. The law that was applied to the sit-in demonstrators there conformed closely to the norms and precedents articulated in similar controversies by the high courts of Alabama, Arkansas, Florida, Georgia, Maryland, North Carolina and Virginia and by many federal district courts throughout the South. Put simply, American law (state and federal) protected the owner of private property against any trespasser. One who remained on the premises against the wishes of the owner, after having been warned, subjected himself to arrest and to criminal penalties; in the absence of statutes to the contrary, the owner of a restaurant could select his customers "on purely personal grounds." Nothing in the due process of law or equal protection clauses of the Fourteenth Amendment commanded the owner of a private establishment to admit Negroes or any other persons whom he did not wish to serve or with whom he did not wish to conduct business. A restaurant located in a privately-owned building did not make the owner an innkeeper at common law which imposes a duty of serving all travelers without discrimination; he could legally eject those whom he had not invited or licensed to remain. Should the owner require the assistance of the police to carry out the ejection of unwanted customers, this was construed judicially as not constituting state involvement in the enforcement of discriminatory policies; under such conditions the police functioned solely as agents of the owner who was legally entitled to protect his private property.

Reversals of Peterson and Lombard, May 21, 1963

In striking down the *Peterson* convictions, the United States Supreme Court addressed itself to one question only. Did the management's denial to serve Negroes at lunch counters constitute state action violative of the Fourteenth Amendment?

The concept of "state action" has had a long and complex constitutional development. Beginning with the Civil Rights Cases (1883) and extending through *Shelley* v. *Kramer* (1948) where it was said that the Fourteenth Amendment "erects no shield against merely private conduct, however discriminatory or wrongful," courts had emphasized that the Amendment was restricted in its applications to only those activities which involved state governmental actions or sanctions.

Chief Justice Warren speaking for a unanimous court in *Peterson* had no difficulty in holding that the City of Greenville, an agency of the State of South Carolina, through its ordinance had in fact taken the decision of serving Negroes "from the sphere of private choice." Even if the manager had acted independently of the ordinance "in deciding to exclude Negroes . . . [he] did precisely what the city law required." Under such conditions the state was significantly involved in an unconstitutional act of discrimination and no attempt "to separate the mental urges of the discriminators" could sustain the convictions.

Lombard had posed a somewhat different legal issue. Here the Louisiana State Supreme Court, in affirming the convictions of four lunch counter sit-in demonstrators, emphasized that there was no city ordinance or state law requiring segregation and that the actions of the manager were based on considerations of a personal or business nature. As seen by that court, the equality requirements of the Fourteenth Amendment did not reach this type of private managerial decision and policy based on the customs of the people of the state.

On review, the extent of Louisiana's involvement in the discriminatory exclusion of the defendants became the central concern of the majority opinion written by Chief Justice Warren. Testimony had been presented to the effect that defendants conducted themselves in an orderly manner, that they caused no disturbances and that they were asked "to leave because they were Negroes." Was this request by the management a *bona fide,* independently arrived at business decision as the lower courts had ruled? Warren thought not, and for this reason: One week prior to the sit-in demonstration at McCrory's store, the New Orleans Superintendent of Police, responding to a similar incident at Woolworth's, had issued a widely publicized statement including the following text:

> We wish to urge the parents of both white and Negro students who participated in today's sit-in demonstration to urge upon these young people that such actions are not in the community interest. . . .

> [W]e want everyone to fully understand that the police department and its personnel is ready and able to enforce the laws of the city of New Orleans and the State of Louisana. . . .

Some days later, the mayor of New Orleans reinforced this announcement with a similar warning, adding that, "the community interest, the public safety, and the economic welfare of

the city" required an end to all such demonstrations and that
"they be prohibited by the police."

As to the role of the manager, he was found to have told the
sit-in demonstrators "I am not allowed to serve you here. . . . We
have to sell to you at the rear of the store [*emphasis supplied by
court*] . . . [and that] he called the police '(a)s a matter of routine
procedure.' " There was further evidence in the record that the
store manager " 'conceded' " that his decision to operate the
segregated facilities " 'conform[ed] to state policy and practice' as
well as local custom." This and some other minor factors seemed
sufficiently compelling to Warren to cause him to conclude "that
the store officials' actions were coerced by the city."

New Orleans had enacted no segregation ordinance while
Greenville had; still a state "cannot achieve the same results by
an official command which has at least as much coercive effect as
an ordinance." Although the directives of the mayor and police
officials spoke of preserving public peace and order "in a non-
discriminatory fashion . . . , the official command here was to
direct continuance of segregated service in restaurants, and to
prohibit any conduct directed toward its discontinuance." Tested
by the effect, this indeed was the "voice of the state" and not
merely that of McCrory's manager.

In his concurrent opinion, Justice Douglas preferred to rest his
agreement with the majority on the broader constitutional claim
which holds that "[w]hen the doors of a business are open to the
public, they must be open to all regardless of race if *apartheid*
is not to become engrained in our public places." Moreover, the
action of the Louisiana courts in imposing criminal penalties
"wholly apart from the activity of mayor and police," were state
actions which by themselves were entirely irreconcilable with the
requirements of the Fourteenth Amendment.

With the United States Supreme Court taking this kind of
judicial stance vis-à-vis the sit-in convictions, there were bound
to be many additional reversals. Taken together they shattered
some, but not all, of the legal immunities which most Southern
courts attempted to preserve for "private" acts of business discrimination. What a majority of the Supreme Court failed to

embrace, however, was Douglas' position that discrimination in public accommodations was constitutionally impermissible standing by itself even in the absence of "state action."

Division on the Court

A sit-in case from Baltimore, *Bell* v. *Maryland* (1964), illustrated quite distinctly the extent of the schism on this point among the liberal members of the Court. Douglas concurred with the majority which had reversed the Maryland convictions on mostly procedural grounds and which preferred perhaps to await the outcome of public accommodation legislation which at that time was pending before Congress. At the same time, he left no doubt about his impatience with the Court for its refusal to meet head-on the central constitutional question which was at the root of the conflict between Negro customers and white restaurant owners.

> We have in this case a question that is basic to our way of life and fundamental in our constitutional scheme. No question preoccupies the country more than this one; it is plainly justiciable; it presses for a decision one way or another; we should resolve it. The people should know that when filibusters occupy other forums, when oppressions are great, when the clash of authority between the individual and the State is severe, they can still get justice in the courts. When we default, as we do today, the prestige of the law in the life of the Nation is weakened.

Four major contentions provided the legal basis of his argument. First, the overriding purpose of the Thirteenth, Fourteenth and Fifteenth Amendments was to strip from the Constitution the relics of slavery and to establish first class citizenship for all. Second, through the development of the common law, courts have imposed a duty on all common carriers and inns to serve all travelers regardless of race, creed or color. "Is the right of a person to eat less basic than his right to travel?" To the modern traveler "restaurants . . . are as essential . . . as inns and carriers." This should be the common law of public accommodation within the framework of the three great amendments. Third, the restaurant property involved here is private property put to public service. Actually most of the sit-in demonstrations were staged in restaurants corporately owned, often members of national corporate chains. Rights belonging to such corporations or "absentee owners" do not stand on the same constitutional plane as do personal rights of association traditionally linked with the private property of the individual store owner. One cannot properly speak of "infringing" personal rights "when a corporate chain store . . . is forced to open its lunch counter to people of all races." Fourth, in *Shelley* v. *Kramer* (1948), the Supreme Court had struck down the enforcement of restrictive covenants against non-Caucasians in deeds of residential properties. If it was unconstitutional there for state courts to enforce private discriminatory policies, how could this then be reconciled with permitting corporate management here to invoke the aid of the State of Maryland—police, prosecutors, and judges—to send to jail those who "defy 'its' will"?

Justice Goldberg (who had joined in the Douglas concurrence) also wrote a separate opinion setting forth his additional views. He stressed that the Constitution and the Fourteenth Amendment obligated the states to maintain a system of laws in which Negroes were treated as equal members of the community; that criminal trespass laws could not be employed to deprive the Negro of his nationally guaranteed rights; and that a proprietor's choice of business clientele would have to be subordinated under the history, purpose and logic of the Fourteenth Amendment to the Negro's superior right to equal treatment in places of public accommodations.

A long and forceful dissent was entered by Justice Black joined by Justices Harlan and White. Black saw the constitutional question which the case presented in these terms:

> [W]hether the Fourteenth Amendment, of itself, forbids a State to enforce its trespass laws to convict a person who comes into a privately owned restaurant, is told that because of his color he will not be served, and over the owner's protest refuses to leave.

This was the issue which, according to Black, the Court should have faced and should have answered in the negative. More particularly, he found himself in fundamental disagreement with Justices Douglas and Goldberg concerning the rights of private property in sit-in controversies, the significance and nature of "state action" under the *Shelley* doctrine, the legislative history of the Fourteenth Amendment and the constitutional status of public accommodations.

An orderly and tranquil society requires that citizens call for the assistance of the police rather than take the law into their own hands when their freedoms and property are in need of protection. "The Amendment does not forbid a State to prosecute for crimes committed against a person or his property, however prejudiced or narrow the victim's views may be." *Shelley* v. *Kramer* has been "misapplied." The reason why the judicial enforcement of the restrictive covenants was held to violate the Constitution was "not merely the fact that a state court had acted" but that the state in this manner allowed racial considerations to preclude two willing parties from enjoying property rights assured to them by the Civil Rights Acts of 1866 and 1870. In the present case, no action or policy of Maryland, no municipal ordinance or public proclamation brought the officials of the state or city into discriminatory conduct against Negroes. If sit-in petitioners were permitted to prevail here this would mean that the rights of the restaurant owner "must be cut down, and he be compelled—though no statute said he must—to allow people to force their way into his restaurant and remain there over his protest." There is nothing in the wording of the Fourteenth Amendment that singles out peoples or properties that are or are not to be protected. "Equal treatment under law" is at the very heart of the federal guarantee.

As to the legislative history of the Amendment, it is simply not true, argued Black, that Congress in enacting the Amendment and the Civil Rights Acts of the 1860's meant to compel the admission of Negroes on equal terms to privately-owned public accommodations. While legislation in 1875 specifically prohibits discrimination against Negroes "by inns, conveyances, theaters and other places of public amusement," restaurants were not included, either in statutes or in the Fourteenth Amendment. "Confining ourselves to our constitutional duty to construe, not to rewrite or amend the Constitution . . . ," concluded Black, "we believe that Section 1 of the Fourteenth Amendment does not bar Maryland from enforcing its trespass laws so long as it does so with impartiality."

By the end of 1963, this much seemed certain. Future sit-in campaigns against discriminatory practices by privately-owned public accommodations could win the required majority on the Court necessary to reverse convictions only in those situations where state law enforcement officials took affirmative action to urge or compel such unequal treatment.

Demonstration—Breach of the Peace

One of the least complicated cases from the factual point of view arose in Savannah, Georgia when a group of six Negroes playing basketball in a park customarily reserved for whites was arrested and convicted for unlawful assembly, disturbing the public peace and failing to disperse when "commanded by an officer of" the law. Their conviction was affirmed by the Supreme Court of Georgia although there was no crowd, no evidence of resistance to arrest or of disorderly conduct. Chief Justice Warren in *Wright* v. *Georgia* (1961), reversing the convictions for a unanimous Court, held the police order violative because it was intended to enforce racial segregation and because the "possibility of disorder by others" could not justify their exclusion, especially "if they otherwise have a constitutional right [founded on the equal protection clause] to be present."

A much more complex set of circumstances was involved in *Edwards* v. *South Carolina* (1963). Following a meeting at the Zion Baptist Church in Columbia, South Carolina, a group of nearly two hundred Negro students walked in "separate groups of about 15" to the statehouse grounds in order to declare before the people and legislature their "dissatisfaction" with the discriminatory actions and laws of the state. They were met by city and county law officers and informed that as long as their conduct was peaceful they were entitled to parade around the Capitol grounds. They walked around the building, "single file or two abreast," carrying placards and signs with such messages as "I am proud to be a Negro" and "Down with Segregation." This continued for about forty-five minutes without interference. Next followed a series of events that persuaded the South Carolina Supreme Court to affirm the arrest and convictions of 187 Negroes for breach of peace and trespass.

[I]n addition to the approximately 200 paraders in the area, there had gathered approximately 350 onlookers and the crowd was increasing. With the paraders and the increasingly large numbers of onlookers congregated in the . . . area seriously affecting the flow of pedestrian and vehicular traffic, the officers approached the admitted leader of the paraders and informed him that the situation had reached the point where the activities of the group should cease. They were told through their leader that they must disperse within fifteen minutes. The parade leader, accompanied by the police authorities, went among the paraders and informed them of the decision and orders of the police. The leader of the group refused to instruct or advise them to disperse but instead began a fervent speech to the group and in response they began to sing, shout, clap their hands and stamp their feet, refusing to disperse. After about fifteen minutes of this noisy demonstration, the appellants, who were engaging in the demonstration, were arrested by State and City officers and charged with the crime of breach of peace.

Without questioning the right of defendants to parade and give expression to their views, the South Carolina court saw the facts and circumstances as sufficiently constituting the critical elements of the common law breach of peace offense. While this "offense was 'not susceptible to exact definition'," its general import was clear. After adequate notice defendants willfully ignored reasonable orders of the police which were "motivated solely by a proper concern for the preservation of order and prevention of further interference with traffic upon the public streets and sidewalks." Such conduct disrupted "the tranquility enjoyed by citizens of a municipality or community where good order reigns among its members. . . ."

On review before the United States Supreme Court, Justice Douglas, writing for the majority, pointed to testimony which to him significantly changed the factual picture.

The Police Chief of Columbia testified as follows:

Q. Did any of your men make a report that any of these persons were disorderly in walking around the State House grounds?
A. They did not. . . .

Q. There was ample room for other persons going in the same direction or opposite direction to pass on the same sidewalk?
A. I wouldn't say they were blocking the sidewalk. . . .
A. At times they blocked the sidewalk and we asked them to move over and they did.

Q. They obeyed your commands on that?
A. Yes.

Q. So that nobody complained that he wanted to use the sidewalk and he could not do it?
A. I didn't have any complaints on that.

The City Manager testified:

Q. You had ample time, didn't you, to get ample police protection, if you thought such was necessary on the State House grounds, didn't you?
A. Yes, we did.

Additional testimony by the city manager indicated that what he had termed as "boisterous," "loud" and "flamboyant" conduct ". . . consisted of listening to a 'religious harangue' by one of their leaders, and loudly singing 'The Star-Spangled Banner' and other patriotic and religious songs while stamping their feet and clapping their hands."

To Justice Stewart the setting and manner in which defendants carried out their protest constituted "an exercise of . . . basic constitutional rights in the most pristine and classic form." At no time did they engage in or threaten violence; they assembled peacefully to bring their grievances to the attention of the South Carolina Legislature. They were convicted not of violating traffic regulations or of disobeying laws reasonably limiting the hours during which the statehouse grounds could be visited but "of an offense so generalized as to be, in the words of the South Carolina Supreme Court, 'not susceptible of exact definition'." The evidence against them "showed no more than that the opinions which they were peaceably expressing were sufficiently opposed to the view of the majority of the community to attract a crowd and necessitate police protection." Therefore, under the Fourteenth Amendment which "does not permit a State to make criminal the peaceful expression of unpopular views," the state "infringed the petitioners' constitutionally protected rights of free speech, free assembly and freedom to petition for redress of their grievances." The convictions had to be reversed.

Dissenting, Justice Clark found still additional testimony in the record to convince him that state authorities could have properly concluded that "traffic was materially impeded," that there was imminence of danger to peace and safety and that during the last fifteen minutes the leaders of the demonstrators had aroused the group to "a fever pitch causing this boisterousness, this singing and stomping."

Citing for supportive precedent a concurrent opinion of Justice Frankfurter in *Feiner* v. *New York* (1951) that in reviewing state cases "the due process clause must not be construed in an abstract and doctrinaire way by disregarding local conditions . . . ," Clark would have affirmed the convictions.

A majority of the Court however had been consistently unwilling ever since *Thompson* v. *City of Louisville* (1960) and *Garner* v. *Louisiana* (1961) to sustain in cases such as these breach of peace convictions which would have allowed local police and courts to substitute opinion for lack of evidence. Due process of law standards of the Fourteenth Amendment and the value of free speech were held to demand proof of outward and tumultuous conduct causing public disorder or disturbance.

This decisional trend was reinforced in *Cox* v. *Louisiana* (1964). A group of twenty-three students from Southern University, a Negro college, was arrested on December 14, 1961, for picketing stores with segregated lunch counters in downtown Baton Rouge. That evening plans were made at a meeting held on the campus to conduct a mass demonstration in front of the courthouse to protest against the arrest and against segregation. The next morning about 2,000 students walked to the city, assembling at the Old State Capitol some two blocks from the courthouse. When the sheriff and police officers met the group their leader, Reverend B. Elton Cox, a field secretary of CORE, explained the purpose of the demonstration. An official request by the officers of the law to disband the marchers and "to take them back whence they came" was rejected by Cox. According to state's witnesses, the students proceeding towards the courthouse seemed well behaved, orderly and not "objectionable." They sang songs, carried placards, shouted and clapped. The incarcerated group responded with song, yells, cheers and applause. What happened next, however, seemed to be in dispute. Louisiana's version of the facts is given first.

> Cox added to the situation that had by then reached a high pitch of emotional tension by making an "inflammatory" speech, causing some of the officers to feel this now disorderly and seething mob intended to storm the court house and liberate the twenty-three people there incarcerated, and that a riot was inevitable. . . .

> The Sheriff, sensing the seriousness of the explosive situation, by means of a loudspeaker ordered the demonstrators to move on. However Cox, and, on his instructions, the group, openly defied this command and continued the "fiery" and "frenzied" demonstration. . . .

> It was only by the use of tear gas that the Sheriff, his deputies, and other law enforcement officers were able to disperse the group.

> The trial judge who presided over the proceedings against Cox . . . stated that he was so "fearful" and "apprehensive" of the outcome of this demonstration . . . in fact intimidated . . . [that he] . . . closed his office and left the building.

After stressing that in cases involving claims of constitutional rights it is the duty of the United States Supreme Court to examine the whole record independently, Justice Goldberg arrived at the following assessment of facts and testimony:

> The students . . . were lined up . . . across the street from the courthouse. . . . The group did not obstruct the street . . . . It is true that the students, in response to the singing of their fellows who were in custody, cheered and applauded. However, the meeting was an outdoor meeting and a key state witness testified that while the singing was loud, it was not disorderly. . . . There [was] . . . no indication that the mood of the students was ever hostile, aggressive

or unfriendly. Our conclusion that the entire meeting from the beginning until its dispersal by tear gas was orderly and not riotous is
confirmed by a film of the events taken by a television news photographer, which was offered in evidence as a state exhibit. . . .

There . . . [was] no indication . . . that any members of the white
group threatened violence. . . . This small crowd, estimated at
between 100 and 300 was separated from the students by "seventy-five
to eighty" armed policemen. . . . As Inspector Trigg testified, they
could have handled the crowd. . . .

Failure of Cox and the students to disperse in accordance with
the sheriff's instructions was then followed, within minutes, by
the police setting off tear gas bombs and breaking up the demonstration. Cox was arrested the following day, charged and convicted of obstructing the sidewalks, obstructing justice and breach
of the peace. On appeal these judgments were affirmed by the
Louisiana Supreme Court.

In reversing all three convictions, it was only the breach of
peace issue, the one most relevant for this discussion with respect
to which Goldberg was able to retain the unanimous backing
of the Court. As in *Edwards* this event was held to have been a
peaceful demonstration of students advocating unpopular views
which attracted crowds and necessitated police protection. It was
this constitutional responsibility to protect the expressions of
opinions antagonistic to the community consensus which the
state failed to assume. Also operating against Louisiana was the
extremely vague breach of peace statute which its Supreme Court
defined in such terms as "to agitate, to arouse from a state of
repose, to molest, to interrupt, to hinder, to disquiet." Such a
law, Goldberg argued, allows punishment of anyone who challenges what a predominant majority considers sacred and unas-
sailable. This makes it incompatible with the First Amendment
freedoms which bind the states through the Fourteenth Amendment. Citing language from *Terminiello* v. *Chicago* (1949), the
essence of free speech is seen by its invitation to unrest, its prone-
ness to anger people, its provocative quality and its tendency to
expose community prejudices and preconceptions. Louisiana's
breach of peace statute, concluded Goldberg, cannot be permitted

to stand because "it sweeps within its broad scope activities that are constitutionally protected. . . ."

Still another test of a Louisiana breach of peace statute resulted from a sit-in demonstration by five Negroes at the Audubon Regional Library at Clinton. Even more significantly, it brought out into the open some of the deep divisions which were forming among the members of the Supreme Court concerning the constitutional protections that could reasonably be afforded certain types of anti-segregation protests. As the majority perceived the factual setting, CORE had planned and organized the demonstration for the express purpose of integrating a public library (serving only white persons) operated jointly by three Louisiana parishes. Negroes wishing to borrow books could obtain them from a blue bookmobile. A red bookmobile and additional branch libraries provided services for the white clientele. On Saturday, March 7, 1964, five young men went into the reading room, where they were met by the Assistant Librarian. Petitioner Brown asked for a book which was not available. He was informed courteously that the book would be requested from the state library and that "he could either pick it up or it would be mailed to him." Instead of leaving the premises, the group remained, one of them sat down, the others stood silently near by. "They said nothing; there was no noise or boisterous talking." Again they were asked to leave and refused. The sheriff "who had received information that 'they [CORE] . . . were going to sit-in . . .' " also had "noticed the petitioners when they went by his office on the way to the library. . . ." He came in ten or fifteen minutes later and after being told by the petitioners that they would not leave, arrested all of them. According to the judicial findings, their behavior throughout this confrontation was orderly and unprovocative.

After convictions for breach of peace by a Louisiana district court and a denial of appeal by the state Supreme Court, the United States Supreme Court granted certiorari and reversed the judgment in a five to four decision, *Brown* v. *Louisiana* (1966). Four separate opinions were written, three of them supporting reversal, one dissenting.

Louisiana's breach of peace statute provides:

Whoever with intent to provoke a breach of the peace, or under circumstances such that a breach of the peace may be occasioned thereby . . . crowds or congregates with others . . . in or upon . . . a public street or public highway . . . or any other public place or building . . . and who fails or refuses to disperse and move on . . . when ordered to do so by any law enforcement officer of any municipality or parish . . . shall be guilty of disturbing the peace.

Justice Fortas, joined by Chief Justice Warren and Justice Douglas, delivered the "prevailing" majority opinion. His argument, in essence, was this:

The library was operated on a racially segregated basis. Petitioners, although quiet, polite and orderly, were convicted of an intentional breach of peace in the absence of any showing of any criminal conduct. Without disturbing anyone else, or violating any regulations, they simply exercised their right of protest against practices denying them equal access to a public facility.

Justice Brennan concurring:

Louisiana's breach of peace statute was so overly broad "requiring instantaneous and unquestioning compliance" that it could be employed to suppress inoffensive conduct (though "arguable" as to its constitutional protection) aimed at seeking constitutionally safeguarded equality of governmental service.

Justice White also concurring in the result:

The brief period petitioners remained after ordering the book did not depart sufficiently from "normal library use." Had they been white they would "not have been asked to leave on such short notice, much less asked to leave by the sheriff and arrested. . . ." On the record, they were requested to leave the library "because they were Negroes" with their conviction denying them the equal protection of the laws.

Justice Black, joined by Justices Clark, Harlan and Stewart, dissented with an eloquent attack on "the novel constitutional doctrine of the prevailing opinion [which] . . . exalts the power of private nongovernmental groups to determine what use shall be made of governmental property over the power of the elected officials of the States and Nation."

Free speech was not violated by the Louisiana breach of peace statute which made "it an offense to congregate in a public library refusing to leave when asked to do so by an authorized person." Peace and order are necessary in a public library and the state has a right to adopt regulations to so enforce it. There was "no racial discrimination practiced in this case." Petitioners remained not to learn but as "monuments of protest" to use the library for dramatizing particular views. There is nothing in the Fourteenth Amendment that gives this Court power to paralyze the states "with reference to control of their libraries for library purposes;" nor does the Amendment give "any person or group of persons the constitutional right to go wherever they want, whenever they please, without regard to the rights of private or public property or to state law."

If there was still a question about how the eighty-year-old civil libertarian felt about this case, the concluding sentences of his opinion exuded a fervor that left no room for doubt or dialectic.

But I say once more that the crowd moved by noble ideals today can become the mob ruled by hate and passion and greed and violence tomorrow. . . . The peaceful songs of love can become as stirring and provocative as the Marseillaise did in the days when a noble revolution gave way to rule by successive mobs until chaos set in.

Nine months later another student demonstration case, *Adderley* v. *Florida,* finally gave Black the opportunity to speak for the Court. Justice White, whose own proclivities towards a more restrictive interpretation of the "rights of protest" which could be discerned from his concurrence to *Brown* v. *Louisiana,* became the fifth member of the new coalition. Could Florida be permitted to prosecute and convict for trespass with malicious and mischievous intent thirty-two Negro students from Florida A and M University out of a group of nearly two hundred who had entered the premises of the Leon County jail in order to protest against previous arrests as well as to demonstrate against the state's discriminatory practices? Black joined by Harlan, Stewart, Clark and White decided to affirm the convictions; Douglas, with whom Warren, Brennan and Fortas concurred, favoring a reversal, dissented.

Here was a large group of people, some of them wanting to be arrested, "singing, clapping and dancing" on the jail premises. Whether or not they actually blocked the driveway and entrance to the jail was not clear from the testimony. Black seemed satisfied that they did, while Douglas contended that they did not. As to the issue of law, Black saw nothing in the Constitution to prevent Florida and any other state "from even handed enforcement of its general trespass statute . . . to preserve the property under its control for the use to which it is lawfully dedicated." Protesters have no constitutional right "to propagandize . . . [their views] whenever and however and wherever they please."

To Douglas, Florida should not have been allowed to use its trespass law "to bludgeon those who peacefully exercise a First Amendment right to protest to government against one of the most grievous of all modern oppressions. . . ." In the absence of any form of violence, threats of violence, attempts at jail break, or "plan or plot to do anything but protest," demonstrations before a jailhouse were no different in nature than those before a courthouse, legislature or executive mansion. Petitions for the redress of grievances have a long and honorable history and are not limited to writing letters to public officials or to "appearing before the local city council." Douglas continued:

> Conventional methods of petitioning may be and often have been, shut off to large groups of our citizens. Legislators may turn deaf ears; formal complaints may be routed endlessly through a bureaucratic maze; courts may let the wheels of justice grind very slowly. Those who do not control television and radio, those who cannot afford to advertise in newspapers or circulate elaborate pamphlets may have only a more limited type of access to public officials. Their methods should not be condemned as tactics of obstruction and harassment as long as the assembly and petition are peaceable, as these were.

What split the Court, aside from differing assessments of facts, was a fundamental disagreement about values. Just as old as the history of petitions for grievances is the clash of views in and out of government about the priorities that must be assigned to public order and tranquility on the one hand and the demands for freedom and revolutionary change on the other. This conflict, relating to basic considerations of political philosophy as well as to deeply rooted psychic predispositions and elasticities within the decision-maker himself, has divided the Court in the past and will probably continue to do so in the future.

Justice Black's position defied easy categorization or classification. His strong libertarian stand in the anti-Communist cases and his adherence to the "absoluteness" of First Amendment freedoms are a matter of record and general knowledge. Less well understood, however, is his equal concern with the rule of the mob and with the kind of mass conduct which in the name of freedom deprived others of theirs. With this qualification in mind, it can be argued that the Court's enduring conservative-liberal bloc alignment reasserted itself in *Cox, Brown* and *Adderley*. As might have been noted from the facts, these were also the controversies in which a conservatively inclined judge could have more easily found blatant forms of racial discrimination to be less crucial and overt while considerations of preserving order and peace more so. Where, however, the evidence seemed clearer, as in *Peterson, Wright* and *Edwards,* that states used their law enforcement machinery to discriminate against or oppress Negroes and where statutes or local ordinances, in some instances, required unequal treatment between the races, most of the members of the Court, liberals and conservatives alike, voted to reverse. In such cases there was obviously no hesitancy to move Southern law and Southern courts toward compliance with the egalitarian concepts of the Fourteenth Amendment and with the constitutional revolution that their implementation entailed.

That the United States Supreme Court did in fact lay a heavy hand on the Southern judiciary in trespass and breach of peace convictions of civil rights demonstrators between 1960 and 1966 is not too difficult to verify. Based on compilations in the *Race Relations Law Reporter,* state supreme court decisions unfavorable to Negro defendants were reversed by the nation's highest court in 94% of the cases. How unwilling, even in the face of such a record of reversal, state supreme courts were in accepting the changing legal norms is further illustrated in ten instances, where on remand orders by the United States Supreme Court, they reaffirmed eight of the convictions. When these defendants afterwards went to the United States Supreme Court for the second time, their convictions were promptly reversed.

Quite a different relationship existed between the state supreme courts of the South and their local courts. Table 1 reflects the strength of the consensus that prevailed between these two levels of the Southern judiciary in decisions affecting interests of Negro defendants who had been convicted of demonstrating on behalf of their civil rights.

TABLE 1

AFFIRMATIONS OF TRESPASS, SIT-IN AND BREACH OF PEACE
CONVICTIONS BY STATE APPELLATE COURTS, 1960–1966

States	Total Number of Decisions	Per Cent Favorable to Negroes
Alabama	37	35%
Arkansas	2	50
Florida	7	0
Georgia	11	18
Louisiana	11	27
Mississippi	7	43
North Carolina	7	0
South Carolina	26	27
Tennessee	2	0
Texas	5	20
Virginia	5	0
N=120	Average for the Southern States	27%

There was little in their experience that could encourage Negro demonstrators and their supporters to expect much help from Southern courts. Local and state judges and lawyers reflected customs and prejudices of communities that strongly resented the challenges that the civil rights movement directed at the traditional way of life. Although generally more sophisticated and better educated than city officials, sheriffs, county boards or legislators, these judicial decision-makers were tied closely into the political system by background, recruitment and election. Trained to admire the law and its great reliance on precedent and procedure, most of them found it impossible to sympathize with those who with moral fervor violated the law which systematically excluded and oppressed them. It was apparent, that Southern courtrooms, generally, were ill equipped to serve as promising forums within which to reconcile such deeply conflicting perceptions of social justice.

Congress Takes a Hand—The Public Accommodations Section of the Civil Rights Act of 1964

Demands for Congress to pass a comprehensive civil rights law had greatly increased in the years following World War II. Negro leaders, liberal politicians, organized labor, church spokesmen, segments of the press and interest groups seeking social justice assailed the continuance of racial discrimination as morally and politically indefensible, as economically and socially detrimental and as immensely harmful to America's image abroad. After issuing an executive order barring segregation in the military forces, President Truman in 1948 added his support to the Negro's cause by urging that Congress adopt far-reaching civil rights measures in law enforcement, voting, employment and interstate transportation facilities.

Intransigence of Southern senators reinforced by committee seniority, the filibuster rule and Northern conservatism held back congressional action for nearly ten more years. Some partial successes, however, were scored in the House. Anti-poll tax bills were passed a number of times, an anti-lynching bill was reported by a committee (but defeated on the floor) and a weak Fair Employment Practices measure was approved in 1950. Finally, in 1957 despite threats of a filibuster, Congress, with the aid of President Eisenhower and after bypassing the Senate Judiciary Committee, enacted the first Civil Rights Act in seventy-five years. Among its major provisions was the establishment of an executive commission on civil rights (with powers to investigate alleged discriminations against voters and to collect information concerning denials of equal protection of laws), the extension of federal district court jurisdiction in certain civil rights controversies and the grant of authority to the Attorney General to seek injunctions against those who deprived persons of their right to vote.

Three years later, a working coalition between Senators Lyndon B. Johnson and Everett M. Dirksen proved successful in maneuvering a moderate civil rights bill through lengthy parliamentary obstructions and filibusters. The 1960 law was aimed primarily at strengthening the Attorney General's role in those instances where a court found a "pattern or practice" of depriving Negroes of their right to vote. It also became a federal crime "to cross state lines to avoid prosecution or punishment for, or giving evidence on, the bombing or burning of any building, facility or vehicle. . . ." Other titles of the act (1) empowered the Civil Rights Commission "to administer oaths and take sworn statements," (2) required the preservation of "voting records and registration papers for all federal elections" and (3) provided for educational and financial assistance for "children of members of the armed forces . . . [whose] schools had been closed to avoid integration. . . ."

That the Civil Rights Act of 1960 could accomplish little in the face of the ever-widening gap between the momentum of the Negro revolution and the resistance to it by powerful interests in Southern communities became quickly apparent. Protests against segregation before courthouses, state legislatures and business establishments began to involve hundreds, even thousands, of demonstrators. Hearings conducted by the Civil Rights Commission documented a rising number of incidents of violence, intimidation and police brutality against civil rights workers, both Negro and white. In more extreme cases, racial moderates among the white leaders of the South encountered economic or social pressures and reprisals. Under such circumstances it seemed imperative to the national civil rights leadership and their supporters that the federal government would have to assume a much more aggressive role if a catastrophe was to be avoided.

On August 28, 1963, a dramatic "March on Washington for Jobs and Freedom," by 200,000 demonstrators underscored the unity of the civil rights movement and its agreement on the urgent need of additional federal action. Earlier that summer President Kennedy had warned the nation in a television address that "[t]he fires of frustration and discord are burning in every city, North and South, where legal remedies are not at hand." On June 19 he submitted to Congress a strong civil rights bill which contained as one of its principal provisions a section on public accommodations aimed at offering legal redress in place of demonstrations, parades and protests.

Clearly beyond the scope of this study would be an analysis of all the factors which combined to finally persuade Congress and especially the Senate to accept the substance of most of the Kennedy proposals and enact the Civil Rights Act of 1964. What led to victory was a paradigm of situations and actions which in barest outline would have to include these elements: the phenomenon of a martyred President inspiring support for a cause he had judged morally right; the receptive mood of a country having watched a number of televised police excesses against peaceful demonstrations; the most intensive lobbying by churches, labor unions and other civil rights supporters; the highly skillful parliamentary leadership of Senators Hubert H. Humphrey and Everett M. Dirksen building an overwhelming coalition of Northern Democrats and Republicans; and the mistaken judgment of strategy by Southern senators that cloture would once again fail to terminate their filibuster.

On July 2, 1964, President Johnson signed the nation's most comprehensive civil rights measure since the days of Reconstruction. In eleven titles the Act

> greatly enhanced the authority of the Attorney General over the administration of voting requirements (especially literacy tests); barred discrimination in public accommodations; authorized the Attorney General to assist in the desegregation of public facilities and in suits aimed at desegregating public schools at all levels; strengthened the civil rights commission; prohibited discrimination in federally assisted programs; established an equal employment opportunities commission; facilitated the review in higher federal courts of certain types of cases involving petitions for "removal"; established a community relations service to assist communities with the resolution of disputes arising out of practices of discrimination or segregation.

Injunctive relief against discrimination or segregation in places of public accommodation "on grounds of race, color, religion or national origin" was made available under Title II of the Act. Constitutionally predicated on the commerce clause, the kinds of establishments to be affected by the new law were defined to include

> any inn, hotel, motel, or other establishment which provides lodging to transient guests, other than an establishment located within a building which contains not more than five rooms for rent or hire and which is actually occupied by the proprietor of such establishment as his residence;

> any restaurant, cafeteria, lunchroom, lunch counter, soda fountain, or other facility principally engaged in selling food for consumption on the premises, including, but not limited to, any such facility located on the premises of any retail establishment; or any gasoline station;

> any motion picture house, theater, concert hall, sports arena, stadium or other place of exhibition or entertainment.

Private clubs and establishments "not in fact open to the public" were exempted from coverage.

Even before the Civil Rights Act of 1964 became law, voluntary desegregation of some public facilities had been peacefully accomplished in a number of Southern cities through the determined efforts of biracial committees, chambers of commerce and civic action groups. In other instances, however, it took formal litigation in federal district courts to assure Negroes even limited access to previously segregated public accommodations. (See Table 2.)

That progress was slow and quite uneven was further emphasized in committee testimony and congressional debate. It was pointed out, for example, by Senator Jacob Javits of New York that as of July 1963, in the fifteen Southern and border States "of some 275 cities with populations of over 10,000, in 65%, all or part of the hotels and motels were still segregated" and so were nearly 60% of "all or part" of the restaurants and theaters. In ninety-eight cities with under 10,000 population, 85% to 90% of "all or part of these types of establishments remained segregated." On a trip from Washington, D.C. to Miami, the average distance between hotel-motel accommodations of "reasonable quality" available to Negroes was estimated to be 141 miles. Traveling from Washington, D.C. to New Orleans, the average between "locations" amounted to 174 miles. Aside from considerations of personal indignity and community race relations, supporters of the public accommodations sections, keeping in mind questions of constitutionality, placed heavy stress in their arguments not only on the Fourteenth Amendment but on the economic burdens segregation laid on interstate commerce.

T A B L E 2

NUMBER OF FEDERAL DISTRICT COURT ACTIONS FACILITATING
EQUAL ACCESS TO PUBLIC ACCOMMODATIONS, 1960–1964

	1960	*1961*	*1962*	*1963*	*1964*	*Total*
Transportation and Transportation Facilities	3	9	10	3	0	25
Public Recreational, Cultural and Health Facilities	5	4	9	8	6	32
Restaurants and Theater	2	0	3	5	6	16
Motels, Hotels and Barber Shops	0	0	0	3	3	6

For example, S. 1732, the interstate public accommodations bill reported by the Senate Commerce Committee and quite similar in its major provisions to Title II, began with a long statement of congressional findings, among which were these:

> Negroes and members of other minority groups who travel interstate are frequently unable to obtain adequate food service at convenient places along their routes, with the result that many are dissuaded from traveling interstate. . . .

> Goods, services and persons in the amusement and entertainment industries commonly move in interstate commerce, and the entire American people benefit from the increased cultural and recreational

opportunities afforded thereby. Practices of audience discrimination and segregation artificially restrict the number of persons to whom the interstate amusement and entertainment industries may offer their goods and services. . . .

Retail establishments in all states of the Union purchase a wide variety and a large volume of goods from business concerns located in other states and in foreign nations. Discriminatory practices in such establishments, which in some instances have led to the withholding of patronage by those affected by such practices, inhibit and restrict the normal distribution of goods in the interstate market. . . .

Business organizations are frequently hampered in obtaining the services of skilled workers and persons in the professions who are likely to encounter discrimination based on race, creed, color or national origin in restaurants, retail stores and places of amusement in the area where their services are needed. Business organizations which seek to avoid subjecting their employees to such discrimination and to avoid the strife resulting therefrom are restricted in the choice of location of their offices and plants. Such discrimination thus reduces the mobility of the national labor force and prevents the most effective allocation of national resources, including the interstate movement of industries, particularly in some of the areas of the nation most in need of industrial and commercial expansion and development.

Opponents of the public accommodation sections of the Civil Rights Act emphasized the danger of permitting federal intervention into the affairs of the states and of private enterprise. They held this to constitute an unconstitutional enlargement of central governmental authority and an irresponsible invitation to further violence between the races.

In the course of the floor debate Senator Spessard L. Holland of Florida anticipated years of litigation:

In the interval, the owners of the thousands of fine hotels, motels, restaurants, boarding houses, and so forth, might be deprived of their constitutional rights to manage their own businesses which they have built up by hard work, sacrifice, and investment of their own hard earned money.

In addition to that economic tragedy, which also is a personal tragedy to me, the point of even greater significance is that enactment of this vicious, socialist legislation strikes at the very heart of the Constitution. . . .

Senator J. Strom Thurmond of South Carolina warned of the Act's broader implications:

The public accommodation proposals give legal sanction to a totally new and dangerous principle. It constricts the personal and property rights of all American individuals in an attempt to create a privilege for a favored few. Those who would patronize these private establishments would retain their right to pick and choose among the many. However, the counterbalancing right, the right to pick and choose one's customers would forever be done away with. . . . Who can deny that this amounts to "involuntary servitude."

And as to the constitutional authority for the public accommodations section, Senator Ervin of North Carolina concluded that

Title II of the bill represents a brazen effort on the part of the Congress to regulate local activities which have not the remotest connection with interstate commerce. It is an attempt to regulate local activities long after interstate commerce has totally ceased.

The Civil Rights Act of 1964 in the Courts

Only five months after the Civil Rights Act of 1964 left the President's desk, the United States Supreme Court unanimously upheld Title II in *Heart of Atlanta Motel, Inc.* v. *United States* and in *Katzenbach* v. *McClung.*

Could Congress through its power over commerce reach a privately-owned 216-room motel in downtown Atlanta located near major highways and bar the establishment from refusing to rent rooms to Negroes? Congress could do just that, decided Justice Clark in upholding the public accommodation sections. Ruled as inapplicable were the old Civil Rights Cases (1883) which had declared unconstitutional the Federal Civil Rights Act of 1875. This Act endeavored to prohibit even then discrimination in "inns, public conveyances on land or water, theaters, and other places of public amusement." What distinguished the legislation of 1964 from its predecessor was the newly added limiting requirement that such regulated establishments had to stand in "a direct and substantial relation to the interstate flow of goods and people."

As to the commerce clause itself, Clark pointed to such cases as *National Labor Relations Board* v. *Jones and Laughlin* (1937) and *United States* v. *Darby* (1941) as having made it unmistakably clear that the "power of Congress to promote interstate commerce also includes the power to regulate the local incidents thereof, including local activities in both the states of origin and destination which might have a substantial and harmful effect upon that commerce." Since Congress in a contemporary setting of high mobility of persons, goods and services could find a "rational basis" that commerce was affected by racial discrimination and since the "means it selected to eliminate that evil are reasonable and appropriate," defendants could not complain of having had their rights of liberty and property taken in violation of the Fifth Amendment.

Nor can the due process and equal protection of the law clauses of the Fourteenth Amendment be invoked against this public accommodation section. Such regulations, repeatedly sustained in the Supreme Court, have been adopted by thirty-two states and many cities. These laws merely "codify the common law innkeeper rule"; they impose no "involuntary servitude"; and possibilities of suffering economic losses as a result of such measures have never been judicially admitted as a barrier to prohibitions against racial discrimination. There was nothing, concluded Justice Clark, to prevent Congress from adopting policies for removing obstacles to commerce by means which are "reasonably adapted to the end permitted by the Constitution."

Differing with Clark and Black, Douglas and Goldberg preferred to build their support for the constitutionality of the accommodation section not so much on the commerce clause as on Section Five of the Fourteenth Amendment. This provides Congress with the power to "enforce by appropriate legislation . . ." the provisions of the Amendment. Such a construction, argued Douglas, would make "unnecessary litigation over whether a particular restaurant or inn is within the commerce definitions of the Act . . ."; it would also allow "every person—whatever his race, creed or color—to patronize all places of public accommodation, whether he travels interstate or intrastate." The right of people to move freely "occupies a more protected position in our constitutional system than does the movement of cattle, fruit, steel and coal across state lines!" Goldberg, citing hearings in Congress and statements by the administration, seemed similarly convinced that there was ample legislative authority in Section Five of the Fourteenth Amendment. "The primary purpose of the Civil Rights Act of 1964," began his concurrence, ". . . is the vindication of human dignity and not mere economics."

In *Katzenbach* v. *McClung*, Clark held that Title II also validly covered Ollie's Barbecue, a small, family-owned, segregated restaurant in Birmingham serving only intrastate travelers and specializing in barbecued meats and homemade pies. Considered significant in this instance were annual meat purchases of approximately $70,000 through local suppliers "who had procured it from outside the state." Relying on the basic case developed in *Heart of Atlanta Motel, Inc.,* these transactions were considered sufficiently substantial to bring even this restaurant within the broad sweep of congressional power over interstate commerce.

While the volume of food purchased was undeniably small to the total flow of commerce, the Court was willing to accept congressional findings that this type of widely practiced discrimination constituted, in the aggregate, a significant burden on travel and on the economic life of the nation.

Compliance and Commentary on Changes in the Civil Rights Movement

Enactment of the public accommodations section provided the forces of protest with additional federal support and with a more helpful legal climate. A closely divided Court in a case from South Carolina, *Hamm* v. *City of Rock Hill* (1964), construed Section 203 (c) to have "abated" any further prosecution and conviction under state criminal trespass or breach of peace statutes of demonstrators who had been seeking peaceful admission to segregated establishments covered under the new law.

In *State* v. *Rachel* (1966) the Court increased the possibilities for "removal" of cases from state to federal courts under those conditions where any attempt is made to "punish" individuals "for exercising rights of equality conferred upon them by the Act."

Senators Richard Russell of Georgia and Allen J. Ellender of Louisiana despite their own previous opposition were reported to have urged quiet compliance in talks with business groups, local officials and community leaders. According to *Congressional Quarterly,* cities in which "early compliance" was also observed included New Orleans, Baton Rouge and Monroe, Louisiana; Albany, Atlanta and Savannah, Georgia; Jacksonville and St. Augustine, Florida; Birmingham, Montgomery and Mobile, Alabama; Jackson, Biloxi, Natchez and McComb, Mississippi.

There were some other legal and political developments. *Dombrowski* v. *Pfister* (1966) modified substantially a well-established principle of constitutional law, the doctrine of "equitable abstention," according to which federal courts were not to interfere with state criminal law administration except in very unusual circumstances. In this case the Court held that a federal district court "erred" in refusing to grant injunctive relief to petitioners (promoting civil rights causes in the South) who had challenged the constitutionality of Louisiana laws "as abridging free expression . . . or discouraging protected activities."

Federal efforts to assist Negroes to register and obtain their suffrage in the South were greatly strengthened when the Court sustained the Voting Rights Act of 1965 in *South Carolina* v. *Katzenbach* (1966). Finding that case-by-case litigation proved ineffective—especially in Alabama, Georgia, Louisiana, Mississippi and South Carolina—Congress, under power granted it by the Fifteenth Amendment, provided for the suspension of literacy tests, for the appointment of federal examiners, for federal review of state election rules that might perpetuate voting discrimination and for additional authority with which the Attorney General could expeditiously enforce the Act which sought "to banish the blight of racial discrimination in voting."

All in all, however, progress was slow. Charged by the Civil Rights Act with assisting communities in resolving disputes relating to discrimination and segregation, the Community Relations Service achieved some agreements after difficult and protracted negotiations. Its director, Roger W. Wilkins observed in 1966:

> While it is true that there have been significant moves toward compliance, by and large this is limited to the downtown sections of larger communities and along the interstate highways. This change has been more meaningful for the traveler than for the local community residents. It has been observed that Negro residents of many of the smaller communities are prevented from eating in restaurants and going to theaters by threats and acts of violence, even though the owner, or manager may be willing to provide service.

Noted as particularly helpful to the cause of integrating public accommodations was the cooperation of national motel and restaurant chains and the pressure of the convention trade.

Putting an end to discrimination and segregation in public accommodation and facilities represented at best only particular facets of the much broader objectives and currents of the Negro revolution. Even the Voting Rights Act of 1965 which followed the turbulent events of the freedom march from Selma to Montgomery and the substantial increase in voting throughout the South to which it contributed failed to assuage the widespread dissatisfaction and hostility among Negro youth. A new era of the struggle for equal justice was in gestation; its aims were national rather than regional; its leadership was changing and far from unified; its traditional tactics of non-violence underwent serious challenge and reassessment.

In the North, Negro frustration with slum living and the urban ghettoes led to riots in Los Angeles, New York, Rochester, Chicago, Newark, Detroit and many other cities. While white America became more affluent, Negro wages remained stubbornly low, unemployment climbed disproportionately and segregation in housing and schools continued unabated. Broken families, insufficient skills, inadequate education and a sense of futility deeply rooted in a culture of poverty compounded the problems.

Impatience with the slowness of reform, with "bureaucratic welfarism," with what was termed "the hypocrisy of the white power structure," and with the legislative and litigational achievements of the N.A.A.C.P. and the Southern Christian Leadership Conference (S.C.L.C.) turned some segments of the civil rights movement, notably SNCC and CORE, appreciably to the political left. Appeals for integration among the various groups and for the discipline of peaceful protests no longer seemed to inspire the masses. New slogans, symbols and leaders competed for loyalties and attention. Less limited goals called for charismatic leaders who spoke less of conciliation and more of power— "black power," especially. Stokely Carmichael of the Student Nonviolent Coordinating Committee better than anyone else was able to infuse the provocative concept of black power with the kind of psychological magnetism that attracted Negroes by the thousands. A position paper by SNCC spelled out its understanding of black power. Black people must find their own identity without the aid of whites; before Negroes can enter into political coalitions with whites they will have to organize themselves, learn political skills, attain self-confidence; blacks must staff the organization; blacks must furnish the brains; blacks must finance and control the movement; only after this has been achieved can there be talk of alliance and brotherly unity; "the broad masses of black people react to American society in the same manner as colonial people react to the West . . . that of the colonized toward the colonizer."

Roy Wilkins of the N.A.A.C.P. and Dr. Martin Luther King of the S.C.L.C., as well as others in the civil rights movement, have not hesitated to criticize the radical and separationist implications of "black power." Committed to the coalition strategy and to the tactics of non-violence, they see in the doctrines of SNCC an ill-concealed form of racism-in-reverse which could only seriously exacerbate white reaction and jeopardize the substantial gains which the Negro has already made. Not unmindful of the widening gap between the Negro proletariat and the middle class and of the politically explosive quality of the cities' teeming tenements, Roy Wilkins, Dr. King and their followers have so far been unwilling to join Carmichael in the wholesale indictment of American society. They still indicate faith in the goals of first class citizenship for all regardless of race and color and in the possibilities of fighting slums and poverty in partnership with government. They still express confidence in America's capacity to rid itself of its racist social and institutional traditions if not through persuasion and the maturation of the individual conscience then through the force of law and of the ballot.

Whatever the outcome of the ideological and leadership struggle within the civil rights movement, Americans irrespective of race cannot help but be affected by it. Should it become impossible to offer genuine equality of opportunity and social justice to the Negro quickly enough, mass alienation could easily be turned by demagogues into mass hostility. Under such circumstances there would be no similarity between the relatively peaceful demonstrations and sit-ins of the past and the kind of armed confrontations that would result if ten per cent of this nation were to believe that it no longer had a stake in society.

Equally alarming to those who seek the peaceful and progressive expansion of civil liberties for all has been the notable erosion of white empathy and support for Negro aspirations as mass protests became a national phenomenon. Extremist appeals for bigger and more paralyzing demonstrations and the cry for "black power" intensified white apprehensions of lawlessness, job displacement and neighborhood "inundations."

White reaction and backlash manifested itself politically in the 1964 Democratic presidential primary vote of Governor George Wallace in Wisconsin, Indiana and Maryland, in some of the angry outbursts at the Republican Convention in San Francisco and to some degree in the 1966 gubernatorial victories of Lurleen Wallace in Alabama and of Lester Maddox in Georgia. Whether resentment at Washington's role in civil rights and hostility to the Negro revolution can furnish sufficient regional and national strength for a third party constituency may be tested again in future elections.

SUGGESTED READINGS

Alexander M. Bickel. *The Politics of the Warren Court.* New York, 1965.

Charles L. Black, Jr. "Mr. Justice Black, the Supreme Court and Bill of Rights," *Harpers Magazine,* February, 1961, 63–68.

Harcop A. Freeman. "The Right of Protest and Civil Disobedience," *Indiana Law Journal,* Winter, 1966, 228–254.

Martin G. Gilbert. "Theories of State Action as Applied to the 'Sit-In' Cases," *Arkansas Law Review,* Summer, 1963, 147–162.

Martin Luther King, Jr. *Stride Toward Freedom.* New York, 1958.

Burke Marshall. "Federal Protection of Negro Voting Rights," *Law and Contemporary Problems,* Summer, 1962, 455–467.

Burke Marshall. *Federalism and Civil Rights.* New York, 1964.

Jerome H. Skolnick. *Justice Without Trial: Law Enforcement in Democratic Society.* New York, 1966.

Irene Tinker. "Nationalism in a Plural Society: The Case of the American Negro," *Western Political Science Quarterly,* March, 1966, 112–122.

James W. Vander Zanden. *Race Relations in Transition.* New York, 1966.

Kenneth N. Vines. "Southern State Supreme Courts and Race Relations," *Western Political Quarterly,* March, 1965, 5–18.

Clement E. Vose. "Interest Groups, Judicial Review, and Local Government," *Western Political Quarterly,* March, 1966, 85–100.

Roy Wilkins. "The Riots of 1964: The Causes of Racial Violence," *Notre Dame Lawyer,* July, 1965, 552–557.

Index

Clock Without Hands

by Carson McCullers

CLOCK

WITHOUT HANDS

by Carson McCullers

Houghton Mifflin Company, Boston

The Riverside Press Cambridge

SELECTIONS FROM *Clock Without Hands* HAVE PREVIOUSLY APPEARED IN *Botteghe Oscure, Harper's Bazaar,* AND *Mademoiselle.*

FOURTH PRINTING

for Mary E. Mercer, M.D.

Clock Without Hands

1

DEATH is always the same, but each man dies in his own way. For J. T. Malone it began in such a simple ordinary way that for a time he confused the end of life with the beginning of a new season. The winter of his fortieth year was an unusually cold one for the Southern town — with icy, pastel days and radiant nights. The spring came violently in middle March in that year of 1953, and Malone was lazy and peaked during those days of early blossoms and windy skies. He was a pharmacist and, diagnosing spring fever, he prescribed for himself a liver and iron tonic. Although he tired easily, he kept to his usual routine: He walked to work and his pharmacy was one of the first businesses open on the main street and he closed the store at six. He had dinner at a restaurant downtown and supper at home with his family. But his appetite was finicky and he lost weight steadily. When he changed from his winter suit to a light spring suit, the trousers hung in folds on his tall, wasted frame. His temples were shrunken so that the veins pulsed visibly when he chewed or swallowed and his Adam's apple struggled in his thin neck. But Malone saw no reason for alarm: His spring fever was unusually severe and he added to his tonic the old-fashioned course of sulphur and molasses — for when all was said and done the old remedies were the best. The thought must have solaced him for soon he felt a little better and started his annual vegetable garden. Then one day as he was compounding a prescription he swayed and fainted. He visited the doctor after this and there followed some tests at the City Hospital. Still he was not much worried; he had spring fever and the weakness of that complaint, and on a warm day he had fainted — a common, even natural thing. Malone had never considered his own death except in some twilight, unreckoned future, or in terms of life insurance. He was an ordinary, simple man and his own death was a phenomenon.

Dr. Kenneth Hayden was a good customer and a friend who had his office on the floor above the pharmacy, and the day the reports were due on the tests Malone went upstairs at two o'clock. Once he was alone with the doctor he felt an undefinable menace. The doctor did not look directly at him so that his pale, familiar face seemed somehow eyeless. His voice as he greeted Malone was strangely formal. He sat silent at his desk and handled a paper knife, gazing intently at it as he passed it from hand to hand. The strange silence warned Malone and when he could stand it no longer he blurted:

"The reports came in — am I all right?"

The doctor avoided Malone's blue and anxious gaze, then uneasily his eyes passed to the open window and fixed there. "We have checked carefully and there seems to be something unusual in the blood chemistry," the doctor said finally in a soft and dragging voice.

A fly buzzed in the sterile, dreary room and there was the lingering smell of ether. Malone was now certain something serious was wrong and, unable to bear the silence or the doctor's unnatural voice, he began to chatter against the truth. "I felt all along you would find a touch of anemia. You know I was once a med student and I wondered if my blood count was not too low."

Dr. Hayden looked at the paper knife he was handling on the desk. His right eyelid twitched. "In that case we can talk it over medically." His voice lowered and he hurried the next words. "The red blood cells have a count of only 2.15 million so we have an intercurrent anemia. But that is not the important factor. The white blood cells are abnormally increased — the count is 208,000." The doctor paused and touched his twitching eyelid. "You probably understand what that means."

Malone did not understand. Shock had bewildered him and the room seemed suddenly cold. He understood only that something strange and terrible was happening to him in the cold and swaying room. He was mesmerized by the paper knife that the doctor turned in his stubby, scrubbed fingers. A long dormant memory stirred so that he was aware of something shameful that had been forgotten, although the memory itself was still unclear. So he suffered a parallel distress — the fear and tension of the doctor's words and the mysterious and unremembered shame. The doctor's hands were white and hairy and Malone could not bear to watch them fooling with the knife, yet his attention was mysteriously compelled.

"I can't quite remember," he said helplessly. "It's been a long time and I didn't graduate from medical school."

The doctor put aside the knife and handed him a thermometer. "If you will just hold this underneath the tongue — " He glanced at his watch and walked over to the window where he stood looking out with his hands clasped behind him and his feet placed well apart.

"The slide shows a pathological increase in the white blood cells and intercurrent anemia. There is a preponderance of leucocytes of a juvenile character. In short — " The doctor paused, reclasped his hands and for a moment stood on tiptoe. "The long and short of it is, we have here a case of leukemia." Turning suddenly, he removed the thermometer and read it rapidly.

Malone sat taut and waiting, one leg wrapped around the other and his Adam's apple struggling in his frail throat. He said, "I felt a little feverish, but I kept thinking it was just spring fever."

"I'd like to examine you. If you will please take off your clothes and lie down a moment on the treatment table — "

Malone lay on the table, gaunt and pallid in his nakedness and ashamed.

"The spleen is much enlarged. Have you been troubled with any lumps or swellings?"

"No," he said. "I'm trying to think what I know about leukemia. I remember a little girl in the newspapers and the parents had her Christmas in September because she was expected soon to die." Malone stared desperately at a crack in the plaster ceiling. From an adjacent office a child was crying and the voice, half strangled with terror and protest, seemed not to come from a distance, but to be part of his own agony when he asked: "Am I going to die with this — leukemia?"

The answer was plain to Malone although the doctor did not speak. From the next room the child gave a long, raw shriek that lasted almost a full minute. When the examination was over, Malone sat trembling on the edge of the table, repulsed by his own weakness and distress. His narrow feet with the side calluses were particularly loathsome to him and he put on his gray socks first. The doctor was washing his hands at the corner washbasin and for some reason this offended Malone. He dressed and returned to the chair by the desk. As he sat stroking his scant, coarse hair, his long upper lip set carefully against the tremulous lower one, his eyes febrile and terrified, Malone had already the meek and neuter look of an incurable.

The doctor had resumed his motions with the paper knife, and again Malone was fascinated and obscurely distressed; the movements of the hand and knife were a part of illness and a part of some mysterious and half-remembered shame. He swallowed and steadied his voice to speak.

"Well, how long do you give me, Doctor?"

For the first time the doctor met his gaze and looked at him steadily for some moments. Then his eyes passed on to the photograph of his wife and two small boys that faced him on his desk. "We are both family men and if I were in your shoes, I know I would want the truth. I would get my affairs in order."

Malone could scarcely speak, but when the words came they were loud and rasping: "How long?"

The buzzing of a fly and the sound of traffic from the street seemed to accent the silence and the tension of the dreary room. "I think we might count on a year or fifteen months — it's difficult to estimate exactly." The doctor's white hands were covered with long black strands of hair and they fiddled ceaselessly with the ivory knife, and although the sight was somehow terrible to Malone, he could not take his attention away. He began to talk rapidly.

"It's a peculiar thing. Until this winter I had always carried plain, straight life insurance. But this winter I had it converted to the sort of policy that gives you retirement pay — you've noticed the ads in the magazines. Beginning at sixty-five you draw two hundred dollars a month all the rest of your life. It's funny to think of it now." After a broken laugh, he added, "The company will have to convert back to the way it was before — just plain life insurance. Metropolitan is a good company and I've carried life insurance for nearly twenty years — dropping a little during the depression and redeeming it when I was able. The ads for the retirement plan always pictured this middle-aged couple in a sunny climate — maybe Florida or California. But I and my wife had a different idea. We had planned on a little place in Vermont or Maine. Living this far south all your life you get pretty tired of sun and glare — "

Suddenly the screen of words collapsed and, unprotected before his fate, Malone wept. He covered his face with his broad acid-stained hands and fought to control his sobbing breath.

The doctor looked as though for guidance at the picture of his wife and carefully patted Malone's knee. "Nothing in this day and age is hopeless. Every month science discovers a new weapon against disease. Maybe soon they will find a way to control diseased cells. And meanwhile, everything possible will be done to prolong life and make you comfortable. There is one good thing about this disease — if anything could be called good in this situation — there is not much pain involved. And we will try everything. I'd like you to check in at the City Hospital as soon as possible and we can give some transfusions and try X-rays. It might make you feel a whole lot better."

Malone had controlled himself and patted his face with his handkerchief. Then he blew on his glasses, wiped them, and put them back on. "Excuse me, I guess I'm weak and kind of unhinged. I can go to the hospital whenever you want me to."

Malone entered the hospital early the next morning and remained there for three days. The first night he was given a sedative and dreamed about Dr. Hayden's hands and the paper knife he handled at his desk. When he awoke he remembered the dormant shame that had troubled him the day before and he knew the source of the obscure distress he had felt in the doctor's office. Also he realized for the first time that Dr. Hayden was a Jew. He recalled the memory that was so painful that forgetfulness was a necessity. The memory concerned the time he had failed in medical school in his second year. It was a Northern school and there were in the class a lot of Jew grinds. They ran up the grade average so that an ordinary, average student had no fair chance. The Jew grinds had crowded J. T. Malone out of medical school and ruined his career as a doctor — so that he had to shift over to pharmacy. Across the aisle from him there had been a Jew called Levy who fiddled with a fine-blade knife and distracted him from getting the good of the class lectures. A Jew grind who made A-plus and studied in the library every night until closing time. It seemed to Malone that also his eyelid twitched occasionally. The realization that Dr. Hayden was a Jew seemed of such importance that Malone wondered how he could have ignored it for so long. Hayden was a good customer and a friend — they had worked in the same building for many years and saw each other daily. Why had he failed to notice? Maybe the doctor's given name had tricked him — Kenneth Hale. Malone said to himself he had no prejudice, but when Jews used the good old Anglo-Saxon, Southern names like that, he felt it was somehow wrong. He remembered that the Hayden children had hooked noses and he remembered once seeing the family on the steps of the synagogue on a Saturday. When

Dr. Hayden came on his rounds, Malone watched him with dread — although for years he had been a friend and customer. It was not so much that Kenneth Hale Hayden was a Jew as the fact that he was living and would live on — he and his like — while J. T. Malone had an incurable disease and would die in a year or fifteen months. Malone wept sometimes when he was alone. He also slept a great deal and read a number of detective stories. When he was released from the hospital the spleen was much receded, although the white blood cells were little changed. He was unable to think about the months ahead or to imagine death.

Afterwards he was surrounded by a zone of loneliness, although his daily life was not much changed. He did not tell his wife about his trouble because of the intimacy that tragedy might have restored; the passions of marriage had long since winnowed to the preoccupations of parenthood. That year Ellen was a high school junior and Tommy was eight years old. Martha Malone was an energetic woman whose hair was turning gray — a good mother and also a contributor to the family finances. During the depression she had made cakes to order and at that time it had seemed to him right and proper. She continued the cake business after the pharmacy was out of debt and even supplied a number of drugstores with neatly wrapped sandwiches with her name printed on the band. She made good money and gave the children many advantages — and she even bought some Coca-Cola stock. Malone felt that was going too far; he was afraid it would be said that he was not a good provider and his pride was affronted. One thing he put his foot down on: he would not deliver and he forbade his children and his wife to deliver. Mrs. Malone would drive to the customer and the servant — the Malone servants were always a little too young or too old and received less than the going wage — would scramble from the automobile with the cakes or sandwiches. Malone could not understand the change that had taken place in his wife. He had married a girl in a chiffon dress who had once fainted when a mouse ran over her shoe — and mysteriously she had become a gray-haired housewife with a business of her own and even some Coca-Cola stock. He lived now in a curious vacuum surrounded by the concerns of family life — the talk of high school proms, Tommy's violin recital, and a seven-tiered wedding cake — and the daily activities swirled around him as dead leaves ring the center of a whirlpool, leaving him curiously untouched.

In spite of the weakness of his disease, Malone was restless. Often he would walk aimlessly around the streets of the town — down through the shambling, crowded slums around the cotton mill, or through the Negro sections, or the middle class streets of houses set in careful lawns. On these walks he had the bewildered look of an absent-minded person who seeks something but has already forgotten the thing that is lost. Often, without cause, he would reach out and touch some random object; he would veer from his route to touch a lamppost or place his hands against a brick wall. Then he would stand transfixed and abstracted. Again he would examine a green-leaved elm tree with morbid attention as he picked a flake of sooty bark. The lamppost, the wall, the tree would exist when he was dead and the thought was loathsome to Malone. There was a further confusion — he was unable to acknowledge the reality of approaching death, and the conflict led to a sense of ubiquitous unreality. Sometimes, and dimly, Malone felt he blundered among a world of incongruities in which there was no order or conceivable design.

Malone sought comfort in the church. When tormented by the unreality of both death and life, it helped him to know that the First Baptist Church was real enough. The largest church in town, taking up half a city block near the main street, the property on offhand reckoning was worth about two million dollars. A church like that was bound to be real. The pillars of the church were men of substance and leading citizens. Butch Henderson, the realtor and one of the shrewdest traders in the town, was a deacon and never missed a service from one year to the next — and was Butch Henderson a likely man to waste his time and trouble on anything that was not as real as dirt? The other deacons were of the same caliber — the president of the Nylon Spinning Mill, a railroad trustee, the owner of the leading department store — all responsible and canny men of business whose judgment was foolproof. And they believed in the church and the hereafter beyond death. Even T. C. Wedwell, one of the founders of Coca-Cola and a multimillionaire, had left the church $500,000 for the construction of the right wing. T. C. Wedwell had the uncanny foresight to put his faith in Coca-Cola — and T. C. Wedwell had believed in the church and the hereafter to the tune of half a million dollars bequeathal. He who had never made a bad investment had so invested in eternity. Finally, Fox Clane was a member. The old Judge and former congressman — a glory to the state and the South — attended often when he was in town and blew his nose when his favorite hymns were sung. Fox Clane was a churchman and believer and Malone was willing to follow the old Judge in this as he had followed him in his politics. So Malone went faithfully to church.

One Sunday in early April Dr. Watson delivered a sermon that impressed Malone deeply. He was a folksy preacher who often made comparisons to the business world or sports. The sermon this Sunday was about the salvation that draws the bead on death. The voice rang in the vaulted church and the stained glass windows cast a rich glow on the congregation.

Malone sat stiff and listening and each moment he expected some personal revelation. But, although the sermon was long, death remained a mystery, and after the first elation he felt a little cheated when he left the church. How could you draw a bead on death? It was like aiming at the sky. Malone stared up at the blue, unclouded sky until his neck felt strained. Then he hurried toward the pharmacy.

That day Malone had an encounter that upset him strangely, although on the surface it was an ordinary happening. The business section was deserted, but he heard footsteps behind him and when he turned a corner the footsteps still followed. When he took a short cut through an unpaved alley the steps no longer sounded, but he had the uneasy sense of being followed and glimpsed a shadow on the wall. He turned so suddenly that he collided with his follower. He was a colored boy that Malone knew by sight and in his walks he seemed always to run across him. Or perhaps it was simply that he noticed the boy whenever he saw him because of his unnatural appearance. The boy was medium-sized with a muscular body and a face that was sullen in repose. Except for his eyes, he looked like any other colored boy. But his eyes were bluish-gray, and set in the dark face they had a bleak, violent look. Once those eyes were seen, the rest of the body seemed also unusual and out of proportion. The arms were too long, the chest too broad — and the expression alternated from emotional sensitivity to deliberate sullenness. The impression on Malone was such that he did not think of him in harmless terms as a *colored boy* — his mind automatically used the harsh term *bad nigger*, although the boy was a stranger to him and as a rule he was lenient in such matters. When Malone turned and they collided, the nigger steadied himself but did not budge, and it was Malone who stepped back a pace. They stood in the narrow alley and stared at each other. The eyes of both were of the same gray-blue and at first it seemed a contest to outstare each other. The eyes that looked at him were cold and blazing in the dark face — then it seemed to Malone that the blaze flickered and steadied to a look of eerie understanding. He felt that those strange eyes knew that he was soon to die. The emotion was so swift and shocking that Malone shuddered and turned away. The stare had not lasted more than a full minute and there was no seeming consequence — but Malone felt that something momentous and terrible had been accomplished. He walked unsteadily the remaining length of the alley and was relieved to find ordinary friendly faces at the end. He was relieved to get out of the alley and enter his safe, ordinary, familiar pharmacy.

The old Judge often stopped by the pharmacy to have a drink before Sunday dinner, and Malone was glad to see that he was there already, holding forth to a group of cronies who stood before the fountain counter. Malone greeted his customers absently but did not linger. The electric fans on the ceiling churned the mixed odors in the place — syrupy smells from the fountain with the bitter medicinal smells from the compounding section in the rear.

"Be with you in a minute, J.T.," the old Judge interrupted himself to say as Malone passed on his way to the back room. He was an enormous man with a red face and a rough halo of yellow-white hair. He wore a rumpled linen white suit, a lavender shirt, and a tie adorned with a pearl stickpin and stained with a coffee spot. His left hand had been damaged by a stroke and he rested it cautiously on the counter edge. This hand was clean and slightly puffy from disuse — while the right one, which he used constantly as he talked, was dingy-nailed, and he wore a star sapphire on the ring finger. He was carrying an ebony cane with a silver crooked handle. The Judge finished his harangue against the Federal Government and joined Malone in the compounding section.

It was a very small room, separated from the rest of the store by a wall of medicine bottles. There was just enough room for a rocking chair and the prescription table. Malone had brought out a bottle of bourbon and unfolded a desk chair from a corner. The Judge crowded the room until he lowered himself carefully into the rocking chair. The smell of sweat from his huge body mingled with the smell of castor oil and disinfectant. The whiskey splashed lightly against the bottom of their glasses when Malone poured.

"Nothing is so musical as the sound of pouring bourbon for the first drink on a Sunday morning. Not Bach or Schubert or any of those masters that my grandson plays . . ." The Judge sang:

"Oh, whiskey is the life of man . . . Oh, whiskey! Oh, Johnny!"

He drank slowly, pausing after each swallow to move his tongue in his mouth and take a little after-swallow. Malone drank so quickly that the liquor seemed to blossom in his belly like a rose.

"J.T., have you ever stopped to consider that the South is in the vortex of a revolution almost as disastrous as the War Between the States?" Malone had not considered, but he turned his head to one side and nodded gravely as the Judge went on: "The wind of revolution is rising to destroy the very foundations on which the South was built. The poll tax will soon be abolished and every ignorant Nigra can vote. Equal rights in education will be the next thing. Imagine a future where delicate little white girls must share their desks with coal-black niggers in order to learn to read and write. A minimum-wage law so outrageously high that it will be the death knell of the rural South may be forced on us. Imagine paying a passel of worthless field hands by the hour. The Federal Housing Projects are already the ruination of the real estate investors. They call it slum clearance — but who makes the slums, I ask you? The people who live in slums make the slums themselves by their own improvidence. And mark my words, those same Federal apartment buildings — modern and Northern as they are — will be turned into a slum in ten years' time."

Malone listened with the trustful attentiveness that he had given the sermon at church. His friendship with the Judge was one of his great prides. He had known the Judge ever since he had come to Milan and had often hunted at his place during the hunting season — he was there the Saturday and Sunday before the death of the Judge's only son. But a special intimacy had flowered after the Judge's illness — when it seemed for a time that the old congressman was finished politically. Malone would visit the Judge on Sundays bringing a mess of turnip greens from his garden or a certain waterground cornmeal that the Judge liked. Sometimes they would play poker — but usually the Judge would talk and Malone would listen. At these times Malone felt near the center of power — almost as though he too was a congressman. When the Judge was up and around, he came often on Sunday to the pharmacy and they would drink together in the compounding room. If Malone ever had misgivings about the ideas of the old Judge, he smothered them immediately. For who was he to cavil with a congressman? And if the old Judge was not right, who could be right? And now that the old Judge was talking about running for Congress again, Malone felt that the responsibility would be where it ought to be and he was content.

With the second drink the Judge brought out his case of cigars and Malone prepared both of them because of the Judge's handicap. The smoke rose in straight lines to the low ceiling and broke there. The door to the street was open and a slice of sunlight made the smoke clouds opalescent.

"I have a serious request to ask you," Malone said. "I want to draw up my will."

"Always glad to oblige you, J.T. Is there anything particular?"

"Oh, no, just the usual thing — but I want it done as soon as you can get around to it." He added in a flat voice, "The doctors say I don't have too long to live."

The Judge stopped rocking and put down his glass. "Why, what on earth! What's wrong with you, J.T.?"

Malone was speaking of his illness for the first time and the words somehow relieved him. "Seems I have a blood disease."

"A *blood* disease! Why, that's ridiculous — you have some of the best blood in this state. I well remember your father who had his wholesale pharmacy on the corner of Twelfth and Mulberry in Macon. And your mother I remember, too — she was a Wheelwright. You have the best blood in this state in your veins, J.T., and never forget that."

Malone felt a little chill of pleasure and pride that passed almost immediately. "The doctors —"

"Oh, doctors — with all due respect to the medical profession, I seldom believe a word they say. Never let them intimidate you. Some years ago when I had that little seizure, my doctor — Doc Tatum over at Flowering Branch — began this alarmist talk. No liquor or cigars or even cigarettes. Seemed like I had better learn to pick a harp or shovel coal." The Judge's right hand plucked on imaginary strings and made a shoveling gesture. "But I spoke up to Doc and followed my own instincts. Instincts, that's the only thing a man can follow. And here I am as hale and hearty as a man my age could wish to be. And poor Doc, the irony — I was a pallbearer at his funeral. The irony was that Doc was a confirmed teetotaler who never smoked — although he occasionally enjoyed a chew. A grand fellow and a glory to the medical profession, but like every man-jack of them, alarmist in judgment and fallible. Don't let them intimidate you, J.T."

Malone was comforted, and as he began another drink he began to consider the possibility that Hayden and the other doctors had made a mistaken diagnosis. "The slide showed it was leukemia. And the blood count showed a terrible increase in leucocytes."

"Leucocytes?" asked the Judge. "What are they?"

"White blood cells."

"Never heard of them."

"But they're there."

The Judge massaged the silver handle of his cane. "If it was your heart or liver or even your kidneys I could understand your alarm. But an insignificant disorder like too many leucocytes does seem a little farfetched to me. Why I've lived for more than eighty years without ever considering if I have any of those leucocytes or not." The Judge's fingers curved with a reflexive movement, and as he straightened them again he looked at Malone with wondering blue eyes. "All the same it's a fact that you look peaked these days. Liver is excellent for the blood. You ought to eat crisp fried calf liver and beef liver smothered in onion sauce. It's both delicious and a natural cure. And sunlight is a blood moderator. I bet there's nothing wrong with you that sensible living and a spell of Milan summer won't cure." The Judge lifted his glass. "And this is the best tonic — stimulates the appetite and relaxes the nerves. J.T., you are just tense and intimidated."

"Judge Clane."

Grown Boy had entered the room and stood there waiting. He was the nephew of Verily, the colored woman who worked for the Judge, and he was a tall fat boy of sixteen who did not have his share of sense. He wore a light blue suit that was too tight for him and pointed tight shoes that made him walk in a gingerly crippled way. He had a cold and, although a handkerchief showed in his breast pocket, he wiped his running nose with the back of his hand.

"It's Sunday," he said.

The Judge reached in his pocket and gave him a coin.

As Grown Boy limped eagerly toward the fountain, he called back in a sweet slow voice, "Much obliged, Judge Clane."

The Judge was looking at Malone with quick sad glances but when the pharmacist turned back to him he avoided his eyes and began to massage his cane again.

"Every hour — each living soul comes closer to death — but how often do we think of it? We sit here having our whiskey and smoking our cigars and with each hour we approach our final end. Grown Boy eats his cone without ever wondering about anything. Here I sit, a ruin of an old man, and death has skirmished with me and the skirmish has ended in a stalemate. I am a stricken field on death's old battleground. For seventeen years since the death of my son, I have waited. Oh, Death, where is thy victory now? The victory was won that Christmas afternoon when my son took his own life."

"I have often thought of him," Malone said. "And grieved for you."

"And why — why did he do it? A son of such beauty and such promise — not yet twenty-five and graduated *magna cum laude* at the University. He had already taken his law degree and a great career could have been open to him. And with a beautiful young wife and a baby already on the way. He was well-to-do — even rich — that was the zenith of my fortunes. For a graduation present I gave him Sereno for which I had paid forty thousand dollars the year before — almost a thousand acres of the best peach land. He was the son of a rich man, fortune's darling, blessed in all ways, at the threshold of a great career. That boy could have been President — he could have been anything he wanted. Why should he die?"

Malone said cautiously, "Maybe it was a fit of melancholia."

"The night he was born I saw a remarkable falling star. It was a bright night and the star made an arc in the January sky. Miss Missy had been eight hours in labor and I had been groveling before the foot of her bed, praying and crying. Then Doc Tatum collared me and jerked me to the door saying, 'Get out of here you obstreperous old blunderbuss — get drunk in the pantry or go out in the yard.' And when I went out in the yard and looked at the sky, I saw the arc of that falling star and it was just then that Johnny, my son, was born."

"No doubt it was prophetic," Malone said.

"Later on I bustled into the kitchen — it was four o'clock — and fried Doc a brace of quail and cooked grits. I was always a great hand at frying quail." The Judge paused and then said timidly, "J.T., do you know something uncanny?"

Malone watched the sorrow on the Judge's face and did not answer.

"That Christmas we had quail for dinner instead of the usual turkey. Johnny, my son, had gone hunting the Sunday before. Ah, the patterns of life — both big and small."

To comfort the Judge, Malone said: "Maybe it was an accident. Maybe Johnny was cleaning his gun."

"It wasn't his gun. It was my pistol."

"I was hunting at Sereno that Sunday before Christmas. It was probably a fleeting depression."

"Sometimes I think it was — " The Judge stopped, for if he had said another word he might have cried. Malone patted his arm and the Judge, controlling himself, started again. "Sometimes I think it was to spite me."

"Oh, no! Surely not, sir. It was some depression that no one could have seen or controlled."

"Maybe," said the Judge, "but that very day we had been quarreling."

"What about it? Every family quarrels."

"My son was trying to break an axiom."

"Axiom? What kind of axiom?"

"It was about something inconsequential. It was a case about a black man it was my duty to sentence."

"You are just blaming yourself needlessly," Malone said.

"We were sitting at the table with coffee and cigars and French cognac — the ladies were in the parlor — and Johnny got more and more excited and finally he shouted something to me and rushed upstairs. We heard the shot a few minutes later."

"He was always impetuous."

"None of the young people these days seem to consult their elders. My son up and got married after a dance. He woke up his mother and me and said, 'Mirabelle and I are married.' They had eloped to a justice of the peace, mind you. It was a great grief to his mother — although later it was a blessing in disguise."

"Your grandson is the image of his father," Malone said.

"The living image. Have you ever seen two boys so shining?"

"It must be a great comfort to you."

The Judge mouthed his cigar before he answered: "Comfort — anxiety — he is all that is left."

"Is he going to study for the law and enter politics?"

"No!" the Judge said violently. "I don't want the boy in law or politics."

"Jester is a boy who could make his career in anything," Malone said.

"Death," said the old Judge, "is the great treachery. J.T., you feel the doctors believe you have a fatal disease. I don't think so. With all due respect to the medical profession, the doctors don't know what death is — who can know? Even Doc Tatum. I, an old man, have expected death for fifteen years. But death is too cunning. When you watch for it and finally face it, it never comes. It corners around sideways. It slays the unaware as often as it does the ones who watch for it. Oh, what, J.T.? What happened to my radiant son?"

"Fox," Malone asked, "do you believe in the eternal life?"

"I do as far as I can encompass the thought of eternity. I know that my son will always live within me, and my grandson within him and within me. But what is eternity?"

"At church," Malone said, "Dr. Watson preached a sermon on the salvation that draws a bead on death."

"A pretty phrase — I wish I had said it. But no sense at all." He added finally, "No, I don't believe in eternity as far as religion goes. I believe in the things I know and the descendants who come after me. I believe in my forebears, too. Do you call that eternity?"

Malone asked suddenly, "Have you ever seen a blue-eyed Nigra?"

"A Nigra with blue eyes you mean?"

Malone said, "I don't mean the weak-eyed blue of old colored people. I mean the gray-blue of a young colored boy. There's one like that around this town, and today he startled me."

The Judge's eyes were like blue bubbles and he finished his drink before he spoke. "I know the nigger you're thinking of."

"Who is he?"

"He's just a nigger around the town who's of no interest to me. He gives massages and caters — a jack-of-all-trades. Also, he is a well-trained singer."

Malone said, "I ran into him in an alley behind the store and he gave me such a shock."

The Judge said, with an emphasis that seemed at the moment peculiar to Malone, "Sherman Pew, that's the nigger's name, is of no interest to me. However, I'm thinking of taking him on as a houseboy because of the shortage of help."

"I never saw such strange eyes," Malone said.

"A woods colt," the Judge said; "something wrong between the sheets. He was left a foundling in the Holy Ascension Church."

Malone felt that the Judge had left some tale untold but far be it from him to pry into the manifold affairs of so great a man.

"Jester — speaking of the devil —"

John Jester Clane stood in the room with the sunlight from the street behind him. He was a slight limber boy of seventeen with auburn hair and a complexion so fair that the freckles on his upturned nose were like cinnamon sprinkled over cream. The glare brightened his red hair but his face was shadowed and he shielded his wine-brown eyes against the glare. He wore blue jeans and a striped jersey, the sleeves of which were pushed back to his delicate elbows.

"Down, Tige," Jester said. The dog was a brindle boxer, the only one of its kind in town. And she was such a fierce-looking brute that when Malone saw her on the street alone he was afraid of her.

"I soloed, Grandfather," Jester said in a voice that was lifted with excitement. Then, seeing Malone, he added politely, "Hey, Mr. Malone, how are you today?"

Tears of remembrance, pride and alcohol came to the Judge's weak eyes. "Soloed did you, darling? How did it feel?"

Jester considered a moment. "It didn't feel exactly like I had expected. I expected to feel lonely and somehow proud.

But I guess I was just watching the instruments. I guess I just felt — responsible."

"Imagine, J.T.," the Judge said, "a few months ago this little rapscallion just announced to me that he was taking flying lessons at the airport. He'd saved his own money and already made the arrangements for the course. But with not so much as by-my-leave. Just announced, 'Grandfather, I am taking flying lessons.'" The Judge stroked Jester's thigh. "Didn't you, Lambones?"

The boy drew up one long leg against another. "It's nothing to it. Everybody ought to be able to fly."

"What authority prompts the young folks these days to act on such unheard of decisions? It was never so in my day or yours, J.T. Can't you see now why I am so afraid?"

The Judge's voice was grieving, and Jester deftly removed his drink and hid it on a corner shelf. Malone noticed this and was offended on the Judge's behalf.

"It's dinnertime, Grandfather. The car is just down the street."

The Judge rose ponderously with his cane and the dog started to the door. "Whenever you're ready, Lambones." At the door he turned to Malone. "Don't let the doctors intimidate you, J.T. Death is the great gamer with a sleeve of tricks. You and I will maybe die together while following the funeral of a twelve-year-old girl." He pressed his cheek to Malone and crossed the threshold to the street.

Malone went to the front of the place to lock the main door and there he overheard a conversation. "Grandfather, I hate to say this but I do wish you wouldn't call me Lambones or darling in front of strangers."

At that moment Malone hated Jester. He was hurt at the term "stranger," and the glow that had warmed his spirit in the presence of the Judge was darkened instantly. In the old days, hospitality had lain in the genius of making everyone, even the commonest constituents at a barbecue, feel that they belonged. But nowadays the genius of hospitality had disappeared and there was only isolation. It was Jester who was a "stranger" — he had never been like a Milan boy. He was arrogant and at the same time overpolite. There was something hidden about the boy and his softness, his brightness seemed somehow dangerous — it was as though he resembled a silk-sheathed knife.

The Judge did not seem to hear his words. "Poor J.T.," he said as the door of the car was opened, "it's such a shocking thing."

Malone quickly locked the front door and returned to the compounding room.

He was alone. He sat in the rocking chair with the compounding pestle in his hands. The pestle was gray and smooth with use. He had bought it with the other fixtures of the pharmacy when he had opened his business twenty years ago. It had belonged to Mr. Greenlove — when had he last remembered him? — and at his death the estate sold the property. How long had Mr. Greenlove worked with this pestle? And who had used it before him? . . . The pestle was old, old and indestructible. Malone wondered if it wasn't a relic from Indian times. Ancient as it was, how long would it still last? The stone mocked Malone.

He shivered. It was as though a draft had chilled him, although he noticed that the cigar smoke was undisturbed. As he thought of the old Judge a mood of elegy softened his fear. He remembered Johnny Clane and the old days at Sereno. He was no stranger — many a time he had been a guest at Sereno during the hunting season — and once he had even spent the night there. He had slept in a big four-poster bed with Johnny and at five in the morning they had gone down to the kitchen, and he still remembered the smell of fish roe and hot biscuits and the wet-dog smell as they breakfasted before the hunt. Yes, many a time he had hunted with Johnny Clane and had been invited to Sereno, and he was there the Sunday before the Christmas Johnny died. And Miss Missy would sometimes go there, although it was mainly a hunting place for boys and men. And the Judge, when he shot badly, which was nearly all the time, would complain that there was so much sky and so few birds. Always there was a mystery about Sereno even in those days — but was it the mystery of luxury that a boy born poor will always feel? As Malone remembered the old days and thought of the Judge now — in his wisdom and fame and inconsolable grief — his heart sang with love as grave and somber as the organ music in the church.

As he stared at the pestle his eyes were brilliant with fever and fear and, transfixed, he did not notice that from the basement underneath the store there was a knocking sound. Before this spring he had always held to a basic rhythm about life and death — the Bible rhythm of the three-score years and ten. But now he dwelt on the inexplicable deaths. He thought of children, exact and delicate as jewels in their white satin coffins. And that pretty singing teacher who swallowed a bone at a fish fry and died within the hour. And Johnny Clane, and the Milan boys who died during the first war and the last. And how many others? How? Why? He was aware of the knocking sound in the basement. It was a rat — last week a rat had overturned a bottle of asafetida and for days the stench was so terrible that his porter refused to work in the basement. There was no rhythm in death — only the rhythm of the rat, and the stench of corruption. And the pretty singing teacher, the blond young flesh of Johnny Clane — the jewel-like children — all ended in the liquefying corpse and coffin stench. He looked at the pestle with a sick surprise for only the stone remained.

There was a footstep on the threshold and Malone was so suddenly unnerved that he dropped the pestle. The blue-eyed nigger stood before him, holding in his hand something that glinted in the sun. Again he stared into those blazing eyes and again he felt that look of eerie understanding and sensed that those eyes knew that he was soon to die.

"I found this just outside the door," the nigger said.

Malone's vision was dimmed by shock and for a moment he thought it was the paper knife of Dr. Hayden — then he saw it was a bunch of keys on a silver ring.

"They're not mine," Malone said.

"I noticed Judge Clane and his boy was here. Maybe they're theirs." The nigger dropped the keys on the table. Then he picked up the pestle and handed it to Malone.

"Much obliged," he said. "I'll inquire about the keys."

The boy went away and Malone watched him jay-walk across the street. He was cold with loathing and hatred.

As he sat holding the pestle there was in him enough composure to wonder at those alien emotions that had veered so violently in his once mild heart. He was split between love and hatred — but what he loved and what he hated was unclear. For the first time he *knew* that death was near him. But the terror that choked him was not caused by the knowledge of his own death. The terror concerned some mysterious drama that was going on — although what the drama was about Malone did not know. The terror questioned what would happen in those months — how long? — that glared upon his numbered days. He was a man watching a clock without hands.

There was the rhythm of the rat. "Father, Father, help me," Malone said aloud. But his father had been dead for these long years. When the telephone rang Malone told his wife for the first time that he was sick and asked her to drive to the pharmacy and take him home. Then he sat stroking the stone pestle as a sort of comfort as he waited.

2

THE JUDGE kept the old-fashioned dinner hours and dinner on Sundays was at two o'clock. Shortly before the time to ring the dinner chimes, Verily, the cook, opened the shutters of the dining room which had been closed all morning against the glare. The midsummer heat and light beat at the windows and beyond there was the burnt lawn and the fever-bright border of flowers. Some elm trees at the end of the lawn were dark and breezeless in the lacquered brightness of the afternoon. Jester's dog responded first to the dinner summons — he walked slowly under the table, letting the long damask cloth linger against his spine. Then Jester appeared and stood waiting behind his grandfather's chair. When the old Judge entered, he seated him carefully and then took his own place at the table. The dinner began according to custom and as usual vegetable soup was the first course. With the soup two breads were served — beaten biscuits and cornsticks. The old Judge ate greedily, sipping buttermilk between swallows of bread. Jester could manage only a few spoonfuls of the hot soup and he drank iced tea and held the cold glass to his cheek and forehead from time to time. According to the habits of the house, there was no conversation during the soup course except for the Judge's customary Sunday remark: "Verily, Verily, I say unto you: you shall dwell in the house of the Lord forever." He added his little Sunday joke: "If you cook this well."

Verily said nothing — only pursed her purplish wrinkled lips.

"Malone has always been one of my most loyal constituents and best supporters," the Judge said when the chicken was brought and Jester had stood up to carve. "You keep the liver, Son, you ought to have liver at least once a week."

"Yes, Grandfather."

So far the meal was consonant with habits and the customs of the house. But later a strange dissonance appeared, a jolt in the usual harmony, a sense of cross purposes and communication deflected and estranged. Neither the old Judge nor his grandson realized what happened at the time, but at the end of the long, hot, customary meal they both felt that something had altered so that their relationship could never again be the same.

"The *Atlanta Constitution* today referred to me as a reactionary," the Judge said.

Jester said softly: "I'm sorry."

"Sorry," said the old Judge. "It's nothing to be sorry about. I'm glad!"

Jester's brown eyes exchanged a long, asking stare.

"You must take the word 'reactionary' literally these days.

A reactionary is a citizen who *reacts* when the age-long standards of the South are threatened. When States' rights are trampled on by the Federal Government, then the Southern patriot is duty-bound to react. Otherwise the noble standards of the South will be betrayed."

"What noble standards?" Jester asked.

"Why, boy, use your head. The noble standards of our way of life, the traditional institutions of the South."

Jester did not say anything but his eyes were skeptical and the old Judge, sensitive to all his grandson's reactions, noticed this.

"The Federal Government is trying to question the legality of the Democratic Primary so that the whole balance of Southern civilization will be jeopardized."

Jester asked, "How?"

"Why, boy, I'm referring to segregation itself."

"Why are you always harping on segregation?"

"Why, Jester, you're joking."

Jester was suddenly serious. "No, I'm not."

The Judge was baffled. "The time may come in your generation — I hope I won't be here — when the educational system itself is mixed — with no color line. How would you like that?"

Jester did not answer.

"How would you like to see a hulking Nigra boy sharing a desk with a delicate little white girl?"

The Judge could not believe in the possibility of this; he wanted to shock Jester to the gravity of the situation. His eyes challenged his grandson to react in the spirit of Southern gentlemen.

"How about a hulking white girl sharing a desk with a delicate little Negro boy?"

"What?"

Jester did not repeat his words, nor did the old Judge want to hear again the words that so alarmed him. It was as though his grandson had committed some act of incipient lunacy, and it is fearful to acknowledge the approach of madness in a beloved. It is so fearful that the old Judge preferred to distrust his own hearing, although the sound of Jester's voice still throbbed against his eardrums. He tried to twist the words to his own reason.

"You're right, Lambones, whenever I read such communist ideas I realize how unthinkable the notions are. Certain things are just too preposterous to consider."

Jester said slowly: "That's not what I meant." From habit Jester glanced to see if Verily was out of the room. "I can't see why colored people and white people shouldn't mix as citizens."

"Oh, Son!" It was a cry of pity, helplessness, and horror. Years ago when Jester was a child he had been occasionally subject to sudden vomiting fits at the table. Then, tenderness had overcome disgust, and afterward the Judge had felt himself sickish in sympathy. Now the old Judge responded to this sudden situation in the same way. He held his good hand to his ear as if he had an earache and he stopped eating.

Jester noticed the old Judge's distress and he felt a tremor of sympathy. "Grandfather, we all have our own convictions."

"Some convictions are not tenable convictions. After all, what are convictions? They're just what you think. And you are too young, Son, to have learned the pattern of thought. You are just deviling your grandfather with foolish words."

Jester's emotion of sympathy withered. He was staring at a picture over the mantelpiece. The picture was a Southern scene of a peach orchard and a Negro shack and a cloudy sky.

"Grandfather, what do you see in that picture?"

The Judge was so relieved that the tension had snapped that he chuckled a little. "The Lord knows it ought to remind me of my folly. I lost a small fortune with those pretty peach trees. Your Great-aunt Sara painted it the year she died. And then right along afterward the bottom dropped out of the peach market."

"I mean, what do you actually see in the picture?"

"Why, there's an orchard and clouds and a Nigra shack."

"Do you see there between the shack and the trees a pink mule?"

"A *pink mule?*" The Judge's blue eyes popped in alarm. "Why naturally not."

"It's a cloud," Jester said. "And it looks to me exactly like a pink mule with a gray bridle. Now that I see it that way, I can't see the picture any other way any more."

"I don't see it."

"Why you can't miss it, galloping upward — a whole sky of pink mules."

Verily came in with the dish of corn pudding: "Why, mercy, what's the matter with you all. You ain't scarcely touch your dinner."

"All my life I had seen the picture like Aunt Sara had intended it. And now this summer I can't see what I'm supposed to see in it. I try to look back as I used to see it — but it's no good. I still see the pink mule."

"Do you feel dizzy, Lambones?"

"Why no. I'm just trying to explain to you that this picture is a sort of — symbol — I guess you might say. All my life I've seen things like you and the family wanted me to see them. And now this summer I don't see things as I used to — and I have different feelings, different thoughts."

"That's only natural, Son." The Judge's voice was reassuring, but his eyes were still anxious.

"A symbol," Jester said. He repeated the word because it was the first time he had spoken it in conversation, although it was one of his favorite words in school compositions. "A symbol of this summertime. I used to have ideas exactly like everybody else. And now I have my own ideas."

"Such as?"

Jester did not answer for a moment. And when he spoke his voice broke with tension and adolescence. "For one thing, I question the justice of white supremacy."

The challenge was plain as a loaded pistol flung across the table. But the Judge could not accept it; his throat was dry and aching and he swallowed feebly.

"I know it's a shock to you, Grandfather. But I had to tell you, otherwise you would have taken it for granite I was like I used to be."

"Take it for granted," the Judge corrected. "Not *granite*. What kind of wild-eyed radicals have you been consorting with?"

"Nobody. This summer I've been very —" Jester was going to say *I've been very lonely,* but he could not bring himself to admit this truth aloud.

"Well, all I say is, this talk about mixed races and pink mules in the picture are certainly — abnormal."

The word struck Jester like a blow in the groin and he flushed violently. The pain made him strike back: "All my life I have loved you — I even worshiped you, Grandfather. I thought you were the wisest, kindest man on earth. I listened to everything you said like gospel truth. I saved everything in print about you. My scrapbook on you was started as soon as I began to read. I always thought you ought to be — President."

The Judge ignored the past tense and there was the warmth of self-pride in his veins. A mirrorlike projection reflected his

own feelings for his grandson — the fair, unfolding child of
his fair doomed son. Love and memory left his heart open and
unaware.

"That time I heard about when that Negro from Cuba was
making a talk in the House I was so proud of you. When the
other congressmen stood up you sat back farther in your chair,
propped your feet up and lighted a cigar. I thought it was
wonderful. I was so proud of you. But now I see it differently.
It was rude and bad manners. I am ashamed for you when
I remember it. When I think back how I used to worship
you —"

Jester could not finish, for the distress of the old Judge was
obvious. His crippled arm tightened and his hand curled hard
and spastic while the elbow joint crooked uncontrollably. The
shock of Jester's words interacted with his disorder so that
tears of emotional and physical hurt started. He blew his nose
and said after some moments of silence: "Far sharper than
a serpent's tooth it is to have a thankless child."

But Jester resented the fact that his grandfather was so
vulnerable. "But Grandfather, you've talked all you want to
always. And I have listened and believed. But now that I
have a few opinions of my own, you won't stand for it and
start quoting the Bible. That isn't fair because it automatically
puts a person in the wrong."

"It's not the Bible — Shakespeare."

"Anyway I'm not your child. I'm your grandson and my
father's child."

The fan turned in the breathless afternoon and the sun
shone on the dining table with the platter of carved chicken
and the butter melted in the butter dish. Jester held the cool
tea glass to his cheek and fondled it before he spoke.

"Sometimes I wonder if I'm not beginning to suspect why
my father — did what he did."

The dead still lived in the ornate, Victorian house with the cumbersome furniture. The dressing room of the Judge's wife was still kept as it was in her lifetime with her silver appointments on the bureau and the closet with her clothes untouched except for occasional dusting. And Jester grew up with his father's photographs, and in the library there was the framed certificate of admittance to the bar. But though all through the house there were reminders of the lives of the dead, the actual circumstance of death was never mentioned, even by inference.

"What did you mean by that?" the old Judge asked with apprehension.

"Nothing," Jester said. "Except it is natural to wonder about my father's death under the circumstances."

The Judge tinkled the dinner bell and the sound seemed to gather the tension in the room. "Verily, bring a bottle of that elderberry wine Mr. Malone brought me for my birthday."

"Right now, today, sir?" she asked, as wine was usually served only at Thanksgiving and Christmas dinners. She took the wineglasses from the sideboard and wiped off the dust with her apron. Noticing the platter of uneaten food, she wondered if a hair or a fly had been cooked in the candied yams or dressing. "Is anything wrong with the dinner?"

"Oh, it's delicious. I just have a mite of indigestion, I suppose."

It was true that when Jester talked of the mixing of races his stomach seemed to churn and all appetite had left him. He opened and poured the unaccustomed wine, then drank as soberly as if he had been drinking at a wake. For the break in understanding, in sympathy, is indeed a form of death. The Judge was hurt and grieving. And when hurt has been caused by a loved one, only the loved one can comfort.

Slowly he put his right hand palm upward on the table toward his grandson, and after a moment Jester placed his own palm on his grandfather's. But the Judge was not satisfied; since words had hurt him, his solace lay in words. He grasped Jester's hand in desperation.

"Don't you love your old grandfather any more?"

Jester took his hand away and drank some swallows of wine. "Sure I do, Grandfather, but —"

And though the Judge waited, Jester did not finish the sentence and the emotion was left qualified in the strained room. The Judge's hand was left extended and the fingers fluttered a little.

"Son, has it ever occurred to you that I am not a wealthy man any longer? I have suffered many losses and our forebears suffered losses. Jester, I'm worried about your education and your future."

"Don't worry. I can manage."

"You've heard the old saw about the best things in life are free. It's both true and false like all generalizations. But this one thing is true: you can get the best education in this country absolutely and entirely free. West Point is free and I could get you an appointment."

"But I don't want to be an army officer."

"What do you want to be?"

Jester was perplexed, uncertain. "I don't know exactly. I like music and I like flying."

"Well go to West Point and enter the Air Corps. Anything you can get from the Federal Government you ought to take advantage of. God knows the Federal Government has done enough damage to the South."

"I don't have to decide about the future until I graduate from high school next year."

"What I was pointing out, Son, is my finances are not what

they used to be. But if my plans materialize, then one day you will be a wealthy man." The Judge had often made vague hints from time to time of future wealth. Jester had never paid much attention to these intimations, but now he asked:

"What plans, Grandfather?"

"Son, I wonder if you are old enough to understand the strategy." The Judge cleared his throat. "You're young and the dream is big."

"What is it?"

"It's a plan to correct damages done and to restore the South."

"How?"

"It's the dream of a statesman — not just a cheap political scheme. It's a plan to rectify an immense historical injustice."

Ice cream had been served and Jester was eating, but the Judge let it melt in his saucer. "I still don't get the drift, sir."

"Think, Son. In any war between civilized nations what happens to the currency of the country who didn't win? Think of World War I and World War II. What happened to the German mark after the armistice? Did the Germans burn their money? And the Japanese yen? Did the Japanese make bonfires of their currency after their defeat? Did they, Son?"

"No," Jester said, bewildered by the vehemence of the old man's voice.

"What happens in any civilized nation after the cannons are silenced and the battlefields are quiet? The victor allows the vanquished to rest and restore in the interests of the common economics. The currency of a conquered nation is always redeemed — devalued, but still redeemed. Redeemed: look what is happening now in Germany — in Japan. The Federal Government has redeemed the enemy money and helped the vanquished restore itself. From time immemorial the currency of a defeated nation has been left in circulation.

And the lira in Italy — did the Federal Government confiscate the lira? The lira, the yen, the mark — all, all were redeemed."

The Judge was leaning forward over the table and his tie brushed his saucer of melted ice cream, but he did not notice.

"But what happened after the War Between the States? Not only did the Federal Government of the United States free the slaves which were the *sine qua non* of our cotton economy, so that the very resources of the nation were gone with the wind. A truer story was never written than *Gone With the Wind*. Remember how we cried at that picture show?"

Jester said: "I didn't cry."

"You certainly did," the Judge said. "I wish I had written that book."

Jester did not comment.

"But back to the issue. Not only was the economy of the nation deliberately wrecked, but the Federal Government completely invalidated all Confederate currency. Not one cent could be redeemed for the wealth of the entire Confederacy. I have heard of Confederate bills used as kindling for fires."

"There used to be a whole trunk of Confederate bills in the attic. I wonder what happened to them."

"They're in the library in my safety box."

"Why? Aren't they worthless?"

The Judge did not answer; instead, he pulled from his vest pocket a Confederate thousand-dollar bill. Jester examined it with some of the wonder of his attic-playing childhood. The bill was so real, so green and believable. But the wonder illumined him only for a few instants, then was extinguished. Jester handed the bill back to his grandfather.

"It would be a lot of money if it was real."

"One of these days it might be 'real' as you say. It will be, if my strength and work and vision can make it so."

Jester questioned his grandfather with his cold clear eyes. Then he said: "The money is nearly a hundred years old."

"And think of the hundreds of billions of dollars squandered by the Federal Government during those hundred years. Think of the wars financed and public spending. Think of the other currencies redeemed and put back into circulation. The mark, the lira, the yen — all foreign currencies. And the South was, after all, the same flesh and blood and should have been treated as brothers. The currency should have been redeemed and *not* devalued. Don't you see that, Lamb?"

"Well it wasn't and it's too late now."

The conversation made Jester uneasy and he wanted to leave the table and go away. But his grandfather held him with a gesture.

"Wait a minute. It's never too late to redress a wrong. And I am going to be instrumental in allowing the Federal Government to redress this historic and monumental wrong," the Judge stated pontifically. "I am going to have a bill introduced in the House of Representatives if I win the next election that will redeem all Confederate monies, with the proper adjustment for the increase of cost-of-living nowadays. It will be for the South what F.D.R. intended to do in his New Deal. It will revolutionize the economy of the South. And you, Jester, will be a wealthy young man. There are ten million dollars in that safety box. What do you say to that?"

"How did that much Confederate money accumulate?"

"There are ancestors of vision in our family — remember that, Jester. My grandmother, your great-great-grandmother, was a great lady and a woman of vision. When the war was over she traded for Confederate money, swapping now and then a few eggs and produce — once I remember her telling me she even swapped a laying hen for three million dollars. Everybody was hungry in those days and everybody had lost faith. All except your great-great-grandmother. I will never forget her saying: 'It will come back, it's bound to.'"

"But it never has," Jester said.

"Until now — but you wait and see. It will be a New Deal for the economy of the South and benefit the nation as a whole. Even the Federal Government will be benefited."

"How?" Jester asked.

The Judge said calmly, "What benefits one benefits the whole. It's simple to understand; if I had a few million, I would invest, employ a lot of people and stimulate local business. And I'm just one individual to be reimbursed."

"Another thing," Jester said. "It's been about a hundred years. And how could the money be traced?"

The Judge's voice was triumphant. "That's the least of our worries. When the Treasury announces that Confederate money is being redeemed, the money will be found all right. Confederate bills will be cropping up in attics and barns all over the South. Cropping up all over the nation and even in Canada."

"What good would it do to have money cropping up in Canada?"

The Judge said with dignity: "That's just a figure of speech — a rhetorical example." The Judge looked hopefully at his grandson. "But what do you think of the legislation as a whole?"

Jester avoided his grandfather's eyes and did not answer. And the Judge, desperate for his approval, persisted. "What, Lamb? It's the vision of a great statesman," he added more firmly. "The *Journal* has many times referred to me as a 'great statesman' and the *Courier* always speaks of me as the first citizen of Milan. Once it was written I was 'one of the fixed stars in that glorious firmament of Southern statesmen.' Don't you admit I am a great statesman?"

The question was not only a plea for reassurance, but a desperate command for emotional annealment. Jester could not answer. For the first time he wondered if his grandfather's reasoning power had been affected by the stroke. And his heart balanced between pity and the natural instinct for separation that divides the sound from the infirm.

The veins of age and excitement crawled in the Judge's temple and his face flushed. Only twice in his life had the Judge suffered from rejection: once when he was defeated in an election for Congress, and again when he sent a long story he had written to the *Saturday Evening Post* and it was returned to him with a form letter. The Judge could not believe this rejection. He read the story again and found it better than all the other stories in the *Post*. Then, suspecting that it had not been properly read, he glued certain pages of the manuscript together and when it was returned another time he never read a *Post* again, and never wrote another story. Now he could not believe that the separation between himself and his grandson was a reality.

"Do you remember how, when you were a little boy, you used to call me Grandy?"

Jester was not moved by the recollection and the tears in his grandfather's eyes irritated him. "I remember everything." He rose and stood behind the Judge's chair, but his grandfather would not get up and would not let him leave. He grasped Jester's hand and held it to his cheek. Jester stood stiff with embarrassment and his hand did not respond to the caress.

"I never thought I'd hear a grandson of mine speak as you have done. You said you didn't see why the races shouldn't mix. Think of the logical outcome. It would lead to inter-

marriage. How would you like that? Would you let your
sister marry a Nigra buck if you had a sister?"

"I'm not thinking of that. I was thinking of racial justice."

"But if your so-called 'racial justice' leads to intermarriage
— as it will according to the laws of logic — would you marry
a Nigra? Be truthful."

Involuntarily, Jester was thinking of Verily and the other
cooks and washwomen who had worked at home, and of Aunt
Jemima of the pancake ads. His face flushed bright and his
freckles darkened. He could not answer immediately, so much
did the image appall him.

"You see," the Judge said. "You were only making empty
lip-service — for the Northerners, at that."

Jester said: "I still think that as a judge you judge one crime
in two different ways — according to whether it is done by a
Negro or a white man."

"Naturally. They are two different things. White is white
and black is black — and never the two shall meet if I can
prevent it."

The Judge laughed and held Jester's hand when he tried
to pull away again.

"All my life I have been concerned with questions of justice.
And after your father's death I realized that justice itself is
a chimera, a delusion. Justice is not a flat yardstick, applied in
equal measure to an equal situation. After your father's death
I realized there was a quality more important than justice."

Jester's attention was always held by any reference to his
father and his death. "What is more important, Grandfather?"

"Passion," the Judge said. "Passion is more important than
justice."

Jester stiffened with embarrassment. "Passion? Did my
father have passion?"

The Judge evaded the question. "Young people of your

generation have no passion. They have cut themselves off from the ideals of their ancestors and are denying the heritage of their blood. Once when I was in New York, I saw a Nigra man sitting at a table with a white girl and something in my bloodstream sickened. My outrage had nothing particularly to do with justice — but when I saw those two laughing together and eating at the same table, my bloodstream — I left New York that same day and never went back to that Babel, nor will to my dying day."

"I wouldn't have minded at all," Jester said. "Soon, as a matter of fact, I am going to New York."

"That's what I meant. You have no passion."

The words affected Jester violently; he trembled and blushed. "I don't see —"

"One of these days you may have this passion. And when it comes to you, your half-baked notions of so-called justice will be forgotten. And you will be a man and my grandson — with whom I am well pleased."

Jester held the chair while the Judge pushed himself up from the table with his stick and stood upright for a moment facing the picture above the mantelpiece. "Wait a minute, Lamb." He sought desperately some words that would abridge the chasm that had opened in the last two hours. And finally he said: "You know, Jester, I can see the pink mule you were talking about — there in the sky over the orchard and the shack."

The admission altered nothing and they both knew it. The Judge walked slowly and Jester stood near him ready to steady him if necessary. His pity mingled with remorse and he hated pity and remorse. When his grandfather was settled on the library sofa, he said: "I'm glad you know how I stand. I'm glad I told you." But the tears in his grandfather's eyes unnerved him so that he was forced to add: "I love you anyway — I do love you — Grandy." But when he was embraced, the smell of sweat and the sentimentality disgusted him, and when he had freed himself he felt a sense of defeat.

He ran out of the room and bounded up the staircase three steps at a time. At the head of the upstairs hall there was a window of stained glass which brightened Jester's auburn hair but cast a sallow light on his breathless face. He closed the door of his room and flung himself on the bed.

It was true he had no passion. The shame of his grandfather's words pulsed in his body and he felt that the old man knew that he was a virgin. His hard boy's hands unzipped his fly and touched his genitals for solace. Other boys he knew boasted of love affairs and even went to a house run by a woman called Reba. This place fascinated Jester; on the outside it was an ordinary frame house with a trellis on the porch and a potato vine. The very ordinariness of the house fascinated and appalled him. He would walk around the block and his heart felt challenged and defeated. Once, in the late afternoon, he saw a woman come out of the house and he watched her. She was an ordinary woman wearing a blue dress and with her lips gummed up with lipstick. He should have been passionate. But as she glanced at him casually, the shame of his secret defeat made him draw up one foot against the other leg and stand stricken until the woman turned away. Then he ran all the six blocks to his house and flung himself on the same bed where he lay now.

No, he had no passion, but he had had love. Sometimes, for a day, a week, a month, once for a whole year. The one year's love was for Ted Hopkins who was the best all-around athlete in the school. Jester would seek Ted's eyes in the corridor and, although his pulses pounded, they only spoke to each other twice in that year.

One time was when they entered the vestibule together on a raining day and Ted said, "It's foul weather."

Jester responded in a faint voice, "Foul."

The other conversation was longer and less casual but completely humiliating. Because Jester loved Ted, he wanted more than anything to give him a gift and impress himself upon him. In the beginning of the football season, he saw in a jeweler's a little golden football. He bought this but it took him four days to give it to Ted. They had to be alone for him to give it and after days of following, they met in the locker room in Ted's section. Jester held out the football with a trembling hand and Ted asked, "What's this?" Jester knew somehow, someway, he had made a mistake. Hurriedly, he explained, "I found it."

"Why do you want to give it to me?"

Jester was dizzy with shame. "Just because I don't have any use for it and I thought I would give it to you."

As Ted's blue eyes looked mockingly and suspiciously, Jester blushed the warm painful blush of the very fair and his freckles darkened.

"Well thanks," Ted said, and put the gold football in his trousers pocket.

Ted was the son of an army officer who was stationed in a town fifteen miles from Milan, so this love was shadowed by the thought that his father would be transferred. And his feelings, furtive and secret as they were, were intensified by the menace of separation and the aura of distance and adventure.

Jester avoided Ted after the football episode and afterward he could never think about football or the words "foul weather" without a cringing shame.

He loved, too, Miss Pafford who taught English and wore bangs but put on no lipstick. Lipstick was repulsive to Jester, and he could not understand how anyone could kiss a woman who wore gummy smeary lipstick. But since nearly all girls and women wore lipstick, Jester's loves were severely limited.

Hot, blank and formless, the afternoon stretched ahead of him. And since Sunday afternoons are the longest afternoons of all, Jester went to the airport and did not come back until suppertime. After supper, he still felt blank, depressed. He went to his room and flung himself on his bed as he had done after dinner.

As he lay there sweating and still unsolaced, a sudden spasm lifted him. He was hearing from far away a tune played on the piano and a dark voice singing, although what the tune was or where it was coming from he did not know. Jester raised up on his elbow, listening and looking into the night. It was a blues tune, voluptuous and grieving. The music came from the lane behind the Judge's property where Negroes lived. As the boy listened the jazz sadness blossomed and was left unshattered.

Jester got up and went downstairs. His grandfather was in the library and he slipped into the night unnoticed. The music came from the third house in the lane, and when he knocked and knocked again the music stopped and the door was opened.

He had not prepared himself for what he would say, and he stood speechless in the doorway, knowing only that something overwhelming was about to happen to him. He faced for the first time the Negro with the blue eyes and, facing him, he trembled. The music still throbbed in his body and Jester quailed when he faced the blue eyes opposite him. They were cold and blazing in the dark and sullen face. They reminded him of something that made him quiver with sudden shame. He questioned wordlessly the overwhelming feeling. Was it fear? Was it love? Or was it — at last, was it — passion? The jazz sadness shattered.

Still not knowing, Jester went into the room and shut the door.

3

THE SAME midsummer evening while the scent of honey-
suckle lingered in the air, J. T. Malone made an unexpected
visit to the old Judge's house. The Judge went early to bed
and was an early riser; at nine in the evening he sloshed
mightily in his evening bath and the same procedure happened at four in the morning. Not that he liked it. He would
have liked to be safe in the arms of Morpheus until six o'clock
or even seven like other people. But the habit of being an early
riser had got into him and he couldn't break it. The Judge
held that a person as corpulent and free-sweating as he was
needed two baths a day, and those who were around him
would agree with this. So at those crepuscular hours the old
Judge would be splashing, snorting and singing . . . his favorite
bathtub songs were "On the Trail of the Lonesome Pine"

and "I'm a Rambling Wreck from Georgia Tech." That evening he did not sing with the usual gusto, as his talk with his
grandson had troubled him, nor did he put toilet water behind each ear as he might have done. He had gone to Jester's
room before his bath but the boy was not there, nor did he
answer from the yard. The Judge was wearing a white dimity
nightshirt and clutching a dressing gown when the doorbell
rang. Expecting his grandson, he went downstairs and crossed
the hall barefooted and with his robe slung negligently on his
arm. Both friends were surprised to see each other. Malone
tried to avoid looking at the too-small bare feet of the very fat
Judge, as the Judge struggled into his robe.

"What brings you here this time of the night?" the Judge
said in a tone as though midnight had long since passed.

Malone said, "I was just out walking and thought I might
step in for a moment." Malone looked frightened and desperate and the Judge was not deceived by his words.

"As you see I've just finished with my bath. Come up and
we can have a little nightcap. I'm always more comfortable
in my own room after eight o'clock. I'll pile in my bed and you
can lie in the long French chair . . . or vice versa. What's
bothering you? You look like you've been chased by a banshee,
J.T."

"I feel like it," Malone said. Unable to bear the truth alone,
that evening he had told Martha about the leukemia. He had
run from his own house in terror and alarm, fleeing for comfort or solace anywhere. He had dreaded in advance the intimacy that tragedy might have restored from the distant
casualness of his married life, but the reality of that soft summer evening was worse than any dread. Martha had cried,
insisted on bathing his face with cologne and talked of the
children's future. In fact, his wife had not questioned the
medical report and behaved as though she believed that her

husband was incurably sick and was in fact a slowly dying man. This grief and credence exasperated and horrified Malone. As the hours passed the scene grew worse. Martha talked about their honeymoon at Blowing Rock, North Carolina, and the births of the children and the trips they had taken and the unexpected changes in life. She even mentioned, in connection with the children's education, her Coca-Cola stock. Modest, Victorian lady — almost sexless it had seemed to Malone at times. This lack of interest in sex had often made him feel gross, indelicate, almost uncouth. The final horror of the evening was when Martha unexpectedly, so unexpectedly, referred to sex.

Martha was embracing the unnerved Malone when she cried, "What can I do?" And she used the phrase that had not been said for years and years. It used to be the phrase for the act of love. It originated when Ellen was a baby who watched the older children do handsprings on the Malone summer lawn. The small Ellen would call out when her father came home from work, "You want me to do a handspring for you, Daddy?" and that phrase of summer evenings, wet lawns and childhood had been their word for the sexual act when they were young. Now the twenty-years-married Martha used the word, her bridges carefully placed in a glass of water. Malone was horrified knowing that, not only was he going to die, but some part of him had died also without his having realized. So quickly, wordlessly, he hurried out into the night.

The old Judge led the way, his bare feet very pink against the dark blue carpet, and Malone followed. They were both glad of the comfort of each other's presence. "I told my wife," Malone said, "about that . . . leukemia."

They passed into the Judge's bedroom where there was an immense four-poster bed with a canopy and feather pillows.

The draperies were rich and musty and next to the window there was a chaise longue which he indicated to Malone before he turned his attention to the whiskey and poured drinks. "J.T., have you ever noticed that when someone has a failing, that fault is the first and foremost thing he attributes to another? Say a man is greedy . . . greed is the first thing he accuses in others, or stinginess . . . that is the first fault a stingy man can recognize." Warming to his subject the Judge almost shouted his next words, "And it takes a thief to catch a thief . . . a thief to catch a thief."

"I know," Malone replied, somewhat at a loss to find a hinge to the subject. "I don't see . . ."

"I'm getting around to that," the Judge said with authority. "Some months ago you were telling me about Dr. Hayden and thoses little peculiar things in the blood."

"Yes," Malone said, still puzzled.

"Well, this very morning while Jester and I were coming home from the drugstore, I chanced to see Dr. Hayden and I was never so shocked."

"Why?"

The Judge said: "The man was a sick man. I never saw a man fall off so rapidly."

Malone tried to digest the intimations involved. "You mean . . . ?"

The Judge's voice was calm and firm. "I mean, if Dr. Hayden has a peculiar blood disease, it is the most likely thing in the world to diagnose onto you instead of himself." Malone pondered over this fantastic reasoning, wondering if there was a straw to grasp. "After all, J.T., I have had a great fund of medical experience; I was in Johns Hopkins for close on to three months."

Malone was remembering the doctor's hands and arms. "It's true that Hayden has very thin and hairy arms."

The Judge almost snorted: "Don't be silly, J.T., hairiness has nothing to do with it." Malone, abashed, was more willing to listen to the Judge's reasoning. "The doctor didn't tell you that out of meanness or spite," the Judge went on. "It's just the logical, human way of contaging bad things away from yourself. The minute I saw him today, I knew what had happened. I knew that look of a mortally sick man . . . looking sideways, his eyes averted as though ashamed. I have seen that look many a time at Johns Hopkins where I was a perfectly well, ambulatory patient who knew every soul at that hospital," the Judge said truthfully. "Whereas your eyes are straight as a die, although you're thin and ought to eat liver. Liver shots," he said almost shouting, "aren't there things called liver shots for blood trouble?"

Malone looked at the Judge with eyes that flickered between bewilderment and hope. "I didn't know you were in Johns Hopkins," he said softly. "I suppose you didn't bruit it around because of your political career."

"Ten years ago I weighed three hundred and ten pounds."

"You've always carried your weight well. I've never thought of you as a fat man."

"Fat man: of course not. I was just stout and corpulent . . . the only thing, I would just have falling-out spells. It worried Miss Missy," he said with a glance at his wife's portrait on the wall across from him. "She even spoke about doctors . . . harped on the subject, in fact. I had never gone to a doctor in my adult life, feeling instinctively that doctors meant either cutting or, just as bad, diet. I was close friends with Doc Tatum who used to fish and hunt with me, but he was in a different category . . . otherwise I just let doctors alone and hoped they would leave me alone. Except for the falling-out spells I was in the pink of health. When Doc Tatum died I had a terrible toothache . . . I think it was psychosomatic, so I went to Doc's brother who was the best mule doctor in the county. I drank."

"Mule doctor!" His faith in the Judge's reasoning echoed with a sick dismay. The old Judge did not seem to notice.

"Naturally, it was the week of Doc's funeral, and what with the wake and cortege and all, my tooth hurt like an electric bell . . . so Poke, Doc's brother, just drew the tooth for me . . . with novocain and antibiotics which he uses for mules anyhow, as their teeth are strong and they are very stubborn about anybody fooling with their mouths and very sensitive."

Malone nodded wonderingly, and as his disappointment still echoed, he changed the subject abruptly. "That portrait is the living image of Miss Missy."

"Sometimes I think so," the Judge said complacently, as he was one of those persons who felt that anything he owned was greatly superior to the possessions of others . . . even if they were identical. He added reflectively:

"Sometimes when I am sad or pessimistic I think that Sara made a bad mistake with the left foot . . . at my worst moments it sometimes resembles a kind of odd tail."

"I don't see that at all, sir," Malone said comfortingly. "Besides it's the face, the countenance that matters."

"All the same," the Judge said passionately, "I wish my wife's portrait had been painted by Sir Joshua Reynolds or one of the great masters."

"Well that's another story," Malone said, looking at the badly drawn portrait done by the Judge's elder sister.

"I have learned not to settle for the cheapest, homemade product . . . especially when it comes to art. But at that time I never dreamed that Miss Missy was going to die and leave me."

Tears brightened the dim, old eyes and he was silent, for the garrulous old Judge could never speak about his wife's death.

Malone was also silent, remembering. The Judge's wife had died of cancer and it was Malone who had filled the doctor's prescriptions during her long illness, and he often visited her — sometimes bringing flowers from his garden or a bottle of cologne as though to soften the fact that he was delivering morphine. Often the Judge would be lumbering bleakly about the house, as he stayed with his wife as much as possible even, Malone thought, to the detriment of his political career. Miss Missy had developed cancer of the breast and it had been removed. The Judge's grief was boundless; he haunted the halls of the city hospital, harrying even doctors who had nothing to do with the case, weeping, questioning. He organized prayers at the First Baptist Church and put a hundred dollars in her envelope every Sunday. When his wife returned home, apparently recovered, his joy and optimism were boundless; also, he bought a Rolls-Royce and hired a "safe, colored driver" for her daily airings. When his wife knew she was ill again she wanted to spare her husband the truth, and for a while he went on with his joyous extravagant ways. When it was apparent that his wife was failing, he didn't want to know and tried to deceive both her and himself. Avoiding doctors and questions, he accepted the fact that a trained nurse had become a member of the household. He taught his wife to play poker and they played frequently when she was well enough. When it was obvious that his wife was in pain, the Judge would tiptoe softly to the refrigerator, eat without tasting what he ate, thinking only that his wife had been very sick and was just recovering from a serious operation. So he steadied himself to his secret everyday grief, and would not let himself understand.

The day she died was a frosty day in December, with a cloudless blue sky and the sound of Christmas carols chiming in the icy air. The Judge, too dazed and worn to cry properly, had a terrible case of hiccups which let up, thank God, during the reading of the funeral service. Late that winter's day, when the ceremonies were finished and the guests were gone, he went alone in the Rolls-Royce to the cemetery (he sold the car the week afterward). There, as the first frosty stars were appearing, he poked the newly laid cement of the grave with a walking stick, pondered over the workmanship of the job, and very slowly went back to the car driven by the "safe, colored driver," and there exhausted, he went to sleep.

The Judge gave a final look at the portrait before he turned his brimming eyes away. A purer woman never lived.

After a proper time of mourning, Malone and the rest of the town expected that the Judge would marry again; and even he himself, lonesome and grieving as he rattled around the enormous house, felt a feeling of unknown expectancy. On Sunday he dressed very carefully and attended church, where he sat demurely on the second pew, his eyes glued to the choir. His wife had sung in the choir and he loved to watch the throats and bosoms of women when they sang. There were some lovely ladies in the First Baptist's choir, especially one soprano whom the Judge watched constantly. But there were other church choirs in the town. With a feeling of heresy, the Judge went to the Presbyterian church where there was a blond singer . . . his wife had been blond . . . whose singing throat and breasts fascinated him, although otherwise she was not quite to his taste. So, dressed to kill and sitting on one of the front rows, the Judge visited the various churches of the town and watched and judged the choirs, in spite of the fact that he had very little ear for music and was always singing off key and very loudly. No one questioned him about his changes of churches, yet he must have had some guilt for he often would declare in a loud voice, "I like to be informed about what goes on in various religions and creeds. My wife and I have always been very broad-minded."

The Judge never thought consciously of marrying again; indeed, he often spoke of his wife as though she were alive. Still there was this hollow yearning that he tried to fill with food or alcohol or watching choir ladies. And there had begun a veiled, subconscious search for his dead wife. Miss Missy was a pure woman, and automatically he considered only the pure. A choir singer, only choir singers attracted him. Those requirements were not too hard to fill. But Miss Missy had also been an excellent poker player, and unmarried, pure choir singers who are also canny poker players are somewhat rare. One evening about two years after Miss Missy's death, the Judge invited Miss Kate Spinner for Saturday night supper. He also invited her elderly aunt as a chaperon and planned the supper with the forethought that was exactly like his wife's. The supper started with oysters. This was followed with a chicken dish and a curry of tomatoes, currants and almonds stewed together which was one of Miss Missy's favorite company dishes. Wine was served at each course and brandy followed the ice cream dessert. The Judge fidgeted over the preparations for days, making sure that the best plate and silver were used. The supper itself was a keen mistake. To begin with, Miss Kate had never eaten an oyster and was deadly afraid of having to eat one when the Judge tried to coax her. The unaccustomed wine made Miss Kate giggle in what seemed to the Judge a somewhat suggestive manner which obscurely offended him. On the other hand, the old maiden aunt said she had never touched a drop of spirits in her life and was surprised that her niece would indulge. At the end of that dismal supper, the Judge, his hopes shaken but not yet gone, brought out a new deck of cards to have a game with the ladies. He had in mind his wife's slender fingers

ringed with the diamonds he had given her. But it materialized that Miss Kate had never held a card in her life, and the
old aunt added that, to her, cards were the entrance to the
devil's playground. The party broke up early and the Judge
finished the bottle of brandy before he went to bed. He
blamed the fact that the Spinners were Lutherans and not
quite expected to be in the same class as those who attended
the First Baptist Church. So he consoled himself and soon
his natural optimism returned.

However, he did not go so far afield in his broadmindedness
about sects and creeds. Miss Missy had been born Episcopalian, changing over to First Baptist when they were married.
Miss Hettie Peaver sang in the Episcopal choir and her throat
was pulsing and vibrant as she sang. On Christmas the
congregation stood up at the Hallelujah passage . . . year after
year he was fooled by this passage, sitting there like a ninny
until he realized that every soul had stood up and then trying
to make amends by the loudest singing in the church . . . but
this Christmas the Hallelujah section came and went unnoticed as the Judge craned his neck at Miss Hettie Peaver.
After church he scraped his feet and invited her and her aged
mother to Saturday night supper the following week. Again he
agonized over preparations. Miss Hettie was a short stout
woman of good family; she was no spring chicken as the
Judge well knew, but then neither was he, pushing seventy
years old. And it was of course not a question of marriage as
Miss Hettie was a widow. (The Judge had automatically in
this unconscious search for love excluded widows and, of
course, grass widows, as he had held it as a principle that
second marriages were most unbecoming for a woman.)

That second supper was quite different from the Lutheran
one. It turned out Miss Hettie adored oysters and was trying
to get up nerve to swallow one whole. The old mother told

a story about when she cooked an all-oyster dinner . . . raw oysters, scalloped oysters and so forth, which the old lady named in detail . . . for the business partner of Percy, "my beloved spouse," and how it turned out that the partner couldn't eat oysters at all. As the old lady drank her wine, her stories grew longer and more tedious and the daughter would try to change the subject with little success. After dinner when the Judge brought cards, the old lady said she was too blind to make out the cards and she would be perfectly satisfied just finishing her port and looking at the fire. The Judge taught Miss Hettie blackjack and found her an able pupil. But he so much missed Miss Missy's slender hands and diamond rings. And another thing, Miss Hettie was a little buxom to his taste and he could not but compare his wife's slender bosom to her somewhat hefty form. His wife had had very delicate breasts, and indeed, he never forgot that one had been removed.

On Valentine's Day, sick with that hollow feeling, he bought a five-pound box of heart-shaped candy, much to the interest of J. T. Malone, who made the sale. On the way to Miss Hettie's house he reconsidered judiciously and walked slowly home. He ate the candy himself. It took two months. However, after some other little episodes like this that came to nothing, the Judge devoted himself solely to his grandson and his love for him.

The Judge spoiled his grandson beyond reason. It was the joke of the town that once at a church picnic the Judge had carefully picked the grains of pepper out of his small grandson's food, as the child did not like pepper. When the child was four years old he could recite the Lord's Prayer and the Twenty-Third Psalm, thanks to his grandfather's patient coaching, and it was the old man's delight when townspeople gathered to hear this prodigy perform. Absorbed in his grandson, his hollowness of grief diminished, as well as his fascination for choir ladies. In spite of advancing age, which indeed the Judge did not admit, he went early every morning to his office in the courthouse — walking the morning way, being driven back at noon for a long midday dinner, and being driven back for the afternoon work hours. He argued vociferously in the court house square and in Malone's drugstore. On Saturday night he played poker in a game held in the back room of the New York Café.

All these years the Judge had as his motto: "Mens sana in corpore sano." His "stroke" did not alter this as much as would have been supposed. After a cantankerous convalescence, he returned to his usual ways; although he went to the office only in the morning and did little but open his diminishing mail and read the *Milan Courier*, the *Flowering Branch Ledger* and, on Sundays, the *Atlanta Constitution*, which infuriated him. The Judge had fallen in the bathroom and had lain there for hours until Jester, sleeping his sound boy's sleep, finally heard his grandfather's cries. The "little seizure" had happened instantaneously so that the Judge had at first hoped that his recovery would come about with the same instant speed. He would not admit it was a true stroke — spoke of "a light case of polio," "little seizure," etc. When he was up and around, he declared he used the walking stick because he liked it and that the "little attack" had probably benefited him as his mind had grown keener because of contemplation and "new studies."

The old man waited restlessly for the sound of a doorlatch. "Jester is out so late," he said, with a note of complaint. "He's usually such a thoughtful boy about letting me know where he is when he goes out at night. Before my bath, when I heard some sound of music from not far away, I wondered if he had not stepped out in the yard to listen. But the music stopped and when I called there was only silence, and although it's past his bedtime, he has not come home."

Malone put his long upper lip against his mouth, as he did not like Jester, but he only said mildly: "Well, boys will be boys."

"Often I have worried about him, brought up in a house of sorrow. If ever there was one. Sometimes I think that's why he loves sad music, although his mother was a great one for music," the Judge said, forgetting he had skipped a generation. "I mean of course his grandmother," he corrected. "Jester's mother was with us only at that time of violence, sorrow and confusion . . . so much so that she passed through the family almost unnoticed, so that now I can hardly remember her face. Light hair, brownish eyes, a nice voice . . . although her father was a well-known rum runner. In spite of our feelings she was a blessing in disguise if ever there was one.

"The trouble was, she was just sandwiched in between Johnny's death, Jester's birth, and Miss Missy's second failing. It would take the strongest personality to not blur against all this and Mirabelle was not strong." Indeed, the only memory that stood out was one Sunday dinner when the gentle stranger said: "I love baked Alaskas" and the Judge took it upon himself to correct her. "Mirabelle," he said sternly, "you love me. You love the memory of your husband. You love Miss Missy. But you don't love baked Alaskas, see?" He pointed out, with a most loving glance at the piece he was cutting, "You like baked Alaskas. See the difference, child?" She saw, but her appetite had quite left her. "Yes sir," she said as she put down her fork. The Judge, feeling guilty, said angrily: "Eat, child. You've got to eat in your condition." But the idea of being in her condition only made her cry, and leave the table. Miss Missy, with a glance of reproach to her husband, followed soon after, leaving him to eat in solitary fury. As a punishment to them he deliberately deprived them of his presence most of the afternoon, playing solitaire in the library behind locked doors; it was a great satisfaction when the doorknob was rattled and he refused to budge or answer. He even went so far as to go to the cemetery alone instead of escorting his wife and daughter-in-law on the customary Sunday visit to Johnny's grave. The jaunt to the cemetery restored his usual good temper. After a stroll in the April twilight, he went to Pizzalatti's which was always open and bought sacks of candy, tangerines, and even a coconut, which the family enjoyed after supper.

"Mirabelle," he said to Malone. "If she had only been taken to Johns Hopkins for the confinement. But Clanes have always been born at home, and who could know how it would turn out, besides. Hindsight is always better than foresight," he finished, dismissing his daughter-in-law who had died in childbirth.

"Such a sad thing about Mirabelle," Malone said, just in order to say something. "Women seldom die in childbirth in this generation, and when they do it's especially sad. She used to come to the drugstore every afternoon for an ice cream cone."

"She craved sweets," the Judge said with a peculiar satisfaction, as he had profited by this circumstance and would often say, "Mirabelle is craving strawberry shortcake," or some such delicacy, passing on his own desires to his pregnant daughter-in-law. Tactfully but firmly, his wife had kept the Judge within the three-hundred-pound weight range during her lifetime, although the words calorie or diet were never used. Secretly she read up on calorie lists and planned the meals accordingly, without the Judge's knowledge.

"Every baby doctor in town was consulted toward the end,"

the Judge said almost defensively, as though he was being reproached for not caring for his kin. "But it was some rare complication that had not been foreseen. To my dying day I will regret that we had not taken her to Johns Hopkins to begin with. They specialize in complications and rare complaints. If it hadn't been for Johns Hopkins, I would be under the sod today."

Malone, who found solace in this talk of the sickness of others, asked delicately: "Was your complaint complicated and rare?"

"Not so much complicated and rare, but curious," the Judge said complacently. "When my beloved wife died I was so miserable I began digging my grave with my teeth."

Malone shuddered, having an instant, vivid image of his friend chewing gritty dirt in the graveyard, crying with misery. His own illness had left him defenseless against such sudden, random images, no matter how repellent. The subjectivity of illness was so acute that Malone responded violently to whole areas of the most placid and objective concepts. For instance, the mere mention of a commonplace thing such as Coca-Cola suggested shame and the disgrace of not being thought a good provider, just because his wife had some shares of Coca-Cola stock which she had bought with her own money and kept in a safety deposit box at the Milan Bank and Trust. These reactions, cavernous and involuntary, were hardly realized by Malone as they had the volatile vigor and backward grace of the unconscious.

"There came a time when I weighed at your drugstore and I weighed three hundred and ten pounds. But that didn't bother me particularly, and I was only troubled by those falling-out spells. But something outlandish had to happen before I took much serious notice. And finally the outlandish thing happened."

"What?" Malone asked.

"It was the time when Jester was seven." The Judge broke off his story to complain of those years. "Oh, the trouble for a man to raise a motherless child, and not only to raise but to rear him. Oh, the Clapps baby food, the sudden earaches in the night which I stopped with paregoric soaked in sugar and sweet oil dropped in his ear. Of course his nurse, Cleopatra, did most of the doing, but my grandson was my responsibility and no question about it." He sighed before he continued his story. "Anyway, when Jester was still a little nipper I decided to teach him to play golf, so one fair Saturday afternoon we set out to the Milan Country Club course. I was just playing away and showing Jester the various holds and positions. We came to that . . . that little pond near the woods . . . you know it, J.T."

Malone, who had never played golf and was not a member of the Country Club, nodded with a certain pride.

"Anyway, I was just swinging away when I suddenly had one of those falling-out spells. And I fell right spang into the pond. There I was drowning with nothing but a seven-year-old boy and a little colored caddy to save me. How they hauled me out I don't know, being too drenched and confused to help myself much. It must have been a job, my weighing over three hundred, but that colored caddy was both shrewd and smart and I was finally safe. However, that falling-out spell made me think seriously enough to consider going to a doctor. Since I didn't like or trust any doctor in Milan, it came to me in a divine flash . . . Johns Hopkins. I knew they treated rare, uncommon diseases like mine. I gave the caddy who had saved me a solid gold watch engraved in Latin."

"Latin?"

"Mens sana in corpore sano," the Judge said serenely, as that was the only Latin he knew.

"Most appropriate," said Malone, who did not know Latin either.

"Unbeknownst to me, I had a peculiar and you might say tragic connection with the colored boy," the Judge said slowly; and he closed his eyes as a kind of curtain for the subject, leaving Malone's curiosity unsatisfied. "Nonetheless," he went on, "I'm hiring him as a body servant." The old-fashioned term struck Malone.

"When I fell in the pond, I was sufficiently alarmed to take myself to Johns Hopkins, knowing they studied rare and curious diseases. I took little Jester with me to broaden his education and as a reward for helping that caddy save me." The Judge did not admit that he could not face such a horrendous experience as a hospital without his seven-year-old grandson. "So the day came I faced Dr. Hume."

Malone paled at the unconscious image of a doctor's office with the smell of ether, the children's cries, Dr. Hayden's knife and a treatment table.

"When Dr. Hume asked if I overate, I assured him I ate just an ordinary amount. Then his questions chiseled finer. He asked, for instance, how many biscuits I had at a meal and I said, 'Just the ordinary amount.' Chiseling in closer in the way that doctors do, he inquired what was the 'ordinary amount.' When I told him, 'Just a dozen or two,' I felt right then and there I had met my Waterloo."

In a flash Malone saw soaked biscuits, disgrace, Napoleon.

"The doctor said I had two choices . . . either to go on living as I had been, which would not be for long, or to go on a diet. I was shocked, I admit. And I told him it was much too serious a question to decide offhand. I told him to let me think it over for twelve hours before my final decision. 'We won't find the diet too hard, Judge.' Don't you loathe it when doctors use the word 'we' when it applies only and solely to yourself? He could go home and gobble fifty biscuits and ten baked Alaskas . . . while me, I'm starving on a diet, so I meditated in a furious way."

"I hate that 'we' doctors use," Malone agreed, feeling the sickening ricochet of his own emotions in Dr. Hayden's office and the doomed words, "We have here a case of leukemia."

"Furthermore," the Judge added, "I hate it, God damn it, when doctors presume to tell me the so-called truth. I was so angry meditating about that diet problem I might have then and there had a stroke." The Judge hastily corrected himself, "A heart attack or a 'little seizure.' "

"No, it's not right," Malone assented. He had asked for the truth, but in asking, he had asked only for reassurance. How could he dream that an ordinary case of spring fever would be a fatal disease? He had wanted sympathy and reassurance, and he got a death warrant. "Doctors, by God; washing their hands, looking out windows, fiddling with dreadful things while you are stretched out on a table or half undressed on a chair." He finished in a voice that wailed with weakness and fury: "I'm glad I didn't finish medical school. I wouldn't have it on my soul nor conscience."

"I meditated the full twelve hours as I said I would do. One portion of me said to go on the diet while another portion said, to hell, you live only once. I quoted Shakespeare to myself, 'To be or not to be,' and cogitated sadly. Then toward twilight a nurse came to the room with a tray. On the tray there was a steak twice as thick as my hand, turnip greens, lettuce and tomato salad. I looked at the nurse. She had dainty bosoms and a lovely neck . . . for a nurse, that is. I told her about my problem and asked her truthfully what that diet was. You could have struck me over with a feather when she said: 'This, Judge, is the diet.' When I was sure it was no trick, I sent word to Dr. Hume that I was on the diet and I fell to. I had forgotten to mention liquor or little toddies. I managed that."

"How?" asked Malone, who knew the Judge's little weaknesses.

"The Lord works in strange ways. When I took Jester out of school to accompany me to the hospital, everybody thought it was mighty strange. Sometimes I thought so too, but secretly I was afraid I would die up North in that hospital. I didn't know the design beforehand, but a seven-year-old boy is just right to go to the nearest liquor store and get a bottle for his sick grandfather.

"The trick in life is to change a miserable experience into a happy one. Once my gut was shrunk, I got along fine in Johns Hopkins and I lost forty pounds in three months."

The Judge, seeing Malone's long-eyed wistfulness, felt suddenly guilty because he had talked so much about his own health. "You may think everything is roses and wine with me, J.T., but it's not and I'm going to tell you a secret I never breathed to a soul in this world, a serious, awful secret."

"Why, what on earth . . ."

"I was pleased after the diet to lose all that corpulence, but that diet had got in my system and just a year later, on my annual visit to Johns Hopkins, I was told I had sugar in the blood and that means diabetes." Malone, who had been selling him insulin for years, was not surprised but he did not comment. "Not a fatal disease but a diet disease. I cussed out Dr. Hume and threatened to bring suit but he reasoned with me and as a dyed-in-the-wool magistrate, I realized it wouldn't stand up in court. That brought certain problems. Do you know, J.T., while it's not a fatal disease, you have to have an injection every day. There is nothing catching about it but I felt there were too many health marks against me to make it known to the general public. I'm still in the zenith of my political career whether anybody recognizes it or not."

Malone said, "I won't tell anybody, although it is no disgrace."

"Corpulence, that little seizure, and then on top of everything, diabetes . . . that's too much for a politician. Although there was a cripple in the White House for thirteen years."

"I have every confidence in your political astuteness, Judge." He said this, but that evening he had strangely lost faith in the old Judge . . . why he didn't know . . . medical faith anyhow.

"For years I put up with those public nurses for the injections and now chance has led me to another solution. I have found a boy who will look after me and give me those needles. He is the same boy you inquired about in the spring."

Malone, suddenly remembering, said, "Not the Nigra with the blue eyes."

"Yes," the Judge said.

"What do you know about him?" Malone asked.

The Judge was thinking about the tragedy of his life and how that boy had centered in it. But he only said to Malone, "He was the colored caddy who saved my life when I fell into that pond."

Then came about between the two friends that laughter of disaster. It was focused consciously on the image of the three-hundred-pound old man being dragged out of a golf pond, but the hysterical laughter was reverberated in the gloom of the evening. The laughter of disaster does not stop easily, and so they laughed for a long time, each for his own disaster. The Judge stopped laughing first. "Seriously, I wanted to find someone I could trust, and who else could I trust more than that little caddy who saved my life? Insulin is a very delicate, mysterious thing and has to be administered by someone who is mighty intelligent and conscientious, needles boiled and so forth."

Malone thought the boy might be intelligent, but isn't there such a thing as a too intelligent colored boy? He feared for the Judge, seeing those cold, blazing eyes and associating them with the pestle, rats and death. "I wouldn't have hired that colored boy, but maybe you know best, Judge."

The Judge was back with his own worries. "Jester doesn't dance, he doesn't drink liquor, he doesn't even go with girls, as far as I know. Where is that Jester? It's getting late. J.T., do you think I ought to call the police?"

The idea of calling the police and such commotion unnerved Malone. "Why it's not late enough to worry about, but I think I'd better go home."

"J.T., take a taxi at my expense and tomorrow we'll talk more about Johns Hopkins because, seriously, I think you ought to go there."

Malone said, "Thanks, sir, but I don't need a taxi — the fresh air will do me good. Don't worry about Jester. He'll be home soon."

Although Malone said the walk would do him good, and although the night was warm, he was cold and weak as he walked home.

Noiselessly, he crept into the bed he shared with his wife. But when her warm buttocks touched his own, sick with the vibrance of their past livingness, he jerked away — for how can the living go on living when there is death?

4

IT WAS scarcely nine when Jester and Sherman first met that
midsummer evening and only two hours had passed. But in
first youth two hours can be a crucial period that can warp
or enlighten a whole lifetime, and such an experience happened to Jester Clane that evening. When the emotion of the
music and the first meeting steadied, Jester was aware of the
room. The green plant growing in a corner. He steadied himself to realize the stranger had interrupted. The blue eyes
challenged him to speak, but still Jester was silent. He blushed
and his freckles darkened. "Excuse me," he said in a voice
that trembled. "Who are you and what was that song you
were singing?"

The other youth, who was the same age as Jester, said in a
voice meant to be creepy, "If you want the sober ice-cold

truth, I don't know who I am or any of my antecedents."

"You mean you are an orphan," Jester said. "Why, so am I," he added with enthusiasm. "Don't you think that's sort of a sign?"

"No. You know who you are. Did your grandfather send you here?"

Jester shook his head.

When Jester first entered, Sherman had expected some message, then as the moments passed, some trick. "Then why did you come busting in here?" Sherman said.

"I didn't come busting in. I knocked and said 'Excuse me,' and we got into a conversation."

Sherman's suspicious mind was wondering what trick was being played on him, and he was very much on guard. "We didn't get into any conversation."

"You were saying how you didn't know about your parents. Mine died. Did yours?"

The dark boy with the blue eyes said, "The sober ice-cold truth is, I don't know anything about them. I was left in a church pew and therefore I was named Pew, in that somewhat Negroid and literal manner, according to the Nigerian race. My first name is Sherman."

It would take a person far less sensitive than Jester to realize that the other youth was being deliberately rude to him. He knew he ought to go home, but it was as though he was hypnotized by the blue eyes set in the dark face. Then without a word, Sherman began to sing and play. It was the song Jester had heard in his own room and he felt that he had never been so moved. Sherman's strong fingers seemed very dark against the ivory keyboard and his strong neck was thrown back as he sang. After the first stanza of the song, he jerked his head and neck toward the sofa as an indication for Jester to sit down. Jester sat down, listening.

When the song was finished Sherman made a playful glissando before he went to the kitchenette in the next room and returned with two drinks already poured. He offered one to Jester who asked what it was as he took his glass.

"Lord Calvert's, bottled in bond, ninety-eight per cent proof." Although Sherman did not say it, he had bought this whiskey for the year he had been drinking because of the advertisement, "The Man of Distinction." He had tried to dress with the negligent care of the man in the ad. But on him it only looked sloppy, and he was one of the sharpest dressers in town. He had two Hathaway shirts and wore a black patch on his eye, but it only made him look pathetic instead of distinguished and he bumped into things. "The best, the most distinguished," Sherman said. "I don't serve rotgut to my guests." But he was careful to decant the drinks in the kitchen in case some juicehead would gobble it up; also he did not serve Lord Calvert's to known juiceheads. His guest tonight was no juicehead; in fact, he had never tasted whiskey before. Sherman began to think that there was no dark plot on the Judge's behalf.

Jester held out a package of cigarettes, which he proferred courteously. "I smoke like a chimney," he said, "and drink wine practically every day."

"I only drink Lord Calvert's," Sherman said staunchly.

"Why were you so rude and ugly when I first came in here?" Jester asked.

"You have to be mighty careful about skitzes these days."

"About what?" Jester asked, feeling somewhat at a loss.

"That means schizophrenics."

"But isn't that a medical disease?"

"No, mental," said Sherman with authority. "A skitz is a crazy person. I actually knew one."

"Who?"

"Nobody you would know. He was a Golden Nigerian."

"A golden what?"

"That's a club I belonged to. It was started as a kind of protest club protesting against racial discrimination and with the very highest aims."

"What highest aims?" Jester asked.

"First we registered for the vote in a body and if you don't think that takes nerve in this county you don't know nothing. Each member got a little cardboard coffin with his name in it and a printed sign, 'A voting reminder.' That actually happened," Sherman said with emphasis.

Later Jester was to learn the significance of that little phrase, but not until he knew more about Sherman and the facts and phantasies of his life. "I wish I had been there when you registered as a body," Jester said wistfully. The phrase "as a body" particularly appealed to him and heroic tears came suddenly to his eyes.

Sherman's voice was raw and cold, "No you wouldn't. You would of been the first to chicken. Besides, you're not old enough to vote . . . the first to chicken."

"I resent that," Jester said. "How do you know?"

"Little Bo-Peep told me so."

Although Jester was hurt, he admired that answer, and thought he would use it himself very soon. "Did many club members chicken?"

"Well," Sherman said hesitantly, "under the circumstances, with cardboard coffins slipped under doors . . . we continued our voting studies, learned the names and dates of all the Presidents, memorized the Constitution and so forth, but we had been aiming to vote, not aiming to be no Joan of Arc, so under the circumstances . . . " His voice trailed off. He did not tell Jester of the charges and countercharges exchanged as voting day neared. nor did he tell him that he was a minor and could not have voted anyhow. And that autumn day, Sherman exactly, with such lingering and exact detail, voted . . . in phantasy. He was also lynched in that phantasy to the tune of "John Brown's Body," which always made him cry anyway and made him cry double that day, a martyr to his race. No Golden Nigerian voted and the subject of voting was never mentioned again.

"We had Parliamentary Procedure and were active in the Christmas Club which delegated in charge of donations for poor children. That's how we all knew Happy Henderson was a skitz."

"Who's that?" Jester inquired.

"Happy was the chief active member in charge of the Christmas donations and he mugged an old lady on Christmas Eve. He was just skitz and didn't know what he was doing."

"I've often wondered if crazy people know if they are crazy or not," Jester said softly.

"Happy didn't know, or any of the Golden Nigerians either, otherwise we wouldn't have voted him into the club. Mugging an old lady in a fit of insanity."

"I feel the sincerest sympathy for crazy people," Jester said.

"The profoundest sympathy," Sherman corrected. "That's what we said on the flowers . . . I mean wreath, we sent his folks when he was electrocuted in Atlanta."

"He was electrocuted?" Jester asked, appalled.

"Naturally, mugging an old white lady on Christmas Eve. Turned out Happy had been in institutions half of his life. There was no motive. In fact, he didn't snatch the old lady's purse after he mugged her. He just suddenly blew a fuse and went skitz . . . the lawyer made a case about the mental institutions and poverty and pressures . . . the lawyer the state hired to defend him, I mean . . . but anyway in spite of everything, Happy was fried."

"Fried," Jester exclaimed with horror.

"Electrocuted in Atlanta, June sixth, nineteen fifty-one."

"I think it's simply terrible for you to refer to a friend and fellow member as being 'fried.' "

"Well he was," Sherman said flatly. "Let's converse about something more cheerful. Would you like me to show you Zippo Mullins' apartment?"

With pride he pointed out each piece in the crowded, fancy, dreary room. "This rug is pure Wilton and the hide-a-bed sofa cost one hundred and eight dollars secondhand. It can sleep four if necessary." Jester eyed the three-quarter-size sofa, wondering how four people could sleep in it. Sherman was stroking an iron alligator with an electric light bulb in its gaping jaws. "A house-warming present from Zippo's aunt, not too modern or attractive, but it's the thought that counts."

"Absolutely," Jester agreed, cheered by any spark of humanness in his new-found friend.

"The end tables are genuine antique as you can see. The plant was a birthday gift for Zippo." Sherman did not point out the red lamp with ragged fringes, two obviously broken chairs and other pieces of sad-looking furniture. "I wouldn't have anything to happen to this apt" (he said the abbreviation). "You haven't seen the rest of the apt . . . just gorgeous." Sherman's voice was proud. "When I'm alone here at night I don't hardly open the door."

"Why?"

"Afraid I might be mugged and the muggers would haul off Zippo's furniture." He added, in a voice that almost broke with self-pride, "You see, I'm Zippo's house guest." Until six months ago he had said he boarded with Zippo, then he heard the phrase "house guest" which enchanted him and he used it frequently. "Let's proceed to the rest of the apt," Sherman said with the air of a host. "Look at the kitchenette," he said ecstatically, "see the most modern conveniences." Reverently he opened the door of the refrigerator for Jester. "The bottom compartment is for crispies . . . crisp celery, carrots, lettuce, etc." Sherman opened the door to the compartment, but there was only a head of wilted lettuce there. "We keep caviar in this section," he said emptily. Sherman gestured to the other parts of the magical box. Jester saw only a dish of cold black-eyed peas jelled in their own grease, but Sherman said, "Last Christmas we had champagne iced in this compart-ment." Jester, who seldom opened his own well-stocked refrigerator, was mystified.

"You must eat caviar and drink loads of champagne at your grandpapa's house," Sherman said.

"No, I never tasted caviar, nor champagne either."

"Never drank Lord Calvert's bottled in bond, nor had champagne, nor eaten caviar . . . personally, I just guzzle it," Sherman said, having tasted caviar once, and having wondered silently why it was supposed to be so high-class. "And look," he said with enthusiasm, "a genuine electric beater . . . plugs in here." Sherman plugged in the beater and it began to beat furiously. "A Christmas gift for Zippo Mullins from yours truly. I bought it on credit. I have the best credit record in town and can buy anything."

Jester was bored standing in the cramped dingy kitchenette, and Sherman soon sensed it, but his pride was undaunted; so they went into the bedroom. Sherman indicated a trunk against the wall. "This is the trunk," he said superfluously, "where we keep our valuables." Then he added, "I shouldn't have told you that."

Jester was naturally offended by that last remark, but he said nothing.

In the room there were twin beds, each with a rose-colored spread. Sherman stroked the spread appreciatively and said, "Pure rayon silk." There were portraits over each of the beds, one of an elderly colored woman, the other of a dark young girl. "Zippo's mother and sister." Sherman was still stroking the bedspread and the Negro-colored hand against the rose gave Jester an inexplicable creepy thrill. But he dared not touch the silk, and he felt that if his own hand would touch the outspread one he would feel a shock like an electric eel, so carefully he placed both his own hands against the headboard of the bed.

"Zippo's sister is a nice-looking girl," Jester remarked, as he felt that Sherman was expecting some comment about his friend's relatives.

"Jester Clane," Sherman said, and though his voice was hard, Jester felt again the creepy thrill from the simple calling of his name, "if you ever, ever," Sherman continued in a voice that lashed at Jester, "if you ever, ever have the teeniest least lewd lascivious thought about Cinderella Mullins I'll string you up by your heels, tie your hands, light fire to your face and stand there and watch you roast."

The sudden fury of the attack made Jester hold on tight to the headboard. "I only said . . ."

"Shuddup, shuddup," Sherman shouted. He added in a low hard voice, "When you looked at the picture I didn't like the look on your puss."

"What look?" asked Jester, baffled. "You showed me the picture and I looked at it. What else could I have done? Cry?"

"Any further wisecrack and I will string you up and make the slowest barbecue that anybody ever made, smothering up the flames so it will last and keep on lasting."

"I don't see why you talk so ugly, especially to somebody you just met."

"When it's a question of Cinderella Mullins' virtue, I talk how I please."

"Are you in love with Cinderella Mullins, passionately, I mean?"

"Any further personal questions and I'll have you fried in Atlanta."

"How silly," Jester said. "How could you? It's a matter of legality."

Both boys were impressed by that last phrase, but Sherman only muttered, "I'll turn the juice personally and set it for very slow."

"I think all this talk about electrocution and roasting people is childish." Jester paused to deliver a stinging blow. "In fact, I suspect it's because you have a limited vocabulary."

Sherman was properly stung. "Limited vocabulary," he shouted with a little quiver of rage. Then he paused for a long time before he asked, belligerently, "What does the word 'stygian' mean?"

After Jester thought for a while he had to admit, "I don't know."

" . . . and epizootical and pathologinical," Sherman went on, making up phony words like crazy.

"Isn't pathologinical something about being sick . . ."

"No," Sherman said, "I just made it up."

"Made it up," Jester said, shocked. "It's utterly unfair to make up words when you are testing another person's vocabulary."

"Anyway," Sherman concluded, "you have a very limited and putrid vocabulary."

Jester was left in the situation of trying to prove his vocabulary; he tried in vain to make up long fancy words but nothing that made sense occurred to him.

"Forchrissake," Sherman said, "less change the subject. You wish me to sweeten your Calvert's?"

"Sweeten it?"

"Yes, goofy."

Jester sipped his whiskey and choked on it. "It's kind of bitter and hot . . ."

"When I said sweeten it, did your dim mind suppose I was going to put sugar in this Calvert's whiskey? I wonder more and more if you come from Mars."

That was another remark Jester thought he would use later.

"What a nocturnal evening," Jester said to prove his vocabulary. "You are certainly fortunate," he added.

"You mean about Zippo's apt?"

"No, I was just thinking . . . ruminating you might say . . . about how fortunate it is when you know what it is you're going to do in life. If I had a voice like yours I would never have to worry about that particular headache any more. Whether you know it or not, you have a golden voice, where I don't have any talent . . . can't sing or dance and the only thing I can draw is a Christmas tree."

"There are other things," Sherman said in a superior voice, as Jester's praise had been sweet to hear.

" . . . not too good at math, so nuclear physics are out."

"I suppose you could do construction work."

"I suppose so," Jester said dolefully. Then he added in a suddenly cheerful voice: "Anyway, this summer I'm taking flying lessons. But that's just an advocation. I think every person ought to learn to fly."

"I utterly disagree with you," said Sherman, who was afraid of heights.

"Suppose your baby was dying, like say one of those blue babies you read about in the paper, and you have to fly to see him before the end, or suppose your crippled mother was sick and wanted to see you before she died; besides, flying's fun and I look on it as a kind of moral obligation that everyone ought to learn to fly."

"I utterly disagree with you," said Sherman, who was sick about talking about something he couldn't do.

"Anyway," Jester went on, "what was that song you were singing this evening?"

"This evening I was singing just plain jazz, but earlier this afternoon I was practicing genuine Simon-pure German lieder."

"What's that?"

"I knew you would ask me that." Sherman's ego was glad to get on the subject. "Lieder, goofy, means song in German and German means German, like in English." Softly he began to play and sing and the new strange music throbbed in Jester's body and he trembled.

"In German," Sherman boasted. "They tell me I don't have a trace of accent in German," he lied.

"What does it mean in English?"

"It's a kind of love song. This youth is singing to his maiden . . . goes something like this: 'The two blue eyes of my beloved, I've never seen anything like them.' "

"Your eyes are blue. It sounds like a love song to yourself; in fact, when I know the words of the song it makes me feel creepy."

"German lieder is creepy music. That's why I specialize in it."

"What other music do you like? Personally, I adore music, passionately, I mean. Last winter I learned the 'Winter Wind' etude."

"I bet you didn't," Sherman said, unwilling to share his musical laurels with another.

"Do you think I would sit here and tell you a lie about the 'Winter Wind' etude?" said Jester who never lied under any circumstances.

"How would I know?" answered Sherman who was one of the world's worst liars.

"I'm out of practice."

As Jester went to the piano Sherman watched intently, hoping Jester couldn't play.

Loudly and furiously the "Winter Wind " etude thundered into the room. When, after the first few bars, Jester's furiously playing fingers faltered, he stopped. "Once you get off the track of the 'Winter Wind' it's hard to get back on."

Sherman, who had been listening jealously, was relieved when the music stopped. Furiously Jester attacked the etude at the beginning.

"Stop it," Sherman shouted, but Jester played on, the music punctured frantically with Sherman's shouted protests.

"Well that's pretty fair," Sherman said at the frantic, rickety end. "However, you don't have tone."

"Didn't I tell you I could play it?"

"There are all kinds of ways of playing music. Personally, I don't like yours."

"I know it's just an advocation, but I enjoy it."

"That's your privilege."

"I like the way you play jazz better than the way you play German lieder," Jester said.

"When I was a youth," Sherman said, "for a while I played in this band. We had hot sessions. The leader was Bix Beiderbecke and he tooted a golden horn."

"Bix Beiderbecke, why, that impossible."

Sherman lamely tried to correct his lie. "No, his name was Rix Heiderhorn. Anyway, I really wanted to sing Tristan at the Metropolitan Opera House but the role is not adaptable to me. In fact, most of the roles of the Metropolitan are severely limited for people of my race; in fact, the only role I can think of offhand is the role of Othello who was a Negro Moor. I like the music all right, but on the other hand, I don't dig his feeling. How anybody can be that jealous over a white dame is beyond me. I would think about Desdemona . . .

me . . . Desdemona . . . me . . . ? No, I can't dig it." He
began to sing, "O! now, for ever farewell the tranquil mind."

"It must give you a funny feeling, not to know who your
mother was."

"No it don't," said Sherman, who had spent all his childhood trying to find his mother. He would pick out one
woman after another who had a gentle touch and a soft voice.
Is this my mother? he would think in wordless expectancy that
ended always in sorrow. "Once you get accustomed to it,
it don't bother you at all." He said this because he had never
gotten accustomed to it. "I loved very much Mrs. Stevens, but
she told me outright I wasn't her son."

"Who is Mrs. Stevens?"

"A lady I was boarded out with five years. It was Mr.
Stevens who boogered me."

"What does that mean?"

"Sexually assaulted, goofy. I was sexually assaulted when
I was eleven years old."

Jester was speechless until he finally said, "I didn't know
anybody ever sexually assaulted a boy."

"Well they do, and I was."

Jester, who always had been subject to propulsive vomiting,
suddenly began to vomit.

Sherman cried, "Oh, Zippo's Wilton rug," and took off his
shirt to scrub the rug. "Get towels in the kitchen," he said to
Jester who was still vomiting, "or get out of this house."

Jester, still vomiting, stumbled out. Jester sat on the porch
until he stopped vomiting, then he came back to help Sherman clean up the mess, although the smell of his own vomit
made him feel sickish again. "I was just wondering," he
said, "since you don't know who your mother is, and since
you have a voice like yours, if your mother wouldn't be Marian
Anderson?"

For the first time Sherman, who soaked up compliments like a sponge because he had had so few, was truly impressed. In all of his search for his mother he had never thought about Marian Anderson.

"Toscanini said she had a voice like once in a century."

Sherman, who felt it was almost too good to be true, wanted to think about it alone, and as a matter of fact, hug the idea to himself. Sherman changed the subject abruptly. "When I was boogered by Mr. Stevens" — Jester turned white and swallowed — "I couldn't tell nobody. Mrs. Stevens asked why I was always hitting Mr. Stevens. I couldn't tell her. It's the kind of thing you can't tell a lady, so at that period I began to stammer."

Jester said, "I don't see how you can even bear to talk about it."

"Well, it happened, and I was just eleven years old."

"What a queer thing to do," Jester said, who was still wiping the iron alligator.

"I'll borrow a vacuum tomorrow and vacuum this rug," Sherman said, who was still concerned about the furniture. He flung a towel at Jester: "If you feel anything like that is coming on again, kindly use this . . . Since I was stammering and always hitting Mr. Stevens, Reverend Wilson talked to me one day. At first he would not believe me, as Mr. Stevens was a deacon in the church and as I had made up so many things."

"What other things?"

"Lies I would tell people about my mother." The thought of Marian Anderson returned to him and he wanted Jester to go home so he could brood about it. "When are you going home?" he asked.

Jester, who was still feeling sorry for Sherman, did not want to take the hint. "Have you ever heard Marian Anderson sing

'Were You There When They Crucified My Lord'?" he asked.

"Spirituals, that's another item that makes me blow a fuse."

"It occurs to me your fuses blow awfully easy."

"What's that to you?"

"I was just commenting how I love 'Were You There When They Crucified My Lord' sung by Marian Anderson. I practically cry every time I hear it."

"Well, cry ahead. That's your privilege."

". . . in fact, most spirituals make me cry."

"Me, I wouldn't waste my time and trouble. However, Marian Anderson sings a creepy species of German lieder."

"I cry when she sings spirituals."

"Cry ahead."

"I don't understand your point of view."

Spirituals had always offended Sherman. First, they made him cry and make a fool of himself which was mortally hateful to him; second, he had always lashed out that it was nigger music, but how could he say that if Marian Anderson was his true mother?

"What made you think up Marian Anderson?" Since that worry-wart Jester wouldn't take the hint and go home to let him daydream in peace, he wanted to talk about her.

"On account of your voices. Two golden, once-in-a-century voices are quite a coincidence."

"Well, why did she abandon me? I read somewhere where she loves her own old mother," he added cynically, unable to give up his marvelous dream.

"She might have fallen in love, passionately, I mean, with this white prince," Jester said, carried away with the story.

"Jester Clane," Sherman's voice was mild but firm, "never say 'white' just out like that."

"Why?"

"Say Caucasian, otherwise you would refer to my race as colored or even Negro, while the proper name is Nigerian or Abyssinian."

Jester only nodded and swallowed.

". . . otherwise you might hurt people's feelings, and you're such a tenderhearted sissy, I know you wouldn't like that."

"I resent you calling me a tenderhearted sissy," Jester protested.

"Well, you are one."

"How do you know?"

"Little Bo-Peep told me so." Jester's admiration for this remark was not lessened because he had heard it before.

"Even if she had fallen for this Caucasian, I wonder why she left me in a church pew at the Holy Ascension Church in Milan, Georgia, of all places."

Jester, who had no way of sensing the anxious, fallow search which had lasted all Sherman's childhood, was worried that a random suggestion on his part could have been blown up to such certainty. Jester said conscientiously, "Maybe she wasn't exactly Marian Anderson; if it was, she must have considered herself wedded to her career. Still it would be a kind of crummy thing to do and I never thought of Marian Anderson as the least bit crummy. In fact, I adore her. Passionately, I mean."

"Why are you always using the word 'passionately'?"

Jester, who had been drunk all evening and for the first time with passion, could not answer. For the passion of first youth is lightly sown but strong. It can spring into instant being by a song heard in the night, a voice, the sight of a stranger. Passion makes you daydream, destroys concentration on arithmetic, and at the time you most yearn to be witty, makes you feel like a fool. In early youth, love at first sight, that epitome of passion, turns you into a zombie so that you don't realize if you're sitting up or lying down and you can't remember what you have just eaten to save your life. Jester, who was just learning about passion, was very much afraid. He had never been intoxicated and never wanted to be. A boy who made A grades in high school, except for a sprinkling of B's in geometry and chemistry, he daydreamed only when he was in bed and would not let himself daydream in the morning after the alarm clock went off, although sometimes he would have dearly liked to. Such a person is naturally afraid of love at first sight. Jester felt that if he touched Sherman it would lead to a mortal sin, but what the sin was, he didn't know. He was just careful not to touch him and watched him with the zombie eyes of passion.

Suddenly Sherman began to pound on middle C, over and over.

"What's that?" asked Jester, "just middle C?"

"How many vibrations are there in the treble?"

"What kind of vibrations are you talking about?"

"The teeny infinitesimal sounds that vibrate when you strike middle C or any other note."

"I didn't know that."

"Well, I'm telling you."

Again Sherman pounded middle C, first with the right forefinger, then with the left. "How many vibrations do you hear in the bass?"

"Nothing," Jester said.

"There are sixty-four vibrations in the treble and another sixty-four in the bass," Sherman said, magnificently unaware of his own ignorance.

"What of it?"

"I'm just telling you I hear every teeniest vibration in the whole diatonic scale from here," Sherman struck the lowest bass note, "to here," the highest treble note was sounded.

"Why are you telling me all this? Are you a piano tuner?"

"As a matter of fact, I used to be, smarty. But I'm not talking about pianos."

"Well, what the hell are you talking about?"

"About my race and how I register every single vibration that happens to those of my race. I call it my black book."

"Black book? . . . I see, you are talking of the piano as a sort of symbol," Jester said, delighted to use the brainy word.

"Symbol," repeated Sherman, who had read the word but never used it, "yeah man, that's right . . . when I was fourteen years old a crowd of us got in a rage against the Aunt Jemima signs, so we suddenly decided to tear them off. We scraped and chiseled away to get the sign off. Upshot . . . cops caught us in the middle and all four of the gang was sent to jail, sentenced to two years on the road for destroying public property. I wasn't caught because I was just a lookout, but what happened is in my black book. One guy died from overwork, another came back a living zombie. Have you heard of the Nigerians and that quarry in Atlanta, who broke their legs with hammers so they wouldn't be worked to death? One of them was one that was caught on the Aunt Jemima signs."

"I read that in the paper and it made me sick, but is that the solemn truth, was he one of those Golden Nigerian friends of yours?"

"I didn't say he was a Golden Nigerian, I just said he was somebody I knew, and that's what I mean by vibrations. I vibrate with every injustice that is done to my race. Vibrate . . . vibrate . . . and vibrate, see?"

"I would too, if I were of your race."

"No you wouldn't . . . tenderhearted, chicken, sissy."

"I resent that."

"Well resent . . . resent . . . resent. When are you going home?"

"You don't want me?"

"No. For the last time, no . . . no . . . NO." He added lowly in a venomous voice, "You fatuous, fair, redheaded boy. Fatuous," Sherman said, using a word that had been hurled at him by a brainy vocabulary-wise boy.

Jester automatically ran his hand down his rib cage. "I'm not a bit fat."

"I didn't say fat . . . I said fatuous. Since you have such a putrid and limited vocabulary, that means fool . . . fool . . . fool."

Jester held up his hand as though warding off a blow as he backed out of the door. "Oh, sticks and stones," he screamed as he ran away.

He ran all the way to Reba's house and when he reached the door he rapped with the firm rap of anger.

The inside of the house was not like he had expected. It was an ordinary house, and a whore-lady asked him, "How old are you boy?" and Jester, who never lied, said desperately, "Twenty-one."

"What would you like to drink?"

"Thanks a million, but nothing, nothing at all, I'm on the wagon tonight." It was so easy he did not tremble when the whore-lady showed him upstairs, nor did he tremble when he lay in bed with a woman with orange hair and gold in her teeth. He closed his eyes, and having in mind a dark face and blue flickering eyes, he was able to become a man.

Meanwhile, Sherman Pew was writing a letter in ice-cold sober black ink; the letter started, "Dear Madame Anderson."

5

ALTHOUGH the Judge was up the night before until far past his bedtime and had spent a restless night, he awakened at four in the morning as usual. After sloshing in the bathtub so mightily that he waked his grandson, who was also having a restless night, he dried himself, dressed slowly, using mainly the right hand because of his infirmity . . . he could not manage the shoestrings so he left them flopping . . . and bathed, dressed and in command of himself, he tiptoed down to the kitchen. It promised to be a fair day; the gray of the dawn sky was changing to the rose and yellow of sunrise. Although the kitchen was still gray, the Judge did not turn on the light, as he liked to look at the sky at this hour. Humming a little song without a tune, he put on the coffee and began preparing his breakfast. He selected the two brownest eggs in the icebox as he had convinced himself that brown eggs were more nourishing than the white ones. After months of practice, with many a gooey slip, he had learned to crack an egg and slip it carefully into the poacher. While the eggs were poaching he buttered his bread lightly and put it in the oven as he disliked toaster toast. Finally, he put a yellow cloth on the breakfast table and blue salt and pepper shakers. Although it was a solitary meal, the Judge did not want it to be a dismal one. The breakfast finished, he carried it item by item to the table, using only the good hand. Meanwhile the coffee was perking merrily. As a final touch he brought mayonnaise from the refrigerator and put a careful dollop on each poached egg. The mayonnaise was made of mineral oil and had, thank God, few calories. The Judge had found a wonderful book, *Diet Without Despair*, which he read constantly. The only trouble was that mineral oil was laxative and it behooved you to be careful not to eat too much for fear of sudden bathroom accidents, bathroom accidents which he knew were unbecoming to a magistrate . . . especially if it occurred in the courthouse office as it had two times. Being sensitive to his own dignity, the Judge was careful to ration the helpings of the delicious, low-calorie mayonnaise.

The small yellow tablecloth and others of the same size which he used and cherished, having them carefully hand laundered, were the ones that had been used on his wife's breakfast trays that he had brought up to her every morning. The robin's-egg blue salt and pepper set had been hers too, as well as the silver coffeepot the Judge now used for his own breakfast. In the old days when he became, little by little, an early riser, he would make his own breakfast, then lovingly prepare his wife's tray, often stopping to go out into the garden and pick some posies to decorate the tray. Then he would walk up carefully, bearing her breakfast, and if his wife was sleeping he would awaken her with kisses, as he was loath to start the day without her gentle voice and encouraging smile before he left for the office. (Except when she became ill he did not waken her; but he could not start out on his day until he saw her, which meant that sometimes toward the end he did not get to the office until afternoon.)

But surrounded by his wife's possessions, his grief subdued by the years, the Judge seldom thought consciously of Miss Missy, especially at breakfast time. He just used her things and sometimes would stare at the blue salt and pepper set with the stun of grief in his eyes.

Anxiety always put a keen edge on the Judge's appetite, and he was especially hungry this morning. When his grandson had come in at nearly one the night before, he had gone straight to bed, and when the Judge had followed, the boy had said in a cold, angry voice, almost shouting: "Don't bother me, for Christ sake, don't bother me. Why can't I ever be left in peace?" The explosion was so loud and sudden that quietly, almost humbly, the Judge went away in his bare, pink feet and his dimity nightshirt. Even when he heard Jester sobbing in the night he was too timid to go in to him.

So for these due and good reasons the Judge was ravenous this morning. He ate the whites of his eggs first . . . the least delicious part of his breakfast . . . then he carefully mashed up the peppered and mayonnaised yolks and spread them delicately on his toast. He ate with careful relish, his maimed hand curved lovingly around the rationed food as though to defend it from some possible aggressor. His eggs and toast finished, he turned now to the coffee which he had carefully decanted into his wife's silver pot. He loaded the coffee with saccharine, blew on it to cool it somewhat, and sipped it slowly, very slowly. After the first cup, he prepared his first morning cigar. It was now going on seven and the sky was a pale tender blue that precedes a fair bright day. Lovingly, the Judge alternated his attention between his coffee and his first cigar. When he had that little seizure and Doc Tatum took him off cigars and whiskey, the Judge had been worried to death at first. He slipped around smoking in the bathroom, drinking in the pantry. He argued with Doc, and then came the irony of Doc's death . . . a confirmed teetotaler who never smoked and only enjoyed a chew on rare occasions. Although the Judge was overwhelmed by grief and an inconsolable mourner at the wake, when the shock of death was over, the Judge felt a secret, such a secret relief that he was almost unaware of what had happened and never acknowledged it. But within a month after Doc's death he was smoking cigars in public and drinking openly as before, but prudently he cut down to seven cigars a day and a pint of bourbon.

Breakfast over, the old Judge was still hungry. He picked up *Diet Without Despair* which was on the kitchen shelf and commenced to read studiously, hungrily. It almost comforted him to know that anchovies, large-sized, were only twenty calories and a stalk of asparagus only five, and that a medium-sized apple was a hundred. But though this knowledge almost comforted him, he was not quite soothed, for what he wanted was more toast, dripping with butter and spread with the homemade blackberry jam that Verily had made. He could see in his mind's eye the delicately browned toast and feel in his mouth the sweet, grainy blackberries. Although he had no intention of digging his grave with his teeth, the anxiety that had sharpened his appetite had at the same time weakened his will; stealthily he was limping to the breadbox when a low growl in his stomach made him stop, his hand outstretched toward the breadbox, and start toward the bathroom which had been put in for him after the 'little seizure.' He veered on his way to pick up *Diet Without Despair* in case there should be any waiting.

After slipping down his trousers hastily, he balanced himself with his good hand and sat gingerly on the stool; then when he was sure of himself, his great buttocks relaxed and he settled. There was not long to wait; he had only time to read the recipe for lemon crustless pie (only ninety-six calories when made with sucaryl) thinking with satisfaction that he would have Verily make the dish for lunch that noon. He was also satisfied when he felt his bowels open noiselessly, and thinking of "mens sana in corpore sano," he smiled a little. When the odor in the bathroom rose, he was not annoyed by this; on the contrary, since he was pleased by anything that belonged to him, and his feces were no exception, the smell rather soothed him. So he sat there, relaxed and meditative, pleased with himself. When he heard a noise in the kitchen, he wiped himself hastily and put himself right before leaving the bathroom.

His heart, suddenly light and volatile as a boy's, had expected Jester. But when, still struggling with his belt, he reached the kitchen no one was there. He could just hear Verily doing her Monday morning cleaning in the front part of the house. A little cheated (he could have stayed longer in the bathroom) he looked at the sky which now had the blaze of full morning, the blue unbroken by a cloud, and he smelled from the open window the fresh, faint smell of summer flowers. The old Judge regretted the fact that the routine of breakfast and bowels was over because there was nothing to do now but wait for the *Milan Courier*.

Since waiting is as tedious in old age as it is in childhood, he found his kitchen spectacles (he had spectacles in the library, the bedroom, aside from his pair at the courthouse) and began to read the *Ladies' Home Journal*. Not to read, really, but to look at the pictures. There, for instance, was a marvelous picture of a chocolate cake, and on the following page a mouth-watering picture of a coconut pie made with condensed milk. Picture after picture the Judge scrutinized wistfully. Then, as though ashamed for his greed, he reminded himself of the truth that, quite aside from the pictures, the *Ladies' Home Journal* was a very superior magazine. (Far, far superior to that dreadful *Saturday Evening Post* whose good-for-nothing editors had never read the story he had once sent them.) There were serious articles about pregnancy and childbirth which he enjoyed, also sound essays on child rearing which the Judge knew were sound because of his own experience. Also articles on marriage and divorce which might well have benefited him as a magistrate if his mind had not been occupied by the plans of a great statesman. Finally, in the *Ladies' Home Journal* there were little extra lines, blocked and inserted in the stories — sayings of Emerson, of Lin Yutang, and the great sages of the world. Several months ago he had read in these bylines the words: "How can the dead be truly dead when they are still walking in my heart?" It was from an old Indian legend and the Judge could not forget it. He had seen in his mind's eye a barefooted, bronzed Indian walking silently in the forest and heard the silent sound of a canoe. He never cried about his wife's death, never even cried about the diet any more. When his nervous system and tear ducts made him cry, he thought of his brother Beau, and Beau was like a lightning rod that could ground and safely conduct his tears. Beau was two years older than he was and had died when he was eighteen years old. As a young boy, Fox Clane had worshiped his brother, yea, worshiped the ground he walked on. Beau acted, could recite, was the president of the Milan Players Club. Beau could have been anything. Then one night he had come in with a sore throat. The next morning he was delirious. It was an infected throat, and Beau was muttering, "I am dying, Egypt, dying, ebbs the crimson lifetide fast." Then he began to sing, "I feel, I feel,

I feel like the morning star; I feel, I feel, I feel like the morning star. Shoo, fly, don't bother me; shoo, fly, don't bother me." At the end Beau had begun to laugh although it wasn't laughter. The young Fox had shuddered so violently that his mother had sent him to the back room. It was a bare bleak room that was a sickroom playroom where the children had their measles, mumps and childhood diseases, and where they were free to roughhouse when they were well. The Judge remembered an old forgotten rocking horse, and a sixteen-year-old boy had put his arms around the wooden horse and cried — and even as an eighty-five-year-old man he could cry whenever he wanted to, just thinking about that early sorrow. The Indian walking silently in the forest and the silent sound of the canoe. "How can the dead be truly dead when they are still walking in my heart?"

Jester came clattering down the stairs. He opened the icebox and poured himself some orange juice. At the same time Verily came to the kitchen and began to prepare Jester's breakfast.

"I want three eggs this morning," Jester said. "Hey, Grandfather."

"Are you all right today, Son?"

"Natch."

The Judge did not mention the crying in the night and neither did Jester. The Judge even restrained himself from asking where Jester had been the night before. But when Jester's breakfast was served, his will broke and he took a golden brown piece of toast, added more butter and spread it with blackberry jam. The forbidden extra toast broke his will even further so that he asked, "Where were you last night?" well knowing as he spoke he shouldn't have asked the question.

"Whether you realize it or not, I'm a grown man now,"

Jester said in a voice that squeaked a little, "and there's such a thing called sex." The Judge, who was prudish about such topics, was relieved when Verily poured him a cup of coffee. He drank silently, not knowing what to say.

"Grandfather, have you ever read the *Kinsey Report?*"

The old Judge had read the book with salacious pleasure, first substituting for the jacket the dust cover of *The Decline and Fall of the Roman Empire.* "It's just tomfoolery and filth."

"It's a scientific survey."

"Science, my foot. I have been an observer of human sin and nature for close on to ninety years, and I never saw anything like that."

"Maybe you ought to put on your glasses."

"How dare you sass me, John Jester Clane."

"Close to ninety years old," the Judge repeated, for now he was a little coquettish about his advancing age, "I've observed human sin as a magistrate and human nature as a man with natural curiosity."

"A bold invaluable scientific survey," said Jester, quoting from a review.

"Pornographic filth."

"A scientific survey of the sexual activities in the human male."

"The book of an impotent, dirty old man," said the old Judge who had relished the book as he marveled behind the covers of *The Decline and Fall of the Roman Empire,* which he had never read but kept in his law office library for show.

"It proves that boys my age have sexual affairs, boys even younger, but at my age it's a necessity — if they're passionate I mean." Jester had read the book in the lending library and it had shocked him. He had read the report a second time and worried terribly. He was afraid, so terribly afraid, that he was not normal and the fear corkscrewed within him. No matter how many times he circled Reba's house, he had never felt the normal sexual urge and his heart quaked with fear for himself, as more than anything else he yearned to be exactly like everyone else. He had read the words "jewel-eyed harlot" which had a beautiful sound that tingled his senses; but the eyes of the woman he had seen leaving Reba's place that spring afternoon were not "jewel-eyed" but only dull and baggy, and yearning to lust and be normal he could only see the gooey lipstick and the vacant smile. And the orange-haired lady he had slept with last night was not a bit "jewel-eyed." Secretly Jester thought sex was a fake, but this morning, now that he had become a man, he felt cocksure and free.

"That's all very well," the Judge said, "but in my youth we went to church and attended B.Y.P.U. meetings and had a raring good time. We went courting and dancing. Believe it or not, Son, in those days I was one of the best dancers in Flowering Branch, limber as a willow and the very soul of grace. The waltz was fashionable those days. We danced to 'Tales of the Vienna Woods,' 'The Merry Widow,' 'Tales of Hoffman' . . . " The old, fat Judge broke off to wave his hands in waltz time and sang in a monotone he imagined was the tune . . .

"Lovely night, oh, lo-o-vely night."

"You're not a bit introverted," Jester said when his grandfather had put down his waving hands and stopped that croaking singing.

The Judge, who had felt this as a criticism, said, "Son, everybody has a right to sing. Every mortal has the right to sing.

Lovely night, oh, lo-o-vely night."

That was all the beautiful tune he could remember. "I danced like a willow and sang like an angel."

"Possibly."

"No possibly about it. In my youth I was as light and radiant as you and your father until the layers of corpulence began to hold me down, but I danced and sang and had a raring good time. I never moped around reading dirty books on the sly."

"That's what I say. You're not a born introvert." Jester added, "Anyway I didn't read the *Kinsey Report* on the sly."

"I had it banned at the public library."

"Why?"

"Because I am not only the leading citizen in Milan but the most responsible one. I am responsible that innocent eyes are not offended nor the calm heart troubled by such a book."

"The more I listen to you the more I wonder if you came from Mars."

"Mars?" The old Judge was bewildered and Jester let it go.

"If you were more introverted you could understand me better."

"Why are you so hipped on that word?"

Jester, who had read the word and never spoken it, deeply regretted he had not used it the night before.

"Lovely night, oh, lov-ely night."

Not being introverted, his grandfather had never wondered if he himself was normal or not. It had never entered his singing and dancing mind if he was normal or queer.

If it turned out he was homosexual like men in the *Kinsey Report*, Jester had vowed that he would kill himself. No, his grandfather was utterly not an introvert, and Jester dearly wished he had used the word the night before. Extrovert, that was the opposite word . . . while he was an introvert. And Sherman? Anyhow, he would use both words.

"I could have written that book myself."

"You?"

"Why certainly. The truth is, Jester, I could have been a great, great writer if I had put my mind to it."

"You?"

"Don't sit there saying, 'You? You?' like an imbecile, Son. All you have to have to be a great writer is application, imagination, and a gift for language."

"You have imagination all right, Grandfather."

The Judge was thinking of *Gone With the Wind* which he could have written easily. He wouldn't have let Bonnie die and he would have changed Rhett Butler; he would have written a better book. He could have written *Forever Amber* with his left foot . . . a much better book, more refined. *Vanity Fair* he could have written too; why, he saw through that Becky as slick as a whistle. He could have written Tolstoy, for although he had not actually read the books, he had seen them in the picture shows. And Shakespeare? He had read Shakespeare at law school and even seen *Hamlet* in Atlanta. An English cast, speaking with English accents, naturally. It was the first year of their marriage and Miss Missy had worn her pearls and her first wedding rings. After three performances of the Atlanta Shakespeare Festival, Miss Missy had enjoyed it so much and was so impressed that she picked up an English accent which lasted a month after they had come home to Milan. But could he have made up "To be or not to be"? Sometimes when he considered the question he thought so, and sometimes he thought not; for after all, even a genius can't do everything and Shakespeare had never been a congressman.

"There have been learned arguments about the authorship

of Shakespeare. It was argued that an illiterate strolling player could never have written poetry like that. Some say it was Ben Jonson who wrote the plays. I know durn well I could have written 'Drink to me only with thine eyes, and I will drink with mine.' I'm sure I could have done that."

"Oh, you can do wonders and eat rotten cucumbers," Jester muttered.

"What's that?"

"Nothing."

". . . and if Ben Jonson wrote 'Drink to me only with thine eyes' and wrote Shakespeare too, then . . ." After a great leap of the imagination, the Judge pondered.

"You mean you are comparing yourself to Shakespeare?"

"Well, maybe not the Bard himself, but after all Ben Jonson was a mortal too." Immortality, that was what the Judge was concerned with. It was inconceivable to him that he would actually die. He would live to a hundred years if he kept to his diet and controlled himself . . . deeply he regretted the extra toast. He didn't want to limit his time for just a hundred years, wasn't there a South American Indian in the newspaper who lived to be a hundred and fifty . . . and would a hundred and fifty years be enough? No. It was immortality he wanted. Immortality like Shakespeare, and if "push came to shovel," even like Ben Jonson. In any case he wanted no ashes and dust for Fox Clane.

"I always knew you were the biggest egotist in the round world, but in my wildest dreams it never occurred to me you could compare yourself to Shakespeare or Ben Jonson."

"I was not comparing myself to the Bard himself; in fact, I have the proper humility. Anyway, I never set out to be a writer and you can't be everything."

Jester, who had been cruelly hurt the night before, was cruel to his grandfather, deliberately ignoring the fact that he was old. "Yes, the more I hear you, the more I wonder if you come from Mars." Jester got up from the table, his breakfast almost untouched.

The Judge followed his grandson. "Mars," he repeated, "you mean you think I'm off on another planet?" His voice was suddenly high, almost shrill. "Well, let me tell you this, John Jester Clane, I'm not off on another planet, I'm right here on this earth where I belong and want to be. I'm rooted in the very center of the earth. I may not be immortal yet, but you wait and see, my name will be synonymous with George Washington or Abraham Lincoln . . . more beloved than Lincoln's, for I am the one who will redress the wrongs in my country."

"Oh, the Confederate money . . . I'm off now."

"Wait, Son, this colored boy is coming today and I thought you would screen him with me."

"I know about that," Jester said. He did not want to be there when Sherman arrived.

"He's a responsible boy, I know all about him, and he will help me with my diet, give me my injections, open my mail, and be my general amanuensis. He will be a comfort to me."

"If that Sherman Pew is a comfort to you, just let me know."

"He will read to me . . . an educated boy . . . immortal poetry." His voice was suddenly shrill. "Not dirty trash like that book I banned at the public library. I had to ban it because as a responsible man I'm determined that things in this town and state are going to be in order, and this country too, and the world if I can accomplish it."

Jester slammed out of the house.

Although he had not set the alarm clock and could very well have daydreamed for a long time before getting out of bed, the spring of energy and life stirred violently that morning. The golden summer was with him and he was still free. When he slammed out of the house, Jester did not race but took his mortal time, for after all it was summer vacation and he was not going to any fire. He could stop to look at the world, he could imagine, he could look with summer vacation freedom at the border of verbena that lined the drive. He even stooped down and examined a vivid flower and joy was with him. Jester was dressed in his best clothes that morning, wearing a white duck suit and even a coat. He just wished his beard would get a hump on and grow so he could shave. But suppose he never grew a beard, what would people think of him? For a moment the vacation joy darkened until he thought of something else.

He had dressed fit to kill because he knew that Sherman was coming, and he had slammed out of the house because he did not want to meet Sherman that way. Last evening he had not been the least bit witty or sparkling; in fact, he had just goofed off, and he did not want to meet Sherman until he could be witty and sparkling. How Jester was going to accomplish that this morning he didn't know, but he would talk about introverts and extroverts . . . where that would lead him, he wondered. In spite of the fact that Sherman utterly disagreed with him about his theories of flight and was unimpressed about Jester's flying, he walked automatically to J. T. Malone's pharmacy and stood at the corner waiting for the bus that went to the airport. Happy, confident, free, he lifted his arms and flapped them for a moment.

J. T. Malone, who saw that gesture through the window of the pharmacy, wondered if, after all, the boy was dotty.

Jester was trying to be witty and sparkling and he thought that being alone in the airplane would help him in this. It was the sixth time that he had soloed. A great part of his mind was taken up with the instruments. In the blue, wind-rushing air his spirits lifted, but witty and sparkling in his conversation . . . he didn't know. Of course it would depend a great deal on what Sherman said himself, so he would have to hinge the conversation and he just dearly hoped that he would be witty and sparkling.

It was an open Moth Jester was flying and the wind pulled his red hair backward from his scalp. He deliberately had not worn a helmet because he liked the sensation of wind and sun. He would put on the helmet when he went to the house and met Sherman there. Careless he would be, and busy, a helmeted aviator. After a half an hour of wind-rushing cobalt and sun, he began to think of landing. Zooming carefully, circling to get just the proper distance, he had no room in his thoughts for Sherman even, because he was responsible for his own life and for the training Moth. The landing was bumpy, but when he put on his helmet and jumped out with careful grace he wished somebody could have seen him.

The bus ride back from the airport always made him feel squashed, and the old bus itself was plodding and terribly re-stricted compared to the air; and the more he flew the more he was convinced that every adult had the moral obligation to fly, no matter what Sherman Pew's convictions were about this matter.

He left the bus at the corner of J. T. Malone's drugstore which was in the center of town. He looked at the town. On the next block was the Wedwell Spinning Mill. From the open basement window the heat from the dye vats made wavy lines in the sweltering air. Just to stretch his legs, he strolled around the business section of town. Pedestrians stayed close to the awnings and it was the time of late morn-ing when their shadows cast on the glittering sidewalk were blunt and dwarfed. His unaccustomed coat made him very hot as he walked through town, waving to people he knew and blushing with surprise and pride when Hamilton Breedlove of the First National Bank tipped his hat at him — very likely because of the coat. Jester circled back to Malone's drugstore thinking of a cherry coke with cool crushed ice. On the corner, near where he had waited for the bus, a town character called Wagon sat in the shade of the awning with his cap on the sidewalk next to him. Wagon, a light-colored Negro who had lost both legs in a sawmill accident, was toted every day by Grown Boy and transported in the wagon where he would beg before awninged stores. Then when the stores closed, Grown Boy would wheel him back home in the wagon. When Jester dropped a nickel in the cap, he noticed that quite a few coins were there, and even a fifty-cent piece. The fifty-cent piece was a decoy coin Wagon always used in hope of further generosity.

"How you do today, Uncle?"

"Just tollable."

Grown Boy, who often showed up at dinnertime, was standing there just watching. Wagon today had fried chicken instead of his usual side-meat sandwich. He ate the chicken with the lingering delicate grace with which colored people eat chicken.

Grown Boy asked, "Why don you gimme a piece of chicken?" although he had already eaten dinner.

"Go on, nigger."

"Or some biscuits and molasses?"

"I ain payin no min to you."

"Or a nickel for a cone?"

"Go on, nigger. You come before me like a gnat."

So it would go on, Jester knew. The hulking, dimwitted colored boy begging from the beggar. Tipped panama hats, the separate fountains for white and colored people in the courthouse square, the trough and hitching post for mules, muslin and white linen and raggedy overalls. Milan. Milan. Milan.

As Jester turned into the dim, fan-smelling drugstore, he faced Mr. Malone who stood behind the fountain in his shirt-sleeves.

"May I have a coke, sir?"

Fancy and overpolite the boy was, and Malone remembered the dotty way he flapped his arms when he was waiting for the airport bus.

While Mr. Malone made up the Coca-Cola, Jester moseyed over to the scales and stood on them.

"Those scales don't work," Mr. Malone said.

"Excuse me," Jester said.

Malone watched Jester and wondered. Why did he say that, and wasn't it a dotty thing to say, apologizing because the pharmacy scales didn't work. Dotty for sure.

Milan. Some people were content to live and die in Milan with only brief visits to relatives and so forth in Flowering Branch, Goat Rock, or other smaller towns near by. Some people were content to live their mortal lives and die and be buried in Milan. Jester Clane was not one of those. Maybe a minority of one, but a definitely *not* one. Jester pranced with irritation as he waited and Malone watched him.

The coke was frosty-beaded on the counter and Malone said, "Here you are."

"Thank you, sir." When Malone went to the compounding room, Jester sipped his icy coke, still brooding about Milan. It was the broiling season when everybody wore shirtsleeves except dyed-in-the-wool sticklers who put on their coats when they went to lunch in the Cricket Tea Room or the New York Café. His Coca-Cola still in hand, Jester moved idly to the open doorway.

The next few moments would be forever branded in his brain. They were kaleidoscopic, nightmare moments, too

swift and violent to be fully understood at the time. Later
Jester knew he was responsible for the murder and the knowledge of that fact brought further responsibility. Those were
the moments when impulse and innocence were tarnished, the
moments which end the end, and which, many months later,
were to save him from another murder — in truth, to save
his very soul.

Meanwhile Jester, Coca-Cola in hand, was watching the
flame-blue sky and the burning noonday sun. The noon
whistle blew from the Wedwell Mill. The millworkers strag-
gled out for lunch. "The emotional scum of the earth," his
grandfather had called them, although he had a great hunk
of Wedwell Spinning Mill stock which had gone up very
satisfactorily. Wages had increased, so that instead of bringing lunch pails the hands could afford to eat at luncheonettes.
As a child, Jester had feared and abhorred "factory tags," appalled by the squalor and misery he saw in Mill Town. Even
now he didn't like those blue-denimed, tobacco-chewing mill
hands.

Meanwhile, Wagon had only two pieces of fried chicken
left . . . the neck and the back. With loving delicacy he
started on the neck which has as many stringy bones as a
banjo and is just as sweet.

"Just a teeny bit," Grown Boy begged. He was looking
yearningly at the back and his rusty black hand reached toward it a little. Wagon swallowed quickly and spat on the
back to insure it for himself. The phlegmy spit on the crusty
brown chicken angered Grown. As Jester watched him, he
saw the dark, covetous eyes fix on the change in the begging
cap. A sudden warning made him cry, "Don't, don't," but
his stifled warning was lost by the clanging of the town clock
striking twelve. There were the scrambled sensations of glare
and brassy gongs and the resonance of the static midday;
then it happened so instantly, so violently, that Jester could

not take it in. Grown Boy dived for the coins in the begging cap and ran.

"Git him. Git him," Wagon screamed, histing himself on his sawed-off legs with the leather "shoes" to protect them, and jumping from leg to leg in helpless fury. Meantime Jester was chasing Grown. And the hands from the mill, seeing a white-coated white man running after a nigger, joined in the chase. The cop on Twelfth and Broad saw the commotion and hastened to the scene. When Jester caught Grown Boy by the collar and was struggling to seize the money from Grown's fist, more than half a dozen people had joined in the fray, although none of them knew what it was about.

"Git the nigger. Git the nigger bastard."

The cop parted the melee with the use of his billy stick and finally cracked Grown Boy on the head as he struggled in terror. Few heard the blow, but Grown Boy limpened instantly and fell. The crowd made way and watched. There was only a thin trickle of blood on the black scalp, but Grown Boy was dead. The greedy, lively, wanting boy who had never had his share of sense lay on the Milan sidewalk . . . forever stilled.

Jester threw himself on the black boy. "Grown?" he pleaded.

"He's dead," somebody in the crowd said.

"Dead?"

"Yes," said the cop after some minutes. "Break it up you all." And doing his duty, he went to the telephone booth at the pharmacy and called an ambulance, although he had seen that look of death. When he came back to the scene, the crowd had drifted back closer to the awning and only Jester remained near the body.

"Is he really dead?" Jester asked, and he touched the face that was still warm.

"Don't touch him," the cop said.

The cop questioned Jester about what had happened and took out his notebook and paper. Jester began a dazed account. His head felt light like a gas balloon.

The ambulance shrilled in the static afternoon. An intern in a white coat leaped out and put his stethoscope on Grown Boy's chest.

"Dead?" the cop asked.

"As a doornail," the intern said.

"Are you sure?" Jester asked.

The intern looked at Jester and noticed his panama hat that had been knocked off. "Is this your hat?" Jester took the hat, which was grimy now.

The white-coated interns carried the body to the ambulance. It was all so callous and swift and dreamlike that Jester turned slowly toward the drugstore, his hand on his head. The cop followed him.

Wagon, who was still eating his spat-on back, said, "What happened?"

"Dunno," said the cop.

Jester felt lightheaded. Could it be possible he was going to faint? "I feel funny."

The cop, glad to be doing something, steered him to a chair in the pharmacy and said, "Sit down here and hold your head between your legs." Jester did so and when the blood rushed back to his head he sat up, although he was very pale.

"It was all my fault. If I hadn't been chasing him and those people piling in on top of us," he turned to the cop, "and why did you hit him so hard?"

"When you are breaking up a crowd with a billy stick you don't know how hard you are hitting. I don't like violence any more than you do. Maybe I shouldn't even have joined the force."

Meantime Malone had called the old Judge to come and get his grandson and Jester was crying with shock.

When Sherman Pew drove up to bring him home, Jester, who was not thinking about impressing Sherman any more, was led to the car while the cop tried to explain what had happened. After listening, Sherman only commented, "Well, Grown Boy has always been just a feeb, and in my case, if I was just a feeb, I'd be glad if it happened to me. I put myself in other people's places."

"I do wish you would shut up," Jester said.

At the Judge's household there were tears and disorder when they arrived. Verily was sobbing for her nephew and the Judge patted her with awkward little pats. She was sent home to her own people to mourn over that sudden noonday death.

Before the news came, the Judge had had a happy fruitful morning. He had been working joyfully; there had been none of the idle tedium that day, that endlessness of time that is as hard to bear in old age as it is in early childhood. Sherman Pew was panning out to his utmost expectations. Not only was he an intelligent colored boy who understood about insulin and the needles as soon as he was told and sworn to secrecy, he also had imagination, talked of diet and substitutions for calories, and so forth. When the Judge had impressed on him that diabetes was not catching, Sherman had said: "I know all about diabetes. My brother had it. We had to weigh his food on a teensy little balancing scale. Every morsel of food."

The Judge, who suddenly recalled that Sherman was a foundling, wondered a second about this information but said nothing.

"I know all about calories too, sir, on account of I am a house guest of Zippo Mullins and his sister went on a diet. I whipped the fluffy mashed potatoes with skimmed milk for her and made sucaryl jello. Yessireebob, I know all about diets."

"Do you think you would make me a good amanuensis?"

"A good what, Judge?"

"An amanuensis is a kind of secretary."

"Oh, a super-dooper secretary," Sherman said, his voice soft with enchantment. "I would adore that."

"Harrumph," said the Judge, to hide his pleasure. "I have quite a voluminous correspondence, serious, profound correspondence and little niggling letters."

"I adore writing letters and write a lovely hand."

"Penmanship is most indicative." The Judge added, "Calligraphy."

"Where are the letters, sir?"

"In my steel file in my office at the courthouse."

"You want me to get them?"

"No," the Judge said hastily, as he had answered every letter; indeed, that was his chief occupation when he went in the morning to his office — that and the perusal of the *Flowering Branch Ledger* and the *Milan Courier*. Last week there had come a day when not a letter of moment had been received — only an advertisement for Kare Free Kamping Equipment which was probably meant for Jester anyway. Cheated that there were no letters of moment, the Judge had answered the ad, posing trenchant questions about sleeping bags and the quality of frying pans. The static tedium of old age had troubled him so often. But not today; this morning with Sherman he was on a high horse, his head literally teeming with plans.

"Last night I wrote a letter that lasted to the wee hours," Sherman said.

"A love letter?"

"No." Sherman thought over the letter which he had posted on the way to work. At first the address had puzzled him, then he addressed it to: "Madame Marian Anderson, The steps of the Lincoln Memorial." If she wasn't right there, they would forward it. Mother . . . Mother . . . he was thinking, you are too famous to miss.

"My beloved wife always said I wrote the most precious love letters in the world."

"I don't waste time writing love letters. This long letter I wrote last night was a finding letter."

"Letter writing is an art in itself."

"What kind of letter do you wish me to write today?" Sherman added, timidly, "Not a love letter, I presume."

"Of course not, silly. It's a letter concerning my grandson. A letter of petition, you might say."

"Petition?"

"I am asking an old friend and fellow congressman to put my boy up for West Point."

"I see."

"I have to draft it carefully in my mind beforehand. They are the most delicate letters of all . . . petition letters." The Judge closed his eyes and placed his thumb and forefinger over his eyelids, thinking profoundly. It was a gesture almost of pain, but that morning the Judge had no pain at all; on the contrary, after the years of boredom and endless blank time, the utter joy of having important letters to compose and a genuine amanuensis at his disposal made the Judge as buoyant as a boy again. He sat furrowed and immobile so long that Sherman was concerned.

"Head hurt?"

The Judge jerked and straightened himself. "Mercy no, I was just composing the structure of the letter. Thinking to whom I'm writing and the various circumstances of his present and past life. I'm just thinking of the individual I'm writing to."

"Who is he?"

"Senator Thomas of Georgia. Address him: Washington, D.C."

Sherman dipped the pen in the inkwell three times and straightened the paper very carefully, thrilled at the thought of writing to a senator.

"My Dear Friend and Colleague, Tip Thomas."

Again Sherman dipped the pen in ink and began to write with a flourish. "Yes, sir?"

"Be quiet, I'm thinking . . . Proceed now."

Sherman was writing that when the Judge stopped him. "You don't write that. Start again. When I say 'proceed' and things like that, don't actually write them."

"I was just taking dictation."

"But, by God, use common sense."

"I am using common sense, but when you dictate words I naturally write them."

"Let's start at the very beginning. The salutation reads: My Dear Friend and Colleague, Tip Thomas. Get that?"

"I shouldn't write the get that, should I?"

"Of course not."

The Judge was wondering if his amanuensis was as brilliant as he first supposed, and Sherman was wondering privately if the old man was nuts. So both regarded each other with mutual suspicions of mental inadequacy. The work went badly at first.

"Don't write this in the letter. I just want to level with you personally."

"Well, level personally."

"The art of a true amanuensis is to write down everything in the letter or document, but not to record personal reflections or, in other words, things that go on in my mind that are more or less extraneous to the said letter. The trouble with me, boy, is my mind works too quick and so many random thoughts come into it that are not pertinent to any particular train of thought."

"I understand, sir," said Sherman, who was thinking that the job was not what he had imagined.

"Not many people understand me," the Judge said simply.

"You mean you want me to read your mind about what to write in the letter and what to not."

"Not read my mind," the Judge said indignantly, "but to gather from my intonations which is personal rumination and which is not."

"I'm a wonderful mind reader."

"You mean you are intuitive? Why so am I."

Sherman did not know what the word meant, but he was thinking that if he stayed on with the old Judge he would pick up a grand vocabulary.

"Back to the letter," the Judge said sternly. "Write after the salutation, 'It has recently come to my attention that . . .'" The Judge broke off and continued in a lower voice which Sherman, who was reading the Judge's mind, did not write down. "How recently is recently, boy? One — two — three years? I guess it happened ten years ago."

"I wouldn't say recently in that case."

"You are quite correct," the Judge decided in a firm voice. "Start the letter on a completely different tack."

The gilt clock in the library sounded twelve strikes. "It's noon."

"Yea," said Sherman, pen in hand and waiting.

"At noon I interrupt my endeavors to have the first toddy of the day. The privilege of an old man."

"Do you wish me to prepare it for you?"

"That would be most kindly, boy. Would you like a little bourbon and branch water?"

"Bourbon and branch water?"

"I'm not a solitary drinker. I don't like to drink alone."
Indeed, in the old days he used to call in the yardman, Verily,
or anyone else to drink with him. Since Verily did not drink
and the yardman was dead, the Judge was many times forced
to drink alone, but he didn't like it. "A little toddy to keep me
company."

This was the delightful part of the job that Sherman hadn't
thought about. He said, "I'd be very pleased, sir. What
measure drink do you like?"

"Half and half, and don't drown it."

Sherman bustled to the kitchen to make the drinks. He
was already worrying about dinner. If they had the drink
together and became friends, he would hate to be sent to the
kitchen to have dinner with the cook. He knew it would
happen, but he would hate it. He rehearsed carefully what he
would say. "I never eat dinner," or "I ate such a hearty
breakfast I'm not hungry." He poured the half and halfs,
both of them, and returned to the library.

After the Judge had sipped his drink once and smacked his
lips, he said, "This is ex cathedral."

"What?" Sherman said.

"That's what the Pope says when he's speaking frankly. I
mean that nothing that I say to you now while we're drinking
is in the letter. My friend Tip Thomas took to himself a
helpmeet . . . or is it helpmate. I mean by this, he took to himself a second wife. As a rule I don't approve of second marriages, but when I think about it I just think, 'Live and let
live.' You understand, boy?"

"No, sir. Not exactly, sir."

"I wonder if I should overlook the second marriage and talk
about his first wife. Talk in praise about his first wife and not
mention the second."

"Why mention either one of them?"

The Judge leaned his head back. "The art of letter writing is like this; you first make gracious personal remarks about health and wives and so forth, and then when that's covered, you come plumb to the subject of what the letter is really about."

The Judge drank blissfully. As he drank a little miracle was happening.

When the telephone rang, the Judge could not understand all at once. J. T. Malone was talking to him, but what he was saying seemed to make no sense. "Grown Boy killed in a street fight . . . and Jester in the fight?" he repeated. "I'll send somebody to get Jester at the drugstore." He turned to Sherman. "Sherman, will you go drive to Mr. Malone's drugstore and pick up my grandson?" Sherman, who had never driven a car in his life, agreed with pleasure. He had watched people drive and thought he knew how it went. The Judge put down his drink and went to the kitchen. "Verily," he started, "I have some serious news for you."

After one look at the old Judge's face, Verily said, "Somebody daid?" When the Judge did not answer she said, "Sister Bula?"

When the Judge told her it was Grown Boy, she flung her apron over her head and sobbed loudly. "And in all these years he never had his share of sense." She told this as though it was the most poignant and explicable truth about the unreasonable fact that was shattering her.

The Judge tried to comfort her with little bearlike pats. He went to the library, finished his drink and the drink that Sherman had left unfinished and then went to the front porch to wait for Jester.

Then he realized the little miracle that had happened. Every morning for fifteen years he had waited so tediously for the delivery of the *Milan Courier*, waiting in the kitchen or in the library, his heart leaping up when he heard that little plop. But today, after all these years, his time was so occupied he had not even thought about the paper. Joyfully, the old Judge limped down the steps to pick up the *Milan Courier*.

6

SINCE livingness is made up of countless daily miracles, most of which are unnoticed, Malone, in that season of sadness, noticed a little miracle and was astonished. Each morning that summer he had waked up with an amorphous dread. What was the awful thing that was going to happen to him? What was it? When? Where? When consciousness finally formed, it was so merciless that he could lie still no longer; he had to get up and roam the hall and kitchen, roaming without purpose, just roaming, waiting. Waiting for what? After his conversation with the Judge, he had filled the freezing compartment of the refrigerator with calf liver and beef liver. So morning after morning, while the electric light fought with the dawn, he fried a slice of the terrible liver. He had always loathed liver, even the Sunday chicken liver that the children squabbled over. After it was cooked, smelling up the whole house like a stink bomb, Malone ate it, every loathsome bite. Just the fact that it was so loathsome comforted him a little. He swallowed even the gristly pieces that other people removed from their mouths and put on the sides of their plates. Castor oil also had a nasty taste, and it was effective. The trouble with Dr. Hayden, he had never suggested any cures, nasty or otherwise, for that . . . leukemia. Name a man a fatal disease and not recommend the faintest cure . . . Malone's whole being was outraged. A pharmacist for close on to twenty years, he had listened to and prescribed for trillions of complaints: constipation, kidney trouble, smuts in the eye, and so forth. If he honestly felt the case was beyond him he would tell the customer to consult a doctor, but that was not often . . . Malone felt he was as good as any bona fide M.D. in Milan, and he prescribed for trillions of complaints. A good patient himself, dosing himself with nasty Sal Hepatica, using Sloan's Liniment when needed, Malone would eat every living bite of the loathsome liver. Then he would wait in the brightly lighted kitchen. Waiting for what? And when?

One morning toward the end of summer, Malone was wakening and fought against wakening. He struggled for the soft, sweet limbo of sleep, but he could not recapture it. The shrill birds were already up and at him, slicing to shreds his soft, sweet sleep. That morning he was exhausted. The terror of consciousness washed over his tired body and limpened spirit. He was going to force himself to sleep. Think of counting sheep — black sheep, white sheep, red sheep all hippity-hoppity and with plumping tails. Think of nothingness, oh, soft sweet sleep. He would not get up and turn on lights and roam the hall and kitchen, and roam and wait and dread. He would never fry that loathsome liver at dawn, smelling up the whole house like a stink bomb. Never no longer. Never no more. Malone switched on the bedside lamp and opened the drawer. There were the Tuinal capsules he had prescribed for himself. There were forty of them, he knew. His trembling fingers slid amongst the red and green capsules. Forty of them, he knew. He would no longer have to get up at dawn and roam the house in terror. No longer go to the pharmacy just because he had always gone to the pharmacy as it was his living and the support of his wife and family. If J. T. Malone was not the sole support, because of those shares of Coca-Cola stock his wife had bought with her own money and because of the three houses she had inherited from her mother — dear old Mrs. Greenlove who had died fifteen years ago — if because of his wife's various resources he was not the utter and sole provider, the pharmacy was the mainstay of the family and he was a good provider, no matter what people might think. The pharmacy was the first store open in Milan and the last to close. Standing faithfully, listening to complaints, prescribing medicine, making cokes and sundaes, compounding prescriptions . . . no more, no more! Why had he done it so long? Like a plodding old mule going round and round a sorghum mill. And going home every night. And sleeping in bed with his wife whom he had long since ceased to love. Why? Because there was no fitting place to be except the pharmacy? Because there was no other fitting place to sleep except in bed beside his wife? Working at the pharmacy, sleeping with his wife, no more! His drab livingness spread out before him as he fingered the jewel-bright Tuinal.

Malone put one capsule in his mouth and drank half a glass of water. How much water would he have to drink to swallow the forty capsules?

After the first capsule he swallowed another, then a third. Then he stopped and refilled the water glass. When he came back to bed again he wanted a cigarette. As he smoked it he grew drowsy. While he was smoking his second cigarette it fell from between his lifeless fingers for J. T. Malone at last had gone to sleep again.

He slept until seven that morning and the household was awake when he went into the busy kitchen. For one of the few times in his life he failed to bathe and shave, for fear of being late at the pharmacy.

That morning he saw with his eyes the little miracle, but he was too swivetty and occupied to take it in. He took the short cut through the back yard and back gate, the miracle was there but his eyes were blind as he loped toward the gate. Yet when he reached the pharmacy he wondered why he had been hurrying so; no one was there. But already he had begun his day. He let down the awnings with a slam and turned on the electric fan. When the first customer entered his day had begun, although the first customer was only Herman Klein, the jeweler next door. Herman Klein was always in and out of the drugstore all day long, drinking Coca-Colas. He also kept a bottle of liquor in the compounding room of the pharmacy, as his wife hated liquor and did not allow it in the home. So Herman Klein spent the whole day at his shop doing his watchwork and visiting the drugstore frequently. Herman Klein did not go home for noonday dinner as did most Milan businessmen; he had a little snifter, then ate one of the neatly wrapped chicken sandwiches that Mrs. Malone supplied. After Herman Klein had been attended to, a flurry of customers came in all at once. A mother came in with a bed-wetting child, and Malone sold her a Eurotone, a device that rings a bell when the bed is being wet. He had sold Eurotones to many parents, but privately he wondered why the ring of the bell would really be effective. Privately he wondered if it might not scare the be-Jesus out of a sleeping child, and what good would it do if the whole house was alarmed just because little Johnny made some quiet little pee-pee in his sleep? He thought privately it would be better to let Johnny just pee in peace. Malone advised the mothers sagely: "I've sold a lot of these devices but the main thing I've always felt about toilet training is the cooperation of the child." Malone scrutinized the child, a squarish little girl who did not look at all cooperative. He fitted a woman who had varicose veins with a surgical stocking. He listened to complaints of headaches, backaches and bowel trouble. He studied each customer carefully, made his diagnosis and sold the medicines. Nobody had leukemia, nobody went away empty handed.

By one o'clock when that wife-ridden, hag-ridden, little Herman Klein came in for his sandwich, Malone was tired. He was also meditating. He wondered who else in the world was worse off than he was. He looked at that little Herman Klein munching his sandwich at the counter. Malone loathed him. Loathed him for being so spineless, for working so hard, for not going to the Cricket Tea Room or the New York Café like other decent businessmen who did not go home for dinner. He did not feel sorry for Herman Klein. He just despised him.

He put on his coat to go home to dinner. It was a sweltering day, with a sky like white lightning. He walked slowly this time, feeling the weight of his white linen coat or a weight somehow on his shoulders. He always took his time and had a home-cooked dinner. Not like that mousy little Herman Klein. He went through the back-yard gate and then, though he was tired, he recognized the miracle. The vegetable garden, which he had sown so carelessly and forgotten in that long season of fear, had grown up. There were the purple cabbages, little frills of carrots, the green, green turnip greens and tomatoes. He stood looking at the garden. Meanwhile, a crowd of children had entered the open gate. They were the Lank brood. It was a curious thing about the Lanks. They had one multiple birth after the other. Twins. Triplets. They rented one of his wife's houses that she had inherited — a crummy, beatup house, as you would expect with all those hoards of children. Sammy Lank was a foreman at the Wedwell Spinning Mill. When at times he was laid off, Malone did not press him for the rent. Malone's house, which Martha had also inherited from old Mrs. Greenlove, God bless her, was the corner house facing a very respectable street. The other three houses which adjoined each other were around the corner, and the neighborhood there was running down. The Lank family house was the last house, that is, the last house in the row of three that Mrs. Malone had inherited. So Malone saw the Lank brood frequently. Grimy, sniffly-nosed, they just hung around since there was nothing at home to do. One especially cold winter when Mrs. Lank was confined with twins, Malone had sent some coal to their house because he was fond of children and knew they were cold. The children were called Nip and Tuck, Cyrily and Simon, and Rosemary, Rosamond, and Rosa. The children now were growing up. The eldest triplets, who were already married and having babies on their own, were born the night the Dionne quints were born and the *Milan Courier* had had a little article about "Our Milan Trio" which the Lanks framed and put in their sitting room.

Malone looked again at the garden. "Sugar," he called.

"Yes, Hon," Mrs. Malone answered.

"Have you seen the vegetable garden?" Malone went into the house.

"What vegetable garden?" Mrs. Malone asked.

"Why, our vegetable garden."

"Of course I've seen it, Hon. We've been eating out of it all summer. What's the matter with you?"

Malone, who had no appetite these days and never remembered what he ate, said nothing, but it was indeed a miracle that that garden, planted so carelessly and never tended, had flourished. The collards were growing like crazy as collards will do. Plant a collard in the garden and they just grow like crazy, pushing out the other plants. The same as morning-glories . . . a collard or a morning-glory.

There was little conversation at the noonday dinner. They had meat loaf and double-trouble potatoes, but although the meal was well cooked, Malone did not taste it. "I've been telling you all summer that the vegetables were home grown," Mrs. Malone said. Malone heard the remark but paid no attention, let alone replied; for years his wife's voice had been like a sawmill to him, a sound you hear but pay no attention to.

Young Ellen and Tommy bolted their dinner and were about to run.

"You ought to chew, darlings. Otherwise nobody knows what intestinal trouble lies in wait for you. When I was a girl they had what they called the Fletcher cure, you were supposed to chew seven times before you actually swallowed. If you continue to eat like firehorses . . ." But already the Malone children had said "Excuse me," and had run from the house.

From then on the dinner was a silent one, and neither voiced their thoughts. Mrs. Malone was thinking about her "Mrs. Malone Sandwiches" . . . plump kosher chickens (it did not matter if the fowls were Jewish), the A & P hens she prodded carefully, midget turkeys, twenty-pound turkeys. She labeled the turkey sandwiches "Mrs. Malone's Turkey Salad Sandwich," although it was an amazing thing how many people could not taste the difference between turkey salad and chicken salad. Meanwhile, Malone was occupied with his own professional considerations; should he have sold the Eurotone this morning? It had slipped his mind that a few months ago a woman had complained about the Eurotone. It seemed that her little Eustis had slept through all the bells of the Eurotone, but the family had waked up and stood around watching the quietly peeing and sound asleep little Eustis, while the Eurotone bells were ringing like mad. Finally, it seemed, the daddy had yanked the child out of the wet bed and warmed his behind in front of the whole family. Was that fair? Malone pondered the subject and decided it was definitely not fair. He had never laid a hand on his children, whether they deserved it or not. Mrs. Malone disciplined the children, as Malone felt it was the wife's duty, and she always cried when it was her clear duty to spank one of the children. The only time Malone felt impelled to act in such a manner was the time the four-year-old Ellen built a secret fire under her grandmother's bed. How old Mrs. Greenlove had cried, both for her own terror and for the fact that her favorite grandchild was being chastised. But playing with fire was the only misbehavior that Malone dealt with, as it was too serious a thing to trust to a tenderhearted mother who invariably cried as she chastised. Yes, forbidden matches and fires were the only things he had to handle. And the Eurotone? Although it was a recommended product, he regretted having sold it that morning. With a painful, final swallow that made his Adam's apple struggle in his frail throat, Malone excused himself and rose from the table.

"I'm going to call Mr. Harris to take over the pharmacy for the balance of the day."

Anxiety flickered across Mrs. Malone's placid face. "Aren't you feeling well, Hon?"

Rage made Malone fist his hands until the knuckles whitened. A man with leukemia not feeling well? What the hell did the woman think he had . . . chicken pox or spring fever? But although his fisted knuckles were white with rage, he only said, "I feel no better nor no worse than I deserve."

"You work too hard, Hon. Altogether too hard. You're a regular workhorse."

"A mule," Malone corrected. "A mule going round and round a cane mill."

"J.T., don't you want me to put you in a tub of nice, tepid water?"

"I certainly do not want it."

"Don't be mulish, Hon. I'm just trying to comfort you."

"I can be mulish as I please in my own house," Malone said stubbornly.

"I was just trying to comfort you, but I see it's no use."

"No use at all," he answered bitterly.

Malone took a steaming shower, washed his hair, shaved, and darkened the bedroom. But he was too angry to rest. From the kitchen he could hear Mrs. Malone beating batter for a wedding cake or something, and this made him still angrier. He went out into the glaring afternoon.

He had lost the summer that year; the vegetables had grown and been eaten unnoticed. The hard blaze of summer shriveled his spirit. The Judge had insisted that nothing ailed him that a spell of Milan summer would not cure. Thinking of the old Judge, he went to the back porch and found a paper sack. Although he was free for the afternoon, there was no sense of freedom in him. Wearily he began to pick a mess of greens for the Judge, both turnip greens and collards. Then he added the largest tomato and stood for a moment weighing it in his hand.

"Hon," Mrs. Malone called from the kitchen window, "what are you doing?"

"What? What?"

"What are you doing just standing there in the heat of the afternoon?"

Things had come to a pretty pass when a man has to account for himself for just standing alone in his own back yard. But though his thoughts were brutal he only answered, "Picking greens."

"You ought to have a hat on if you are going to linger long in this broiling sun. Might save you a sunstroke, Hon."

Malone's face paled as he shouted, "Why is it your God-damn business?"

"Don't swear, J.T., for mercy's sake."

So Malone stayed longer in the broiling heat, just because his wife had questioned and interfered. Then, hatless, and carrying the sack of vegetables, he trudged over to the Judge's house. The Judge was in the darkened library and the nigger with the blue eyes was with him.

"High-ho, J.T., high-ho, my hearty. You're just the man I was looking for."

"What for?" For Malone was both pleased and taken aback by this hearty reception.

"This is the hour for immortal poetry. My amanuensis reads to me."

"Your what?" Malone asked sharply, as the word suggested to him Eurotone and bed-wetting.

"My secretary here. Sherman Pew. He is an excellent reader, and the reading hour is one of the pleasantest portions of the day. Today we're reading Longfellow. Read on, MacDuff," the Judge said jovially.

"What?"

"I was just paraphrasing Shakespeare, so to say."

"Shakespeare?" Sherman felt out of his element, left out

and cloddish. He hated Mr. Malone for coming in at the poetry hour. Why wasn't that old sourpuss at the drugstore where he belonged?

"Go back to:

> By the shore of Gitche Gumee,
> By the shining Big-Sea-Water,
> At the doorway of his wigwam . . ."

The Judge's eyes were closed and his head gently wagged with the rhythm. "Proceed, Sherman."

"I don't want to," said Sherman sullenly. Why should he make a monkey of himself in front of that fuss-body Mr. Malone? He'd be damned if he would.

The Judge felt something amiable was going amiss. "Well, just recite, 'I shot an arrow into the air.' "

"I don't feel like it, sir."

Malone watched and listened to the scene, his sack of greens still in his lap.

The Judge, feeling that something *very* amiable was going amiss, and craving to finish the lovely poem, continued himself:

> "Daughter of the moon, Nakomis
> Dark behind it rose the forest
> Rose the black and gloomy pine-trees
> Bright before it beat the water
> Beat the clear and sunny water
> Beat the shining big sea water . . .

My eyes are tired in this darkened room. Can't you take over, Sherman?"

"No, sir."

> "Ewa yea, my little owlet
> Who is this that lights the wigwam
> With his great eyes lights the wigwam . . .

Oh the tenderness, the rhythm and tenderness of this. Why can't you feel it, Sherman? You always read immortal poetry so beautifully."

Sherman scrooched up his behind and did not comment.

Malone, still with the sack of greens in his lap, felt the tension in the room. It was apparent that this sort of thing went on every day. He wondered who was crazy. The old Judge? The nigger with the blue eyes? Himself? Longfellow? He said with careful tact, "I brought you a mess of turnip greens from my garden, and a mess of collards."

With arrogant rudeness Sherman said, "He can't eat them."

The Judge's voice was dismayed. "Why, Sherman," he said pleadingly, "I adore turnip greens and collards."

"It's not on the diet," Sherman insisted. "They belong to be cooked with side meat, streak of lean and streak of fat. And that's not on the diet."

"How about just a slither of the lean portion of streak of lean, streak of fat?"

Sherman was still mad that Mr. Malone had come in at the reading hour which he loved, and the sourpuss old drugstore man had looked at the two of them like they were loony and spoiled the immortal poetry hour. However, he had not read Hiawatha aloud. He had not made himself a monkey; he had left that to the old Judge who did not seem to care if people thought he had just escaped from Milledgeville or not.

Malone said soothingly, "Yankees eat greens with butter or vinegar."

"While I'm certainly no Yankee, I'll try the greens with vinegar. On our honeymoon in New Orleans I ate snails. One snail," the old Judge added.

From the parlor, there was the sound of the piano. Jester was playing the "Lindenbaum." Sherman was furious because he played it so well.

"I eat snails all the time. Picked up the habit when I was in France."

"I didn't know you were ever in France," Malone said.

"Why certainly. I had a brief stint in the service." Zippo Mullins had been in the service, and that was the actual truth, and had told Sherman many stories, most of which Sherman took with a grain of salt.

"J.T., I'm sure you need some refreshment after your broiling walk. How about some gin and quinine water?"

"That would be most acceptable, sir."

"Sherman, will you make Mr. Malone and me some gin and quinine water?"

"Quinine, Judge?" His voice was incredulous, for even if that old Mr. Malone was a drugstore man, he surely wouldn't like bitter quinine on his day off.

The Judge said in a bossy voice, as if to a servant, "It's in the refrigerator. On the bottle it says 'tonic.' "

Sherman wondered why he had not said so at first. Tonic water was not the same as quinine. He knew because he had tasted little drinks ever since he had been with the Judge.

"Put plenty of ice in it," the Judge said.

Sherman was fit to be tied, not only because the reading hour was spoiled but because he had been ordered around like a servant. He hurried in to take it out on Jester. "Is that 'Rockabye Baby' you're playing?"

"No, it is 'Lindenbaum'; I borrowed it from you."

"Well, it is the utter end in German lieder."

Jester, who had been playing with tears of emotion in his eyes, stopped playing, to Sherman's content because he had been playing much too well, especially for a sight-reading job.

Sherman went to the kitchen and fixed the drinks with very little ice. Who was he to be ordered around? And how was it that that puny-faced Jester could play genuine German lieder so well, especially on a sight-reading job?

He had done everything for the old Judge. The afternoon when Grown Boy died, he had cooked supper himself, waiting on the table; however, he would not eat the supper he had cooked. He would not eat the supper, even at the library table. He had found a cook for them. He had found Cinderella Mullins to pinch-hit for them while that Verily was away.

Meanwhile, the Judge was telling his friend Malone, "That boy is a veritable treasure, a jewel. Writes letters for me, reads for me, let alone giving me the injections and making me toe the line on my diet."

Malone's skepticism showed on his face. "How did you happen to run across this paragon?"

"I didn't run across him. He has affected my very life since before he was born."

Malone was hesitant even to conjecture about this mysterious remark. Could it be that the snooty blue-eyed nigger was the Judge's natural son? Improbable as it seemed, it could be possible. "But wasn't he found in a pew at one of the colored churches?"

"He was."

"But how does this affect your very life?"

"Not only my very life but my life's blood — my own son."

Malone tried to think of Johnny having a sexual relation with a colored girl. The fair-haired, decent Johnny Clane with whom he had many times gone hunting at Sereno. It was highly improbable but again not impossible.

The Judge seemed to read his puzzled mind. With his good hand he gripped his stick until the hand turned purple. "If you think for one single moment that my Johnny ever slept with nigger wenches or such immoral doings . . ." The Judge could not finish for rage.

"I never supposed any such thing," Malone said soothingly. "You just put it so mysteriously."

"It is a mystery, if ever there was one. But it's such a bad business that even a garrulous old man like myself can hardly discuss it."

Yet Malone knew he wanted to discuss it further, but at that moment Sherman Pew banged two glasses on the library table. When Sherman bolted out of the room, the Judge continued: "However, now that boy is a golden skein in my old age. Writes my letters with the calligraphy of an angel, gives me my injections and makes me toe the line on the diet. Reads to me in the afternoon."

Malone did not point out that the boy had refused to read that afternoon, so that the old Judge himself had had to finish Longfellow.

"Sherman reads Dickens with such pathos. Sometimes I cry and cry."

"Does that boy ever cry?"

"No, but often he smiles at the humorous places."

Malone, puzzled, waited for the Judge to say something more pertinent about the mystery he had intimated, but he only said, "Well it only goes to show again that 'out of this nettle, danger, we pluck this flower, safety.' "

"Why, what's the matter, sir? Were you in danger?"

"Not exactly in danger . . . that's just the expression of the Bard. But since my dear wife's death I've been so much alone."

Malone was not only puzzled about the Judge, but suddenly worried. "Alone, sir? You have your grandson, and you're the most revered citizen in all Milan."

"You can be the most revered citizen in town, or in all the state, and still feel alone. And *be* alone, by God!"

"But your grandson who is the apple of your eye?"

"It's the nature of young boys to be selfish. I know boys through and through. The only thing that's the matter with Jester is . . . adolescence. I have a profound knowledge of all boys and it all comes down to . . . selfish, selfish, selfish."

Malone was pleased to hear Jester criticized, but very properly he said nothing. He only asked, "How long have you had the colored boy?"

"About two months."

"That's a short time for him to be so well established in the household . . . so cozily settled, one might say."

"Sherman is cozy, thank God. Although he's an adolescent like my grandson, we have a quite different relationship."

Malone was thankful to hear this, but again very properly said nothing. Knowing the capriciousness of the Judge, his fits of instant delight and instant disappointment, he wondered how long this situation would last.

"A veritable jewel," the Judge was saying enthusiastically. "A treasure."

Meanwhile, "the veritable jewel" was reading a movie magazine and drinking gin and tonic with loads of ice. He was alone in the kitchen as that old Verily was cleaning upstairs. Although he was replete with the comforts of taste and imagination . . . it was a very good article about one of his favorite movie stars . . . he was very, very mad. Not only had his special hour of the day been spoiled by the fusspot Mr. Malone, he had lived for three months in suspense, suspense that little by little grew into anxiety. Why hadn't Madame Anderson replied to his letter? If it had been wrongly addressed, it could have been forwarded, for his mother was too famous to miss. When Jester's dog, Tige, walked into the room, Sherman kicked him.

Verily came down from upstairs and looked at Sherman reading the magazine, drinking the gin and tonic. She was going to comment about him but the look of the fierce eyes in the dark face silenced her. She only said, "In my day I never sat around reading books and drinking liquor."

Sherman said, "You were probably born a slave, old woman."

"Slave I was not, my grandfather was."

"They probably put you on the block in this very town."

Verily began to wash the dishes, turning on the water spigot very loud. Then she said, "If I knew who your mother was I would tell her to switch you to a frazzle."

Sherman went back into the parlor to rile Jester for a while, having nothing else to do. Jester was playing again, and he wished he knew what the name of the music was. Suppose he said something bad about the composer and it was the wrong composer. Was it Chopin, Beethoven, Schubert? Because he did not know he could not trust himself to be insulting and that made him more furious. Suppose he said, "That's terrible Beethoven you're playing," and Jester said, "It's not Beethoven, it's Chopin." Sherman, out of pocket, did not know what to do. Then he heard the front door open and close and knew that that busybody, Mr. Malone, had gone. Having embarrassed himself, he went in, meek as Moses, to the Judge. On his own accord he resumed Longfellow, starting with:

"I shot an arrow into the air."

Malone had never felt the heat so much as he had this summer. As he walked he felt the blazing sky, the sun, weigh down his shoulders. An ordinary, practical man who seldom daydreamed, he was daydreaming now that in the autumn he was going to a northern country, to Vermont or Maine where again he would see snow. He was going alone without Mrs.

Malone. He would ask Mr. Harris to take over the pharmacy and he would stay there for two weeks, or who knows, two months, alone and at peace. He saw in his mind's eye the polar enchantment of snow and felt the cool of it. He would stay in a hotel by himself, which he had never done before, or would it be a ski resort? As he thought of snow he felt a freedom, and a guilt gnawed him as he walked, shoulders bent, under the terrible heat of the day. Once, and only once, he had had the guilt of freedom. Twelve years ago he had sent his wife and the small Ellen to Tallulah Falls for a cool summer vacation, and while they were gone Malone chanced to meet Malone's sin. At first he did not think it was a sin at all. It was just a young lady he met at the drugstore. She had come in with a cinder in her eye and very carefully he had removed the cinder with his clean linen handkerchief. He remembered her trembling body and the tears in her black eyes as he held her head to remove the cinder. She left and that night he thought of her, but that seemed to be the end. But it happened they met the next day when he was paying the dry goods bill. She was a clerk in the office. She had said, "You were so sweet to me yesterday. I wonder what I could do for you now?" He said, "Why, why don't you go to lunch with me tomorrow?" and she had accepted, a little slip of a young thing, working in the dry goods store. They had lunch in the Cricket Tea Room, the most respectable place in town. He talked to her about his family and he never dreamed it would come to anything else. But it did, and at the end of two weeks he had sinned and the awful thing was, he was glad. Singing as he shaved and putting on his finest garments every day. They went to the picture show in town, and he even took her to Atlanta on the bus and took her to the cyclorama. They went to the Henry Grady Hotel for dinner and she ordered caviar. He was strangely happy in this transgression, although he knew it was soon to end. It ended in September when his wife and child came back to town, and Lola was very understanding. Maybe a thing like that had happened to her once before. After fifteen years he still dreamed of her although he had changed dry goods stores and never saw her. When he learned that she had married he was sad, but in another portion of his soul, relieved.

Thinking of freedom was like thinking of snow. Surely, in the autumn of that year, he would have Mr. Harris take over the pharmacy and he would take a vacation. He would know again the secret stealth of snow and feel the blessed cold. So Malone walked wearily to his own home.

"When you have a vacation like this, Hon, I don't think it's a real vacation just to trudge around town, not in this heat."

"I wasn't thinking of the heat, although this town in summer is hot as the hinges of hell."

"Well, Ellen's been trying herself."

"What do you mean?" Malone said alarmed.

"Just trying herself, and crying, crying all afternoon in her bedroom."

Quickly Malone went up to Ellen's bedroom and Mrs. Malone followed. Ellen was in the bed in her pretty little blue and pink girl's room, sobbing. Malone could not bear to see Ellen cry, for she was his heart. A little tremor came over his tired body. "Baby, baby, what is it?"

Ellen turned her face to him, "Oh, Daddy, I'm so much in love."

"Well, why does that make my heart-child cry?"

"Because he doesn't even know I'm on the earth. We pass on the street and everywhere and he just waves in a casual way and goes on."

Mrs. Malone said, "That's all right, darling, one of these

days when you are older you will meet Mr. Right and all will end well."

Ellen sobbed more vehemently and Malone hated his wife for it was the silliest thing a mother could say. "Baby, baby, who is it?"

"Jester. I'm so much in love with Jester."

"Jester Clane!" Malone thundered.

"Yes, Jester. He is so handsome."

"Darling, love," Malone said, "Jester Clane is not worth one inch of your little finger." As Ellen still sobbed, he regretted that he had toted the turnip greens to the old Judge, although the old Judge was innocent of all this. Trying so much to make amends, he said, "And after all, heart-child, this is only puppy love, thank goodness." But as he said these words he knew they were just as silly and comfortless as Mrs. Malone's were. "Darling, in the cool of the afternoon, why don't we go to the pharmacy and pick up a quart of that ripple-fudge ice cream for supper." Ellen cried for a while, but later in the afternoon, which was not cool, they went in the family car to the pharmacy and picked up some ripple-fudge ice cream.

7

J. T. Malone was not the only one who was worried about
the Judge those months; Jester had begun to be concerned
about his grandfather. Selfish, selfish, selfish as he was, with
a hundred problems of his own, he still worried about his
grandfather. The Judge's wild enthusiasm for his "amanuensis" just carried him away. It was Sherman this, Sherman that,
all day long. His grandfather dictated letters in the morning,
then at noon they had a drink together. Then when he and
his grandfather had their dinner in the dining room, Sherman
made himself a "slight sandwich" and ate it in the library.
He had told the Judge that he wanted to think over the
morning's correspondence, that he didn't want to be distracted
by conversations with Verily in the kitchen, and that a heavy
noon dinner was bad for his work and concentration.

The Judge had agreed with this arrangement, pleased that his correspondence was pondered so seriously, pleased as pie about everything these days. He had always spoiled servants, giving them costly, but often very peculiar, gifts for Christmas and birthdays. (A fancy dress nowhere near the right size or a hat nobody would be caught dead in or brand new shoes that did not fit.) Although most of the servants had been female churchgoers who never drank, a few had been in a different category. Yet whether they were teetotalers or the drinking kind, the Judge never checked his liquor shelf in the sideboard. Indeed, Paul, the old gardener (a wizard with roses and border flowers), had died of cirrhosis of the liver after gardening and drinking twenty years at the Judge's.

Although Verily knew the Judge was a born spoiler, she was amazed at Sherman Pew and the liberties he took in the Judge's household.

"Won't eat in the kitchen because he says he wants to think about letters," she grumbled. "It's because he's too uppity to eat with me in the kitchen as he belongs. Fixing himself party sandwiches and eating in the liberry, if you please! He's going to ruin the liberry table."

"How?" the Judge asked.

"Eating them party sandwiches on them trays," Verily said stubbornly.

Although the Judge was very sensitive to his own dignity, he was not so sensitive to the dignity of others. Sherman stifled his sudden rages in the Judge's presence and took them out on Gus, the new yardman, Verily, and most of all on Jester. But although the actual rage fits were smothered, the anger remained, and indeed increased. For one thing he hated reading Dickens, there were so many orphans in Dickens, and Sherman loathed books about orphans, feeling in them a reflection on himself. So when the Judge sobbed aloud over orphans, chimney sweeps, stepfathers, and all such horrors,

Sherman read in a cold, inflexible voice, and glanced with cool superiority when the old fool acted up. The Judge, obtuse to the feelings of others, noticed none of this and was as pleased as pie. Laughing, drinking, sobbing at Dickens, writing whole mailsacks of letters, and never an instant bored. Sherman continued to be a jewel, a treasure, and no word could be said against him in the house. Meanwhile, in Sherman's dour but quailing heart things went steadily from bad to worse so that by the middle of autumn his feelings for the Judge were those of veiled but ever present hate.

But in spite of the soft, clean, bossy job; in spite of the fun of riling that soppy, chicken-outing Jester Clane, that autumn was the most miserable one in Sherman's entire life. Day after day he waited, his very livingness suspended in the blank vacuum of suspense. Day after day he waited for the letter, and day after day, week after week, there was no answer. Then by chance one day he met a musician friend of Zippo Mullins' who actually knew Marian Anderson, owned a signed photograph of her and everything, and from this hideous stranger he learned the truth: Madame Anderson was not his mother. Not only was she wedded to her career and too busy studying to have had the time for love affairs with princes, let alone borning him and leaving him so peculiarly in a church pew, she had never once been to Milan and could not possibly have touched his life in any way. So the hope that had lifted and made so luminous his searching heart was shattered. Forevermore? He thought so at that time. That evening he took down his records of German lieder sung by Marian Anderson and stomped on them, stomping with such despair and fury that not a groove of the records remained unshattered. Then, as the hope and the music could not be altogether silenced, he threw himself with his muddy shoes on the fine rayon bedspread and scraped his body on it as he wailed aloud.

Next morning he could not go to work as his fit had left

him exhausted and hoarse. But at noon when the Judge sent him a covered tray of fresh vegetable soup with piping hot cornsticks and a lemony dessert, he was sufficiently recovered to eat the food slowly, languidly . . . glad with the feeling-sick feeling and eating the cornsticks with his little finger delicately crooked. He stayed home a week and somebody else's cooking and the rest restored him. But his smooth, round face hardened and, although he did not think consciously about that cheating creep of a Madame Anderson after a while, he yearned to rob as he had been robbed.

The first of that fall was the happiest time Jester had ever known. At first lifted by the wings of song, his passion now had quieted to friendship. Sherman was in his home every day, and the security of constant presence alters passion which is fed by jeopardy and the dread of change, of loss. Sherman was at his house every day and there was no reason to believe it would not go on forever. True, Sherman went out of his way to insult him, which wounded Jester. But as the weeks passed he had learned not to let the wounding remarks be felt too deeply or too long; indeed, he was learning to defend himself. Hard as it was for Jester to make up jazzy hurtful remarks, he was learning to do it. Furthermore he was learning to understand Sherman, and understanding which conflicts with the ruthless violence of passion leads to both pity and love. Nevertheless, when Sherman was away that week, Jester was a little bit relieved; he did not have to be on his P's and Q's every instant and could relax without the fear of having to defend his pride at any moment. Another element of their relationship was Jester's dim awareness that he was the chosen one; that he was the one that Sherman used to lash out against when he wanted to lash out against the world. For Jester knew dimly that fury is unleashed more freely against those you are most close to . . . so close that there is the trust that anger and ugliness will be forgiven. Jester, himself, would be angry only with his grandfather as a child . . . his fits of head-banging temper were directed only toward his grandfather — not Verily, Paul, or anybody else — for he knew that his grandfather would forgive and love. So while Sherman's wounding remarks were certainly no blessing, he sensed in them a kind of trust for which he was grateful. He had bought the score of *Tristan*, and when Sherman was away it was a relief to practice it without fear of belittling wisecracks. However, when his grandfather roamed the house like a lost soul and almost couldn't eat, Jester was concerned. "I just don't see what you see in Sherman Pew."

"That boy's a jewel, a veritable treasure," the Judge said placidly. His voice changed when he added, "Besides, it's not a short time I've known the boy and I feel responsible for him."

"Responsible how?"

"It's because of me that the boy is an orphan."

"I don't dig it," Jester protested. "Don't talk in riddles."

"It's too sorry a business to be discussed, especially between you and me."

Jester answered, "Anything I despise is for somebody to tell just half a story, work up a person's interest and then don't go on."

"Well, forget it," his grandfather said. He added with a glib addendum that Jester knew was only a sort of camouflage to the truth, "After all, he was the colored caddy who saved my life when I was flailing and drowning in the golf pond."

"That's just a detail and not the real truth."

"Ask me no questions and I'll tell you no lies," the Judge said in a maddening voice.

Deprived of the joys and the busyness of Sherman, the Judge wanted to rope in Jester, who was too busy with his own life and school to be roped in. Jester would not read immortal poetry, or play poker, and even the correspondence did not interest Jester a hoot. So the sadness and tedium returned to the Judge. After the manifold interests and activities of those months, solitaire bored him and he had read every speck of all the issues of the *Ladies' Home Journal* and *McCall's.*

"Tell me," Jester said suddenly, "since you imply you know so much about Sherman Pew, did you ever know his mother?"

"Unfortunately, I did."

"Why don't you tell Sherman who she is. Naturally he wants to know."

"That is a pure case where ignorance is bliss."

"One time you say knowledge is power and another time you say ignorance is bliss. Which side are you on? Anyway I don't believe a particle in any of those old saws."

Absentmindedly Jester was tearing up the spongy rubber ball the Judge used to exercise his left hand. "Some people think it's the act of a weakling . . . to commit suicide . . . and other people think it takes a lot of guts to do it. I still wonder why my father did it. And an all-around athlete, graduated with all honors from the University of Georgia, why did he do it?"

"It was just a fleeting depression," the Judge said, copying J. T. Malone's words of consolation.

"It doesn't seem an all-around athlete thing to do."

While his grandfather carefully laid out the cards for a game of solitaire, Jester wandered to the piano. He began to play *Tristan*, his eyes half closed and his body swaying. He had already inscribed the score:

> For my dear friend Sherman Pew
> Ever faithfully,
> John Jester Clane

The music gave Jester goose pimples, it was so violent yet shimmering.

Nothing pleased Jester more than giving a fine present to Sherman, whom he loved. On the third day of Sherman's absence Jester picked some mums and autumn leaves from his garden and bore them proudly to the lane. He put the flowers in an iced-tea pitcher. He hovered over Sherman as though he was dying, which annoyed Sherman.

Sherman lay languidly on the bed and when Jester was arranging the flowers he said in a sassy, languid voice: "Have you ever stopped to consider how much your face resembles a baby's behind?"

Jester was too shocked to take it in, let alone reply.

"Innocent, dopey, the very living image of a baby's behind."

"I'm not innocent," Jester protested.

"You certainly are. It shows in your dopey face."

Jester, like all young things, was a great one for gilding the lily. Hidden in his bouquet of flowers was a jar of caviar which he had bought from the A & P that morning; now with the violence and insolence of this new attack he did not know what to do with the hidden caviar which Sherman claimed to eat by the ton-fulls. Since his flowers had been set so peculiarly at nought . . . not a word of thanks or even an appreciative look . . . Jester did wonder what to do with the hidden caviar, for he could not stand to be humiliated further. He hid the caviar in his hip pocket. So he had to sit gingerly in a sideways position. Sherman, with pretty flowers in the room which he appreciated but didn't bother to thank Jester for or mention, well fed with somebody else's cooking, and rested, felt well enough to tease Jester. (Little did he know that he had already teased himself out of a jar of genuine caviar which he would have displayed in the most conspicuous shelf in the frigidaire for many months before serving it to his most distinguished guests.)

"You look like you have tertiary syphilis," Sherman said as a starter.

"Like what?"

"When you sit wonkensided like that it's a sure sign of syphilis."

"I'm just sitting on a jar."

Sherman did not ask why he was sitting on a jar and naturally Jester did not volunteer. Sherman only wisecracked: "Sitting on a jar . . . a slop jar?"

"Don't be so crude."

"People in France sit like that a lot of times on account of they have syphilis."

"How do you know?"

"Because in my brief stint in the service I was in France."

Jester suspected this was one of Sherman's lies but said nothing.

"When I was in France I fell in love with this French girl. No syphilis or anything like that. Just this beautiful, lily-white French virgin."

Jester changed his position because it's hard to sit long on a jar of caviar. He was always shocked by dirty stories and even the word "virgin" gave him a little thrill; but shocked or no he was fascinated so he let Sherman go on and he listened.

"We were engaged, this lily-white French girl and I. And I knocked her up. Then, like a woman, she wanted to marry me and the wedding was going to take place in this ancient old church called Notre Dame."

"A cathedral," Jester corrected.

"Well, church . . . cathedral . . . or however you call it, that's where we were going to be married. There were loads of invited guests. French people have families like carloads. I stood outside the church and watched them coming in. I didn't let anybody see me. I just wanted to see the show. This beautiful old cathedral and those French people dressed to kill. Everybody was chick."

"You pronounce the word 'sheik,' " Jester said.

"Well, they were sheik and chick too. These carloads of relatives all waiting for me to come in."

"Why didn't you go in?" Jester asked.

"Oh, you innocent dope. Don't you know I had no intention of marrying that lily-white French virgin? I just stayed there the whole afternoon watching these dressed up French people who were waiting for me to marry the lily-white French virgin. She was my 'feancee' you understand, and come night they realized I was not going to be there. My 'feancee' fainted. The old mother had a heart attack. The old father committed suicide right there in the church."

"Sherman Pew, you're the biggest liar who ever walked in shoe leather," Jester said.

Sherman, who had been carried away with his story, said nothing.

"Why do you lie?" Jester asked.

"It's not exactly lying, but sometimes I think up situations that could very well be true and tell 'em to baby-ass dopes like you. A lot of my life I've had to make up stories because the real, actual was either too dull or too hard to take."

"Well, if you pretend to be my friend, why try to make me be a sucker?"

'You're what the original Barnum described. Barnum and Bailey Circus, in case you don't remember. 'A sucker is born every minute on this earth.' " He could not bear to think of Marian Anderson. And he wanted Jester to stay but he did not know how to ask him. Sherman had on his best blue rayon pajamas with white piping, so he was glad to get out of bed to show them off. "Would you like a little Lord Calvert's bottled in bond?"

But whiskey and best pajamas were far away from Jester. He was shocked by the dirty story, but he was touched by Sherman's explanation of why he lied. "Don't you know that I'm one friend you don't have to lie to?"

But gloom and rage had settled in Sherman. "What makes you think you're a friend?"

Jester had to ignore this and he only said, "I'm going home."

"Don't you want to see the fine food Zippo's Aunt Carrie sent to me?" Sherman walked to the kitchen and opened the icebox door. The frigidaire had a faintly sour smell. Sherman admired Aunt Carrie's fancy food. "It's a tomato aspic molded ring with cottage cheese in the middle."

Jester looked dubiously at the food and said, "Do you lie to Aunt Carrie, Cinderella Mullins, and Zippo Mullins?"

"No," Sherman said simply. "They got my number."

"I've got your number too, and I do wish you wouldn't lie to me."

"Why?"

"I hate stating obvious facts and the fact why I don't like you to lie to me is too obvious for me to state."

Jester squatted by the side of the bed and Sherman lay in his best pajamas, propped with pillows and pretending to be at ease.

"Have you ever heard the saying that truth is stranger than fiction?"

"Of course I've heard it."

"When Mr. Stevens did that thing to me it was a few days before Halloween and it was my eleventh birthday. Mrs. Stevens had given me this wonderful birthday party. Many invited guests attended, some wearing party clothes and other people Halloween outfits. It was my first birthday party and was I thrilled. There were guests in witches' costumes and in pirates' outfits as well as party best clothes they wore to Sunday School. I started the party wearing my first brand new pair of navy blue long trousers and a new white shirt. The state paid my board, but that didn't include birthday parties nor brand new birthday clothes. When the invited guests brought presents, I minded what Mrs. Stevens said, didn't snatch at the presents but said 'Thank you' and opened them very slowly. Mrs. Stevens always said I had beautiful manners and I truly had beautiful manners on that birthday party. We played all kinds of games." Sherman's voice trailed off and finally he said, "It's a funny thing."

"What's funny?"

"From the time the party began until in the evening after it was over I don't remember hardly a single thing. For it was the evening of the fine party that Mr. Stevens boogered me."

In a swift unconscious gesture Jester half raised his right hand as though warding off a blow.

"Even after it was done and over and the real Halloween had already gone, I remembered only snitches and snatches of my b-bi-birthday p-party."

"I wish you wouldn't talk about it."

Sherman waited until his stammer was under control, then went on fluently: "We played all kinds of games, then refreshments were served. Ice cream and white iced cake with eleven pink candles. I blew out the candles and cut the birthday cake as Mrs. Stevens said for me to do. But I didn't eat a bite on account of I wished so much to have beautiful manners. Then after the refreshments we played running and hollering games. I had put on a sheet like a ghost and a pirate hat. When Mr. Stevens called out behind the coal house I ran to him quickly, my ghost sheet flying. When he caught me

I thought he was just playing and I was laughing fit to kill. I was still laughing fit to kill when I realized he wasn't playing. Then I was too surprised to know what to do but I quit laughing."

Sherman lay on the pillow as if he were suddenly tired. "However, I have a charmed life," he continued with a tone of zest that Jester found hard to believe at first. "From then on I never had it so good. Nobody ever had it so good. Mrs. Mullins adopted me . . . not a real adoption, the state still paid for me, but she took me to her bosom. I knew she wasn't my mother, but she loved me. She would beat Zippo and spank Cinderella with a hairbrush, but she never laid a hand on me. So you see I almost had a mother. And a family too. Aunt Carrie, Mrs. Mullins' sister, taught me singing."

"Where is Zippo's mother?" Jester asked.

"Died," Sherman said bitterly. "Passed on to glory. That's what broke up the home. When Zippo's father remarried, neither Zippo or I liked her a bit so we moved out and I've been Zippo's house guest ever since. But I did have a mother for a little while," Sherman said, "I did have a mother even though that cheating creep of a Marian Anderson is not my mother."

"Why do you call her a cheating creep?"

"Because I prefer to. I've ripped all thought away from her. And stomped on all her records." Sherman's voice broke.

Jester, who was still squatting by the bed, steadied himself and suddenly kissed Sherman on the cheek.

Sherman rared back in the bed, put his feet down for balance and slapped Jester, using his whole arm.

Jester was not surprised although he had never been slapped before. "I only did that," he said, "because I felt sorry for you."

"Save your peanuts for the zoo."

"I don't see why we can't be serious and sincere," Jester said.

Sherman, who was half out of the bed, slapped him again on the other cheek so hard that Jester sat down on the floor. Sherman's voice was strangled with rage. "I thought you were a friend and you turn out like Mr. Stevens."

The slap and his own emotions stunned Jester, but quickly he got up, his hands clenched, and biffed Sherman straight in the jaw, which surprised Sherman so that he fell on the bed. Sherman muttered, "Sock a fellow when he's down."

"You weren't down, you were sitting on the bed so's you could slap me hardest. I take a lot of things from you, Sherman Pew, but I wouldn't take that. Besides you slapped me when I was squatting."

So they went on arguing about sitting up and squatting and which was a more sportsmanlike position to slap or to punch somebody. The argument went on so long that they quite forgot the words that had preceded the blows.

But when Jester went home he was still thinking: I don't see why we can't be serious and sincere.

He opened the caviar, but it smelled like fish which he didn't like. Neither did his grandfather like fish, and Verily just said "Ugh" when she smelled it. The part-time yardman, Gus, who would eat anything, took it home.

8

In November Malone had a remission and was admitted for a second time to the City Hospital. He was glad to be there. Although he had changed doctors, the diagnosis had not changed. He had changed from Dr. Hayden to Dr. Calloway and changed again to Dr. Milton. But though the last two doctors were Christians (members of the First Baptist and Episcopal churches) their medical verdict was the same. Having asked Dr. Hayden how long he would live, and having received the unexpected and terrifying answer, he was careful not to ask again. Indeed, when he changed to Dr. Milton, he had insisted he was a well man and just wanted a routine checkup and that one doctor had said that there was just a slight suspicion of leukemia. Dr. Milton confirmed the diagnosis and Malone asked no questions. Dr. Milton suggested that he check in at the City Hospital for a few days. So Malone again watched the bright blood dripping drop by drop, and he was glad because something was being done and the transfusions strengthened him.

On Mondays and Thursdays an aide wheeled in some shelves of books and the first book Malone selected was a murder mystery. But the mystery bored him and he could not keep track of the plot. The next time the aide came around with the books, Malone returned the mystery and glanced at the other titles; his eyes were drawn to a book called *Sickness unto Death*. His hand had reached for the book when the aide said, "Are you sure you want this one? It doesn't sound very cheerful." Her tone reminded him of his wife so that he immediately became determined and angry. "This is the book I want and I'm not cheerful and don't want to be cheerful." Malone, after reading for a half hour, wondered why he had made such a fuss about the book and dozed for a while. When he awoke he opened the book at random and began to read just to be reading. From the wilderness of print some lines struck his mind so that he was instantly awake. He read the lines again and then again: *The greatest danger, that of losing one's own self, may pass off quietly as if it were nothing; every other loss, that of an arm, a leg, five dollars, a wife, etc., is sure to be noticed.* If Malone had not had an incurable disease those words would have been only words and he wouldn't have reached for the book in the first place. But now the thought chilled him and he began to read the book from the first page. But again the book bored him so that he closed his eyes and thought only of the passage he had memorized.

Unable to think of the reality of his own death, he was thrown back into the tedious labyrinth of his life. He had lost himself . . . he realized that surely. But how? When?

His father had been a wholesale druggist from Macon. He had been ambitious for J.T., his eldest son. Those years of boyhood were good for the forty-year-old Malone to dwell on. He had not been lost then. But his father was ambitious for him, too ambitious it seemed later to Malone. He had decided that his son would be a doctor as that had been his own youthful ambition. So the eighteen-year-old Malone matriculated at Columbia, and in November he saw snow. At that time he bought a pair of ice skates and he actually tried to skate in Central Park. He had had a fine time at Columbia, eating the chow mein he had never tasted before, learning to ice skate, and marveling at the city. He had not realized he had started to fail in his studies until he was already failing. He tried to bone up . . . studying until two o'clock on examination nights . . . but there were so many Jew grinds in the class who ran up the average. Malone finished the first year by the skin of his teeth and rested at home, a bona fide premedical student. When the fall came round again the snow, the ice, the city was not a shock to him. When he failed at the end of his second year at Columbia, he felt himself to be a no-good. His young man's pride would not let him stay in Macon, so he moved to Milan and got a job as a clerk with Mr. Greenlove, in the Greenlove drugstore. Was it this first humiliation that made him fumble in the beginning of life?

Martha was the daughter of Mr. Greenlove and it was only natural, or seemed natural, when he asked her to a dance. He was dressed up in his best blue suit and she had on a chiffon dress. It was an Elk's Club dance. He had just become an Elk. What had he felt as he touched her body and why had he asked her to the dance? After the dance he had dated her a number of times because he knew few girls in Milan and her father was his boss. But still he never thought of love, let alone marriage, with Martha Greenlove. Then suddenly old Mr.

Greenlove (he was not old, he was only forty-five but the young Malone thought of him as old) died of a heart attack. The drugstore was put up for sale. Malone borrowed fifteen hundred dollars from his mother and bought it on a fifteen-year mortgage. So he was saddled with a mortgage, and before he even realized it his own self, with a wife. Martha did not actually ask him to marry her, but she seemed to assume so much that Malone would have felt an irresponsible man if he had not spoken. So he spoke to her brother who was now the head of the family, and they shook hands and had a drink of Blind Mule together. And it all happened so naturally that it seemed supernatural; yet he was fascinated by Martha who wore afternoon dainty dresses and a chiffon dress for dances and who, above all, restored the pride he had lost when he failed at Columbia. But when they were married in the Greenloves' living room in the presence of his mother, her mother, the Greenlove brothers, and an aunt or two, her mother had cried, and Malone felt like crying also. He didn't cry, but listened to the ceremony, bewildered. After the rice had been thrown they had gone on the train to their honeymoon in Blowing Rock, North Carolina. And ever afterward there was no particular time when he regretted marrying Martha, but regret, or disappointment was certainly there. There was no particular time when he asked, "Is this all there is of life?" but as he grew older he asked it wordlessly. No, he had not lost an arm, or a leg, or any particular five dollars, but little by little he had lost his own self.

If Malone had not had a fatal disease he would not have brooded about this. But dying had quickened his livingness as he lay in the hospital bed, seeing the bright blood drop, drop by drop. He said to himself he didn't care about the hospital expenses, but even while he was there he was worried about the twenty-dollars-a-day bill.

"Hon," Martha said on one of her daily visits to the hospital, "why don't we take a nice relaxing trip?"

Malone stiffened on his sweaty bed.

"Even resting here at the hospital you always seem tense and worried up. We could go to Blowing Rock and breathe the nice mountain air."

"I don't feel like it," Malone said.

" . . . or the ocean. I've seen the ocean only once in my life and that was when I was visiting my cousin, Sarah Greenlove, in Savannah. It's a nice climate at Sea Island Beach, I hear. Not too hot, not too cold. And the little change might perk you up."

"I've always felt that traveling is exhausting." He did not tell his wife about the trip he was planning later on to Vermont or Maine where he could see snow. Malone had carefully hidden *Sickness unto Death* beneath the pillow for he did not want to share anything that was intimate with his wife. He did say fretfully, "I'm sick of this hospital."

"One thing I'm sure you ought to do," Mrs. Malone said, "you ought to make a habit of turning the pharmacy over to Mr. Harris in the afternoons. All work and no play makes Jack a dull boy."

Home from the hospital with every afternoon off, Malone blundered through his days. He thought of the mountains, the North, snow, the ocean . . . thought of all the life he had spent unlived. He wondered how he could die since he had not yet lived.

He took hot baths after his morning work and even darkened the bedroom to try to take a nap, but it had never been his habit to sleep in the middle of the day and he could not sleep. Instead of waking at four or five o'clock in the morning to roam the house in fear, the flashes of terror had flickered for a season, leaving boredom and a dread that he could not formulate. He hated the blank afternoons when Mr. Harris took over the pharmacy. He was always fearing that something might go wrong, but what could go wrong? The loss of another Kotex sale? A bad judgment on a physical complaint? He actually had no reason to advise in the first place, having never finished medical school. Other dilemmas plagued him. He was now so thin that his suits hung in baggy folds. Should he go to a tailor? Though the suits would long outlast him, he did go to a tailor instead of going to Hart, Schaffner & Marx, where he had always gone, and ordered an Oxford gray suit and a blue flannel suit. The fittings were tiresome. Another thing, he had paid so much on orthodontist's bills for Ellen that he had neglected his own teeth, so that suddenly so many teeth had to be pulled that the dentist gave him a choice of pulling twelve teeth and having false teeth or making expensive bridges. Malone decided on the bridges, even knowing he couldn't get the good of them. So dying, Malone took more care of himself than he had done in life.

A new chain drugstore opened in Milan which did not have the quality and trustworthiness of Malone's pharmacy, but it was a competitor which undercut fair prices and this annoyed Malone immoderately. Sometimes he even wondered if he shouldn't sell the pharmacy while he could supervise the sale. But the thought was more shocking and bewildering than the thought of his own death. So he did not dwell on it. Besides, Martha could be trusted to dispose of the property, including stock, good will and reputation, when the occasion arose. Malone spent whole days with a pencil and paper, writing down his assets. Twenty-five thousand (it comforted Malone that his figures were conservative) for the pharmacy, twenty thousand life insurance, ten thousand for the home, fifteen thousand for the three run-down houses

Martha had inherited . . . while the combined assets were
not a fortune, they were considerable when added up; Malone
totaled the figures several times with a fine-sharpened pencil
and twice with a fountain pen. Deliberately he had not
included his wife's Coca-Cola stock. The mortgage on the
pharmacy had been burned two years ago and the insurance
policy converted from retirement insurance to plain life
insurance, as it had been to begin with. There were no outstanding debts or mortgages. Malone knew that his financial
affairs were in better order than they had ever been before, but
this comforted him little. Better, perhaps, if he had been
harried by mortgages and unpaid bills than to feel this flat
solvency. For Malone still felt he had unfinished business
which the ledgers and his figuring did not show. Although he
had not talked more about his will with the Judge, he felt
that a man, a breadwinner, should not die intestate. Should
he set five thousand legally aside for the children's education,
the residue going to his wife? Or should he leave it all to
Martha, who was a good mother if she was anything? He had
heard of widows buying Cadillac cars when their husbands
had died and left them in full charge of the estate. Or widows
being rooked into phony oil well deals. But he knew that
Martha would neither breeze around in Cadillac cars nor buy
any stock more chancy than Coca-Cola or A. T. & T. The
will would probably read: To my beloved wife, Martha Greenlove Malone, I bequeath all monies and properties that com-
prise my entire estate. Although he had long since ceased
loving his wife, he respected her judgment, and it was the
ordinary will to make.

Until that season, few of Malone's friends or relatives had
died. But his fortieth year seemed a time for death. His
brother from Macon died of cancer. His brother had been
only thirty-eight years old and he was the head of the Malone

Wholesale Drug Company. Also, Tom Malone had married a beautiful wife and J.T. had often envied him. But blood being thicker than jealousy, Malone began packing his suitcase when Tom's wife telephoned he was failing. Martha objected to the trip because of his own ill health, and a long argument followed which made him miss the Macon train. So he was unable to see Tom again in life, and in death the body was too much rouged and terribly shrunken.

Martha came the next day when she had arranged for someone to care for the children. Malone, as the elder brother, was the chief spokesman in financial matters. The affairs of the Malone Wholesale Drug Company were in worse shape than anyone had imagined. Tom had been a drinking man, Lucille extravagant, and the Malone Wholesale Drug Company was faced with bankruptcy. Malone went over the books and figured for days. There were two boys of high school age and Lucille, when faced with the necessity of earning a living, said vaguely that she would get a job in an antique shop. But there were no vacancies in an antique shop in Macon, and besides, Lucille didn't know scat about antiques. No longer a beautiful woman, she cried less for her husband's death than that he had managed the Malone Wholesale Drug Company so badly, leaving her a widow with two growing children and no ideas about work or jobs. J.T. and Martha stayed for four days. After the funeral when they left, Malone gave Lucille a check for four hundred dollars to tide the family over. A month later Lucille got a job in a department store.

Cab Bickerstaff died, and Malone had seen and talked with him that very same morning before he just fell over dead at his desk in the Milan Electric and Power Company. Malone tried to remember every act and word of Cab Bickerstaff that morning. But they were so ordinary that they would have been unnoticed if he had not slumped at his desk at eleven o'clock, dying instantly of a stroke. He had seemed perfectly well and absolutely ordinary when Malone had served him the coke and some peanut butter crackers. Malone remembered that he had ordered an aspirin along with the coke, but there was nothing unusual about that. And he had said on entering the pharmacy, "Hot enough for you, J.T.?" Again perfectly ordinary. But Cab Bickerstaff had died an hour later and the coke, the aspirin, the peanut butter crackers, the hackneyed phrase were fixed in an inlay of mystery that haunted Malone. Herman Klein's wife died and his shop was closed for two full days. Herman Klein no longer had to hide his bottle in the compounding room at the pharmacy, but could drink at his own home. Mr. Beard, a deacon at the First Baptist Church, died also that summer. None of these people had been close to Malone, and in life he had not been interested in them. But in death they were all fixed in the same curious inlay of mystery that compelled an attention that they had not exerted in life. So Malone's last summer had passed in this way.

Afraid to talk to the doctors, unable to speak of anything intimate with his own wife, Malone just blundered silently. Every Sunday he went to church, but Dr. Watson was a folksy preacher who spoke to the living and not to a man who was going to die. He compared the Holy Sacraments with a car. Saying that people had to be tanked up once in a while in order to proceed with their spiritual life. This service offended Malone, although he did not know why. The First Baptist Church was the largest church in town with a property worth, offhand, two million dollars. The deacons were men of substance. Pillars of the church, millionaires, rich doctors, owners of utility companies. But though Malone went every Sunday to church, and though they were holy men, in his judgment, he felt strangely apart from them. Though he shook hands with Dr. Watson at the end of every church service, he felt no communication with him, or any of the other worshipers. Yet he had been born and reared in the First Baptist Church, and there was no other spiritual solace he could think of, for he was ashamed and timid to speak of death. So one November afternoon, shortly after his second stay at the hospital, he dressed up in his new tailored Oxford gray suit and went to the parsonage.

Dr. Watson greeted him with some surprise. "How well you are looking, Mr. Malone." Malone's body seemed to shrink in the new suit. "I'm glad you've come. I always like to see my parishioners. What can I do for you today? Would you like a coke?"

"No thanks, Dr. Watson. I would like to talk."

"Talk about what?"

Malone's reply was muted and almost indistinct. "About death."

"Ramona," Dr. Watson bawled to the servant who quickly answered him, "serve Mr. Malone and me some cokes with lemon."

As the cokes were served, Malone crossed and uncrossed his withered legs in their fine flannel pants. A flush of shame reddened his pale face. "I mean," he said, "you are supposed to know about things like that."

"Things like what?" Dr. Watson asked.

Malone was brave, determined. "About the soul, and what happens in the afterlife."

In church, and after twenty years of experience, Dr. Watson could make glib sermons about the soul; but in his own home, with only one man asking, his glibness turned to embarrassment and he only said, "I don't know what you mean, Mr. Malone."

"My brother died, Cab Bickerstaff died in this town, and Mr. Beard died all in the course of seven months. What happened to them after death?"

"We all have to die," said the plump, pale Dr. Watson.

"Other people never know when they are going to die."

"All Christians should prepare for death." Dr. Watson thought the subject was getting morbid.

"But how do you prepare for death?"

"By righteous living."

"What is righteous living?" Malone had never stolen, had seldom lied, and the one episode in his life that he knew was a mortal sin had happened years ago and lasted only one summer. "Tell me, Dr. Watson," he asked, "what is eternal life?"

"To me," Dr. Watson said, "it is the extension of earthly life, but more intensified. Does that answer your question?"

Malone thought of the drabness of his life and wondered how it could be more intensified. Was afterlife continual tedium and was that why he struggled so in order to hold onto life? He shivered although the parsonage was hot. "Do you believe in heaven and hell?" Malone asked.

"I'm not a strict fundamentalist, but I believe that what a man does on earth predicates his eternal life."

"But if a man does just the ordinary things, nothing good, nothing bad?"

"It's not up to man's judgment to decide what is good and what is bad. God sees the truth, and is our Saviour."

These days Malone had often prayed, but what he was praying to he did not know. There seemed no sense in continuing the conversation, for he was getting no answer. Malone put the Coca-Cola glass carefully on the doily beside him and stood up. "Well, thanks very much, Dr. Watson," he said bleakly.

"I'm glad you dropped in to talk with me. My home is

always open to my parishioners who want to speak of spiritual things."

In a daze of weariness and vacuity, Malone walked through the November twilight. A bright woodpecker pecked hollowly at a telephone pole. The afternoon was silent except for the woodpecker.

It was strange that Malone, who loved singsong poetry, would think of those memorized lines: *The greatest danger, that of losing one's own self, may pass off quietly as if it were nothing; every other loss, that of an arm, a leg, five dollars, a wife, etc., is sure to be noticed.* The incongruity of these ideas, fateful and ordinary as his own life, sounded like the brassy clamor of the city clock, uncadenced and flat.

9

THAT WINTER the Judge made a grave mistake about Sherman and Sherman made a still graver mistake about the Judge. Since both mistakes were phantasies which flowered as richly in the senile brain of the old man as they did in the heart of the thwarted boy, their human relationship was going very much amiss, choked as it were with the rank luxuriance of their separate dreams. So that the relationship which had begun with such joy and lucidity was, by the end of November, already tarnished.

It was the old Judge who spoke first of his dream. One day with an air of secrecy and zest he opened his safety deposit box and handed Sherman a sheaf of papers. "Read carefully, boy, for this may be my final contribution as a statesman to the South."

Sherman read and was puzzled, less by the ornate and badly spelled manuscript than by the contents of what he read. "Don't bother about the calligraphy or spelling," the Judge said airily. "It's the trenchancy of ideas that matters." Sherman was reading about the Confederate money while the Judge looked on, glowing with pride and anticipated compliments.

Sherman's delicately fluted nostrils widened and his lips fluttered but he said nothing.

Passionately the old Judge began to speak. He described the history of devaluations of foreign monies and the rights of conquered nations to the redemption of their own currencies. "In every civilized nation the currencies of defeated nations have been redeemed . . . devaluated, to be sure, but redeemed. Look at the franc, the mark, the lira and look at, by God, even the yen." This last redemption particularly infuriated the old man.

Sherman's slate-blue eyes stared at the deeper blue eyes of the old Judge. At first bewildered by the talk of all the foreign money, he wondered if the Judge was drunk. But it was not yet twelve o'clock and the Judge never started his toddies until noon. But the old Judge was speaking passionately, drunk with his dream, and Sherman responded. Knowing nothing about what the Judge was discussing, Sherman responded to rhetoric, repetition and rhythm, to the language of passionate demagoguery, senseless and high flown, of which the old Judge was a past master. So Sherman's delicately fluted nostrils widened and he said nothing. The Judge, who had been hurt by his grandson's casual indifference to his dream, knew a spellbound listener when he had one and pressed on triumphantly. And Sherman, who seldom believed a word that Jester said, listened to the Judge's tirade, heedful and wondering.

It happened that some time ago the Judge received a letter from Senator Tip Thomas in reply to the first petition letter that Sherman had written concerning Jester's admittance to West Point. The senator had replied with cumbersome courtesy that he would be glad to put his old friend and fellow statesman's grandson up at his first opportunity. Again the old Judge and Sherman had struggled with a letter to Senator Tip Thomas. This time with the same cumbersome courtesy the old Judge wrote of the dead Mrs. Thomas, as well as the living Mrs. Thomas. It always seemed a miracle to Sherman that the old Judge had actually been a congressman in the House of Representatives in Washington, D.C. The glory was reflected in Sherman, the genuine amanuensis who had his trays on the library table. When Senator Thomas replied, referring to past favors the Judge had shown him and promising that Jester would get an appointment at West Point — playing footsie with the old Judge — it seemed magical to Sherman. So magical that he even fought down his rebellious jealousy that his own letter to Washington had not been answered.

The Judge, in spite of his oratory, was a great one for putting his own foot in his mouth, and soon, sure enough, his foot was in the middle of his mouth. He began to talk about reparation for burnt houses, burnt cotton, and to Sherman's shame and horror, of reparation for slaves.

"Slaves," Sherman said in a voice almost inaudible with shock.

"Why certainly," the old Judge continued serenely. "The institution of slavery was the very cornerstone and pillar of the cotton economy."

"Well Abe Lincoln freed the slaves and another Sherman burnt the cotton."

The Judge, fixed in his dream, had forgotten that his

amanuensis was colored. "And a sad time that was, to be sure."

The Judge wondered helplessly why he had lost his spellbound listener, for Sherman, far from being spellbound, was now trembling with insult and fury. Deliberately, he picked up one of the pens and broke it in two. The Judge did not even notice. "It will take a lot of statistical work, a pile of arithmetic, in fact a lot of doing. But my motto for my election campaign is 'rectify' and justice is on my side. I only have to get the ball rolling, so to say. And I'm a born politician, know how to work with people and handle delicate situations."

The Judge's dream had flattened for Sherman, so he could see it in all its detail. The first flush of enthusiasm with which he had responded to the Judge's dream had faded utterly. "It would take a lot of doing," he said in a dead voice.

"What strikes me is the simplicity of the whole idea."

"Simplicity," Sherman echoed in the same dead voice.

"Yes, the simplicity of genius. Maybe I couldn't have thought up 'To be or not to be,' but my ideas of the restoration of the South are sheer genius." The old voice quivered for confirmation. "Don't you think so, Sherman?"

Sherman, who was looking round for a fast escape in case the Judge did anything suddenly wild, said simply: "No. I don't think it's genius or even common sense."

"Genius and common sense operate at two different polarities of thought."

Sherman wrote down the word "polarities" thinking he would look it up later; he was benefiting from the Judge's vocabulary if nothing else. "All I would say is that your plan would turn back the clock for a hundred years."

"I would like nothing better," said the mad old foolhardy Judge. "And furthermore I think I can do it. I have in high places friends who are deadly sick of this so-called liberalism and who are only waiting for a rallying cry. I am after all one of the Senior Statesmen in the South and my voice shall be attended; maybe some weak sisters will hesitate because of the details of statistics and bookkeeping involved. But, by God, if the Federal Government can screw every nickel out of me for income tax, my plan will be child's play to carry out."

The Judge lowered his voice. "I never filed state income tax yet and never will. I wouldn't bruit this around, Sherman, as I tell you in strictest confidence. And I pay the Federal Income Tax under the utmost duress and mighty unwillingly. As I say, many a Southerner in high power is in my same boots and they will harken to the rallying call."

"But what does your income tax have to do with this?"

"A lot," the old man said. "A mighty lot."

"I don't dig it."

"Of course the N.A.A.C.P. will be dead set against me. But the brave long for battle if the battle is just. For years I've yearned to tangle with the N.A.A.C.P., force them to a showdown, put them out of business."

Sherman just looked at the blue and passionate eyes of the old Judge.

"All Southern patriots feel the same about the scurrilous pressure group that aims to destroy the very axioms of the South."

Sherman's lips and nostrils fluttered with emotion when he said: "You talk like you believe in slavery."

"Why of course I believe in slavery. Civilization is founded on slavery."

The old Judge, who still thought of Sherman as a jewel, a treasure, continued to forget, in his passionate prejudice, that Sherman was colored. And when he saw his jewel so agitated he tried to make amends.

"If not actual slavery at least a state of happy peonage."

"Happy for who?"

"For everybody. Do you believe for a single instant that the slaves wanted to be freed? No, Sherman, many a slave remained faithful to his old master, would not be freed till the day he died."

"Bullshit."

"Beg your pardon," said the old Judge, who was conveniently deafer at times. "Now I've been told that the conditions of the Negro in the North are appalling — mixed marriages, nowhere to live and lay his head, and just downright appalling misery."

"Still a nigger would rather be a lamppost in Harlem than the Governor of Georgia."

The Judge inclined his good ear. "Didn't quite catch," he said softly.

All Sherman's life he had thought that all white men were crazy, and the more prominent their positions the more lunatic were their words and behavior. In this matter, Sherman considered he had the sober ice-cold truth on his side. The politicians, from governors to congressmen, down to sheriffs and wardens, were alike in their bigotry and violence. Sherman brooded over every lynching, bombing, or indignity that his race had suffered. In this Sherman had the vulnerability and sensitivity of an adolescent. Drawn to broodings on atrocities, he felt that every evil was reserved for him personally. So he lived in a stasis of dread and suspense. This attitude was supported by facts. No Negro in Peach County had ever voted. A schoolteacher had registered and been turned down at the polls. Two college graduates had been turned down likewise. The Fifteenth Amendment of the American Constitution had guaranteed the right to vote to the Negro race, yet no Negro Sherman had known or heard

tell of had ever voted. Yes, the American Constitution itself
was a fraud. And if his story he had told Jester was not true,
about the voting of the Golden Nigerians and the cardboard
coffins, he had heard the actual story about a club in another
county; and if it had not actually happened to the Golden
Nigerians of Milan, he knew it had happened to others somewhere else. Since his imagination enveloped all disasters, he
felt that any evil he read or heard about could just as well have
happened to himself.

This state of anxiety made Sherman take the old Judge more
seriously than he would have under calmer conditions. Slavery!
Was the old Judge planning to make slaves of his race? It did
not make sense. But what the fuckin hell made sense in the
relation between the races? The Fifteenth Amendment had
been put at nought, the American Constitution was a fraud as
far as Sherman was concerned. And justice! Sherman knew
of every lynching, every violence that had happened in his
time and before his time, and he felt every abuse in his own
body, and therefore lived in his stasis of tension and fear.
Otherwise he would have thought of the plans of the old
Judge as the product of a senile mind. But as a Negro in
the South, an orphan at that, he had been exposed to such
real horror and degradation that the wildest phantasies of the
old Judge seemed not only possible, but in Sherman's lawless
land, almost inevitable. Facts combined to support his
phantasies and fears. Sherman was convinced that all white
Southerners were crazy. Lynching a Negro boy because a
white woman said he had whistled at her. A Judge sentencing
a Negro because a white woman said she didn't like the way
he looked at her. Whistling! Looking! His prejudiced mind
was inflamed and quivering like some tropical atmosphere that
causes mirages.

At noon Sherman made the drinks and neither he nor the

old Judge spoke. Then at dinnertime an hour later, Sherman was reaching for a can of lobster when Verily said: "You don't need that, Sherman."

"Why not, old woman?"

"Yestidy you opened a can of tuna fish and made yourself a tuna fish sandwich mess. There's ample plenty of the tuna fish to make a sandwich today."

Sherman kept right on opening the lobster can. "Besides," Verily went on, "you ought to be eating collards and corn-pones in the kitchen like anybody else."

"Nigger doings!"

"Well, who do you think you are? The Queen of Sheba?"

Sherman was mashing the lobster with hunks of mayonnaise and chopped pickles. "Anyway I'm not pure nigger like you are," he said to Verily who was very dark. "Look at my eyes."

"I seen them."

Sherman was busily spreading his lobster sandwich.

"That lobster was supposed to be for Sunday night supper when I'm off. I got a good mind to tell the Judge on you."

But since Sherman was still the jewel, the treasure, the threat was an empty one and they both knew it.

"Go on and tell him," Sherman said as he garnished his sandwich with bread and butter pickles.

"Just because you have them blue eyes is no reason to act so high and mighty. You nigger like the rest of us. You just had a white pappy who passed on them blue eyes to you, and that's nothin to put on airs about. You nigger like the rest of us."

Sherman took his tray and stalked carefully through the hall to the library. But in spite of the party sandwiches he could not eat. He was thinking about what the Judge had said and his eyes were fixed and bleak in his dark face. His mind felt that most of the Judge's words were crazy, but Sherman, slanted by anxiety, could not think rationally; he could only feel. He remembered the campaign addresses of certain Southerners, cunning, violent, menacing. To Sherman the Judge talked no crazier than many another Southern politician. Crazy, crazy, crazy. All of them!

Sherman did not forget that the Judge had once been a congressman, thus holding one of the highest offices in the United States. And he knew people in high places. Just look at his answer from Senator Tip Thomas. The Judge was smart — mighty foxy — he could play a soft game of footsie. In dwelling on the power of the old Judge, he forgot his sicknesses; it did not even occur to Sherman that the brain of the old man who had once been a congressman could have deteriorated in old age. Zippo Mullins had a grandfather who had lost his mind in his old age. Old Mr. Mullins ate with a towel around his neck, could not pick out the watermelon seeds but swallowed them whole; he had no teeth and would gum his fried chicken; at the end he had to go to the county home. The old Judge on the other hand carefully unfolded his napkin at the beginning of a meal and had beautiful table manners, asking Jester or Verily to cut up the food he couldn't manage. Those were the only two very old men that Sherman had actually known, and there was a world of difference between them. So Sherman never considered the possibility of brain-softening in the old Judge.

Sherman stared for a long time at the fancy lobster sandwich, but anxiety would not let him eat. He did eat one bread and butter pickle before going back to the kitchen. He wanted a drink. Some gin and tonic, half and half, would settle his spirits so that he could eat. He knew he faced another run-in with Verily, but he went straight to the kitchen and grasped the gin bottle.

"Look yonder," she said, "look what the Queen of Sheba is up to now."

Sherman deliberately poured his gin and added cold tonic.

"I try to be kind and pleasant to you, Sherman, but I knew from the first it was no use. What makes you so cold and airy? Is it them blue eyes passed on from your pappy?"

Sherman walked stiffly from the kitchen, his drink in hand, and settled himself again at the library table. As he drank the gin his inward turbulence increased. In his search for his true mother, Sherman had seldom thought about his father. Sherman thought only that he was a white man, he imagined that the unknown white father had raped his mother. For every boy's mother is virtuous, especially if she is imaginary. Therefore, he hated his father, hated even to think about him. His father was a crazy white man who had raped his mother and left the evidence of bastardy in Sherman's blue and alien eyes. He had never sought his father as he sought his mother, the dreams of his mother had lulled and solaced him, but he thought of his father with pure hate.

After dinner when the Judge was taking his usual nap, Jester came into the library. Sherman was still sitting at the table, his tray of sandwiches untouched.

"What's the matter, Sherman?" Jester noticed the gin-drunk somnolence in the rapt eyes and he was uneasy.

"Go fuck," Sherman said brutally, for Jester was the only white person to whom he could use words like that. But he was in a state where no words could relieve him now. I hate, I hate, I hate, he thought as his unseeing eyes fixed, brooding and drunk, at the open window.

"I have often thought that if I had been born a Nigerian or colored, I couldn't stand it. I admire you, Sherman, the way you stand up to it. I admire you more than I can say."

"Well save your peanuts for the zoo."

"I have thought often," went on Jester who had read the idea somewhere, "that if Christ was born now he would be colored."

"Well he wasn't."

"I'm afraid . . ." Jester began and found it hard to finish.

"What are you afraid of, chicken-out sissy?"

"I'm afraid that if I were a Nigerian or colored, I would be neurotic. Awfully neurotic."

"No you wouldn't." His right forefinger cut swiftly across his neck in a slashing gesture. "A neurotic nigger is a dead nigger."

Jester was wondering why it was so hard to make friends with Sherman. His grandfather had often said: "Black is black and white is white and never the two shall meet if I can prevent it." And the *Atlanta Constitution* wrote of Southerners of good will. How could he tell Sherman that he was not like his grandfather, but a Southerner of good will?

"I respect colored people every whit as much as I do white people."

"You're one for the birds all right."

"Respect colored people even more than I do white people on account of what they have gone through."

"There's plenty of bad niggers around," Sherman said as he finished his gin drink.

"Why do you say that to me?"

"Just warning the pop-eyed baby."

"I'm trying to level with you about how I feel morally about the racial question. But you don't pay any mind to me."

His depression and rage accented by alcohol, Sherman only said in a threatening voice, "Bad niggers with police records and others without records like me."

"Why is it so hard to be friends with you?"

"Because I don't want friends," Sherman lied, because next to a mother, he wanted a friend the most. He admired and feared Zippo who was always insulting him, never washed a dish even when Sherman did the cooking, and treated him very much as he now treated Jester.

"Well, I'm going to the airport. Want to come along?"

"When I fly, I fly my own planes. None of those cheap, rented planes like you fly."

So Jester had to leave it at that; and Sherman watched him, brooding and jealous, as he walked down the drive.

The Judge awoke from his nap at two o'clock, washed his sleep-wrinkled face, and felt joyful and refreshed. He did not remember any tensions of the morning and as he went downstairs he was humming. Sherman, hearing the ponderous tread and the tuneless voice, made a face toward the hall door.

"My boy," said the Judge. "Do you know why I would rather be Fox Clane than Shakespeare or Julius Caesar?"

Sherman's lips barely moved when he said, "No."

"Or Mark Twain or Abraham Lincoln or Babe Ruth?"

Sherman just nodded no without speaking, wondering what the tack was about now.

"I'd rather be Fox Clane than all these great and famous people. Can't you guess why?"

This time Sherman only looked at him.

"Because I'm alive. And when you consider the trillions and trillions of dead people you realize what a privilege it is to be alive."

"Some people are dead from the neck up."

The Judge ignored this and said, "To me it is simply marvelous to be alive. Isn't it to you, Sherman?"

"Not particularly," he said, as he wanted very much to go home and sleep off the gin.

"Consider the dawn. The moon, the stars and heavenly firmaments," the Judge went on. "Consider shortcake and liquor."

Sherman's cold eyes considered the universe and the comforts of daily life with disdain and he did not answer.

"When I had that little seizure, Doc Tatum told me, frankly, if the seizure had affected the left part of the brain instead of the right, I should have been mentally and permanently afflicted." The Judge's voice had dropped with awe and horror. "Can you imagine living in such a condition?"

Sherman could: "I knew a man who had a stroke and it left him blind and with a mind like a two-year-old baby. The county home wouldn't even accept him. Not even the asylum. I don't know what happened to him finally. Probably died."

"Well, nothing like that happened to me. I was just left with a slight motor impairment . . . just the left arm and leg, ever so slightly damaged . . . but the mind intact. So I reasoned to myself: Fox Clane, ought you to cuss God, cuss the heavenly elements, cuss destiny, because of that little old impairment which didn't really bother me anyhow, or ought I to praise God, the elements, nature and destiny because I have nothing wrong with me, my mind being sound? For after all, what is a little arm, what's a leg, if the mind is sound and the spirit joyful. So I said to myself: Fox Clane, you better praise and keep on praising."

Sherman looked at the shrunken left arm and the hand permanently clenched. He felt sorry for the old Judge and hated himself for feeling sorry.

"I knew a little boy who had polio and had to wear heavy iron braces on both legs and use iron crutches . . . crippled for life," said Sherman who had seen a picture of such a boy in the newspapers.

The Judge was thinking that Sherman knew a whole galaxy of pitiful cases, and tears came to his eyes as he murmured, "Poor child." The Judge did not hate himself for pitying others; he did not pity himself, for by and large he was quite happy. Of course, he would love to eat forty baked Alaskas every day, but on the whole he was content. "I'd rather stick to any diet than have to start shoveling coal or picking a harp. I never could manage even my own furnace and I'm not the least bit musical."

"Yes, some people can't carry a tune in a basket."

The Judge ignored this, as he was always singing and the tunes seemed all right to him. "Let's proceed with the correspondence."

"What letters do you want me to write now?"

"A whole slew of them, to every congressman and senator I know personally and every politician who might cotton to my ideas."

"What kind of letters do you wish me to write?"

"In the general tenor of what I told you this morning. About the Confederate money and the general retribution of the South."

The zip of gin had turned to dour anger. Although he was emotionally keyed up, Sherman yawned and kept on yawning just to be rude. He considered his soft, clean, bossy job and the shock of the morning's conversation. When Sherman loved, he loved, when he admired, he admired, and there was no halfway emotional state. Until now he had both loved and admired the Judge. Who else had been a congressman, a judge; who else would give him a fine, dainty job as an amanuensis and let him eat party sandwiches at the library table? So Sherman was in a quandary and his mobile features quivered as he spoke, "You mean that part even about slavery?"

The Judge knew now that something had gone wrong. "Not slavery, Son, but restitution for slaves that the Yankees freed. Economic restitution."

Sherman's nostrils and lips were quivering like butterflies. "I won't do it, Judge."

The Judge had seldom been said "no" to, as his requests

were usually reasonable. Now that his treasure, his jewel, had refused him, he sighed, "I don't understand you, Son."

And Sherman, who was always pleased with any term of affection, especially since they were so seldom addressed to him, basked for a moment and almost smiled.

"So you refuse to write this series of letters?"

"I do," said Sherman, as the power of refusal was also sweet to him. "I won't be a party to turning the clock back almost a century."

"The clock won't be turned back, it will be turned forward for a century, Son."

It was the third time he had so called him and the suspicion that was always dormant in Sherman's nature stirred wordlessly, inchoate.

"Great change always turns forward the clock. Wars particularly. If it weren't for World War I, women would still be wearing ankle-length skirts. Now young females go around dressed like carpenters in overalls, even the prettiest, most well-bred girl."

The Judge had noticed Ellen Malone going to her father's pharmacy in overalls and he had been shocked and embarrassed on Malone's behalf.

"Poor J. T. Malone."

"Why do you say that?" asked Sherman who was struck by the compassion and the tone of mystery in the Judge's voice.

"I'm afraid, my boy, that Mr. Malone is not long for this world."

Sherman, who didn't care about Mr. Malone one way or the next and was in no mood to pretend to feelings he didn't truly feel, only said, "Gonna die? Too bad."

"Death is worse than too bad. In fact, no one on this earth knows what death is really about."

"Are you awfully religious?"

"No, I'm not a bit religious. But I fear..."

"Why have you often referred to shoveling coal and picking harps?"

"Oh, that's just a figure of speech. If that's all I feared and if I was sent to the bad place, I would shovel coal along with the rest of the sinners, a lot of whom I would have already known beforehand. And in case I'm sent to heaven, by God I'd learn to be as musical as Blind Tom or Caruso. It's not that I fear."

"What is it you do fear?" asked Sherman who had never thought much about death.

"Blankness," said the old man. "An infinite blankness and blackness where I'd be all by myself. Without loving or eating or nothing. Just lying in this infinite blankness and darkness."

"I would hate that too," said Sherman casually.

The Judge was remembering his stroke, and his thoughts were stark and clear. Although he minimized his illness to others as a "little seizure" or "slight case of polio," he was truthful to himself; it was a stroke and he had nearly died. He remembered the shock of falling. His right hand felt the paralyzed one and there was no feeling, just a weighty clamminess without motion or sensation. The left leg was just as weighty and without feeling, so in the hysteria of those long hours he had believed that half of his body was mysteriously dead. Unable to wake Jester, he had cried to Miss Missy, to his dead father, his brother Beau — not to join them, but for solace in his distress. He was found in the early morning and sent to the City Hospital where he began to live again. Day by day his paralyzed limbs awakened, but shock had dulled him, and cutting off liquor and tobacco added to his misery. Unable to walk or even raise his left hand, he busied himself by working crossword puzzles, reading mysteries, and playing solitaire. There was nothing to look forward to but meals, and the hospital food also bored him although he ate every bite that was put on his tray. Then suddenly the idea of the Confederate money came to his mind. It just came; it happened like the song a child might sing that was suddenly made up. And one idea brought the next idea, so that he was thinking, creating, dreaming. It was October and a sweet chill fell upon the town in the early morning and at twilight. The sunlight was pure and clear as honey after the heat and glare of the Milan summer. The energy of thought brought further thoughts. The Judge explained to the dietitian how to make decent coffee, hospital or no, and soon he was able to lumber from the bed to the dresser and from there to the chair with the help of a nurse. His poker cronies came and they played poker, but the energy of his new life came from his thinking, his dream. He sheltered his ideas lovingly, telling them to no one. What would Poke Tatum or Bennie Weems know about the dreams of a great statesman? When he went home he could walk, use his left hand a little, and carry on almost as before. His dream remained dormant, for whom could he tell it to, and old age and shock had made his handwriting deteriorate.

"I would probably never have thought of those ideas if it hadn't been for that stroke that paralyzed me so that I was half dead in the City Hospital for close on to two months."

Sherman rooted in his nostrils with a Kleenex but said nothing.

"And paradoxically, if I hadn't gone through the shadow of death I might never have seen the light. Don't you understand why these ideas are precious beyond reason to me?"

Sherman looked at the Kleenex and put it slowly back in his pocket. Then he began to gaslight the Judge, cupping his chin in his right hand and looking into the pure blue eyes with his own creepy stare.

"Don't you see why it is important for you to write these letters I'm going to dictate?"

Sherman still did not answer, and his silence irritated the old Judge.

"Aren't you going to write these letters?"

"I told you 'no' once and I'm telling you 'no' again. You want me to tattoo 'no' on my chest?"

"At first you were such an amenable amanuensis," the Judge observed aloud. "But now you're about as enthusiastic as a gravestone."

"Yeah," said Sherman.

"You are so contrary and secretive," the Judge complained. "So secretive you wouldn't give me the time of day if you were just in front of the town clock."

"I don't blah-blah everything I know. I keep things to myself."

"You young folks are secretive — downright devious to the mature mind."

Sherman was thinking of the realities and dreams he had guarded. He had said nothing about what Mr. Stevens had done until he had stuttered so much that his words seemed to make no sense. He had told no one about his search for his mother, no one about his dreams about Marian Anderson. No one, nobody knew his secret world.

"I don't 'blah-blah' my ideas. You are the only person I've discussed them with," said the Judge, "except in a glancing way with my grandson."

Secretly Sherman thought Jester was a smart cookie, although he would never have admitted it. "What is his opinion?"

"He too is so self-centered and secretive he wouldn't give

anyone the time of day even if he was just in front of the town clock. I had expected something better of you."

Sherman was weighing his soft, bossy job against the letters he was asked to write. "I will write other letters for you. Letters of acceptance, invitations, and so forth."

"Those are insignificant," said the Judge, who never went anywhere. "A mere bagatelle."

"I will write other letters."

"No other letters interest me."

"If you are so hipped on the subject you can write the letters yourself," Sherman said, well knowing the condition of the Judge's handwriting.

"Sherman," the old man pleaded, "I have treated you as a son, and sharper than a serpent's tooth it is to have a thankless child."

Often the Judge quoted this line to Jester, but with absolutely no effect. When the boy was small he had plugged his ears with his fingers, and when he was older he had cut up in one way or another to show his grandfather he didn't care. But Sherman was deeply affected; his gray-blue eyes fixed wonderingly on the blue eyes opposite him. Three times he had been called "Son," and now the old Judge was speaking to him as though he was his own son. Never having had parents, Sherman had never heard the line that is the standard reproach of parents. Never had he sought his father, and now, as always, he kept the conjured image at a distance: blue-eyed Southerner, one among all the blue-eyed South. The Judge had blue eyes and so had Mr. Malone. And so, as far as that goes, had Mr. Breedlove at the bank, and Mr. Taylor, and there were dozens of blue-eyed men in Milan he could think of offhand, hundreds in the county nearby, thousands in the South. Yet the Judge was the only white man who had singled out Sherman for kindness. And Sherman, being suspicious of kindness, wondered: Why had the Judge given him a watch with foreign words, engraved with his name, when he had hauled him out of that golf pond years ago? Why he had hired him for the cush job with the fancy eating arrangements haunted Sherman, although he kept his suspicions at arm's length.

Troubled, he could only skip to other troubles, so he said: "I wrote Zippo's love letters. He can write, of course, but his letters don't have much zip, they never sent Vivian Clay. Then I wrote 'The dawn of love steals over me' and 'I will love thee in the sunset of our passion as much as I do now.' The letters were long on words like 'dawn' or 'sunset' and pretty colors. I would sprinkle in 'I adore thee' often, and soon Vivian was not only sent but rolling in the aisles."

"Then why won't you write my letters about the South?"

"Because the idea is queer and would turn back the clock."

"I don't mind being called queer or reactionary either."

"I just wrote myself out of a fine apartment, because after the love letters, Vivian herself popped the question and Zippo accepted very gladly. That means I will have to find another apartment; I wrote the very planks out of the floor."

"You'll just have to find another apartment."

"It's hard."

"I don't think I could endure moving. Although my grandson and I racket around this big old house like two peas in a shoebox."

The Judge, when he thought of his ornate Victorian house with the colored windows and the stiff old furniture, sighed. It was a sigh of pride, although the people in Milan often referred to the house as "The Judge's White Elephant."

"I think I would rather be moved to the Milan Cemetery than have to move to another house." The Judge considered what he had said and took it back quickly, vehemently:

"Pshaw, I didn't mean that, Son." He touched wood carefully. "What a foolish thing for a foolish old man to say. I was just thinking that I would find it mighty hard to live elsewhere on account of the memories."

The Judge's voice was wavering, and Sherman said in a hard voice, "Don't bawl about it. Nobody makin *you* move."

"I dare say I'm sentimental about this house. A few people can't appreciate the architecture. But I love it, Miss Missy liked it, and my son Johnny was brought up in this house. My grandson, too. There are nights when I just lie in the bed and remember. Do you sometimes lie in the bed and remember?"

"Naw."

"I remember things that actually happened and things that might have happened. I remember stories my mother told me about the War Between the States. I remember the years when I was a student at law school, and my youth, and my marriage to Miss Missy. Funny things. Sad things. I remember them all. In fact I remember the far-off past better than I recall yesterday."

"I've heard that old people are like that. And I guess I heard right."

"Not everyone can remember exactly and clear as a picture show."

"Blah-blah," said Sherman under his breath. But although he spoke toward the deaf ear, the old Judge heard and his feelings were hurt.

"I may be garrulous about the past, but to me it is just as real as the *Milan Courier*. And more interesting because it happened to me, or my relatives and friends. I know everything that has happened in the town of Milan since long before the day you were born."

"Do you know about how I was born?"

The Judge hesitated, tempted to deny his knowledge; but since he found it difficult to lie, he said nothing.

"Did you know my mother? Did you know my father? Do you know where they are?"

But the old man, lost in the meditations of the past, refused to answer. "You may think me an old man who tells everything, but as a jurist I keep my council and on some subjects I am as silent as a tomb."

So Sherman pleaded and pleaded, but the old Judge prepared a cigar and smoked in silence.

"I have every right to know."

As the Judge still smoked on in silence, Sherman again began to gaslight. They sat like mortal enemies.

After a long time, the Judge said, "Why what's the matter with you, Sherman? You look almost sinister."

"I feel sinister."

"Well, stop looking at me in that peculiar way."

Sherman kept right on gaslighting. "Furthermore," he said, "I've got a good mind to give you quit notice. And how would you like that?"

And on these words, in the middle of the afternoon, he stomped away, pleased that he had punished the Judge and brushing aside the thought that he also punished himself.

10

ALTHOUGH the Judge seldom spoke about his son, he was with him often in his dreams. Only in the dream, that phoenix of remembrance and desire, could his memory live. And when he woke up he was always cross as two sticks.

As he lived very much in the here and now except for pleasant daydreams just before he went to sleep, the Judge seldom brooded over the past in which, as a judge, he had almost unlimited power . . . even the power of life and death. His decisions always were preceded by long cogitations; he never considered a death sentence without the aid of prayer. Not that he was religious, but it somehow siphoned the responsibility away from Fox Clane and dribbled it to God. Even so, he had sometimes made mistakes. He had sentenced a twenty-year-old Nigra to death for rape, and after his death another Nigra confessed to the crime. But how was he, as a judge, to be responsible? The jury after due consideration had found him guilty and had not recommended mercy; his decision just followed the law and the customs of the state. How could he know when the boy kept saying, "I never done it," that he was saying the God's truth? It was a mistake that might have put many a conscientious magistrate under the sod; but although the Judge regretted it deeply, he kept reminding himself that the boy had been tried by twelve good men and true and that he, himself, was only an instrument of the law. So, no matter how grave the miscarriage was, he could not pine forever.

The Nigra Jones was in another category. He had murdered a white man and his defense was self-defense. The witness of the murder was the white man's wife, Mrs. Ossie Little. It had come about in this way: Jones and Ossie Little were sharecroppers on the Gentry farm, close to Sereno. Ossie Little was twenty years older than his wife, a part-time preacher who was able to make his Holy Roller congregation talk in strange tongues when the spirit came upon them. Otherwise he was a shambling, no-good tenant who let the farm rot. Trouble started as soon as he married a child-bride wife whose folks came up from around Jessup where their farm was in a ruined dust bowl area. They were traveling through Georgia in an old jalopy on the way to hope and California when they met up with Preacher Little and forced their daughter, Joy, to marry him. It was a simple, unsavory story of the depression years and nothing good could reasonably be expected, and surely nothing good came of any part of the sorry affair. The twelve-year-old child-bride had character seldom met with in one so young. The Judge remembered her as a pretty little thing, at first playing dolls with a cigar box of doll's clothes, then having a little baby of her own to bear and care for when she was not yet thirteen. Then trouble, having started, compounded as trouble always does. First, it was rumored that young Mrs. Little was seeing more of the colored tenant on the adjacent farm than was right and proper. Then Bill Gentry, provoked by Little's laziness, threatened to turn him off the farm and hand over his share to Jones.

The Judge pulled up a blanket on his bed as the night was very cold. And how did his fair-born, darling son get mixed up with Nigra murderers, shiftless preachers, child-brides? How? Oh how? And in what a mangled maw it was to lose his son!

Self-defense or no, the Nigra was doomed to die and Johnny knew it as well as anybody else. Why then did he persist in taking the case, which was a lost cause from the beginning? The Judge had argued to dissuade him. What would it fetch him? Nothing but failure. Yet, little had the Judge known that it would lead to more than a young man's hurt pride, more than a fledgling lawyer's failure — but that it would lead to obscure heartbreak and death. But how, oh how? The Judge groaned aloud.

Except for having to impose sentence, he had kept out of the case as much as possible. He knew that Johnny was all too deeply involved with the case, burned the midnight oil till daylight, and boned up on law as though in defending Jones he was defending his own blood brother. During the six months Johnny was working on the case, the Judge reproached himself, he should have known. But how could he have known, not being a mind reader? In the courtroom Johnny was as nervous as any other fledgling lawyer at his first murder trial. The Judge had been distressed when Johnny agreed to take the case, was amazed at first at the way he handled it — hot potato that it was. Johnny was eloquent, just speaking the truth as he believed it. But how could you sway twelve good men and true like that? His voice did not rise and fall like most trial lawyers. He did not shout, then sink to a whisper at the incriminating point. Johnny just talked quietly as though he was not in court at all — how could that sway twelve good men and true? He was talking about justice with a voice that broke. He was also singing his swan song.

The Judge wanted to think of something else — to daydream of Miss Missy and to go to sleep, but most of all he wanted to see Jester. In old age or invalidism, stories once remembered cast a spell on the mind. Useless to think about the time he had a box at the Opera; it was the first time the Atlanta Opera opened. He had invited his brother and sister-in-law as well as Miss Missy and her father for the gala occasion. The Judge had invited a whole box of friends. The first performance was *The Goose Girl*, and well did he remember Geraldine Farrar coming across the stage with two live geese on a kind of harness. The live geese said "Quack, quack," and old Mr. Brown, Miss Missy's father, had said, "First damned thing I've understood this evening." How embarrassed Miss Missy was, and how pleased he had been. He had listened to the Germans squalling their heads off in German — the geese quacking — while he just sat there looking musical and learned. Useless to think of all these things. His mind came back to Ossie Little, the woman, and Jones — it would not let him rest. He struggled against it.

When was Jester ever coming home? He had never been hard on the boy. True, there was a peach switch in a vase on the diningroom mantelpiece, but he had never used it on Jester. Once when Johnny had been cutting up and throwing bread at the servant and his parents, he had lost his temper, taken down the peach switch, and dragged his

young son to the library where, amid the wails of the entire
household, he had cut him two or three times on his bare
and jumping legs. After that, the switch remained stark in the
vase on the mantelpiece as a threat but never once used from
that day to this. Yet the Scripture itself said: "Spare the rod
and spoil the child." If the peach switch had been used more
often, would Johnny still be alive? He doubted it, but still he
wondered. Johnny was too passionate; although it was not the
passion he could readily recognize — the passion of the posse,
the passion of the Southerner who defends his womankind
against the black and alien invader — it was passion nonetheless, as strange as it had seemed to him and other Milan citizens.

Like a tedious tune that pounds in a fevered brain, the
story insisted. The Judge turned mountainlike in his huge
bed. When was Jester coming home? It was so late. Yet
when he turned on the light he saw that it was still not nine
o'clock. So Jester was not out so late after all. On the mantel
to the left of the clock there was Johnny's photograph. The
vigor of the young lost face seemed to blossom in the lamp
light. On Johnny's left chin there was a small birthmark. This
imperfection served only to sum up the beauty of Johnny's face,
and when he noticed it the Judge felt closer to heartbreak.

Yet in spite of the spasm of grief that always came when he
looked at the little birthmark, the Judge could not cry for his
son. For underneath his emotions there was always resentment — a resentment that had been lulled at Jester's birth,
softened a little by the passage of time, but always and forever there. It was as though his son had cheated him by depriving him of his beloved presence, the sweet and treacherous
thief had plundered his heart. If Johnny had died in any
other way, cancer or leukemia — the Judge knew more of
Malone's illness than he let on — he could have grieved with

a clear heart, cried also. But suicide seemed a deliberate act of spite which the Judge resented. In the photograph Johnny was faintly smiling and the little birthmark summed up the radiant face. The Judge folded back his twisted sheet and lumbered out of bed, steadying himself with his right hand as he crossed the room. He took down Johnny's photograph and put it in a bureau drawer. Then he steered himself into bed again.

There was the sound of Christmas chimes. For him, Christmas was the saddest season. The chimes, the Joy to the Worlds . . . so sad, so left, so lonesome. A flash of lightning lit up the dark sky. Was there a storm coming? If only Johnny had been struck by lightning. Yet one cannot choose. Either at birth or death one cannot choose. Only suicides could choose, disdaining the living quick of life for the nothing nothing of the grave. Another flash of lightning was followed by thunder.

True, he had almost never used the peach switch, but he had counseled Johnny as a lad. He had been concerned about Johnny's admiration of Bolshevism, Samuel Liebowitz, and radicalism in general. He had always consoled himself by the fact that Johnny was young, was a quarterback on the University of Georgia football team, and that the fads and fancies of the young pass quickly when reality must be faced. True, Johnny's youth was so different from his father's waltzing, singing-and-dancing days when he was the beau of Flowering Branch and courted and won Miss Missy. He could only say to himself that "Yond Cassius has a lean and hungry look; He thinks too much: such men are dangerous" — but he did not dwell on it, because in his wildest dreams he could not associate Johnny with danger.

Once he had said aloud that first year Johnny was in the firm, "I have often noticed, Johnny, that when one is too much involved with the underdog, one is apt to go under oneself."

Johnny had only shrugged his shoulders.

"When I first began to practice, I was a poor boy. Not a rich man's son like you." Although he had noticed the embarrassment that flickered over Johnny's face, he had gone right on: "I eschewed court charity cases which fall to the lot of a poor lawyer at first. My practice increased and soon I was able to defend the cases that brought in considerable financial returns. Financial returns or political prestige was, and always has been, a prime consideration."

"I'm not that kind of lawyer," Johnny said.

"I'm not trying to persuade you to emulate me," the Judge said untruthfully. "One thing — I have never taken a crooked case. I know when a client is lying and wouldn't touch the case with a ten-foot pole. I have a sixth sense in such matters. Remember the man who murdered his wife with a mashie on the golf course at the country club? The fee would have been princely, but I refused it."

"As I remember it, there were witnesses."

"Johnny, a lawyer of genius can bamboozle witnesses, convince the jury they were not where they swore they were, and could not possibly have seen the things they saw. However, I refused the case and many another like it. I have never committed myself to unsavory cases, no matter how princely the fee."

Johnny's smile was as ironical as the one in the photograph. "Well, isn't that handsome of you!"

"Of course, when lucrative cases combine with a just cause, it is just sheer heaven for Fox Clane. Remember how I defended the Milan Power Company? Sheer heaven and a whopping fee."

"The rates went way up."

"You cannot sell your birthright for electricity and gas. I never had them as a child. Had to trim lamps and stoke stoves. But I was free."

Johnny said nothing.

Often the Judge had taken down the photograph when paroxysms of emotion were caused by the little birthmark or when the smile seemed to mock him like a sneer. The photograph would be kept in the drawer until his mood changed or until he could no longer bear the absence of the likeness of his son. Then it would appear in the silver frame and he would gaze at the little blemish and even tolerate the remote and lovely smile.

"Don't misunderstand me," he had counseled those years ago, "I take lucrative cases but not out of self-interest." The mature lawyer and ex-congressman had yearned for some word of appreciation from his young son. Had his honesty in saying home truths seemed like cynicism to Johnny?

After some time Johnny had said: "Often this past year I have wondered how responsible you are."

"Responsible!" The Judge flushed quickly, violently. "I am the most responsible citizen in Milan, in Georgia, in all the South."

To the tune of "God Save The King," Johnny chanted, "God help the South."

"If it weren't for me, where do you think you would be?"

"A little scrap hanging out on the washline of heaven." Johnny's voice changed. "I never wanted to be your son."

The Judge, still flushed with emotion, wanted to blurt, "But I always wanted you to be my son." Instead he asked, "What kind of son do you think would be about right for the old man?"

"How about . . ." Johnny's mind turned over imaginary sons. "Why, how about Alec Sisroe?" Johnny's light laugh blended with his father's bass guffaws. "Motheromine, oh Motheromine," the Judge quoted through his spittle and wild laughter. For Alex Sisroe quoted that poem every Mother's Day at the First Baptist Church. He was a prissy, weedy mother's boy, and Johnny would take off the performance to the delight of his father and disapproval of his mother.

The sudden, off-beat hilarity ended as quickly as it had begun. Often the father and son who responded to the ridiculous in the same manner were caught by such laughter. This side of their relationship had prompted the Judge to a further assumption, to a fallacy often common in fathers. "Johnny and I are more like two brothers than father and son. The same love of fishing and hunting, same sterling sense of values — I have never known my son to tell a lie — same interests, same fun." So the Judge would harp on such fraternal similarities to his audiences in Malone's pharmacy, in the courthouse, in the back room of the New York Café and in the barbershop. His listeners, seeing little relation between the shy young Johnny Clane and his town-character father, made no comment. When the Judge himself realized the widening difference between his son and himself, he harped on the father-son theme even more than ever, as though words could turn the wish into reality.

That last laugh about the "Motheromine Boy" had been perhaps the last joke shared between them. And hacked about Johnny's reference to responsibility, the Judge had cut the laughter short and said: "You seemed to criticize me for taking the case for the Milan Electric and Power Company. Am I right, Son?"

"Yes sir. The rates went up."

"Sometimes it is the painful choice of the mature mind to have to choose the lesser of two evils. And this was a case where politics were involved. Not that I had any brief for

Harry Breeze or the Milan Electric and Power, but the Federal Government was rearing its ugly head. Imagine when TVA and such like power plants control the entire nation. I could smell the stink of creeping paralysis."

"Creeping paralysis doesn't stink," Johnny had said.

"No, but socialism does to my nostrils. And when socialism takes away self-initiative and . . ." the Judge's voice meandered until he found a sudden image, "puts people into cookie cutters, standardization," the Judge said wildly. "It might interest you to know, Son, that I once had a scientific interest in socialism and even communism. Purely scientific, mind you, and for a very brief time. Then one day I saw a photograph of dozens of young Bolshevik women in identical gymnastic costumes, all doing the same exercise, all squatting. Dozens and dozens of them doing the same gymnastics, breasts the same, the hams the same, every posture, every rib, every behind the same, the same. And although I have no aversion to healthy womanflesh, whether Bolshevik or American, squatting or upright, the longer I studied the photograph the more I was revolted. Mind you, I might well have loved a single one among all those dozens of exuberant womanflesh — but seeing one after another, identical, I was revolted. And all my interest, however scientific, quite left me. Don't talk to me of standardization."

"The last track I followed was that of the Milan Electric and Power raising the rates on utilities," Johnny had said.

"What's a few pence to preserve our freedom and escape the creeping paralysis of socialism and the Federal Government? Should we sell our birthright for a mess of pottage?"

Old age and loneliness had not yet fixed the Judge's hostilities upon the Federal Government. He had spread his huffs of passing anger to his family, as he still had a family, or among his colleagues, as he was still an able, hard-working jurist who

was not above correcting young trial lawyers when they mis-
quoted Bartlett, Shakespeare, or the Bible, and his words were
still weighed and heeded whether on the bench or not. It was
the time when his chief concern had been the widening rift
between Johnny and himself, but the concern had not yet
changed to worry, and indeed he had mistaken it for youthful
folly on the boy's part. He had not worried when Johnny had
upped and got married after a dance, not worried that her
father was a well-known rum runner — preferring in his secret
heart a well-known rum runner to a preacher who might spoil
the family feasting or try to crimp his style. Miss Missy had
been brave about the matter, giving Mirabelle her second best
string of pearls and a garnet brooch. Miss Missy had made
much of the fact that Mirabelle had gone two years to Hollins
College where she was a music major. Indeed, the two practiced duets together, and memorized the "Turkish March."

The Judge's concern had not yet changed to worry until,
after no more than a year of practice, Johnny had chosen to
take the case of Jones *versus* the People. To what avail had
Johnny graduated *magna cum laude* at the University, if he
did not have a grain of common sense? To what avail had
been Johnny's legal knowledge and education when he stepped
on the bunions, corns, and calluses of every one of that jury of
twelve good men and true?

Refraining from discussing the case with his son, he had
cautioned him about a lawyer's sensitivity to jurors. He said,
"Talk on their own level and for God's sake don't try to lift
them above it." But would Johnny do that? He argued as if
those Georgia crackers, millhands, and tenant farmers were
trained jurors of the Supreme Court itself. Such talent. But
not a grain of common sense.

It was nine-thirty when Jester came into the Judge's room.
He was eating a double-decker sandwich which, after those

hours of remembered anxiety and grief, the old man eyed hungrily.

"I counted on you for supper."

"I took in a show and made myself a sandwich when I got home."

The Judge put on his spectacles and peered at the thick sandwich. "What's in it?"

"Peanut butter, tomatoes, and bacon and onions."

Jester took a gaping bite of the sandwich and a chunk of onion fell to the carpet. To quell his appetite, the Judge shifted his eager gaze from the delicious sandwich to the onion which was stuck to the carpet with mayonnaise. His appetite still remained, and so he said: "Peanut butter is loaded with calories." Opening the liquor chest he poured some whiskey. "Just eighty calories an ounce. And more what I wanted anyhow."

"Where is my father's picture?"

"In the drawer over there."

Jester, who knew well his grandfather's habit of hiding the photograph when he was upset, asked, "What's the matter?"

"Mad. Sad. Cheated. When I think of my son I often feel so."

A certain stillness fell on Jester's heart, as it always did when his father was mentioned. The Christmas chimes were silvery in the frosty air. He stopped eating and silently placed the scallop-bitten sandwich on the end table beside the bed. "You never talk about my father to me," he said.

"We were more like brothers than father and son. Blood twin brothers."

"I doubt it. Only introverts commit suicide. And you're no introvert."

"My son was not an introvert I'll have you know, sir," the Judge said with a voice that was shrill with rage. "Same sense of fun, same mental caliber. Your father would have been a genius if he'd lived, and that's not a word I bandy about lightly." (This was truer than anyone could have imagined, as the Judge used the word only when it applied to Fox Clane and William Shakespeare.) "Like blood twin brothers we were until he got involved with the Jones case."

"Is that the case where you always said my father was trying to break an axiom?"

"Laws, blood customs, axioms indeed!" Glaring at the bitten sandwich, he seized and ate it hungrily; but because his emptiness was not a hunger of the belly he remained uncomforted.

Since the Judge seldom talked about his son to Jester or satisfied his grandson's natural curiosity, Jester was used to asking angled questions, and so he asked: "What was that case about?"

The Judge responded at so wide an angle that the answer and question did not directly meet. "Johnny's adolescence was passed when communism was blaring wide and handsome in the grandstand. High muckety-mucks squatting in the very White House itself; the time of TVA, FHA, and FDR, all those muckety-muck letters. And one thing leading to another, a Negress singing at the Lincoln Memorial and my son . . . !" The Judge's voice soared with rage, "and my son defending a Nigra in a murder case. Johnny tried to . . ." Hysteria overcame the old man, the hysteria of the fantastic incongruity which strikes upon the heart's chagrin. He could not finish for the painful cackles and flying spittle.

"Don't," Jester said.

The rasping cackles and spittle continued while Jester watched soberly, his face white. "I'm not," the Judge managed to articulate until hysteria mounted again, "not laughing."

Jester sat upright in the chair, and his face was white.

Alarmed, he began to wonder if his grandfather was having an apoplectic fit. Jester knew that apoplectic fits were queer and sudden. He wondered if people turned red as fire and laughed like that in an apoplectic fit. He knew, also, that people died from apoplectic fits. Was his grandfather, red as fire and choking, laughing himself to death? Jester tried to raise the old man so he could slap him on the back, but the weight was too heavy for him, and at last the laughter weakened and finally stopped.

Bewildered, Jester considered his grandfather. He knew that schizophrenia was a split personality. Was he acting crisscrossed in his old age, laughing fit to kill when he ought to be crying? He knew well that his grandfather loved his own son. A whole section of the attic was kept for his dead father: ten knives and an Indian dagger, a clown costume, the Rover Boy series, Tom Swift series, and stacks of child's books, a cow skull, roller skates, fishing tackle, football suits, catchers' mitts, trunks and trunks of fine things and junk. But Jester had learned that he must not play with the things in the trunks, fine things or junk, for once when he tacked the cow's skull to the wall of his own bedroom, his grandfather had been furious and threatened to switch him with the peach switch. His grandfather had loved his own and only son, so why did he laugh with hysterics?

The Judge, seeing the question in Jester's eyes, said quietly: "Hysterics is not laughter, Son. It's a panic reaction of confusion when you cannot grieve. I was hysterical for four days and nights after my son's death. Doc Tatum helped Paul haul me into the bathtub for warm water baths and gave me sedatives and I kept on laughing — not laughing, that is — hysterical. Doc tried cold showers and more sedation. And there I was hysterical and the corpse of my son laid out in the parlor. The funeral had to be held over a day and I was so weak it took two big, strong men to hold me up when we went down the church aisle. Tight fit we must have been," he added soberly.

Jester asked in the same quiet voice: "But why do you get hysterical now? It's over seventeen years since my father died."

"And in all those years not a day has passed that I didn't think about my son. Sometimes for a glancing time, others for a brooding spell. I seldom ever trusted myself to speak of my son, but today most of the afternoon and the long evening I have been remembering — not only the skylarking times when we were young but the grown-up gravities that split and vanquished us. I was seeing my son at that last trial as plainly as I see you right now — plainer, in fact. And hearing his voice."

Jester was holding the chair arms so tightly his knuckles whitened.

"His defense was masterly except for one fatal flaw. The fatal flaw was that the jurors never got the gist at all. My son argued the case as though he was talking to a panel of New York Jew lawyers instead of the panel of twelve men good and true of the Circuit Court in Peach County, Georgia. Illiterate, one and all. Under the circumstances my son's opening move was a stroke of genius."

Jester opened his mouth and breathed through it, so tense was his silence.

"My son's first motion was to request the jurors to rise and pledge allegiance to the American flag. The jurors shambled to their feet and Johnny read them through the rigamarole, the pledge. Both Nat Webber and I were caught flatfooted. When Nat objected, I rapped the gavel and ordered the words struck from the record. But that didn't matter. My son had already made his point."

"What point?"

"At one stroke my son had joined those twelve men and prompted them to function at their highest level. They had been taught in school the pledge of allegiance and in speaking it, they were participating in some kind of holy exercise. I rapped the gavel!" The Judge grunted.

"Why did you strike it from the record?"

"Irrelevance. But my son, as defense lawyer, had made his point and lifted a sordid, cut-and-dried murder case to the level of constitutional law. My son went right on. 'Fellow jurors and your honor . . .' My son looked hard at each juror as he spoke, and at me. 'Each one of you twelve jurors has been lifted to an immense responsibility. Nothing takes precedence over you and your work at this hour.'" Jester listened with his hand and forefinger propping up his chin, his wine-brown eyes wide and asking in his listening face.

"From the beginning, Rice Little maintained that Mrs. Little had been raped by Jones, and his brother had every right to attempt to kill him. Rice Little just stood there like a little dirty feist dog guarding his brother's property line and nothing could shake him. When Johnny asked Mrs. Little, she swore it wasn't so and that her husband had tried to kill Jones out of deliberate malice . . . and in the struggle for the gun her husband was killed . . . a strange thing for a wife to swear. Johnny asked if Jones had ever treated her in any way that was not right and proper and she said, 'Never,' that he had treated her always like a lady."

The Judge added, "I should have seen something. But then eyes had I, but saw not.

"Plainer than yesterday I hear their words and see their faces. The accused had that peculiar color of a Nigra who is deathly scared. Rice Little in his tight, Sunday suit and his face as hard and yellow as a cheese paring. Mrs. Little just sat there, her eyes blue, blue and brazen, brazen. My son was trembling. After an hour my son shifted from the particular to the general. 'If two white people or two Negro people were being tried for this same accident, there would have been no case at all, for it was an accident that the gun went off when Ossie Little was trying to kill the defendant.'

"Johnny went on: 'The fact is that the case involves a white man and a Negro man and the inequality that lies between the handling of such a situation. In fact, fellow jurors, in cases like this, the Constitution itself is on trial.' Johnny quoted the preamble and the amendments freeing the slaves and giving them citizenship and equal rights. 'These words I quote now were written a century and a half ago and spoken by a million voices. These words are the law of our country. I, as a citizen and lawyer, can neither add to nor subtract from them. My function in this court is to underscore and try to implement them.' Then carried away, Johnny quoted 'Four score and seven years ago . . .' I rapped."

"What for?"

"These were just private words that Lincoln spoke, words that every law student memorizes, but I was not bound to hear them quoted in my courtroom."

Jester said, "My father wanted to quote them. Let me hear it now." Jester did not know clearly what the quote would be, but he felt nearer to his father than he had ever been, and the riddling skeleton of suicide and the old glory hole trunks were being fleshed by a living image. In his excitement Jester rose and stood with one hand on the bedpost, one leg drawn up against the other, waiting. Since the Judge never needed a second invitation to sing or recite or otherwise exercise his voice for an audience, he gravely quoted the Gettysburg Address while Jester listened with tears of glory in his eyes, his foot drawn up and his mouth open.

At the end, the Judge seemed to be wondering why he was quoting that. He said, "One of the greatest pieces of oratory ever spoken, but a vicious rabble-rouser. Shut your mouth, boy."

"I think it was terrible that you struck that from the record," Jester said. "What else did my father say?"

"His closing words, which should have been his most eloquent, petered out sadly after the high-flown impractical words of the Constitution and the Gettysburg Address. His own words drooped like a flag on a windless day. He pointed out that the amendments that followed the Civil War had not been implemented. But when he spoke of civil rights, he was so wrought up he pronounced it 'thivil' which made a bad impression and naturally undercut his own confidence. He pointed out that the population of Peach County was almost equally balanced between the Nigra and white races. He said he noticed that there was no Nigra represented on the jury and the jurors looked quickly at each other, suspicious and puzzled.

"Johnny asked, 'Is the defense being accused of murder, or of rape? The prosecution has tried to smear the defendant's honor and the honor of Mrs. Little with sly and evil insinuations. But I am defending him against the accusation of murder.'

"Johnny was trying to get to a climax. His right hand grabbed as though to conjure some word. 'For more than a century these words of the Constitution have been the law of our land, but words are powerless unless they are enforced by law, and after this long century our courts are stately halls of prejudice and legalized persecution as far as the Negro is concerned. The words have been spoken. The ideas have been shaped. And how long will be the lag between the words and the idea and justice?'

"Johnny sat down," the Judge added bitterly, "and I unscrooched my behind."

"You what?" Jester asked.

"My behind, which had been scrooched up ever since that mistake about 'thivil' instead of civil. I relaxed when Johnny's speech was finished."

"I think it was a brilliant defense," Jester said.

"It didn't work. I retired to my chambers to await the verdict. They were out just twenty minutes. Just time enough to troop down to the courthouse basement and to check their decisions. I knew what the verdict would be."

"How could you know?"

"When rape is even rumored under such circumstances, the verdict is always guilty. And when Mrs. Little was so quick to speak up for her husband's killer, it just looked downright strange. Meanwhile, I was as innocent as a newborn babe, and so was my son. But the jury smelled a rat and returned a guilty verdict."

"But wasn't it a frame-up?" Jester said angrily.

"No. The jury had to decide who was telling the truth, and in this case they decided right, although little did I reck at the time. When the verdict was announced there was a great wail from Jones's mother in the courtroom, Johnny turned ghost pale, and Mrs. Little swayed in her chair. Only Sherman Jones seemed to take it like a man."

"Sherman?" Jester paled and flushed in quick succession. "Was the Negro named Sherman?" Jester asked in a vacant voice.

"Yes, Sherman Jones."

Jester looked puzzled and his next question was widely angled, tentative. "Sherman is not a common name."

"After Sherman marched through Georgia many a colored boy was named for him. Personally I have known half a dozen in my lifetime."

Jester was thinking about the only Sherman he knew, but he kept silent. He only said, "I don't see it."

"Neither did I at the time. Eyes had I and did not see. Ears had I and did not hear. If I had just used my God-born sense in that courtroom, or if my son had confided in me."

"Confided what?"

"That he was in love with that woman, or thought he was."

Jester's eyes were suddenly still with shock. "But he couldn't be! He was married to my mother!"

"Like blood twin brothers we are, Son, instead of grand-father and grandson. Like two peas in a pod. Same innocence, same sense of honor."

"I don't believe it."

"I didn't either when he told me so."

Jester had often heard about his mother so that his curiosity about her had been satisfied. She had been, as he knew, fond of ice cream, especially baked Alaskas, she played the piano and was a music major at Hollins College. These scraps of information had been told him readily, casually, when he was a child, and his mother had not elicited the awe and mystery the boy felt for his father.

"What was Mrs. Little like?" Jester asked finally.

"A hussy. She was very pale, very pregnant, very proud."

"Pregnant?" Jester asked, repelled.

"Very. When she walked through the streets it was as though she expected the crowds to part for her and her baby like the Red Sea parted for the Israelites."

"Then how could my father have fallen in love with her?"

"Falling in love is the easiest thing in the world. It's stand-ing in love that matters. This was not real love. It was love like you are in love with a cause. Besides, your father never acted on it. Call it infatuation. My son was a Puritan and Puritans have more illusions than people who act out every love at first sight, every impulse."

"How terrible for my father to be in love with another woman and be married to my mother, too." Jester was thrilled with the drama of the situation and felt no loyalty to his baked-Alaska mother. "Did my mother know?"

"Of course not. My son only told me the week before he killed himself, he was so upset, so shocked. Otherwise, he would never have told me."

"Shocked about what?"

"To make an end to the story, after the verdict and execution, Mrs. Little called for Johnny. She had had her baby and she was dying."

Jester's ears had turned very red. "Did she say she loved my father? Passionately, I mean?"

"She hated him and told him so. She cursed him for being a fumbling lawyer, for airing his own ideas of justice at the expense of his client. She cursed and accused Johnny, maintaining that if he had conducted the case as a cut-and-dried matter of self-defense Sherman Jones would be a free man now. A dying woman, ranting, wailing, grieving, cursing. She said that Sherman Jones was the cleanest, most decent man she had ever known and that she loved him. She showed Johnny the newborn baby, dark-skinned and with her own blue eyes. When Johnny came home he looked like that man who went over Niagara Falls in a barrel.

"I just let Johnny talk away, then I said, 'Son, I hope you have learned a lesson. That woman couldn't possibly have loved Sherman Jones. He is black and she is white.'"

"Grandfather, you talk like loving a Negro is like loving a giraffe or something."

"Of course it wasn't love. It was lust. Lust is fascinated by the strange, the alien, the perverse and dangerous. That's what I told Johnny. Then I asked him why he took it so to heart. Johnny said: 'Because, I love Mrs. Little, or would you have me call it lust?'

" 'Either lust or lunacy, Son,' I said."

"What happened to the baby?" Jester asked.

"Evidently, Rice Little took the baby after Mrs. Little died and left it on a pew of the Holy Ascension Church in Milan. It must have been Rice Little, he's the only one I can figure out."

"Is it our Sherman?"

"Yes, but don't tell him of any of this," the Judge warned.

"Did my father kill himself the day Mrs. Little showed him the baby and cursed him and accused him?"

"He waited until Christmas afternoon, a week later, after I thought I had knocked some sense into his head and it was all over and done with. That Christmas started like any other Christmas, opening presents in the morning, and piled up Christmas wrapping under the Christmas tree. His mother had given him a pearl stickpin and I had given him a box of cigars and a shockproof, waterproof watch. I remember Johnny banged the watch and put it in a cup of water to test it. Over and over I have reproached myself that I didn't notice anything in particular that day, since we were like blood twin brothers I should have felt the mood of his despair. Was it normal to horse around with the shockproof, waterproof watch like that? Tell me, Jester."

"I don't know, but don't cry, Grandfather."

For the Judge, who had not cried in all these years, was weeping for his son at last. The journey into the past which he had shared with his grandson had mysteriously unlocked his stubborn heart so that he sobbed aloud. A voluptuary in all things, he now sobbed with abandon and found it sweet.

"Don't Grandfather," Jester said. "Don't Grandy."

After the hours of remembrance, the Judge was living in the here and now again. "He's dead," he said. "My darling is dead but I'm alive. And life is so full of a number of things.

Of ships and cabbages and kings. That's not quite right. Of
ships and, and —"

"Sealing wax," Jester prompted.

"That's right. Life is so full of a number of things, of ships
and sealing wax and cabbages and kings. This reminds me,
Son, I've got to get a new magnifying glass. The print of the
Milan Courier gets wavier every day. And last month a straight
was staring me straight in the face and I missed it — mistak-
ing a seven for a nine. I was so vexed with myself I could have
burst out bawling in the back room of the New York Café.

"And furthermore, I'm going to get a hearing aid although
I've always maintained that they were oldladyish and did not
work. Besides, one of these years I am going to get second
senses. Improved eyesight, hearing, a vast improvement of
all the senses." How this would come about the old Judge
did not explain, but living in the here and now and dreaming
of a more vivid future, the Judge was content. After the emotions of the evening he slept peacefully all through the winter
night, and did not wake up until six the next morning.

11

Who am I? What am I? Where am I going? Those questions, the ghosts that haunt the adolescent heart, were finally answered for Jester. The uneasy dreams about Grown Boy which had left him guilty and confused, no longer bothered him. And gone were the dreams of saving Sherman from a mob and losing his own life while Sherman looked on, broken with grief. Gone also were the dreams of saving Marilyn Monroe from an avalanche in Switzerland and riding through a hero's ticker tape parade in New York. That had been an interesting daydream, but after all, saving Marilyn Monroe was no career. He had saved so many people and died so many hero's deaths. His dreams were nearly always in foreign countries. Never in Milan, never in Georgia, but always in Switzerland or Bali or someplace. But now his dreams had strangely shifted. Both night dreams and daydreams. Night after night he dreamed of his father. And having found his father he was able to find himself. He was his father's son and he was going to be a lawyer. Once the bewilderment of too many choices was cleared away, Jester felt happy and free.

He was glad when the new term of school opened. Wearing brand new clothes he had got for Christmas (brand new shoes, brand new white shirt, brand new flannel pants), he was free, surehearted now that the "Who am I? What am I? Where am I going?" was answered at last. He would study harder this term, especially English and history — reading the Constitution and memorizing the great speeches whether they were required in the course or not.

Now that the deliberate mystery of his father had been dispelled, his grandfather occasionally spoke of him; not often, not weeping, but just as though Jester had been initiated like a Mason or Elk or something. So Jester was able to tell his grandfather about his plans, to tell him that he was going to study law.

"The Lord knows I never encouraged it. But if that's what you want to do, Son, I will support you to the best of my ability." Secretly the Judge was overjoyed. He could not help showing it. "So you want to emulate your grandfather?"

Jester said, "I want to be like my father."

"Your father, your grandfather . . . we were like blood twin brothers. You are just another Clane off the old block."

"Oh, I'm so relieved," said Jester. "I had thought about so many things that I could do in life. Play the piano, fly a plane. But none of them exactly fitted. I was like a cat always climbing the wrong tree."

In the beginning of the New Year the even tenor of the Judge's life was abruptly shattered. One morning when Verily came to work she put her hat on the back porch hatrack and did not go into the front of the house to start the day's house cleaning as usual. She just stood in the kitchen, dark, stubborn, implacable.

"Judge," she said, "I want them papers."

"What papers?"

"The govment papers."

To his outraged amazement and the ruin of his first cigar, Verily began to describe social security. "I pays part of my salary to the govment and you supposed to pay a part."

"Who's been talking all that stuff to you?" The old Judge thought probably this was another Reconstruction, but he was too scared to let on.

"Folks was talking."

"Now, Verily, be reasonable. Why do you want to pay your money to the government?"

"Because it's the law and the govment is catching folks. Folks I knows. It's about this here income tax."

"Merciful God, you don't want to pay income tax!"

"I does."

The Judge prided himself on understanding the reasons of Nigras and said with soothing firmness, "You have got this all mixed up. Forget it." He added helplessly, "Why, Verily, you have been with us close on to fifteen years."

"I wants to stay in the law."

"And a damn interfering law it is."

The truth of what Verily wanted finally came out. "I wants my old age pension when the time comes for it."

"What do you need your old age pension for? I'll take care of you when you are too old to work."

"Judge, you're far beyond your three score years and ten."

That reference to his mortality angered the Judge. Indeed the whole situation made him fit to be tied. Moreover, he was puzzled. He had always felt he understood Nigras so well. He had never realized that every Sunday morning when at dinner time he had said, "Ah, Verily, Verily, I say unto you, you will live in the Kingdom of Heaven . . ." he had not noticed how, Sunday after Sunday, that had irritated Verily. Nor had he noticed how much affected she had been since the death of Grown Boy. He thought he understood Nigras, but he was no noticer.

Verily would not be side-tracked. "There's a lady will figure out them govment papers, pay me forty dollars a week, and give me Saturday and Sunday free."

The Judge's heart was beating fast and his face changed color. "Well, go to her!"

"I can find somebody to work for you, Judge. Ellie Carpenter will take my place."

"Ellie Carpenter! You know good and well she doesn't have the sense of a brass monkey!"

"Well, how about that worthless Sherman Pew?"

"Sherman is no servant."

"Well, what do you think he is?"

"No trained servant."

"There is a lady will figure out the govment papers, pay me forty dollars a week, and give me Saturday and Sunday free."

The Judge grew angrier. In the old days a servant was paid three dollars a week and felt herself well paid. But each year, year after year, the price of servants had gone up so that the Judge was now paying Verily thirty dollars a week, and he had heard that well-trained servants were getting thirty-five and even forty. And even then they were scarce as hen's teeth these days. He had always been a servant-spoiler; indeed, he had always believed in humanity — did he have to believe in such high wages too? But, wanting peace and comfort, the old Judge tried to back down. "I will pay the social security for you myself."

"I don't trust you," Verily said. He realized for the first time that Verily was a fierce woman. Her voice was no longer humble, but fierce. "This woman will figure out my govment papers, pay me forty dollars a week . . ."

"Well, go to her!"

"Right now?"

Although the Judge had seldom raised his voice to a servant, he shouted, "Now, God dammit! I'll be glad to be rid of you!"

Although Verily had a temper, she would not let herself speak. Her purplish, wrinkled lips just grimaced with anger. She went to the back porch and carefully put on her hat with the pink roses. She did not even glance around the kitchen where she had worked for nearly fifteen years, nor did she tell the Judge goodby as she stomped away through the back door.

The house was absolutely silent and the Judge was afraid. He was afraid that if he was left alone there in his own house he would have a stroke. Jester would not be back from school until afternoon and he could not be left alone. He remembered that as a little boy Jester would scream in the darkness, "Somebody! Anybody!" The Judge felt like screaming that now. Until the house became silent, the Judge never knew how necessary the voice of the house was to him. So he went to the courthouse square to pick up a servant, but times had changed. No longer could one pick up a Nigra in the courthouse square. He asked three Nigras but they were all employed, and they looked at the Judge as though he was out of his mind. So he went to the barbershop. He had a haircut, a shampoo, a shave and, to kill time, a manicure. Then when everything had been done for him at the barbershop, he went to the Green Room at the Taylor Hotel to kill some more time. He took two hours over his lunch at the Cricket Tea Room and then he went around to see J. T. Malone at the pharmacy.

Rootless and dismal, the Judge passed three days in this way. Because he was afraid to be alone at home, the Judge was always on the streets of Milan or in the Green Room at the Taylor Hotel, at the barbershop, or sitting on one of the white benches of the courthouse square. At suppertime, he fried steaks for himself and Jester, and Jester washed the dishes.

As servants had always been available to him as a part of his way of life, it never occurred to him to go to an agency. The house got dirty. How long this sad state of affairs would have lasted is hard to say. One day he went to the pharmacy and asked J. T. Malone if Mrs. Malone could help him out in finding a servant. J.T. promised to talk with Mrs. Malone.

The January days were glossy blue and gold and there was a warm spell. In fact, it was a false spring. J. T. Malone, revived by the new turn of the weather, thought he was better and planned a journey. Alone and secretly he was going to Johns Hopkins. On that first fatal visit Dr. Hayden had given him a year or fifteen months to live, and already ten months had passed. He felt so much better that he wondered if the Milan GP's hadn't been mistaken. He told his wife that he was going to Atlanta to attend a pharmaceutical convention, and the secrecy and deceit pleased him so that he was almost gay when he set out on his northward journey. With a feeling of guilt and recklessness he traveled pullman, killed time in the club car, ordered two whiskeys before lunch and the seafood platter, although liver was the special on the menu.

The next morning it was raining in Baltimore and Malone was cold and damp as he stood in the waiting room explaining to the receptionist what he wanted. "I want the best diagnostician in this hospital because the GP's in my hometown are so far behind the times I don't trust them."

There followed the now familiar examinations, the wait for slides and tests, and finally the too-familiar verdict. Sick with rage, Malone took the day coach back to Milan.

The next day he went to Herman Klein and put his watch down on the counter. "This watch loses about two minutes every week," he said pettishly to the jeweler. "I demand that my watch keep strict railroad time." For in his limbo of waiting for death, Malone was obsessed with time. He was always deviling the jeweler, complaining that his watch was two minutes too slow or three minutes too fast.

"I overhauled this watch just two weeks ago. And where are you going that you have to be on strict railroad time?"

Rage made Malone clench his fists until the knuckles whitened and swear like a child. "What the hell business is it of yours where I'm going! What the fuckin hell!"

The jeweler looked at him, abashed by the senseless anger.

"If you can't give me proper service I'll take my trade elsewhere!" Taking his watch, Malone left the shop, leaving Herman Klein to stare after him with puzzled surprise. They had been mutually loyal customers for close on to twenty years.

Malone was going through a time when he was often subject to these fits of sudden rage. He could not think directly of his own death because it was unreal to him. But these rages, unprovoked and surprising even to himself, stormed frequently in his once calm heart. Once he was picking out pecans with Martha to decorate some cake or other when he hurled the nutcracker to the floor and jabbed himself viciously with the nut picker. On tripping over a ball that Tommy had left on the stairs, he threw it with such force that it broke a pane of the front door. These rages did not relieve him. When they were over, Malone was left with the feeling that something awful and incomprehensible was going to happen that he was powerless to prevent.

Mrs. Malone found the Judge a servant, so he was rescued from the streets. She was nearly full Indian and very silent. But the Judge was no longer afraid to be alone in the house. He no longer wanted to call, "Somebody! Anybody!" for the presence of another human being consoled him so that the house with the stained glass window, the pier table with the mirror, the familiar library and dining room and parlor was no longer silent. The cook was named Lee, and the meals were sloven, badly cooked and badly served. When she served soup at the beginning of dinner, her thumbs were stuck a half inch into the sloshing soup. But she had never heard of social security and could neither read nor write, which gave the Judge some subtle satisfaction. Why, he did not question.

Sherman did not altogether make good his threat of leaving the Judge, but the relation had much deteriorated. He came every day and gave him his injections. Then, sullen and looking put upon, he would idle in the library, sharpening pencils, reading immortal poetry to the Judge, fixing their noon toddies and so forth. He would not write any letters about the Confederate money. Although the Judge knew he was deliberately acting ugly and he was not getting a lick of work out of him, except for the injections, the Judge let him stay on, hoping things might change for the better. He would not even allow the old Judge the pleasure of bragging about his grandson and his decision to go into law. When he would mention the subject, Sherman would hum rudely or yawn like an alligator. The Judge often repeated, "The devil has work for idle hands." When the Judge said that, he looked directly at Sherman, but Sherman only looked directly back at him.

One day the Judge said, "I want you to go to my office in the courthouse and look in the steel filing case under 'Clippings.' I want to read my clippings from the newspapers. Little as you know it, I am a great man."

"The steel filing case under 'C' for 'Clippings,'" Sherman repeated, for he was delighted with the errand. He had never been in the Judge's office and he had yearned to.

"Don't monkey around with my important papers. Just take the newspaper clippings."

"I don't monkey around," Sherman said.

"Give me a toddy before you go. It's twelve o'clock."

Sherman did not share the noon toddy, but went straight to the courthouse. On the door of the office there was printed on the frosted glass a sign saying: CLANE & SON, ATTORNEYS-AT-LAW. With a little thrill of pleasure, Sherman unlocked the door and went into the sunny room.

After taking out the file marked "Clippings," he took his time to meddle with other papers in the steel cabinet. He was not looking for anything in particular, just a born meddler, and he was mad that the Judge had said "Don't monkey around." But at one o'clock that afternoon, while the Judge was eating his dinner, Sherman found the folder which held the papers from Johnny's brief. He saw the name Sherman. Sherman? Sherman? Except for this Sherman, I am the only one I know of who has that name. How many Shermans are there in town? As he read the papers, his head swayed. At one o'clock that afternoon he found out that there was a man of his own race whom the Judge had had executed, and his name was Sherman. And there was a white woman who was accused of fucking the Negro. He could not believe it. Could he ever be sure? But a white woman, blue eyes, was all so

otherwise than he had dreamed. It was like some eerie, agon-
izing crossword puzzle. And he, Sherman . . . Who am I?
What am I? All that he knew at that hour was that he was
sick. His ears were waterfalls of disgrace and shame. No,
Marian Anderson had not been his mother, nor Lena Horne,
nor Bessie Smith, nor any of the honeyed ladies of his childhood. He had been tricked. He had been cheated. He wanted
to die like the Negro man had died. But he would never
fool around with a white person, that was for sure. Like
Othello, that cuckoo Moor! Slowly he replaced the folder,
and when he returned to the Judge's house he walked like
a sick man.

The Judge had just waked from his nap; it was afternoon
when Sherman came back. Not being a noticer, the Judge did
not notice Sherman's shaken face and trembling hands. He
asked Sherman to read the files aloud and Sherman was too
broken not to obey.

The Judge would repeat phrases Sherman read, such as:
*A fixed star in the galaxy of Southern statesmanship. A man
of vision, duty and honor. A glory to this fair state and to the
South.*

"See?" the old Judge said to Sherman.

Sherman, still shaken, said in a quavering voice, "You have
a slice of ham like a hog!"

The Judge, still wrapped up in his own greatness, thought
it was some compliment and said, "What's that, boy?" For
although the Judge had bought a hearing aid and a new
magnifying glass, his sight and hearing were failing rapidly
and he had not got second sight and the improvement of
all his senses.

Sherman did not answer, because having a slice of ham
like a hog was one thing, but it was not insult enough for his
life and the fucking blue eyes and who they came from. He

was going to *do something, do something, do something.*
But when he wanted to slam down the sheaf of papers he
was so weak that he just put them limply on the table.

When Sherman had gone, the Judge was left alone. Putting
his magnifying glass close to the clipping, he read out loud
to himself, still wrapped up in his greatness.

12

THE GREEN-GOLD of the early spring had darkened to the dense, bluish foliage of early May and the heat of summer began to settle over the town again. With the heat came violence and Milan got into the newspapers: *The Flowering Branch Ledger, The Atlanta Journal, The Atlanta Constitution,* and even *Time* Magazine. A Negro family moved into a house in a white neighborhood and they were bombed. No one was killed, but three children were hurt and vicious feeling mounted in the town.

At the time of the bombing, Sherman was in trouble. He wanted to *do something, do something, do something,* but he did not know what he could do. The bombing went into his black book. And slowly he started to go out of line. First he drank water at the white fountain in the courthouse square.

No one seemed to notice. He went to the white men's room at the bus station. But he went so hurriedly and furtively that again no one noticed. He sat on a back pew at the Baptist Church. Again, no one noticed except at the end of the service, and an usher directed him to a colored church. He sat down in Whelan's drugstore. A clerk said, "Get away, nigger, and never come back." All these separate acts of going out of line terrified him. His hands were sweaty, his heart lurching. But terrified as he was, he was more disturbed by the fact that nobody seemed to notice him except the clerk at Whelan's. Harassed and suffering, *I've got to do something, do something, do something* beat like a drum in his head.

Finally he did something. When he gave the Judge his injections in the morning, he substituted water instead of insulin. For three days that went on and he waited. And again in that creepy way nothing seemed to happen. The Judge was as crickety as ever and did not seem sick at all. But although he hated the Judge and thought he ought to be wiped from the face of the earth, he knew all along it should have been a political murder. He could not kill him. If it were a political murder, maybe with a dagger or with a pistol he could have, but not in that sneaky way of substituting water for insulin. It was not even noticed. The fourth day he went back to insulin. Urgent, unceasing the drum beat in his head.

Meanwhile, the Judge, no noticer, was pleasant and unusually agreeable. This infuriated Sherman. It got to the point that with the Judge, as well as other white men, there was no motive for his hate, just compulsion. Wanting to go out of line and afraid, wanting to be noticed and afraid to be noticed, Sherman was obsessed those early May days. *I have got to do something, do something, do something.*

But when he did something it was so strange and zany that even he could not understand it. One glassy late afternoon while he was passing through the Judge's backyard going to the lane, Jester's dog, Tige, jumped on his shoulders and licked his face. Sherman would never know why he did what he did. But deliberately he picked up a clothesline, made a noose of it, and hanged the dog on an elm branch. The dog struggled only for a few minutes. The deaf old Judge did not hear his strangled yelps and Jester was away.

Yet, early as it was, Sherman went to sleep without supper and slept like the dead that night and only woke up when Jester pounded at the door at nine in the morning.

"Sherman!" Jester was calling in a voice that was shrill with shock. While Sherman took his time dressing, dabbling water on his face, Jester was still pounding at the door and screaming. When Sherman came out, Jester half dragged him to the Judge's yard. The dog, stiff in death, hung against the blue May sky. Jester was crying now. "Tige, Tige. How? What?" Then he turned to Sherman who stood looking at the ground. A nightmare suspicion came to Jester which was suddenly affirmed by Sherman's downward-staring face.

"Why, Sherman? Why did you do this insane thing?" He stared at Sherman in the stun of not yet realized truth. He was hoping he would know the right thing to say, the right thing to do, and hoping he would not vomit. He did not vomit, but went to the shed to get a shovel to dig the grave. But as he lowered the body, cut the noose and placed Tige in the grave, he felt he was going to faint.

"How did you know right away I done it?"

"Your face, and I just knew."

"I see you walking that white man's dog, getting all dressed up in them seersucker pants, going to the white man's school. Why don't nobody care about me? I do things, don't nobody notice. Good or mean, nobody notices. People pet that goddamned dog more than they notice me. And it's just a dog."

Jester said, "But I loved him. And Tige loved you too."

"I don't love no white man's dog and I don't love nobody."

"But the shock. I can't get over it."

Sherman thought of the May sun on the courthouse papers. "You're shocked. You ain't the only one who has been shocked."

"A thing like this makes me think you ought to be in Milledgeville."

"Milledgeville!" Sherman mocked. His limp hands waggled in an imitation of an idiot. "I'm too smart, kid, to get in Milledgeville. Nobody else would have believed what I done about the dog. Even a crazy-doctor. If you think that is something crazy, you wait and see what else I am going to do."

Arrested by the threat in his voice, Jester couldn't help but say, "What?"

"I am going to do the craziest thing I have ever done in my life before, me or any other nigger."

But Sherman would not tell Jester what he was planning to do, nor could Jester make Sherman feel guilty about Tige's death or even realize that he was acting creepy. Too upset to go to school that day, too restless to hang around the house, he told his grandfather that Tige was dead, had died in his sleep and that he had buried him, and the old Judge did not question further. Then for the first time in his life, Jester played hooky from school and went to the airport.

The old Judge waited in vain for Sherman, but Sherman was writing a letter with the "calligraphy of an angel." He was writing an Atlanta agency in order to rent a house in Milan in the white man's section. When the Judge called him, Sherman said that he was not going to come to work any longer and His Honor could get his injections somewhere else.

"You mean you're leaving me high and dry?"

"That's right. High and dry, Judge."

The Judge was left on his own again without Sherman. Reading the *Milan Courier* with the new magnifying glass, with the silent half-Indian servant who never sang and Jester away at school, the Judge was tired and idle. It was a blessing when a veterinarians' convention was held in the town. Poke Tatum attended and he and a half-dozen other delegates stayed at the Judge's house. Mule doctors, pig doctors, dog doctors, they drank up a storm and slid down the banisters. The Judge felt that sliding down the banisters was going a little bit too far, and he missed his wife's dainty church conventions when the preachers and church delegates sang hymns and minded their P's and Q's. When the veterinarians' convention was over and Poke gone, the house was lonelier than ever and the emptiness of the old Judge blanker, more dismal. He blamed Sherman for leaving him. He thought back to the times when there was not only one servant in the house, but two or three, so that the voices of the house were like mingling brown rivers.

Meanwhile, Sherman had got a reply from the agency and sent a money order for the rent. His race was not questioned. He began to move in two days later. The house was around the corner from Malone's house, next door to the three little houses that Mrs. Malone had inherited. A store was beyond the house that Sherman had rented, and after that the neighborhood was Negro. But shabby and beaten up as it was, his house was in a white section. Sammy Lank and the Lank brood lived next door. Sherman bought on time a baby grand piano and beautiful genuine antique-y furniture and had a mover move them to his new house.

He moved in the middle of May and at last he was noticed. The news spread like wildfire through the town. Sammy Lank went to Malone to complain and Malone went to the Judge.

"He's left me high and dry. I am too furious to fool with him any longer."

Sammy Lank, Bennie Weems and Max Gerhardt, the chemist, milled around the Judge's house. The Judge began to work on Malone. "I don't hold with violence any more than you do, J.T., but when a thing like this comes up I feel it is my duty to act."

Secretly the Judge was excited. In the old days the Judge had been a Ku Kluxer and he missed it when the Klan was suppressed and he could not go to those white-sheeted meetings at Pine Mountain and fill himself with a secret and invisible power.

Malone, no Ku Kluxer, was feeling unusually peaked these days. The house was not his wife's property, thank goodness, and besides, it was a sagging, waucome-sided house.

The Judge said, "It's not people like you and me, J.T., who will be affected if things like this go on. I have my house here and you have your house on a very good street. We are not affected. Nigras are not likely to be moving in on us. But I am speaking as a chief citizen of this town. I am speaking for the poor, for the unprofited. We leading citizens have to be the spokesmen for the downtrodden. Did you notice Sammy Lank when he came to the house? I thought he was going to have apoplexy. All worked up, as what he should be since his house is the house next door. How would you like to be living next door to a Nigra?"

"I wouldn't like it."

"Your property would depreciate, the property that old Mrs. Greenlove left your wife would depreciate."

Malone said, "For years I have advised my wife to sell those three houses. They have turned into nothing but a slum."

"You and I as foremost citizens of Milan . . ." Malone

was meekly proud that he was bracketed with the Judge.

"Another thing," the Judge went on, "you and I have our property and our positions and our self-respect. But what does Sammy Lank have except those slews of children of his? Sammy Lank and poor whites like that have nothing but the color of their skin. Having no property, no means, nobody to look down on — that is the clue to the whole thing. It is a sad commentary on human nature but every man has to have somebody to look down on. So the Sammy Lanks of this world only have the Nigra to look down on. You see, J.T., it is a matter of pride. You and I have our pride, the pride of our blood, the pride in our descendants. But what does Sammy Lank have except those slews of white-headed triplets and twins and a wife worn out with child-bearing sitting on the porch dipping snuff?"

It was arranged that a meeting would be held in Malone's pharmacy after hours, and that Jester should drive the Judge and Malone to the meeting. That night there was a moon serene in the May night. To Jester, to the old Judge, it was just a moon, but Malone looked at the moon with a hollow sadness. How many May nights had he seen the moon? And how many more moons like this would he ever see? Would this be the last one?

While Malone sat quiet and wondering in the car, Jester was wondering also. What was this meeting all about? He felt it had something to do with Sherman moving into the white section.

When Malone opened the side door to the compounding room, he and the Judge went inside. "You go on home, son," the Judge said to Jester. "Some of the boys will bring us back."

Jester parked the car around the corner while Malone and the Judge went into the pharmacy. Malone turned on the

fan so that the warm stale air was churned to a breeze. He
did not fully light the drugstore and the half-light gave a sense
of conspiracy.

Assuming that the arrivals would come through the side
door, he was surprised when there was a loud knock at the
front. It was Sheriff McCall, a man with dainty purplish
hands and a broken nose.

Meanwhile, Jester had come back to the drugstore. The
side door was closed but not locked and he entered very
quietly. At the same moment, a group of new arrivals were
knocking at the front and being admitted, and Jester's presence was unnoticed. Jester was very silent in the darkness of
the compounding room, afraid of being discovered and sent
away. What were they doing at this hour when the drugstore
was closed?

Malone did not know what the meeting would be like. He
had expected a group of leading citizens, but except for Hamilton Breedlove, the cashier at the Milan Bank & Trust Company, and Max Gerhardt, the chemist at the Nehi plant, there
were no leading citizens. There were old poker cronies of the
Judge, and there was Bennie Weems and Sport Lewis and
Sammy Lank. Some of the other new arrivals Malone knew
by sight, but they were nameless. A group of boys arrived
in overalls. No, they were not leading citizens, but ragtag
and bobtail for the most part. Moreover, on arrival they were
halfway liquored up and there was the atmosphere of a
carnival. A bottle was passed around and put on the counter
of the fountain. Before the beginning of the meeting, Malone was already regretting that he had lent his pharmacy to it.

It may have been Malone's frame of mind, but he recalled
something unpleasant about each of the men he met that
night. Sheriff McCall had always sucked up to the old Judge
so obviously that it had offended Malone. Besides, he had

once seen the sheriff beat a Negro girl with his billy stick on the corner of Twelfth Street and Main. He looked hard at Sport Lewis. Sport had been divorced by his wife for extreme mental cruelty. A family man, Malone wondered what extreme mental cruelty could be. Mrs. Lewis had got a Mexican divorce and later on she had married again. But what was that — extreme mental cruelty? He realized he himself was no saint, and once he had even committed adultery. But no one was hurt and Martha never knew. An extreme mental cruelty? Bennie Weems was a deadbeat and his daughter was sickly so that he was always in debt to Malone and the bills were always unpaid. And it was said that Max Gerhardt was so smart that he could figure out how long it took a toot to get to the moon. But he was German, and Malone had never trusted Germans.

Those gathered in the drugstore were all ordinary people, so ordinary that he usually didn't think of them one way or the other. But tonight he was seeing the weaknesses of these ordinary people, their little uglinesses. No, none of them were leading citizens.

The round yellow moon made Malone feel sad and chilly although the night was warm. The smell of whiskey was strong in the drugstore and this faintly nauseated him. There were more than a dozen people there when he asked the Judge: "Is everybody here that's coming?"

The Judge himself seemed a little disappointed when he said, "It's ten o'clock; I guess so."

The Judge began in his old grandiloquent speech voice. "Fellow citizens, we are gathered here together as leading citizens of our community, as property owners and defenders of our race." There was a hush in the room. "Little by little we white citizens are being inconvenienced, even gravely put upon. Servants are scarce as hen's teeth and you have to pay them an arm and a leg to keep them." The Judge listened to himself, looked at the people, and realized he was off on the wrong tack. Because by and large these were not the people who kept servants.

He started again. "Fellow citizens, are there no zoning laws in this town? Do you want coal-black niggers moving in right next door to your house? Do you want your children crowded in the back of the bus while coal-black niggers sit in the front? Do you want your wife carrying on behind the back fence with nigger bucks?" The Judge posed all the rhetorical questions. The crowd muttered among themselves and from time to time there were shouts of "No. Goddammit, no."

"Are we going to let the zoning of our town be decided by niggers? I'm asking you, are we or are we not?" Balancing himself carefully, the Judge pounded his fist on the counter. "This is the hour of decision. Who is running this town, us or the niggers?"

Whiskey was freely passed around and there was in the room a fraternity of hate.

Malone looked at the moon through the plate glass window. The sight of the moon made him feel sickish, but he had forgotten why. He wished he was picking out nuts with Martha, or at home with his feet on the banisters of the porch drinking beer.

"Who's going to bomb the bastard?" a hoarse voice called.

Malone realized that few in the crowd actually knew Sherman Pew, but that a fraternity of hate made them all act together. "Should we draw lots, Judge?" Bennie Weems, who had done this sort of thing before, asked Malone for a pencil and paper and began to tear strips of paper. Then he marked an X on one strip. "The X is the one."

Cold, confused by the bustle, Malone still looked at the moon. He spoke in a dry voice: "Can't we just talk with the

Nigra? I never liked him, even when he was your houseboy, Judge. Just a biggity, disrespectful, and a thoroughly bad Nigra. But violence or bombing I don't hold with."

"No more do I, J.T. And I am fully cognizant that we, as members of this citizens' committee, are taking the law into our own hands. But if the law doesn't protect our interests and the interests of our children and descendants, I am willing to go around the law if the cause is just and if the situation threatens the standards of our community."

"Everybody ready?" Bennie Weems asked. "The X mark is it." At that moment Malone particularly loathed Bennie Weems. He was a weasel-faced garage man and a real liquor-head.

In the compounding room, Jester sat hugging the wall so closely that his face was pressed against a bottle of medicine. They were going to draw lots to bomb Sherman's house. He would have to warn Sherman, but he didn't know how to get out of the drugstore, so he listened to the meeting.

Sheriff McCall said, "You can take my hat," as he proffered his Stetson. The Judge drew first and the others followed. When Malone took the balled-up paper his hands were trembling. He was wishing he was home where he belonged. His upper lip was pressed against the lower. Everybody unrolled his paper under the dim light. Malone watched them and he saw, one after another, the slackened face of relief. Malone, in his fear and dread, was not surprised when his unrolled paper had an X mark on it.

"I guess it is supposed to be me," he said in a deadened voice. Everybody looked at him. His voice rose. "But if it's bombing or violence, I can't do it.

"Gentlemen." Looking around the drugstore, Malone realized there were few gentlemen there. But he went on. "Gentlemen, I am too near death to sin, to murder." He was excruciatingly embarrassed, talking about death in front of this crowd of people. He went on in a stronger voice, "I don't want to endanger my soul." Everybody looked at him as though he had gone stark raving crazy.

Somebody said in a low voice, "Chicken."

"Well, be durned," Max Gerhardt said. "Why did you come to the meeting?"

Malone was afraid that in public, in front of the crowd in the drugstore, he was going to cry. "A year ago my doctor said I had less than a year or sixteen months to live, and I don't want to endanger my soul."

"What is all this talk about soul?" asked Bennie Weems in a loud voice.

Pinioned by shame, Malone repeated, "My immortal soul." His temples were throbbing and his hands unnerved and shaking.

"What the fuck is an immortal soul?" Bennie Weems said.

"I don't know," Malone said. "But if I have one, I don't want to lose it."

The Judge, seeing his friend's embarrassment, was embarrassed in turn. "Buck up, Son," he said in a low voice. Then in a loud voice he addressed the men. "J.T. here doesn't think we ought to do it. But if we do do it, I think we ought to do it all together, because *then* it's not the same thing."

Having made a fool and a spectacle of himself in public, Malone had no face to save, so he cried out, "But it is the same thing. Whether one person does it or a dozen, it's the same thing if it's murder."

Crouched in the compounding room, Jester was thinking that he never thought old Mr. Malone had it in him.

Sammy Lank spat on the floor and said again, "Chicken." Then he added, "I'll do it. Be glad to. It's right next to my house."

All eyes were turned to Sammy Lank who was suddenly a hero.

13

JESTER went immediately to Sherman's house to warn him. When he told about the meeting at the pharmacy, Sherman's face turned grayish, the pallor of dark skin in mortal fright.

Serves him right, Jester thought. Killing my dog. But as he saw Sherman trembling, suddenly the dog was forgotten and it was as though he was seeing Sherman again for the first time as he had seen him that summer evening almost a year ago. He, too, began to tremble, not with passion this time, but from fear for Sherman and from tension.

Suddenly Sherman began to laugh. Jester put his arms around the shaking shoulders. "Don't act like that, Sherman. You've got to get out of here. You've got to leave this house."

When Sherman looked around the room with the new furniture, the bought-on-time baby grand piano, bought-on-time genuine antique sofa and two chairs, he began to cry. There was a fire in the fireplace, for although the night was warm, Sherman was cold and the fire had looked cozy and homelike to him. In the firelight the tears were purple and gold on his grayish face.

Jester said again, "You've got to leave this place."

"Leave my furniture?" With one of the wild swings of mood that Jester knew so well, Sherman began to talk about the furniture. "And you haven't even seen the bedroom suit, with the pink sheets and boudoir pillows. Or my clothes." He opened the closet door. "Four brand new Hart, Schaffner & Marx suits."

Wheeling wildly to the kitchen, he said, "And the kitchen, with all modern conveniences. And all my own." In an ecstasy of ownership, Sherman seemed to have forgotten all about the fear.

Jester said, "But didn't you know this was going to happen?"

"I knew and I didn't know. But it's not going to happen! I have invited guests with RSVP invitations to a house-warming party. I bought a case of Lord Calvert's bottled in bond, six bottles of gin, six bottles of champagne. We are having caviar on crisp pieces of toast, fried chicken, Harvard beets, and greens." Sherman looked around the room. "It's not going to happen because, boy, you know how much this furniture cost? It's going to take me more than three years to pay for it and the liquor and the clothes." Sherman went to the piano and stroked it lovingly. "All my life I have wanted an elegant baby grand."

"Stop all this goofy talk about baby grands and parties. Don't you realize this is serious?"

"Serious? Why should they bomb me? Me who is not even noticed. I went to the dime store and sat down on one of those stools. That is the actual truth." (Sherman *had* gone to the dime store and sat down on one of the stools. But when the clerk approached threateningly, Sherman said, "I'm sick. Will you give me a glass of water, miss?")

"But now you've been noticed," Jester said. "Why can't you forget all this mania about black and white, and go North where people don't mind so much? I know that if I were a Negro, I'd certainly light out for the North."

"But I can't," Sherman said. "I have rented this house with my good money and moved in this beautiful furniture. For the last two days I have been arranging everything. And if I do say so myself, it's elegant."

The house was suddenly all of Sherman's world. He never thought consciously about his parentage these days, since his discovery in the Judge's office. There was just a sense of murk and desolation. He had to busy himself with furniture, with things, and there was always this ever present sense of danger and the ever present sense that he would never back down. His heart was saying, *I have done something, done something, done something.* And fear only buoyed his elation.

"You want to see my new green suit?" Sherman, wild with tension and excitement, went to the bedroom and put on his new Nile green silk suit. Jester, trying desperately to cope with the veering Sherman, watched while Sherman pranced through the room in the new green suit.

Jester could only say, "I don't care about all this furniture and suits but I do care about you. Don't you realize this is serious?"

"Serious, man?" Sherman began to pound middle C on the piano. "Me who has kept a black book all my life, and you talk about serious? Did I tell you about vibrations? I vibrate, vibrate, vibrate!"

"Stop pounding the piano like a lunatic and listen to me."

"I have made my decision. So I am going to stay right here. Right here. Bombing or no. Besides, why the fucking hell do you care?"

"I don't know why I care so much, but I do." Over and over Jester had asked himself why he cared for Sherman. When he was with him, there was a shafting feeling in the region of his belly or his heart. Not all the time, but just in spasms. Unable to explain it to himself, he said, "I guess it's just a matter of cockles."

"Cockles? What are cockles?"

"Haven't you ever heard the expression, cockles of your heart?"

"Fuck cockles. I don't know anything about cockles. All I know is, I have rented this house, paid my good money, and I am going to stay. I'm sorry."

"Well you have got to do better than be sorry. You have got to move."

"Sorry," Sherman said, "about your dog."

As Sherman spoke, the little spasm of sweetness shafted in that region of Jester's heart. "Forget the dog. The dog is dead. And I want for you to be living always."

"Nobody lives for always, but when I live I like to live it up." And Sherman began to laugh. Jester was reminded of another laughter. It was the laughter of his grandfather when he talked about his dead son. The senseless pounding on the piano, the senseless laughter, jangled his grief.

Yes, Jester tried to warn Sherman, but he would not be warned. It was up to Jester now. But who could he turn to? What could he do? He had to leave Sherman sitting there, laughing and pounding on middle C of the baby grand piano.

Sammy Lank had no idea how to make a bomb so he went to the smart Max Gerhardt who made him two. The explosive feelings of the last days, the shame, the outrage, the insult, the hurt and fearful pride had almost gone away, and when Sammy Lank stood with the bomb that soft May evening looking at Sherman through the open window, his passion had been almost spent. He stood numb of any feelings except a feeling of shallow pride that he was doing what had to be done. Sherman was playing the piano and Sammy watched him curiously, wondering how a nigger could learn how to play the piano. Then Sherman began to sing. His strong dark throat was thrown back, and it was at that throat that Sammy aimed the bomb. Since he was only a few yards away, the bomb was a direct hit. After the first bomb was thrown a feeling savage and sweet came back to Sammy Lank. He threw the second bomb and the house began to burn.

The crowd was already in the street and yard. Neighbors, customers at Mr. Peak's, even Mr. Malone himself. The fire trucks shrilled.

Sammy Lank knew he had got the nigger, but he waited until the ambulance came and he watched them cover the torn dead body.

The crowd outside the house stayed on to wait. The fire department put out the fire and the crowd moved in. They hauled the baby grand out in the yard. Why, they did not know. Soon a soft drizzling rain set in. Mr. Peak who owned the grocery store adjoining the house had a very good business that night. The news reporter on the *Milan Courier* reported the bombing for the early edition of the paper.

Since the Judge's house was in another part of town, Jester did not even hear the bombing, and only heard the news the next morning. The Judge, emotional in his old age, took the news emotionally. Uneasy and nostalgic, the softhearted, soft-brained old Judge visited the morgue at the hospital. He did not look at the body, but had it removed to an under-taking establishment where he handed over five hundred dollars in United States greenbacks for the funeral.

Jester did not weep. Carefully, mechanically he wrapped the *Tristan* score he had inscribed to Sherman and placed it in one of his father's trunks up in the attic and locked it.

Rain had fallen all night but had now stopped, and the sky was the fresh and tender blue that follows a long rain. When Jester went to the bombed house, four of the Lank brood were playing "Chopsticks" on the piano which was now ruined and out of tune. Jester stood in the sunlight hearing the dead and no-tune "Chopsticks" and hatred was mingled with his grief.

"Is your father there?" he called to one of the Lank brood.

"No he ain't," the child answered.

Jester went home. He took the pistol, the one that his father had used to shoot himself, and put it in the glove compartment of the car. Then cruising around town slowly, he first went to the mill and asked for Sammy Lank. He was not there. The nightmare feeling of out-of-tune "Chopsticks," the little Lanks, added to his feeling of frustration that he could not find Sammy Lank and made him beat the steering wheel with his fists.

He had been afraid for Sherman but he never really felt it would ever happen. Not a real happening. It was all just a nightmare. "Chopsticks" and ruined pianos and the determination to find Sammy Lank. Then when he started driving again, he saw Sammy Lank lounging before Mr. Malone's drugstore. He opened the door and beckoned. "Sammy. You want to come with me to the airport? I'll take you on an airplane ride."

Sammy, sheepish and unaware, grinned with pride. He was thinking: Already I'm such a famous man in town that

Jester Clane takes me for an airplane ride. He jumped in the car joyfully.

In the training Moth, Jester seated Sammy first, then scrambled around to the other side. He had put the pistol in his pocket. Before taking off, he asked, "Ever been in an airplane before?"

"No sir," said Sammy, "but I'm not scared."

Jester made a perfect take-off. The blue sky, the fresh windy atmosphere, quickened his numbed soul. The plane climbed.

"Was it you who killed Sherman Pew?"

Sammy only grinned and nodded.

At the sound of Sherman's name there was again the little cockles spasm.

"Do you have any life insurance?"

"Nope. Just younguns."

"How many younguns are there?"

"Fourteen," said Sammy. "Five of them grown."

Sammy, who was petrified of a plane, began to talk with nervous foolishness. "Me and my wife almost had quints. There were three younguns and two things. It was right after the quints in Canada were born and they were our first younguns. Every time me and my wife used to think of the quints in Canada — rich, famous, mother and daddy rich and famous too — a little quinch came in us. We almost hit the jackpot, and every time we did it we thought that we were making quints. But we only had triplets and twins and little ole singles. Once me and my wife took all the younguns to Canada to see the quints in their little glass playhouse. Our younguns all got the measles."

"So that's why you had so many children."

"Yep. We wanted to hit the jackpot. And me and my wife were naturals for borning twins and triplets and such. But we never hit it. However, there was an article in the *Milan Courier* about our Milan triplets. It's framed and on our living room wall. We've had a hard time raising those younguns but we never gave up. And now that my wife has changed life, it's all over. I'll never be nothing but Sammy Lank."

The grotesque pity of the story made Jester laugh that laughter of despair. And once having laughed and despaired and pitied, he knew he could not use the pistol. For in that instant the seed of compassion, forced by sorrow, had begun to blossom. Jester slipped the pistol from his pocket and dropped it out of the plane.

"What's that?" said Sammy, terrified.

"Nothing," Jester said. He looked across at Sammy who had turned green. "Do you want to go down?"

"No," said Sammy. "I ain't scared."

So Jester circled on.

Looking downward from an altitude of two thousand feet, the earth assumes order. A town, even Milan, is symmetrical, exact as a small gray honeycomb, complete. The surrounding terrain seems designed by a law more just and mathematical than the laws of property and bigotry: a dark parallelogram of pine woods, square fields, rectangles of sward. On this cloudless day the sky on all sides and above the plane is a blind monotone of blue, impenetrable to the eye and the imagination. But down below the earth is round. The earth is finite. From this height you do not see man and the details of his humiliation. The earth from a great distance is perfect and whole.

But this is an order foreign to the heart, and to love the earth you must come closer. Gliding downward, low over the town and countryside, the whole breaks up into a multiplicity of impressions. The town is much the same in all its seasons, but the land changes. In early spring the fields here are like patches of worn gray corduroy, each one alike. Now you could begin to tell the crops apart: the gray-green of cotton, the dense and spidery tobacco land, the burning green of corn. As you circle inward, the town itself becomes crazy and complex. You see the secret corners of all the sad back yards. Gray fences, factories, the flat main street. From the air men are shrunken and they have an automatic look, like wound-up dolls. They seem to move mechanically among haphazard miseries. You do not see their eyes. And finally this is intolerable. The whole earth from a great distance means less than one long look into a pair of human eyes. Even the eyes of the enemy.

Jester looked into Sammy's eyes which were popped with terror.

His odyssey of passion, friendship, love, and revenge was now finished. Gently Jester landed the airplane and let Sammy Lank out — to brag to his family that he is such a well-known man now that even Jester Clane had taken him up on an airplane ride.

14

AT FIRST Malone cared. When he saw that Bennie Weems had taken his trade to Whelan's and that Sheriff McCall did not drink his customary cokes at the pharmacy, he cared. In the front of his mind he said, "To hell with Bennie Weems; to hell with the sheriff." But deep down he worried. Had that night at the drugstore jeopardized the good will of the pharmacy and a sale for the good will? Was it worth taking the stand he did at the meeting? Malone wondered and worried and still he did not know. Worry affected his health. He made mistakes — mistakes in bookkeeping that were unusual with a good figuring bookkeeper like Malone. He sent out inaccurate bills which customers complained about. He did not have the strength to push sales properly. He himself knew that he was failing. He wanted the shelter of his home, and often he would stay whole days in the double bed.

Malone, dying, was sensitive to sunrise. After the long, black night, he watched the false dawn and the first ivory and gold and orange of the eastern sky. If it were a fair and blossomy day, he sat up on the pillows and eagerly awaited breakfast. But if the day was gloomy with sour skies or rain, his own spirits were reflected in the weather so that he turned on the light and complained fretfully.

Martha tried to comfort him. "It's just this first hot spell. When you get accustomed to the weather you will feel better."

But no, it was not the weather. He no longer confused the end of life with the beginning of a new season. The wisteria trellis like lavender waterfalls had come and gone. He did not have the strength to plant the vegetable garden. And the gold-green willows were turning darker now. Curious, he had always thought of willows in connection with water. But his willows had no water, although there was a spring across the street. Yes, the earth had revolved its seasons and spring had come again. But there was no longer a revulsion against nature, against things. A strange lightness had come upon his soul and he exalted. He looked at nature now and it was part of himself. He was no longer a man watching a clock without hands. He was not alone, he did not rebel, he did not suffer. He did not even think of death these days. He was not a man dying . . . nobody died, everybody died.

Martha would sit in the room knitting. She had taken up knitting and it soothed him to see her there. He no longer thought about the zones of loneliness that had so bewildered him. His life was strangely contracted. There was the bed, the window, a glass of water. Martha brought him meals on a tray and nearly always she had a vase of flowers on the bed table — roses, periwinkle, snapdragons.

The love for his wife that had so receded returned to him.

As Martha thought of little dainty things to tempt his appetite or knitted in the sickroom, Malone felt a nearer value of her love. It touched him when she bought from Goody's Department Store a pink bedrest so he could sit propped up in bed without being supported by only the damp sliding pillows.

Since that meeting at the pharmacy, the old Judge treated Malone as an invalid. Their roles were now reversed; it was the Judge now who brought sacks of water-ground meal and turnip greens and fruit as one brings to a sick man.

On May fifteenth the doctor came twice, once in the morning and again in the afternoon. The current doctor was now Dr. Wesley. On May fifteenth, Dr. Wesley spoke with Martha alone in the living room. Malone did not care that they were talking about him in another room. He did not worry, he did not wonder. That night when Martha gave him his sponge bath, she bathed his feverished face and put cologne behind both his ears and poured more cologne in the basin. Then she washed his hairy chest and armpits in the scented water, and his legs and callused feet. And finally, very gently, she washed his limp genitals.

Malone said, "Darling, no man has ever had such a wife as you." It was the first time he had called her darling since the year after they were married.

Mrs. Malone went into the kitchen. When she came back, after having cried a little, she brought with her a hot water bottle. "The nights and early dawns are chilly." When she put the hot water bottle in the bed, she asked, "Comfy, Hon?"

Malone scrounged down from his bedrest and touched his feet to the hot water bottle. "Darling," he said again, "may I have some ice water?" But when Martha brought the ice water the cubes of ice bumped against his nose so he said, "This ice tickles my nose. I just wanted plain cold water."

And having taken the ice from the water, Mrs. Malone withdrew into the kitchen to cry again.

He did not suffer. But it seemed to him that his bones felt heavy and he complained.

"Hon, how can your bones feel heavy?" Martha said.

He said he was hungry for watermelon, and Martha bought shipped watermelon from Pizzalatti's, the leading fruit and candy store in town. But when the slice of melon, pink with silvery frost, was on his plate, it did not taste like he thought it would.

"You have to eat to keep up your strength, J.T."

"What do I need strength for?" he said.

Martha made milkshakes and surreptitiously she put an egg in them. Two eggs in fact. It comforted her to see him drink it.

Ellen and Tommy came back and forth in the sickroom and their voices seemed loud to him, though they tried to talk softly.

"Don't bother your father," Martha said. "He is feeling pretty peaked now."

On the sixteenth Malone felt better and even suggested that he shave himself and take a proper bath. So he insisted on going to the bathroom, but when he reached the washbasin he only grasped the basin with his hands and Martha had to lead him back to the bed.

Yet the last flush of life was with him. His spirit was strangely raw that day. In the *Milan Courier* he read that a man had saved a child from burning and had lost his own life. Although Malone did not know the child or the man, he began to cry, and kept on crying. Raw to anything he read, raw to the skies, raw to the world outside the window — it was a cloudless, fair day — he was possessed by a strange euphoria. If his bones weren't so heavy, he felt he could get up and go down to the pharmacy.

On the seventeenth he did not see the May sunrise for he was asleep. Slowly the flush of life he had felt the last day was leaving him. Voices seemed to come from far away. He could not eat his dinner, so Martha made a milkshake in the kitchen. She put in four eggs, and he complained of the taste. The thoughts of the past and this day were commingled.

After he refused to eat his chicken supper, there was an unexpected visitor. Judge Clane suddenly burst into the sickroom. Veins of anger pulsed in his temples. "I came to get some Miltown, J.T. Have you heard the news on the radio?" Then he looked at Malone and was shocked by his sudden feebling. Sorrow battled with the old Judge's fury. "Excuse me, dear J.T.," he said in a voice that was suddenly humble. Then his voice rose: "But have you heard?"

"Well, what is it, Judge? Heard what?" Martha asked.

Sputtering, incoherent with anger, the Judge told about the Supreme Court decision for school integration. Martha, flabbergasted and taken aback, could only say "Well! I vow!" as she had not quite taken it in.

"There are ways we can get around it," cried the Judge. "It will never happen. We will fight. All Southerners will fight to the last ditch. To the death. Writing it in laws is one thing but enforcing it is another. A car is waiting for me; I am going down to the radio station to make an address. I will rally the people. I want something terse and simple to say. Dramatic. Dignified and mad, if you know what I mean. Something like: 'Four score and seven years ago . . .' I'll make it up on the way to the station. Don't forget to hear it. It will be a historic speech and will do you good, dear J.T."

At first Malone hardly knew the old Judge was there. There was just his voice, his huge sweaty presence. Then the words, the sounds, ricocheted in his un-understanding ears: integration . . . Supreme Court. Concepts and thought washed in his mind, but feebly. Finally Malone's love and friendship for the old Judge called him back from his dying. He looked at the radio and Martha turned it on, but since a dance band was playing, she turned it down very low. A newscast that announced again the Supreme Court decision preceded the speech by the Judge.

In the soundproof room of the radio station, the Judge had latched onto the microphone like a professional. But although he had tried to make up a speech on the way to the station, he had not been able to. The ideas were so chaotic, so inconceivable, he could not formulate his protests. They were too passionate. So, angry, defiant — expecting at any moment a little seizure, or worse — the Judge stood with the microphone in his hand and no speech ready. Words — vile words, cuss words unsuitable for the radio — raged in his mind. But no historic speech. The only thing that came to him was the first speech he had memorized in law school. Knowing dimly somehow that what he was going to say was wrong, he plunged in.

"Fourscore and seven years ago," he said, "our fathers brought forth on this continent a new nation, conceived in liberty, and dedicated to the proposition that all men are created equal. Now we are engaged in a great civil war, testing whether that nation, or any nation so conceived and so dedicated can long endure."

There was the sound of scuffling in the room and the Judge said in an outraged voice: "Why are you poking me!" But once you get on the track of a monumental speech, it's hard to get off. He went on, louder:

"We are met on a great battlefield of that war. We have come to dedicate a portion of that field as a final resting place for those who here gave their lives that that nation might live. It is altogether fitting and proper that we should do this."

"I said, quit poking me," the Judge shouted again.

"But, in a larger sense, we cannot dedicate — we cannot consecrate — we cannot hallow this ground. The brave men living and dead who struggled here have consecrated it far above our poor power to add or detract. The world will little note nor long remember what we say here . . ."

"For chrissakes!" somebody shouted, "cut it!"

The old Judge stood at the microphone with the echo of his own words ringing in his ears and the memory of the sound of his own gavel rapping in his courtroom. The shock of recognition made him crumble, yet immediately he shouted: "It's just the other way around! I mean it just the other way around! Don't cut me off!" pleaded the Judge in an urgent voice. "Please don't cut me off."

But another speaker began and Martha switched off the radio. "I don't know what he was talking about," she said. "What happened?"

"Nothing, darling," Malone said. "Nothing that was not a long time in the making."

But his livingness was leaving him, and in dying, living assumed order and a simplicity that Malone had never known before. The pulse, the vigor was not there and not wanted. The design alone emerged. What did it matter to him if the Supreme Court was integrating schools? Nothing mattered to him. If Martha had spread out all the Coca-Cola stocks on the foot of the bed and counted them, he wouldn't have lifted his head. But he did want something, for he said: "I want some ice-cold water, without any ice."

But before Martha could return with the water, slowly, gently, without struggle or fear, life was removed from J. T. Malone. His livingness was gone. And to Mrs. Malone who stood with the full glass in her hand, it sounded like a sigh.

Basket Case

The Frenetic Life of
Michigan Coach Bill Frieder

Bill Frieder with Jeff Mortimer

Bonus Books, Chicago

92   91   90   89   88   5   4   3   2   1

Library of Congress Catalog Card Number: 88-71563

International Standard Book Number: 0-933893-67-1

Bonus Books, Inc.
160 East Illinois Street
Chicago, Illinois 60611

Printed in the United States of America

To my mom, my brother Larry, Laura,
and Don Canham, who hired me.
        — B.F.

———————————————

To my mother, and to L.K., Theo,
and Adriana.
        —J.M.

Contents

1 •

Growing Up

I wasn't supposed to be a basketball coach.

And for me to be the basketball coach at the University of Michigan, compared to the type of person who normally is a basketball coach at a major institution, is just unheard of.

In the first place, coaches are supposed to have been great, or at least very good, players. Or at least starters. I started once in a while for Saginaw High School in the 1958–60 seasons, but mostly I was the sixth man. And I didn't play at all in college, not even intramurals. I was too busy getting my degrees, a bachelor's and a master's in business administration, and a teaching certificate, too.

The summer before my senior year in college, I took 19 hours at three different places—the University of Michigan campuses at Ann Arbor and Flint and Delta College in Bay City—so I could graduate through business administration and have a teaching certificate. Ridiculous.

I got my teaching certificate so I could coach, but I better backtrack here a bit. I was so busy taking all those courses and studying that I wouldn't have had time to play basketball even if I had been good enough, and I certainly wasn't recruited, I can tell you that.

I was supposed to be a businessman, like my dad. That's the way it was always told to me—you've got to go to college, you've got to get into business so you don't have to work so hard in the fruit market. So it was going to be management or marketing or finance or something in the business field. My dad owned a produce business, the Florida Fruit Market. It had been his father's business before him. He worked hard. He didn't want me to work that hard. The funny thing is, I do. I'm just like him. But I'm working at being a coach instead of selling watermelons.

Being a businessman. That's the environment I was raised in. That was what I went to college for. That was all I heard when I was growing up.

Then Cazzie Russell came along. When Cazzie was a freshman and Bill Buntin was a sophomore, this would be in the 1962–63 season, I didn't go to a Big Ten game until well after the season started. I mean, I was so engrossed in studying and doing well in school that I didn't follow basketball until the tail end of what was my first year at Michigan. I was always busy studying.

Then my roommate, Bill Beck, a friend of mine from Saginaw, got me to go to a game. It was when Michigan upset Creighton when they had Paul Silas. Buntin had a great game, and I became a Michigan basketball fan.

I think I'm just an ordinary guy who works hard. There's no question I have a lot of motivation to succeed. I have a lot of pride, a lot of determination and enthusiasm for what I do.

I can remember in second grade being the only kid in the class who could make baskets when we went out to recess, but by then I was already working for my dad at the market. And when I worked in the fruit market, I was the same type of guy I am now. Everything was organized, and if the people were gonna start coming at eight in the morning, I was there at five to get everything on display.

When I was a kid, the fruit market was wholesale and retail both. We'd go to the Saginaw city market. We'd buy from farmers at the markets in Grand Rapids, Benton Harbor, Bay City, and the Eastern Market in Detroit. We'd buy from up north and from California. We'd go to stockyards throughout the state and in Ohio, where farmers would bring their cattle to auction them off and then buy fruits and vegetables on the grounds. And the community people would come to get their stuff, too. Later on, it was just wholesale, primarily servicing restaurants, small stores and factories. The retail business became much tougher because people were canning fewer peaches, going to the supermarkets more and things like that.

I was very much involved from the age of 13 or 14 until I went to college. I learned you just had to go out and dig and work hard if you were going to make it. You had to outhustle the other guy. If it's Saturday noon and there's no more customers and you're sitting with 200 bushels of peaches, you gotta sell 'em somehow. I learned buying and selling.

(Says boyhood pal Tom Billy: "He was a legend for his sales abilities. He was known throughout the farmers' market. His dad had a booth and Bill was down there selling when he was six, seven years old. People were amazed at how well he could sell something and then make change and handle the whole transaction at such a young age. And that ability that he developed very early has stuck with him through his whole life. He's phenomenal with the numbers he can hold in his head and how he can deal with statistics.

"Hard work is a trait of his family. His father was an extremely hard worker. He worked long hours to make his business a success. Bill's uncle Sam was the same. He was kind of a role model. His grandfather, his father, his uncle—he just followed in their footsteps and adopted that hard work ethic and approach and it stuck with him.")

We used to buy watermelons by the carload, bananas, everything. I loved it. It was a big thrill going and buying 600 crates of peaches, bringing them back and selling them and making money. That was fun. You'd buy and sell, depending on supply and demand. It was pure capitalism. I learned how to make money in that business, but it was a tough business. If you didn't sell that stuff, it would spoil. That stuff had to be there. If there was going to be a rush at eight o'clock Saturday morning and the strawberries didn't come in until 11, you were dead.

One time, we heard about a farmer in Grand Rapids who had peaches at a good price, but he wouldn't sell to us because our order wasn't big enough to make the trip worthwhile for him. We knew there were no peaches in town and we had a big week coming up, so we — my dad and my brother and I — called him a dozen times, disguising our voices: "Hey, Aloise, got any peaches? I need about a hundred crates."

Finally, he decided he had enough people in Saginaw to bring in a thousand crates. When he got to the market, he couldn't find any of these customers except us, so we offered to help him out by buying all his crates at a reduced price. My brother Larry was only eight or nine years old, and he masterminded it. He was on the phone more than I was. Now he's a professor of finance at Florida A&M University in Tallahasse, Florida, and one of the country's leading experts on bank mergers.

I grew up in that business, and I don't know exactly where sports became involved. My dad, who never participated in sports himself because of a heart condition, always coached my teams, summer leagues and stuff, when I was in fifth and sixth grades. Then, when I got to junior high, I started coaching my brother's teams.

Right after I first got my driver's license, one of our players went up north for the weekend. We had a big game, so I drove up and got the guy. I mean, that was unheard of in a summer recreation league, to drive up to Higgins Lake to get a kid who's 12 years old to play in some pee wee basketball contest and then take him back. I mean, you've gotta be out of your mind. But I did it because I wanted to win. We always had good teams. We were organized, even back then, and I think I learned the organization from the fruit business.

That's where the organization was in my life, not at home. I moved around. My first eight years, I lived with my mom and dad on State Street in Saginaw. When they first got divorced, my mom, for some reason, went to Montreal with a friend, and I went with her. I don't even know what she did up there. All I remember about Montreal is being up there and peddling papers and not going to school.

Then we came back to Saginaw and moved over on the east side to an apartment. My mom started working and I moved in with my aunt. Then I moved back with my mom, and then my mom moved in with her dad and I lived there, still on the east side. I spent the eighth grade at Howe Military Academy in Howe, Indiana. That was my dad's idea. He knew I was struggling and he felt that maybe that would be good for me.

But I always resented that. I didn't like that. I went, and I did a good job. I was a standout basketball player. I was a top guy on campus and I did well in school. But I resented being sent away, and I just went one year.

I ended up, my last two years of high school and my first couple of years of college, living where I started, where my dad was. He got the house.

It wasn't the normal home life. For several years, I just kind of raised myself. My mother worked a couple of jobs. My brother was in a nursery. I don't remember him that much until he was about seven, and I was in college by the time he was in junior high. We're very close now, but all those years we were both like only children. We weren't together a lot.

(Says Tom Billy: "He played some baseball, what we called Knothole Baseball, when he was a young kid, although I think that eventually interfered with his involvement in his dad's business, so he dropped that.

"We used to play a lot of basketball. We'd play at Central Junior High School, which was about two blocks from our houses. He and I used to go over there and play pickup games. When we were in high school, we had a standing bet that we would take on any two people in the city for five dollars, full-court basketball, up to 24 points, with each basket counting a point. Bill's about 5'9", I guess, and I'm 5'11". We never lost.

"I was a worker like him and we were both in excellent shape. We just would never give up. We stayed the course and we'd run 'em until they dropped. It didn't matter how tall or how short they were. Oftentimes, it'd come up when we were at a dance or some social event in high school and a bunch of us would go down there and two guys would challenge us. We'd drive down there and use the headlights from the car to light up the court so we could play.")

I played on great teams at Saginaw High. Two years after I graduated, in 1962, they won the state championship. I was in my second year at Delta College (it was Bay City Junior College when I started there), and I went right up to Alpena one night after class to scout Alpena High for Saginaw. Janice's dad, Larry Laeding, was the Saginaw coach—he had been my coach, in fact—and I just wanted to stay involved somehow.

(Says Larry Laeding: "I'm surprised he actually took time off to play basketball, because he was working all the time for his dad at the Florida Market. The odds of him ever getting to be the basketball coach at a place like the University of Michigan were insurmountable, a million to one, like Lehigh winning the national championship.

"I'm not going to tell you he was a great basketball player because he wasn't. When he came off the bench, he was just like he is now, which is very, very intense. Whatever he did, he did with a vengeance. You knew good and well the level of play when he went in was going to stay where it was or get better, one or the other. That's the reason he was on the team, not because he was a great basketball player, but because he had a great desire to win, which fit right into my way of thinking.")

I was around blacks a lot when I was growing up and I think that's been a big help to me, because not all white coaches are that comfortable around blacks. But I went to a junior high that was primarily black and Saginaw High, which was probably 60 percent black, and I never, ever even thought about it, really. There were the typical problems that most schools have, fights and things like that, but no racial problems.

Maybe because I was involved with sports and playing with black kids, I didn't notice what was going on outside of sports. In sports, you're always involved with the team concept. The Saginaw High team I was on, I'd say there were three white kids in the top six or seven.

(Says Janice Frieder: "Bill was accepted into the honors program at Michigan State. I wanted to go to Northwestern but my dad taught and coached high school basketball and there was no way that I could afford it. I became involved in a co-op program where you worked half days at Dow Corning and went to school half days at Bay City Junior College.

"A high school counselor told Bill about the program and he also became involved. I'm not sure what really made him decide to go to junior college with me, but I have a suspicion he saw the opportunity to make money while he was going to school. There were six of us that commuted back and forth. We left Saginaw in the morning about seven o'clock, went to Bay City for classes until noon, drove an hour to Midland and worked for four hours, and then drove back to Saginaw at night. We were gone from seven in the morning until seven at night.

"We did that for two full years, and then we came down to Michigan as juniors.")

Sometime during my junior year, my first year at Michigan, I decided I wanted to be a coach. Maybe I always liked coaching or maybe watching Cazzie and that team reconfirmed it or got me to thinking about it more, I don't know. That summer and the next year I started working on my teaching certificate, because you had to have that to be a coach and business administration would not accept any of the education hours, so I took 20 extra hours. That was the summer I took courses at three different places. I was all over the place to pick up extra hours so that I could still graduate through business administration and also have my teaching certificate at the end of my senior year. I wanted to stay with business because I knew I probably would not like teaching, so it was a matter of whether I would stay in coaching if I got into it.

I did well in everything in school and graduated from Michigan with honors. If I went to college again, I wouldn't work nearly as hard. I really wouldn't. The amount of extra hours you had to spend to go from a "B" to an "A" is phenomenal. I could have cut maybe 12 hours a week taking "B's" instead of getting "A's," but I always wanted to get everything right.

At the end of my senior year, I passed up a lot of jobs because I decided to stay and get my master's in business administration. Janice was going to Northwestern to get her master's, plus Cazzie was back and Buntin was back and I wanted to follow the basketball team. I was going to all those games, home and away. Bill Beck and I were going all over the place. We had even gone to Kansas City for the Final Four in 1964.

Janice got her master's in learning disabilities and language therapy. At that time, that field was really in demand, and I was getting a lot of job offers, primarily junior varsity jobs, because they wanted Janice to coordinate their speech and language therapy program for the whole school system. We got married the summer after we both got our master's degrees, and they'd take me to get her. I was even offered head coaching jobs, which was unheard of for a kid out of college who didn't play in college, because they wanted her. It was great.

I accepted one of those jobs, as head coach at Rudyard High in the Upper Peninsula. On the way back to Saginaw, I stopped at Alpena High, only because I had scouted them three years before for Janice's dad. I told them they had a great program up there. They didn't have any openings at the time, but about 10 days later, the head coach, Dick Dennis, called me. I was just getting ready to mail the signed contracts to Rudyard, until Dennis talked me into going to a Class A school to coach the jayvee rather than going to the U.P. And they had a job for Janice, so we started in Alpena. I was offered a job with Standard Oil in 1964, after I got my bachelor's degree, for $14,000. Now I was going to Alpena, with a master's, for $4,700. That shows you how nuts I really am.

2

College to Head Coach

Going to Alpena was the first lucky move that I made when it comes to basketball, because Dick Dennis was a successful coach who had brought teams from the north through that tough Flint–Saginaw regional and beat those teams to get to the quarterfinals. He had good players, and here I am with him for two years and he gets the Flint Northern job offered to him and he brings me with him. What a great, great break. The rest kind of fell into place.

My first year at Alpena, my jayvee team lost its first five games and eight of its first nine. I was a basket case up there. I worked so hard and we just kept losing, mostly because we weren't any good. Then Dick gave me a couple of his juniors for the later part of the season and we won seven straight and wound up 8–8.

The second year, I was 14–3. We even beat some varsity teams. There were Class C and D schools not far from Alpena that never filled their schedules because they were so far north. They were looking for games and, as the jayvee team of a Class A school, there wasn't that much difference in competition. And sometimes there were situations, like when Alpena played Highland Park at Cobo Hall in Detroit, when the jayvees didn't play and the varsity did, so we had games to fill, too.

One day, Dick Dennis came up to me and said, "Congratulations."

I said, "For what?"

He said, "You're our new head tennis coach."

He was the athletic director, too, see. I told him I didn't know anything about tennis and he said not to worry, I'd do a good job.

And I did do a good job, except I got in trouble because I scouted. I didn't know you couldn't scout and then stack your lineup. I stacked mine. I took my five and six men and started them at one and two, then went one-two-three-four after that. I didn't know anything about tennis. I didn't know how to coach it, I didn't know how to play it and I didn't know you weren't supposed to do that.

Some of those teams up there were pretty good, like East Jordan. They were always good in tennis. Their coach started talking to me about strategy one day. He said, "Do you take two to the net or do you stay one up?"

I said, "Well, we do it both ways." I didn't know what he was talking about.

I talked Dennis into taking the Flint Northern job. I don't think he wanted to go. Here was a guy from outside of Grand Rapids who had never been in the big cities, who had never coached black kids. Before going to Alpena, he'd been up in Carson City, where he coached with Bob Leach, who was Flint Central's football coach and the brother of Dick Leach, the athletic director for the Flint school system and Rick's dad. Bob Leach was pushing Dick Dennis for the job in Flint and I was pushing from the Alpena end that he should take it.

He had turned it down the year before so they decided to stay with the same guy for another year, then it came up again and they stayed after Dick. I wanted him to go so badly because I knew he would take me as his assistant. I kept telling him how he was going to win a state championship and how great the talent was and finally he decided to do it. I think my nagging was an influence.

When we got the job in Flint, I moved immediately. I took a trailer and my car to Alpena High the day I got my last paycheck and went right from there to Flint. When we found out in April we had the job, we started going to Flint, which was like a five-hour drive then, twice a week for six straight weeks. I'd meet with kids in the high schools, get announcements in the junior highs —"if anybody is interested in going out for Flint Northern basketball next season, there'll be a meeting, come with your gym shoes"— and then I'd meet with those kids and tell them when I would be back and it grew and grew and led right into the summer program.

By the time summer came about, all the elementary and junior highs that fed into Northern were playing some form of basketball and working under me. Now basketball has become year-round but when I brought that concept to Flint, that was a new thing, for a coach to be working in the off season with his players. I was one of the first guys I know of to take a team from Flint and go down to Detroit and scrimmage a Detroit team in the summertime. They never did stuff like that.

I thought that was the way you got ahead, by working with the kids year-round, so that's what I did. The summer I got to Flint, I must have worked 60 to 80 hours a week on basketball, but it was all my own program. I wasn't working for anybody or getting paid for it. I just did it. All I wanted was the use of the facilities. I had leagues. I had the potential varsity, the potential jayvee, the ninth grade team, and elementary kids. I had instruction some days. I had leagues some days. When you put it all together, we were busy all the time. I was always a go-getter for youth programs and keeping basketball in front of everybody. I did the same thing in Alpena.

I was really lucky to be hired by Dick Dennis. I was inexperienced. I didn't know a lot. I thought I did, but I didn't. Had I gone to the wrong place and not done well, it could have been over. Here I got with a guy that was successful and knew basketball and I got other opportunities because of his success. And I took advantage of it. But I was lucky, too.

Working hard in the summer paid off. For the first time in a long while, kids in that area developed some confidence in the coaches. We were sincere about them, we were working with them in the summertime, and that hadn't been going on. That, plus the fact that we picked up a few kids who wouldn't necessarily have been in school otherwise, led to a decent season. Dick's varsity went 11–6 and finished second in both the unofficial city standings and the Saginaw Valley Conference before losing to Flint Northwestern by a point in the first game of the state tournament. My jayvees went 13–3.

I told you I didn't remember any problems when I was a student at Saginaw, but when I went to Flint as a coach and teacher, there were a lot of problems. I went from Alpena, where the fight at recess is your biggest problem, to Flint Northern, where they're telling you what to do if the police are in the building, what to do if there's tear gas, what to do if there's a bomb scare.

It was a big difference. Our first year, the principal was fired, a new principal came in, there were fights, there were outsiders in the building every day, and we had the riots after Martin Luther King was assassinated.

I can remember one day in the spring of our first year. The fire siren was going and there were fights and tear gas and police and people running around all over. It was just chaotic. Dick and I were standing in the hall, just watching it, and our athletic director, Bill Adams, runs up and says, "You know what the problem is? People just haven't seen a .500 season here in so long that they don't know how to act."

A group of us played poker every Wednesday night. One night, these two guys with a shotgun and a pistol and wearing ski masks broke in. As soon as they came through the door, I threw my keys under the table. I figured they were going to take everything, and damned if they didn't—watches, wallets, everything. They even made us take off our pants, so we couldn't chase 'em, I guess.

I had a big, red Flint Northern parka that I wore every day.

And this guy who was taking the coats and stuff recognized it. He said, "Hey, this looks like Frieder's. Is that you, Frieder?"

And I said, "Yeah, man."

And he said, "You're doing a good job with the brothers. Keep it up, man. We like your team. You're doing a great job."

I said, "Hey, man, since I'm doing such a good job with the brothers, do me a favor."

He said, "What's that?"

I said, "Take my money but leave my license and all that."

So he went back through the pillowcase and pulled out my wallet and took out the money and left the wallet. That saved me some money, which I had underneath the flap. But the big thing was I got my license and stuff.

Well, maybe the second biggest thing. That was the most scared I've ever been. You talk about your heart beating. That heart really beats when there's a shotgun at your head.

The third year I was at Flint, there was a teachers' strike. I was coming off of a 16–0 season with the jayvees the year before, but I was out of coaching for a year because I resigned from my teaching job on Oct. 20, 1969, rather than be a party to that strike. I resigned and assailed the teachers for going on strike. I sold mutual funds that year. I was the top salesman in Michigan for First Investors and one of the top five or ten in the country. I made five times what I did as a teacher, but I really missed coaching.

Then Dick Dennis quit as head coach to become business manager for the school system. He recommended me strongly for the job, and Don Gaviglio, the principal, had a conference with the returning players and they were behind me, too. So they hired me back to be head coach. It was kind of a tough situation because a lot of people didn't want me back. When I was introduced at the first teachers' meeting of the school year, they booed me. But they cheered when we won the state championship.

We went 14–2 during the regular season, the best Northern had done in years. Both of our losses were to Campy Russell's Pontiac Central team, which was ranked first in the state. The second one really hurt. They beat us—in Flint—by 33 points, 88–55, in the last game of the season. It wasn't a great way to go into the tournament, but we managed to win our first six and make it to the semifinals.

The other three teams in the semifinals were Kalamazoo Central, Detroit Kettering and, yup, Pontiac Central, which was still unbeaten. They had a draw in Lansing to determine the pairings. They just wrote the name of each school on a piece of paper, folded it and dropped it into a hat. Then a representative from each school picked out one slip. The first two teams picked would be one semifinal pairing and the next two would be the other.

I was the only coach of the four who went to the drawing and I watched carefully as they put the names into the hat. They didn't fold them too much and they didn't shake them up too good. I wanted Kalamazoo. I figured we could handle them but I knew for a fact we probably couldn't handle Pontiac. And if we got to Kettering, we'd take our chances.

Pontiac Central was the first name in the hat, then Kettering, Kalamazoo Central and Northern. The first guy to pick got Northern. I was second. I figured they were going to come out in the opposite order they went in and I was right. I got Kalamazoo. It was just a matter of being observant. We beat them in the semis and Kettering upset Pontiac Central, handing them their only loss of the year.

Kettering was no pushover, you understand. They had Lindsay Hairston, Eric Money and Coniel Norman, three guys who went on to play pro ball. And they had Joe Johnson, who went on to Michigan and was the captain of the 1974–75 team.

For the first time that year, 1971, the finals of the state tournament were held in Ann Arbor, instead of Michigan State's Jenison Fieldhouse in East Lansing, where they had always been. I took the team to the Campus Inn, which is where I now keep my Michigan players on the nights before weekend afternoon games. It had snowed on the day of every tournament game we played that year, and our players cheered when they saw it start to snow on the afternoon of the championship game.

I was leaving nothing to chance. I was going to wear the same clothes — red blazer, blue shirt, checked pants and loafers — that I had for the previous seven tournament games. And I took the same suitcase that my father-in-law used when his Saginaw High team won the title in 1962. Nonetheless, the late Hal Schram of the *Detroit Free Press*, who was the leading authority on prep sports in the state, called us "one of the tournament's biggest underdogs in memory." And that was *before* we beat Kettering, 79–78. We had a nine-point lead with 2:50 to go and almost blew it. That was also my first victory ever at Crisler Arena.

Four starters from that team graduated — Tom McGill, who was an all–stater, Ron Polk, James Britt (Wayman's older brother) and Barry Menefee. The next season we weren't even supposed to be contenders for the city title, much less anything more than that. But Wayman Britt, the one returning starter, developed into a true leader, Dennis Johnson came up from the jayvees to be our center and leading scorer, and a kid named Terry Furlow, a senior who had hardly played before due to personal and academic problems, finally began to fulfill the potential that made him a star at Michigan State and in the NBA before his tragic death in an auto accident.

We went undefeated. Our 25–0 record was the best ever for a Class A high school team in Michigan up until then. And we got our revenge on Pontiac Central. We beat them three times that season, the only games they lost all year. We beat them twice in the regular season (including a win at their place by 15 points, the first time in 16 years Northern had won on that court) and the third time in the state championship game, 74–71. I don't have to tell you how hard it is to beat the same team three times in one season, but that 1972 team was a cool, mature bunch. Where the guys on the '71 team would throw up before the games, the '72 team just sort of came to work, if you know what I mean. I think Wayman Britt had a lot to do with that.

That was a great rivalry, let me tell you, between Northern and Pontiac Central. In those two seasons, we were 47–2 and the only losses were to them, and they were 41–4, with three of the losses to us and the other to Detroit Kettering in the state semifinals in 1971.

There's a clipping in one of my scrapbooks of an interview I did with Pete Sark, a Flint sports broadcaster, early in 1972. He was curious about how I had managed to discipline my kids in a situation where it had been a problem before, and at a time in history, looking back at it, when there was a lot of unrest. Some of the things I told him then are still true today, even though my circumstances have changed so dramatically:

"I think probably getting their confidence, this is the big thing. We start on our basketball program almost as soon as the basketball season ends, and on getting to know the youngsters that are coming into Northern. We work with them, and I don't work with them just as getting something out of them basketball-wise. I want them to go to classes. I want them to get good grades. If it means coming out on a Thursday night to school and demanding that five of them are there to do homework assignments for two hours, then we do that.

"I want them to learn to be gentlemen. They know I'm sincere, that I'm more than a coach. I have a sincere interest in the guys getting through high school, doing a good job in school and on the court, going on to college and getting an education. They know if something comes up they can come to me and they'll get my support."

Northern went into the 1972–73 season with a 33-game winning streak and two state titles in my first two years as head coach. I was wearing out my lucky outfit, but I didn't have to wear it much longer. Even though we lost all five starters from the 1972 team, we still managed to win our first four games to run our unbeaten streak to 37 games (a record for Class A schools that stood for 13 years) before Flint Southwestern finally beat us.

I also had to kick two kids off the team, which I hated to do, but I couldn't have individuals undermining the team concept. That was particularly important that year because we didn't have much talent and needed a lot of defensive tenacity and offensive discipline if we were going to win. We won games by scores of 41–33, 42–41, 50–46 and 49–47 with a bunch of guys who would have loved to run up and down the court but knew what it took to win.

We wound up 14–6 in the regular season and got all the way to the regional finals, including a 46–31 upset of Flint Northwestern in the district final, before losing to, of all people, Saginaw.

That was my last game as a high school coach. In three seasons at Flint Northern, my teams won 65 of 74 games. Even more impressive, in my opinion, was the fact that our record was better in the tournament (21–1) than it was during the regular season (44–8). That loss to Saginaw was the only tournament game we lost in my three years. We won 21 consecutive tournament games, which was also a record at the time.

I actually had a head coaching job at a college offered to me while I was still at Northern. It was in 1973, not long before the Michigan assistant's job opened up. Muddy Waters, who later became the football coach at Michigan State, was the athletic director at Hillsdale College and he offered me the job there. I was still considering it when I met Gene Bartow for the first time at the 7-Up National Basketball Coaches Clinic in Grand Rapids. He was at Memphis State at the time and had just finished second to UCLA in the NCAA tournament.

I asked Bartow what he thought and he said, "You're going to do better than Hillsdale. I'd hire a guy like you. You just stay at the high school level and keep getting to know college coaches." Not long after that, he was the head coach at Illinois and I was an assistant at Michigan.

When I became the varsity coach, they made me the co-op education coordinator, where I could get release time, work with kids, run the sales and marketing program, teach advanced classes and then place kids in jobs and supervise them. I went out and hustled jobs for them. I liked that. It was better than teaching business math and typing, which I did as a jayvee coach.

But I didn't have a certificate to be a coordinator—I had a teaching certificate—so while I was the head coach at Northern, I was running down to Eastern Michigan taking courses to get my state certificate. By the time I finally got my certificate to be a coordinator, I got the assistant's job at Michigan.

John Orr was taking a lot of heat at the time. After two years of contending for the Big Ten championship, everybody had picked Michigan to win it and instead they finished sixth and lost their last four in a row and six of their last eight. They had an atrocious season. When Dick Honig resigned as one of Orr's assistants on Aug. 1, 1973, I don't think U of M Athletic Director Don Canham intended to replace him. He was just going to go with Richard Carter and Jim Dutcher as Orr's assistants.

Honig resigned on a Sunday. On the following Tuesday, they had some sort of U of M outing in Flint and Orr was there. I was there when he arrived and I chased him all around. I said, "John, you gotta hire me. I've won state championships. I'm ready to go into college coaching." I begged him.

Well, you know how John was. He'd rather socialize and go hit the golf ball. "You've got tenure," he said to me. "Stay where you are. I'm gonna get fired anyway."

I hung around all day, followed him around on the golf cart, was with him at dinner, with him after he spoke, after him, after him, after him. Rommie, his wife, was up in Gaylord and he was supposed to meet her there, but I knew he wasn't going to make it because he'd had a long day, so when he left, I followed him.

Sure enough, he stopped at the Holiday Inn in Saginaw. I followed him into the lobby. When he turned around after registering, there I was. I finally got him to commit to me that when he got back to Ann Arbor, he would go to Canham and try to hire me. But he just wanted to get rid of me. He was not going to hire me. I think he had been told that he wasn't going to get a replacement, but I had a tie with Dutcher. He and I had become good friends when he was the coach at Alpena Community College and I was at Alpena High. Then he went to Eastern Michigan while I was at Flint Northern and he recruited Wayman Britt and Tom McGill and some of my players, and then he came to Michigan. He and Honig signed Britt for Michigan, so I had a lot of ties with Dutcher.

And Dutcher really felt I was the guy they should hire. He was for me. And John was for me, but he just didn't think Canham was going to do it, and he wasn't going to fight with Canham. Then, after John told me they weren't going to hire me, I tried to make an appointment with Canham, but Canham wouldn't really make an appointment. He would say he would see me but he wouldn't give me a time.

Finally, I just showed up at eight o'clock one morning and sat in his office until he would see me. I told Janice, "You check at Ulrich's [a landmark student bookstore] every half hour. I don't know when I'll be done. When I'm ready to go, we'll go."

He finally saw me, it must have been about 11 or 11:30 a.m., and I talked to him for an hour about why I had to be hired at Michigan.

I told him I was married but I didn't have any kids and my wife worked, so money wasn't a problem. "This is my life," I said. "I'm a Michigan man. I went to Michigan. I've done everything that I can do in high school and I want to be a college assistant."

Then he gives me the budget business. He says they're running a deficit and this is a way for them to save $15,000. I said, "Hey, if that's the only reason you can give me for not hiring me, that's not good enough, because I'll work for nothing. I don't need the money, I need the job."

And he said, "I'll talk to the board. I'll let you know."

I had met Canham a couple of times before, and I knew he was impressed with our state championships and the good discipline and supervision that we had, which was far ahead of other schools at that time. "I know you can do it," I said.

"Well," he said, "that's a fair assessment," as if to say he could do it but he didn't know if he would.

So that was that. I was really dejected. I left his office and I didn't even go up to the basketball office to see Orr and Dutcher, I was so dejected. I went to Ulrich's, picked up Janice, and drove home to Flint.

When I got there, the phone was ringing. It was Dutcher.

He said, "Where'd you go?"

I said, "I drove home."

He said, "Right after you left, Canham came up and told Orr he liked you, he liked your enthusiasm, you're a good guy for Michigan, and to hire you and give you $14,000."

So that's how I got the job at Michigan. I called Orr and he said, "Don't come down. I'll see you Monday." I said, "No, I'm coming down. Stay there." And I jumped in the car and drove right back down.

They told me not to say anything for a month because the job had to be posted. Well, this was the middle of August. School was starting in two weeks and I had to let Northern know I was leaving, so that was a problem. So I went in and resigned "for personal reasons." I said my dad was sick and I was going to help out in the fruit business.

I was incredible when I first came here. I ran from my office to the car. I ran up the stairs. I was flying. I'd knock people over in the athletic office if they weren't careful, but that's how excited I was. It was a big, big break for me, but I had to work to get it. Winning the state championships helped, but John truly thought if he had another bad year, he'd be gone. He wasn't interested in hiring anybody.

I've been lucky, but you make your own luck sometimes. When opportunity knocks, you better take advantage of it, because it doesn't knock all the time. I felt at the time, "I love basketball. I hate teaching. Now I've gotta get into college, and this is the time to do it." And what better place to do it than a place you love and where you went to school?

I had to do it. Hell, if Canham wouldn't have hired me, I might have just packed up and come down here anyway. I was determined.

Being an assistant taught me the things I needed to know at the college level that didn't really relate or weren't pertinent at the high school level, like recruiting, handling alumni, dealing with the media, the sophistication of the offenses and defenses, handling kids. I did a lot of that in high school, anyway, but it was on a much lower level. It's magnified at this level and seven years at Michigan as an assistant taught me the things that I had to know to make the transition from head coach in high school to head coach in college.

I got the reputation of being a great recruiter very fast, even though I had no experience at it. I just approached it the same way I approached helping Dick Dennis build the basketball program at Flint Northern: with a lot of work. I didn't know any other way to do it. I outworked people at the high school level, no question. But when you get to college, they're all working that hard themselves, for the most part. In high school, I was ten years ahead of my time because I went year-round and I was all basketball and I didn't care whether I was paid when I worked in the summer, but in college they're all doing that, so you don't have that edge.

So my edge had to come from other things, like calling ahead to make appointments when I went to see a kid, and planning trips so I could see as many kids as possible in a given time span.

I worried a lot more then than I do now. I'll say, "Aw, who gives a damn?" about something that, when I was an assistant, would have seemed like the biggest thing in the world. I see that with my assistants today. They remind me of me sometimes.

I admired John Orr because he could say the hell with basketball and go out and have a good time and still run a good program. Of course, he knew Frieder would usually be watching the Indiana film, anyway. I just can't do it the way he did it. I can't allow myself that kind of thing.

He could put basketball aside for the summer and enjoy life. That's hard for me to do. I was just nervous and worried all the time. John wasn't. I wish I could be like him, but I can't. John gave me more authority and more credit than I deserved, which was a credit to him. It showed he wasn't insecure.

There were two big things I learned from John Orr: number one, you can't do everything yourself, and number two, if you do everything yourself, you're gonna lose your good people. You've got to surround yourself with good people and you've got to give them authority.

I always felt bad for John. First, it was Fred Snowden that was coaching the team, then it was Jim Dutcher, then it was Frieder. Hell, I didn't understand that. Sooner or later, they've got to give the guy credit. I think it finally came to him. He's certainly gotten plenty of credit at Iowa State.

I continued to play 21, as I had since about 1968. I'd go out to Las Vegas for a week and make a handsome profit. That was a big thing because I needed the money. I didn't do it recreationally but as a business. I couldn't afford to lose. I had to go out and make money. It was a big thrill, too, but now it's no longer important. When I became the head coach at Michigan, both Don Canham and Bo Schembechler cautioned me about the negative consequences of being involved with cards in a big way. Except for a half hour for fun here and there, I haven't played since.

My first two years on Orr's staff were when I really made my reputation as a recruiter. I bet I saw Phil Hubbard play or practice a hundred times. I once saw Bruce Flowers, a suburban Detroit kid who wound up going to Notre Dame, at least once a day for 36 straight days. You could do those things then. I wore out at least two cars, just wore them out.

What I didn't see was the Michigan basketball team and Wayman Britt, who did just the kind of job for the Wolverines that he had done for me at Flint Northern: unbelievable defense, especially for a 6'2" kid playing the other team's toughest forward and sometimes giving away seven or eight inches, clutch offense, a surprising number of rebounds, and all-around inspiration. It was hard for other guys to slack off when they saw how hard Wayman always worked.

At the end of my second year at Michigan, two major things happened. One was that we signed Hubbard, capping a recruiting year that also included Alan Hardy, Tom Staton and Rickey Green. The other was that Dutcher left to become the head coach at Minnesota. Not only were there no longer two Alpena "alums" on the staff, but I became Orr's number one assistant. I worked with travel arrangements, scheduling, budgets and game preparation, and I sat next to John on the bench.

That was the year we finished second to Indiana in the Big Ten and the nation. I remember Detroit sportswriter Joe Falls being amazed when I told him about driving to Metro Airport at one in the morning to personally pick up film on Rutgers, which was our opponent in the semifinals. He was even more amazed that I then went straight to the office to watch it, study it and break it down. If some people think I don't get much sleep now, they should have seen me at tournament time when I was an assistant.

That was the year I coached Michigan at Crisler Arena for the first time. One night near the end of the season, when Illinois was in town, Orr came down with the flu. He had it really bad, and I had to coach the team. Well, we took a 17–1 lead after three minutes and 19 seconds and wound up winning, 90–75. Somebody asked Steve Grote afterward what I had said to them and he said, "After you get ahead, 17–1, what can any coach say to you?"

I filled in for Orr one other time, in the Big Ten opener in 1978. We beat Northwestern, 80–65, so I was 4–0 in Crisler Arena — Northern won a state semifinal game there in 1972 in addition to the state championship game in 1971 — before I ever became head coach.

That win over Northwestern came right about the time Dick Vitale was campaigning for the Pistons' job. He had quit coaching at the University of Detroit because of health problems, but when the Pistons fired Herb Brown, he announced that his problems weren't all that bad, after all. I told the press conference after the Northwestern game that when Orr got well, he wasn't going to be a candidate to coach the Pistons.

The players used to call me "Snoop" and "Columbo" because I would wander around hotels on the road in the middle of the night, wearing my pajamas and slippers and knocking on doors to see who was awake. Rickey Green once told a reporter, "If he tells you he's gone to bed, don't believe him." But I wasn't really spying on them; I just wanted to talk basketball. I did the same thing to the writers.

I started getting offers after the 1976 season. Fordham was the first but it didn't look like a good situation to me, with no facilities to speak of and stuck in the middle of New York City. I figured being the head assistant at Michigan was good enough that I wasn't going to take any job just to be a head coach.

There was some interest in me over the next five years, from feelers to offers: Evansville, Marshall, Washington and several teams in the Mid-American Conference at one time or another.

The two jobs I think I came the closest to getting were Vanderbilt and Nevada-Las Vegas, two very different situations. This was after the 1979 season, just a year before Orr left for Iowa State. I was definitely in the running with Vanderbilt and there were a lot of things I liked, but their academic situation was just too difficult to deal with. It looked like Northwestern: It would just be too hard to get the kids I needed into school. That shows you what a terrific job Vanderbilt's head coach C. M. Newton has done there.

UNLV officials talked to me because Jerry Tarkanian was going to the Lakers, but that deal hit a snag at the last minute. Tark stayed put and so did I.

3

Jan: My Side

Bill first noticed me in the ninth grade, but that was probably because my dad was the basketball coach at the high school. It was March and he wanted tournament tickets. He came up to me one day and pulled on my ponytail. "Hey, girl," he said, "do you suppose your dad could get me some tickets for the state tournament?"

I went home and asked my dad. I said, "Bill Frieder would like some tickets for the state tournament." My dad's response was "Absolutely not."

Bill's dad had a sister to whom he was very attached, and the two of them lived with their father, Bill's grandfather. When Bill was in junior high, he lived with his mother on Gage Street, but he moved in with his dad in the tenth grade and stayed for three years.

Bill was lucky that he didn't get into trouble because I can remember he had a lot of freedom. I think he went through a period where he didn't get a lot of direction.

I can remember Bill telling me that when he was in seventh grade, he and a friend—maybe this was why his dad sent him to military school, I don't know—would go down the street and put kerosene on the sidewalk and light it up. Another time, he and two friends took a train to Texas and they ended up with more money than they started out with because Bill played cards on the train and the three of them would go into grocery stores and take things like bread and cheese. So he's very lucky that he didn't get into trouble. His dad was concerned about him. When you're bright, you have a great potential for both good and bad. Fortunately, Bill has focused his potential in the right direction.

He always worked hard. When we were in high school, I believed that Bill was poor. I knew he bought his clothes at rummage sales, and he got his shoes at a shoe store where they were two or three dollars a pair.

Then one of his buddies called me up one night and said, "Bill would like to go with you but he really wants to make sure that you're not after his money."

And I started to laugh. I said, "What money?"

The friend said, "Well, Bill has $10,000 of his own personal money. He just wants to make sure you're not after it."

I didn't believe it, so he got the bank book and showed me. Bill had worked for his dad from the time he was about eight years old. I know how hard he worked because I used to work with him. We would get up at two or three o'clock in the morning and drive into Sandusky. We'd get there, unload the truck, start selling about eight in the morning, then leave Sandusky at five or six at night and drive back and unload the truck.

Bill had always done that kind of thing, and I assumed that anyone who was doing that wouldn't have much money. But he saved absolutely every dime. He wouldn't even eat lunch when we were in high school. That saved him 35 cents.

So with that and all the other deals—selling peaches, hustling concessions at sports events, selling candy at military school, playing cards—he had accumulated $10,000.

I can remember a truckload of charcoal came into Saginaw. The driver approached Bill's dad about buying it and he was not interested. They were broken bags. Bill said, "How much will you sell 'em to me for?" The man said 10 cents a bag.

So Bill bought the whole truckload and went out and got people like our younger brothers, who were less than 10 at the time, to go door to door selling the charcoal at 60 cents a bag. Bill made 50 cents a bag and gave Larry and Mike a nickel a bag each. He was always out to see how he could make money.

He enjoyed seeing money form money. He never really did anything with it. He wasn't saving it for something. He just liked to see it accumulate.

I really became aware of Bill in our junior year at Saginaw High, when we had a chemistry class together. I just waited around until after basketball practice and then he took me home. That's how I began dating him.

Bill had a car. I think his dad bought it for him. Saginaw, at that time, was pretty much divided between the west side, which was fairly wealthy, and the east side. My family lived on the east side, which was the Saginaw High district. Kids from the west side went to Arthur Hill High.

Bill was living with his dad on the west side, but his dad's fruit store was not far from Saginaw High on the east side. Bill went there to school even though he lived in the Arthur Hill district, and nobody ever questioned it. Who would want to go to Saginaw High when they could go to Arthur Hill? But Bill wanted to because he had always pretty much associated with east side kids.

Bill kidded me a lot when we were in high school. One day, we were driving down Washington Street, where a cathedral and a synagogue are across the street from each other. I don't know why, but I asked him, "Where does your dad go to church?"

He said, "Right here on Washington."

I said, "He's not Catholic."

He said, "No, he doesn't go there. He goes over here."

"That's the synagogue."

"Yeah."

"That means you're Jewish."

"Yeah, my dad is."

And I said, "Bill, you shouldn't tell people that. It's okay to kid people but you shouldn't kid people about stuff like that."

Then we went to dinner at his house with his dad and his aunt, who more or less looked after his dad and ran the household, and I told her, "You want to hear the craziest thing? Bill tried to tell me you people are Jewish!"

And his aunt said, "We are."

Now where does a conversation go from there? "Pass the potatoes"?

I went home and told my mom. "Did you know that Bill's dad is Jewish?" I asked.

She said she did.

"Why didn't you tell me?"

"I don't know," she said. "It doesn't make that much difference."

Deep down, it was probably more important to his dad and his aunt than Bill thought it was. They identified strongly with their cultural heritage. It caused some problems when we were married. When my mother called his aunt to make plans for the wedding, she said, "We assumed he would marry a Jewish girl." Bill's dad and aunt were upset when we didn't get married in the synagogue.

There was another time, years later, when I fell for one of Bill's jokes and it ended up making me look good. After the 1976 season, when Fred Taylor was released at Ohio State, Bill told me that Eldon Miller, who was then the coach at Western Michigan, was going to get the job.

Jerry Tarkanian called our house that night. He was writing a column for a Las Vegas newspaper and he wanted to talk to Bill. I said, "He's not here, but let me give you some news. Eldon Miller is going to be the next head coach at Ohio State. Bill told me this afternoon."

Jerry thanked me and said he would put it in his column.

When Bill came home, I told him Jerry called and I had shared the information about Eldon getting the job at Ohio State.

He said, "Jan, I was just telling you that. That's nonsense. He's not gonna get that job."

But Jerry had already put it in his column. And, of course, it turned out to be true.

Bill and I were in the co-op program at Dow Corning and Delta College for two years. He had a marketing instructor at Delta named Mr. Gordon for whom he did a report on companies of the future. The first K mart store had just opened in Garden City, Michigan, and Bill wrote about it. He explained what this was going to lead to, the free-standing stores in the suburbs with big parking lots, how much money they would make and the fact that the downtown Kresges would be closing and the big K marts on the outskirts would be opening up.

His final recommendation was to buy all the Kresge stock you can and become an instant millionaire. Mr. Gordon knew Bill had some money, and he told him that he was right, that Kresge would be a good investment. Bill met me in the hallway one day about lunch time and said, "Janice, Mr. Gordon thinks I should take my $10,000 and invest it in Kresge stock."

I told him, "Don't be a fool, Bill. That's just the way people lose their money. If you lose this $10,000, how are you going to go on to Michigan?"

He figures that if he had bought the stock with that money that it would be worth at least $6 million today, but he also says he wouldn't be as happy.

We attended Michigan for two years after leaving Delta. I thought that we would get married after graduation, but Bill was giving serious thought to law school. They had a program at that time where, if you graduated from business school, you could have a law degree in two years instead of three. He went into graduate school in business at Michigan and I did my graduate work at Northwestern.

As a project for a business administration course, Bill essentially generated the idea for the all-purpose credit cards, like Master Card and Visa, before they ever came out. He called it the Continental Credit Card. You would deposit your paycheck with CCC and they would pay your bills for you and give you credit at stores and keep track of it all on computers. I think his professor was behind the eight-ball when he didn't pick up on this—he wasn't like Mr. Gordon—but I have to admit that I didn't, either.

I had completely forgotten about it when, years later, my sister Joan called and asked me if I had seen or heard about Visa and Master Card. "Wasn't that Bill's idea?" she said.

When I came home for the Christmas vacation of our first year in graduate school, Bill was still interested in law school and tried to persuade me to come back to Michigan to get my doctorate. I told him if I were going to do that, I would stay at Northwestern. I had a scholarship and it would be foolish not to take advantage of that.

One night, right after Christmas, we had just come home from a Michigan basketball game—I think it was against Butler—and we were parked in front of my parents' house.

He reached into this cardboard box full of basketball statistics that he always carried around with him and fished out an engagement ring. "Here," he said, and handed it to me. I ran into the house screaming. We were married the following summer, after we both had our master's degrees.

When we were first married, we traveled quite a bit throughout the United States. I think some of his interest has decreased because we've traveled so much the last few years, although if you see him in Europe or on vacation, he really has a great time. It's amazing. He gets into it if he's in a place where he's not easily recognized.

Bill knows a lot more about different things than you would think. When we were in Paris with an alumni group 10 years ago, we went into the Louvre. I don't know artists that well, but before he saw the nameplate on a painting, as soon as we walked into the room, Bill could identify the artist. Doesn't that blow your mind?

And—I could not believe this—we walked into one gallery and he said to me, "I want to take your picture in front of the *Mona Lisa*." I was shocked. I said, "Why would you care if I had my picture taken with the *Mona Lisa*?" But, you see, he had a really great art history instructor in junior college who made art come alive for him, and he remembered a tremendous amount.

Once he had worked in an office at Dow, he knew he did not want to be confined to a desk job. We talked one night right after we graduated and he said, "Janice, your family seems really happy. Your dad doesn't make a lot of money but you seem happy and your dad is doing what he really likes to do. What would you think if I thought about coaching? With the idea that we probably wouldn't make a lot of money." I said I thought it would be fine, that I would enjoy it.

We did have a lot of good times centered around basketball when we were going together. My brother and Bill would come home after my dad's high school games when we were in junior college and play what we called Living Room Basketball. We lived in an old house with high ceilings, and they'd roll up a sock and twist a coat hanger for a basket and hang it on the door to the stairs. They completely wore out our carpet.

Bill never would have gotten the job in Alpena if it hadn't been for me. I was home for spring break from Northwestern and they called from Alpena and wondered if I would come in for an interview and I said I didn't think so because my fiance was looking for a job as an assistant basketball coach and since Alpena hadn't contacted him I was pretty sure we were going to Rudyard.

And the secretary said, "Bill Frieder! We've been trying to call him all week long! The phone is continually busy."

"I know what the problem is," I said. "He's studying for exams and he takes the phone off the hook. But I'm going to see him. Do you want me to have him call you?"

She said she did, so we went up and had our interviews and were hired.

Bill always used to take the telephone off the hook and he'd probably have an unlisted number now, but I strongly object to that, and I always answer the telephone. I never let it ring. Sure, we get some crank calls, but the public really supports him to a large extent and he has done as well as he has, in terms of money as well as coaching, because of the public and their interest. So I think if somebody wants to call him and talk to him, they are entitled to do so. Where would he be if no one were interested in basketball?

I think, for the most part, Bill genuinely enjoys being with the players. A lot of coaches don't enjoy the kids that much. Bill is much more apt to go along with what they want than with what I want. Bill has not enjoyed young children, like three- or four-year-olds but, for example, when Jim Dutcher was in town and his son, Brian, who is now an assistant coach, was in the seventh or eighth grade, Bill would play card games and board games with him.

He does that with our daughter Laura, too. She and I were playing crazy eights once. Bill watched for a while, then he said, "Move aside. I'll show you how to play this game." And he started teaching her strategy. For crazy eights! He was an excellent bridge player, too, in addition to poker.

He and Laura think a lot alike. She's really great with math but I have to encourage her to read. One time, she was complaining about having to study history. I said, "Laura, don't you like to learn about different people in history?" And she said, "Who wants to learn about dead people?" That sounds a lot like Bill.

Laura knows the basketball stuff. She wants to get a hold of those stat sheets as soon as she can. I'm amazed, when she talks with the kids on the team, how much she's been paying attention to what's going on during the game. I don't really watch the game that way, to be able to analyze it, but she does.

One big difference between Bill and myself is that I've always been very interested in people and how they react, and I can enjoy being with people even if I don't particularly like them. I figure maybe they'll offer me a new insight. But Bill thinks, "Why waste the time?" Maybe it's because he has to be involved with people and I don't. When he has free time, he doesn't want to be with people he doesn't enjoy. I've done a lot of things like bicycle trips and hiking in Europe, and I will go by myself or with Laura. Bill would never take a chance on going on a vacation and being put with a group of people that he might not like.

Bill keeps his circle of friends pretty small, pretty limited, and a lot of those friends were initially my friends, like Nan and Steve Gill and even John Sposito, who is Bill's accountant. Bill is very good friends with him now but I was the one who initially sat down with him and his wife. It was at the NCAA regional in Lexington, Kentucky, in 1977, when John Orr was still head coach.

John said there was this great restaurant we had to go to. Bill said he wasn't going to go because he had film to look at and so on. I said, "Well, that doesn't prevent me from going." So I went with the Orrs and the Spositos were there and I got to know them and enjoyed them and encouraged Bill to develop a friendship with them.

The same thing happened with Don Fitch, who is an administrator at University Hospital. His wife and I had worked together and I invited them over for dinner one evening. Don loves sports and was asking Bill all kinds of questions. You know how Bill is. Sometimes when he's meeting people, his mind is elsewhere. He's off in a different world even when they're talking to him. He never asks about anything that he's not really interested in; no polite questions.

After they went home, I said, "Gee, you know, you should be more friendly when we have people for supper. Ask some questions and try to get involved in the conversation."

He said, "Janice, you know, he's a nice guy, but he asks so many questions, and I get those same questions over and over again." But somehow we had them over again and Bill did learn to adjust. Now they're great friends.

Once we were at Bogey Busters, that's a big golf tournament in Dayton, and they had a buffet with about 800 people, a lot of whom were big-name entertainers such as Bob Hope. We happened to be seated with one of the Secret Service agents assigned to President Ford. Bill was asking this man all sorts of questions because he was intrigued by the Secret Service. As a matter of fact, Bill and I at one time talked about becoming FBI agents.

And I said to the agent, "Your job must really be intriguing. You get to meet so many different people from all walks of life.

You come to events like this where you have the opportunity to meet celebrities."

He said, "Well, not really. After a while, it's just so many questions." I nudged Bill.

But when Bill does become involved with people, I think he becomes involved on a much deeper level than I do. He has a tremendous thing about loyalty and I think, for those people he really gets to know, he would probably be more loyal to them than I would be. When he gets to the people he really cares about, he's really sincere and he becomes involved.

He has some strange quirks. When we went to Las Vegas, for example, he would try to get autographs from entertainers. I would never do that. Bill made an effort to have Laura have her picture taken with President Ford. I had nothing to do with that. I didn't even really cooperate that much, but it was important to him.

He can't sit still. Almost the only time I can get him to go out to eat is in the summertime, when we can go to an outdoor cafe. He's a little more willing to sit in a situation like that, where he can watch people on the street and be diverted. He does not like being confined in a restaurant.

In church, he'll pull out the bulletin and start writing things down. He always has his mind on three things at once. I think one of the reasons he doesn't like to travel is because he doesn't like to be confined on a plane. And he doesn't read. I tried to encourage him to read because he would become interested and lose track of the time, lose himself in a book. But I don't think that happens with him. I don't think he ever gets that involved in a book. I don't know if he doesn't permit himself to do it or if he really can't.

The only thing he can lose himself in is playing cards. When he used to go out to Las Vegas and play blackjack, he could totally forget the basketball. That was the only thing that allowed him to block it out.

He does relax a little bit sometimes. I just never know when, like when we were in New Orleans for the NCAA championships in 1987. He loved Bourbon Street, absolutely loved it. We went down there several nights and it's like a continuous circus. They have mimes and tap dancers and all kinds of street entertainers, and the streets are very narrow, so they kind of blend in with the crowd. And right there in the middle of the French Quarter, Bill starts acting like a mime as he walks down Bourbon Street. I could not believe it. That's the kind of thing he does, and it's the kind of stuff he does with Laura, too. It occurs within the context of the situation. He doesn't go out and make plans. It just sort of happens. It's not structured or premeditated. Scheduled activities are not the way his fun happens, for the most part.

He has a lot of childlike qualities and that's one of the reasons he enjoys the players so much, because he can do that kind of thing with them all the time. I don't think he's an easy person to characterize because he has different aspects to his personality and sometimes they don't appear to fit.

Bill has always liked his players but, since we've had Laura, he's become more sensitive to the different needs that they have. He sees different aspects of their personalities. He sees them as more than just players, more as a total person. And I think he can appreciate their differences more and understand some of their behavior better than he did before.

He does a lot of surprise things, and he really comes through in important times. When we came to Ann Arbor, we started going to the First Congregational Church because Bill liked Terry Smith, the pastor there, so much. Bill had never been baptized and I had tried to convince him at different times that he should really think about it, but he never wanted to. I think it was sort of embarrassing to him.

So the day Laura was born, he came in and said, "You'll never guess where I was today."

I said, "How would I know?"

He said, "I went over and I had Terry baptize me."

I said, "You're kidding."

He said, "No, I went up to see Terry to see what I'd have to do and Terry was painting and he said, 'Come on, we'll just do it right now.' "

But that's the way Bill does things. He decides and then he does it. And he knew that was an important thing to me.

He was always a little bit apprehensive about having children, possibly because he didn't really remember his own childhood as being that happy. When I would read to Laura when she was little, I would mention different story book characters or nursery rhymes to him, and he had no idea what I was referring to. He had never heard of Cinderella or Jack in the Beanstalk or Hansel and Gretel. I don't know what he did as a youngster.

I'm sure he played games with the kids in his neighborhood but I think it was much more loosely structured than the situation I grew up in. Then, too, he spent a lot of time in his dad's store. He had a lot of "different" in his childhood, like going from no school for a year in Montreal to spending a year in a military academy. That's a big difference.

He was real concerned about being there when Laura was born. He said, "Gee, Janice, your dad wasn't there when you were born. Why should I be there?"

He was eating soup when I told him Laura was about due, and his hand just started shaking. I said, "What's wrong with you?"

He said, "I just don't know about this, Janice. Why am I going?"

I said, "You're going as a coach, to help out and provide me with support and encouragement. It's like your team, Bill. Do you think they need you there the day of the game?"

And he said, "Well, yeah."

And I said, "It's the same sort of deal. A lot of the work is done and you are prepared, but when you're going through something, you need that moral support and the direction that the head guy can give you."

It turned out he was on the road when I had Laura. He was calling in periodically to check on me and learned that I was on the way to the hospital. He literally came whipping into the delivery room. Because it was a Caesarean section, he was supposed to just sit at the head of the table and keep me company.

But, as usual, he started walking around and saying, "What's this? What's that?"

I said, "Bill, you've got to come up here and sit down."

He came and sat down and then he said, "Boy, Janice, are you going to be sore tomorrow!"

About a week later, he was going through the mail and he said, "Who's this Laura Frieder?"

I said, "Bill, that's our daughter." He comes and goes, if you know what I'm saying.

He never really wants any arguments from me. I remember one time when we were having an argument and he said, "Hey, Janice, look, we're supposed to be on the same team," as if to say, "Why are we arguing if we're husband and wife?" We can discuss but not argue.

The second year we were married, we realized that any time we had an argument it revolved around how he spent time and how I spent money. Bill would play poker twice a week until six in the morning and I would buy—remember we were only making about $5,000 a year each—$100 dresses. Bill could not understand that. Here was a man who bought two-dollar shoes. But I couldn't understand why he couldn't come home at three instead of six.

He said, "What you don't understand, Janice, is that when you are playing poker, you have to wait for certain hands, and it might not be until three in the morning that the cards start to change and you can make some money." Bill's not a gambler in the real sense. He only used cards to make money. It was a business.

I told him it was obvious we really didn't understand or appreciate each other's values in terms of time and money and that we had to do something about. It seemed foolish to continue to argue about these things when we could really identify it.

I said, "If that's the case, then you really only need to stay if you're making money. And if you're making that much money, you should be willing to share some of it with me if I'm willing to let you stay out until 6 a.m."

So we agreed that he could play cards as late as he wanted but he owed me five dollars for every 15 minutes he was out after 3 a.m. Remember, this was back in 1967. It added up to a fair amount of money. If he didn't come home until 6 a.m., I had $60, which I could apply to a dress that I wanted. Since Bill doesn't play cards anymore, my wardrobe is suffering.

A lot of people say to me, "I would never marry a coach." Some coaches' wives say that they might not do it again, that they don't get any recognition or it's too stressful or whatever, but I don't really feel that way. I think that Bill's job is something I've truly enjoyed. We've had shared values and we've worked together for a common goal.

There are tremendous benefits to being in this position. One is that Bill and I have something in common that we're both interested in and enjoy giving a good amount of our attention. Another is the travel, which we've been able to do much more extensively than we would in most other professions. And we've met a lot of interesting people — presidents, governors, senators — that we wouldn't have had the opportunity to meet, and Laura has been exposed to these people, too.

But beyond that, I've really enjoyed the relationships that we've been able to establish with the players' parents, particularly the mothers — Verna Bodnar, Lois Heuerman, Jan Henderson, Mary Grant, Saliner Tarpley and Helen Ford, Rumeal Robinson's mother. They are all special to me. They know that we're just as interested in their sons' education and personality and interests as we are in basketball. When I'm with the mothers, we hardly even mention basketball. We're more involved in conversations about other areas of interest.

Speaking of relationships, I have to mention John Orr. We really had a good time with John. He was hysterically funny. And when we came down to Ann Arbor, he was concerned about our living arrangements and the like. It wasn't just, "Here's your salary; find a place to live." John helped us secure a loan. He didn't just give us the name of someone to call but, when it looked like we might not get the loan at a good interest rate, he hopped in and said, "C'mon, I know you can do better than this." He stuck his neck out for us.

Bill was fortunate in the people he worked under. Both Dick

Dennis and John Orr gave him what he needed when he needed it. Part of the reason Bill relates to the players so well is that the way he grew up wasn't unlike the way some of them have grown up. I think he gives kids more opportunities and chances than another coach might because of some of the opportunities and chances he had himself.

Of all the different fields that one's husband could be in, this is one that allows more active participation than most. Basketball really serves as a common ground, and when the end of the year comes, you can start over and make plans for the new season. There's always hope. There's always renewal.

4

Rocky Start to the NIT

To me, there was little adjustment in becoming head coach. At least, I can't think of much. I had been a head coach in high school. Even with the jayvees, I had been in charge of my own team. I wasn't just assisting somebody with a team. And my seven years as an assistant at Michigan taught me the things I needed to know specifically about the college situation.

The job happened so fast. John left and almost everybody thought I was going to be the head coach and I was right in the middle of recruiting, which was principally Tim McCormick, and we went through the summer and into the fall and into the season and I never stopped to think about it.

I knew I could coach. I knew I could handle kids. And I knew I could do all the other things that had to be done. Going from high school to college was a bigger adjustment. I think there might be some difficulty going from assistant to head coach if the assistant had never had head coaching experience, but I think the fact that I had

had that experience and won the state championships gave me the confidence I needed.

That first summer I was head coach, I made 42 home recruiting visits. You could go on the road then through all of July, August and September, but I was stupid because I just went in everywhere. You can still go into as many homes as you want, but you can only make three visits for each kid, and the time span is limited. It's a lot different from the old days.

The way my first season started, it almost looked too easy. I think part of it was we had four seniors who started—Mike McGee, Marty Bodnar, Paul Heuerman and Johnny Johnson. We won nine straight in the non-conference for the best start by a Michigan team in 17 years, lost at Purdue in the Big Ten opener, then took seven of the next nine. McGee was playing the best basketball of his career. Three of our first six Big Ten games went into overtime and we won all three (although, ironically, we lost the three that were regulation games), including beating Indiana, the eventual national champion, at Crisler in the third conference game of the season. We eventually played five overtime games that season and won four of them.

So there I was, a rookie head coach at the college level, with my team 7–3 in the Big Ten, 16–3 overall and ranked 10th or 12th in the country in most polls. And then the wheels came off. We lost six in a row, starting with an 18-point licking at home by Ohio State and including a four-point defeat at home by Northwestern. That's the only time Northwestern has ever won at Crisler Arena.

I'll be the first to admit that if it were me right now, somehow we would have prevented the six-game losing streak. We're doing things now that we didn't do that first year. I think our mental and physical approach and preparation are much improved since then.

We lost a tough one at Illinois, when we didn't even get there until the day of the game because of weather problems, before coming back to play Northwestern. We came home and I let them go and took off recruiting when we should have talked about getting mentally ready for Northwestern and not allowing the Illinois trip to cost us a victory. Maybe we should have come back at night and gotten a good 30 minutes of serious shooting. There are so many things we probably should have done that we didn't, but that's how you learn.

We beat Minnesota at home to end the streak, lost to Purdue in overtime on the road to end the regular season, and got invited to the NIT for the second year in a row. They gave us two games at home, just like the year before, and we beat Duquesne and Toledo. Then they sent us on the road, just like the year before, and we lost, just like the year before, except to Syracuse instead of to Virginia.

The trouble with having so many seniors in the lineup is that you have so many players to replace the next season, and then I wound up having even more to replace than I had expected. Tim McCormick's knees gave him trouble all through his freshman year and he finally had surgery over the summer, which meant he would miss the entire season. Then Jon Antonides, a 7-footer from Sarnia, Ontario, got stepped on at practice the day before the season opener, suffered a scrotum hematoma, and was also out for the season.

They were our only players over 6'7". We had already lost our experience, and now our size was gone, too. Our pre-season practices were lousy and so was the season, the worst of my career and Michigan's worst since 1960. After the Ohio State football game, Bo gave me Greg Washington and Dave Hall as he was very concerned about our situation. He took Hall back for the Bluebonnet Bowl, but at least I had enough players to hold a practice. M. C. Burton left the team right before Christmas and Joe James was suspended right after.

We actually managed to play pretty tough at Arkansas on national TV in the opener but then we came home and lost to Eastern Michigan. We beat Northern Michigan, a Division II school, but we lost at Western Michigan, and then at home to Detroit (by four) and Louisiana Tech (by one) and then in a Christmas tournament in Los Angeles to Southern Cal and Alabama-Birmingham (by one).

The kids showed a lot of class. There was no friction in the locker room, no carping or squawking. My hat is off to Thad Garner. It was his senior year and he was the captain and I know it had to be a disappointment to him, to say the least, but he hung in and hung in and just never quit.

Once we got to be 1–10, which happened after we lost at Indiana by 30 points, we just wrote it off as 1–26. Laura was two years old and I'd go home and she'd smile and say, "Hi, daddy." She didn't know my record. I think, if nothing else, it gave me a different perspective on life. I had fun the rest of the year.

We'd play a game on Saturday, then I'd give the players Sunday and Monday off. On Tuesday, I'd let the assistants handle practice so I could recruit, then I'd practice with them on Wednesday and we'd play on Thursday.

I think keeping those kids together after losing four players was a fantastic job. After we were 1–13, we came back to win five of the next eight, and we upset Ohio State and Iowa when they were leading the league and Illinois (we came from eight behind, I think it was, to win by two) when they were challenging for the lead. We helped Minnesota slip into the championship.

The Ohio State game was unforgettable. Eric Turner missed two free throws after time expired in regulation time and I thought we were done. Then, when the kids went back on the court for the overtime, the fans gave 'em a standing ovation. If you don't think that makes a difference, you're wrong. Dan Pelekoudas beat 'em at the buzzer in overtime. We just hung in and hung in and hung in.

The day of the Ohio State game, a big piece by Lynn Henning appeared in the *Detroit News* on what was wrong with the Michigan program. The illustration with it was this huge, crumbling block "M." I'll give Henning credit. He opened the press conference by saying, "This doesn't look like a crumbling program to me."

I respected those kids for the way they stayed together when they could have gone in the tank or started playing for themselves. They were still trying at the end, winning at Wisconsin on the next-to-last day of the season, then coming home and battling Notre Dame right down to the buzzer at the Silverdome before losing by a point.

Considering how the season started, it felt pretty positive by the end. Part of it was the way the team hung in there, and part of it was the recruiting year we had, getting Roy Tarpley (although he was not the most publicized of the group), Richard Rellford, Butch Wade, Robert Henderson and Paul Jokisch. Tim McCormick would be coming back, and so would Turner and Leslie Rockymore, who had matured fast as freshmen in that situation.

Nine games into the 1982–83 season, we were 8–1, which meant we had already won one more than all of the previous season. But other than Kansas, we hadn't really beaten anybody, and we still hadn't when we went into the Big Ten opener at Northwestern with a 9–1 record and promptly lost. We were 2–7 halfway through the conference season and wound up ninth with a 6–12 record.

I think some coaches might have panicked in that situation and started fooling around with the lineup or looking at jaycees or whatever, but I hung in there with those guys. I knew they'd be good someday and I wasn't going to jeopardize their future, or the program's, by demoralizing them. If it meant accepting a ninth-place finish, so be it.

As it was, we were a lot harder to beat than we had been the year before. It took Purdue three overtimes to beat us at Crisler, and we upset Indiana, which was ranked fourth at the time, by 13 points late in February. They went on to win the league championship.

Iowa coach George Raveling said at the beginning of the 1983–84 season that we had the best talent in the league from one through 15. I said they should make a rule that new coaches in the league know how to count, since I only had 14 players on my roster.

I had that team spend a bigger share of its practice time on defense than any team of mine before it, high school or college. We worked on a skill drill, which is just fundamentals and positioning in relation to where the ball is.

And we worked much harder on all types of defensive situations. A guy gets beaten; now what are the other four supposed to do? A guy takes a charge and falls down but it's not called; now what are the other guys supposed to do? A guy fronts and there's a good lob; what are the other four guys supposed to do? We tried to teach defense as a team as it relates to all kinds of situations, rather than just doing one-on-one, which was the old, conventional way of working on defense.

We won our first eight that year, then lost to Texas-El Paso and Texas Tech by a point each in the Sun Bowl Classic. We beat Northwestern at home to start the Big Ten season, then almost blew a 20–3 lead over Iowa before winning, 53–49. Our next game was on the road at Minnesota and it was notable on two counts: It was only our fifth win in three years on the road in the Big Ten, and it was Roy Tarpley's first start.

Rick Olson scored 39 points against us at Wisconsin and we lost by seven (although the Badgers later had to forfeit that game and all the others they played in 1982, '83 and '84), then we came home and Ohio State beat us.

Two days later, we played Indiana. This was the day Bobby Knight disrupted my post-game press conference after we beat them, 55–50, with a great effort. That's pretty much the order in which the media covered the stories, too. Indiana shot only 42 percent from the field, and Rockymore, Joubert, Pelekoudas and Eric Turner took turns guarding Steve Alford, holding him to 12 points.

We were 4–2, our best start in the Big Ten since my first year.

Then we went to Purdue and lost by four (really only two; we scored and didn't have any timeouts left so we took a technical and they made two free throws). We went to Illinois from there and lost in four overtimes. We went to Michigan State and lost by five. All of a sudden, we were 4–5 and everybody wanted to know what was wrong. Nothing was wrong except that we'd been playing on the road in the Big Ten.

Sure enough, we turned around and beat Michigan State at home a week later, then beat Illinois at Crisler, too, before Purdue beat us by three in overtime. We had lost eight games at this point— two by a point in El Paso, one at the buzzer to Ohio State, one in one overtime, one in four overtimes, one by four on the road and one by five on the road. Our worst loss had been by seven points. Some of the writers were nervous wrecks, but we were playing good basketball. I was satisfied with my team. We were there. We were just young, but I knew we were going to be all right.

After Purdue, Indiana beat us in Bloomington by 15, but we came back from that to win in Columbus, the first time in six years that Michigan had beaten a first-division team on the road in the Big Ten. We only lost one more after that. . .and that was in overtime, too. I knew these guys were knocking on the door.

One of the negative aspects of the season was the way some of the fans booed Dan Pelekoudas. They just couldn't understand why he would be out there instead of Joubert, who was a freshman. It wasn't who he was, but who he wasn't. The same people probably booed Joubert three years later. I was upset about that.

Dan Pelekoudas is what college athletics is all about, or at least what it was originally intended to be: 4.0 students out there doing extra-curricular activities.

In retrospect, the greatest thing that ever happened to this program was losing at Northwestern in the last Big Ten game of the 1984 season, even though we got screwed in the game and we got screwed by the NCAA selection committee. We were 18–9 going into that game and we figured a win would lock up a tournament berth. But we always seem to have a tough time there, and here we were in overtime against them.

We had the ball with about 14 seconds to go and the score tied and we were going for the winning shot. Rockymore missed one and Ralph Rosser, one of the officials, came running from midcourt to call a foul on Tarpley on the rebound with two seconds to go. It was a bad call. It was a call you don't make in that situation, especially the official out of position. Northwestern makes both ends of the one-and-one and we lose by two.

We still thought we had a shot. We were 18–10, 16–2 at Crisler Arena, and we finished fourth in the Big Ten. I never said anything before, but we really got treated unfairly. They took teams with 17 wins, they took teams with 11 losses, and we played a tougher schedule than half the teams they took, most notably Dayton, who was also 18–10 and whom we beat by 22 points. The *Sporting News* ranked us 26th in the country and we couldn't make a 53-team field.

I never said a word about it. I was positive about it. I said we're going to go into the NIT with enthusiasm, and it ended up being great for us because we won the NIT, we got tremendous exposure and it set the stage for winning back-to-back Big Ten championships. From the day they won the NIT, all those kids talked about was winning the league. They gained a world of confidence. Not only that, but we won 20 games. We wound up 23–10. (Wisconsin's forfeit later changed it to 24–9.) If we had gone to the NCAA tournament, we probably would have won one and lost one and finished 19–11.

So if Bobby Knight engineered us going to the NIT that year, it came back to haunt him, and I think he probably was involved. He told the Associated Press that only three Big Ten teams — Purdue, Illinois and Indiana — deserved to go, and I heard he was on the phone to some people on the committee. You know how strong he is with the head honchos, so I think he had some influence.

I took the team to Europe for the first time that spring. We went to Luxembourg; Amsterdam; Athens; and Nice, France. I came up with the idea after we recruited that class with Tarpley, Henderson, Jokisch, Wade and Rellford. I knew that it would be important for them to get that type of experience, and get that experience at the right time.

I thought the right time was between their sophomore and junior years, when they'd been through enough at this end to know what it took to be successful. They'd matured some within my system, so now this was another step in the right direction at the right time in their development.

Of course, just how much they were about to develop exceeded even my expectations.

5

"Guaranteed" to Win?

Eric Turner went hardship during the off season and Tim McCormick, who had been redshirted the year he was injured, decided not to use his last year of eligibility. The night we won the NIT, both his mom and his dad came up to me and said it was a good way for Tim to end his career, so I knew he was gone. He was upset when he wasn't accepted in graduate school at Michigan, which I think was the main reason he played so poorly at Northwestern. He got the letter the day before we went there, just a cold, hard rejection letter. And this was a kid who did so much for so many, spoke at every banquet and attended any function to which he was asked. He was an outstanding citizen at the university. I tried to talk him out of leaving, but I couldn't.

For the second year in a row, we won our first eight games, but then we lost on the road at Tennessee and Indiana came in and trounced us by 25 points in Crisler in the Big Ten opener. The Hoosiers had upset the North Carolina team with James Worthy, Sam Perkins and Michael Jordan in the NCAA tournament the previous spring.

They looked like the national champs. We looked like a seventh-place team.

That was on a Thursday night. On Saturday afternoon, not much more than 40 hours later, we came back to beat a good Ohio State team, 87–82. I think the loss to Indiana woke the kids up. They realized, "Hey, the coach is right. We aren't very good on defense." That turned out to be the most points we allowed anybody all season.

Beating Ohio State was pivotal, because then we went on the road to Champaign and lost in overtime, so we could have been 0–3 in the league real quick. Instead, we were 1–2, and then we won 15 straight games (16 overall, including beating 15th-ranked Kansas by 19 at home on national television; we were up by 31 before they scored the last 12 points) and the Big Ten championship, our first in eight years.

There were two other especially significant games in that streak: coming back to win at Purdue after starting the first road trip with a loss at Illinois, and the triple overtime win over Iowa at home. We beat Purdue decisively, by 16, and it showed we could win on the road and that we weren't going to let one loss lead to another, like we used to do before.

Beating Iowa, the third victory in the streak, set the stage for our success. The Hawkeyes were supposed to be the team to beat, and we were down, 12–0, right at the start and 30–18 at the half. Tarpley made the winning shot at the buzzer and said later that he ran off the court so fast afterward because he didn't want anyone to see him cry. If we had lost that game, who knows where the Big Ten race would have gone?

We came a long, long way. And the 15th one was right there on Indiana's court. That was sweet, and there's no better way than at the buzzer. The man who made the shot, of course, was Gary Grant, who was the main reason we came back to win the title. That was the first time in 20 years a Michigan team had won in Bloomington, and the first time any Michigan team had ever beaten Indiana in Assembly Hall. It was also the first time in the game we had the lead.

And guess who wound up the seventh-place team? Indiana, that's who.

I was so wrapped up in the season that I didn't pay that much attention while it was going on, but when I looked back at it, I was awed by that winning streak. I'd look at the films and just be amazed at how easy they made it look. And seven of our 16 Big Ten victories were by five points or less. We were winning the close games we had lost the year before.

We went to Dayton for the first round of the NCAA tournament. We were ranked second in the country and seeded first in the Southeast Region. In our first game, we struggled and struggled and struggled and finally beat Fairleigh Dickinson, 59–55. In our second game, we struggled and struggled and struggled and finally lost to Villanova by the same score.

What people don't understand is I knew Villanova was a great team when I scouted them. I didn't care that they had 10 losses. Six of them were to Georgetown and St. John's, which were the best teams in their league, and they were all one-pointers or overtime. Then they lost at Maryland by three. They did get blown out by Pittsburgh early in the season, but they came back to beat Pitt in the conference tournament. So most of their losses could be discounted, and they were playing very well at the time. They also had four senior starters and we had none, and they were in their sixth straight NCAA tournament, where we hadn't been to one in eight years.

We actually played pretty good basketball, but they dictated tempo and our guards didn't shoot well. If there's one thing I've learned from the tournament, it's that you've gotta watch freshmen. Gary Grant hurt us against Villanova and Glen Rice hurt us the next year against Iowa State. Gary had no points, no rebounds, no steals, one assist and three turnovers before fouling out with five minutes to go.

Our front line was good and we hung in there, but we got a bad call, a terrible call, when we had a chance to go ahead by three. They called a block on Butch Wade instead of a charge on Villanova, and we just couldn't get over the hump down the stretch.

But Villanova proved they were a team because they went on to win the national championship.

Repeating as Big Ten champs was a great job. We were the only team to do it since Indiana in 1975–76. And we were the only Division I team in the country to repeat as regular-season champs. In fact, no pro team—in any sport—repeated that year, either. Everybody was having trouble.

We started off by winning the Chaminade Tournament in Hawaii, the first time a Michigan team ever won a tournament, other than an NCAA regional, outside the state. We beat a good Virginia Tech team by a point when Gary Grant tipped in a missed free throw by Wade with 17 seconds to go, then blocked a shot by Dell Curry with three seconds left to clinch it. We ripped Kansas State for the title, and then came one of the big, big victories of my career at Michigan.

After seven or eight days in Hawaii, we came back to Ann Arbor for one day and then went to Springfield, Massachusetts, to play Georgia Tech in the Hall of Fame game. So we've traveled about 7,000 miles in two days and we're playing the top-ranked team in the country. People looked on it as a terrible game because the final score was 49–44 and we shot 31.1 percent and they shot 29.6 percent. At one point, we went 18 straight possessions without scoring.

But it was a hard-fought game, a great defensive game. We were down by eight at the half and we won by five. The media and many other people missed the key point, as they never mentioned a 13-point turnaround in a game that ended in the 40s with the number-one team in the country. What a great job, to come back with that kind of swing in such a low-scoring game.

We were 16–0 and 4–0 in the Big Ten before losing at Minnesota. We went to Iowa and won there, but then lost three of the next eight, two of them to Michigan State. The Spartans even beat us by 15 at home. This was after Joubert "guaranteed" that we would beat Michigan State at home. I closed the locker room to the press after that. I also "guaranteed" we would win the Big Ten title, just to take the pressure off the players and put it on me. Luckily, we did win it. That was a strange season in one respect—we lost only four games before the tournament and three of them were by 10 or more points.

After the second loss to MSU, we came back to play Alabama-Birmingham on national television, one of those teams that the fans don't think is any good but you, as a coach, know better. The season could have gone down the tubes right there. We were struggling. The fans were booing. But we hung in there and hung in there and finally got the lead and beat 'em down the stretch, 62–54.

Hanging in when things aren't going well is a key. You do that with substitutions, with timeouts, with changing your offenses and defenses, and you hope something will jell. Hanging in is so important, especially because you can have bad calls, you can have a bad break, you can have a bad spurt, and you've gotta hang in like gangbusters when that's going on.

So we come in to the last game of the regular season and we're playing Indiana in Crisler and we're both 13–4. It's one game to decide the outright championship and the two teams in contention are playing each other. How often do you get to see something like that, much less take part in it?

And, boy, were we ready. It was such a big game and we beat 'em by 28 points. That's the worst beating that a Bobby Knight Indiana team ever took. Mort says he still has a copy of the final stat sheet. He's going to get it framed. That was the greatest victory in Crisler Arena ever. It was for the Big Ten championship. It was the last game of the season. It was on national television. It was the largest crowd here ever—14,198—and it was the best crowd here ever.

That's something they can't take away from me, or from any other Michigan fan, even though the NCAA tournament was a disappointment again. We went to Minneapolis, we were seeded second in the Midwest Region, and we had trouble in the first game again, this time edging Akron, 70–64, before losing in the second game again, this time to Iowa State, 72–69.

That was one of those emotional things. They had a lot of Michigan kids, it was Johnny Orr, and they played their butts off. They shot 60 percent, played over their heads, and we made some freshman errors. If I had that to do over again, I might have Glen Rice out of there in the last couple of minutes.

I was happy for Johnny Orr that they beat us, I really was, because they never gave him the credit he deserved here. But then in the next game, they were awful. They shot 32 percent or something and North Carolina State beat 'em. You've got to be lucky in tournaments. Anybody can get you any time, and I'm not going to jump off a bridge when they do.

Richard Rellford and Butch Wade were good kids, tough kids, hard-nosed competitors. They found a way, defensively or on the boards or whatever. Wade was a terrible foul shooter, but he never went to the line in a crucial situation and lost us a game. He made big free throws for us. Those guys would rebound and be tough and take charges, and that's what our inside guys didn't do enough of in 1987–88.

Rellford was never hurt. In four years at Michigan, he was never hurt. Those guys always played over that stuff. It didn't matter what happened to Butch. He could run into a train today and be ready to play tomorrow. My kids last year weren't as tough, and that was part of the problem.

Don't sell those two Big Ten championship teams short. Hardly anyone worked harder than they did, especially the second year.

I didn't just lose four great players between seasons. I lost my dad, too. He passed away on Sept. 23, 1986, less than a month before his 68th birthday. He supposedly had retired when he was 65, but he still put in lots of hours at the Florida Market. He'd had heart trouble all his life. When I was in Flint, a cardiologist my doctor sent me to said I had a defective mitral valve in my left ventricle. I was still seeing the cardiologist regularly, sort of having him monitor it, after I became an assistant at Michigan. But then he was killed in an auto accident and, quite frankly, I figured it was one less thing I had to deal with, and it was years before I consulted anyone else about it.

That 1986–87 team was a roller coaster. They really didn't have a whole lot more potential than the 7–20 team of 1981–82. Gary Grant and Antoine Joubert were back, of course, but expecting a guard, even one as good as Gary, to be your top scorer, leading defender, team leader, playmaker and so on is asking a lot, and Joubert was playing out of position at forward.

So what we had, basically, was a three-guard (Grant, Joubert and Garde Thompson), three-sophomore (Mark Hughes, Glen Rice, Loy Vaught) team. And Vaught had been redshirted as a freshman, so he was really a rookie.

But they were a lot of fun. Thompson had a lot to do with that, both by being such a loose, fun-loving operator off the court and an explosive three-point threat on it. He almost single-handedly brought us back against Indiana at Crisler Arena. They led us by 17 at the half but with Garde popping in three-pointers from everywhere, we actually were ahead by a point before Steve Alford beat us with a basket with one second to go. And Garde set an NCAA tournament record with nine three-pointers against Navy in the first game of the tournament.

Those guys were performers, no doubt about that. Every time the TV lights went on, so did they. Three times, we played teams ranked in the top five on national television in Crisler. Three times we won. We beat Syracuse, 91–88. We beat Iowa, 100–92. And, in one of the most amazing performances by any Michigan team ever, we just destroyed Purdue, which was ranked third in the country and gunning for an undisputed Big Ten title, by 36 points in the last game of the regular season.

The day before the Iowa game, I almost killed my top assistant, Steve Fisher. We weren't practicing well. There was not enough concentration and I really got mad at the team, yelling and swearing and ranting and raving. I was on 'em something fierce. They were facing me in a semicircle, and Fisher was on my left, part of the way between me and the players. There was a basketball sitting on the floor and, when I got good and worked up, I took one step and hauled off and kicked it as hard as I possibly could.

Fisher couldn't have been more than five feet away from me,

and it caught him point-blank in the face. He went down for the count and we all thought he was dead. I didn't know whether to laugh or cry. Fortunately, and almost miraculously, all he had was a black eye and a bunch of bruises. But I guess I got their attention.

I got their attention before we played Purdue to end the regular season, too. On the Wednesday before that game, which was on a Saturday, Illinois came into Crisler and beat us by 14 points. That should never happen, never. Everyone loses at home once in a while. In fact, next to winning the NCAA tournament, my biggest unmet goal is winning every Big Ten home game in a season. We've gone 8–1 four times but never 9–0. But the point is, you shouldn't lose at home by 14.

My staff and I stayed at Crisler until 4 a.m. after that game, looking at film. We were back at 6 a.m. to go another six hours. By the time the players arrived for practice that afternoon, we had a show for them. We showed them five possessions against Syracuse, then five possessions against Illinois, then five possessions against Iowa, then five possessions against Illinois.

I don't think I ever watched so much film in my life. I know the players hadn't. But it paid off. It was all worthwhile. We appealed to their pride and what Michigan is all about. We reminded them they were here for the purpose of playing to their potential. And it was a credit to them that they responded the way they did.

What the heck, they were overachievers all year. A lot of people forget that Navy, whom we played in the first round of the NCAA East Regional at Charlotte, North Carolina, was seeded higher than we were. Sure, David Robinson scored 50 points, but the rest of his team only scored 32 and we won by 15. That gave us 20 wins for the season and I was pretty happy about that, too.

I wasn't even that unhappy about losing to North Carolina. They scored the first 12 points of the game and then we played them even the rest of the way. They were up by 17 at the half and we cut it to six in the first four minutes of the second half before running out of gas. Even the North Carolina players said we gave them one of their hardest games of the season.

For a year that I thought would be a throwaway, we did pretty well. But the fact remains that I would rather have all the great expectations and have people say I can't coach, as long as we win the Big Ten. I'd rather do that than finish fifth and have people say what a great job I did.

Two days after we beat Purdue, and a day after we found out that the NCAA had nullified Sean Higgins' commitment to UCLA, I flew to Holland, which is on the other side of the state, to watch Matt Steigenga, at that time a junior at Grand Rapids South Christian. What with one thing and another, I was so jacked up when we landed back in Ann Arbor that I took off running across the landing strip toward my car.

You know those blocks of wood that keep the plane's wheels in place? I tripped on one and somersaulted a couple of times and scraped my arms and legs and knees and hands. I was a bloody mess. Even worse, my briefcase flew open and all my folders — on recruiting, on Navy, on my investments — started blowing around in the wind. I chased down as much as I could, wiped the blood off my hands, jumped into my car and started going 70 in a 30 m.p.h zone.

Then I thought to myself, "Maybe that fall was a warning. Maybe I should slow down."

So I buckled my seat belt.

6

Six Days in the Life of Bill Frieder

On the morning of Monday, Dec. 7, 1987, Bill Frieder sits in his office in the University of Michigan athletic administration building, flipping through several sheets of closely typed paper.

It's not a big office, perhaps 12 feet by 16 feet, and it's dominated by his desk, which is perpetually strewn with a layer of papers about half an inch deep. There are pictures on the wall of Laura riding horseback, of Gerald Ford, of the 1984 NIT champions and the 1985 and '86 Big Ten champions. Opposite his desk, between the door and the wall, is a color television monitor connected to a satellite dish. He often comes in here at night after his own game to watch somebody else's.

There is at least one good reason why the desk is positioned so that his back is to the window: The view is of a parking lot and the wall of another wing of the building. No wonder he'd rather face the TV set.

Four of the pages Frieder is studying are stapled together: the day-by-day schedules, from

Dec. 11–30, of all the high school players he and his staff are currently courting. There are also two loose sheets, one each for assistant Mike Boyd's recruiting schedule and Frieder and top assistant Steve Fisher's schedule. Assembling these calendars is complicated—for example, certain coaches need to be at Michigan's practices or games on certain days—and they remain maddeningly tentative. The staff might decide to "get off" some players before they're scheduled to see them (if, say, someone else commits to the Wolverines and obviates the need to find another shooting guard, or someone commits to another school) or get on the trail of others they hadn't previously considered (if, say, a player who committed somewhere else changes his mind, or a source calls with a tip on some youngster who's suddenly blossoming).

Boyd's calendar shows him seeing at least one player every day, in either a game or a practice, from the 11th through the 30th, with the exception of Christmas Day. Several days he's scheduled to see two players, either one in the afternoon and one in the evening or one in each game of a tournament doubleheader. If all goes according to plan, he will see 15 players, some of them twice, in the 20-day stretch.

Such planning was less vital prior to the 1987–88 season, when new NCAA rules limited both the number of times a coach or his staff could see a player and the dates during which they were permitted to do so.

"You can only see four games a year per player," Frieder explains. "You don't go on the road so much but you've really gotta plan. You don't want to see anybody more than twice in December. I don't like all this record-keeping. Before, if I decided to see a game, I'd just go see it. But I think they're all good rules."

Assistant Athletic Director Will Perry comes in to tell Frieder that the carpeting for the weight room has been approved and to complain about the money he's spending on videotape. He points out that the idea of videotape is to save money by reusing it. "Can you stand an audit?" he asks.

Frieder says a lot of tape has gone out to other schools in film exchanges (coaches, for some reason, persist in calling tape "film," the way people still "dial" push-button phones).

Not only that, points out Steve Fisher, who has come into the office for a meeting, but "the football guys were down here borrowing tapes the other day."

Momentarily mollified, Perry leaves. "He okayed $2,500 for carpeting, then he complains about a $12 videotape," Frieder says.

Boyd joins them and the meeting begins. "Okay," says Frieder, "five minutes on Kirk Taylor. We've gotta decide today. He plays tonight [against Western Michigan] or we redshirt him. One reason for that is it's best for Kirk Taylor. It would help in recruiting Jimmy Jackson [a junior guard from Toledo ranked as one of the top prospects in the country], and then we can concentrate on Rumeal and Sean playing more, and that's all good. But if we do that and redshirt him and it costs us a ball game or two, I don't want that.

"Iowa and Ohio State...their pressure defense is pretty good, and then watchin' our bleepin' practice yesterday...I guess if I had to vote this minute, I'd say let's redshirt him."

"You can make a case either way," says Fisher. "One thing we talked about before is will it cost us a game? Kirk Taylor, at this point, is not a ball-handling guard. But what if Rumeal goes down? What if Gary goes down?"

"If Gary goes down," says Frieder, "the season is over."

"The thing is," says Boyd, "if you don't redshirt him, you have to give him playing time. You've gotta give him more than three or four minutes a game in the non-conference."

"If you had to vote, how would you vote?" Frieder asks.

"I'd say redshirt him," says Fisher. "In fairness to Kirk Taylor. It's the best thing for him."

"I agree," says Frieder. "I think that's what we're gonna do. Gary's a 40-minute player, Rumeal is getting better, Griffin is steady, and Higgins, we just gotta get Higgins better."

"If the decision is made to redshirt Kirk," says Boyd, "we have to get Higgins better at ball handling."

Frieder points out that Griffin "is smart enough not to hurt us if he's rested. In a 90-second game, he gives us no minuses."

"Can he bring it up?" Boyd asks.

"In a delay game," Frieder answers.

"Hughes is smart enough, Mills is big enough, and we've gotta have Gary," says Fisher, speculating on a possible delay game lineup.

"It depends on how quick and what the defense is," says Frieder. "Okay. Mike. Where do we stand on this?" He brandishes the recruiting schedules.

Boyd ticks off a condensed version of his itinerary. "Mitchell is playing a big game on the 18th," he notes. Sam Mitchell is a junior from Kalamazoo; Boyd will be in New Albany, Indiana, that day to see a prospect named Pat Graham. "Steve could see [Tony] Tolbert [a Detroit prospect] and you could go see Mitchell on the 18th," Boyd says to Frieder.

"I was going to see Mitchell on the 11th," says Fisher. "Now we're changing that?"

Frieder notes that Boyd is in Toledo on the 22nd with the 23rd and 24th up in the air, although he might fly down to Florida to watch a couple of players practice. "You taking Christmas off?" Frieder asks Boyd.

"There's no game," he shrugs. "When is Steve gonna see that kid in Texas?"

"You're gonna see him on the 22nd," Frieder tells Fisher. "Schoettelkott. Todd Schoettelkott, in Texas. You tell her on those airline tickets not to get you tied up with that 100 percent cancellation stuff. Those are gonna change."

"Okay," says Frieder, "I'm seeing Weber on the 11th, Jackson on the 15th, Tolbert the afternoon of the 18th. . . ." He has two more questions for Boyd.

"Anything on Boykin's transcripts?"

"He's still not playing?" That one gets answered with another question.

"Did you talk to the admissions office about [Eric] Riley [a seven-footer from Cleveland who just signed with Michigan]?"

"I talked to Torres. He said he'd have all the information."

The conversation turns to that night's game. It means more than most non-conference games with intrastate rivals because Western Michigan beat the Wolverines — in Crisler, no less — the year before.

"You have to make the point, again, that this Western team had a 16-point lead on us," Fisher says. "We came back, got in the game, then lost it at the end."

" 'Cause we didn't have anything left," says Frieder.

"We dug too deep a hole," agrees Fisher.

"We gotta come out and play like we did against Central [Michigan, whom the Wolverines beat by 30 points the previous Saturday afternoon]," says Frieder. "I shouldn't sub as soon. If they're not ready early, we should get 'em out of there quick. I think they're ready."

"We've gotta get the ball inside," says Fisher. "Mills has gotta have the ball."

"We called Central right, didn't we?" Frieder whoops with pleasure. "They played man all year and they came out in a zone. Hammer! Hammer!"

Assistant Coach Dave Hammer's voice floats in from the next room. "He's dead."

"You gotta get in here," says Frieder, as Boyd and Fisher depart. "I'm calling Bill Dunifan [the vice president at Augusta College in Georgia, where Hammer has applied for the head coaching job]. Anything you want me to emphasize?"

"Just tell him the job I've done," says Hammer modestly. "Tell him my bags are packed."

Frieder can't get through to Dunifan, so he calls the Michigan sports information office to complain about not having updated statistics to peruse before he goes to the University of Michigan Club of Ann Arbor's Monday luncheon at Weber's Inn, a hotel on the western edge of town. Frieder speaks there every week during the season.

"Who's this?" he demands when his call is answered. "Frank? Well, listen, Frank, this is Frieder. I'm putting you in charge of getting those statistics over here." His impatience stems from the fact that while the head coach can't seem to obtain the statistics, he's absolutely convinced that there will be a copy of them at each place setting in Weber's banquet room.

When he arrives at Weber's after a six-minute drive that would have taken anyone else at least 10 minutes, a huge salad and two iced teas are waiting for him. So are the statistics.

This week, every week, the format calls for an opening speaker, usually the coach of a so-called minor sport like volleyball or swimming, followed by a few warmup remarks from Frieder, an interview with local sportscaster Jeff DeFran that's broadcast live (and also taped for rebroadcast later) on WPZA, Domino's Pizza magnate Tom Monaghan's radio station, more of Frieder's comments, and then what is often a surprisingly free-wheeling question-and-answer session with the assembled alums.

In addition to a side order of platitudes —"We'll take 'em one at a time," "You have to take each team individually"— Frieder fields queries about the Proposition 48 players ("We thought we'd have a problem with Terry Mills somewhere —being coachable, social life —but we haven't. Cliff [Sjogren, U of M's director of admissions] and his staff admitted him under a special arrangement. Our people won't admit anybody if they don't feel they have a chance to succeed. Mills is a dedicated kid. The kid we got off was Derrick Coleman [a Detroiter who went to Syracuse] because we thought he couldn't pass the [SAT] test. He passed. The kid we thought would pass it was Mills. He didn't. And the media cannot believe what a kid Rumeal Robinson is: dedicated, personable, he does nothing but school and basketball. He's really a beautiful kid and he's getting better and better. If Rumeal makes a mistake, he goes home and thinks about it. He got stripped of the ball at the half Saturday. He came to practice Sunday and the first thing, he apologized for it. That shows you he's gonna make it."), the schedule ("Our schedule is exactly the way we want it and exactly what we need. I will not travel in December. You cannot believe how much we're doing academically. We had nine kids at study table yesterday from 1:30 to 5 p.m. Then we practiced at 6 p.m., and a couple of kids stayed after practice. You don't need 31 tough games. Last Friday, from 7 to 11 p.m., they were all studying. You cannot believe how busy they all are.") and about keeping the players happy ("I don't have to keep these kids happy. I have to keep myself happy.")

That night, the Wolverines pay back Western in style, beating the Broncos, 113–66. The 47-point margin will turn out to be their second largest of the season.

At the post-game press conference, Western Coach Vern Payne is asked if there's any consolation he can take from the game. "Yeah," he says. "I get to leave Crisler Arena in about half an hour."

Michigan's schedule is always a hot topic in December, and tonight is no exception. "Ninety percent of those type of programs in the country play similar schedules to Coach Frieder," says Payne, "and they do that because they want to establish how they want to play, and there's nothing wrong with that."

Like a good politician, Frieder knows that the best way to head off stupid, unanswerable or repetitive questions is to set the agenda himself. His first words into the microphone are, "Is Jack Saylor [veteran reporter for the *Detroit Free Press* and a Frieder favorite] in the room?"

Saylor waves. "Saylor," says Frieder, a statement rather than a direct address. "In 1976 or 7, Saylor wrote an article at the *Free Press* about what a disgrace it was the University of Michigan wasn't playing state schools. And Jack Moss [long of the *Kalamazoo Gazette*] did, too. Remember, Jack? So that's why we're playing the state schools. I don't want to hear about it, okay?"

There isn't much more to say. After 10 minutes or so of *pro forma* interrogation, Frieder walks out of the interview room and fights his way across the crowded hallway and up the stairs into the locker room, shaking hands with well-wishers, pausing to stroke recruits, trying to shake off his mother and getting in a few phone calls before some members of the print media corner him as he comes out of his office (the one in the locker room, not the one in the athletic administration building). Later in the season, he will wonder out loud why they bother with press conferences when every reporter winds up talking to him in the locker room to get his "own" story, anyway.

He notes that this is the best passing team he's ever had. "I think that should make you fairly happy," says one writer.

"If you're happy for long in this business," the coach says, "I'll show you losses."

"You can be happy for five minutes," the writer says.

"I'm happy," Frieder says. "I shouldn't say this because it'll come back to haunt me, but I think our depth is good enough to give 'em a rest and we're not losing a lot."

It does, of course, come back to haunt him. Sean Higgins is declared ineligible three weeks later and his absence, more than any other factor, reduces the Wolverines from a top-five team nationally to perhaps top-12 status.

Like all good coaches, Frieder is able to analzye his team's performance apart from the outcome of the game, discerning the pluses in a loss and the minuses in a win. He tells how one of his rookies responded when the coach pointed out a minus: "Mills looked at me like I was nuts when I got on his butt for letting one of those guys get two in a row on him. He goes, 'Coach, first of all, you got me on the perimeter guarding a guard, and secondly, you told me he couldn't shoot.' "

Frieder laughs humorlessly. "I keep hearing this stuff about needing more than one basketball. That's so much bull it makes me sick. Terry Mills played on a state championship team. He scored nine points in the state final. He's unselfish. He passes the ball. This is ridiculous for people to say that. We don't have a problem with that here. We might overpass it sometimes."

John Beckett of the *Ann Arbor News* tells Frieder that Austin Peay, Thursday night's opponent, is playing Illinois the next night. Frieder has been miffed at Beckett since he wrote a series of stories on Roy Tarpley's drug use as a Wolverine. A chance for a tweak has presented itself.

"Good," Frieder says to Beckett. "Hey, Hammer."

"Yeah?"

"Who's scouting Austin Peay?"
"I am."
"When?"
"Tomorrow night."
"Where?"
"Illinois."

It is almost midnight on Monday, Dec. 7. Frieder can't sleep. He gets up and watches the tape of the Western Michigan game.

By 6 a.m., he's back in his office on campus, writing letters to recruits. Most of the time, he does not send full-fledged missives but rather photocopies of clippings with notes attached: "I saw your game Friday. Keep up the good work. Here's what the *Detroit News* had to say about our program. Hope you can be a part of it."

Boyd and Fisher show up and he meets with them again, fine tuning the schedules they worked on the day before. They plan the afternoon's practice, then Frieder returns phone calls (coaches wanting to schedule games, writers and broadcasters wanting to schedule interviews, someone from Canham's office wanting to check on a purchase order) and answers his mail (much of this is from fans: Why don't you make your players tuck in their jerseys? Why can't I get a ticket in the blue seats? Why did the scorer credit Mills with a basket that was really made by Loy Vaught?).

Then it's time for practice, then a team meeting in the locker room after practice, then Austin Peay "films," then a review of the Austin Peay personnel, then a review of the team's schedule—individually and collectively—for the rest of the week, then training table.

As the players begin to eat, Frieder heads downtown for the WPAG studio to do one of his weekly radio shows. He finishes at 8:30 p.m., just in time to go back to his office to watch the second half of the Austin Peay–Illinois game, during which he calls recruits. No sense letting any part of his consciousness lie fallow.

He goes home at 10:30 p.m. to say good night to Janice and

Laura, then returns to the office for two more hours of "odds and ends." He finally calls it a day at 1 a.m., 19 hours after his first appearance in his office. Tonight, he sleeps.

At 9 a.m. Wednesday, Frieder is settled behind his desk, reading Hammer's scouting report on Austin Peay. He summons Fisher, his second in command, to discuss what Hammer has learned and talk about possible matchups and tactics. Boyd comes in and another recruiting meeting is convened. The schedules will have to be changed. Some kids are not going to be seen a second time so that others can be fit in. Frieder reminds them that Fisher's presence is required at practice Friday, the only practice between the Austin Peay and Eastern Michigan games, so Boyd will have to see the player Fisher was planning to see.

The assistants retreat to their offices to continue the planning their nomadic feats require. Although Pat Perry, Will Perry's wife and the athletic department's business manager, actually makes the final arrangements, the coaches themselves must determine which flights they need, check on the availability of rental cars, pick motels, inform the schools that they're coming, arrange for passes to the games and fill out expense reports.

Frieder calls Norm Stewart, the Missouri coach, to get tapes of the Tigers' game with Eastern Michigan. The Hurons took them into overtime in Columbia before losing and, not surprisingly, Frieder likes to show his team its opponents at their best. Normally, such a task would not be Frieder's but, as he explains, "It's a situation where graduate assistants and assistant coaches working with graduate assistants and assistant coaches couldn't get it accomplished. You have assistants and you set policies so you don't have to do things yourself, and you wind up with assistants to supervise and policies to administer and you still have to do those things."

He leaves the office at 11:30 a.m. to go to the bank and Thano's, the old-time downtown pizzeria owned by longtime Frieder (and, before him, Johnny Orr) pal Thano Masters. When the players don't have training table at the arena, they have it at Thano's. On the rare occasions when Frieder actually eats lunch, he eats it at Thano's.

Within an hour, he's back at the office. A half hour after that and he's at the arena for practice and the beginning of a sequence much like that of the day before, except that the discussions of Austin Peay are fortified by Hammer's report, the evening radio show is on WAAM instead of WPAG, and Frieder goes to scout Eastern Michigan in its game at the University of Detroit instead of watching a future opponent on television.

Glen Rice scores 11 points, matching his eventual low for the season (he also scores 11 at Purdue in the penultimate Big Ten game), Austin Peay uses a lot of moving screens, à la Indiana, to free former Hoosier Andre Harris, who finishes with 21 points, and the Wolverines can't shake the Governors until midway through the second half, finally posting an 88–67 victory. Gary Grant's near-perfect shooting (9 of 11 from the field, 10 of 10 from the foul line) and Loy Vaught's 14 points off the bench make the difference.

Frieder sounds both exhausted and wired in the post-game press conference. "Then we've got Eastern Michigan on Saturday and I don't know how many damn games we've played here in a row, but we've been playing a lot of games [this is the fourth in nine days since returning from the Great Alaska Shootout], really too many but, you know, it's 100 grand a game plus parking, concessions and programs. . ." The reporters laugh ". . .and I've gotta keep Canham happy, but we really needed about two less games in here. I don't know how many games we've played and now we've got another one Saturday and I just hope they have enough left in 'em."

He bristles at a reference to his team's apparent sluggishness. "Mills was up until five this morning studying. Hughes didn't get any sleep at all. You guys don't realize it, man. That's a tough school. They've got papers, articles, projects, exams, review sessions. . .it's a tough time. That's why you'll never see me on the road this time of year."

Back in the locker room, he calls Mills into his office and shuts the door for a private chat. He tells Mills that after the Bowling Green game, the first home game, Mills' father called Boyd and "really got on his butt." This nettles Frieder on two counts. The first is that he does not permit basketball-related conversations between parents and staff members during the season. If they want to talk about academic matters, social problems, visits home, fine. If they want to talk about playing time or how much their boy is scoring, forget it. The second is that he doesn't like people who get free tickets to be critical. He tells Mills he called his father back and assaulted an analogous part of his anatomy.

"I said, 'Hey, Tree, I'm a great basketball coach and Mills is gonna be a good player, but he's got a lot of learning to do and I . . .' Did he tell you I called him?"

"Yeah," says Mills, looking thoughtfully neutral. "I talked to him."

"So I said, 'Hey, you just get out there and cheer and don't listen to your buddies and when your buddies get up there and holler and rant and rave, you tell 'em Frieder's doing a great job. And that's all there is to it.' And he was super, okay? He was really good. Then he waited for me after the game and he's 'Hey, coach', and all that, and that's super. Now Morris tonight, your brother-in-law, he jumps on Boyd out there. We don't need that, see? We don't need other parents hearing that, you know what I'm saying? You don't need parents out there hearing one family complaining. You don't need it to carry over into the team. See, they're all excited because they're used to you getting 30 every game. . . ."

"That's what I talked to my father about," Mills says.

"See, they don't understand, see?" says Frieder. "You're here every day. You understand it. They don't. So you gotta tell Morris, 'Hey, man, I'll get you the tickets but I don't want to hear anything bad about Michigan or the coaches or the players. You be supportive.' You just tell him, 'Hey, I'm coming along fine. And the coaches even want me to shoot more than I'm shooting. You just let them handle the team and you cheer for Michigan.' Tell him or we're not going to leave him tickets."

"Okay."

"You can handle him, but you just gotta tell him yourself. It's a typical thing with a guy when they're scoring 30 in high school, now they don't get their 30 and everybody wants to know what's the matter. Well, nothing's the matter, but they gotta hear it from you, see?"

"Okay," says Mills. "I'll do that."

In this, as in other matters, Mills' word is completely reliable. It may or may not be a result of losing a year to Proposition 48 but, for one of the most highly touted high school stars in the country, he is remarkably gracious, pleasant, eager to learn and genuinely humble. By the end of the season, Frieder will have only one complaint about his off-court performance, and it is a curious one: He tends to assume too much personal responsibility for the team's shortcomings.

After the players and the media and the managers and even the maintenance people have left, Frieder and company meet to start their final preparations for Eastern Michigan. Even though this is, to the casual fan, just another non-conference game in December, the staff is giving it "Big Ten-style" preparation. They know the game matters much more to the Hurons than it does to the Wolverines, which is always a dangerous situation, and they also know how tired their team is, both from academic pressures and the hectic schedule of games.

They meet again the next day, minus Boyd, who has left for Syracuse to begin his recruiting expedition. Two managers have "cut out" the tape of the Eastern Michigan–Missouri game. This means they have transferred particular sequences to separate tapes for more concentrated study: offensive plays, defensive sets, individual players and, says Hammer, "the parts where we want to build them up. It's easy to do that in the Big Ten."

It's fairly easy to do that for Eastern, too, a team that will go on to win both the regular-season and tournament titles in the Mid-American Conference before losing a tight battle to Pittsburgh in the opening round of the NCAA tournament.

At 2:45 p.m. on Friday, December 11, Frieder sits on a court-side table at Crisler Arena, watching his players emerge from the tunnel between the locker room and the court. They start pre-practice, the time before the beginning of regular practice that is set aside for players to get loose and warm by working on their personal games: one-on-one technique, post moves, perimeter shooting, free throws and other individual responsibilities.

"Every day we spend time on this," Frieder tells a visitor. "The worst thing that I've ever seen is when I go recruiting and I walk into a gym and practice starts at three and it's twenty to three and the coach is sitting down and the kids are just out there screwing around. They get six, eight shots and talk to their buddy and get a drink of water, etc. So their responsibility from 2:50 to 3:20 is to get all their individual things done."

He says it will be "a short, short practice. In fact, we're gonna take 'em inside first to emphasize the Eastern Michigan game. We'll come out and go six–eight minutes on a warmup just to get loose. Maybe ten minutes on defensing Eastern Michigan and breaking out (walking through individual matchups, switches and the like). Maybe six–eight minutes on our half-court offense, which was awful last night. Maybe five minutes on last-second plays, which we've been doing a terrible job at. And that's about it. Maybe some free throws. And then we'll go back in, watch some film, shower, have training table at five o'clock, get 'em out of there early.

"Then they gotta be at the Campus Inn at 7:00 for study table and usually after study table at 9:00, I let 'em go until 11:00, but tonight they've gotta stay in and watch film and stuff like that, and they'll have just an hour to go, whenever they want, 9:00 to 10:00 or 9:30 to 10:30 or 10:00 to 11:00. Just so they're not cooped up. I like 'em to get out if they want to walk around or go see their girlfriend or run home or whatever they want to do. Then everyone's in at 11:00, have another short meeting, hopefully get a good night's rest."

Frieder is constantly checking, double-checking, synchronizing and reciting schedules, like an incantation against the devil of uncertainty, as if he could, by being persistent and methodical enough, finally surprise and unschedule defeat itself.

Keeping the players on a shorter leash than usual is another indication of the special treatment Saturday's game is receiving.

"The biggest thing here is you know Eastern will come to play but my players still don't realize what they're capable of doing," Frieder says. "They don't think for a minute that they could be upset, but they can. Right now, Eastern is more enthused about the game than we are. They've had more time to prepare since their last game, they haven't had as many as we've had in the last two or three weeks, plus they've been thinking about it since last summer. These guys haven't. They've been thinking about Indiana and Michigan State and Western Michigan, because those teams beat us last year."

Frieder has decided to start Vaught at center in place of Hughes. "I talked to Mark about it," he says. "Mark's a good kid. You can see right now [by the intensity of his practice] that he's not affected by it. He certainly doesn't like it, but Loy's deserving of it; he's done a good job. We've gotta give him a shot in there, so we're gonna go with him. I hope he plays well because sometimes he has a tough time putting two or three games together."

Fisher conducts the meeting that comes between pre-practice and practice, using the cut-out tape and wall charts for visual aids in a crash course on the Hurons. "Glen, you'll have Grant Long. He's a Big Ten-type player. . . ."

When the team goes back on the floor, Frieder goes out the exit at the opposite end of the tunnel to check on the installation of a remote-control starter in his car. "This way, I can get out of the shower in the morning and start the car, so it's warm when I'm ready to go." For a man who never wears an overcoat, this is important, not that Frieder would be able to resist the lure of any time-saving gizmo. His foray fulfills another agenda, too.

"I purposely do things like this during practice because I want them, whether I'm there or not, to be in the habit of working hard," he says. "That, I think, teaches character, not the old junior high school deal— 'When the coach leaves, we can screw around.' "

They are hard at a full-court scrimmage when he returns. Fisher is coaching the white shirts, the starters, and Hammer is handling the blue shirts, the subs, whose job it is to impersonate the next opponent. Frieder likes to start practice this way. His theory is that the game is played five-on-five, full-court, and that's how the bulk of practice should be conducted. Starting out full-tilt also encourages a more painstaking pre-practice.

The blues are giving the whites a hard time, spreading out their man-to-man, sending cutters through the lane and making them play 30 to 35 seconds of defense on almost every possession. Play is surprisingly spirited, perhaps too much so. Chris Seter whacks Bob Tait in the mouth in a struggle for a rebound. Trainer Dan Minert takes Tait to a dentist. He's gone no more than five minutes when Rumeal Robinson somehow reinjures the ligament in his right thumb while guarding Demetrius Calip. Assistant trainer Jim Berry accompanies Robinson to the locker room.

Frieder sees Vaught, the new starter, make a defensive move he likes. "That's pretty good," he says. "That's pretty good. Make the step out more emphatic, Loy, more meaningful, like you're goin' after him."

Next is a rebounding drill; more precisely, a boxing-out drill, an area Freider was displeased with the night before against Austin Peay. He stops the drill often and is on the floor for most of it, within teaching and preaching distance.

"The hardest thing to teach," he says when he returns to the sidelines, "is when you give defensive help on the ball side, when the shot goes up, to come back and keep your man off the boards. That's one of the toughest things."

On the next run-through, sure enough, nobody keeps the man who was abandoned off the boards. "Loy started to," Frieder says, "but he got on the wrong side. Usually, if a shot's missed on that side, it's gonna rebound on this side. Four out of five times. Most people don't realize we teach little things like that."

Another little thing that seems even harder to teach is the willingness to put flesh to varnish, to risk a floor burn. Frieder tries setting an example, hurling himself to the floor in front of his startled players. "If you just do that," he says, "you've got the ball."

J. P. Oosterbaan goes down. Nobody is even close to the burly backup center. His right knee simply collapses. Frieder is almost out of trainers, not to mention players, but Minert gets back from the dentist's just in time to examine Oosterbaan.

"We practiced 45 minutes and got three guys hurt," Frieder laments.

Robinson leans against a table on the sidelines, shivering. It is not entirely because of the ice pack wrapped around his thumb. "This is the coldest gym I've ever been in in my life," he says. "When you got greyhounds, you know, you need a gym to keep 'em warm so they can run. We'll have to get some Clydesdales." Frieder blows his whistle and heads for the locker room. "Coach," says Robinson, "you need a gym for greyhounds, not Clydesdales."

"Tell me about it," Frieder says.

Not only that, but the players' dinner is already cooling in the Crisler Arena lounge and they haven't even showered yet. "If I ever get the two of them here at the same time—the team just coming out of the shower and Romanoff [the company that caters training tables and a number of other athletic department functions] ready to feed 'em—it'd be a miracle. Either they're waiting for us for 15 minutes or we're done and waiting for them for 15 minutes."

Nonetheless, the players eat. Jerry Ashby, Frieder's constant recruiting companion, and a visitor are waiting for the coach. It's the first night that coaches are allowed to see high school players play, and Frieder is like a rock in a slingshot.

The trio clamber into Frieder's New Yorker. It's a foggy, rainy, inhospitable night, with the temperature barely above freezing. Frieder, in the back seat, has unloaded his omnipresent attache case and set up a virtual office. He's signing brochures for his summer basketball camp — that's what he hands to anyone who asks for an autograph — and doing the complimentary tickets for tomorrow's game.

Ashby invariably drives to the game. Frieder invariably drives back. "That's because it matters if we get there but it doesn't matter if we get back," says Ashby. He was a Michigan fan in the 1960s and remained one after he moved to Las Vegas in 1970. He befriended Frieder when the latter accompanied the Wolverines to a tournament there in 1975. "He had the Nevada–Las Vegas job all locked up in '79," Ashby says. "Tarkanian was gonna take the Lakers job and Frieder was gonna get the UNLV job."

But the deal fell through on the Laker end, Tarkanian stayed put, and Ashby moved back. That was eight years ago, and he has made virtually every recruiting trip with Frieder since. He also goes to every road game as a sort of volunteer assistant, sitting behind the bench, handing out towels, going to the scorer's table to ask questions, wearing a participant pass. He is agreeable with virtually anyone on virtually any subject, unless someone criticizes the Michigan program or its coach.

That very afternoon, at the weekly luncheon meeting of the "Friday Club," an informal group with a fluctuating membership that has been getting together for a good 20 years at various Ann Arbor restaurants, such an event had occurred. A fellow member asserted that Mark Hughes started only because Frieder had promised him as much when he was recruiting him. Such tactics are anathema to Frieder, and Ashby said as much in response. Word of the tiff had reached the coach's ears.

"He and I have been friends for years," Ashby says, "but you're either for the program or against it. There's no damn in-between. You can't be for a program and criticize the coaching and the players. It's been building up. I just had enough of it."

Frieder is busy writing names on envelopes, tucking complimentary tickets into them and then crossing those same names off a checklist. "I've been doing the tickets a long time," he says. "I don't spend over half an hour a day on 'em, but it's good relaxation in the car. One thing I've learned on the tickets—there are never enough blue seats. I determine who gets what, but you like to put all the parents in the blues, and you like to have all the recruits in the blues, and the coaching staff's family requests, and there just isn't enough blues, so someone's gotta bite the bullet and go to the gold."

The car inches through Ann Arbor's outbound rush-hour traffic. It's the first night of recruiting, after all, and both of them have lost their traffic chops. Neither has given any thought to how crowded the route to Detroit Country Day School is at this time of day, and the weather is further locking the grid.

Their destination is a pre-holiday tournament at the private school in Southfield, an aging suburb due north of Detroit's west side. Their quarry is Chris Weber, a 6'9" freshman, only the second ninth grader Frieder has ever gone to see. The first was Terry Mills.

Frieder says that one time when he was in Tampa, he read about a fourth grader in Clearwater and went to see him play, but he doesn't count that.

The talk turns to the two consecutive Big Ten championship teams. Somebody in front points out that Roy Tarpley is the only player from those teams to have made it in the NBA. Frieder is quick to elaborate on the implications. "Those two Big Ten title teams, we did a great job," he says. "They had a lot of deficiencies. Wade couldn't shoot. Rellford was an in-betweener. Joubert was slow. There were a lot of deficiencies and we did a great job. But the whole thing on that comes back to the NCAA. They're not giving enough credit for getting through the Big Ten schedule."

At this particular moment, Frieder would settle for getting through the traffic. His normal impatience is exacerbated by the fact that such occasions are largely ceremonial anyway.

"Our purpose is to get there early and everybody will see that I'm there," he says. "To me, that's the main thing—that they know Bill Frieder is there. When I recruit, especially juniors and seniors, I already know they can play. I know whether I want a kid or not, so it's a matter of getting there and saying hello to the coaches and the people involved and making sure the kid and the family see you. And that's that. We'll probably leave at halftime of the kid's game. You can't talk to them. You can't have any contact off campus with any kid that's not at least in his senior year."

Ashby finally leaves the freeway and tools north on Lahser Road. The school is reportedly clearly marked and located at a major intersection, Lahser and Fourteen Mile Road. There's plenty of time. More than plenty, in fact—the car's computerized, digital-readout clock, the one nestled amid a display of lights that also tells the outside temperature, relative humidity and wind velocity and direction, is 10 minutes fast. While it seems consistent with Frieder's character, he claims it's inadvertent.

"It's because I could never really set it," he says. "I don't know how to set it. A couple of other people have played with it. We finally got the hour right but we could never get the minutes changed." His claim gains credibility in context: This man also does not know how to pump his own gas at a self-service filling station or play a tape in a cassette deck without assistance.

He and Ashby speculate on the parking situation at Country Day, finally concluding that there's likely to be plenty of space and, if there isn't, that they are equal to the task.

"The best way to get a good parking spot is to pull in a lot and hold up traffic and argue with the guy," Frieder says. "I used to always get into Michigan State when I didn't have a pass for the J [premium] lot. 'They told me I could park here,' I'd say. 'I talked to [then Coach] Gus [Ganakas] myself. He was gonna leave me a pass to the J lot and now he hasn't.' By then, people would be hollering and honking and he would say, 'Aw, go on in.' "

Guess what? The school isn't where it's reputed to be. At least, not so these latter-day Marco Polos can find it. Parking is suddenly a back-burner issue.

"I've been so busy I haven't had a chance to double-check everything," says Frieder. "I just figured I knew this one. How in the hell did this school disappear, men?" He looks anxiously at churches, modest suburban homes, convenience stores. "We gotta stop and ask somebody. Is this . . . maybe it's down at Eleven Mile."

"We found it a hundred times when we weren't looking for it," says Ashby.

Several trips back and forth on the stretch of Lahser between Eleven and Fourteen Mile and two pauses for directions later, Frieder spies the sign.

"There it is," he cries. "How in the hell did we miss it?"

They park—uneventfully—and dash through the rain into the school. The first game, not the one in which Weber is playing, is already under way in the poorest lighting that any of them has ever seen for a basketball game. Perhaps it is to obscure the fact that there are only about 60 people sitting in a gym that could hold a thousand.

The coach of one of the teams in the opener is Cliff Turner, father of Eric Turner, who played for Frieder at Michigan in the early '80s. Cliff was the coach at Flint Central when Frieder was at Flint Northern and has a son in junior high who is reputed to be a hot prospect. But when Frieder is asked about him, or any other boy that young, he has begun telling people: "I won't be coaching that long."

The game lures Frieder as irresistibly as a mongoose lures a snake. Not *this* game, but *the* game. Even though the outcome of Flint Academy vs. Detroit Renaissance means about as much to him as the political situation in the outer Hebrides, he can't help watching, reacting, perceiving, analyzing. "That's it," he says to no one in particular, having seated himself as conspicuously as possible in the second row of a nearly empty section. "The best way to keep the clock going is by scoring points. No rebounds. It goes through, the people are retrieving. . . .You miss, now you've got chances to foul. . . ."

There is a terrible call, and then another. If it is true that a large component of humor is relief that the event perceived as funny is happening to someone else, then there is almost no laughter like the laughter of a coach at terrible officiating in someone else's game.

The Flint team's lead fluctuates between five and nine points. "You always used to tell 'em to stay on the odd number to avoid overtime," Frieder says. "Now, with the three-point shot, you've got that to worry about, too." Almost the only thing Frieder doesn't worry about is how much he worries.

Right now, for example, his cold caffeine craving is kicking in. "Did you see a concession stand on the way in?" he asks.

"I didn't see anything that looked like one," says the tagalong.

"Guys are sitting around with bottled pop," Ashby notes. Frieder's face falls.

It is brighter later. After the first game ends, after the intermission, after the players in the featured game take the floor, it is positively radiant. "He saw me," says Frieder. "He saw me from the window in the door to the locker room. The main thing is he knows I'm here. That's all that counts."

The game certainly doesn't count for much. Country Day's opponent is a team of nice Canadian kids from across the river in Windsor, the kind of cannon fodder host teams feed themselves in tournament openers.

"It's going to be an awful game," Frieder says, "but we'll have to sit through it for a half anyway."

It's as safe a prediction as a coach can ever make. The Ontario kids can barely get the ball over the 10-second line. Weber scores his team's first five baskets, virtually unopposed. The Windsor coach calls his second timeout with a minute left in the first quarter and Country Day leading, 19–4.

"If you're a high school coach and you're down 19–4 seven minutes into the game, what do you do?" Frieder is asked.

"I don't think that's ever happened to me," he answers.

Frieder says he ran into an assistant coach from the University of Detroit between games. He is there to look at a senior guard from Country Day.

"He says, 'I don't like seeing you here; it scares me,'" Frieder reports. "He thought I'm after Bolden, see. I said, 'I don't know why. I'm looking at a ninth grader, Weber.' 'Oh,' he said. 'We're still after seniors. That's how far ahead of our program your program is.'" Frieder is delighted. It may be obvious to even the most casual fan that the Michigan program is light years ahead of Detroit's, but that doesn't diminish Frieder's pleasure in fresh evidence.

At last, the half is over. Frieder gets up just before it ends and positions himself between the court and the locker room, so that Weber will see him once more before he leaves.

On the way back to the car, Frieder explains his priorities. "If this was my assistant, he would be required to stay there the whole game and, at the end, have the kid see him as he comes out of the locker room and talk to the coaches and everyone involved. As the head coach, I've gotten to the point where I just don't think that's necessary for me any more. They know when I'm there and that's what's important and it's important for me to get back with my team. And then I can always tell those kids, 'When you come to Michigan, I'm not going to be out there all the time; I'm going to be with you.' "

Frieder is at the wheel for the trip back to Ann Arbor. Partly because it's the first recruiting venture of the season and partly because the way Frieder drives makes people sentimental about their lives, tales of past recruiting feats fill the car.

"One time when we flew to see Gary Grant [in Canton, Ohio] in an ice storm, they had to fly to Toledo and turn left because it was too dangerous to fly over the lake," says Ashby. "They were afraid to go over it. The pilot kept looking out the window with a flashlight at the wings. And when we flew down to see [Steve] Stoyko [in Bay Village, Ohio, a Cleveland suburb] for the first time, we got down to the car rental place to rent a car and we didn't have billfolds or money."

"I left everything in my briefcase," says Frieder, "which was in the car back in Ann Arbor."

"Bill says, 'Give 'em your driver's license,' " says Ashby. "I said, 'I can't. It's back in Ann Arbor.' "

"I had to talk that guy into letting us take the car with nothing and then sending everything to him when I got back," says Frieder. "He gave us a car without any identification, any credit card, anything. A guy at a Standard gas station in Elyria, Ohio. Plus he wasn't gonna be there when we got back. He stuck the keys under the seat. Drive it to the airport, he says, and we'll get it tomorrow."

Michigan has recently raised the speed limit on its interstates to 65, which means Frieder is going only 20 miles over the maximum instead of 30. The passenger in front notes that with an analog speedometer, it would be possible from his position to misread their speed and enjoy some false security, but with the digital speedometer in the New Yorker, there's no way to avoid knowing, with aching clarity, that they are going 89.

Ashby says that there seems to be no speed limit whatsoever on the stretch he drives between his home in Chelsea, about 15 miles west of Ann Arbor, and his office. "In the morning, I'm going 75 and they pass me like I'm standing still," he says.

"If you have any problems," Frieder kids, "I know the governor."

The coach recalls that in the days of unlimited recruiting, he made 100 trips to Canton to woo Phil Hubbard.

"What's that, about four or five hours each way?" he's asked.

"Three-ten," Frieder says. "Two hundred thirteen miles. I got it down to a science. It's amazing I'm still living, I'm tellin' ya."

"Tell him about the trip to Kalamazoo," says Ashby. "Two and a half hours up, an hour and a half back."

"In the ice," Frieder chuckles. "Ashby thought he did a good job getting there in two and a half."

"What's your best time to Chicago?"

"Chicago? Uh, three hours. Two hundred seventy-five miles. Hey, Mike Boyd drove from Pittsburgh to Detroit in less than four hours. That's impossible. Boyd and I made it from Spring Lake, which is on the water by Muskegon, in an hour and 50 minutes. It's two-ten from Grand Rapids and we're an hour on the other side of Grand Rapids. We were flying 100 miles an hour, man, but ya gotta when you're on the road that much.

"I was coming from the Akron Classic once and Campy [Russell] was playing at the Cleveland Coliseum, so I thought I'd shoot in there on the way home and watch the last part of the game. And I wheeled around on that street and went through New Boston and as soon as I went around the corner, some cop stops me, gives me a summons and says, 'You gotta follow me now to the courthouse to see the justice of the peace and pay it.' So now I follow him 11 miles. We go in. He takes off his police hat, puts it on a chair, goes behind the desk, runs off, comes back with a different kind of jacket on, takes his gavel, hits the thing and says, 'Can I help you?' I said, 'Yeah, I got this ticket.' He gets out this book with all the fines in it, looks all through it, goes through all this crap, then says, '$50.' Then, after I pay, he says, 'You got any questions?' I say, 'Yeah. Why don't you carry that damn book with you in your car?' "

Frieder is so preoccupied with his reminiscences that he misses the exit he wants and has to take a more circuitous route back to the arena, where Ashby's car is parked. Even so, he makes the return trip in 34 minutes, roughly half what the outbound journey required. He drops off Ashby and arrives at the Campus Inn moments before study table ends at 9 p.m.

"Swamped again," he says as he pulls into the lot. "Look at the cars. I bet it's a Christmas party. That ticks me off 'cause I don't like to give 'em my key." He slams the car into park, jumps out, moves a "Lot Full" sign and parks his car where it had been.

Up on the 15th floor, most of the players have returned to their rooms from study table. The lone exception is Sean Higgins, the freshman from Los Angeles. Frieder has been alerted to the fact that Higgins' absences from one of his classes have jeopardized the 2.0 average he needs to stay eligible, so he and his sister Jamie, an honors student with a 3.8 average, are studying together in the coach's suite under Jan's watchful eye.

Frieder makes the rounds of the rooms, asking each player what his grades are likely to be, what tests and papers he has left and, in general, where he stands. The courses they discuss — psychology, art history, religion, natural resources, urban planning — come as a bit of a shock to a visitor who thought most athletes majored in gut courses.

Loy Vaught, the new starter, is a bright, well-spoken young man with a reputation among his teammates for a somewhat skewed perspective. When he tells Frieder he's getting an "A" in logic, the coach and the other players in the room hoot and slap their thighs. "I can't begin to comprehend that," says Frieder. "Loy getting an 'A' in logic."

He stops at the room Steve Stoyko shares with J. P. Oosterbaan. The TV is on, Oosterbaan is gone and Stoyko is stretched diagonally across the bed with a ponderous looking volume propped up on his chest. "Here's my number one man," says Frieder. "This is my favorite, right here. Good guy, hell of a guy. How we doin', pal? Got everything handled? What are your classes this year?"

"Let's see," Stoyko says. "Endocrinology, cellular physiology, physiological psychology, introduction to sociological medicine. . . ."

"These other guys are all about done and he's got five tough exams next week," says Frieder, shaking his head. "He's loaded."

"How can you study that stuff with the TV on?" Stoyko is asked.

"Is it still on?" Stoyko says. "I didn't even notice. J. was watching it."

"They hated October," Frieder says en route back to his suite. "We didn't leave the practice floor until twenty to seven, then we ate, then there was study table from 8:15 to 10:15, so they were at the arena from 1:00 or 1:30 until 10:30."

Frieder gets on the phone as soon as he's back in his room. He orders pizzas from Thano's and hot chocolate from room service for the players' bedtime snack, hoping they'll arrive as close to the same time as possible. He calls his own answering machine and dictates a letter to Weber for his secretary to type.

Meanwhile, Jan is trying to commandeer his leftover attention for a discussion of Christmas plans. She talks about a guest list, the dinner menu, when they'll go to church. He talks about going to the arena around 3:30 or 4:00 Christmas afternoon and having a practice at 7:00.

An English instructor phones Frieder's room, returning a call from Terry Mills. Mills is summoned and takes the receiver: "A lot of people looked at it. . . . It's my own thoughts. . . . Brainstorming technique....Yes, it does....Guess I'll have to try harder next course. I really have learned a lot...."

He hangs up and turns to Frieder. "I passed," he says, exhaling softly. "With a 'D.'" His voice drops. "She said, 'Is this your work?' I said, 'yes.' She said, 'I didn't know you could write this well.' I said, 'Well, it came down to a pass or fail, so I had to do my best work.' She said, 'It's disappointing because you could do an "A" in this course if you're capable of writing like this.'"

Sean Higgins comes in from taking his sister back to her dormitory. "I've gotta get a 'D' in psychology," he says. "If I had been in class, I wouldn't be in jeopardy."

"I've got a shot at a 'B' in natural resources," Mills says.

They make plans to study after the game on Saturday and again on Sunday afternoon. "Just tell her how much you learned and how it helped you as a person," Mills advises Higgins.

His canniness provokes Jan. "That makes me mad, Terry," she says. "You have the skills."

Mills smiles enigmatically. "I have the schemes," he says.

A VCR has been hooked up to the TV in one of the rooms to present continuous showings of Eastern Michigan's greatest hits. At any given time, half a dozen or so players are crowded in, oohing and aahing over the exploits of the next day's opponents.

At about 10:30, the pizza and hot chocolate arrive, as simultaneously as possible, another good omen. The players gather in the hall—the team has the floor to itself—to eat and listen to the professorial Fisher review the material he covered that afternoon following practice.

As soon as the players are bedded down, Frieder leaves to take his other fellow traveler back to the Crisler Arena parking lot. He uses the short trip to explain the rationale behind the constant meetings and review sessions.

"I just think mental is so much of the game," he says. "Mental. To get 'em concentrating and thinking about their opponents. These kids, they're not like [Marty] Bodnar, they're not like [Paul] Heuerman [two stalwarts of Frieder's first teams as head coach]. Their concentration drifts in a hurry. You can see it in their play, so it's important to keep harping on concentration, mental toughness, fighting fatigue, etc., etc., and that's what we do.

"We had a meeting before practice. We had a meeting after practice. We had a meeting at the Campus Inn. We had a meeting again at the Campus Inn. And this is for Eastern Michigan. We don't put near the emphasis on Eastern that we'll put on a Big Ten game, but more on Eastern than we do most non-conference games."

In Frieder's view, playing a non-conference neighbor is fraught with far more peril than playing some less familiar team.

"They don't respect Eastern Michigan like I do," he says. "They know those kids. Mills thinks he's better than Grant Long. Gary Grant *knows* he's better than Goheen, and you go right through the lineup. They don't understand that they can get their butts beat by this team. They see it happen to Missouri or somebody else, but it's not going to happen to them. I think they were impressed with the film clips. That got their attention, see, when they saw those three-pointers starting to go in regular.

"So you do different things. You can't be monotonous. You can't do the same things over and over. You've just gotta keep it fresh."

It is nearly midnight on Friday, Dec. 11, and Frieder seems as fresh as a newly laundered pillowcase. His visitor is somewhat less so. They agree to meet at 12:30 p.m. the next day, an hour and a half before game time, and go their separate ways.

It is 12:35 p.m. on Saturday, December 12. Frieder exits the locker room in a swirl of managers, assistants and pals, and heads to a radio show.

This is the first season of the Michigan basketball team's first exclusive radio contract. In the past, any station willing to pay the rights fee could broadcast the games. To the surprise of absolutely no one, Detroit's affluent and sports-saturated WJR (which also carries the Tigers, the Red Wings, the Lions and Michigan football) won Don Canham's auction and became the sole carrier, except for WWJ, a lower-powered, all-news station in Detroit that was "grandfathered" because it had been the first station ever to beam Michigan sports.

Frieder originally planned to do his pre- and post-game shows with comparable exclusivity on WJR, but WWJ, which had been doing such programs with him since he became head coach, complained, and he yielded. Now he does two pre-game shows and two post-game shows.

He finds Larry Henry, the WJR announcer, at his courtside location. "Larry, you ready? Let's go."

He finishes with Henry and moves to the other end of the table. Vince Doyle, WWJ's color man, is there, but not Dale Conquest, the play-by-play announcer who conducts the interview. Then he appears. "You ready, Dale? These guys are usually breathin' down my neck. Today I couldn't find 'em."

His mother, a tiny, plump, birdlike woman with snow-white hair, intercepts him on his way back to the locker room. She asks for three autographed programs. "When you get time," she says. "I know you're busy." She turns to the man shadowing her son. "Aren't mommies terrible?"

Back in his office, he confers with Dan Minert on Robinson's condition ("His concern is whether he can take a pass," says Minert; "He's gonna play, I'm tellin' ya," says Frieder) and posts the week's schedule for study table, weight work, films, stretching, pre-game taping and free throws.

Frieder is asked if he ever taught driver education. "No," he says, "but someone in this room did."

"He's the guy we showed the movies about," says Fisher, who is leaving immediately after the game for Tilsonburg, Ontario, where he will see a prospect from Sarnia play a road game.

"So you've got a three-and-a-half-hour drive?" says Frieder.

"You didn't bring your fuzzbuster, did you?" Fisher asks.

"It's in my car," says Frieder.

"Can I borrow it?" says Fisher.

"You should take Ashby," says Frieder. "Why don't you call up Ashby?"

Minert returns. "Whadda you think?" Frieder asks. "Whadda *you* think?"

"He's in pretty good shape," says Minert. "He's not having a lot of trouble with it. He says it's where it was when he came back to practice [after hurting it the first time]."

"Tell him to let us know if he has any trouble."

"I already did."

There is an almost preternatural calm in the locker room. It is as quiet as it ever gets. The players are out on the court shooting around, and the only sound is the distant drone of VCRs taping other games. Frieder seems almost tranquil. Here, there are no well-wishers, autograph seekers, recruits, hangers-on, reporters, fans or parents. There aren't even any players. For a man who professes to enjoy his solitude, Frieder lives a life where it's hard to come by.

"This is why a lot of guys stay in the locker room," he says. "They don't come out until their team goes back [on the court at game time]."

That time is getting closer. He goes out to watch the final few minutes of pre-game shooting. Stoyko swishes a three-pointer from deep in the corner.

"Hey, Stoyk!" Frieder yells. "Why don't you shoot it like that in games?"

"I'm too nervous," Stoyko replies.

"Their concentration is good," Frieder says after watching for a minute or so. "They're not out there screwing around. They're shooting 'em in. They're business." It is just another little bit of data wriggling in Frieder's net.

He waves the team in to the locker room. As they're getting settled, he tries to find the programs for his mother. "It takes an act of Congress to get programs around here," he grouses. "People think the coach has an unlimited supply of everything."

He stops at Robinson's locker for a report.

"He said I could go but if it starts hurting to come out," the first-year guard says.

"How does it feel now?"

"It's stiff in the joints, like it was before."

"Don't overhandle it. Take wide-open jumpers. Play defense."

Back in the coaches' office, Frieder tells Fisher about a woman behind the bench who was bugging him about a scorer's mistake in last Monday's game. Fisher is reminded of a time when the team was at Iowa. A distinguished-looking man, who looked familiar enough that Fisher returned his greeting, took him by the arm behind the bench during a timeout and said, "You're doing a great job, a great job, but can't the guys stop standing up during the games? They're blocking my view."

A voice from the locker room urges, "Shut the door!" and Frieder obliges.

Rhythmic, insistent chants are heard through the door: cheers, songs, some homemade rap music. "Our house, our house, blue-blue-blue-blue, let's get geeked, let's get pumped."

Frieder smiles. "Gary's really trying to be a good captain," he says. "He always takes a few minutes before the game to talk to them. We never had one, even when Orr was here, who talked to 'em before a game. He came to me before the opener and said, 'When are you gonna talk?' I told him. He said, 'Is it all right if I talk to 'em for a few minutes before the game?'"

The chorus quiets. The door opens. Frieder stands at the front of his team. "Carry your concentration and enthusiasm onto the floor," he says. "They're starting Soucie instead of Henderson for a little more offense. Make sure they don't make you play defense for a long time. Run the plays. And run the plays to completion."

Fisher—again—goes over individual matchups and specific tendencies. This is the third time in 24 hours the players have been exposed to this material. Then Frieder has the floor one last time.

"There are two or three things on my mind," he says. "Long shots mean long rebounds. They're starting Soucie, besides for offense, because they want to spread the floor. The main thing is to contain so they don't have us five on four. Kick it in, kick it out, basket. Their defense is good man-to-man. They don't give up many layups. You've gotta make them play defense and exploit them some. They've gotta be worried about us. We don't want to be hearing from Ypsilanti. Let's go do the job."

In keeping with a tradition that is, as far as anyone knows, eternal, each player and coach slaps the "Go Blue" sign above the doorway as he exits.

"We're taking no prisoners," says Higgins, with a prescience that he probably doesn't imagine himself.

The game is almost unbelievably easy, a virtual highlight film for the Wolverines. The Hurons' three-point game abandons them, Michigan's hitherto suspect inside defense chokes off Grant Long, and the long shots that result do indeed mean long rebounds, most of which become Wolverine baskets. Michigan shoots 68 percent in the first half to 28 percent for Eastern Michigan, which also makes only 7 of 13 free throw attempts. The margin in rebounds is 2 to 1, in assists 4 to 1. The halftime score is 66–27.

The players are as high as a ski lift as they roll into the locker room. The coaches pile into their cubicle for the customary conference, but there isn't a great deal to say.

"I knew they were ready," says Frieder, "but I didn't think it was going to be this easy."

He goes out for his first set of remarks to the players. "Men, that was a great first half," he says. "Now listen. This next 20 minutes, I'm gonna tell you right now, it's 0–0 on that scoreboard and it's like practice. And if this 20 minutes of practice isn't good, we're gong to practice Sunday and/or Monday. This is important. Every four minutes when we have a television timeout, I want to see good results and a bigger spread. We don't bullshit out there. We're gonna play the game the way it's supposed to be played. But that was a great effort and congratulations to all of you."

Back in the office, Frieder is almost exuberant. "Sonofa. . .they were. . .well, see, we got 'em startin' to shoot that long shot quicker and then it's over. It's over when they did that."

"Well," says Dave Hammer, "it helps to have Long on the bench for the last eight and a half minutes, too."

"You might want to give some thought to running some different plays," says Fisher. "If we don't have anything out of transition, run a set play and make it work. Run it to completion before you get into motion. . . ."

"I'll tell 'em that," says Frieder. "We're gonna run each set play at least once to completion. If somebody doesn't do what they're supposed to do, we're gonna take him out."

There are a few technical problems to discuss, but not many. Robinson has played so well that the pre-game concerns about his thumb have been all but forgotten. The primary fear is that the big lead will vitiate motivation for the second half. Beyond that, the coaches sound like a bunch of guys talking sports in a bar.

Frieder notes that the Mills–Long confrontation (they are cousins and former high school teammates) has been a bust so far. "That's typical of all that bull," he says. "Remember last year— Anthony Robinson and Gary Grant? They got a lousy three points between 'em."

"You can bet, though, that Grant Long is gonna come out and try to get his points," says Fisher.

"If we do the job," says Frieder, "we'll make him look bad. If we're in there diggin' and helpin' . . ."

". . .doublin' . . ." says Hammer.

"Yeah," says Frieder. "That's a pretty awesome display of basketball, I have to admit that. That was pretty impressive. How in the hell can that team go into Missouri. . ."

". . . 'Cause Missouri's not that good, Bill," says Hammer. "You can't tell the kids that, but Missouri's no damn top 10 team. Those people are crazy puttin' that crap in there."

"We may have screwed up five or six things, but, boy, we did a lot of things well," says Frieder. "Gary gave it up at the right time. We overpassed two or three times, but I'd rather have 'em overpass than underpass."

He goes out to talk to the team:

"Three or four things. One, I want us to do things the right way. I'm not gonna let you play if you don't. I don't want to turn three-point plays into turnovers when we could have baskets. And I got on Mills' butt when he got a charge. All he had to do was give the ball back to the guy who gave it to him, or go up and dunk it, and we'd have had the three-point play. But he spun and made a fancy move and he ends up with his third foul and could have been hurt. I got on Calip, same thing. Gary, I've been on his butt many times because of that. That's not teaching us anything. If you want to go in and dunk one and you can do it and it's a natural thing to do, fine. I don't care. But I want baskets when we're in transition. I don't read the scoreboard. I evaluate you on every play, so make sure. If you're running the floor hard, you're gonna have all kinds of opportunities to get great baskets and great plays.

"He's [EMU Coach Ben Braun] gonna try to regroup 'em and they might regroup for five minutes, but if you keep playing the way you've been playing, it'll get back to the same way. They'll start shootin' it quickly and you're gonna get transition stuff. Now all you gotta do is stay in there and rebound, run the floor. We want it done the right way.

"The other thing, in this half, we're gonna run each play, when we get to do a set play, we're gonna run each play at least once to completion, like it was a practice situation, so this can help us prepare for Big Ten teams. So we're gonna run corner and option and blue and high and low and special and x, etc. We'll call 'em out. We're gonna run 'em all to completion, so we want you to be thinking out there so we can work that in.

"We want our defense to be good, so work hard. We'll come with new people when you get tired. We want the same type of half the second half as we had in the first half. I'm gonna let you play, as long as you do things the right way, because you need to play. I'm not worried about that. It's good for them to have you play against 'em. They need to go against good players. So that's not a problem.

"But I want you to do the things the right way out there. I want Gary to lead this team like he did in the first half. He made good baskets, he cashed in on the transition stuff, he passed the ball — he must have had a dozen assists — and ran our plays to completion. Mark, you did good off the bench. Loy did a nice job. Grant Long is gonna try to get his points, you know that. They're gonna go in to him, Loy, so you've gotta key on him. Glen or whoever, you've gotta help on him and everybody board, 'cause he'll probably force some and again you'll be off to the races.

"When you go back out there, if there's four or five minutes on the clock (until the horn for the second half), get good, hard shots. Gary, get 30 seconds of good, hard layups to get as loose as you can. Make sure you come ready to play the second half. All right, let's go."

And they do. Ironically, Frieder's wrath seems to mount in direct proportion to the lead, as if he can't stand to let his players enjoy this until it's really over.

"Get after those loose balls, men," he implores, with the margin at 49 points. Lest anyone wonder why a coach even notices such a flaw in such a context, it should be noted that this becomes a problem of no little importance later on.

He complains to Art Willard, one of the three Mid-American Conference officials working the game, about lane violations, which have been legion. Says Willard, in an exaggerated display of mock humility: "That's what we do in the Mid-Am. We don't know how to play."

With the score 98–51, Eastern puts in an offensive rebound. "We're givin' 'em up in bundles down here. Let's play smart defense and get some rebounds."

With the score 104–57, Bob Tait misses a free throw. "Well, re-bound the SOB!"

The final score is 115–63, the most lopsided defeat in Eastern Michigan history. No one is more surprised than Frieder. "Maybe this team is a little better than I thought," he tells Larry Henry on the WJR post-game show.

He does his other radio show. On the way to the locker room, he stops to sign autographs, stops to shake hands, stops to get his picture taken with a fan, stops to say hello to Gary Grant's high school coach, finally gets to the locker room stairs, which he takes two at a time.

"Congratulations," he says to the team. "You did a great job playing. You did a great job preparing. The first half was phenomenal. In spite of exams and all the games, you did a phenomenal job."

He makes a few announcements about training and study table schedules, concluding with, "Take a couple of days away from basketball. And be humble when you talk to the press."

Boyd is on the phone from Washington, D.C. Fisher is already on his way to Ontario. A group of kids from Angell Elementary School, where Jan's friend, Nan Gill, is the principal, are milling around the locker room.

At 4:18, Frieder bounds out of the locker room and, escorted by Sports Information Director Bruce Madej, makes his way across the hall to the lounge, where the post-game press conference is conducted in one of the last of the smoke-filled rooms.

"I was shocked," he tells the reporters. "I was really shocked. We were really concerned about this team. We gave it Big Ten-type preparation—stayed in the Campus Inn, extra free throws, extra meetings. But I knew they were ready."

"How?" asks a writer.

"From the way they ate their pizza last night."

There isn't much more to say. Most of the writers probably began composing their stories at halftime and need only pick up a few quotes to fill in the blanks. The press conference is shorter than usual and Frieder crosses the hall again.

"I should have asked Canham," Jan says.

"She wanted 'em [the Angell School kids] in the press conference," Bill says, his face a mask of pop-eyed disbelief.

"Did you stop coaching?" asks Charlie Vincent of the *Detroit Free Press*.

"I just watched the last six or seven minutes," says Frieder, an assertion some witnesses might challenge. "I didn't enjoy it but I wasn't gonna get mad at my kids."

He goes to the supply room for a box of wristbands and hands them out to the Angell School brigade. "Is it an NCAA violation to give wristbands to elementary kids?" he wonders out loud. Coaches talk about the NCAA the way disgruntled employees talk about the boss in a particularly dimwitted bureaucracy. It is the butt of jokes, the target of insults and abuse. Nobody says anything nice about it—about individuals, perhaps, but never about the institution.

Frieder shepherds Higgins into his office. "You're so much better when you let your shots come from the offense," he tells him.

"That was high school stuff coming back," Higgins says. "I'm aware of what I'm doing."

Frieder excuses Higgins as Minert enters to give the coach a medical update. "Rumeal will be in a cast until Friday," he says. "He can do defensive work. Terry has a bruise of his lower back [from the charging call Frieder disdained so]. J. P. has a cartilage tear in his right knee [from Friday's practice]. We'll do arthroscopic surgery Monday afternoon if it's no better or worse."

"So we're talking three weeks?"

The players drift out. They are going to do something they haven't done in almost two months, since practice started on Oct. 15. They are going to spend 48 hours away from basketball.

Eventually, Frieder leaves, too. He is going to do the things he always does this time of year—watch the tape of the game, watch a little Nickelodeon (other than hoops, his favorite TV fare is reruns of shows from the '50s and '60s), try to sleep, fail, spend Sunday afternoon at the arena. . . .

7

I Wish Next Year Started Tomorrow

I had told them before the game not to fall behind early. They'd been doing it all year and Assembly Hall in Champaign, Illinois, was no place to continue.

So here we were, six minutes into the game, and Illinois was leading, 13–4. It was a two-point game the rest of the way but, like they say, close only counts in horseshoes and grenades. Three of our last four games had been on the road and we'd lost all of them. Whatever slim chance we had of tying Purdue for the Big Ten title was gone, and our NCAA seed was sinking fast. Part of it was the schedule; we played three of our four toughest road games within 11 days at the end of the season. Part of it was inexperience; the biggest difference between us and Purdue was Melvin McCants teaching Terry Mills the things Roy Tarpley taught him. And part of it was fatigue; younger players are more prone to that, and it makes them persist in habits that they know they should break.

I told them right after the game, "We're not working hard enough as a group, and it starts with Gary. We're not working hard enough to get that ball where we have to get it, under control and under pressure. We're too eager to deviate, put it on the floor and do stupid things. You've got to dig in there under pressure.

"You're not dedicated to being as good a rebounding team as you can be. You've given away too many second and third shots. You big guys, it's going to force us to a smaller lineup if you don't dominate the boards. You've got to say they're not going to get second and third shots on me and you've got to go hard after that basketball.

"The third thing is you've got to decide how badly you want it. You've got to decide are we going to bounce back here and beat the hell out of Ohio State on Saturday. It's no disgrace losing to this team on the road. But it is a disgrace to play the way that we played at times, not using good judgment and not paying attention at timeouts. Those are the things you've got to get corrected.

"I've got great faith in you. Those are three tough games on the road. I'm really disappointed we didn't win at least one of them. But to say it's no disgrace and not do anything about correcting it is not doing our job. You're too good a basketball team not to be ready to go. If anybody's got any suggestions for me, you talk to me on the plane on the way home, because I'm open to suggestions.

"Hell, if you want until Saturday off, to not practice tomorrow and Friday, if you think that's what the best thing is, you can have it. But we can't have guys coming into Crisler Arena saying I'm tired. Illinois wasn't tired. Purdue wasn't tired. Iowa wasn't tired. We shouldn't be tired.

"If anybody's got any suggestions, I want to hear from you on that plane, so by the time we talk when we get back in Ann Arbor, we know exactly what we have to do tomorrow and Friday to get ready for Saturday and the NCAA tournament."

Some sniping and bickering had flared up at halftime of the Indiana game at Crisler three weeks before. We were up by two, but it had been a lot more, and there was some name-calling and finger-pointing and so forth as we came into the locker room. I thought we coaches did a good job with it. We addressed it. We let them know we noticed. But we didn't chew them out about it until the next day. First, we had to win that game.

Gary was still fuming when we left the locker room, so I talked with him individually before we went back out. I said, "You've got to lead now. This is where you've got to lead. That's why you're the captain. They're not going to do it to you. You've got to do it to them. Hey, man, forget it and win this game." And we did, by 20 points. We were just frustrated because we knew we'd blown that lead.

But the season really seemed to wear on this team. I don't know if it was because of the new Big Ten schedule format, where we basically made eight road trips instead of four, or because they were so young and not used to the pressure and grind of the Big Ten, or because there was so much media focus on things happening off the court, but they were turning into basket cases themselves. I know I was so worn out by the end of the year that I caught the flu at the NCAA regional in Seattle and spent most of my time lying down when I wasn't coaching or at a press conference.

After the Illinois game, a few of the players did come up to talk, and I called a few more up myself. I think it helped them to talk about their concerns and how they saw the situation.

Something helped because we beat Ohio State and then we went to Salt Lake City and beat Boise State and Florida before North Carolina ended our season for the second year in a row, this time in Seattle. We made it to the Sweet Sixteen for the first time since I was head coach, and we did it in a year when we were picked by almost everybody, including me, to finish fourth or fifth in the Big Ten.

That, to me, should have been the story of the season. We had two starters, Rumeal Robinson and Terry Mills, who had never played college ball before. In 20 of our games, we had another starter, Loy Vaught, who had averaged only 12 minutes per game the year before. And we won 26 of 34 and finished second in the Big Ten and 10th in the nation. In its own way, it was as big an accomplishment as winning 20 the year before, but what got all the attention?

Roy Tarpley revealing that he was undergoing treatment for a drug problem. Sean Higgins becoming academically ineligible. Me pushing a camera out of my face at halftime of the Iowa game. Using two players who had sat out a year because of Proposition 48. Rumors about Glen Rice going pro. Rumors about me going to Texas.

The Tarpley story broke less than a week after practice started. It seems like his problem must really have taken hold over the summer after his rookie year, which was the first summer he had a lot of money, a lot of freedom and a lot of time. Far from avoiding it, I put the clippings up in the locker room so the kids could read it. I wanted them to know about it and to know about the consequences. We talk about that type of stuff all the time.

I called Roy as soon as I could get a hold of him. I told him I was really sorry to hear about his problem, but it was necessary for him to take all the steps that he had to take to make sure it never occurred again. I told him, "Roy, you know you love basketball and you're in the position now that your second contract will be so great that it's going to set you up for life. You'll be able to live the rest of your life the way you want to. You can't allow something like this to destroy your life."

Of course, he agreed. He promised me. "Coach," he said, "I just ran with the wrong people. My mom's coming down to Dallas to live, and I'm going to do everything I have to do to get it done."

He told me he had to go to meetings, get in a conditioning program and so on. He couldn't even have one beer. "Do it, Roy," I said. "You've got too much to lose. If you lose your career, you're out on the streets and you're going to give up doing what you enjoy doing."

"It's not a problem," he said. "I'm going to handle it."

The way he played last year sure made it look like he is. That's what gets me about all these rumors about my program. How do they think we won two straight Big Ten titles if we had a drug problem? It can't be done. That doesn't mean there isn't a positive test once in a while. But if there is, we deal with it. We bring in the family and we require mandatory counseling and we give them a chance.

The day the Tarpley story came out, I got to practice and Dan Minert said, "We're testing 'em today." I said, "Fine." I decide in general when we'll test and then Minert finalizes the day, which I thought he had done. But it turned out the test had been ordered by someone in university administration, who then called me over the weekend with a lot of insinuations and allegations that were not true.

On Monday, I talked to Canham about it because I was mad. Don said, "Did you know they're testing 'em again today?"

I said, "They are?"

He said, "Yeah. They wanted to test 'em Monday thinking they'd lower their guard after being tested Friday."

And then they came back and tested them a third time on Thursday. And everything was negative, like it was the entire season.

We started the season at the Great Alaska Shootout in Anchorage. It took us 20 hours to get there due to plane problems. We were five hours late getting out of Detroit, missed our direct flight from Chicago to Anchorage, wound up going through Seattle and had to fight for seats every step of the way. I told a press conference after we got there that if it took us that long to get back, we were going to miss our first two home games.

It wouldn't have been worth it, except for what we learned in the three games we played. It was dark 18 hours a day, the crowds were small, there were prostitutes and a million bars and it was just depressing.

I said at a press conference that I wouldn't come back even if they held the Final Four there, which wasn't sticking my neck out much, but the Sporting News picked up my comment and I started getting a lot of mail from Alaska. Actually, everybody's mood in Alaska improved a great deal by Monday. We had won two of our three games and then enjoyed a fantastic side trip that included airplane rides, snowmobiling and dog sledding. The kids had a super time.

After it rained the whole time we were in Seattle for the regional, I felt like apologizing to Alaska. At least, the snow looks better than the rain.

But Alaska was a good experience. We had three different types of games with three different types of opponents — an easy win over Miami and Tito Horford, a tough loss to a veteran Arizona team, and then a come-from-behind win in a close game with Alabama-Birmingham.

That last one was so important. Consolation games are the toughest in the business, especially the third game in three days. We got a lead and we didn't sustain it but it wasn't because we weren't working. We got tired and we made mistakes but we played with great unity. Our unity was a hundred percent better than in the Arizona game. It didn't look good, but we came back and won it.

We left Alaska at 1:20 on a Tuesday morning, got back to Ann Arbor late Tuesday afternoon and opened at home against Bowling Green on Wednesday night. We must have shaken off the jet lag, because the way we rolled through the rest of the pre-conference schedule was almost scary. My Big Ten championship teams sometimes played just well enough to beat the teams we played in December. Last year's team went after 'em like they were Big Ten opponents. We beat Bowling Green by 21, Central Michigan by 30, Western Michigan by 47, Austin Peay by 21, Eastern Michigan by 52, Northern Michigan by 24 and Grambling by 17 before we went down to Tampa and won the South Florida Tournament.

At one point, Steve Fisher ran into Jud Heathcote at Metro Airport. Fisher said, "How ya doin', Jud?"

Jud said, "How'm I doin'? We're on our way to Austin Peay to lose to another team you beat by 50." They did, too.

One morning I was on the radio and the announcer started getting on my schedule. I said, "Let me ask you something. Have you said anything about Michigan State losing to Eastern Michigan?"

He said, "No."

I said, "Have you said anything about them losing to Austin Peay?"

He said, "No."

I said, "Then why in the hell would you rip me for beating them? I don't understand this. We're playing teams that everybody else in the league is playing and because we go out and play hard for 40 minutes and have impressive victories, you want to rip our schedule, but you don't say anything about someone else losing to the same teams."

By Christmas, I thought this could be my best team ever. I knew it was the quickest Michigan team I had ever seen, going back to the days when I went to Yost Fieldhouse to see Cazzie Russell and Bill Buntin. We were quick at every position. And even though we were expecting everything of Gary—beat the presses, score, guard the toughest offensive player, be the captain, provide leadership—he was doing it. We weren't good on defense because we were young, but we were getting better. We went eight deep. We had a great scoring forward in Glen Rice and three good players off the bench in Mike Griffin, Sean Higgins and either Vaught or Mark Hughes, depending on who started. We could be patient. We could run. And we looked like we'd outrebound everybody.

And then Sean Higgins became ineligible. So did Demetrius Calip, another freshman, but Sean was the one who got all the publicity. Sean was the big recruiting prize that we had apparently lost to UCLA until the NCAA voided his tender. And Sean was the one whose grades became front-page news.

It was the first time in eight years as head coach that I had a shock like that. If we had somebody in trouble before, I always knew. But I was thrown off guard because I was seeing his papers and his grades in his communications class and they were "B's" and "B+'s" and "B−'s," so I figured that class was in good shape, a "B−" or a "C+" at worst. We knew he wasn't doing well in psychology but we figured his other courses would pull him up to a 2.0 with no problem. His other courses were English and sociology, by the way. He wasn't taking any cake courses.

But he missed some classes in communications and they lowered him half a grade for every two misses and they wouldn't allow him to do any extra credit work. I guess the attendance requirement was in the syllabus, but I didn't know about it. Every class is different about attendance. It goes right back to no matter how much you delegate, unless you're checking everything yourself, that's what you can run into. I should have read the syllabus myself.

All of a sudden, he was in trouble in two courses instead of one. I let him out of practice several days to do extra studying for his finals but it wasn't enough. He just missed a 2.0 and, really, when you think about it, what the hell is wrong with that? If you checked all the other freshmen at Michigan who aren't athletes, how many of them went under a 2.0 their first term? Ten percent? Twenty percent?

But this freshman was on the front page of the *Ann Arbor News* for three straight days. This freshman had letters to the editor written about him. It goes along with having a big-time program, I suppose, but it seems so unfair to the kid.

I think it's clear we just weren't as good without Sean. He could play both guard and forward, so he gave us more versatility and maneuverability. He gave us more depth. And he was our best three-point shooter. In fact, he was the Big Ten's best three-point shooter at the time he became ineligible. He's great at that because he has no conscience. He'll only shoot if he has the ball.

I don't think I'm going to shock anybody when I say that Gary Grant was a big reason we still did as well as we did. But I don't think most people truly appreciate how many ways he can have a positive effect on your game.

Two games from last year are good examples. After our first Big Ten loss of the season, at Ohio State, we came home to play Wisconsin. This is a tough situation, not only coming back from a loss but also playing a team you know you're supposed to beat.

And it wasn't easy. We were up by 15 at the half but they just wouldn't die. We finally beat them by 11. Gary scored "only" 13 points and everyone wanted to know why he had such a bad game.

The national pee wee bowling champion of 1948. You could look it up.

One of Saginaw's leading tap dancers. You could look that up, too.

When I was 4, they could still get me to sit still.

Cadet Frieder, Mar. 15, 1956. That's a brand new Ford, you know.

I really did play basketball. I'm number 30.

That's me at top left. And you didn't believe I was ever a tennis coach.

At the 1971 state finals, I watched the game from a fresh perspective.

John Orr and I hug each other after beating Missouri to qualify for the Final Four in 1976.

Dick Vitale proves once and for all he's a Michigan fan.

I guess I am a basket case.

Gary Grant comes off the Crisler Arena court for the last time.

Laura with her program before an Iowa game.
You don't think she knows what's going on?

One of the things I love about my job is that it enables me to provide experiences like this for Laura.

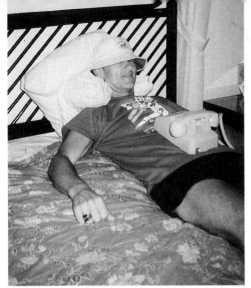

This is how I relax on vacation.

Celebrating the NIT championship with Janice.

Bobby and I in Bloomington, and in Crisler Arena (below), in friendlier days.

I said, "What bad game? He had six assists, four steals, only one turnover and held Trent Jackson, their leading scorer, to nine points. And he had seven rebounds, including the last three of the game when they were coming at us. You think he didn't play well because he didn't score 23 points, but he did play well. He played great."

The other game I'm thinking of was at home against Michigan State. Again, he "only" scored 17 and Glen Rice got the headlines for scoring 33, which is fine. He's a great shooter and a great scorer. But look at the stretch of that game where we went on a 12–3 run to go from a 51–48 lead to a 63–51 lead. Our offensive sequence was Grant layup, Grant layup, Grant one and one, Robinson layup from Grant, Grant one and one, Grant layup. He scored 10 of the points and assisted on the other two, and that was the game.

Right about this time, Gary and Glen were battling for the Big Ten scoring championship. Glen, of course, eventually won it, becoming the first Michigan player to lead the league since Campy Russell in 1974, and Glen and Gary were the first teammates ever to finish one-two in the conference in scoring. Jim Spadafore of the *Detroit News* asked Glen about winning the scoring title and he said he didn't care as long as someone from Michigan won it, and that a senior ought to win it, anyway.

"You've got him trained," Spad said to me.

"He's not trained," I said. "That's the kind of kid he is. That's the way he feels. He really believes that. He's a sincere kid."

I don't like to make excuses, but I think if Gary had been healthy down the stretch in the regular season, we might have won one of those three road games that we lost. With that groin injury, he just couldn't get any legs into his shot. He made only 7 of 20 shots at Purdue and scored just eight points at Illinois. He was 16 of 46 from the field in the last three games before the tournament.

And, I hate to say it, he wasn't that much better in the tournament. He played good defense against Boise State but he also had six turnovers and only nine points. He had his best game against Florida—19 points and 11 assists—and I thought he'd turned it around, but then he was so bad against North Carolina that I only played him for 29 minutes. He finally fouled out with 36 seconds to go, with almost as many turnovers (five) as points (seven), one steal and 3 for 10 shooting.

It's too bad. I thought he would play extremely well and I can't tell you why he didn't. I think he tries too hard and when he doesn't start well, he thinks too much about it. North Carolina can do that to you.

But at least we made it past the second round. I can't tell you what a relief that was, especially after the problems we had getting to Salt Lake City and the problems Boise State caused us once we got there.

The trip to Utah was typical of what happens when you don't do things yourself. You are required to use the travel arrangements the NCAA makes for you for the tournament. You've got to go through its travel agency. You call and then you wait to hear back. They finally got us 33 seats on a flight, but what they didn't tell us was that 27 of them were middle seats.

Well, that's ridiculous. It's another example of how even though the NCAA is making a fortune on college basketball, it really doesn't care about the kids. Here's Terry Mills and here's Loy Vaught and they're doing a great job, and when we send them to the West Regional, we put them in a middle coach seat. How stupid can you be? It took about two hours to get that straightened out. To make a long story short, I bought some first-class seats so we could operate and at least have our team in decent aisle seats. Stuff like that doesn't even enter the NCAA's mind.

When we got to Salt Lake City, there were two reminders, one pleasant and one unpleasant, of Michigan basketball history. The pleasant reminder was the game that night at the Salt Palace between the Dallas Mavericks, Roy Tarpley's team, and the Utah Jazz, Rickey Green's team. That was a great treat, to arrive so far from home and see two guys in the NBA who had such great success at our institution. The unpleasant reminder was Boise State, which played like it wanted to be the 1988 version of Fairleigh Dickinson or Villanova.

They were a tough, veteran, well-coached, disciplined team that did everything they had to do to cause us trouble, but we still would have put them away sooner if we had made our free throws. We were up by eight, 59–51, when Griffin missed a one and one and then Grant missed a one and one. We were up by six, 61–55, when Gary missed another one and one, and by three, 61–58, when Terry Mills did the same. Griffin finally made two free throws to finish them off, 63–58. At that point, I was really worried about Florida, our next opponent, who had beaten St. John's.

I needn't have worried. Before the first TV timeout, we had them, 18–7, and the lead just kept getting bigger. The kids were determined to get that second-round monkey off our backs and they did, 108–85. The thing that pleased me as much as anything else was that it was the 100th Michigan win in Gary Grant's career. I think I wanted that as much as I wanted to get to the Sweet Sixteen.

I loosened up the curfew a little bit that night so the players could celebrate. We didn't have to play again for six days, after all. I originally set it for 11 p.m., then a couple of players would come up and dicker and I'd make it half an hour later, then an hour and so on. It eventually got to 1 a.m., but I knew what I was doing: Because of the Sunday liquor laws in Utah, last call on Saturday night is 11:30 p.m. Some of the writers were complaining about that, but I wasn't. That's why I gave in.

The dream ended in Seattle with nonstop rain and me sick as a dog the whole time. Frankly, it was a little less realistic than most dreams. North Carolina was a winnable game that we didn't win, which was true of several of our late-season games, but I doubt we could have beaten Arizona in any event.

We figured if it was a transition and backcourt game, we could win, but if it became an inside game, they would win. And they did what we like to do. They were the aggressor. They dictated the tone of the game. A good chunk of our inside game disappeared along with Gary, and a brilliant, even heroic, performance by Rumeal Robinson just couldn't offset what Carolina had to throw at us.

But we just didn't make the big plays consistently over the last third of the season. We had problems finding ways to win against good teams on the road, which meant we weren't a top 10 team but more like a top 15 team. The top five to eight teams find a way to win those games. We're only talking about a difference of maybe 10 points, but 10 points can mean three games and three games is the difference between 24–7, which is how we finished the regular season, and 27–4, which is a top five kind of record.

On the plus side, we scored more field goals than our opponents in 30 of 34 games, the exceptions being at Syracuse, at Illinois, at Minnesota and home against Michigan State. That shows we can improve if we learn to be a little smarter about being physical and get to the line more. We were 8–0 against the bottom four teams in the league and 9–1 against the bottom five. We didn't lose any games we weren't supposed to lose and, believe me, the second-division clubs the second time around are the toughest to prepare for. When you play Northwestern and Wisconsin in February and March, you've gotta make sure your kids don't overlook them and that they're mentally ready to go.

On the minus side, we never came back from a halftime deficit all season. We were behind at halftime in five games and lost all of them. And it was really more of an offensive failure than a defensive one. We kept giving ourselves chances that we couldn't cash in on. I look back especially at the late-season losses at Illinois, Purdue and Iowa and see where we had three possessions, four points down, and didn't score, four possessions, six points down, and didn't score, and so on.

But you'd have to say Rumeal Robinson came into his own in the Carolina game. It was almost as if he saw that no one else was taking charge and took it upon himself. Tired as I was, sick as I was, he almost made me wish that next year started tomorrow. He was quick, aggressive, played good defense and took the ball to the hole stronger than any other Michigan guard since, I don't know, maybe Steve Grote. He's a beautiful kid, too. He has a learning disability, and he has to work twice as hard as anybody else to get his schoolwork done, but he does it and he never complains.

He gives you hope, and that's why you keep coming back.

8

Selling the Program

They put a label on you. They've got a label on me as a recruiter, but I'm not as good a recruiter as they think.

My first eight recruiting years as a head coach, I got exactly three high school All-Americans. And two of them—Terry Mills and Antoine Joubert—played within an hour's drive of the campus. Mills' home is in Romulus, which is only 17 miles away. It was easy to see him or go to his high school. Really, we didn't spend nearly as much time on him as we have on other recruits. By the time Terry played his first game for Michigan, I had known him about seven years.

But we've never really gotten what we've wanted. We've never really signed a big-time center out of high school. They talk about me being a great recruiter, but I've never gotten a big-time center, and I'm still trying. Now Tim McCormick and Roy Tarpley developed into good Big Ten centers, but I'm talking about an Olajuwon, a Sampson, a Benoit Benjamin, a Patrick Ewing, and you can go on and on. We've never signed anyone like that.

The only way that's ever going to happen with Michigan is if a player like that grows up in Michigan. Otherwise, you're not going to see that type of player here because it usually involves something extra. Maybe not necessarily cheating—although it might involve cheating—but it might involve something like hiring the high school coach or a parent or something like that, and we're not going to do that. Michigan would not stand for that.

If I had gone in and told Canham I was going to hire some guy that doesn't have his degree, or even somebody's high school coach, he would not have gone along with that. And we're certainly not going to pay out big bucks, so the only way it's going to happen is if some big guy grows up in Michigan. Now you've got a guy familar with Michigan. You've got all the advantages of a kid staying in the state, which are very important if a guy can think ahead. But there always seems to be something, with big-time players.

If you get right down to it, in my years as head coach at Michigan, who have I gotten outside of the Midwest? Sean Higgins, but he spent 11 years in Ann Arbor and his dad is in Detroit. That was a Michigan tie. We got Richard Rellford from Florida because we had the Anthony Carter connection there; they went to the same high school. We got Butch Wade from Boston, but Butch wasn't highly recruited. The biggest name people I've gotten have been Michigan people—Joubert, Mills—or Midwest people, like Gary Grant.

But I don't want to underestimate the significance of successfully recruiting McCormick. If you had to say who was the most important kid I ever signed as head coach, I'd have to say him, because he was the first player I signed as head coach, he was from Michigan, he was a 7-footer, and he said, "Hey, I don't care if Bill Frieder is a first-year head coach. I've got confidence in him."

It was extremely important that I get Tim. We had to have a good recruiting year because people were wondering if we were going to get kids like that or not with me as head coach. When he's considering guys like Dean Smith and Digger Phelps and some of these guys that have been established as head coaches, I think it meant a lot to convince him to come to Michigan.

That was funny, too. See, when Johnny Orr took the Iowa State job in the spring of 1980, I found out about it the morning before the day it was going to be announced. Canham was in Florida. Orr finally got a hold of him later that day, like five or six in the evening. Canham tells Orr to tell me I've got the job but not to do anything until he gets back.

The next morning, I'm leaving for the MacDonald's all-star game and McCormick's in the MacDonald's. I thought it was important for me to call everybody I was recruiting to let them know. I didn't want them to read in the paper that Orr was leaving and not know who the head coach is, so I called everybody that night. I didn't want to call them until I talked to Canham, but I couldn't get a hold of him anywhere, so I finally said, what the hell, I'm going to call them and tell them Orr's leaving, I'm the new head coach, it's going to be announced in a week. Because if I'm not the head coach, what difference does it make? And if I am the head coach, this is what I need to do. So that's what I did. I called all my recruits and told them that.

Then when I got to Washington, the press was all over the place because the word was now out that Orr was going to Iowa State. So I had to get a hold of Canham to find out what he wanted me to say to the press. And I finally did; he had come back that morning. He said, "You tell 'em that it's probably going to take a week before we get this settled but, sure, you're interested in the job and you would hope that you're a leading candidate." The following Monday is when they announced it, at the basketball bust, but everybody knew it by then.

All the Michigan kids we got were very important. Joubert was very important. We had had the good class the year before—Wade, Robert Henderson, Tarpley, Rellford and Paul Jokisch— but now here comes a great player out of Detroit. Even though I felt he wasn't going to be the savior that they were building him up to be, I think he was important for our credibility.

You have to remember that when I took over as head coach, there wasn't a single player from Michigan on the roster. Not one.

Mike McGee was from Omaha, Johnny Johnson from Buffalo, Thad Garner from Indiana, Ike Person from Illinois, and the Bodnars, Paul Heuerman and Joe James were from Ohio.

Then we signed McCormick and that started it. The next year we got Eric Turner from Flint and Leslie Rockymore from Detroit, and we just went from there. This season, we have Mills from Romulus, Mark Hughes from Muskegon, J. P. Oosterbaan from Kalamazoo, Glen Rice and Demetrius Calip from Flint and Loy Vaught from Grand Rapids.

I think sometimes when you're too close to a situation, you get too critical of it and you assume something farther away is much better. We had this happen in recruiting, where we recruited kids farther away because we didn't know them as well and we thought they were better than the ones we were passing up close by, because we knew them too well.

The big thing in recruiting is reading situations and not wasting time. You've gotta have a feeling that you're gonna have a chance. We might have lost a kid or two because we got him off early but if you think back to when I was an assistant, we lost a lot of kids. We were always second, and that was because we were wasting too much time on kids where we didn't have a chance.

For example, we did a great job on Derrell Griffith, but if we had read it right, we would have known in the fall that he was going to Louisville. Anybody could have pushed their way into second if they'd worked as hard as we did, but nobody was going to beat Louisville on Derrell Griffith. So I think what I've done is learn to read the situations better and just do a much better job on kids where we've got a legitimate chance.

I would say my best recruiting job had to be Rellford, Tarpley, Wade, Henderson and Jokisch, because it was a time when our program was floundering. We were having an atrocious year—the record books now say 8–19 but it was actually 7–20 because one of the wins was a forfeit from Wisconsin that came years later— and there were a lot of doubters out there. Can this guy coach? Does he have a good staff? What's going on at Michigan? How can they be 1–13, which we were at one point?

Well, it got us off our butt and we worked the hardest we ever worked in our entire life and we had a good recruiting year. It was crucial to get it. All those kids heard was, "Michigan's program is bad, they're not gonna win there, Frieder can't coach, Frieder's gonna get fired," and we recruited them anyway and we got them and then we won with them.

And we did it just right. We organized the whole thing so that each month, even though the season was bad, we were getting good news. First there was Tarpley's commitment, then there was Jokisch's commitment, then in February was Rellford's commitment. Every time we got a commitment, it took everybody's mind off the season and started building anticipation for the next year. Even though we were losing, we were getting good news and positive publicity. By the end of the year, the team came along and we were heroes again. We took a bad situation and we became heroes.

How we got some of those guys is pretty interesting. Like Tarpley, who had moved around so much—from New York to Alabama to Detroit—that people kind of lost track of him. Nobody had ever heard of the guy the summer before his senior year. He attended some camps and the scouts didn't even know he was there. Neither did we.

But late that summer, we saw this skinny kid with the long arms and we decided to take a chance. We had a lousy team coming back with a 6'2" forward and a 6'6" center, so we could afford to gamble. We got him to commit early and he never visited a school, not even ours. He was just kind of flabbergasted Michigan was interested, then he grew up to 6'11" and became a great player.

And then there were Rellford and Wade. I first met them in 1981 when they were playing for the New York Gauchos, a summer AAU team, at the Las Vegas Invitational. The coach got Richard because Richard's brother Cecil played at St. John's, and he got Butch from Boston somehow.

I did not know either kid, although Mike Boyd had recruited Richard, but we had never, ever seen Butch or anything.

They happened to be at the blackjack table at the Aladdin Hotel, and I just happened to be in there, too, so I just saw it as an opportunity to make sure they knew who I was. But the rules say you can't have any contact with the players until the start of their senior year. Technically, I could not talk to them.

So I went in and sat right between 'em, and I started talking to the dealer. I said, "Hey, I'm Bill Frieder, the basketball coach at Michigan, and on my right here is Richard Rellford and over here is Butch Wade. I cannot talk to these kids right now because of NCAA rules, but I can talk to you, and I just want you to know I'm recruitin' the hell out of 'em, and I want 'em to come to Michigan. I think they're great players," and so on.

That got those guys jacked up and jivin'. That might have been the whole key to their coming to Michigan, I don't know. Then when they got back to New York, I called them. They really liked that. Then I confirmed visits with both of them. I confirmed official visits for both of them, and they wanted to visit on the same date. And they were roommates when they came. But up to that day at the blackjack table, I had never had any contact with either one of them in any way, shape or form.

Recruiting was easy when had the bad year but the good years are a help, too. You have a Glen Rice watching our guys win a Big Ten championship and he wants to be a part of it. Terry Mills grew up watching Michigan be successful, so he wanted to be a part of it, so the bottom line is that every situation is completely different and you really don't know.

My second best recruiting job—and it wasn't far behind—came when the program was going good, only Orr was the head coach and I was the assistant, but I was very much involved. That was Phil Hubbard and Rickey Green. Hubbard was the first of a lot of great players we've gotten from Ohio: Steve Grote, the Bodnars, Paul Heuerman, Gary Grant and maybe Kirk Taylor and Eric Riley. I don't mean maybe they're from Ohio but maybe they'll be great.

We shouldn't beat Ohio State on those kids and it goes back to when Fred Taylor was the coach. He won five Big Ten titles in his first six years and seven altogether, but when the recruiting game changed, he didn't adjust. Fred was from the old school and rarely left his office to recruit kids. Well, that was Phil Hubbard.

We got Phil because he didn't think they really wanted him down there. Grote was recruited for football and then his basketball team went on and won the state championship, and Orr expressed an interest, but he wasn't really being recruited as a basketball player.

The Bodnars and Heuerman were great students, interested in law and professional schools and things like that. Gary came because of the Hubbard connection. They went to the same school in Canton, Phil's uncle still lives in the same town, Phil and Gary knew each other, plus Ron Stokes and Troy Taylor had just gone to Ohio State from his school and he really didn't want to compete against them, so we had a kind of a tie and an edge there.

The problem with Gary was that his high school coach had his own son as the other starting guard on the team. He wanted a scholarship for his son or he wanted a job for himself. Remember when he supposedly blew the whistle on us? Grant narrowed his choices to us, Illinois, Kentucky and Ohio State, and I think that somebody among those three, or all of them, must have offered his coach a job or offered his coach's son a scholarship: "If Gary comes to our school, we scholarship your boy." Well, that's a big financial thing to the coach. So he tried to engineer Gary going to some other school.

We eventually had to go around his coach, set up appointments in the house without him knowing, stuff like that. Then when Gary chose Michigan, he's the one who said we cheated, and we didn't. No one turned us in or anything. Then he later apologized to us. I've got the letter. I sent a copy to the NCAA. It got kind of nasty but we ended up getting Gary anyway.

That's when I started documenting everything. If the NCAA wants to know what we've done, I want to be able to tell them. That happens whenever you go after highly recruited kids. There are just so many rumors in something like this. We heard them again when we signed Terry Mills. You don't know what the temptations are like. Someone offered to see that Mills passed his SAT for $2,500. I didn't inquire as to how it would be done, and, obviously, I didn't do it.

Probably the biggest surprise was Glen Rice. We did very little on him. We were recruiting Roy Marble and we lost him to Iowa. We lost Lowell Hamilton to Illinois. And we lost Melvin McCants to Purdue. Those were our three main guys that year, and we didn't get any of them. So here we jumped on Glen, who was leaning toward Central Michigan or somewhere, and then Iowa State was coming in, but we just went hard and got him. You could see him coming along, getting better, and he was always a good shooter.

We got Kirk Taylor and we never even knew Kirk Taylor. He called us. I knew nothing about him. All I knew was Mike Boyd got word to me that we had to take a look at this kid. Then Kirk called and said he wanted to come to Michigan. I stalled for time, set up a visit with him, then sent someone to Toledo to get films on the state championship, so I could see him play, and he was a great player. We knew about him a week before we got him. We knew about Terry Mills for six years. Recruiting is funny.

We were fortunate the year before last with recruiting, with Higgins going to UCLA and then falling out of the sky for Michigan, and then Taylor coming along. Does that sound like great recruiting to you? When November came around, we didn't know about Taylor and, as far as we knew, we'd lost Higgins, so we got two pretty good players on the rebound, really.

We got Eric Riley on the rebound, too. He told us at one time it was down to Syracuse and Ohio State. We said, "It's down to Syracuse, Ohio State and Michigan. Keep us in there. We're not done yet." And by God, if we didn't hang in there and get him.

What we did was we convinced him not to sign on that Wednesday, the first day they could sign letters of intent. That was a great move because Syracuse ended up signing four recruits, three of them big guys, and Ohio State ended up signing four recruits, and by Sunday Eric had changed his own mind about going to those places. This kid decided, "Hey, I'm going to Michigan. These other schools talk about how they want me but they keep signing these other players." If we'd given up when he told us no, he wasn't coming to Michigan, we'd have lost him. He would have signed earlier and it wouldn't have mattered how many guys were signed.

Mike Boyd deserves a lot of credit. Mike was relentlessly on that phone, calling, sending telegrams and messages and notes, double- and triple-checking. It's crazy. You do what the competition does because you have to. You go to games because the other guy is there. You go to camps because the other guy is there. And you call kids because the other guys are calling them.

You've got to juggle home visits, school visits and seeing them play, plus their visits here. There are limits on each, both how many you can have and when you can have them, so you've gotta pinpoint it and you've gotta be really flexible. What if you find out after the first time that you like some other kid better? Or you've been in a home and it looks like a cheating situation and you're just going to get out completely? A lot of times you can tell. A lot of times you just get the feeling that they aren't interested in what you're talking about, academics and so on, that they're waiting to hear what else you can do for them—cars, transportation to games, that kind of thing. They want to hear that that's taken care of. Sometimes a coach wants to hear that you're going to hire him, or the kid wants a scholarship for a friend. A lot of that stuff they want to hear isn't illegal. A lot of people are out hiring high school coaches, but we're not going to do it.

After I lose a kid, I don't spend much time thinking about it. It's just like a game; you lose and you go on and you win the next one. But two recruits do come to mind, Derek Harper and Melvin McCants. We led on Melvin McCants from start to finish, we felt. He told us he was coming. He went to Purdue. Of course, we wound up with Glen Rice instead that year, so I don't feel too bad.

And then there was Derek Harper. We recruited him hard. The reason that hurt is the kid wanted to come, he was going to come, he committed orally, he even talked Harry Gozier, who was his best friend, into signing to play football here without even visiting because this was where Derek was coming, but then he went to Illinois. I've always wondered about that. I can't prove anything, but I think they must have turned his mother against us somehow so she wouldn't let him come here.

The nastiest stuff we hear about is in other conferences. There are conferences in the south and west that are supposed to be pretty bad and Nevada-Las Vegas is often in trouble, but we don't compete against those school for very many kids. Some people in our league seem to think that Illinois cheats but, except for the Harper situation, I've never had a problem with Illinois. I've never seen it. Bobby Knight has made the biggest noise about it but he's never come up with anything specific.

When you look at Lou Henson's roster, they're primarily Illinois kids, and he should get Illinois kids if he works hard, just like I should get Michigan kids.

Basically, you sell your program, you sell Michigan, you try to show everything in the best possible light. There were a lot of similarities in recruiting Gary Grant and Rumeal Robinson and they're good examples of how we go about it and how you have to present all aspects of your program and the university.

With both Gary and Rumeal, we told them we had a style that would showcase their strengths, that they could run and press and play the kind of ball they like to play and that we would stick with them if they had a bad game or a bad couple of games. They wouldn't have to be looking over their shoulder at somebody on the bench or wondering if we were going to go out and get jaycees. And we told them both that they realistically had a chance to be captain some day.

Then we told them about what it means to be with a successful program: the great facilities, the national TV appearances, the NCAA tournament, the trips to Alaska and Hawaii and Europe. And, of course, there's the advantage of having a degree from a school like Michigan. That blended really well with the hometown connections we had with both of them: Phil Hubbard, like I said, came from Canton, Ohio, like Gary, and he got his degree and had a successful career; Butch Wade came from the Boston area, like Rumeal, and he got his degree and had a successful career. In fact, at the time Rumeal came for his visit, there were eight kids from Boston on the football team. We use football a lot in recruiting.

We try to get the seniors who are making official visits, the ones who might be making decisions soon, in here the first three or four weekends of school for football games, when the weather is still nice. And we've done a great job of convincing people this is a great basketball school. We make a point of inviting the underclassmen to the key games with the big crowds and national television. We've got 'em convinced. I'm a salesman, and that's part of the job.

Since we've had a successful program, the recruiting has taken a different cast. It's "come join a great program and learn from the veterans in the program, and when they leave, your opportunity's gonna come. If you want to start and play 40 minutes at a school, go somewhere else. But if you want to play on a team that's going to be nationally ranked and might win the national championship and is going to be on national TV, come to Michigan. The worst thing that's going to happen to you is you're going to have a degree in four years."

I think that's why our transfer rate is low, because I do not talk playing time with anybody. But kids are short-term. They look at "what's in store for me next year" and they don't take into account that the guy who promises you a starting position may go out and take a jaycee kid, and then take a transfer. We don't do that at Michigan. I'm not saying I never will, but we haven't yet and I don't intend to, because I want to recruit freshmen, have them become part of the Michigan family, and when they leave four or five years from now, be happy that they came.

I feel there's an obligation on my part as well as on the player's. I could have panicked after our bad year and gone out and got jaycees and transfers, but I didn't. I went with freshmen, I hung with them and up the line we won a couple of Big Ten championships. I'm not that hungry for the wins.

So in addition to athletic ability, one of the qualities we look for in a kid is that he understands and responds to that. We also look for kids who play on winning teams—every starter on our 1976 NCAA runnerup team played for a state championship team in high school—and kids with room to grow. That might be the hardest thing of all to spot: a kid who has already gotten as good as he's going to get.

Some coaches will always recruit a certain type of player to their system, where I'm the type of guy that if there's a Tim McCormick in the state, I'm going to recruit him. Now if that means you're not going to be as quick as you used to be or want to be in the future, you're still going to coach so you can get McCormick into the game, which might mean more setup offense and stuff like that.

Louisville might not have taken McCormick if he was 10 minutes down the road, because they're going to have much more quickness, much more jumping ability, and they're going to have five guys that have all those characteristics.

When I became head coach, people wondered who was going to be my Bill Frieder, like I had been Johnny Orr's top recruiter. I don't think you can be quite as exact as that because every coach structures his staff differently, but Mike Boyd certainly deserves a lot of credit for this program. He's very involved in recruiting a lot of those kids. He develops relationships early, before I even get involved. He's the advance man.

And Mike knows that when he calls on me, I'll be there. Either other head coaches are coming in or the kid is starting to waver or whatever, but if he says I gotta get down there, I'm gonna be down there at the earliest possible opportunity. You know, John didn't go on the road that much toward the end of his years here, although he started again when he went to Iowa State. He was on the road a lot, because he knew what he had to do and he did it. I used to tease him by telling him, "You're in Michigan more now than you ever were when you lived here."

Mike probably knows who Bo Derek is, too, or whoever's the equivalent now. When I was an assistant, I was recruiting Glenn Rivers in Chicago and I saw a story in one of the papers that said, "If Bo Derek is a '10,' then Rivers is an '11.' " I said to myself, "Well, who in the hell is this Bo Derek?" I called back to the office to find out, because we had to get on this kid. George Pomey, who was doing the games on the radio at the time, was the guy who finally told me who Bo Derek was. I didn't know this person existed.

I don't have time for a whole lot besides basketball, and a lot of the time I put in on basketball is recruiting. You've gotta work hard at it and hang in there. You've gotta be careful, you've gotta be smart and you've gotta be lucky.

And it never ends.

9

Parents, Problems and Progress

The kids don't give me much trouble about playing time because they know who's good and who isn't. It's the parents that cause problems. We'll talk with parents up until the season starts, but then we won't discuss basketball with them until the season is over. That was a decision I made around my second year as head coach.

I'd get a phone call from a parent about playing time and I'd try to answer it, but then I'd get too involved with them and I don't have the time for that. They're all prejudiced. Every parent is prejudiced for his or her son. I can't worry about their problems. I've got the team to worry about. Being a parent myself, I can appreciate their concerns, but it's my job to make decisions for the best interests of the team as a whole.

Parents can't come into the locker room. They cannot contact our staff during the season about basketball matters. If it's a health problem or an academic problem, fine. But we will not discuss basketball with parents.

One parent who was always very much involved in a positive way was Saliner Tarpley, Roy's mom. If Roy missed a class, I called Saliner, and she'd be mad. She'd get on his butt. I got to know her very well through keeping her informed on Roy and because of her reaction. She understood what Roy needed to do to be successful.

Jan Henderson, Robert's mom, was very involved, too. She was a problem sometimes on playing time. One time after a game, Mike Boyd said, "Jan wants to see you." I thought he meant Janice, my wife. I said, "Send her back." This was like 40 minutes after the game, and here comes Jan Henderson rolling in, complaining about playing time for her son. I chewed Boyd out about that.

At the time, it was disturbing and frustrating, but now I look back and laugh. She's a great parent, she cares about her kid, she loves her kid, and that was on her mind. But back at the time, you say, "This is why I don't want the job."

The players love cars. You see this in life: Everybody loves cars. I don't want them to have cars. I get nervous about that. I especially don't want them to have new cars, because people assume, well, how did they get that car? Even though we do not cheat, I get concerned about anything that might bring negative publicity.

Tarpley's senior year, his mom leased him a Bronco from Varsity Ford over the phone. I do not know one person from Varsity Ford. They've never given a car to the university, nothing, but Bill Treml, this reporter from the *Ann Arbor News*, he wanted to know if Michigan bought him the car. He really did. He called Mrs. Tarpley and she set him straight. She's a sharp lady. She called 'em up and made the arrangements and they sent her the papers and she co-signed them and sent them back, because she had great credit, and Roy went in and got the car. You can lease a new car for $1,000 down and $130 a month.

It was ridiculous, but when it showed up, people suspected things. The newspapers did an article on Roy and there was a picture of him with his new Bronco and it's, "Well, who got him that?" There's nothing I can do when a player decides to go get a car or if a parent buys a player a car, but I don't like it. It creates rumors.

But you know what? Gary Grant brought a Fiero last fall and, hell, I found out you could buy one for $10,000 or $11,000. I didn't know that. I thought it was like a $20,000 automobile. Grant went in on his own, got a first-time buyer loan at something like 3.9 percent, and he paid about $200 a month, which he could handle. But freshmen, I don't want them to have cars.

Usually, when they're freshmen, they don't need cars because they're in the dorms and there's no parking anyway. Cars are a pain because, if they have them, sometimes they're doing things in the evenings or on the weekends that I don't want them doing. I don't want them leaving Ann Arbor at all once we start practice, except to make basketball trips.

But they all want cars. When they're juniors and seniors, they think they've got to have something. And when they're juniors and seniors, I don't mind, because now they're more responsible and know how to handle it, and they might move off campus, which I don't mind. That's fine. That's part of growing up.

It's the rumors I want to avoid. When we were recruiting Rumeal Robinson, who's from Boston, we played the Hall of Fame Game in Springfield, Massachusetts, and I knew Rumeal was coming and I wired the NCAA to let them know that he was going to be at the game, that they were paying for their own tickets, that they were coming with their own coach and we had nothing to do with it. I told the NCAA we weren't going to talk to him or recruit him while we were there, and feel free to send someone to monitor the situation, if they want, because I knew if the Boston papers were there, they might write that Rumeal Robinson was there as the Michigan guest or something. So I even communicate with the NCAA to avoid rumors.

I've communicated with the bouncers at the campus bars, too. I heard the same stuff everybody else heard about where they were hanging out—the Nectarine and Dooley's and so forth—so I started going in those places and checking. See, all the bars are off limits. I might occasionally let 'em go in on a Saturday night after an afternoon game, but for the most part all the bars and discos are off limits from the first day of practice to the end of the season. I think

I'm stricter on that now than when I was first head coach.

Number one, I don't like the rumors associated with it. Number two, in all honesty, when they're fighting to win big-time basketball games, there's really nothing they can do to benefit themselves after midnight in some bar. Even if they're just dancing, they don't need to be on their feet at that hour. I still check around and they know it. I call almost every one of 'em at home almost every night, just to make sure.

If I were a drinking guy, I wouldn't mind sitting down after a game and having a drink with one of my players. Some of them are 21, 22, 23. They can drink. It was a tough game, let's talk about it, let's have a beer. But now I've gotten even tougher on that because I just don't think they need it. So I've told 'em that the staff won't have any drinks during the season and we don't expect them to, either.

When I suspended Roy Tarpley for the Akron game in the NCAA tournament in Minneapolis in 1986, I suspected—I tried to prove it and couldn't prove it—that he had had a drink. But then when he was late to the team meeting, I used that as the reason—it was also a valid one—not to play him the first five minutes of each half.

My starting lineup came to me. They wanted me to start him. They said, "Coach, discipline him some other way. Start him and discipline him some other way." Most of our discipline is 6 a.m. or 7 a.m. running or study table. They hate that. I think you've got to set some form of discipline and have it be beneficial, so it's usually running or study table. If anything, I'm probably harder on starters than I am on non-starters, because those are the guys you rely on.

I'll tell you what. There's always so much discussion on drugs but you must also be aware that alcohol in athletics can be a problem because drinking is legal at the age of 21. It can become a very big problem. And you've just got to really talk to them and educate them and work on that. There's so much concern about a Len Bias situation happening again that there's an obsession with cocaine. Alcohol, however, tends to be ignored.

Freshmen haven't learned that a lot of the hurts they get are things you play over instead of getting treatment for. The same kids, when they're juniors, won't even mention some of the injuries that make them think they're all battered up when they're freshmen. Welcome to the Big Ten.

Terry Mills is a good kid, a pleasure. He's going to be a good player. Someday, he's going to be a good pro, if he continues to work. He came to me all the time last season: "Coach, I can't *believe* the difference between high school and college, how hard it is, how hard you work."

It's hard when you're a freshman, or a first-year player, like Terry. You think you know the game and you don't know anything. You never had to be taught how to get open when somebody was trying to prevent you from getting the ball. You were always good enough in high school to get yourself open. You usually had the ball. You'd rebound it, bring it down, shoot it. Here, all of a sudden, when you say, "Okay, let's go," someone prevents you from getting the basketball. You've gotta work your butt off to get open. That's the first thing—how to play against good defense.

And the second thing is how to play defense yourself. That's what the young kids learn because, when they come in, the kids already in the system work defensively. So now, all of a sudden, you've gotta learn two things: how to work hard defensively and how to get yourself open against people who are working hard defensively. In both major aspects of the game, you have to do something you never had to do before.

They have a lot of bad habits. They can spin and take bad shots and get away with it in high school because they're talented. Where they would spin and make a basket a year ago, now if they spin, it's an offensive foul. They could take a bad shot a year ago, because they could go rebound it, but here it's a fast break and a basket the other way. They could throw a careless pass a year ago because the defenses were slow to react, but now a careless pass is a turnover. So all that stuff has to be corrected. Things that they've done all their lives, they're hearing for the first time, "No, you can't do that."

That's why the jury is out on anybody that you sign. Some guys never adapt. Some guys can't work hard enough to get themselves open. They've always been a good player because they're talented enough that when they had the ball, they could shoot it in, but now they've got to work to get the ball. They've got to shoot it in against good defense, and they've never done that before.

Some guys never learn to do it, and you've got the Vitales of the world yelling, "What the hell did Frieder do to that kid?" when you know they know what's going on because they've been through it themselves.

I've probably started more freshmen in the time I've been head coach at Michigan than any other coach in the league, and I don't promise playing time. I've never promised an ounce of playing time, but I tell kids they're going to get every opportunity. I'm not the type of guy that says, "I'm gonna bring you along." I'm going to play you. I'm going to give you an opportunity.

I don't think Bobby Knight would have taken what I had to take with Rellford, Tarpley, Wade and Henderson: a ninth-place finish as freshmen. I think he'd have found a way—jaycees, transfers or going with veterans or something—to avoid that. But that's his philosophy. I'll take my lumps with young kids and let 'em learn.

That's why I started Terry Mills every game last season. Maybe there were times when someone else deserved to start ahead of him, but I went with Terry because eventually he's going to be a great player, and if we lose a game or two along the way, I don't give a damn. I'm going to go with him.

There was one guy that nobody ever questioned my going with as a freshman, and that was Gary Grant. What a complete player he is. That's why he had such success at Michigan—four straight 20-win seasons, two Big Ten championships and one runnerup. He does everything. He can score if you need him to score, yet I remember when he was a freshman, he had nine straight baskets in the first half when we blew Kansas out, and then he didn't take a shot in the second half. He's unselfish.

He can pass the basketball. He can steal it. He's a good assist man. If he's open, he can shoot the jumper in. He's a good penetrator. And he's one of the best defensive players I've ever seen. He was a great defensive player long before he became a real offensive threat in college. He's gonna do what it takes to be successful; that's why I expect him to be a good pro.

We wanted Gary Grant because he loved to play basketball, he was a quality kid and he played both ends of the court. We called everyone in the fall and told them we weren't going to take them because we had a verbal commitment from someone. We actually didn't have the commitment from him; we just banked on the fact that we were going to get him. We stopped recruiting all those other kids, about six or eight, because we felt he was the one we had to have.

From day one, he had an impact. He was the defensive glue as a freshman. I knew he was going to be good. I didn't know he was going to be one of the five best ever to play at Michigan, which he was.

Gary Grant did the best job and, over a four-year period, was the best player I ever coached at Michigan. He did it as a freshman and kept on doing it. He's the guy that's responsible for those banners in Crisler Arena. Those other guys—Tarpley, Rellford, Wade, Henderson, Joubert—were here when he arrived, but he played defense and he got 'em to go.

And here's a great example of the kind of person he is. Right before the NBA draft last summer, he was visiting various NBA teams to talk with them and take physicals and so forth. He was scheduled to be in Chicago the Monday of the week before the draft and in Milwaukee the following Wednesday. On the Tuesday in between, he was scheduled to speak at my basketball camp (for no charge, by the way; he refused to take any money for it). Instead of finding a way to get out of that commitment, he flew here from Chicago to speak and then flew back to Milwaukee. That's Gary Grant.

Roy Tarpley improved the most, by far, of any player I ever coached at Michigan. He wasn't very good coming out of high school. He wasn't highly recruited. He didn't play much at all as a freshman but he started to come on pretty well the middle of his sophomore year. After we lost at Indiana that year, we came into Columbus and he scored 18 or 19 of our first 24 points. By then, you knew he was going to be a player. So he went from not playing as a freshman to the Big Ten's most valuable player as a junior and a factor in the NBA by the end of his rookie year.

You'd have to say Joubert was the biggest disappointment, as far as the fans were concerned, but the fans' expectations were unrealistic. I think Joubert had a good career. In terms of my own expectations, I really haven't had any disappointments. Most of the guys I've recruited hard, I've given them a good opportunity and they've all played and done fairly well.

Even though you have problems with the kids every day, team problems, things that are big, big things at the time, a lot of times you look back at it and it's all part of growing up. You laugh about it.

Like Butch Wade. When he went home for Christmas vacation his freshman year, he did not come back. And he did not play in the two games after Christmas, except maybe a minute in the second game, because it took us three extra days to get him back. He was not going to come back to Michigan. It was a combination of not playing, homesickness and just the typical freshman problems.

We had to send Mike Boyd to Boston to get him, to meet with him and his mom, Dorothy. And his mom was very supportive. She said, "You made the decision to go there. You're going." But he would not have come back had we not pursued it like we did. Now you can't get Butch Wade out of Ann Arbor. He stays here all the time. When he comes back from playing in Europe, he lives here in the summer.

I think I'm the only coach in America that makes recruits sign to give me permission to drug-test them before they even sign the tender to play basketball here. I want the privilege of being able to random sample them throughout their career.

My purpose is not to catch them and kick them off the team. My purpose is, if there's a problem, I want to know about it so I can deal with it. And there is absolutely no distinction made between the first player on the team and the 12th or whatever. We dismissed a player once because of drugs, but in such a way that no one ever knew or will know that that was the reason.

I think you can be too strict. Look at Roy Tarpley and what an outstanding season he had last year. Where would he be today had he been kicked off the team the time he tested positive? Would he be playing in the NBA today? And, if not, what would he be doing? You can destroy people's lives.

I've never had a guy test positive on a regular basis. I've never really had a significant problem on this team. If you have a serious drug problem, you can't win two straight Big Ten championships. It can't happen. Your players can't play to their capabilities and get it done. But the players here have a situation where they go to school, they come to practice, they go to training table, which is right at Crisler Arena, then they stay at the arena for study table.

So we're with them, in effect, from 2:00 to 10:00 p.m., then they're supposed to go back to their apartments and dorms and get a good night's rest and go to school the next morning. We're with them most of the time. We're on road trips with them.

But in the pros, that isn't the case. It's a concern of mine about Gary Grant. Gary and I are great friends, but this year, for the first time, Gary's not gonna have us there for the 10 hours a day that he had us when he was in school, and he's gonna be making $300,000 a year, and so now you've got a different world out there. You've got agents who are phony, you've got people selling cocaine, you've got people selling shady investments.

So how are these players going to survive? You hope they make it, but sometimes they don't. I think that maybe happened to Roy. For the first time, he was out there without a lot of direction and I think maybe that's why that happened to him. I think now, with his mother living in Dallas, I will be surprised if Roy has another problem.

I think it's important not to expect athletics to cure all the evils of society. Drugs are a big, big problem. A junior high kid in Detroit is probably dying right now from an overdose of cocaine, so what are you going to do? It's a big problem and we must be able to deal with it intelligently. We've had a drug education program in place for four years now and we've been pleased with the results.

Every person you've been associated with isn't going to turn out exactly the way you might want. Eventually, some guy out of this program might rob a bank. Well, what am I supposed to do if that happens? Or one of them might not have a good job. Are you accountable for everyone that you've worked with or worked for or who's worked under you? Are you accountable for these guys five years from now?

We make them go to school. We give them all the tutorial support that they need. We do everything that we possibly can to see that they graduate. Twenty-two of my 28 seniors since I've been head coach have gotten their degrees.

At the end of the season, we meet with every player and go over three or four main things—where he's going to live next fall, does he have a lease, does he need a summer job, what kind, is he going to spring term, is he going to summer term—and then give him his summer workout schedule.

We work our butts off to get them good summer jobs, good career jobs and good jobs after they leave. We've educated them. Some of them we've prepared for the NBA. We've made them much better basketball players. When you work at it around the clock, all year long, what else can you do? If you've done the best you possibly can and somebody doesn't turn out exactly the way you want, you cannot be held responsible.

Let's talk about some successes, okay? Not that Roy Tarpley is a failure; he's having a great pro career and he's on track now in his personal life and I'm convinced he's straightened out. But let's talk about some guys that haven't gotten into the papers.

Marty Bodnar is an attorney in Cincinnati and his brother Mark is a financial and business consultant. Mark got his M.B.A. from Michigan but they didn't accept Marty into law school here. I was upset about that at the time and I got in trouble with my comments. I told them that the Bodnars would be much better attorneys than half the ones they turn out. They didn't like it when I said that, but Marty's turned out to be a good attorney.

Paul Heuerman's another one we couldn't get in. He's an attorney down in Naples, Florida. He went to the University of Florida Law School. I was really mad. They were 3.7 students who scored over 600 on the boards but Michigan wanted 4.0s with 725s and they wouldn't budge and they wouldn't accept them. I thought that was wrong. I had to stop Heuerman from going to Ohio State to law school. That's where he wanted to go. I had to get involved and get him a law school. I had to recruit against Ohio State to get him here in the first place and then, four years later, I had to recruit against the same guys again. Ridiculous.

Robert Henderson was playing in Belgium a couple of years ago. Now he's got a security job at Domino's, a great job. He and Butch Wade both bought used Mercedes, then brought them back here and sold them for a profit. Those guys are learning.

There are a lot of great success stories. Mark Lozier is vice president of a marketing firm in Southfield. Thad Garner is in West Palm Beach, Florida, a regional supervisor for Domino's. Wayman Britt is an employee relations executive with Steelcase Furniture in Grand Rapids. Jon Antonides is a franchisee operations director for Domino's of Canada.

Gerard Rudy is in medical school at Michigan. Garde Thompson is with Procter and Gamble in Grand Rapids. Dan Pelekoudas is an attorney in Newport Beach, California. Ike Person is playing in Sweden. He lives in Ann Arbor in the off season. Eric Turner is in Italy.

Rellford finished up last season with the San Antonio Spurs and played for them in the playoffs. He's hanging in there. McGee, Tarpley, McCormick, Hubbard and Green are all still in the NBA.

Glen Rice came out of the inner city of Flint. From the time he was in seventh grade, his mom raised him and his brothers and sister by herself. He grew up in a tough environment with no money and was never pushed academically. If you think that first year with Glen Rice will go perfectly, you're crazy.

At Flint Northwestern, he was closely monitored and supported by his teachers and counselors. His coach was even his biology teacher. I think this is an area where Proposition 48 is super because it has the attention of the younger athletes and the secondary schools. If they keep coming up with kids who are ineligible, they'll start to take some heat. That's embarrassing to the schools, so I think they're making provisions to do a better job preparing these young people. Anything we do to upgrade that is good, and you never heard me say a negative word about it.

So now Glen Rice is at the University of Michigan and, for the first time in his life, mom's not there to get him up for eight o'clock classes, so if he's late for class, he's gonna get told about it and he's gonna have 7 a.m. running or 7 a.m. study table. He has to show up for his tutors. His time is more tightly scheduled and he has a lot of obligations.

But Glen is developing into a mature person. When he was a freshman, he never smiled and he never made eye contact. Now he's matured. He's a leader. He's a veteran. He's clean-cut. He stays in on the weekends. Do you know he's never asked for tickets for anyone but his mom? "Ernestine Rice—three tickets; Ernestine Rice—four tickets." He never asked for anything else. Players get four comp tickets per game and they can dicker and swap with their teammates for more. Guys like Butch Wade and Gary Grant were always looking for more. Garde Thompson was the worst. They always pay for their extras, you understand, but Garde might say, "Hey, I need 85 tickets." I'd say, "We can get you 30." He had a great following in Grand Rapids.

But Glen Rice is a heck of a kid, and it could not have happened had he not been given the opportunity.

It's just like Mills. They complained when we took Mills at Michigan because he didn't make the Proposition 48 minimum on the Scholastic Aptitude Test. Some people said it was an embarrassment to the university. That's a bunch of hogwash. It's far from an embarrassment. Just because you make a special admission doesn't mean he doesn't have to do the work. Anybody we admit, they have to do the work.

They make special admissions in all programs. It's just that the athletes get more attention. Check the music department. Check the art department. There are scholarships for individuals who have the talent but aren't as good academically. Those people still have to do the work once they're here, and it's very hard for them sometimes because they've got to compete with outstanding students. In basketball, at least, they've got the skills to compete with the people they're competing against. In school, they don't. They got in on the tail end of the admission standards and they're competing against people who were the valedictorians of their class and people who are paying their way through school. They need to learn that if they don't work extremely hard at it, they're going to find themselves in a hole in a hurry.

The players learn how to study. They learn how to plan their day. They learn not to let things go until the last second. When you give kids a chance, the positives outweigh the negatives. There'd be a lot more problems if those kids didn't have that chance. They learn the right way. They learn what's good and what's bad. They learn the types of people to develop as friends and the kinds of people to stay away from. They learn to hang with kids that can upgrade them professionally and not people who can pull them down.

And all of that comes about with the opportunity of a scholarship for them. But if you don't work your butt off to develop them and encourage them in the right ways, they're not going to make it. And if you don't spend a lot of time on it, they're not going to make it. And if they don't work at it—well, that's a problem.

But it's like I tell my staff: Why work your butt off to get a kid and then let him become ineligible? This is your number one priority, and you've got to understand there are going to be a million problems the first couple of years. But by the time they're juniors and seniors, they'll be able to take care of themselves and function and there'll be fewer problems.

Sean Higgins and Demetrius Calip, last year, were the first players ever to be academically ineligible at Michigan in my 15 years on the coaching staff. I'm not using this as a defense or a justification, but that's a pretty good record. In a way, it speaks well of the program that everyone was so shocked. Hopefully, Sean and Demetrius learned from it and everybody benefited from it. Life went on. We didn't win as many games as we would have, but so what? Honest to God, that's the way I feel.

If I had kicked Rice off the team when he popped that student when he was a freshman, it would have snowballed. What if I take another Rice a year later and I had the same problem with him? Do I kick him off, too? You've got to work with kids. You've got to feel the accomplishment when they leave with their degree and they can go back to their community and function competently. That's what it's all about.

I'll be honest with you. It used to be easier to keep players eligible. I know about it firsthand: When I was an assistant, one of my jobs was to keep Mike McGee eligible. Everything is so much tougher now because of all the publicity and stuff. Every university is checking to make certain that all athletes are fulfilling all requirements.

Now you're allowed 10 hours of independent study—you know, arranging courses with instructors and things like that—in four years. Back then, it was more like 18. Mike did a good job. One thing he did was he never flunked anything—and, boy, that's such a key. Say you can get two hours of "A" in some easy course and then you get an independent study arranged with an instructor and you get three more hours of "A." Now if you have a tough English or psychology course or the tough physical education courses like kinesiology and physiology, and you get a "D," those are hours toward your degree and they're honor points and you can make it. That's a big thing. That's like saving it out of the garbage. And Mike never flunked anything. He went to class and he worked. And in courses where he had a chance to do well, he did. He was always eligible.

Fall sports don't have to worry about two consecutive semesters of eligibility. Their season's over before the grades come out. They can have incompletes. They can have "E"s. They've got winter term, spring term, summer term to get back to the 2.0 grade-point average. If football had to play a national championship game in the beginning of January, tell me they wouldn't be basket cases in December. The Big Ten is tougher than the NCAA on this. At some schools, if you're eligible in the fall, you're eligible all year. In the Big Ten, you, have to be recertified in January and, at Michigan, you have to have a 2.0.

Athletes are the most discriminated against people around. These poor kids have to go through everything and don't get nearly as many breaks as people think they do. They don't have the free time that other students have. They don't have the privacy that other students have. They have more restrictions on them than other students have. A music professor can give one of his students a hundred bucks and the student doesn't lose his scholarship. An art professor can give a student a Christmas present. A history professor can loan a student the money to go home for the weekend. I can't do any of those things. In short, athletes can't accept favors which are available to other students.

10

On Being a Basket Case

Think about it. A college basketball game lasts about two hours. My team plays 33 or 34 games a season. So I actually only spend fewer than 70 hours a year actually coaching a team during a game. It's the tip of the iceberg.

But if an orchestra hasn't rehearsed properly, there's nothing the conductor can do on the podium at the concert that's going to fix that. It's the same thing with a basketball team. You can't walk in on Saturday morning and say we want to win this game. You have to have worked your tail off previously to get it done.

Everything you do in the off season, in the pre-season, the week of the game, the day before the game, all leads to the product that you put on the floor. Your players have to go out and perform to their capabilities. Once the performance starts, they've got to go out and do it.

The game is the only time when I'm completely occupied, when there's no room left over in my mind. Coaching in a game is total. I don't see or hear anything else. Once that game starts, it's all there is. The most important thing in the world can be forgotten.

I see everything I need to see, and I need to see everything. My assistant coaches watch the off-ball stuff. And I have to be in the habit, too, of not just watching the ball. On defense, especially, you watch away from the ball, because you know your guy is doing the job on the ball. You're watching those guys away from the ball so you can holler, "hey, weak-side help!" or "down a little lower" or "front him" or "beat him over there." You want to make sure your coverages are exactly the way you want, that your weak side people aren't too tight to their man away from the ball and that they are in the help position that they're supposed to be in.

On offense, you're primarily looking to see that they're all executing and doing what they're supposed to do on every pass and every movement. You've got to be able to learn as much as you can about what they're doing right and what they're doing wrong so that when you have that first timeout you can make the biggest corrections that need to be made. You want to make as many adjustments as you can in that 60 to 90 seconds you have with them.

You have to watch a lot of things at the same time. I try to teach my guys on the bench not to watch the ball but to watch their man, the guy they might be guarding or the guy they might be replacing.

You always have to have a basic philosophy you're trying to implement. It isn't really all that important what it is. I might steer a guy to the baseline defensively and you might steer him to the middle, and that doesn't mean I'm wrong or you're wrong. What it comes down to is how well you execute. You don't think the great UCLA teams could have run any kind of halfcourt offense and been successful? They could have. It's just a matter of what they decided to do. It's execution that's important.

We can play any style of ball we have to play. You have to coach to your talent. My philosophy is to get the talent first and then coach according to what they can do. I had slow white kids at Alpena and we held the ball. At Flint Northern, we ran for two years and held the ball the last year.

But all things being equal, and if I could just tailor my personnel to what I like to do, I'd press and run. I like a quick team.

It's easier to score in transition than it is out of a halfcourt offense. I like to press, too, but not to the extent of, say, Iowa. They'll stay in it even after they've given up a bunch of easy baskets. If we give up two or three, the press comes off. I don't like giving up easy baskets. I'm not saying Iowa is wrong; they've had great success with what they do. I'm just saying we won't stay with the press to the extent that they do.

We use all kinds of presses: man-to-man, halfcourt trap, with pressure on the in-bounds passer, without pressure on the in-bounds passer. The press can give you the ball and the three-on-one, four-on-two, five-on-four situations. And we use both kinds of fast break, the traditional kind where the guard brings the ball down the middle with guys on the wings ready for him to dish off to, and the sidelines break where you can bang the ball inside to the big man if they fill up the wings defensively.

We're to the point now where we don't plan ahead of time which one we're going to use. We need a guard who can read the situation, decide which one to use and call it on the fly.

And even though we're basically a man-to-man team defensively (if you look at the Big Ten champions over the years, they've all been man-to-man except for the Magic Johnson teams at Michigan State, and they could have done anything), we always have several zone defenses ready for when we need them, like we did at Indiana last year.

We think the key in the Big Ten is to establish control of the game, to be the aggressor. And you have to maintain that through the cycles of the game, the rallies, the substitutions, the shifts in momentum. Are you letting them make their passes? Are you taking them out of their defense and frustrating them?

You need eight players, your starting five—and you should definitely have a starting five because there are somehow five players that have to be better than the others—plus a backup post man, a backup forward and a backup guard. When you start going to 9, 10, 11 players, you're cutting into the playing time of players who are better than numbers 9, 10, 11, and you can't allow that to happen. You can't get involved in playing kids just to get them playing time. They have to earn it and you have to have some kind of rotation that's sensible and that's been proven to you throughout your practices. When you look at the league champions and the NCAA champions, you see teams that use seven or eight players.

You have to have a game plan and you have to make your team go out and play the way that you've practiced and do things the way you want them done. But in addition to having a plan, you also have to be flexible enough to react to situations. It all gets down to that.

It's also imperative that you have an outstanding staff, and I have one of the best. I've talked about Mike Boyd's role already, but I also want to emphasize the job that Steve Fisher has done. Steve is an excellent bench coach, a very good teacher, thorough and well prepared. He doesn't hesitate to express his opinion on important and delicate matters, but if my decision differs, his loyalty is evident. We have a staff that complements each other very well. That's important. Dan Minert, my trainer, and Gil Zimmerman, my strength coach, have done a great job in their specific areas. It's been a true team effort off the court as well as on.

Not only that, but everyone on my staff has gone out of his way to assist in other areas, such as academics. For example, Dan and Gil spend countless hours helping tutor players in such classes as physiology and kinesiology, in which they are very well trained.

You've got to get to know the officials, too. If you swear at some of them, for example, you get a technical, so you can't swear at them (unless you want the technical; sometimes you do). You scout officials just like you scout teams and players: what they let go, what they won't let go, whether you can talk to them or not, whether you can intimidate them or not. Some officials have a chip on their shoulder. If you say something to them, the next call is going to go against you. They don't want you to talk to them.

We're always aware of who the game officials are and we tell the kids what to look for: "Now this guy's going to call you for a handcheck early, so don't handcheck. Let 'em call the other team for a handcheck."

You can never let the players get involved with the officiating. I tell my players I'll handle the officials. But if you start complaining, they start complaining, and then they're not out there doing what they have to do.

And those officials are human beings. They're not going to let a player make them look bad. They're going to come back and get him. Hell, that's human nature.

Players have to learn that there will be periods of time when you get bad calls, and when those periods come, you've got to get back and play defense and not let those bad calls cost you baskets. When officiating comes your way and the other team doesn't react properly, you take advantage of it.

The bottom line is that the harder you work, the luckier you get and the more you get away with, because the officials can't keep up with the game. A lot of our fans were complaining about the officiating in our loss at Iowa last season, but Iowa got away with a lot more because they worked harder. Period. My two Big Ten champions beat the hell out of teams and we got away with it because we worked harder than they did. Those teams would have won that game at Iowa because they would have done the job in the lane and on the inside. They would not have been outrebounded by 10. They would not have allowed missed free throws to become three-point plays.

It's funny how the former coaches on TV always know better than you do how to coach your team. Former coaches change in a hurry. I probably would never be an announcer simply because I wouldn't criticize the coaches. I know what they're going through. I know they know more about their players than any announcer does.

In my last five years as a head coach, my teams have won two outright Big Ten championships, been to four NCAA tournaments and won the NIT. They're 64–26 in the conference and have never been out of the first division. And they're still trying to find out if I can coach or not.

Just check with all the coaches I've beaten. Call Bobby Cremins and Larry Brown and Gene Bartow and Eddie Sutton and Digger Phelps and ask them if Frieder can coach. I can coach as well as any of them. You can't accomplish what we've accomplished if you're not a good bench coach.

But so much of that is due to the NCAA tournament. That seems to be the most important thing in everybody's minds. It's like you get no credit for what you do during the year. They discount the 18 games you play and fight your guts out for. If you go 2–1 or 1–1 in the tournament, you're a failure. Look at Rollie Massimino. He finally won it, but he'd never been to the Final Four before that and he'd been coaching all his life. When Louie Carnesecca got there a few years ago, he'd been coaching 20-odd years at St. John's. Digger Phelps has only been there once. It took John Wooden almost 20 years to win an NCAA title. These guys are good coaches, you know.

And I'm realistic enough to know that you can work hard and have great talent and do one thing after another all your life and it still may not happen. You've got to be fortunate on top of everything else, so to base your whole life on that one goal would be ridiculous. It would be nice. It's a goal. But if it doesn't happen, it's not going to affect me. There are a lot of outstanding coaches who haven't won the national championship.

Sometimes I think our emphasis on winning the Big Ten does hurt our chances for winning the NCAA. We're so exhausted when the Big Ten is over that it might affect us, but it's my job to guard against that as a coach.

Another thing I have to guard against is the distractions. There are so many of them off the court that sometimes it's hard to remember that coaching in the games is what it's all about. I've got airplane pilots and people who help with summer jobs and recruiting, and with that comes phone calls. But if people help my program, then I want to give them some of my time, not because they demand it but because that's the kind of guy I am. It's hard for me not to answer their phone calls when I know they're behind my team. As Jim Duderstadt said when he was being interviewed for the U of M presidency, the alumni are "an extraordinary network." It's important that we include these people and I do. But, as a result, over a 15-year period, the demands on your time intensify.

And radio shows. I do two pre-game shows and two post-game shows. I do shows on two different Ann Arbor stations the morning after every game and I do a sportswrap show on the same stations once a week, plus doing WJR's sportswrap regularly, plus the weekly U of M Club luncheon at Weber's.

Then there are the national media — *Sports Illustrated*, *Sporting News*, CBS, NBC, ABC, ESPN, *USA Today*. If you don't accommodate them, you're a jerk. If you do accommodate them, it drives you nuts.

I try to delegate, but they all need to talk to Frieder, it seems. I'll have Fisher or somebody return the calls, but they want to talk to Frieder. I've cut way down on my clinics and speaking engagements because I just don't have the time, but they stay after you. If you don't return their calls, they show up and catch you between places.

And if you don't stop and sign an autograph for a kid, what kind of person are you? But then one autograph leads to 50 and it just goes on and on.

It may sound funny, but the main thing you've got to do is make sure you don't neglect your team. You cannot neglect the preparation for a game, and I think I've done a good job at that.

The story behind the towel is that there is no story behind the towel. I think I started doing it when I coached at Flint Northern. When I first started coaching, I used to chew my nails until they were raw. I started holding a program so I'd have something else to do with my hands. But I'd always lose the program for some reason, and that led to holding the towel. But then, of course, when you get up, the towel has to go somewhere, so it went over my shoulder. It just happened. The fact that the towel is over my shoulder is nothing I intended to do, nothing I thought about, nothing that was ever planned. It was a reflex, plus if I put it down, I'd lose it, just like I lost the programs.

Occasionally, I've thrown it. One time during an Iowa game, I got mad and threw the towel and one corner caught Glen Rice on the temple and the rest of it wrapped right around his head. We all just broke up on the bench. It certainly eased the tension.

People complain about our pre-Big Ten schedule. Even Janice complains. She showed up late for our game with Northern Michigan on the Saturday before Christmas last year. When I asked her why, she said, "I was trying to find a *good* game on television."

But what you need those games for, as much as anything else, is so you can practice against somebody other than your own guys; practice, really, against somebody better than your own second five. It's a good deal. You can work on stuff, try different things and still win the ball game, which you have to do. Against Bowling Green last December, we went to the matchup zone on three possessions and gave up three baskets, but when we wanted to put it in for our game at Indiana, it was there for us and helped us win.

And just because they're on your schedule doesn't mean they're automatic wins. You have to go out and beat them. It's easy for Dick Vitale and some others in the media to say what a soft deal it is, but they wouldn't feel that way if they were coaching. They'd be worried. When Vitale was at the University of Detroit, he couldn't even win his own tournament with Eastern Michigan, Western Michigan and us. He lost to Eastern the first night, then he lost to Western the next night in the consolation game.

I usually sit down in August and draw up a master schedule for practice from October 15 until the first game, broken down into 10- or 20-minute segments: how much we'll do on offense, how much we'll do on defense, when we'll bring the zones in, when we start on the presses, etc. But nothing is written in stone. The coaches get together after practice every day and make adjustments if we have to, but this gives us a basic structure.

I like to get into a lot of five-on-five play because that's where the game is played. That's the game. But your emphasis is different depending on the kind of team you have. Last year, we did a lot more breakdown work, which is where you break down into two-on-two or three-on-three and go over particular situations. On post defense, for example, what do you do when the ball is high, when it's at the wing, when it's low? We did a lot more teaching, a lot more fundamentals.

We didn't have the nucleus returning that we had in past years. We had six new players. If you have a situation like we did in 1986, with Robert Henderson, Roy Tarpley, Richard Rellford, Butch Wade, Garde Thompson, Antoine Joubert and Gary Grant all returning, it was more a matter of continuing with what you'd been doing and getting more sophisticated with the offenses and defenses, although you still have to do some breakdown work because otherwise they start to develop bad habits.

We have two practices a day on Sundays and non-football Saturdays until the season starts, usually one late in the morning and one late in the afternoon. In between, there are study table and weights. It's not unusual for freshmen and sophomores to be at Crisler from 10:30 in the morning until 9:00 at night on the weekends.

We don't go hard all of that time, but there's so much to teach. The morning sessions are all teaching: walk through the offense, dummy the offense, show 'em the press, show 'em the out-of-bounds plays. Then, when you work with 'em in the evening, you've already introduced it and now you can go right into it.

Practices have to be well organized. You have to be accomplishing things every day. If the kids are not doing things exactly the way you want them done, you have to be able to communicate that and get it changed.

We always have a good, hard practice right before we go on the road. I started that about six years ago, after it dawned on me that we were always having so many problems on the road: snow, fog, canceled flights. If we got in a practice on the road at all, it usually wouldn't be a good one. But you just can't avoid the weather in the Midwest in the middle of winter, so I decided to get in a good practice right before we leave. The main thing then is just to get on the other team's floor at least once before the game, just to do some shooting and get the feel of it. If you have time for a good practice, so much the better, but you can't depend on it.

I have almost as many managers now as I had players in the 1981–82 season. I had nine last season, and I needed all of them. They're never in the way and they're always busy. There were two who did nothing but tape games all season. Believe me, that came in handy at NCAA tournament time. We had tape on 47 of the 64 teams when the pairings were announced, including two on Boise State.

It's a year-round job. At the end of the season, all the coaches have to watch every film of every game. We break that down into every offensive series and every defensive series. We put that all on a computer. It's big time. It's a lot of work.

But we would know, for example, what happened every time Gary Grant had the ball in transition. We could show the other guards on paper why we wanted Gary Grant to have the ball in the middle, because here's what happened when Grant did it the last 20 times and here's what happened when they did it the last 20 times. There's a reason why everything happens, and we want to know why we were scored on and who's at fault. We want to know how our team does with different combinations on the floor.

You've got your early signings in November, so in June and July, you're going to the camps, trying to get kids interested in visiting in the fall. Then you try to sign them in November, but if you don't, or you only get one, you've got to continue the process through the season and into the second signing, which is in the middle of April.

Immediately after that, you spend the rest of the school year on underclassmen, getting into the schools for visits. Plus you've got your kids here. You've got to make sure they're taking care of business and going to class.

I have clinics and speaking engagements and Michigan outings. I go to about 20 alumni functions every summer. You have to do it. You have to be accessible. These are the people who supply jobs, who can be helpful up the line if they support you. They support the program. I may not see it directly, but they support Michigan behind the scenes.

And then there's my own basketball camp, which runs for five weeks in June and July. I took that over from John Orr when he left, and made it a point to be at the camp every day. I take care of business and, as a result, we have built the camp from 500 kids to about 2,000.

But I'm there. One summer, I talked to every kid in camp. I was in my office in the arena. Each kid would get a tap on the shoulder—"Hey, Coach Frieder wants to see you in his office right away." That kid would come running in and I'd tell him, "You've gotta work on your defense. I watched you play last night. I'm going to watch you play tomorrow." You don't think that pays dividends?

You take care of your own business. If you open a restaurant and you're not there every day, you're going to lose your butt. But if you're there every day, you can make some money. It's the same way with this. We built the camp by me being there every day.

One of the things I learned how to handle was Canham's memos. At first, I responded to them immediately, but that would just lead to another memo and then another and then another. Eventually, I got to the point where I would get a memo and let a week go by, and then hope that I would run into him casually and get the matter settled.

When you work for the University of Michigan athletic department, there are a million checks and balances. Everybody's checking you all the time. If we want to get 20 practice shirts, I have to argue with Will Perry to get the purchase order signed. Then when we get it signed, we have to go over it again when it's typed. When the bill comes, we have to go over it again. What was this for? Why did you need it? Why did you get 20 and who were they for?

I mean, they're tough. But that's why it's a good program. This place is so big and so many people are involved that if they aren't watching it like a hawk, too many things could slip through.

I wish we could slip more towels through, I can tell you that. It's hard to convince them that you need more than 15 towels for

14 players. Hah. You probably need 50. The staff uses them, the trainers, the managers. You use them for the floor.

I do think we argue too much about little things. We'll argue about leaving a pre-paid plane ticket for a recruit because it costs $20 more, so then we mail the ticket and the recruit doesn't get it and now what? You end up paying $200 more for the ticket 10 days later than you would have if you'd left it pre-paid to begin with. It's hard to convince them that I've been to that neighborhood and I don't care how you send it, the kid might not end up with the ticket. The wino down the street might end up with it. Sometimes we're penny wise and pound foolish.

When I came to Michigan, our kids never did one thing with weights. They never stretched, either. We didn't pay a lot of attention to it, especially in the off season. Then, in John Orr's last three years or so, we had them do some stuff over in the football building, like Phil Hubbard would go over there to work on rehabilitating his knee.

Now our guys do weights three times a week all year long until October 15 and twice a week from then until the end of the season. You should see our weight room. I can't tell you what all those machines are, but it's sophisticated, it's organized, the players work their butts off and the results are incredible. When my strength coach and I developed this and we got the first machines, the athletic administration had no idea.

About the fifth year, we needed another six machines. I went to Canham and Perry and said, "We need about $20,000 so we can finish what we need in that weight room."

They wanted to know where all these machines were going. They had no idea that room existed. They said, "Oh, there isn't any place like that."

I said, "There is, too." I had to take them over there and show it to them. They walked in and there were about 10 machines in there. They couldn't believe it. They were stunned. And we'd been operating it for about three years.

Faculty members are just like anybody else. You've got some

who will cooperate, who like athletes, and you've got a lot who couldn't care less. One professor at Michigan still brags about flunking Cazzie Russell in one of his classes. You get cooperation from some people and a hard time from others. I've had a player get an "E" on an exam because an instructor wouldn't excuse him from it when we had a game. It's wrong, but it happens.

One thing we get no cooperation on is registration. Every year, it's the same way. Every year, I make a complaint. Every year, they tell me I'm right and they're going to do something about it. And every year, we have the same problem. Before he moved on to Princeton, President Shapiro appointed a committee to study the way the athletic department was run and how it related to the rest of the university, and one of their recommendations was to allow athletes to register separately. I'm not going to hold my breath.

Right during exams, the players have to pre-register for the winter term. They go see their counselors. They work out their schedules. They get them verified. Then they go to register and half the classes are full. To be eligible, they have to be registered in 12 hours, so they get what they can, maybe six of the 12 hours, and then they take six hours in anything that's open, advanced Russian history or French Six or whatever, just so they're enrolled in enough hours to meet the NCAA rules.

Now they have to try to drop and add. We might talk an instructor into letting a kid into a particular class, but they won't give you an override until the first day of class. Last school year, the first day of class was January 6. We were at Northwestern. When we come back, we go to the teacher and the teacher says, "We told you to see us the first day of class. We can't let you in now. We let these other three in."

Now we have to see what else we can get them in. It seems so unfair. By the time we get it straightened out, they're a week or more behind everybody else and they don't have the courses they want. They're supposed to be here primarily to get an education, and yet they put all these roadblocks in their way. Last year, we only had one player who got his whole schedule the way he wanted it.

The solution is to say, okay, we're starting registration on November 13. Let's get basketball in and get them registered, instead of giving Rumeal Robinson December 10, the last date you can register, which they did last year. Let's tell basketball they can come through that morning. If they get themselves registered by three o'clock, fine. Otherwise, they've got to take their assigned time. But they don't do that for you. Three of our players were given registration days while we were in Alaska. We had a manager go through for them. They'll probably be mad when they find out about that. Some would rather have them miss it so they could complain about athletes. It's frustrating, to say the least.

When coaches, alums and others say they don't understand the NCAA rules, that's a copout. I'm the first to admit that there are many rules that are ambiguous and need interpretations. There are also rules you could make an honest mistake on that are incidental. For example, when the Bodnars came to town for orientation in the summer of 1977, they came out to Concordia College, where John had his basketball camp, to visit the coaches.

They got there at lunch time and just started shooting around. It led to a three-on-three with me and assistant coach Dan Fife and a couple of other guys, and a photographer from the *Michigan Daily*, who had come out to take the weekly camp picture, took some photos. The *Daily* ran them, along with a story.

Well, it turned out we had violated about five rules: prospects at a camp without being charged, practicing out of season, having a tryout for prospects, etc. Even if they've signed, the rules say they're still prospects until they're enrolled, and if they're not prospects, you can't practice with them.

We were playing three-on-three for 15 minutes because they came out to say hello, and the next thing you know, we're fighting five violations. A lot of crazy things can happen in this business.

However, everyone associated with the game knows that giving players cash payments or arranging for cars and stereos and wardrobes and transportation is wrong. That's what we're talking about when we talk about cheating, and everyone has to know that's wrong.

When you hire people, you've got to make their responsibilities clear. And you've got to ask them to understand that you're not hiring them to coach the basketball team. You're hiring an individual as a recruiter, for office work, whatever the role is. One of the biggest problems in the league in recent years was when Bill Norton, the great coach from Birmingham Brother Rice, went to Michigan State as an assistant. He thought he was going to help coach the team. I think Jud Heathcote had different ideas. Evidently, there wasn't good communication and, to make a long story short, Bill left after one year. I remember Bill telling me on one recruiting trip that it was the 50th time that he had left campus and I said to myself, "If he's counting, he's in trouble."

When I came to Michigan from Flint Northern, they made it clear to me that I was the recruiter. I might see Michigan on Saturday afternoon, but I'm not going to be coaching this team. I'm going to be on the road. Then when Jim Dutcher left and John moved me up, that was made clear to the new people. You have to do that or you have problems.

I'll be honest with you. I don't know how Mike Boyd does it, because Mike Boyd has done for nine years now what I did my first two years. And that was a pace. I don't know if I could have ever kept that pace up. Mike has been helped by recruiting rules that have kept people from being on the road all the time but when he's allowed to go, he might be gone for 15 straight days.

Being a good basketball coach is a lot like being a good card player. You need great discipline. You need to be mentally prepared and physically fit. You need a lot of poise. You need to be able to fight adversity and not go off the deep end when things aren't going your way.

The difference between cards and basketball is that you've got more control in cards. They're your cards and it's your money. With a team, you're telling other people what you want them to do. I know I could sit down in a poker game with anybody and win money. I would win at least seven times out of 10 and my winnings would be bigger than my losses. That's the key—limit your losses and don't throw good money after bad.

It's the same thing with basketball. You've got to hang in there when it's not going well. When you lose a game, you can't let it lead to another loss. You've got to recover fast and make your adjustments and get the next one. You can't dwell on victories too long, either. If you waste four hours celebrating a victory, that's four hours that can never be made up.

I had strong rules for myself when I played blackjack. I would only play two or three hours a day, at the very most, because I had to pick and choose my spots and have ideal conditions. You can't just jump in and play. First of all, I don't like it crowded because other people can disturb your concentration. Second, they had single decks back then, so to get a situation where they would deal down with single decks and you could see all the cards, you would want two or three people at the table, possibly four. With three people, sometimes you could get them to deal four times. If there were four people, you could get them to deal a third time. When they dealt that third or fourth time, you could get down toward the end of the deck and have a tremendous advantage by knowing the count.

With five at the table, they would never deal a third time because there weren't enough cards. They'd reshuffle after the second deal and you'd never get to the bottom.

With fewer people at the table, you can sit where you can see the cards. You can study the dealers so you can see the burn card when they flash it. If you were good and the dealers weren't great, you could see both the bottom card and the card they flashed from the top. If you get down to the last dozen cards, knowing what those two are pays big dividends. Sometimes dealers will make mistakes; sometimes dealers will work with you a little if you tip 'em. There are all kinds of things. I became fascinated by all that stuff.

Let's say I've been in Las Vegas for the first two days of a 10-day stay and I haven't played yet and I really want to and the conditions are finally right. Let's say I sit down and I get a pair of threes against something up and the count is such-and-such and I split the threes. Let's say I even won both bets.

Then it dawns on me that I was not, according to the book, supposed to split the threes in that situation. Whether I won or lost is immaterial. I penalize myself now. I cannot play for 24 hours because I did not do the right thing. So now I lay in the hot tub, take a blackjack lesson (Lawrence Revere was the top guy then, and I met with him several times), study my notes and practice, so the next day I'll do a better job. I'm kicking myself that I never gave lessons. I should have. I could have made a fortune.

The casinos saw to it that I couldn't make a fortune at the tables by banning me from them. The bottom line in Las Vegas is that the people who control the casinos consider losing house money to be a serious matter. If you go into a casino and win, that registers with them. If you leave again a winner and again a winner, they're going to do everything they can to stop it, and the ultimate is not letting you play. They want you to come to Vegas and have fun but leave the money behind. It doesn't matter if it's $10, $100 or $1,000, if you regularly beat them, they're not going to let you play. It's as simple as that. And they have the casinos licensed as private clubs, so they have the authority to ban you.

The first time I was banned was when I was an assistant at Michigan. I was shocked. I was just playing $10 or $20 a bet. But when you count cards and the good situations come where you have a big advantage, then you have to bet more, and that's when they detect card counters. On this particular occasion, there were a dozen cards left and 10 of them were aces and 10s. Now the deck was rich. I had like a 60 percent advantage on the house, because if I bet $100, the dealer can get the blackjack as well as me, but if he gets the blackjack, he wins $100, and if I get it, I win $150.

That's a big, big advantage. If I get a pair of 10s, I can split 'em; he can't. If I get a busting hand, I don't have to bust it; he does. You can split, you can double down, you can do all kinds of things. So when it got down to those dozen cards, I played two hands with like $100 on each hand. When you go for that kind of jump, they see it. Any time you make a big increase, the dealer will call it out—"black in action" or "checks in play" or something—to illustrate to the pit that something's going on differently. So now they were watching me, and here I get a blackjack and a 20, and the dealer gets a 20, and they say, "You can't play here anymore."

I went through all the motions of fighting it, but that was the wrong thing to do. That was even before I knew I was a good blackjack player. That led me to taking lessons, in part to learn how to protect my longevity. Revere taught me that there are so many casinos and so many shifts at each one, and you never play the same shift more than once in the summer. If you make a big hit, you walk out and go someplace else. But I still got banned a few more times because they're not gonna let you win. That's why beating them was such a big thrill to me, because I learned how to beat them at their own game.

I stopped playing cards as a business when I became head coach, but I think it's unfair. Anybody else can go out there for four days and drink and have fun and lose money and no one says a word. But if I go out there for a week and work to make some money, I'm bad. Because I can go out and beat those guys, I'm wrong. But if I'm going to go to Las Vegas, I'm going to make money or I'm not going to go. I'm not going to give those bums money. They've got enough money.

I think it was important for Bo Schembechler to get the athletic director's job. With the many problems in intercollegiate athletics today, I thought it was important for, number one, a Michigan man and, number two, a coach or a former coach to be our athletic director. Bo fills the bill.

A good way to describe Bo is to examine what he did in the spring of 1987. When President Shapiro was going to vote for the athletic cuts, the decrease in scholarships, the reduction in the number of games and so forth, Bo went head to head with him and won.

We got the Board in Control of Intercollegiate Athletics on our side and then Bo went to Shapiro. Shapiro said he was still voting for the cuts and the only way he would change his mind would be if the Big Ten presidents, the Council of Ten, voted the opposite way. Bo went to the NCAA convention and convinced those people to do that. If you have a wishy-washy athletic director, that's not going to get done. You're going to have serious problems.

Bo is an advocate of athletics, and he knows the importance of athletics — good, clean athletics — at the University of Michigan. Michigan is a great academic school but it's also a great athletic school, and we've got to maintain that. If we don't, we're in trouble.

Detroit News columnist Joe Falls wrote that I was upset about Bo becoming athletic director because of my rivalry with football. Nothing could be farther from the truth. If I were an athletic director at Michigan, the number one thing I would take care of is football, because if I'm going to be a great athletic director, then we better have 100,000 people for every game. And if we're going to continue to have 100,000 people at every game, then I better do all the things I've got to do to stay ahead of the other football schools. That's just the way the business is.

I was worried about who was going to be our athletic director. I was worried about bringing in an outside guy who didn't understand how successful Michigan has been in athletics over the years and wouldn't be as concerned about having a winning athletic program, someone who might be intimidated by the faculty and the other people on The Hill. Bo's not going to be intimidated. We've allowed our athletic director to run the athletic department. I think that's important, and I think Bo will continue that. With Jim Duderstadt's philosophy of hiring outstanding people and letting them do the job, I feel a lot more confident.

It's the number one academic-athletic institution in the world, and athletics, whether people like it or not, have been a prominent part of the University of Michigan. Maybe that's been the avenue that's united the great alumni body, because what better way to bring hundreds of thousands of people together than a football game?

I thought it would be important for the new president to recognize that, and I think Jim Duderstadt does. I think he's going to want Michigan to be in every top five poll academically, but I think he's also going to want to maintain a quality athletic program. And that's the type of president I want to work for.

We had to go to Duderstadt for decisions on important matters when he was provost and he was always very, very good. He was very much involved in getting Terry Mills accepted at Michigan. That was a big problem. The admissions office did not want to admit Terry, but we had recruited him for five years and I felt we had a moral obligation. They will never admit anyone here unless you can convince them of the student's potential and predict success. But if you can come up with a plan or persuade them that a kid will make it because of his dedication or the type of person he is, then they will always listen to you. From that standpoint, Duderstadt was very much involved.

Shapiro belongs at Princeton. I don't think he's a strong athletic guy. He's a much more academically oriented guy, and that's Princeton, that's the Ivy League. It's a good place for him. It's more his style. If you're the president of the University of Michigan, you have to understand that this is a unique place because of the great academic-athletic tradition, and you have to work hard to maintain both. You can't start voting for things that are going to take away from your athletic program.

At most other places, there is not the loyalty between the school and the coach and between the coach and the school that there is at a place like Michigan. I love Michigan. I'm loyal to Michigan, and I feel Michigan is loyal to Bill Frieder. I don't think there are a lot of places like that. I think there's a lot of mistrust elsewhere. I think many coaches won't work for a place unless they can bring their attorney and have a contract and all that kind of stuff. They'll leave in a second. They don't have loyalty to the school or to the kids.

Not many schools have the stability of the University of Michigan: three athletic directors in 67 years before Bo got the job, two basketball coaches in 21 years, two football coaches in 30 years. I've never had a contract at Michigan. I have a 10-month appointment that's renewed every year. I'm technically unemployed from June 30 until September 1.

I had serious talks with both Washington and Arizona State in the last three or four years, and the advice I got from a lot of people, which I didn't follow, was to go. In this business, you pick up more enemies every year.

Coaches joke that it's like being a sheriff in a town where some guy robs the bank and you chase the guy but can't catch him. Now you go back and get your deputies and the four or five of you chase him, and you still can't get him. Now you go back and deputize more guys, maybe 10 or 12. The posse gets bigger and bigger until pretty soon the whole town is chasing not the bank robber, but you, trying to get you for something. They're trying to get you for cheating. They're trying to get you because your kids don't graduate. They're trying to get you because of rumors about marijuana or alcohol. They're trying to get you for anything they can get you for.

The Lute Olsons, the Gene Bartows, I think their philosophy is to enjoy your honeymoon period for four or five years, then get out and let the new guy fight the pressures you've created for him and start a new honeymoon. The last time Bartow played me here, they were booing us. This was in 1986, and we had lost to Michigan State here on Thursday night and now we were behind Alabama-Birmingham on national TV on Saturday. Gene came into my locker room after the game and told me I should leave right then. "When they do that to you, it's time to go," he said.

But Gene's very sensitive. The boos weren't that bad, maybe a hundred people or so. You've just got to believe that more people support you than don't.

And this is a great job. I love coaching basketball at Michigan. I guess it comes down to the fact that even though there are all these distractions and things that bother you a little, the positives far outweigh the negatives. It isn't even close. I think coaches enjoy the limelight and all that a little more than they let on. I might act like I don't, or even feel like I don't, but I do.

I don't think I would ever coach in the pros. I feel I have a lot more control at this level. I want control of my team. I don't want to be bound by what contracts say in terms of playing time or incentives or not getting cut. I don't want to coach people who are making more money than I am. I'm in complete control here. If I tell someone to do something, they do it.

Another aspect of college coaching I find particularly enjoyable is the good relationships I've enjoyed with competitors in coaching. Gene Bartow spent time with me when I was a high school coach and Eddie Sutton invited Janice and me to dinner when I was an assistant at Michigan. Jerry Tarkanian had me over to his house numerous times before I became head coach.

Even though I've competed with both Bartow and Sutton, our relationships away from basketball have gotten stronger each year. The annual Nike Basketball Coaches Conference and various Nike clinics have helped develop further camaraderie with guys like Gene Keady, Abe Lemons, Rich Falk and Jim Valvano. It's nice to know that you can compete with people like this and still maintain good friendships.

One of the fun things about my job is if I want to go in right now and call somebody important, somebody who's busier than I am, I can get through to them. I don't talk to the secretary. I don't have to fight with anybody. If they get a call from Bill Frieder, it's going to go through or they're going to return it immediately. I love that.

It's a big thrill for me to be able to call Tiger executive Jim Campbell and have him give me four seats in his private box. I went through it the other way. I put my order in the mail for World Series tickets in 1968 and wondered if I would get them or not and would they be in the bleachers. I did that route. Now I'm doing it the other way.

Campbell and Sparky Anderson sent me a telegram after we won the NIT in 1984. Maybe I don't understand the magnitude of my job, but that was a big thrill. I suppose I am to them what they are to me, but I look at them as being so much more famous and important. Here I am, just a little guy, and here are the guys from the Detroit Tigers writing to me. I couldn't believe it.

I haven't even thought about giving it up, because I want to do this. I enjoy it. I probably shouldn't even say this, but the amount of money coaches get paid is incredible. We're stealing it; we really are. I'd do it for a lot less. I did and I would.

11

●

Big News in the Big Ten

People make too big a deal out of Bobby Knight. That goes for me, too, I guess, since here's a whole section of my book about him. You'd think he was the only coach, or maybe the only person, in the league. Whatever Bobby's doing is always the biggest news in the Big Ten. The only thing that comes close is what his team is doing.

The fans at Crisler are always their loudest and most involved for our games with Indiana. And whose face is on the Midwest editions of all the pre-season magazines? They even had a full-page ad for some investment company or something, half of which was a picture of him, in our own Michigan basketball program! I told Madej to get it out of there.

I don't agree with everything Dale Brown says, but the Louisiana State coach was right when he said Bobby tries to get his way by intimidating people—referees, other coaches, his players. Mort says this is because he's (Bobby and Mort both, really) an only child and a Scorpio and that's the way they are. Mort pays attention to that kind of stuff; I don't. It's not gonna help me win games.

Maybe it's only the media that make too big a deal out of Bobby. With them, it's more like manipulation. He gets his tail beat but the whole story is not the game. The whole story is something else, and then nothing happens to him. I've seen that for 15 years.

I remember Iowa was beating him in Bloomington one year and the whole story was about Wayne Duke and the officials. It was the game where he went to Wayne during one of the timeouts and ripped Wayne on the officials.

He picked that fight with me in 1984 after I beat him, or I should say my team beat his team (see how easy it is to fall into that?), and here we go again. Here he was getting beat and the whole story is whether he did me a favor and his breaking into my press conference, and nothing about my players winning a great basketball game. They were young kids, and they had no business beating Indiana that day, but that's Bobby Knight.

And that's always what it seems to come down to. We beat Indiana in Bloomington by 12 points last season and the story was how this was Bobby's worst start ever at Indiana and the program was in ruins and "What's Wrong with the Hoosiers?" and all this bull.

Mort says Hank Hersch of *Sports Illustrated* told him that Knight is like the pivot that the league revolves around. Coaches are judged on how often they beat Knight, or whether they're pro-Knight or anti-Knight, and so on.

And, sure enough, after we beat them again, this time by 20, in Ann Arbor, the story was how I was now 8–8 against Bobby and I had won five of my last seven against Bobby and I had swept Bobby for the second time in three seasons. See? It was like now I was a good coach because I was .500 against Bobby.

Bobby liked me just fine when his teams were beating mine all the time. The trouble started when my teams started beating his. He and Orr were supposedly such great friends, but you notice Bobby beat Orr's butt more than Orr beat his. Now they're still great friends, but they don't play each other, either, do they? I don't think Bobby has too many friends among the coaches he plays regularly.

Some people say he just loses control of himself, but I don't agree. He's setting the agenda and it's calculated. This man knows what he's doing. I don't think Bob Knight has ever lost control.

It's a fact that the Big Ten isn't going to discipline him, and neither is the NCAA. But what would happen if you worked for Don Canham and you threw a chair, or hit a policeman, or pulled your team off the floor? I'll tell you what, you wouldn't do it again. If you were lucky, you might get one warning, but I doubt it.

It's funny that incident with him ever happened. If we'd had the coaching box back then, it probably wouldn't have. I would have had to work another official to get that other official to do what he had to do. I never would have gotten close enough to him for him to hear, or think he heard, what I said.

Even at that, there were a lot of coincidences involved.

First, there was the fact that I was at Crisler the Friday morning before the Indiana game, which was on a Saturday afternoon. We had lost to Ohio State, a team that hadn't won a game in the Big Ten up until then, at the buzzer Thursday night, so I didn't go to the office at all. I was at Crisler until five or six in the morning, might have gone home for a couple of hours, then went right back. Now maybe in another situation, I wouldn't have been at the arena at 11 in the morning, but I was.

Second, Indiana had played at Michigan State Thursday night, so they were here for like a noon practice. Normally, it's 5:30.

And third, John Viges of the *Ann Arbor News* shows up. So for this whole situation to happen required an unusual sequence of events. Usually I would come a little later, usually they would practice later, and usually Viges wouldn't be there, but it all happened.

So I walked out to say hello to Knight and Viges was out there. This was when Knight wasn't talking to anybody in the media, and Viges asked me if I could get him an interview with Bob. He must have found out somehow that they were practicing at noon, so he came over.

So I went out and Bob and I sat on the scorer's table. We got talking and I said, "Bob, they're on my butt because I didn't start McCormick. Viges ripped me for not starting McCormick and the *Daily* ripped me for playing him 28 minutes because I knew he was sick."

McCormick hadn't been playing well. He got one rebound the game before Ohio State. So I said, "Yeah, they're rippin' my butt for changing the lineup."

He said, "Well, I've changed the lineup 17 different times already this year. What the hell has that got to do with it?"

I said, "Well, my guy's out there right now. He wants to interview you. Why don't you talk to him about it?"

He said, "I will."

That was it. That was the favor, okay? That was the favor I asked of him.

He said, "What kind of guy is he?"

I said, "He's a good guy. I want you to do the interview with him."

So that was the favor.

Now, during the game, he was up berating the officials; intimidation, like he always does. None of that bothered me, except that my guy was waiting to shoot a free throw, and we're waiting and we're waiting and we're waiting for Ed Maracich and Knight to finish their conversation.

Finally, I said, "Either sit the SOB down or give him a technical." Probably five or ten seconds before I said that, Maracich had given him a technical, but I didn't know that. I must have been looking back at our end of the floor to see what was going on. Whatever it was, I didn't see it.

Knight claims that I said "give him another technical," which I didn't, but it doesn't really matter what I said because he shouldn't have been taking up the time. We should have been playing. Let the kids decide the game, not him.

Then Knight came after me, calling me a chicken-bleep SOB and that kind of stuff.

He chewed me out all the way into the tunnel at halftime, calling me every name in the book, just like I read he calls his players. My biggest thing then, when I walked in—we were four ahead at the half—was, hey, we're gonna win this game. We are not letting his commotion detract from what we've got to do as basketball coaches. We did a great job in that locker room, putting all this behind us and coaching our team, instead of going in there bitching and complaining about Bobby Knight, which is what he probably wanted.

It's the same old thing. Bob Knight, if he gets beat, he wants to find a way to distract from his loss. Purdue's beating him, he throws a chair. Michigan beats him, he does something like he did here. The Russians are beating him, he pulls his team off the floor. So that when he gets his tail beat and walks into a press conference, the story isn't the game, the story is what Bob Knight did, the story is some of his antics, and that's what it was here.

I started off the press conference by asking for a vote on throwing out Jim Spadafore of the *Detroit News* because he had written a story misquoting my players. I wasn't really serious—Spad's a good guy and I just wanted to have some fun with him—but I like to keep the press a little off balance and I wanted to relieve the mood.

I didn't even know there was a back door to the room where we have the press conferences at Crisler, but I found out soon enough because Knight came storming through it right after I asked about taking that vote. It was quite a shock because, like I said, Knight wasn't talking to the press then, or going to press conferences.

Well, he not only came to this one, but he also started off by making some sarcastic remark about how he didn't like to hear the media criticized. I said I hadn't realized Bobby was there and I'd let him talk and come back later. And then he laid into me, calling me more (but not very different) names, saying I had used him, talking about how much he had done for me, and so on. Lynn Henning, who was covering my team then for the *Detroit News*, wrote that "to anyone there, the whole ugly scene felt like a punch in the stomach." That covers it pretty well.

After he was finished and I came back, they all wanted to talk about Bob Knight. No one wanted to talk about the job my basketball team did in beating Indiana when they had lost by 27 points in Bloomington the year before.

When I got home that day, I told Janice, "You know, this is so ridiculous. As badly as I feel, and as upset as this guy has got me, I wish we'd have lost the game. You shouldn't have to go through something like this."

I honestly felt that. I felt that, hey, I don't want to go through this nonsense. If you can't compete against each other and then be friends afterwards, then who needs it? I was upset because I thought the guy was a friend, and a friend does not act that way.

He called me at my house that night. He called me at my house the next day. I didn't even want to talk to him, but I did, and I tried to defend myself. You could see that he was upset, that he was not going to bend, that he thought I was entirely wrong and disloyal or whatever. I think he wanted an apology.

He was upset at some of the things I said at the press conference, I forget exactly what. He said I lied to the press. I tried not to discuss it, but he had on tape everything that I said. He was upset that I did not admit that he did me a favor, that was the crux of it. We just kind of got into it again, so it just never got settled.

I don't remember ever calling him after that. I answered his calls a couple of times within the next year or so, but I didn't talk to him at the press conferences and meetings. We really haven't talked since then, and that's fine with me.

He did get a hold of me after many attempts in Charlotte at the NCAA tournament in '87 because my manager screwed up and said I was there after I had not taken the call. He wanted to congratulate me for beating Purdue. I'm going to prove to the world that I don't need favors from him to have a successful program.

He's the type of guy who, when this happened, called everybody. Everybody. He called coaches. He called media people. He called mutual friends. He wanted to tell them his side of the story and get their support.

I never called anybody to discuss the matter, but when I would run into a Sparky Anderson—"Oh, Bob Knight called me"—or if I'd run into a coach—"Hey, Bob Knight called me about this." He called everybody, because now he's trying to get support and justify what he did. I think if he did do me a favor, it's not a favor when you call a press conference and talk about it.

If I do anything for anybody, they can stab me in the back, but then I don't go tell other people what I did for them. If I do somebody a favor, it's a favor and it's over.

I made a mistake my third year as head coach when I let him come into my locker room and talk to my team. It seemed like a nice thing at the time because I had great respect for the man, but I would never have allowed it to happen if I knew he was going to call a press conference and tell about it.

He said, "I can't believe Frieder did this to me, when I went into his locker room and talked to his team one time."

Jim Dutcher told me after I did that that I made a mistake. He said, "You should never have let him go in there, because you'll owe him. You'll owe him the rest of your life because he thinks he did you a big, big favor. You're as good a basketball coach as he is. You don't need him."

What it amounts to is, he's your friend as long as he beats your butt every time you compete. And as soon as you start beating him, you're no longer his friend. At least, that's how it was with me.

Knight and I had a great relationship before that incident. I first met him when we were on clinics together when I won the state championship at Flint Northern and he first went to Indiana, which was 1971 or '72. Then I came to Michigan in '73. I always respected him. I always thought he was the finest coach in the country. I knew he was doing a great job. He knew that I liked him, that I was observant of what Indiana basketball was accomplishing and how they were accomplishing it, and that I was trying to learn from him.

You know, we had Orr's 50th birthday party and Janice invited Knight and he came. I don't think he'd have come to many assistants' houses.

When we went to Bloomington, Janice went over to their house.

We had a pretty good friendship going. When the game was over, he'd be patting me on the back, telling me how my kids were coming along and to hang in there, we're getting better.

See, Knight paid me a great compliment once, and maybe that's why he got so upset with me. He sent me a picture of the two of us at the national championship in Philly in 1981, from when I went down and wished him good luck before the game. In fact, they were all amazed that I could get down there, because I didn't have any pass or anything.

Then somehow there was a picture taken of it, of me wishing him good luck before the game. So he got it laminated and wrote on it, "Some day the positions will be reversed" or something like that.

In all honesty, that's a great compliment—isn't it?—from a great coach when I'm a first-year coach. I don't think he would do that for too many people. Now because of all that, maybe he felt that I was in a special category of one of his lieutenants or whatever. I think that's what he imagined. Now all of a sudden these incidents come up and it's something that he can't take because he thinks he's been betrayed. Maybe he's going back to the war or something and he's been betrayed by one of his men, and he can't cope with that. I think that's what he went through with it all, and that wasn't the case at all. I was just trying to win a basketball game.

I think our relationship would probably still be good today if he had just called me afterward and said, "Hey, I think you made a mistake. I'm talking to the official and you shouldn't interfere when I'm talking to the official." I would have agreed with him then. I'm an easy guy to get along with.

I just hope he doesn't go out the way Woody Hayes went out, that's all I care about. He's accomplished too much, but if the United States has the guts to let him coach in the Olympics and nothing happened, maybe he'll make it. What guts that took, huh? And they stood by him, but thank God he won. Thank God something didn't happen where he was getting beat and there was some bad incident.

You can tell by his book (*Season on the Brink*) that he doesn't like me or Michigan. What poetic justice it was to beat him in the first Big Ten game of the 1986 season. Going into that game, he's telling his team we haven't played anybody, and our last non-conference game was who? Cleveland State, who beats them in the first round of the NCAA tournament. I never thought I would see the day when Knight didn't respect opponents, but evidently he didn't respect Cleveland State if he would tell his team we hadn't played anybody and we're fat and lazy.

What an honor it was for me and my team that he prepared for Michigan during his Christmas tournament. That's in the book, about how he didn't worry about San Jose State and all of them, he worried about Michigan, prepared for Michigan, and then we beat 'em down there. That was satisfying, if he put that much into the game.

But, see, then he lost the next game to Michigan State. That's one thing I've learned about this league. That's what happens if you put too much effort into one game. You cannot do that at this level, and he made a serious mistake there.

There are 18 games and you better not get too involved in any one game in this league or it's gonna cost you three up the road. I've never even treated Michigan State any differently because after that Michigan State game, you've gotta go play somebody else. You play 'em all twice and they're all one win only and they're all one loss only, and that's the way you gotta treat it.

It is extremely important to me to get the best kids in Michigan to commit to Michigan. I thought that was a real weakness in the program when I took over, that there wasn't a single Michigan kid on the team, but do you notice how few Indiana kids there are in Knight's program now? Part of the reason for that is the jaycees he's taking.

That shows there's a lot of two-face in Bobby Knight. When I was an assistant, you cannot believe how he ripped the schools that were taking jaycees. How they cheat. How he will never take a jaycee kid because they've got bad attitudes. How there's a reason that they're in junior college, that they can't do the work academically. He went on and on and on, but he went and got jaycees when he had a bad season.

Well, what kind of person is that? He compromised. I don't like people who compromise their principles. And then he wins the national title and he goes out and gets more jaycees. It's almost like once he acquired the taste, he forgot about his principles.

Also in *Season on the Brink* is a scene where Indiana is playing Iowa at home and the referees give George Raveling a technical. Knight comes over and asks them to give him another technical.

That's the same thing he said I did that got him irritated, and it's another example that if Bobby Knight decides to do it, it's okay, but if someone else decides to do it, you're violating the code. It's just like the jaycees. If someone else takes jaycees, it's not good, but if he takes 'em, then it's okay.

And don't ever let him tell people that our fans are the worst, because his fans haven't been that nice to me, even though I entertained 2,000 of them in New Orleans at the national finals in '87, when I saw them up and down Bourbon Street. They were all shaking my hand and being nice to me because we beat Purdue for them to give 'em the co-championship and the number one seed. I mean, I just set the whole national championship up for them.

All those fans were nice to me and promised me a standing ovation in Bloomington, and I did get some cheers when I got introduced—I think it was my boys I met on Bourbon Street—but when I go off that court, I get stuff thrown at me. I hear 'em talking.

How's he think the people are gonna treat him when he walks out here after the way he's acted? You know what I mean? What the hell does he expect?

Now he's griping about our yellow towels. He said something on his television show about that. He said their fans at Indiana wouldn't do that and that's bush league. What the hell, we went down there and they had a red pompom on every seat. Laura was gonna give hers back to Bobby Knight here and I wouldn't let her.

He says he wouldn't let this and he wouldn't let that. Maybe he should walk off with me some night, when his fans are yelling and screaming and throwing crap. Maybe he should protect me, if he's my friend. But that would be another favor, I suppose.

Janice says that if I feel about Bobby the way I say I do, then he shouldn't be included in this book at all, but maybe it's time I did him a favor.

12

Playing to the Cameras

The thing I like the most about coaching that I really don't have anymore is working with 15 guys behind closed doors, day after day. In high school, it was nice not having to deal with anybody else, not having to answer to television people, sports information people, the media, whatever, because to me, that's all a distraction.

You wish you could just walk in, have your 15 guys, your coaching staff, and that's it. But I'm smart enough to know that isn't the way it is anymore. It's here to stay and I work with it and accept it.

You know, one of the reasons we built this program is because we are on national television. I don't like all the nonsense of having to deal with all the TV people when they come in the day before the game with their trucks and cables and lights, but that's all part of the business. Money talks, and despite what everybody else like university presidents or faculty representatives say, money is important in athletics. So when TV comes at you with all this money, you listen.

My experience has been that any time you get exposure, it's good. I can think back to Butch Wade, Richard Rellford and Rumeal Robinson, and I know it certainly didn't hurt that they knew something about Michigan from television. And it doesn't hurt for Michigan kids to see us as they're growing up, either. You can even use it if you don't do well on TV: "You saw us play, didn't you? Then you can see that we need you."

The media's been extremely good to us and Michigan has a great reputation, so you have to work with these people. It's just a necessary evil, I guess, like recruiting's a necessary evil. Sometimes I think everything is a necessary evil in this business.

If you could just coach your 15 guys and see them progress, and not have to account for every little thing, then you would really enjoy it.

I think I've done a great job cooperating with the media and getting along with them, and I like them. I've gone out of my way to be friendly to them and make them feel good and make them feel welcome and so forth.

I enjoy those people, and I've found out they've got their pressures, too. They've got editors who are on their butts to write something controversial, or who change their stories, and I know the writers don't write the headlines or decide how the stories are played. So a lot of times it isn't them, and I understand that.

Plus most people read the paper and then a day or two goes by and it's over with and they're on to something else. They don't even retain it. It's at the bottom of their bird cage. So you can't react to all that.

My biggest complaint about the media is when they write something you did not say or something that's not the truth in order to sell papers. That's my biggest complaint, or if they don't honor some of my requests in dealing with the players. When that happens, I'm just like I would be with my family, my friends or anybody else: I don't treat them quite the same. I get bullheaded. I don't talk to relatives if I think they've been unfair to me, so I do the same thing with the media.

I'll give you an example. Once we got into the season, we did not allow Terry Mills and Rumeal Robinson to talk to the press when they were freshmen because we could not say "yes" to everybody. CBS wanted to do something, NBC wanted to do something, Billy Packer, Al McGuire, Vitale, the *Sporting News*, *Sports Illustrated* and right on down the line. Everybody.

These kids had to go to school! The demands on their time were just too much, so we said nobody could talk to them. Well, the *Detroit Free Press* went around me and went to their dorm and continued to harass them and they finally talked to the *Free Press* and the *Free Press* got a story and it made my credibility look bad with everybody else.

These kids were crawling in and out of their windows to avoid the *Free Press* in the hallway, and then they came back with photographers. So the rest of the year, I didn't provide the *Free Press* with any special considerations. I had my press conferences, I answered their questions, but when they wanted to do features and additional things, I just would not cooperate with them. That's just the way life is, you know. Maybe I'm too stubborn that way, but they didn't honor what I wanted to do for the benefit of those kids.

It makes me mad if I pick up the paper and there's something they say I said that I didn't say, but I've also learned you can't react to that too much. I'm above that and I've got a program to run and if you worry about every little thing that's written, you drive yourself nuts.

I have to admit, though, that I do let some things get to me sometimes. After Illinois beat us at home by 14 in the next-to-last game of the 1987 regular season, I stomped out of my press conference when some guy asked what it did to our chances for the NCAA tournament.

Part of it was that I just get tired sometimes of answering the same questions, especially questions about the tournament because nobody knows what the hell is going to happen until those guys get together in that room. Anyway, our next game, we just annihilated Purdue, 104–68. It was just shocking, to me as well as to Gene Keady, and it knocked them out of an outright Big Ten championship.

So I walked into my press conference, and the same guy is

there, and I ask him, "Now what was your question?"

Another time, I made a statement that when it comes to drugs, I don't care about constitutional rights. When it got printed in the *Sporting News*, it said, "Bill Frieder says, 'I don't care about constitutional rights.'" So now here come all the letters to the editor about Bill Frieder. Even though I might have gotten the same letters either way, there was a big difference between what I said and what was printed.

Dick Vitale can get to me, too. I like Dick, I really do. We've had some good times together, but he can be so unfair. He announced the Great Alaska Shootout games for ESPN at the beginning of last season, and in the Alabama-Birmingham game in particular, he kept talking about our bad post defense. But the main reason it was bad was Terry Mills, who was playing in his third college game.

So down the stretch, when we needed to stop UAB's Larry Rembert, who was killing us, we went with Mark Hughes and Loy Vaught. Vitale kept complaining about how could we have Mills on the bench down the stretch, but he failed to mention that Rembert didn't score in the last five minutes. He failed to mention that we did a great job of coming from behind and winning.

After we got home, Dave Woolford of the *Toledo Blade* and half a dozen other writers called and wanted to do stories on me and Vitale: Why is he doing this to Michigan and Bill Frieder? Why doesn't he go overboard like that with other schools? Does it go back to the Michigan–Detroit deal when he was there?

I told 'em, hey, I have no idea. My job is so tough and I can't get involved in discussing the media. I've got enough problems without worrying about what some broadcaster is doing. I don't know if he's got ulterior motives. I don't know if somebody's put him up to it. But I do know that when he picked us number one in his magazine, that made others raise us because of it. Nobody else picked us number one. I voted in Larry Paladino's magazine, *Sports Fans' Journal*, and picked us 12th, which, as it turned out, is where we wound up.

Vitale is the first guy who ever said we had a cream-puff schedule, and it was not an accurate statement, but because he said it everyone believed it, or at least paid attention. The year he said we had the easiest schedule in the country, it was rated 11th in the country. Besides our Big Ten games we had played Georgia Tech when they were ranked number one, Tennessee and Alabama-Birmingham. We won the Chaminade Tournament and had decent NCAA games. We had those six or seven straight at home in December and he kept alluding to those, but who doesn't do that?

I think Dick was a little envious of Michigan when he was at Detroit. He always brought Michigan into something. I think at one time he would have loved to have the Michigan job. But the way I look at it, he's given us publicity, he's given us exposure, and that's not all bad. He's always got us in the news, he's always talking about us, but I've always looked at that as good.

You know the old saying, "Just spell my name right and keep talking about me." I've gotten a lot of speaking engagements because Dick Vitale is out mentioning my name.

One of the biggest times I was upset about the press was when I was an assistant, this was about 1977, and Larry Keith, who was with *Sports Illustrated,* was pushing me on questions and answers about Johnny Orr. And I might have said something like, "There's no question Orr has always hired good assistants and given them authority," but what Keith said I said was that the reason John was successful was because he had hired me.

I was sick over that. But you know what John did? Three days after the magazine came out, he sent me a note with $300 in it: "This is your bonus for all the extra work you do, and especially for handling my interviews. I love you. Johnny."

Those are things people on the outside don't understand. What a great guy. He knew I was upset. He knew I wasn't wrong. He knew I was a loyal, hard-working assistant, and he knew I had been taken advantage of.

Another thing that bothered me was the *Ann Arbor News* editorial that came out after Roy Tarpley admitted he had used cocaine. The *News'* John Beckett wrote a story that Tarpley had tested positive for cocaine three times at Michigan. The editorial complained about what it called a policy of "protecting the stars" and said "the image of the U-M athletic department and the stature of the university have been damaged by the protection afforded Roy Tarpley during his stay on campus and the confidentiality with which his case was treated."

I don't quite know how to deal with something like that. You know my policies about drugs and confidentiality and having the same rules for all the players. Far from protecting the stars, sometimes my players have thought I went too far the other way. Like I told Janice, sometimes when you say that anything regarding the team is a family matter and it's confidential, sometimes you're penalizing your kids by keeping it confidential. You're better off saying, "Hey, this kid's not gonna start because he didn't go to class last week or because he missed practice or because he was 10 minutes late." If you don't do that, you've got too many reporters digging into it and they're assuming other things: It must have been this, it must have been that, he must be into drugs. And then they start printing it and that's so unfair.

Maybe you're better off just saying what it was and it's over. Like when I suspended Antoine Joubert at Michigan State for being late to practice. I didn't want a bunch of articles on whether he should or shouldn't have been suspended. I didn't want to get into that, so that's why I said he didn't start because of a discipline matter and that's all I'm saying. But then the press started speculating that it must have been worse things, and it wasn't.

I was upset with the way Beckett wrote up the Tarpley situation. Tarpley did not test positive for cocaine three times, yet Beckett reported that he had.

Inaccurate information caused me a lot of problems, because the crux of everybody else's deal was that this kid tested positive for cocaine three times and why wasn't more done? And that didn't happen.

That put me in a tough spot, too, because the basis for the whole testing program is that it's confidential. I couldn't really answer those stories without violating that.

The media are so much more involved today. There's so much coverage and every guy has to have a story. That's why you have to work hard to get good kids with good attitudes. Because even when you have that, you're still going to have your share of problems.

Let me tell you something. I've got 15 kids. Bo's got a hundred. If you have kids, or your kids have kids, you've probably got one or two or three. And just with those two or three, I'll bet you there are pregnancies you're not too happy about, or somebody drinking too much, or somebody that tried marijuana or cocaine, or got in a fight at school, or doesn't go to class, or is seeing a psychiatrist.

These kids aren't any different. A lot of them come from poorer backgrounds than what you have, but they're good kids, they work hard, and that doesn't mean we're not going to have a problem or two along the way, because we do. When you're dealing with 15 kids and you're with them as much as I am, you're going to have problems.

I think, basically, when you rate the media's coverage of the Michigan basketball program, it's been very good. I'm almost tempted to say "excellent," but I think I'll stick with "very good." You know, I went through some bad times and they were good to me. The Detroit papers are powerful papers, big-time papers with big-time writers. When you think of a Jerry Green or a Joe Falls, these guys have been around for a long time and yet, during my bad year, these guys didn't write anything negative. They didn't come in here and demand Frieder be fired or do an in-depth report as to what was wrong.

I think they took the approach that, hey, it's not fair to judge him on that season. You've got to give the guy a chance, and they did. They've been good to me, on the whole. We've had great coverage in our good years. We've been covered well. If we play bad and they want to write that we stink, hell, I've got no objection to that. That's their job.

If someone lies or tries to make me look bad, that really bothers me, but, outside of that, I've really had good success with the press.

I needle some of them but, basically, I've had a good relationship and I've been treated pretty fairly.

I've learned to be flexible, too. I've probably said, "We've had enough press; we've had enough interviews; now no more," a thousand times, but when Charlie Vincent of the *Free Press* calls and says, "I've got to do something for the *Sporting News*. It'll be a nice piece on Gary. Can I get with him for 10 minutes?", what would you do? It's good for the program. It's good for Gary. Charlie's been a good guy for years. You've just got to use good judgment, I think. Make sure it doesn't interfere with basketball, be a good person, and once in a while put your foot down.

When I first started, you had one guy each covering you from the *Detroit Free Press* and the *Detroit News*. Now you might have five guys call you in one day. This guy's doing an advance on the game. This guy's doing a feature on Glen Rice. This guy wants to talk about the Sean Higgins incident. This guy wants to talk about the three-point shot. It's incredible how that's changed, but it's all part of the business. Now, after the post-game press conference, you have to talk to six, eight, 10 guys individually in the locker room because they don't want the stuff from the press conference. They want their own story. They don't want to ask their questions in the press conference. The problem with this is, why did we have the press conference? That gets tiresome, but if you're not winning and you don't have good players, they're not going to be there.

George Puscas, the sports editor of the *Free Press*, told me once that when Michigan signed Cazzie Russell, he wrote a paragraph on getting Cazzie, one paragraph, five or six lines. Then he wrote a second paragraph on the others that we signed, and they cut out the second paragraph. He couldn't get 'em both in. That's how far it's come in 25 years. Now there are books an inch thick on the newsstands just on high school prospects, ranked from one to a million, and who's in on 'em, and everybody's interested.

But that's what's led to television, that's what's led to exposure, that's what's led to me being able to recruit nationally and stay at nice places and go to Alaska and Hawaii and Europe, and to the job being a lot more lucrative than it was when Dave Strack was the coach.

So you get paid for it, but you wonder if maybe it was better the other way. I know I was happier as a high school coach. I know I was happier as an assistant. I can do far more things now. I'm living a more comfortable life, but I know I was happier back then. At least, it seems to me that I was. But I would never go back.

The Fans Speak (and Write)

TV cameras, Iowa and I just don't mix.

Last year, when the Hawkeyes played at Crisler, there was that incident where I pushed the camera out of my face on the way to the locker room at halftime.

The year before, when we were upsetting Iowa in Crisler on national television, Glen Rice was going in for a layup on the front end of a fast break and Jeff Moe just grabbed him around the arms while he was in midair. It was right at the end of the game, we already had the victory clinched, and it served no purpose whatsoever.

I started screaming at Moe, calling him names I hope Laura never hears and just generally berating him. I thought Moe's play was a senseless thing to do. He could have hurt Glen, although he did try to break his fall. What I didn't realize was that the camera was on me the whole time, and nobody in the national TV audience needed any special skills in lip-reading to know what I was saying.

I know Tom Davis doesn't coach that sort of thing and, generally, I like Moe, too. I apologized to both of them later on, but that didn't get enough publicity in Iowa to offset the impression that television gave.

And it didn't help my popularity there, either, when some comments I made at the bust that year got picked up by the papers out there. Referring to Iowa's loss to Nevada-Las Vegas, I said, "I guarantee you that if we have an 18-point lead in the second half of the regional finals, we won't blow it."

I've gotten a lot of interesting letters from Iowa since then. One of them came last February from a man in Garner, Iowa, named Russ Appel. Russ wasn't upset about my pushing the camera, but he was upset that I wanted a technical foul on his team when I had a 35-point lead.

I decided to resolve this personally, so I called him from my hotel room in Madison the night before we played at Wisconsin. Fortunately, Mort was there and had his tape recorder running. This is how it went:

"Is Russ there? Russ, this is Bill Frieder. I'm calling you about the letter. Now, what do you want to discuss?

"Well, let me tell you something, okay? What if you were a coach at a baseball game, and you were ahead, 7–0, okay? And a guy slid into second base and he was clearly out, but the umpire called him safe for the other team. And you question him and he says, 'Hey, Russ, don't worry about it. Settle down. Yeah, he was out, but you're 7–0 ahead, so don't worry about it.'

"You cannot tolerate this as a coach from any official. Scores should never enter the officials' minds. And these officials in the Big Ten, you have to let them know at times when you're unhappy or they're going to screw you all year. You know what I mean?

"So this was my beef with the official. It had nothing to do with anything except it was bad judgment by the official. Maybe even if a technical shouldn't have been called, he shouldn't have told me that. If that's why he didn't make the call, that's completely wrong.

"Okay. So my beef was with the officials because officials cannot look at the score to make calls or not make calls. Secondly, the camera incident. First of all, I was hit by somebody first and when I turned around, there was a camera and I did shove the camera out of the way. I did not touch the cameraman. But I was nicked by either a camera or some person or something as I was arguing with the official.

"Regarding the running up the score, my God, you know what I'm getting ripped on in Michigan? Why I gave up 77 points in the second half. I took a great effort from my team and destroyed it by allowing Iowa to score 77 points in the second half, and I'm gettin' ripped now so, you know, you can't win on that. You guys are mad because we scored 120 and all my people are ticked off at me because we had chances to lead the league in defense.

"I don't know what you can do about that. I played all 11 players in the first half and, hey, the way Iowa's throwing 'em in, you can't fool around. I mean, you can't let them get it under 15 or 12 or they might come back and beat you. So I don't agree with you on that.

"As far as maybe getting a little hot, yeah, that could be true. If I offended anybody, I apologize on that. And I didn't get mad that it wasn't called. If he'd have given me a technical for jumping up and down, I'd have respected the guy. I got mad when he told me, 'Hey, Bill, yeah, it's a technical, but you're 30 ahead.' Then I got . . . then that . . . honest to God, yup, and I really got hot, because that is ridiculous.

"You cannot have officials do that. You know what I'm saying? But I wanted to answer your letter and I figured a phone call would be a lot easier. . . . Well, I'm calling you . . . okay. Now don't be too hard on me in Iowa City. I'm not that bad a guy. . . . Okay, podnuh. . . . take care."

When I told him what the official had told me, Russ said, "Oh, God, did he really say that to you?" I said, "Yeah." He said, "Well, I can really see why you got hot."

He was stunned. He said, "I can't believe you're really calling me."

Then I sent him a letter thanking him for being so

understanding.

I try to answer all my mail, the good, the bad and the ugly, and I'll mix it up with people if they want to mix it up with me. Some of it is unanswerable, however, either because there's no signature, or it's one you can't read, or because, well, there's just no way to answer.

Here's one I got before we went to Seattle last season for the West Regional:

"4 Ways to Beat N. Carolina.
1. Get ball to Mills all night. Head fake drive on him Reid will get in foul trouble.
2. Keep a hand in S. Lebo's face all night. He will hurt you more than R. Smith.
3. Keep an eye open all night for N. Carolina (back door) they are best in country at this.
4. After we make field gold, get back on defense quick. N.C. are real good pushing ball up floor. After a basket is scored. (don't be caught napping). Good Luck. See you in K.C."

I can't say that anything we tried worked any better than what this (anonymous) correspondent recommended.

In a refreshing change of pace, another writer who chose not to sign his or her name offered some fashion notes.

"Some of the larger *class* teams that don't allow their players to wear T-shirts: Virginia, Duke, Ill., Ind., Purdue, N. Carolina, Duke, Kyn., Vanderbilt, Notre Dame, DePaul, Michigan State, Kansas.

"Your team — some with T-shirts others with regular shirts — makes your team look like a pickup group. Where's your discipline? You don't see it in the pros. There is a rule that prohibits that.

"Your towel act is laughable. Why don't you do something original for a change?

"You are embarrassing to 'M' alumni, especially when you are on T.V. Wake up!

"P.S. Maybe you should look in the dictionary and see what UNIFORM really means."

First, I want to find out why Duke has two teams.

After we won at Indiana last year, I kiddingly proposed to Gary Grant in front of the media. It caused problems when he accepted, though, because I already have a wife. Someone signing "D" had a solution.

"Congratulations on your recent announcement of your marriage plans! I am sure the two of you will be very happy. Since I am sure that you, Coach Frieder, are smart enough to know bigamy is illegal, you will have to divorce Janice prior to marrying Gary. Hence, I would like FIRST DIBS on Jan!"

In the middle of March, I got a letter signed by "A Friend," but the greeting, as you will see, was anything but friendly. I'm not going to repeat all the good advice this person gave me, but the letter started like this "Coach: (?)"

March was the month for flattering mail. A trio of alumni in Houston took time out from their busy schedules to send me a page and a half of single-spaced tips on how I could improve the team. Just so I knew they weren't going soft on me, they concluded this way:

"Because of deficiencies such as those listed above, we have to admit we are not your biggest fans. However, as alumni we feel obligated to offer our views on improving the team. We long to see the day when Michigan can obtain a national championship. Unless some changes are made, however, it will never happen."

Sometimes the mail doesn't come directly to me. This one was sent to Don Canham, and he was good enough, and amused enough, to share it with me:

"For God's sake, can't anybody put a muzzle on Frieder. I know he's your fair haired boy and of course you never make a mistake in choosing your assistants. One look at the athletic staff in the football guide, with one or two exceptions, it looks like a rogues gallery. Where in the world did you find them.

"Frieder talks like an old farmer from MSU in the 1890's. He certainly is a hayseed. No wonder no other school wants him. Jeff Heathcote looks like a star from Hollywood by way of comparison. Look out for MSU next winter. At least they will have a couple of white men who won't falter in a crucial contest. Steigenga is the man to watch. So much for Mills. He's very mediocre!

"I hope this letter makes you so mad you want to accuse me again of trying to run the athletic dept. I wouldn't want it under any circumstances!"

Unlike the sentiments (unfortunately), the signature was indecipherable.

The following was addressed to Johnny Orr, but the author sent a copy to me, too:

"We've been reading in the papers that there are three officials in the Big Eight that you would like to send on a slow boat to China—among other things.

"I just want you to know that in the Big Ten we still have Jim Bain (as you might have noticed on the recent CBS game at Iowa City).

"I swear to God the man was born with a whistle in his mouth and the first word he uttered was 'Charge!'. It is only fitting that he be laid to rest with his right hand resting behind his head.

"How's this for a horse trade? Send those three officials over to us and we'll send you Bain. I'm sure you can handle him as he is a step slower since you chased him down the tunnel in Champaign."

The only thing I can tell you for sure about the last letter I'm going to share is that it didn't come from Iowa:

"Because I love God, please forgive me for any and every unkind thought, unkind word, or unkind deed that I have expressed against you, knowingly or unknowingly.
God bless you—I love you."

I get phone calls, too. One time, this guy called me at home about 2:30 in the morning. Naturally, I was up.

"Hey, coach," he said. "We need a question answered. When did Saginaw High win the state championship?"

"1962," I said.

"See," he said. "I told you, man. I told you. My buddy wants to talk to you, coach. Tell my buddy."

His buddy got on the line and said, "Coach, when did they win it?"

I said, "1961," and hung up.

14

●

Basketball à la Frieder

I don't rule the world, or even the basketball world, and I don't want to. I don't usually think about how I would change the rules, either, unless somebody asks me. I'm the type of guy who just wants you to tell me what the rules are and I'll live with them and abide by them and try to figure out how to make the most of them.

But that doesn't mean I don't have opinions, or that I don't think some areas could stand improvement. Here are some changes that I think are worth considering.

Freshmen should not be eligible. Everybody keeps saying it but it never gets voted, because we've got greedy athletic directors and greedy presidents. They want freshmen eligible to help their programs. They want instant help. You don't see the big-time programs, the class programs, voting for freshmen eligibility. They don't need it. But there aren't enough of them, numerically, to vote it down.

The bottom line is that freshmen are not

ready to play. They need that year of adjustment—academically, socially and basketball-wise. From that standpoint, Proposition 48 was good for Terry Mills and Rumeal Robinson. I think that's the way every freshman should have to do it, and they're better off today because of the whole situation.

Sean Higgins is another example. If he hadn't been eligible, he couldn't have become ineligible, right? And he could have learned what it takes to maintain a 2.0 grade point at the University of Michigan without it being on the front page of the *Ann Arbor News.*

I don't think we need a Big Ten tournament, I really don't, but I could accept it if we go back to a 14-game conference schedule. There is so much hype about the post-season tournaments and the NCAA tournament nowadays that maybe it's good for the fans, maybe it's good for the media, maybe it's good for the players, maybe it will help exposure.

On the other hand, I don't think we have to go to it just because most of the other leagues have done it. The Big Ten has always been a leader in everything. We have the largest arenas, the biggest crowds, we hold our own in non-conference and NCAA play, so I don't think we have to do it to impress anybody.

And with a tournament, who's going to be the true Big Ten champion? The regular season winner? If you don't play every other team home and home, how fair is that? The tournament winner? If you have it in Indianapolis every year, how fair is that?

You might be surprised about how a tournament would draw, too. What if it's in Indianapolis and Indiana loses the first round? How many people from Wisconsin or Minnesota, or even Michigan, are going to come and support that tournament? Will what they make on the tournament offset the loss of four Big Ten games by each team? I think there are some "cons."

I don't think you can write a good rule to stop intentional fouls at the end of a game. They certainly haven't done it yet. The rule they have now is dangerous, and it's dangerous because it has to be interpreted and because of the inconsistencies that occur in how the referees call it. Some officials act like they have to call it at least once every game. Others won't call it under any circumstances. And a lot of them seem to call similar plays differently at different times in the game.

When a player makes a pass that leads directly to a shot without a dribble, and the shooter is fouled and makes two free throws, that should be an assist. You get the two points, anyway. Think how many more assists Gary Grant would have had in his career. Guys like Roy Tarpley and Glen Rice were always getting fouled in situations like that.

Did you know that each team that reached the Final Four of the NCAA tournament last season made $1,153,700? That's absolutely incredible. They don't need to get that much. That's twice what we get from television for the entire season.

I think we've got to get more money to the have-nots somehow, whether it's giving them all $25,000 and decreasing the top a little or some other plan, but somehow we've got to include all of them. I'm not for expanding the tournament, but I'm for giving everybody a little share of the money.

Scholarship limits only help the cheaters. The cheaters find a way to have 14, 15, 16 guys in their program. At Michigan, you don't see a lot of transfers, walk-ons or non-predictors, and we have always renewed scholarships, even if the kid is not on the team. We do not take away scholarships. A lot of programs will not renew scholarships and send kids away so they'll have more scholarships to give.

I like the three-point shot line where it is. I agree that maybe it's not worth three points compared to the difficulty of other shots, but I like it where it is. We really didn't benefit from it that much last year, not like the year before when we had Antoine Joubert and Garde Thompson, but I think the fact that you can pop in a three-pointer from out there makes the game exciting.

It's done a great deal for the game of basketball. I know the players like it. Hey, you get seven, eight, nine ahead, then somebody pops in a couple out there and they're back in the game.

I like the 45-second clock. I would even be in favor of a 30-second clock or a 35-second clock. That would make the games exciting, too.

But the rule change I really want to see is, I'd like to go to four baskets. I'd like to have two baskets at each end. You just move the basket from where it is now over to the right and put another basket on the left. You might have to widen the court by 10 feet or so.

This way, if you're playing five-on-five at one basket, you can break a little guy over to the other basket and they've gotta defense him. This would really help the little guy, see.

You could go to all kinds of things. Maybe only 60 percent of the points can be scored at one basket, so that if there's too much play at one basket and you get down to the stretch of the game, you have to score all your points at the other basket. There could be all kinds of things that could happen. You'd really have to be awake, wouldn't you?

Did you know I was kidding on that? The media didn't. The Big Ten has a press conference via telephone every Tuesday afternoon where all the coaches (except Bobby Knight, that is) answer questions in turn. I did that whole spiel during that press conference one day late last season, and nobody said "boo." I don't know if they didn't want to sound like they were taking it seriously by asking a question, or if they were worried that it was something they should know about but didn't, or if they just didn't want to hear me talk about it any more, but nobody said anything.

I am serious about boosters, though. We don't really have any such thing at Michigan, and that's good. The boosters are where a lot of the trouble comes in. They promise kids this and that, that they're gonna be taken care of and so on, and the next thing you know you run into problems.

I'm in favor of no one having boosters at all. They are not a necessary evil. Your program needs loyal friends, not boosters. That's why they shouldn't reduce staff size any more than they already have. If you have enough staff to take care of all the necessary details, there's no need for outsiders to become involved. Dave Hammer was a so-called part-time assistant but he worked at least full-time. I don't know how he managed. You need the staff to do so many things—recruiting, scouting, films, running study table, checking on academics, supervising managers and tutors. A lot of times boosters get involved when there isn't enough staff to do the things that need to be done, then they wind up hanging around with the kids and developing relationships.

Anything that limits recruiting is all right with me. Even though it means more scheduling and planning, it saves a lot of wear and tear on the coaches. And Mike Boyd's kids recognize him now. It used to be you could see a high school kid play as many times as you wanted. I saw almost every game Phil Hubbard, Tim McCormick and Eric Turner—just to name three—played as seniors. Now you can only see a kid four times a year, and then only during certain time periods during the season.

That's why it's not a minor infraction if they catch somebody exceeding that limit or seeing a player during a prohibited period. It's a serious infraction and it should be dealt with seriously. Otherwise, these limits won't work, and it's hard enough to stay ahead of the cheaters as it is.

15

Mortimer Reports

He wasn't supposed to be a basketball coach.

He's cast against type in every way but one: eccentricity, or as Robyn Norwood of the *Los Angeles Times* put it, estrangement from popular culture.

He doesn't know who's running for president, hasn't been to a movie in 20 years and has written one more book than he's read in the same time span.

He's a basketball junkie, a guy who carried a box of statistics around with him when he was in college, who would break from studying only to drive to road games, who scouted for free for his father-in-law, who should have become an insurance agent or investment banker or realtor whose hobby is following his favorite team around. Instead, he became the coach of his favorite team.

He'd go to the games even if he didn't have to. He loves justifying what he does by having it be part of his job, but he'd pay his way in. He'd have a satellite dish in his yard.

After 15 years of college coaching, eight of

them as the head coach at Michigan, he can still barely contain his delight and amazement at finding himself in this situation. He's like a mischievous little kid, soaping windows, listening in on the other line, pushing the doorbell and running away.

Following a singularly dreary victory over Youngstown State in December 1985, he called the local papers and told them he was resigning. John Beckett of the *Ann Arbor News*, who had been on the beat less than two months, admits now that he came dangerously close to believing it.

Jim Spadafore of the *Detroit News* is a favorite target. When the team is on the road, Frieder frequently invites Spadafore to his room, but one time Spadafore returned from a night on the town, unlocked the door to his room, and found Frieder asleep on his bed. That the coach was asleep was more of a surprise than the fact that he had managed to invade Spadafore's quarters.

On another occasion while Spadafore was visiting, Frieder picked up the phone, called his office back in Ann Arbor, and told his secretary, "If that idiot Spadafore calls, tell him I'm out of town."

When the team was in Alaska at the beginning of last season, Frieder conveyed his dislike of the place to Beckett with such comments as, "If you like suicide, alcoholism and prostitution, it's great." Then he told Spadafore what a great time he was having and how much he and his players were enjoying and learning about Alaska. And then he sat back and waited for the writers' editors to wonder what their correspondents had been drinking to produce such wildly disparate stories.

Gary Grant is a prankster, too, which may be why they became such great friends. And make no mistake. They are friends, as we truly understand the term. This is rare between coaches and their players, but it is not rare between Frieder and his players. Of course, he wasn't supposed to be a coach, so maybe he doesn't know.

And Gary Grant's abilities are only incidental to their friendship. His affection for his players is not regulated by their skills. He gives a speech about each senior player at each spring's basketball bust, and he was never more emotional than when he gave his speech about Dan Pelekoudas in 1984.

And he was never more emotional in the locker room than before last year's Ohio State game, the last home game of the season. Tears streaming down his face, his familiar rasp even hoarser than usual, he could barely croak his valedictory for Gary Grant *and* Steve Stoyko, and no one there doubted he would miss the latter as keenly as the former.

One of his main concerns about his book was that somehow the more candid passages would discourage potential recruits, as if an accurate portrayal of his almost obsessive devotion to his players could do that. This devotion endures long after they cease to play for him, long after they are, as a cynic might put it, "of use." He helps them get into graduate school. He helps them get jobs. He spent considerable time last season making phone calls and writing letters on behalf of an ex-Wolverine who graduated several years before and was having trouble finding employment.

He is, in a much less publicized and self-congratulatory way than Bobby Knight, their friend forever. It is a side the public almost never sees.

Sometimes it seems as if the games exist only as raw material for tapes to be cut and studied, for highlight videos to be used as recruiting tools, for newspaper stories, broadcasts, telecasts, his TV show, after-dinner speeches. And the stories, always the stories, in the locker room, in the hotel room, on the plane, in the car, hanging around yet another high school gym, positioning himself to be glimpsed by yet another high school prospect.

The games themselves aren't that much fun for him. They are, in fact, the most demanding part of his job, and the fact that they require his total attention, unlike almost anything else he does, makes them as exhausting as they are exhilarating. He often looks wan and drained afterward and, of course, he's too wired to restore himself with sleep.

He's said that he enjoys landing a big recruit more than he enjoys winning a big game, and it's not hard to see why. For one thing, he wins 20 or more games every year, but he only signs four or five recruits. Recruits may last four or five years. A victory lasts only until the preparation for the next game begins — frequently a matter of hours.

He knows as much about the problems, pressures and perspectives of the working journalist as any coach I've ever known. If he's unhappy about a story, he goes right to the person who wrote it and asks questions, intelligent questions, rather than stewing about it or complaining to his cronies or attacking the writer behind his back.

And if he gets answers, he remembers them. He's surprised me more than once with his thorough knowledge of the newspaper business. He predicted exactly when Joe Falls' column speculating on his relationship with Bo would appear. He heard on a Wednesday that the column had been written, looked at the schedules of the Tigers, Pistons and Red Wings, and told Janice, "They'll run it across the top of the front sports page on Saturday morning." And they did.

I used to admire Joe Falls. He was one of only two people I thanked publicly when I said goodbye to the daily sports writing life. But I was appalled by his treatment of Frieder last season. He seemed to be looking for a cross to crucify him on, and I can't figure out why, unless it was just a case of Joe casting himself as the guardian of jock morality again.

The cameraman incident during the Iowa game was nothing. I was walking right behind Frieder when it happened. I don't know where Falls was but he wasn't in the vicinity. The guy stuck a camera in Frieder's face and he pushed it aside. It was in his path, for heaven's sake. Anybody else would have done the same thing, and nobody else made a big deal out of it except Falls, who persisted in trying to keep the story alive. Every time there was a minute discrepancy or clarification, Falls flew to his computer and tapped out another "story." He has his supervisors, if any, and the people he covers so intimidated that they dare not point out that the emperor is wearing his birthday suit.

Falls did it again with the "scandal" over whether or not Frieder sought the Texas job. The people who originally got that non-story, Jim Spadafore and Jerry Green, were inclined to use it, if at all, in a notes column, but when Falls picked up the scent, he jumped on it like a starving Doberman, shoving Spadafore and Green aside to take charge, Haig-like, himself.

For the most part, Frieder genuinely likes the people in the media. Deep down inside, he's just another statistics nerd who loves to talk sports, except that somehow he wound up as the coach of one of the top college basketball programs in the country and, thus, a producer of sports news as well as a consumer of it. Sometimes that slips his mind, and he starts talking to reporters the way he would talk on the team bus to one of his assistants or in a hotel lounge to one of his cronies.

That propensity was the first thing that got him into trouble. During one of Spadafore's visits to his room when they were in Salt Lake City for the opening rounds of the NCAA tournament, Frieder told him — off the record — that he would be meeting with Texas at the Final Four in Kansas City. He had been given to understand, via a circuitous route, that Texas would not be averse to an inquiry from him, so he had made it.

As Frieder said later, "I thought off the record with Spadafore doesn't go out of the room." Not only did it go out of the room, but within minutes it had traveled all the way to Detroit via Spadafore's telephone. An hour later, he was back in Frieder's room saying his editors wanted more information.

Now came the second thing that got Frieder into trouble: a well-intentioned but clumsy attempt at damage control. He didn't want to give the impression that he was job-hunting, because he wasn't. He didn't want to give the impression that he was trying to leverage Michigan for a better deal, because he couldn't. And he didn't want to reveal the precise sequence of events, because it would needlessly embarrass other people. In the spring of 1986, Mike Boyd went to Kentucky to see Terry Mills play in an all-star game. There were rumors that some Kentucky fans, angered by Mills' decision to spurn the Wildcats for the Wolverines, were, literally, gunning for him. "If that's the case," said Frieder, "Boyd's going to have to step in front of him and take the bullet."

Like all good bosses, Frieder never asks an assistant to do something he wouldn't do himself. He now stepped in and took the bullet. He clammed up. He stonewalled. And he looked bad because he was trying to protect others.

Considering Texas A&M's almost unseemly courtship of Bo Schembechler in 1981, and Princeton's almost equally public wooing of Harold Shapiro six years later, Frieder's flirtation with Texas, such as it was, was trivial and fleeting. Only Falls' vendetta against him sustained its notoriety beyond the day or so it deserved.

He uses timepieces only to keep appointments. He may be the only human being on the face of the earth with no biological clock. He goes and goes and goes until he collapses for a while. Then he gets up and goes some more.

There are two classes that, to the everlasting credit of the school systems of Alpena and Flint, Michigan, he never stood in front of in the days when he "had to teach five classes a day to get to the thing I loved." Those classes were nutrition and driver education.

I have seen him go eight hours without eating, then send a manager to Wendy's under orders to bring back a quadruple chocolate frostee. . . for breakfast. I have heard reports of him slurping down a bowl of scalding hot soup before his colleagues' had cooled to the point where they would even dare to test it. He never blinked. He didn't even notice. What's that got to do with winning games?

And I have ridden with him doing 90 in the fog, and it seems I have never ridden with him doing less than twice the speed limit, and I know I have never ridden with him when he paid more than half his attention to the road (which, in his case, is actually quite a lot).

If you ask him how he's doing, chances are the answer will be, "I'm hangin' in there, coach." It's his defining expression and the one his associates pick up on. He loves pursuits where hangin' in there pays off, and he hates making decisions (although, obviously, he makes them all the time). Recruiting fills the bill on both counts—hangin' in there is its essence, and, ultimately, the recruit makes the decision, not Frieder.

Maybe that's why he's never troubled much by officiating. Oh, he can remember a handful of cases where he thought he was jobbed—at Northwestern in 1984, against Notre Dame in the Silverdome in 1983 and, when he was an assistant, at a tournament in Las Vegas in 1975. But, by and large, he doesn't have much to say about officiating, even in private. His interest is purely practical. He's not interested in justice or the merits of a decision. He just wants to know what he can learn from it—a particular official's response to a particular set of circumstances—that may provide an advantage in the future.

He discounts, even derides, anything outside his realm, because he is uncomfortable with anything he can't control. It makes him feel helpless, and he hates feeling helpless. Perhaps it reminds him of his childhood, when the whole world must have seemed out of control. So he concentrates on one or two pursuits that he can master, where he can make the rules and enforce them, and shies away from those he can't.

And when he does lose control and pushes a camera or blows up at a hotel clerk or a parking lot attendant or a security guard, he either pretends to forget or he doesn't even notice, as if his body did something while his mind was elsewhere. On the night of the camera incident after we got to the coaches' cubicle in the locker room, I asked him if he had hurt his hand.

"No," he said. "What did I do?"

It is another of his anomalies that, as much as he craves control, he is also constantly asking other people for their opinions, even about what he should do. He vacillates over how strictly he should control the media's access and what time to have practice and how long it should be and whether and how he should change his lineup. When Steve Fisher, noting a player error, tells Frieder to "Say something to him right now, coach," he instantly, almost dutifully, says something to him right now. But when the same Fisher, in the same game, tries to talk to an official, Frieder snarls,

"Don't be trying to talk to him when I want to get his attention."

His pre-game and halftime speeches are matter-of-fact, technical, almost pedagogical. There is minimal eloquence and no emotional appeal. He can prepare a team, teach a team, work a team, assemble a team. He rarely makes inspirational speeches. The spiritual component is up to the players, but it almost seems that, in some uncanny way, he recognizes this, for he has recruited some inspirational players.

He's criticized for what are seen as his team's failures in the NCAA tournament, but the hardest work is winning the regular season championship in the Big Ten. It seems there's been a change in emphasis in sports. Performance over the long haul takes a back seat to getting hot and striking it rich. Never mind what you accomplished over the grueling, 18-game Big Ten schedule. What did you do in the sudden-death NCAA tournament? Just be good enough to make the playoffs and then hope you get hot and lucky.

On stage, he hurls his hoarse shriek at the officials, knowing he's got that technical at last. On stage, he is charming and diplomatic in set pieces for the cameras, garrulous and assured in press conferences, in charge of almost all situations and certain that he knows what to do about the ones he isn't in charge of. On stage, he takes turns flattering, cajoling, and browbeating his players. On stage, he pokes fun at Janice and flummoxes the media.

Off stage, he is one of the world's great blackjack players, banned from virtually every Las Vegas casino. It should surprise no one that a man who has made money on everything from peddling produce to bank mergers excels at the purest form of making money there is: no product to provide, no service to render, no distractions between Frieder and the purity of profit.

Off stage, he's still running from something even if he's forgotten what it is now. Off stage, he probably pays more positive attention to his players than some of their parents do, and is more of a pedagogue than many of them would imagine (and more of a teacher, in the truest sense of the term, than some of those coaches who like to boast of their "role as an educator"). Off stage, he defers to Janice in virtually every area of their domestic life and doesn't know how to pump his own gas or play a cassette in his car's tape deck. Off stage, he will pay attention to Laura when he will pay attention to no one else, and his huge hands reach almost unconsciously to stroke her hair.

Off stage, he does not agonize over the possibility that none of this matters; he is certain that it doesn't. Off stage, that is one of the few matters he is certain about.

He stays in hotels even when he's home. He keeps the team in the Campus Inn the night before weekend afternoon games. Sometimes when they have a Sunday game or a game during a vacation, he keeps them there for two nights. Last season, he spent an additional night in an Ann Arbor hotel, the Holidome, because his house was being readied for the Ann Arbor Women's City Club's annual Home Tour.

He actually seems more at home in a hotel. Given his background, that may not be surprising. Who would feel more at home on the road, and more lost at home? Besides, hotels give him space to roam in. He wanders from room to room in his suite, usually talking on the phone all the while. Then he wanders from room to room in the rest of the hotel. Then he's in the lounge, then the restaurant, then the pool, then the halls. No wonder he can't sleep. He can't endure being in an enclosed space, let alone a bed. No wonder he doesn't go to movies. That would require two hours of immobility. One almost imagines that he won't die simply because he could never sit still that long.

Coaching is the absolute focus of his life. He loves it. He gets a kick out of it. He doesn't need food. He doesn't need sleep. He doesn't need culture or art. He might not even need love. But he sure as hell needs basketball.